Contemporary Marriage
Special Issues in Couples Therapy

Contemporary Marriage

Special Issues in Couples Therapy

Edited by Daniel C. Goldberg, Ph.D.

Foreword by Paul J. Fink, M.D.

DORSEY PROFESSIONAL BOOKS

1985

THE DORSEY PRESS

Homewood, Illinois 60430

ISBN 0-256-03484-2

Library of Congress Catalog Card No. 85–70188

Printed in the United States of America

1 2 3 4 5 6 7 8 9 0 K 2 1 0 9 8 7 6 5

To my father and mother

Foreword

This volume is an important contribution to the theory and practice of marital/couples therapy. Dr. Goldberg has attempted to bring together a group of experts from a variety of disciplines and perspectives, which serves as an unspoken demonstration of the complexity of contemporary marriage. The book highlights issues and problems in marriage, child rearing, and divorce that have rapidly moved to center stage. As we continue to have more questions than answers about some areas of human relationships, other aspects of marriage are becoming clarified.

Marriage is so much a part of the social fabric of human life that it is difficult to deal with the topic from the psychological perspective alone. We must also think about the sociological, philosophical, biological, religious, and socioeconomic aspects of marital relations. This book is addressed to professionals who work with couples and provides a great deal of important information about contemporary coupling and uncoupling. The broader perspective must be kept in mind in order that this material fit into an even more comprehensive sociocultural matrix.

The post World War II changes in the roles of both women and men have forced a reexamination of the mores, traditions, and belief systems that governed marriage for centuries. One of the significant factors is that greater freedom for women brought with it a number of previously nonexistent choices. In the past social sanctions for deviant behavior within specific classes were much stronger and these sanctions controlled the destiny of men, women, and their marital relationships. The acceptance of women of all classes in the workplace is a recent phenomenon which has changed the economic status of women and has concomitantly affected the power relationships between marital partners. The rapid introduction of many women into higher education, the professions, and positions of power has caused major disruptions in the traditional views of family, child rearing, roles within the home, and roles in the marketplace.

The demise of the frontier, with its inherent dangers, need for brute strength, and sense of freedom and need for self-sufficiency, has markedly changed the traditional role of men. Today, very few American and European men work the soil. Rather, the corporation, with its hierarchical power structure, confinement, and demand for experience, credentials, competition, and production, has become the new frontier on which both men and women must toil. Many families are fully dependent on two incomes. Many people have discarded religion as the source of moral and social values. Contemporary men and women, threatened by quick and easy methods of annihilation, have moved toward existentialism with its concomitant affluence, hedonism, and narcissism. Almost imperceptibly, these massive and rapid cultural shifts have altered the way young people look at marriage as an institution and have changed their expectations of the marital relationship.

In spite of these changes certain aspects of human relations have remained the same. While the rules of courting have changed, young and not so young couples still court each other. While pragmatism seems a ruling ethic of our times, romance is very much alive and plays a significant role in bringing people together and to the altar. While we speak glibly about modern approaches to marriage including open marriage, togetherness without marriage, and childless marriage by choice, jealousy remains an important human passion, fidelity is still cherished, children are still very much desired, and family continues to be an important, cohesive force in our society. Divorce, while more common and much more accepted, is still traumatic to both parties. Filled with acrimony, hatred, and long-term fallout, divorce usually affects both the partners and the children adversely. Such old institutions as infidelity, extramarital affairs, and misery in marriage are still with us.

How then are we to understand this heterogeneous entity called marriage? Can one write an essay or even a brief foreword such as this without invoking the ethereal, relatively undefinable concept of love? Are there any unifying themes that will tie the subject together into a meaningful theory or group of precepts which workers in the field can use as guidelines?

First, it should be clear that marriage is very hard work. In *Fiddler on the Roof* Tevye asks Golda, his wife of 25 years, if she loves him. He tells her that "the first time I met you was on our wedding day. My father said we'd learn to love each other. Now I want to know, do you love me?" There is no evidence that today's method of choosing one's mate is any more successful than the arranged marriages of yesterday. The hard work does not end when the marital ceremony takes place. That is when it begins. Negotiation of the roles of each partner and the acceptance of each by the other are critical to the creation of a successful marriage.

Second, children change a marriage into a family. Responsibilities and roles are forced out of the realm of rhetoric and into the cold, stark world of reality. The joys of having children are counterbalanced by the personal doubts and inexperience of parents, the new social and scientific influences on the growth and development of children, and the greater number of choices open to children. These choices tend to create a gulf between children and parents with respect to beliefs, values, morals, and attitudes. Nevertheless, human infants and children need to be cared for longer than any other mammal and someone must accept the role of caretaker. Psychoanalytic theory has taught us the importance of object constancy during the first three years of life and Spitz has warned us that "children raised without love become adults full of hate." Thus, the rules of a marriage before the advent of children must inexorably change after they arrive.

Fortunately, attachment theory makes parenting somewhat easier on those mothers who have a choice. Many parents, however, dependent on two paychecks, and/or raised with the idea of husband and wife equality, or ambivalent about family versus career, suffer a tremendous disruption in their relationship when children arrive. And children who suffer damage through genetics or development may cause even greater marital disruption. Over 75 percent of parents with a mentally retarded child experience marital disruption that results in a significantly higher divorce rate. Thus, modern couples must be better prepared for the effects of children on marriage.

Third, power and control issues are part of every marriage. The lack of firm, societal guidelines discussed above has brought these struggles out into the open. The old aphorism, "behind every great man there is a woman," in which the woman's power is implied, has been replaced by the concept of partnership and the acceptance in some quarters that behind every great woman there may be a man, sometimes supportive and helpful and sometimes resentful and furious. Power and control have always been part of every marriage but in the past they were neither recognized nor openly discussed and dealt with. These issues are now an accepted part of negotiations and renegotiations that must take place in a modern marriage if it is to succeed.

Fourth, the concept of "marriage for life" seems to be waning. More and more people enter marriage with the idea that if it doesn't work out divorce is a logical, viable, and acceptable alternative. Thus, fidelity in the fullest sense of the word is not as powerful a force in binding people to each other as it once was. The effort of some religions to interdict divorce as a real and acceptable alternative is weakened by the power of social forces that make divorce easier and by the wave of narcissism which puts the self above the couple.

Narcissism is the true enemy of every couple. In the face of narcissism, concepts like sharing, giving, altruism, for better or for worse, and in sickness and in health are weak and malleable. Educators, theologians, philosophers, and therapists must recognize that a sole focus on self is the greatest enemy of the couple and that we must try to reinstate the couple as the foundation of our society. As long as marriage can be viewed as transient it will be vulnerable to self-interest and separation, disruption, and divorce.

In trying to bring order out of the chaotic state in which the institution of marriage finds itself, data gathered through observation and greater respect for the power of mediation, conciliation, negotiation, and therapy are needed. While marriage will always be a major part of the nature of human relationships, we must be tolerant of its ever changing appearance and accepting of its variety and pitfalls.

"Grow old along with me, the best is yet to be" is a reality for some and could be a meaningful and fulfilling goal for all.

Paul J. Fink, M.D.
Chairman, Department of Psychiatry
Albert Einstein Medical Center
Northern Division
Philadelphia, PA

Preface

The central theme of this book is quite straightforward: Marital life seems to be different today than in years past and the complex of problems manifested by couples today represents a significant challenge for therapists. While a consensus over the dynamics and reasons for this trend may be difficult to achieve, signs that marriage is undergoing a transformation can be easily observed. Divorce rates have climbed to nearly one out of every two marriages, with second marriages faring only slightly better but not as well as one would expect if learning from experience is indeed the valuable social reinforcer it is alleged to be. The traditional nuclear family (i.e., two biological parents with child[ren]) represents an extemely small minority of all households across the country. This change in family structure to more single person households has even begun to make an impact on the types of new homes being constructed. Sexual concerns in marriage seem to be taking a different shape as well. In years past people were concerned with functioning effectively. Today, people seem to be going beyond physiology as evidenced by the degree to which they are troubled by how much they are *interested* in sex with their partner. Sex therapists report that nearly half of their caseload is comprised of people with problems related to sustaining an adequate level of sexual desire.

Unobtrusive observations of daily life events can be used to identify ways in which marriage has changed. If one could have a special, time-lapse movie covering the past 10 years of train station platforms near our major cities during commuter rush hours, one would see a dramatic shift in demographics, one in which the number of women waiting for trains is now almost equal to that of men. One manifest consequence of this role expansion can be seen in the proliferation of child care centers and home care arrangements.

Another, unobtrusive measure of change is the sex and marriage section in bookstores. The growing existence of these sections and the rapid proliferation of the number of books on these topics indicate that there must be an eager market out there. One can infer that people seem to be searching for guidance (or perhaps deeper satisfaction) in their relationships through self-help measures. Moving from bookstores to the video rental center, what shall we make of this new "resource"? Individuals can and do rent X-rated movies for their weekend sexual enhancement. One can only speculate as to whether this phenomenon represents sexual freedom and an avenue for disinhibition or whether these movies signal a search for a way to fill the emptiness in contemporary relationships.

Clearly, the phenomena discussed above represent only a few examples of possible changes in marital interactions. The underlying issues are complex and require extensive elaboration (the task of this volume), but perhaps there is an organizing principle that might help to bring parsimony to our understanding of contemporary marital life. The question, of course, is why has marriage undergone such a transformation in the first place? Why is there so much turmoil around marriage today?

The notions of Emile Durkheim, noted social theoretician, regarding the relationship between society and the individual might help to guide our thinking here. He described how people begin to feel alienated from their social surround and was concerned about the emotional distress caused by their loss of personal identity. Durkheim indicated that if a secure sense of self is to emerge people need relatively clear expectations (reflecting social consensus) from society so that effective guidelines for organizing behavior can be established. A sense of alienation can be described by three concepts: normlessness (the degree to which society agrees to certain normative behaviors); powerlessness (the degree to which individuals can exert control through their own behavior); and meaninglessness (the degree to which people are able to predict their future).

Applying these concepts to contemporary marriage, we might postulate that many individuals are experiencing a feeling of alienation and that there may be some key reasons that explain this phenomenon. Our social environment is fraught with uncertainty regarding questions about our future. For example, nuclear destruction is no longer an unthinkable possibility; hence, the ability to predict the shape of our collective future has become tenuous. Perhaps one consequence of this sense of meaninglessness is the tendency toward impulsive behavior in today's marriages. People want things to happen *now* and see little reason for delaying gratification. This puts pressure on the marriage and may even cause people to seek "greener pastures" in other romantic liaisons. Moreover, we are hard pressed to identify clear, socially derived standards for expected behaviors in marriage. While many may welcome this trend toward a more internally derived source of values and expectations, the current situation carries with it the uncertainty inherent in making choices. Questions proliferate. Should marriage last " 'til death do us part"? Is it reasonable to expect monogamy? Should the roles of men and women in marriage be defined differently? How do individuals pursue self-fulfillment while maintaining a keen sensitivity to their partners' needs, the family unit, and society as a whole? There are no clear guidelines to help us answer questions such as these and thus a sense of normlessness may have developed in many pair-bonded relationships.

Finally, our sphere of influence appears to be shrinking. Societal problems seem vast and political leaders seem able to make only a dent in solving them. People are frustrated and voter dissatisfaction is high. It may be that this sense of powerlessness is leading people to turn to their marriages and to expect more from them than was the case in years past. The marital relationship may symbolize a haven where people do indeed have power if they attend to "cultivating their own garden." If individuals cannot change society they can at least make their own, personal lives as rewarding as possible.

In developing this book I knew that truly capturing the complexities of today's relationships was a hefty, perhaps almost impossible assignment. To make the task manageable, I developed four major sections that I considered salient for clinicians. Some chapters are more educational in focus while others are more oriented around treatment issues. This dual focus is quite intentional since I believe that often, in helping couples, we are asked in effect to be educators as well. The first section reflects my bias toward the usefulness of theoretical reflections to guide our clinical work. I wanted this section to address certain important questions such as whether marriage has indeed changed, what the role of romantic love might be, and how relationships might go through phases as they develop.

The second section examines different issues around lifestyle management. It seems that many couples are contending with a variety of concerns and life stressors and this section covers a number of these including dual professional marriages, infertility, alternative lifestyles, and sexual communication between parent and child. The third section concentrates on clinical extensions. Much more could have been included here, but my focus was primarily on treatment issues that had not recieved as much attention in the existing literature as I felt they deserved. Such topics as extramarital affairs, sexual apathy, experiential work with couples, and couples groups are covered in this section. The final section looks at issues around uncoupling. One chapter focuses on the differences in the way men and women handle the process of divorce. The second chapter concentrates on gender and sex role matters, while other chapters tackle such questions as how divorce affects children and whether second marriages are truly different from first marriages.

In putting this book together a number of people offered invaluable help. My colleagues at Jefferson, Salman Akhtar, M.D. and Arlene Goldman, M.A., provided excellent feedback on various parts of the manuscript and were there to exchange ideas on many occasions. A very special thanks goes to Emily Kahn who participated in much of the day-to-day, "nitty-gritty" work of preparing a book. Her mark on the book will not be as clear to others as it is to me, but her editing skills (not to mention her other administrative assistance) are exemplary and have significantly strengthened the book. Finally, I am quite lucky to have a wife, Marjorie Gutman, Ph.D., who can alternate among the roles of lover, friend, and colleague, and for whom I have much professional respect. She is not only a contributor to the book. She also allowed me to devote many conversations at dinner (and beyond the dinner hour) to gathering her comments on how the book should be conceptualized, as well as to how the book was developing.

Daniel C. Goldberg, Ph.D.

LIST OF CONTRIBUTORS

Salman Akhtar, M.D. Jefferson Medical College	1015 Chestnut Street, Second Floor Philadelphia, PA 19107
Bernard Apfelbaum, Ph.D. Berkeley Sex Therapy Group	2714 Telegraph Avenue Berkeley, CA 94705
Constance Apfelbaum Berkeley Sex Therapy Group	2714 Telegraph Avenue Berkeley, CA 94705
Lillian F. Brunell, Psy. D. Private Practice	25 Scarsdale Drive Livingston, NJ 07039
Albert Ellis, Ph.D. Institute for Rational-Emotive Therapy	45 East 65th Street New York, NY 10021
Lana P. Fishkin, M.D. Jefferson Medical College	Park Towne Place E-104 2200 Benjamin Franklin Parkway Philadelphia, PA 19130
Ralph E. Fishkin, D.O. Jefferson Medical College	Park Towne Place E-104 2200 Benjamin Franklin Parkway Philadelphia, PA 19130
Thomas F. Fogarty, M.D. Center for Family Learning	10 Hanford Avenue New Rochelle, NY 10805
Hettie B. Frank, Ph.D. Private Practice	164 W. 79th St., Apt. 10-A New York, NY 10024
Matti K. Gershenfeld, Ed.D. Temple University	Benson East Suite A-13 Jenkintown, PA 19406
Daniel C. Goldberg, Ph.D. Jefferson Medical College	122A Haddontowne Court Cherry Hill, NJ 08034
Martin Goldberg, M.D. Marriage Council of Philadelphia	4025 Chestnut Street Philadelphia, PA 19104
Marjorie A. Gutman, Ph.D. Downstate Medical Center	42 North Main Street Cranbury, NJ 08512
Janet R. Kahn, Ed.M. American Institute for Research	22 Hilliard Street Cambridge, MA 02138
John W. Santrock, Ph.D. University of Texas at Dallas	P.O. Box 688 Richardson, TX 75080
Marlene Schneider, M.S.W. Mt. Sinai Hospital	3802 Little Avenue Coconut Grove, FL 33133

G. Pirooz Sholevar, M.D.
Jefferson Medical College
1015 Chestnut Street, Second Floor
Philadelphia, PA 19107

Karen Sitterle, Ph.D.
Timberlawn Psychiatric Hospital
5846 McCommas
Dallas, TX 75206

John C. Sonne, M.D.
Jefferson Medical College
214 West Main Street
Moorestown, NJ 08057

William R. Stayton, Th.D.
Jefferson Medical College
14 Elliott Avenue
Bryn Mawr, PA 19010

Wendy Stock, Ph.D.
Texas A & M University
Texas A & M Department of Psychology
College Station, TX 77843

Sandra Strine, Ph.D.
Private Practice
14 Elliott Avenue
Bryn Mawr, PA 19010

Nathan W. Turner, Ed.D.
Jefferson Medical College
14 Elliott Avenue
Bryn Mawr, PA 19010

Daniel B. Wile, Ph.D.
California State University, Hayward
6119 Acacia Avenue
Oakland, CA 94618

CONTENTS

SECTION 1

Theoretical Considerations

SECTION 2

Lifestyle Management

SECTION 3

Treatment

SECTION 4

Uncoupling and Beyond

SECTION 1

Theoretical Considerations

ONE

Contemporary Marriage: The Question of Significant Change in Marital Patterns

John C. Sonne, M.D.
Clinical Professor of Psychiatry and Human Behavior
Jefferson Medical College

*T*his chapter discusses the impact of changes in the systems of psychology, politics, and technology upon marriage; the value placed on several variables active in the composition of marital patterns past and present; and outlines some of the developmental processes operative in the movement toward marital intimacy.

INTRODUCTION

What is happening to the institution of marriage in America today? Why is it that we have a divorce rate of epidemic proportions at a time in our society when we have most of the ingredients one might assume would produce happy marriages and happy families? Why are there so many unhappy marriages, and why is it that the search for a happy marriage seems so like Diogenes' search for an honest man? We see the composition of the American marriage apparently changing today and ask ourselves what the operative variables are. We wonder how changes in the larger society and in the world may be causing changes in marriage and vice versa. We wonder if marital patterns of today are indeed different from those of yesterday, and ask ourselves if all this turbulence represents a creative transition to a higher level of functioning or a destructive descent into chaos.

These are questions we are all asking, questions to which no one has a precise answer. We don't have enough knowledge about the social, marital, and family processes involved. We're unsure about our goals, and even if we think we know what we want, we're not sure of how to go about getting it, whether we have the power, or whether we're caught in a tidal wave of forces beyond our control which, even if understood, may bode ill or well for marriage, family and society over time, regardless of our own small, personal struggles to influence events. We seem to be in the midst of a rapid cultural evolution, a social kaleidoscope in which every man, woman, and child is spinning, a kaleidoscope in which not only do the patterns keep shifting, but the pieces of glass themselves appear to be undergoing metamorphoses of size, shape, and color as well.

Thus, in any present-day study of marriage we must take into account: (1) the relatively stable dynamic interaction of multiple variables both horizontally and vertically in what conceptually we call systems and levels of organization; (2) the oscillations and changes over time which are constantly occurring in the open, negentropic-entropic flux within which we all live; and (3) the possibility of the appearance at any moment of a surprising, unexpected, seemingly nonlinear event occurring in any element or system, which could change our whole state or organization.

In this chapter I shall discuss how psychological insights and psychotherapeutic experiences over the past several decades have changed the way people see themselves and behave as individuals, and in turn how they behave, what they expect, and how they experience themselves in marital relationships. Next I shall present a table comparing the importance or value placed on certain variables in marriage, past and present. Following this I shall discuss several political and technological changes which have occurred in our world that have affected all of us and, hence, our marriages. The subject of marriage is not a closed one, but a complex, open one regarded as highly important and of great interest by millions of people. This is attested to by the tens of thousands of academic papers and books being published on the subject, the attention being given to it in the arts, and the large number of writings in the lay press, writings that are eagerly consumed by a literate public looking for answers, models, and something of value in their lives in a rapidly changing society.

CHANGES IN THE SYSTEM OF PSYCHOLOGY

I would like to focus first on some major variables that are operative in marriage and about which our understanding has been greatly increased by important studies in the fields of psychoanalysis, family therapy, and communication theory over the past century. These studies have not only changed the way we view ourselves but, put into practice in a variety of psychotherapeutic, educational, and social settings, they have changed the way we relate to one another—including the way we relate in the intimacy of marriage.

In the field of psychoanalysis great strides have been made in understanding the mental mechanisms of defense and the developmental stages involved in two main tasks or processes that occupy and interest people: One is the acquisition of a sense of self and the other is a search for gratification of one's desires. In two related articles (Sonne & Swirsky, 1981; Sonne, 1981) the importance of self and desire processes in marital interaction is discussed in depth. Akin to the sense of self, are such concepts as self-esteem, identity, autonomy, individuation, and the idea that we are unique, apart, alone, and yet related to other selves whom we call objects. In our relationships with others, from infancy on, we reciprocally affirm and define our selves, and we gradually develop a refined capacity to give and receive love. In the area of desire we must successfully traverse the stages of psychosexual development in order to develop the capacity to reciprocally give and receive frustration and gratification of our desires in adult life, desires which, although ultimately sexual, can range from seeking ecstasy in orgasm to wanting to enjoy the quiet, contemplative pleasure of a full moon on a clear, balmy summer evening.

The field of family therapy has given us the opportunity to understand the way the individual processes of self and desire interrelate with the familial interactive processes from which they in part derive and to which they reciprocally contribute. In particular, a family system perspective has helped us to see that multiple, actual, or potential triadic relationships are an important part of all monadic or dyadic processes of self and desire, both in childhood and in adult life. This triadic system or contextual concept has enriched the psychoanalytic understanding of the individual, particularly with respect to the process of internalizing a family image (Sonne, Speck & Jungreis, 1962), and has been crucial in facilitating the application of psychoanalytic concepts to an understanding of marital and family dynamics.

The field of communication theory has enriched both psychoanalysis and family therapy by alerting us to the importance of nonverbal communication, of context, and of the nuances and inflections of speech which, often, out of the sender's and/or receiver's awareness, convey how a message is to be received. We think today of communication as an organizing principle that is operative in a multidirectional network of interacting elements, and we regard every movement, action, and posture, including the way we dress, the symptoms we have, and the occupations we choose as having a communication function—both to ourselves and to others. A corollary of a communication view of life is that one cannot *not* communicate or, put differently, one cannot *not respond*. Our increased understanding of communication has made us aware that much of our time is spent repressing, suppressing, or attempting consciously or unconsciously to stop or delay something we consider potentially creative or destructive from happening (Sonne, 1967, 1979). The implications of communication theory for our understanding of self and desire processes in individual, marital, family, and societal life are far reaching, and touch on our topic of changes in marital patterns relative to defining and communicating "who's who and who wants what from whom" in the contemporary marriage. Increased awareness of messages sent from the unconscious can open the way to rational, clear communication and negotiation toward consciously wished for personal and marital goals that were previously unattainable because of unconscious, often destructive and collusively shared dynamics.

PSYCHOLOGY IN PRACTICE

The prospects for applying our understanding of the dynamics of self and desire toward the end of producing happier marriages would seem to have never been better, for most of the pieces are there. Yet, the integration of these pieces does not occur without conflict with internal and external unconscious and conscious resistances: such resistances die hard. It is not easy to change oneself, to truly assimilate new understanding, insight, and awareness. But once a person has changed, he or she relates differently. Sometimes this change is welcomed by the people with whom one is in relation, and sometimes it is met by opposition. Also, in changing, people may become active change agents in intimate relationships or, on a larger scale, they may become social activists. If others don't or won't change, it may be necessary for the person who has changed to establish new relationships with new people in new settings. These alloplastic shifts are fraught with conflict and resistance. It is not surprising that the studies I have outlined have greatly disturbed the status quo; nevertheless, they are here, and hopefully they can be used constructively.

The knowledge obtained from psychoanalytic, family therapy, and communication studies is changing how we see ourselves and the world around us. It is also changing the world, as are art and branches of science other than the humanities. We have listened to the emotionally disturbed and the mentally ill, and we have learned from them. No longer does a "Freudian slip," a parapraxis, or a nonverbal revelation by a politician appearing on TV escape our notice. We have become sophisticated: We are curious about such things as the origins of Hitler's and Stalin's behavior, and we study the family backgrounds of the Baader-Meinhof gang. We question religious and secular authorities and wonder about their concept of self and their level of psychosexual development. Although segments of the general public may no more know that their lives have been changed by psychoanalysis, family therapy, and communication studies than that colored cartoons in the newspaper are derivative from Matisse, this change is happening. Millions of people in America have had some form of psychotherapy, and millions of others have read articles, books, or seen plays, movies, or TV shows that are psychologically sophisticated. Although the knowledge that has been acquired from the mental health sciences may often be misunderstood and misapplied, it is unquestionably massive and voluminous. This knowledge is the result of energetic and intelligent studies by countless brilliant and dedicated men and women and equals or surpasses, in both degree and influence, that seen in any other field of endeavor in recent times. We are living in an age of psychology.

Interestingly, the translation of the insights provided by psychological studies into the language of love and marriage seems to have been done, with a few exceptions, by people other than the mental health scientists who have released human beings from the bondage of psychopathology. A special breed of psychologically sophisticated "lovers" are incorporating the work of scientists into poetic descriptions of love, and communicating these to the public. Studies of the casualties in the areas of self and desire are often so focused on psychopathology that they give minimal emphasis to the positive dimensions of people's capacity for love and sex in marriage. Writings by poets, philosophers and theologians are all too often lacking in the depth which can come from using the tools of psychoanalytic theory, family therapy, and communication studies. Branden (1981), an example of the psychologically sophisticated lover, has likened people's search for romantic love and monogamy to an evolutionary process of movement toward a higher stage of development. He has defined romantic love as "a passionate spiritual-emotional-sexual attachment between a man and a woman that reflects a high regard for the value of each other's person" (p. 3).

CONTEMPORARY MARRIAGE

Although romantic love has long been considered a desirable life experience—and hopefully an ingredient in a happy marriage—its pursuit has often led to such heartbreak, misery, and indifference that many have taken the position that believing such an experience to be possible is only an unrealizable fantasy. Do more of us hold different beliefs today? In focusing on contemporary marriage, let us ask how, in this age of psychology, we view marriage compared to the way we used to view it, and how marriages are constructed and functioning today compared to yesterday. In the past people expected less of marriage than they do today or they expected different things; and if they were in trouble, or if they got less than we now think they should have, they either did not know it or did not know why or what to do about it. They often either endured, developed, or tolerated psychiatric syndromes in themselves and/or in their mates, found extramarital satisfactions as a way of life or, less often, separated.

Today people expect more from marriage; "American Gothic" will not do. They freely choose to marry someone they love. They expect to give and receive life in terms of personal growth and affirmation of self; liberty in terms of freedom from coercion and exploitation; and the pursuit of happiness in terms of pleasant times and sexual satisfaction. They expect equality, reciprocity, sharing, and intimacy. They do not want to possess or be possessed. They expect to fit and be a "couple," but do not expect to lose their separate identities or sense of self. They are not willing to accept a mate who is narcissistic, withdrawn, obsessive-compulsive, depressed, dependent, hysterical, tyrannical, or unable to experience romantic love. They want love more and they want to love more. They have the knowledge, the personal capacity, the time, and the freedom from disease, unplanned pregnancies, and the primitive fight for survival to make "the good life" possible. In short, they want more for themselves and more for their partners.

The loving discontent in our psychological civilization has moved many people and many marriages in the direction of greater fulfillment—with therapy or without it. It has also produced an epidemic of divorce, an increased number of pre and extramarital relationships, an inclination on the part of many couples to live together without marriage, and a reluctance of some to ever marry. One of the problems society is having is defining the new values. Experimentation with our newfound freedom has sometimes led to disaster at worst; a loss of bearings in a "sea of the possible," and a disruption of stable patterns of living at best. All of this has created conspicuous and special problems for children; however, whether their problems would have been worse otherwise or just silently different is debatable. If the old values were not good and the new ones are, our adult responsibility here is to provide the children with a model of a psychological family to help them in their own developmental struggles of self and desire in the midst of the current marital turbulence (Sonne, 1980 a, 1980 b).

MARITAL VALUES AND VARIABLES

In the following table I have listed several variables operative in the composition of marital relationships and the relative value placed on each by men and women, past and present. I have chosen the term *value* rather than *practice* because I believe, of the two, value more accurately reflects motivation and better reveals the essence of a process. People will often admit that what they practice is not consonant with their belief system. What they value, however, reveals a sense of what they aspire to and are

TABLE 1 Marital Values and Variables

Variable	*Present*	*Past*
Romantic love	High value, regarded as attainable.	Low value, regarded as ephemeral and an unrealistic expectation.
Virginity	Low value, often interpreted as a problem.	High value, especially in female.
Fidelity	High value if spontaneous, but not paramount if it interferes with growth. Sometimes seen as a rationalization of inhibition or attempt to control spouse.	High value, by commitment.
Affairs	Either accepted, condoned, valued and respected, or regarded as symptomatic of marital or individual problems that need to be worked on.	Silently accepted or severely criticized as traitorous, cruel, sinful, weak, or irresponsible behavior.
Divorce	Accepted, but not lightly.	Frowned upon. A sign of low moral fiber and betrayal of vows and commitment.
Neurotic symptomatology	Seen as an impediment to experiencing romantic love in marital relationship. At times valued because of positive potential inherent in marital unhappiness and indication for therapy for either or both spouse(s), or marital therapy leading to change or dissolution of marriage. At other times seen as reason for quick divorce.	Accepted, happily or unhappily, as "That's the way he or she is, or I am—for better or worse." Maladaptions were lived out in an "emotional divorce." Pseudo mutuality in marriage was highly valued, along with a variety of rationalized acting-out patterns in relationships with children, relatives, and significant, peripheral persons. Rarely, divorce would occur when one or the other or both spouses "couldn't take it anymore."
Dependency	Low value, each spouse expected to be autonomous and independent. Interdependency, teamwork and sharing evolve from this.	Female dependency valued by male and accepted by female. Male dependency often present in disguise, i.e., wife handles paycheck.
Financial contribution and money management	Both male and female valued as contributors and share responsibility, although male usually expected to be major contributor.	Highly valued from male. Male seen as provider by self and mate.
Protection	Low value.	Female needed protection.

TABLE 1 (*concluded*)

Variable	*Present*	*Past*
Responsibility	Responsibility for self and others balanced.	Responsible for others.
Possessiveness	Low value.	High value. Owned each other.
Control	Low value.	High value. Male often manifestly dominant, female covertly controlling.
Jealousy	Low value.	High value. Assumed to be measure of love.
Cooking and housekeeping	Low value, or shared.	Primarily valued as woman's role.
Child raising	Valued, and shared.	Valued, but seen primarily as woman's role.
Sex roles	Flexibility valued. Recognition and enjoyment of commonalities and "bisexual" nature of men and women, which they accept in themselves and empathically and vicariously enjoy in their mates.	Sharply delineated and brittle.
Experiencing one's own sexual pleasure	Highly valued by both sexes.	Moderately or highly valued by male. Little valued or expected by female.
Mutual enjoyment of both one's own, one's mate's, and "our" sexuality in a shared experience	Highly valued by both sexes. Sexual pleasure is enhanced and escalates by virtue of mutual vicarious identifications and contributions which occur, and there is a special pleasure in the creative, musical togetherness in which one and one are more than two. Competition is minimal and synergistic cooperation maximal. One's pleasure is augmented by the partner's pleasure. What pleases one pleases both.	Male enjoyed his own sexuality but not his wife's. Inequality accepted. Often valued that female was unresponsive. Wife did not enjoy her own sexuality, "did her duty" for her husband without necessarily identifying with him. Servicing, using, and mutual masturbation sanctioned. Covert or overt competition. Lack of cooperation expected.
Shared interests	High value, although respect for and appreciation of independent interests.	Low value.
Ideas and intellect	Valued in both.	Usually valued in male.
Careers	Valued in both.	Usually valued for male.
"What will people say"?	Low value.	High value.

working toward, what their feelings are, how they view matters, and what areas of their behavior they regard as open in terms of negotiation and possible change. The variables I have chosen and the relative values placed on them represent an abstraction and condensation of data obtained from a wide variety of sources. They are not the result of a questionnaire or a methodical, planned, survey that has been statistically tabulated by computer. Rather, they come from my active interest in the subject over many years, from my omniverous reading of thousands of scientific and popular books and articles on the subject, from countless conferences, from my practice and clinical research in psychoanalysis and family therapy, from midnight "bull sessions" with friends and colleagues, from my family, and from my personal experience. To list the numerous pertinent books and articles on this subject that come to mind as I write and the various salient points presented in each, or to give illustrative vignettes or statistical percentages of how many people placed such and such a value on such and such a variable, or to list only a few of my favorite writings, is not my intention in this chapter.

At the risk of being criticized on the basis that the variables chosen and the values placed on them in the following table are "just one man's opinion," I have simply listed them. I leave it to the reader and to time to judge their validity and their durability. The list is not exhaustive, and I make no claim that the description of attitudes about these variables is universal or unchallengeable, or that there are not overlaps and/or exceptions. However, I believe this table conveys the essence of a definite change in how marriage is viewed today versus how it was viewed yesterday by a vocal segment of the American population, and that both marital values and customs are changing.

THE ADDITIONAL INFLUENCE ON MARRIAGE OF CHANGES IN THE SYSTEMS OF POLITICS AND TECHNOLOGY

As mentioned earlier, any study of marriage must take into account the resultant effect of multiple, interpenetrating systems in our living kaleidoscope. Marriage has been affected not only by changes in the field of psychology, but also by the political and technological changes that have occurred in our world in recent years which have taken the form of what might be called mass movements. The changes in the systems of psychology, politics, and technology all have to do with freedom, but the freedom in each system is of a different order from that of the others. Whereas psychology, through the exploration of the unconscious and the lifting of repression, has freed people in terms of autonomy and power over their internal organization, changes in the political system have given them external freedom from oppression and from others' power over them.

Changes in the technological system have given people instrumental ways and means of using the power that has been made available to them via both internal (psychological) and external (political) freedom. Change in any one of these open systems affects the others.

A special point should be made about changes in the technological system, for these changes have distinctive characteristics in regard to their subject matter, timing, integration, and consequences. Changes in the psychological and political systems involve human emotions, concepts, relationships, values, and wisdom and occur relatively slowly, thereby providing time for reflection, discussion, negotiation, balancing, and integration at a pace compatible with man's capacity for creative adaptation relative to marriage in particular and to life in general. Changes in the technological system, however, involving increased knowledge of living and nonliving matter, and of concretely evident physical facts, often occur abruptly and in a seemingly discontinuous manner. They come on the scene as a surprising event, forcing a change in the entire organization of life. They give people increased power, extend the scope and length of life, and speed up life, often at a rate exceeding people's capacity to adapt, both socially and in marriage. Knowledge without wisdom can sometimes lead to a "push-button" exercise of freedom rather than to a creative turbulence resulting in constructive integration and resolution.

Later in this chapter I will discuss some specific changes in technology that have altered American family life dramatically, enhancing the opportunities for the "good life." They have also, however, offered the opportunity for avoidance of time-consuming conflict resolution, and the fostering of unrealistic expectations and omnipotent postures in human marital interaction.

The diagram on the following page schematically illustrates the interplay of marriage and marital partners with various elements or mass movements in the psychological, political, and technological systems.

The first mass movement I wish to discuss occurred during and after World War II when millions of marital partners experienced prolonged separation and many women were widowed. Separation and loss and the needs of war required and offered the opportunity for increased female independence and responsibility at home, in the work force, and in the military, as well as the need and opportunity for extramarital experiences. Males away from home similarly experienced extramarital relationships, more so than their wives and often with partners from cultures quite different from their own. Both men and women lived in fear, and the possibility of a life cut short heightened the importance of the pursuit of romantic love above other values they had been taught and lived by. Their experiences further changed them. The marital reunions following the war were often between two people both of whom or only one of whom had changed. Husbands and wives felt and expressed ambivalence, con-

FIGURE 1 Diagram of Interacting Systems

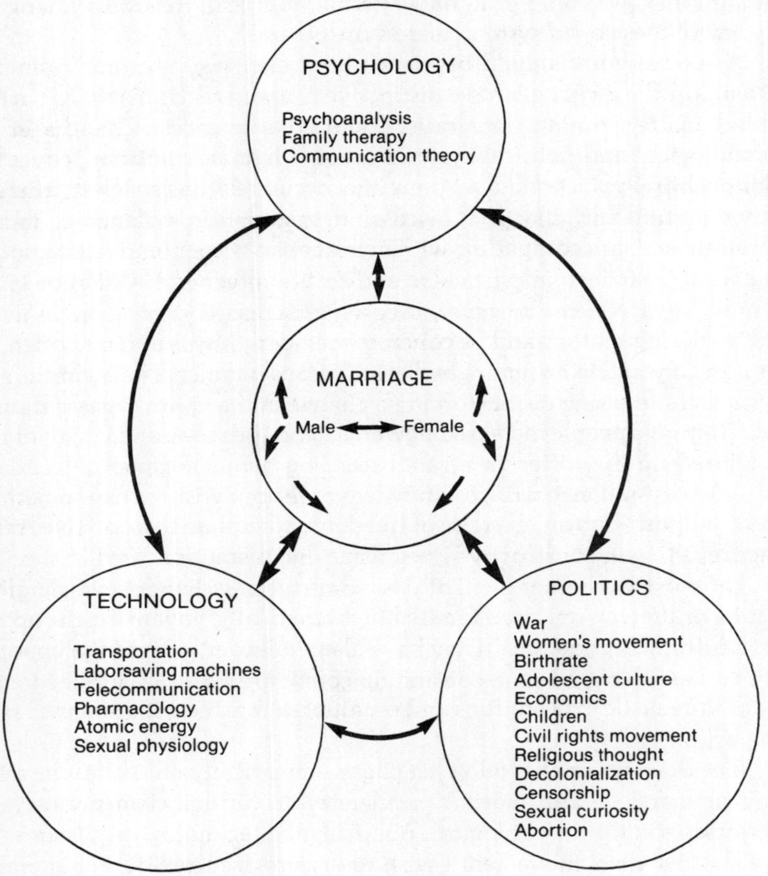

flict, guilt, and recriminations around many of the marital variables listed earlier, and the marriages that could not handle change began to deteriorate or fall apart.

The women's liberation movement gained momentum as women, partly deriving from their involvement in the work force during World War II, became increasingly mobile, moved more into insisting on and enjoying careers of their own, and pursued advanced education. Coincident with this, women experienced a sense of mastery, competence, economic independence, and a broadening of cultural awareness in college and in the marketplace. This autonomy and social freedom led them to expect more in marriage and to give more as well—in relationships of equality rather than dependency. As an outgrowth of this movement, the legal changes which have minimized the difficulty of obtaining an abortion have had far reaching consequences in our society.

Another mass movement that occurred and ultimately affected marriage was the worldwide, 50 percent increase in the birth rate following World War II. These children, possibly spawned out of anxiety about destruction of the world and the atom bomb, began to shake up the world when they arrived on the scene as 17-year-olds in the 1960s opposing the Vietnam war, pollution, male chauvinism, and conscienceless avarice. They espoused freedom, got "high" on drugs, challenged established authority, poked holes in hyprocrisy, and saturated the air with new songs of love and sex. Although some of them, as bound delegates (Stierlin, 1976, 1978), became terrorists and traitors, and some sense of maleness and respect for rational authority may have been temporarily lost, their influence, particularly through their music (lyrics, harmony, melody, and rhythm combined) on society's values regarding love, sex, romantic love, and marital patterns has been enormous. Many of these children did not expect to be alive today.

The economic factors operative in our mélange of psychological, political, and technological variables is complex in origin and effect. Affluence gives people the power to buy what they want and need in services and goods so that they can enjoy their personal lives more. Ideally, both men and women work not solely for money but for personal fulfillment as well. With the increased number of women working, one might expect a happier equality in the marital partnership and more time and leisure for romantic love. However, the tail can lead the dog. Some men, and now more women, work in jobs they do not like because they must in order to have the basic necessities of life rather than for the joyous anticipation of having the finer things in life, personal fulfillment and time and energy for romantic love.

In either case, taxes, inflation, child care costs, unexpected political and technological changes, the media's creation of artificial needs, and the time and energy involved in earning money can sometimes keep people enslaved by the struggle for economic survival or the burden of maintaining a high lifestyle. Working in this fashion can erode any potential gains in the area of time and energy for personal fulfillment, leisure, and romantic love. Although not having enough money can cause difficulties in a couple's creation and enjoyment of their marital relationship, sometimes too much money can also cause problems. Money can be used by either spouse as a means of avoiding resolution of a marital conflict, or it can be used by one or both spouses in the pursuit of ephemeral, relatively meaningless, or extramarital activites.

Changes in children and childhood (and not just those in the adolescent population mentioned earlier) also affect marriage today. In our TV world children have become more sophisticated and self-reliant, and can mobilize marital conflict constructively. Ideally, children who are raised in a "marriage-centered," better-educated, healthier, and smaller family than in the past are unlikely to drain libido from a marriage; rather, they support the marriage and enjoy a family image which they see as a model for themselves as future adults. However, if children are unfairly neglected or unable to adjust, they can destroy their parents' pursuit of adult fulfillment and romantic love and remain on the scene as casualties, poor prospects for marriage. The sometimes "disappearance of childhood," and the unprotected, excessive, or premature exposure to the same psychological, political, and technological changes impacting on their parents, can create problems in children which adversely affect their parents' marriage, and impede their own attainment of the kind of marriage for which parents are striving.

Three additional mass movements, pertinent to our subject of changes in marital patterns, have had at their center a concern for autonomy, equality, respect for personhood, and freedom from oppression, prejudice, and tyranny: the civil rights movement, changes in religious thought, and the dissolution of colonialism. The emergence of blacks to positions of prominence in American life, decisively communicated by Martin Luther King, Jr's. march from Selma to Montgomery, was not only important to blacks. The civil rights movement challenged hypocrisies in religious and civil life, and many women saw in that movement a parallel to their own struggle for emancipation. It also represented an intolerance of the defensive use of prejudice to shore up a pseudomasculine posture by a certain sector of the white male population, and sexual inhibitions in correspondingly fastidious and "pure" sectors of the white female population.

Changes in religious thought, exemplified by Buber's *I and Thou* (1937), Tillich's (1960) *Love, Power and Justice,* Taylor's (1954) *Sex in History,* and Robinson's (1964) *Christian Morals Today,* redefined man's relation to man and to his God by emphasizing the importance of the individual, the importance of love, and the retrieval of sexuality from the realm of sin. In defending *Lady Chatterley's Lover,* Robinson sought to portray the sex act as something sacred, "in a real sense, an act of holy communion."

The last of these three mass movements was the dissolution of colonialism, perhaps most vividly evident in the work of Gandhi. Although Gandhi's ideas on celibacy sound contrary to Robinson's sacred celebration of sex, and, from a psychoanalytic perspective can be seen as self-punitive and indirectly hostile to women's sexual needs, his opposition to the caste system and his and others' opposition to colonial tyranny and violence served the cause of autonomy and freedom and is part of the amalgam of variables discussed in this chapter that have contributed to the composition of contemporary marriage.

Another mass movement I want to consider is the direct insistence of the public and of scientists on the freedom to satisfy their curiosity about the physical aspects of sex. In the area of law, censorship of such books as *Lady Chatterley's Lover, Fanny Hill*, and *The Pearl* was overthrown (Kronhausen & Kronhausen, 1959) and a wide range of tasteful, as well as tasteless, explicitly sexual literary and theatrical productions titillated and educated the public and released in them a desire to experiment. Kinsey's (1948, 1953) contribution, the work of Masters and Johnson (1966), Perry and Whipple (1982), and various surveys on the sexual behavior and attitudes of American men and women came on the scene, as well as books such as *The Harrad Experiment* by Robet Rimmer (1966), *The Groupsex Tapes* by Margolis and Rubenstein (1972), and Gay Talese's (1981) chronicle of the sexual revolution, *Thy Neighbor's Wife*. Although the intense interest in sex per se seemed at times to have left love far behind and mechanics in the ascendency, sanctioned acting out rather than resolution, and caused unexpected guilt and jealousy, it nevertheless played a role in overthrowing puritanical suppression and repression and contributed to the freeing up of sexuality for expression in romantic love relationships.

Another mass movement occurred derivative from the development of antibacterial agents and the invention of the birth control pill. These technological developments gave men and women, particularly women, increased opportunity to experience sexual pleasure and romantic relationships—marital, premarital, or extramarital. Neurotic inhibitions or social prohibitions against the sharing of romantic love could no longer be rationalized by the fear of pregnancy or fear of disease; hence, those responsibly and genuinely concerned about children as well as about each other felt freer to love. That this freedom has been abused by some, and has thus debased love, does not diminish the positive aspects of this movement: more opportunity and a concomitant responsibility to attain and experience romantic love.

A major factor, interwoven into almost all the mass movements I've discussed, is the advance in technology which has facilitated physical mobility and made possible the incredibly rapid transmission of information signals. We have been thrown into what McLuhan (1964) calls "the global village," and our nervous systems have been extended beyond our bodies. As a consequence, in an unfulfilled "closeness," we have suffered both a degree of alienation from one another and from our bodies, plus a compensatory heightening of our need for what Naisbitt (1984) calls "high touch" in a time of "high tech."

Discussion and Summary

I have discussed some of the changes in psychology, politics, and technology that have impacted on marriage, and I have outlined the value changes in reference to several variables in the composition of marriage, past and present. The changes in psychology, politics, and technology have mainly to do with autonomy, freedom from tyranny and irrational authority, and freedom of movement and access to information. The origin of many of these changes is unclear, and the timing of their occurrence is debatable. The turning point would seem to have been around the mid-1960s, when many of these changes began to have a major impact and people began to realize that something was happening to them in their marriages, and that what was happening to them was happening to others as well as part of a large-scale social phenomenon. In the process many marriages fell apart, and only time will tell whether the new marriages, based on new values, will be happier and more enduring. Both John Rock (1966), father of the "pill," and Branden (1980) envision the recent turbulence, disruption, and reorganization in marriage as movement toward a more satisfying or "high" monogamy based on healthy values that are freely chosen.

The cornerstones of modern marriage are autonomy, equality, and freedom. Where we have run into trouble, however, is with our definition of equality. Even though we have come to see the value of accepting our bisexual nature, there is nonetheless truth in Freud's statement that biology is destiny. We are all still struggling with the question of what constitutes true masculinity and true femininity. If what we do with our inherent bisexuality, as a task of adolescence, is for the male to surrender his femininity to the female, and the female to surrender her masculinity to the male (Blos, 1962; Binstock, 1973), this process should not be viewed as one of dominance and submission. It is more akin to a process of quid pro quo as described by Jackson (1965) in his paper on marital rules. In a quid pro quo equality marital partners are equal but different. In the area of sexuality acceptance of this kind of equality should result in the greatest capacity for men and women to experience mutual, synergistic enjoyment of each other. Such acceptance is part of the adolescent resolution of Erikson's (1950) stage of intimacy versus isolation, occurring during what Blos (1962) has called the second individuation process, a futher refinement of the capacity to love that derives from Mahler's (1975) substages of separation/individuation, particularly the rapprochement substage.

All the changes in the psychological, political, and technological systems, all the increased freedom, and all the experimentation should lead to just this: the capacity for the intimate, loving affirmation of two selves, one by the other, one male and one female, and their mutual enjoyment of sexual expression and the quid pro quo exchanges of everyday life.

If autonomy, equality, and freedom are used in a way that detracts from the pleasure of whatever personally and mutually rewarding characteristics of masculinity and femininity we possess, either in the area of romantic love or in the quid pro quo division or balance in other areas of married life such as providing a living, managing a household, or caring for children, we may have come close to "throwing out the baby with the bath water." Many women today are lost with their newfound autonomy, equality, and freedom and many men have become what Robert Bly (Thompson, 1982) calls "soft males," out of touch with the "deep male" in themselves. The deep male, although valuing autonomy, equality, and freedom, does not want a woman who sees liberation in terms of a constant challenge to men rather than as a facilitator of intimate cooperation and sharing. And today's woman is no longer interested in the soft male she previously courted. The soft male no longer finds the challenging female attractive, and the truly liberated woman is unresponsive to him.

Hopefully, autonomy, equality, and freedom, properly understood, will enhance the mutual enjoyment of masculinity and femininity and promote a positive appreciation of the quid pro quo balance in intimate male-female relationships. It would be sad if our hard-won values were to lead us to isolation, competition, meaningless sex (Gilder, 1973), and a dull sameness. It would be equally unfortunate if fear caused us to burn our books and turn back and away from a true appreciation, integration, and application of important concepts, forged over time, which could show us the way toward happier marriages and happier families in a rapidly changing world.

References

Binstock, W. A. (1973). On the two forms of intimacy. *Journal of the American Psychoanalytic Association, 21,* 93–107.

Blos, P. (1962). *On adolescence.* New York: Free Press.

Branden, N. (1981). *The psychology of romantic love.* New York: Bantam Books, Inc. (Originally published, 1980.)

Buber, M. (1957). *I and thou.* New York: Charles Scribner's Sons. (Originally published, 1937.)

Erikson, E. (1950). *Childhood and society.* New York: W. W. Norton.

Gilder, G. F. (1973). *Sexual suicide.* New York: Quadrangle/The New York Times Book Co.

Jackson, D. D. (1965). Family rules: The marital quid pro quo. *Archives of General Psychiatry, 12,* 589–594.

Kinsey, A., Pomeroy, W., & Martin, D. (1948). *Sexual behavior in the human male.* Philadelphia: W. B. Saunders.

Kinsey, A., Pomeroy, W., & Martin, D. (1953). *Sexual behavior in the human female.* Philadelphia: W. B. Saunders.

Kronhausen, P., & Kronhausen, E. (Eds.). (1959). *Pornography and the law.* New York: Ballantine Books.

Mahler, M. S., Pine, F., & Bergman, A. (1975). *The psychological birth of the human infant: Symbiosis and individuation.* New York: Basic Books.

Margolis, H. F., & Rubenstein, P. M. (1972). *The groupsex tapes.* New York: Paperback Library.

Masters, W. H., & Johnson, V. E. (1966). *Human sexual response.* Boston: Little, Brown.

McLuhan, M. (1964). *Understanding media: The extensions of man.* New York: McGraw-Hill.

Naisbitt, J. (1984). *Megatrends.* New York: Warner Books.

Perry, J. D., & Whipple, B. (1982). Multiple components of the female orgasm. In B. Graber (Ed.), *Circumvaginal musculature and sexual function.* New York: S. Karger.

Rimmer, R. (1966). *The Harrad experiment.* Los Angeles: Sherbourne Press.

Robinson, J. A. T. (1964). *Christian morals today.* Philadelphia: The Westminster Press.

Rock, J. (1966, November 5) Remarks made in annual award address. *Ninth Annual Conference of the Society for the Scientific Study of Sex,* New York.

Sonne, J. C. (1967). Entropy and family therapy. In G. H. Zuk & I. Boszormenyi-Nagy (Eds.), *Family therapy and disturbed families.* Palo Alto: Science and Behavior Books.

Sonne, J. C. (1979). Entropic communication in families with adolescents. *International Journal of Family Therapy, 1,* 276–289.

Sonne, J. C. (1980a). The psychological family and family image construction in unrooted children. *Family Therapy, 7,* 255–284.

Sonne, J. C. (1980b). A family system perspective on custody and adoption. *International Journal of Family Therapy, 2,* 176–192.

Sonne, J. C. (1981). Transference considerations in marriage and marital therapy. In G. P. Sholevar (Ed.), *The handbook of marriage and marital therapy.* Jamaica, NY: Spectrum Publications.

Sonne, J. C., Speck, R. V., & Jungveis, J. E. (1962). The absent-member maneuver as a resistance in family therapy of schizophrenia. *Family Process,* 7, 44–62.

Sonne, J. C., & Swirsky, D. (1981). Self-object considerations in marriage and marital therapy. In G. P. Sholevar (Ed.), *The handbook of marriage and marital therapy.* Jamaica, NY: Spectrum Publications.

Stierlin, H. (1976). The adolescent as delegate of his parents. In S. C. Feinstein & P. Giovacchini (Eds.), *Adolescent psychiatry: Vol. 4,* (72–78). New York: Jason Aronson.

Stierlin, H. (1978, November). *Families of terrorists.* Paper presented at 10th Annual Conference of the Family Institute of Philadelphia: Troubled Children, Troubled Families, Philadelphia, PA.

Talese, G. (1981). *Thy neighbor's wife.* New York: Dell Publishing.

Taylor, G. R. (1970). *Sex in history.* New York: The Vanguard Press. (Originally published, 1954.)

Thompson, K. (1982, May). What men really want: A New Age interview with Robert Bly. *New Age, 6*(10), pp. 30 plus.

Tillich, P. (1960). *Love, power and justice: Ontological analyses and ethical applications.* New York: Oxford University Press.

TWO

The Role of Romantic Love in Marriage

Thomas F. Fogarty, M.D.
Associate Director
Center for Family Learning

THE NATURE OF ROMANTIC LOVE

Romantic love can be described as imaginative but impractical, mysterious, and fictitious. It is exciting, adventurous, idealized, and may often be based on a short- as well as a long-lived attachment. It is a socially acceptable deception; yet, because it is a delusion, it is a form of insanity. Romantic love is a deception because it promises more than it can deliver. It is a delusion because the emotional state it represents does not exist.

People tend to react to situations in two kinds of ways—with feelings or with emotions. *Feelings* are predominantly based on "how I feel about you," on the reaction of one person to another. *Emotions* are primarily reactions to "how I feel about me," my own personhood. Romantic love might be called a feeling rather than an emotion because it has more to do with how one feels about the other than "how I feel about me." The intensity of feeling is directed outside self, into other, which helps to avoid the emptiness inside self. The focus is on the other.

Romantic love contains strong elements of *fusion* as one person blends into the other. There is little sense of where I begin and end, an absence of space between self and other. A pain in you is a pain in me. Everything is taken personally; if you go to a movie you are leaving me. In fusion we strive for a sense of togetherness and a longing to be one and complete.

We are, *we* do, *we* feel. Love songs are full of the words of romantic love. "We can build a stairway to the stars." "Heaven is being with you." (But does your mother have to come along?) "When I love, I smile." "Smoke gets in my eyes." "The feeling is indescribable." "I hurt when you hurt." "I can't live without you." All of these expressions of feeling—of reactivity to the other—are an attempt to capture the spirit of romantic love. They try to express the hope for fusion, for the sense of completion and oneness that is simply a human feeling, a universal want.

But wishing for such fusion, while understandable, leads to the opposite—distance—as well as to all the problems that clinicians hear every day: "He doesn't listen." "She makes assumptions." "He tells me what to do." "She wants me to be her father." "She is frigid and demanding." "He turns me down sexually." Eventually, neither member of the couple feels loved, at which point we have the beginning of the death of romantic love.

"I can't live without you" is a promise whose death leads to disappointment, resentment, anger, bitterness, blame, and self-righteousness. A desire that is felt as a need does not die easily because a need does not want to become a want. Romantic love does not want to capitulate to the art of loving. Hence, the desire for fusion is fueled by hope, hope that all the forces in our culture want to hear. As long as there is the hope that romantic love is possible over time, that there is something outside of the self that will make that self complete, human beings will seek fusion.

Needing one another, feeling isolated from the rest of the world, romantic lovers exist in what Erich Fromm called an "egotism à deux" (Fromm, 1956). The twosome tries to "solve the problem of separateness by enlarging the single individual into two. They have the experience of overcoming aloneness; yet, since they are separated from the rest of mankind, they remain separated from each other and alienated from themselves; their experience of union is an illusion" (p. 55).

David McWhirter and Andrew Mattison (1984), in *The Male Couple*, describe their theory of the development of relationships. Although they studied gay, male couples in a narrow socioeconomic setting, their findings may be useful in understanding more about the passing of romantic love in any relationship. A relationship, they believe, is a couple's symbolic offspring. Like a child a relationship grows in stages, each stage building upon the last. Growth is "spiral" rather than linear.

Stage One, which McWhirter and Mattison called the Blending Stage, is the time when romantic love is in full bloom. The partners seek to merge, each taking on those qualities of the other that they had previously felt to be lacking in themselves. One member of a male couple nostalgically remembers this phase: "It was so peaceful. We talked with our eyes. We moved with the same motions. Even when I was at work it felt like Patrick was inside me. The experience was like walking on air—calm, reassuring, I felt whole" (McWhirter & Mattison, 1984, p. 23).

Stage One couples, in the throes of romantic love, tend to focus on their similarities and to minimize or ignore their differences. In this stage each partner seems to find a reflection of self in the other—and likes that reflection. Such couples also often avoid conflict—at any price. "I even thought his squeezing the toothpaste in the middle was cute" (p. 24). Sometimes, they conflict violently and make up intensely.

Stage One is also characterized by the feeling for which Dorothy Tennov (1979) invented the term *limerence.* She coined this word to explain the "crazy in love" feeling that is so often described in poetry, prose, and song. Limerence includes obsessive thinking about the loved one, idealization of this person, extreme emotional swings, and even physical symptoms such as aching in the chest.

Limerent feelings, McWhirter and Mattison believe, should not be trivialized as meaningless and ephemeral, for they will influence the quality of the relationship for as long as it lasts. But when limerence begins to recede many couples may mistake its passing for the death of love. When we are experiencing limerence we sincerely believe the feeling will last forever. A relationship may end because of the "misleading belief that the quieting of limerence signals the end of love" (McWhirter & Mattison, 1984, p. 29).

ORIGINS OF ROMANTIC LOVE

In childhood and adolescence romantic love is a delusion to be believed. It inspires hope and keeps us going. Later, it may be a way of drawing two people together to form a couple, but it is incapable of sustaining a relationship for long.

Everybody wants to feel special and significant in the eyes of someone else. This is so even though—and perhaps because—deep down inside so few of us really believe that we *are* that special. To want the feeling of specialness is simply to be human. Yet, that we are really so important is a delusion existing in our own or someone else's mind. Thus, as romantic love fades, so does the illusion of our specialness.

Behind every romantic fusion is a fear of loneliness and a lack of self-acceptance. The lower one's self-esteem, the higher one's expectations of others are likely to be, and the more one will try and hope to get both survival needs and self-esteem from others. Since these are unrealizable expectations, they lead to great disappointments.

In a sense, romantic love may be a reaction to an inner emptiness, which is experienced as loneliness. Erich Fromm wrote that romantic lovers "take the intensity of the infatuation, this being 'crazy' about each other, for proof of the intensity of their love, while it may only prove the degree of their preceding loneliness" (Fromm, 1956, p. 4).

One's expectations of loving and being loved and lovable are strongly influenced by the parent that one has been closer to (usually but not necessarily the mother). The very closeness to that parent also breeds disrespect for him or her since the over-close parent is often a too sympathetic advocate for the child and bends the truth to protect that overcloseness. A consequence of such advocacy is that what this parent says is hard for the child to believe. When the child grows up he or she is left with expectations that come from this parent, disrespect for this same parent, and fears that he or she will turn out exactly like this parent. "I spent all my life trying to be different than my mother and here, at the age of 40, I end up screaming and behaving just like her."

As people grow and become aware of their emptiness, they often don't realize that it is connected with the parent they were more distant from, usually the father. Their emptiness is connected with this relationship, the one they feel they never had, the love that was never experienced. Often that distant relationship was accompanied by respect but was lacking in love. Those periods of emptiness experienced in the middle phase of the process of adult loving are profound, individual experiences which make one question the purpose and value of marriage, love, life, children, and family.

One woman said, "I grew up understanding that I could depend on my family. After my parents died I wanted to depend on my husband. Then I was devastated and realized that my husband would never be my parents. So I withdrew, alone. I reached out to others but it did not work. There was no peace, even in prayer. I turned away from people. No one seemed to have what I wanted."

From the perspective of transactional analysis, romantic love is the adolescent state, evidenced by statements such as: "You and I will create a world that is different from any before us. And we will do it together." Romantic love, like the adolescent, denies the helplessness of a child and lacks the maturity of an adult. It denies the fact that I see my spouse as a parent and as an equal at the same time; I want you to be my father/lover.

So many unmet needs are invested in romantic love that its death can be a devastating experience. As we feel it die we ask ourselves: Was it all imaginary? Was it a fantasy, an infatuation, an obsession? Was this a promise from my parents, from my family, from my culture, which will never come to be?

Romantic love is an expression of a hope. It feels delightful when it works, devastating when it doesn't. It can fling an exalted lover into the heavens of joy one day and into a whirlpool of despair the next. The feelings it arouses are excruciatingly real, but ironically they are based upon a fiction. Romantic love has little to do with real individuals. It is a drama played out by two characters who exist primarily in one another's imagination.

Romantic love has often been understood as a function of sexual feelings. Freud told us that the amount of "love" we experience is a function of our level of "aim-inhibited instincts of affection" or repressed libido (Freud, 1959, p. 44). Indeed, he went so far as to state that:

> If the sensual impulsions are more or less effectively repressed or set aside, the illusion is produced that the object has come to be sensually loved on account of its spiritual merits, whereas on the contrary these merits may really only have been lent to it by its sensual charm. (p. 44)

Yet the very sexuality in a relationship may have been a poor substitute for, and at worst killed off the possibility of, connectedness.

A couple may have frequent sex as a result of the driving need to merge, to fully *know* the other (think of the biblical meaning of the words *to know*). Sex at first helps a couple to strengthen their bond. McWhirter and Mattison feel it creates a vulnerability that is useful in breaking down emotional barriers so that a couple can begin their pairing. "Merger has its most tangible expression in sexual union, and limerence finds its fulfillment in making love" (McWhirter & Mattison, 1984, p. 35).

But people may use sex to express all kinds of feelings, wants, and needs other than love, yet label their feelings love. Berscheid and Walster (1974) developed a two-part theory to explain romantic love. They believe that a state of intense *physiological arousal* (including but not limited to sexual arousal), combined with *situational cues* that suggest "passionate love" as an appropriate label for this state, will lead to the illusion of love. Their ideas, based on Schachter's (1964) studies of emotion and physiological arousal, suggest that romantic love may be at least in part a product of our culture. Since cultural norms encourage romantic love, particularly with appropriately marriageable partners. When we feel aroused, and the signs are right, we think we're in love. Yet, as Erich Fromm said, "Sexual attraction creates, for the moment, the illusion of union, yet without love this 'union' leaves strangers as far apart as they were before—sometimes it makes them ashamed of each other, or even makes them hate each other, because when the illusion has gone they feel their estrangement even more markedly than before" (Fromm, 1956, pp. 54–55).

Thus, romantic love including fusion, limerence, and sexual interactions can help to start a union. However, it is equally capable of hurting one or both partners. Sooner or later it becomes clear that romantic love lacks consistency.

While it is a pleasant feeling, romantic love makes people terribly vulnerable and is often as painful as it is pleasurable. Some researchers have found that this "agony" may actually help to create the illusion of love. Driscoll, Davis, and Lipsitz (1972; cited in Berscheid & Walster, 1974) found that a sense of uncertainty and challenge is associated with feelings of romantic love, while trust and security lead to feelings of more stable "conjugal love." The power of obstacles is renowned in literature and history. Freud seems to be describing what might be called the "Romeo and Juliet syndrome" when he notes that:

> Some obstacle is necessary to swell the tide of libido to its height; and at all periods of history whenever natural barriers in the way of satisfaction have not sufficed, mankind has erected conventional ones in order to enjoy love. (quoted in Berscheid & Walster, 1974, p. 365)

Romantic love is a form of interpersonal attraction. But unlike the state of interpersonal liking, romantic love does not follow behavioristic principles. We tend to like someone when we are rewarded by them, but we may "love" someone who does nothing but hurt us. Berscheid and Walster point out that romantic love is not a response to *actual* rewards; rather, it is a reaction to the *fantasied* rewards we anticipate receiving from a person who exists only as an ideal image in our minds. Love defies analysis. It cannot be created but it can be encouraged or undermined.

THE RISE AND FALL OF ROMANTIC LOVE

Some general observations can be made about the course of romantic love despite the fact that from couple to couple details may vary, sequences carry their own pattern, the course of time can be one hour or many years, and the erosion may be dramatic or so gradual that it is hardly perceptible.

Because romantic love promises the universal hope for union, completion, and the loss of personal emptiness, it is, by its nature, very exciting—a hard act to follow and maintain. Over time the natural rhythm of that excitement is similar to the natural rhythm in a hysterical person. Gradually, the peaks of excitement become harder to reach, and the low valleys that follow become deeper and longer in duration.

As romance fades the opposite side of the coin appears. Given the intense atmosphere of hoped-for fusion, distance begins to replace closeness and feelings of hate and anger may replace feelings of tenderness. Hope begins to fade into hopelessness, fusion into bickering and distance, and differences become problems rather than simply matters of taste.

Romantic love demands too much. Its unreality carries the expectation that self will give to other completely and that previous relationships and interests will fade into the background. Such an emotional investment is very risky. It can lead to a sense of abandonment in one person and suffocation in the other. Eventually one person becomes the pursuer, desperately trying to maintain the fusion of romantic love, and the other becomes the distancer, protecting self from rejection. Thus, fusion leads to distance and pursuit, ending either in a breakup or in a redefinition of what loving means.

The reactive feelings of romantic love fight for their lives in the face of reality, which dooms those feelings. The time involved in this transition and inner conflict may vary. Distractions abound. These include raising small children and taking care of the many material requirements of the beginning family. Some couples are blind to the demise of romantic love until they have a child. Others expend time and energy disagreeing over the children as a way to avoid confronting each other. Still others are so busy that they do not feel the death of romantic love until the children have grown and left the nest.

Romantic love makes life seem so simple, so clear. Our goals are to get married, have children, pay for the car, get an education and a career, buy a house. The struggle to accomplish these goals may be easy or difficult, accomplished with or without problems. But, even if these goals are attained, they do not substitute for the promise of fusion. They do not deliver what they promised. They do not fill up the gnawing emptiness inside self. Something is missing.

When romantic love collides with reality, as happens when two people live together and, for example, he finds out that she snores or she learns that he slurps his coffee, then "being in love" makes contact with learning how to love. As romantic love and reality come together the hope and promise of fusion become vulnerable. Romantic love tends to be conditional as evidenced by the "if" syndrome: "I will if you will," which often implies, "I won't if you won't." The result can be a paralysis in which one waits for the other to make the first move. Pride and stubbornness override love, and protection of self becomes more important than risk taking.

As the excitement of romantic love wears off, more basic patterns of thinking, feeling, and behaving emerge and dysfunctions of varying severity appear. The issue of responsibility becomes confused with blame. Efforts to forget or forgive become more strained, and the hope that one can change the other stifles acceptance. Over time, small talk begins to die out and be replaced by unresolved arguments and issues, disagreements over responsibility, accumulated resentments, and carefully nurtured hurts. Confusion often results.

We may begin to perceive the hope for romantic love, which is *our* self-deception, as deception by the other. Stated differently, our self-deception is projected onto the other person: "He never told me about this part of himself." "I thought she would be different after marriage." "My parents warned me about in-laws, but I felt mine were different." "Before we married he pursued me but now he is indifferent to me."

As the delusion fades in the face of reality and living experience, people struggle for balance, and the fun, good nature, and good humor of the relationship disappear. The couple may lose its sense of humor, become too rigid, too serious, too problem oriented and pessimistic. There is greater reactivity and hypersensitivity to the hurt, to what the other is or is not doing. This intense focus on self or other leads to less freedom to be oneself, to laugh at oneself. The very lifeblood of the relationship seems to be disappearing as boredom and duty replace enthusiasm.

Love becomes a serious business as each partner runs from inner emptiness and renews the hope for fusion. Some may try to lower their expectations of what they "need" from others. But then they ask, "Why stay connected if I can't expect this from you?" It is as if getting something from the other equals love.

As the emptiness in self becomes more and more covered by protective walls of withdrawal, anger, or substitution, a person experiences a growing sense of doom. As the relationship appears to die, it feels like being at one's own funeral. Even fantasy takes on a gray coloration as it tries to survive and escape a person's sense of being unlovable. One may say: "What a fool I was to fall in love." "Why can't I love like others seem to do?" "If you leave me, you will regret it."

This inner death is very difficult to understand. Faced with confusion, we tend to concretize that which we do not understand. Feeling lonely, one will accuse the other of being overinvolved with extended family or with work. Faced with anxiety and depression over the feeling of inner death, one may develop psychosomatic symptoms and become the identified patient or "physically sick member of the family."

Ghosts of the past intrude on the twosome, making the picture even more complicated because it now involves others. "I wanted to be a different mother from my own mother and yet I find myself doing the same things." Wife speaks to husband and sees her father perched on his shoulder, laughing and saying, "You thought you could get away from me. But look, you married a man just like me."

One's picture of romantic love may be strikingly influenced by family history. The way the child views the father, the way the child's mother views her husband, may affect the way the grown child sees his or her spouse. Trying to escape from or stay stuck in the past, trying to ignore the influence of extended family, we allow romance to linger long after it is really dead.

As these and other complexities intrude on romantic love, one wonders if one is still a child wanting to be cared for, an adolescent struggling for freedom, or an adult, whatever that is. Disappointment in self or spouse is complicated by the unending hope of fusion and by faulty advice from others.

It becomes clear that when we marry, we do not get away from or leave behind the legacy of the past. Marriage is not a green pill that will take that memory away. The imprint of the extended family is brought into the marriage. It is experienced as pressure to be like the family of origin or to be different from them.

Romantic love is seen as a unique relationship between two people. Actually, when we marry another, we marry, to some variable extent, that person's past and the people he or she came from and grew up with. Romantic love, in its ardent desire for togetherness, tends to see values, expectations, wants, and needs as being negotiable due to its aura of "because we love each other, all will be solved." There is little appreciation that these beliefs from the past are almost imprinted on the bones of each individual and romantic love will not modify them. One must begin to see one's spouse not as an isolated episode but as a point in history.

In romantic love the couple tries so hard to be close that it ignores the reality of a system of people that is much larger, much more influential than the two of them. They try to be so close that they don't see or know each other, and seeing only what they want and hope to see, they miss the overview. By losing that overview a twosome tries to be everything to each other. Extended families and old friends lose importance. The world becomes a twosome. After all, if two can become one who needs anybody else?

Yet within this insulated nest, everything becomes too important; hence, small issues tend to be magnified. The painful reality of the separation of self from other becomes apparent. A person thinks, "I can get close, but not close enough. I cannot get inside your skin." "If only I could walk into your eyes and close the lids behind me, and leave all the world outside" (Peele, 1976, p. 77). This kind of desire is not loving but mutual addiction.

In an ironic way the very devotion of one to the other and the hope of completion in a "we-ness" demands more than the ordinary human being can handle. Such devotion is experienced as one person giving up his or her self and transferring it to the other to preserve this "we-ness," the illusion of romantic love. The person who compromises in that way will eventually become a hollow shell, a boring piece of furniture, emotionally or physically disabled. Or he or she will stage an angry revolution that tears romance apart. As the sense of selfhood, of being respected and treated as a significant and acceptable person, is lost, the romance must either die completely, or move on to a less romantic but more caring, consistent, and substantial kind of loving. At this point each partner may go through a reevaluation by facing his or her inner self. Each asks: "What do I really want, what is possible, and do I really love the other person?"

If we focus more on our own needs, romantic love may die completely. If we focus more on our wants our love may enlarge to become the more substantial, consistent, peaceful art of loving.

THE TRANSITION TO SUSTAINING LOVE

Individuals who comprise a couple may at times find themselves out of sync. At different points in their lives each bears different levels of stress, each with different goals. Can love, as the connecting force between people, be sustained if each partner is not able to give equally? Can love become a one-way street for a time and still survive?

As we grow older our inner emotional climate, what we want, hope for, and desire, how we feel about ourselves—our emotionality—all become increasingly important. Passion and intimacy seem to be most important in early adulthood while affection and loyalty may be more highly valued in the second half of life. Romantic love is part of youthful passion. Tender affection and loyalty are aspects of an enduring love, one which can be sustaining yet can also include romance.

As romantic love dies directly or is displaced, desperate efforts are made to restore it. For example, I may feel that I have to "fix" problems in the other, to raise her up when she is down, or to react and go down with her. In this desperate desire to maintain hope and avoid hopelessness and helplessness, romantic love can progress into efforts to control its object. In the name of love, we can have an impact on others that is far beyond what we imagine, know, or even intend. These desperate efforts to perpetuate romantic love, based on a feeling of need and not want, are experienced internally as the death of fantasy, delusion, and of our very own self since they inevitably lead to failure. Soon the emotional climate in the family becomes increasingly reactive, out of control. There is no one who can come in to put out the fire. The climate becomes so hot in fact that no episode or issue can be discussed without increased anxiety, followed by argument or distance.

During this transitional period some people get "stuck" on their expectations. In trying to avoid the emptiness within themselves they continue to seek romantic fusion at the price of anger, argument, pursuit, and distance. Many twosomes get into triangles in an effort to preserve their relationship. They retreat into affairs to fill in missing pieces. One can sustain the hope of romantic love in marriage by blaming the other for the loss of that romance and by getting rid of him or her. The hope for constant romance may be perpetuated by a hysterical search for excitement, affairs, the substitution of work for people, or the popular "alternative lifestyles." Open marriage is an example of disaster caused by the search for romance. Or on the other hand, the relationship may deteriorate into a hopeless pattern of endurance, tolerance, toughing it out.

TREATMENT IMPLICATIONS

For many couples the only alternative is separation and divorce. Some may enter marital therapy. In therapy we tend to see people who are stuck in the transition period. One of the difficulties encountered by therapists is the urgency that many couples feel to accomplish, in a relatively short period of time, the same task that ordinarily requires many years—the transition from romantic love to sustaining love. The layers of bitterness may be so deep and so deeply entrenched that the transition is impossible. For some people the death of romantic love is the death of love.

Unfortunately, marital therapy can sometimes exacerbate the problem. Clinicians tend to be romanticists. They often want to help the couple make contracts and agreements so that the pair will stay together. They tend to side with the one who wants to give, be loving, and perpetuate romance. In so doing, they may ignore the value of respecting the individual, of wanting to know where each one really stands. Seeking a cure, a solution, they sympathize with one member of the couple and begin to form a negative judgment about the other.

The therapist's attitude is influenced by his or her own experiences. His or her hopes, history of loving, and desires for fusion in a relationship will affect how the couple is treated. For example, some therapists may try to restore balance, set up structural rules, and use various techniques to "solve problems." Certainly, the use of structure and techniques is important. However, if the focus remains on them, therapy becomes an endless series of dealing with episodes, one after the other, a series of "tasks" that each member of the couple has to perform, a series of behaviors to be enacted. The focus on pathology, responsibility and duty, and power and control misses the basic question: the inevitable death of romantic love and the ensuing death within the person, as evidenced by feelings of nothingness and purposelessness.

It is essential for the individual to face these feelings in order to deal with the passing of romantic love. Putting words such as *sadness, worthlessness,* and *purposelessness* to the feelings helps. Somehow, specific words enable one to "get his fingers around himself." It also helps if a person can experience feelings of being unloved slowly so that he or she can desensitize gradually to them. If people go into these feelings too rapidly, they tend to lose the ability to connect with others and they drop into despair. Once a person can survive feelings of emptiness, then he or she can begin to learn from them.

In my mind I see emptiness as a stake driven through self. It anchors self in place so that one does not bend with every breeze in life. The anchor allows one to stand for something, to be sensitive to others but not determined by their reactions. Self is the definition of what one stands for and the struggle to live up to that definition. Differentiation is knowing where self ends and others begin and dealing respectfully with both. As a person begins to learn from one's insides, the realization that he or she should not attempt the impossible task of filling in the emptiness of others begins to set in. People realize that to preserve connectedness, they must decrease their expectations of others, that suffering is a part of life, and that it is OK to cry.

As one learns from his insides while staying connected, he learns that hunger for love kills off love. He learns that he can allow others to be empty, that he must stop trying to "fix" people and solve problems, that he can listen without feeling responsible for others. He learns that one is special if he sees himself as "ordinary." This genuine humility distinguishes him. However, it must be genuine and based on living experience or it becomes a manipulation. It is not exactly true that life proceeds in sequence but if it did, it would be fair to say that one must accept (not love) self before one can love others. We are loved partly because of and not in spite of our imperfections.

Because love is inconstant, a sometimes quality, there must be a center of self, a self-integrity, a life for self, a network that allows others to move off and that avoids the suffocation—possessiveness—that drives others away. This center of self, based on emptiness, loneliness, helplessness, and hopelessness allows one to go on with one's own life without resentment because others have left. Just as love is the fuel of connectedness, hope of completion is the fuel of fusion. Emptiness is the fuel of self. As one becomes more familiar with the emptiness inside of self, these empty emotions hold the center of self and give equal respect to the center of self in others.

As one begins to experience emptiness, knowing that he can survive it, realizing from having lived it that it is a universal human experience, he begins to realize that he must have self-respect first. He finds himself talking about and using that word to himself and others. The struggle to define and live up to "what I believe in" becomes the task of many lifetimes. It becomes clear that respect is a vital ingredient of love.

Often people say, "I will respect you if, when, and after I find that I like you." This is putting the cart before the horse. Respect for a person, his time and space, is given automatically. After that it may be possible to like and then love him. Romantic love is riddled with elements of disrespect. It contains strong aspects of an urge and a belief that one person can change the other, that differences will melt away so that a fused "we-ness" can occur.

Disrespect can be subtle or gross. The operating principle of respect is to not tell another person what to do. This is a process principle in that you can't do much directly about the desire to tell others what to do, but you *can* prevent yourself from acting on that desire by refusing to make it known. Acceptance of others means not only tolerance, but also expression of genuine interest in the inner feelings and thoughts, the space and time of the other. This kind of sharing has nothing in common with the "get it off your chest" theory. One must avoid subtle demands, efforts to control, or covert threats of retribution which may be hidden in one's tone of voice or facial expression. Even silence and withdrawal, which may be an attempt at self-control, can come across as rudeness. Disrespect tends to be contagious, to spread through the system. It comes from high expectations of others coupled with the notion that "I can do it better."

Another common form of disrespect in fusion is "mind reading," where one person acts as though she knows the other's motives and purposes better than the other knows herself. To mind read in this fashion usually means ascribing negative motives to the other person. The origin of this kind of mind reading is usually hurt, which leads to anger and then to disrespect. One is protecting self from the experience of hurt by focusing on the other.

One can also use the sexual relationship to show disrespect. Sex may be so attractive that it can mask for some time the absence of a relationship. How many women have said: "He cares about me only for sex." "He uses me." "He never talks to me, shows interest, or listens to me." "After an argument, then he wants sexual relations."

One important element of marital therapy is for each partner to define clearly what he or she means by love and loving. The definition of love, what loving and being lovable means, and the experience of the death of some of these hopes, must be expressed. For example, some people may have the sense that love means that "if you love me, you will agree with me." Romantic love denies differences and accentuates agreement. Yet this is the ultimate disrespect. And in reality, wouldn't it be boring for me to be married to me?

The couple must come to see that romantic love may have been a useful way to get together but that it is not a way to stay together. If romantic love demands that one must give up a part of one's beliefs or self-respect, then it will be poorly tolerated.

Love does not exist as a discrete entity. It is an attribute of connectedness, an emotion that represents a particular form of connectedness. It is not a thing but an attitude, a quality. Love comes from the heart and is sometimes simple, sometimes long-lasting, and sometimes short-lived. Thinking about love can and often does make it complicated, so complex in fact that it never ends or never gets started. Love is not a fixed state, something that one has and owns. Rather, it varies in intensity from time to time. Because the people's insides swirl about with so many conflicting feelings and emotions, one must have some kind of theory of love or one will get lost and that theory of loving must go beyond "being in love." It must get away from a problem orientation despite the fact that problems are easier to talk about than love.

Sustaining love is an emotion and not a feeling. Thus, it is a feeling about me: It basically excludes the other person as if he or she did not exist. This is where the gold of differentiation lies; it gives me a sense of being me.

Sustaining love is not self-centered or other-focused. It contains a keen appreciation of the value to self in giving. Sustaining love does not mean giving up self, becoming a martyr or a nonperson for the sake of the other. It does not mean setting out to please the other person or not to please her. It comes from a genuine acceptance and respect for oneself "the way I am." It is not self-love nor is it selfishness and grandiosity.

"I buy my own package with my warts and limitations." Love is humble. It leads to a redefinition of what is actually good for self, a genuine lack of self-interest when dealing with the time, space, and movement of others, an appreciation that all others are different, that improvement in others brings more self to the family and to the network.

To have sustaining love, one must be able to avoid entanglement with episodes, details, and concrete words. One must not get caught in "the small stuff."

A necessary assumption for the building of sustaining love is that the *direction* of movement is more important than the *nature* of movement. It is predictable that a distant husband will emerge angry and impatient when he first starts moving toward his spouse. None of these moves will be encouraged—by wife or therapist—unless one is determined to place the direction of the move before the nature of the movement. This emphasis on direction places a keen focus on the development of a positive emotional climate, one that will encourage movement. Much of therapy approaches problems when the emotional climate in the family is full of anxiety, hypersensitivity, and self-righteousness. In that context no problem can be solved. The development of a calm, reasonable, respectful emotional climate must take precedence for love to emerge. Then many problems will simply dissolve. The couple must develop an attitude and philosophy that most things don't matter, but connectedness is something that does.

Marriage can be a seesaw. Each person is not only aware of the person seated opposite, but is also partially controlled by the movement of that person. The search for balance may temporarily calm things down. But the attempt to find balance through sensitivity to the other's position will eventually deteriorate into one person being controlled by the other.

In therapy we initially try to work toward this balance in the family. We distribute responsibility, involve everybody in conversation, respect each viewpoint, and ask for concessions. The feelings of each member are treated respectfully, as having significance.

The therapist may help to set up a balance, and then purposefully destroy it after the emotional climate has calmed down. This is done because critical mistakes in living, and in therapy, can be made at either polarity. To work on togetherness in the context of a bitter emotional climate, or to work on individuality in the absence of a calm, loving emotional climate are both risky. To tolerate is not the same as to accept. Romantic love is not the same as loving with romance. Romantic love must give way to respect for differences.

It is important for the therapist to make it absolutely clear to the couple that sustaining love acknowledges the infinite quantity of love but also recognizes its human, time limitations. It acknowledges the human fact that people function on an irregular level and are sometimes distracted by their own personal difficulties, by others, and by stress. Sustaining love allows people to be out of sync, to be inconstant and inconsistent, to realize that a husband, when at work, is more involved with his work than with his children—and that it is OK for him to be that way at that particular moment. The moments in between sustaining love are filled with an acceptance of the suffering and emptiness within self.

The elements described above are only the beginning. They can serve to calm the emotional climate in the family so that the real work of therapy can begin. If the therapy stops at that point, which it often does, the result is an adaptation which is temporary and vulnerable to the everyday stress inherent in people living together. Sooner or later the calm will again be upset by the demands for individuality, togetherness, and differentiation because the members of the twosome have not gone through the process of allowing romantic love to die, and a more substantial form of sustaining love has not been developed.

Sustaining love is a quality that cannot be earned from others. Yet, while it cannot be created, it is still partly the product of hard work. It is learned, suffered through, and worked at in order to prosper. The desire for sustaining love is natural but it is not a naturally occurring phenomenon. It is amazing how many people feel, "I have married, so that is accomplished. Now I must work at my career." Learning to love should be a growth experience, perhaps the most important in life.

Erich Fromm wrote that learning to love is like mastering a difficult art. One cannot "fall into" sustaining love; rather, one must apply emotion, knowledge, and effort. The issue on which to focus is the development of the capacity to love rather than being loved or being lovable. The art of loving demands discipline, concentration, patience; it requires humility, courage, and faith with reason. Love is an activity that must be tirelessly, endlessly practiced (Fromm, 1956). I would add that it must be there and donated.

Sustaining love has its birth in the death of fused romantic love, in the inner death that one experiences as he or she moves into emptiness, a profound, inner, individual experience of loneliness, hopelessness, and helplessness. The urge to run, to triangle, to distance, and to maintain hope outside of oneself fights with the urge to stay in the family, to endure, to sustain. If one can stay with his or her emptiness, learn to gradually survive it, and finally learn and experience wisdom from his or her insides, then one is ready for sustaining love. Such love is impossible without the experience of emptiness.

Summary

The conclusion is clear. Romance does not have to die; love does not have to die. Romantic love may draw people together but it will inevitably fade away. It serves the very useful purpose of giving people aspirations and goals, but it lacks consistency and reality. It must evolve toward a redefinition of love; toward a relationship that includes *respect* for the time and space of *self* and *other;* toward closeness without fusion; toward being with, without trying to get inside the skin of the other.

Hope is the fuel of fusion and emptiness is the fuel of self. Love is the fuel of connectedness. Romantic love is largely based on fusion and disrespect. Romantic love says one plus one equals one. Emptiness begins with the belief that one plus one equals zero. In attempting to run from emptiness, to maintain hope, to triangle, one plus one begins to equal three, four, or five. As one comes to grips with one's feelings of worthlessness, loneliness, and the inner death of hopes, one plus one begins to equal two.

References

Berscheid, E., & Walster, E. (1974). A little bit about love. In T. L. Huston (Ed.), *Foundations of interpersonal attraction* (p. 356–381). New York: Academy Press.

Freud, S. (1959). *Group psychology and the analysis of the ego* (J. Strachey, Trans.). New York: W. W. Norton. (Originally published, 1921.)

Fromm, Erich. (1956). *The art of loving.* New York: Harper & Row.

McWhirter, D. P., & Mattison, A. (1984). *The male couple: How relationships develop.* Englewood Cliffs, NJ: Prentice-Hall.

Peele, S., & Brodsky, A. (1976). *Love and addiction.* New York: Signet Books.

Schachter, S. (1964). The interaction of cognitive and physiological determinants of emotional state. In L. Berkowitz (Ed.), *Advances in experimental social psychology, Vol. I.* New York: Academic Press.

Tennov, D., (1979). *Love and limerence.* New York: Stein & Day.

THREE

Phases of Relationship Development

Daniel B. Wile, Ph.D.
California State University,
Hayward Counseling Services

OVERVIEW

This chapter examines whether relationships have purposes, whether they have phases, and whether they develop. In contrast to the common belief that dependency dooms relationships, I suggest that an important positive purpose of couple relationships in our society is to institutionalize dependency and in general to solve personal problems, correct partners' childhoods, and compensate for personal limitations. The history of a relationship (the sequence of relationship phases) is in large part an account of efforts to fulfill these goals and to deal with intrinsic relationship contradictions. For many couples the relationship does not "develop." Each stage is simply another restricted or abortive attempt to pursue these goals and to deal with these contradictions.

The critical factors in relationship development are *degree of entitlement to feelings* and *action-solutions.* Couple life-cycle transitions become a problem when they expose individuals to feelings to which they feel unentitled. Instead of confiding in their partners, and in so doing appealing to the curative potential of the relationship, individuals engage in action-solutions that often make matters worse. Rather than recognizing and talking to her husband about a momentary, mutual detachment, for example, a wife asks him whether he loves her. This action-oriented attempt to solve the problem produces a compliant response by the husband that increases the sense of detachment and thus exacerbates the problem.

Development or growth of a relationship occurs when partners experience an increased sense of entitlement to their feelings and, as a result, are more likely to confide in one another rather than simply to employ action-solutions. The ultimate goal is to engage the curative potential of the relationship, to enable partners to use the relationship to deal not only with lifelong problems but also with problems produced *by* the relationship.

Relationship phases are often viewed by couples therapists, not merely as descriptive, but as having causal significance, that is, as determining the health or pathology of the relationship. The fate of the relationship is thought to depend on the couple's or family's ability to fulfill the particular tasks of each phase and to accomplish the appropriate family life-cycle transitions; for example, to make the commitment of marriage, to deal with the birth of children, and later, to allow one's grown children to leave home. Relationship problems are thought to occur when couples fail to accomplish the required tasks and when they resist the appropriate transitions.

The effect of focusing on circumscribed stages and stage-specific tasks is to segment and to decentralize relationships. Attention is directed away from the general issues, themes, and purposes of the relationship. I believe that the couple life-cycle can more usefully be conceptualized, not as a set of discrete stages, but as a series of attempts by partners to pursue the goals of their relationship and to deal with the flaws or conflicts intrinsic to the relationship.

Relationship phases have a causal role but one that is different from and in some sense opposite to that generally conceived. Couple life-cycle transitions produce symptomatic behavior *when they expose partners to feelings that they think they should not be having.* The problem is not so much partners' resistance to couple life-cycle transitions as it is the hidden ways in which couples are already criticizing themselves for resisting (i.e., for having difficulty negotiating) their current or unfolding family life-cycle stage. Partners feel uncomfortable with or unentitled to their apprehensions about getting married, their difficulties in adjusting to marriage, their worries whether they will like their new baby, or their ambivalence about their grown children leaving home. Instead of thinking through the issues and confiding in each other about them, they engage in counterproductive action-solutions.

For example, a newly married husband may blame himself for his temporary loss of sexual interest in his wife. He fails to see this as an understandable response to a distressing and unresolved argument with her and instead views it as an indication that he does not love her, that his marriage is a mistake, or that he is unmanly, afraid of closeness, and unable to sustain a relationship. His "solution" is to force himself to engage in sex in the hope of regenerating erotic feeling. Since he is subjecting himself to a performance demand and he is not sexually aroused, he loses his erection. The result of his "solution" is an increase in the problem. He takes his impotence as further evidence that his marriage is a mistake and that he is unmanly and afraid of closeness.

Such action-solutions appear to occur to a lesser or greater degree in everyone's relationships and are my way of understanding the widespread difficulty individuals in our culture have in establishing workable and satisfying relationships. People are unable to think or talk effectively about certain important feelings, in particular those associated with couple life-cycle transitions, because they are so upset about having them and/or because previous attempts to talk just seemed to make matters worse. Instead, they engage in forced action-oriented attempts to resolve the situation. Relationships, whether functional or dysfunctional, are in large part sequences of such action-solutions.

DESTABILIZING AND RESTABILIZING EVENTS IN THE FAMILY LIFE CYCLE

The phases of relationship development are generally discussed from two points of view: how partners deal with the conflicts that emerge when the early romantic glow wears off, and how partners handle shifts in family membership or role (e.g., marriage, birth of children, children turning adolescent, children leaving home, retirement). Attention will be directed first to the latter issue (the family life cycle) and at the end of the chapter to the former.

The notion of a family life cycle (Duvall, 1971) has attracted the recent attention of family and couples therapists. The major idea, originally suggested by Haley (1973), and elaborated by Barnhill and Longo (1978), Hughes, Berger, and Wright (1978), Weeks and Wright (1979), Terkelsen (1980), and Hoffman (1980), is that symptoms occur when families are unable to make family life-cycle transitions; that is, when they have difficulty accomplishing the necessary family tasks associated with the particular developmental phase into which they are moving. Thus, a young adult arriving at the leaving home stage may develop psychotic symptoms and be unable to leave as a consequence of the wish of other family members to keep him at home.

The theory is a natural outgrowth of the systems view and in particular of the notion of family homeostasis or negative feedback. The family, having established a certain stability at a given stage, is seen as resisting changes that might threaten this stability. Family life-cycle transitions are viewed as being disorganizing and aversive to the family.

I suggest that family life-cycle transitions are as likely to be stabilizing and relationship enhancing as they are to be destabilizing and problem generating. Emptying the nest may have advantages for the partners, as several studies have suggested (e.g., Lowenthal & Chiriboga, 1972; Glenn, 1975; Harkins, 1978). A grown child's leaving home can bring an end to the family-splintering arguments that his or her presence provokes. Arguments about a child are not always simply displacements of deep-seated problems between parents.

The following account shows how each successive phase or stage in a relationship may have a destabilizing and/or a stabilizing effect. The account also provides an example of how family life-cycle stages can be viewed in part as phases in a couple's efforts to deal with central and ongoing relational conflicts. This approach contrasts with the traditional conceptualization of the family life cycle as a succession of discrete stages each with its own unique phase-specific problems and tasks.

The central flaw or problem in Joe's and Carol's relationship is, to use Fogarty's (1976) term, their *pursuer/distancer* interaction. Joe feels pressured and withdraws when Carol complains about what seems to her to be Joe's inadequate emotional involvement. Both are worried that Joe is afraid of intimacy and that Carol is a nag. Each stage of their relationship—marriage, birth of children, children turning adolescent, empty nest, and retirement (a modified version of Solomon's, 1973, five family life-cycle stages)—will be discussed in terms of this underlying conflict.

Joe's and Carol's decision to get married is in part an attempt to solve this pursuer/distancer problem. Their unspoken hope is that the commitment of marriage will increase Joe's emotional involvement and at the same time decrease Carol's insecurity and need for reassurance.

While their solution-attempt is partly successful, and they are at first relatively content with each other, the original problem soon reemerges. Joe and Carol are now even more deeply involved (since they are married) in what they begin to fear is an unworkable relationship. After briefly considering one possible family life-cycle transition, divorce, they engage in another, having a baby. The new, unspoken hope is that having a child will cement the relationship.

This solution also produces mixed results. The arrival of a baby, while not resolving Joe's and Carol's conflict, allows it to take a less acute form. The pressure of dealing with the child distracts the couple from their problem with each other, that is, their reduced sense of intimacy, which by this time has affected their sexual life. Carol's major new concern, an offshoot of her previous objection, is the insufficient time she feels Joe spends with the child, and his failure to help with household tasks.

Joe's and Carol's dissatisfactions remain in this chronic, low-key form during the birth of two more babies and throughout their children's preadolescent years. A shift takes place, however, when their children become adolescents. Carol becomes vicariously involved in the intimacy/sexuality of their children, which distracts her from and makes more bearable her lack of intimacy/sexuality with Joe. Joe, however, is affected in the reverse manner. The intimacy that he experiences with their adolescent children (much greater than what he has with Carol) and his sexual feelings toward his daughters simply make him more aware of what he is missing in his relationship with Carol.

Not knowing exactly what he is feeling or how to express it, Joe blurts out a complaint about what seems to him Carol's overinvolvement with their children and her lack of sexual interest in him. Carol is partly pleased (she had begun to think that Joe had lost all interest in her, sexual and otherwise) but she also feels unjustly criticized. She tells Joe that he is jealous of the attention she is giving their children and that he wants to be mothered along with them. Joe grunts a defense and then falls silent; he thinks that Carol might be right. His attempt to talk with her about their problems thus runs aground. Carol devotes even more of her energies to her children and Joe directs his attentions to his work.

When Joe's and Carol's children leave home the problems of their pre-children life reemerge. However, Joe and Carol are now a different couple. Their pursuer/distancer conflict, although remaining, has decreased several degrees in intensity. They have become accustomed to many of the characteristics in one another that they had earlier so detested and have even developed a fondness for some of those characteristics.

Joe's retirement brings an ironic shift. With more time on his hands Joe seeks greater emotional contact with Carol, which is what Carol always thought she wanted. Carol, who has not retired, suddenly finds herself in Joe's position—feeling pressured to express more affection and to spend more time with the other and feeling guilty about not doing so.

A purpose of this extended vignette is to suggest how family life-cycle stages can be viewed as phases in a couple's efforts to deal with the flaws or conflicts inherent in their relationship. Joe's and Carol's decisions to marry and to have children can be seen in part as efforts to solve their pursuer/distancer conflict. The birth of children, while not producing the renaissance of intimacy for which both partners had hoped, temporarily relieved the problem. Carol and Joe had other things to worry about (child care activities) and new family members with whom to be intimate. Their pursuer/distancer conflict took a new form: Carol became concerned about what she saw as Joe's failure to spend time with the family and to help with child care tasks.

The presence of young children served as partial protection against Joe's and Carol's pursuer/distancer conflict. The presence of adolescent children exacerbated the problem and turned it in a new direction. *Joe temporarily became the pursuer.* He complained about what he saw as Carol's overinvolvement with their adolescent children and her underinvolvement with him. However, when Carol defended herself, accusing Joe of wanting to be mothered, Joe adopted his usual stance and withdrew.

Joe became the pursuer in a more permanent way when he retired. He felt that he had overly limited his life by focusing so much on work and achievement. He wanted to reach out to others—in particular, to Carol. Carol, who continued working, felt pressured. This reversal of their usual problem was easier to deal with since, unlike their usual problem, it did not reflect and reinforce these partners' major, private worries about themselves, their historically based, special sensitivities. In fact, both were at least partly amused to find Carol in the position of seeking distance and Joe in the position of seeking contact. After causing severe difficulties throughout this couple's life together, the problem had finally assumed a manageable form.

THE PURPOSE OF RELATIONSHIPS

My major point in discussing Carol and Joe is to suggest that the various stages in their relationship can more usefully be viewed not as discrete causal entities but as phases in these partners' efforts to pursue the goals of *and* to deal with the flaws or contradictions intrinsic to their relationship. My aim in this and in the following section is to discuss these two aspects of relationships. The purpose of relationships is considered in this section and inherent relationship flaws are considered in the next.

The tendency of some therapists to view the goals and purposes of partners as pathological may cause them to discount these goals and purposes. Such therapists distinguish "healthy" relationships from those in which one or both partners enter a relationship to solve personal problems and to compensate for missing elements within themselves. The latter individuals are seen as seeking from each other what they should and can only provide for themselves. They are viewed as inappropriately seeking from their relationships (1) self-esteem (when they need first to learn to love themselves), (2) dependency (when a viable relationship requires an ability to be independent), (3) self-completion (when they need to fill the gaps in their personalities by themselves), and/or (4) resolution of unresolved issues with parents and siblings (when they need to recognize that their problem is with these earlier figures). McGoldrick (1980), Bergner (1977), and Fromm (1956) among others subscribe to elements of this view.

At first glance, this view seems indisputable. Relationships are continuously being destroyed by partners' inabilities to feel loved, which may lead for example to unmanageable jealousy; or by their dependent demandingness, the use of each other to compensate for personal deficiencies, and by childhood-derived conflicts.

On the other hand, relationships are often successful or partly successful in *resolving* personal problems. They are so successful, in fact, that one might reverse the above view and suggest that forming an intimate relationship might be a good way of improving self-esteem, becoming more independent, completing oneself, and working through unresolved issues with one's parents.

My point is that every relationship is founded on critical personal needs. Why else would people form long-term relationships were they not to serve important functions and to solve difficult problems?

Learning to love oneself can be a difficult task; only a lucky few are very good at it. Most people can use all the help they can get. One approach that a person can use is to form an intimate relationship with someone who does love him or her. But this effort can backfire. Doubts about one's own lovability may reemerge as unmanageable jealousy or compulsive, relationship-destroying demands for reassurance. However, in many more cases, the effort is at least partly successful. For a great number of people intimate relationships constitute an important initial step in learning to love themselves.

A major thesis of Fromm's (1956) book, *The Art of Loving,* is that *dependency dooms relationships.* I approach from the opposite direction and suggest that an important, positive purpose of marriage in our society is to *institutionalize dependency,* to establish a relationship on which one can consistently and comfortably depend. The qualities generally associated with "excessive dependency"—desperate pleas, unremitting neediness, self-centered demands, whiny complaints, helpless, longing looks—are, according to Apfelbaum (1977), manifestations of an *inability to be dependent;* that is, an inability to obtain the minimal sense of contact and comfort that anyone might need. Kris (1976, p. 85) points to an "emotional starvation, analogous to diabetes mellitus, where a metabolic block prevents the body from using its available nutrients." Intimate relationships provide a consistent source of dependency gratification to many people who never had such a source. These relationships establish the groundwork or possibility for developing the opposite capacity—independence.

Bergner (1977) questions the health and viability of relationships in which "each partner engages to a greater extent than is usual in what might be termed a search for his missing parts in the person of another" (p. 88). He gives the example of a detached, inhibited man who marries a woman because she is outgoing and spontaneous, and his emotional, disorganized wife, who marries this man because he seems organized and steady.

I view such a marriage as representative of the major motivation behind everyone's relationships. As previously mentioned, people would have no reason to engage in long-term relationships were they not to serve important functions and solve difficult problems. In an experiment conducted by Karp, Jackson, and Lester (1970), engaged women described their fiancés as being closer to their own ideal selves than they were themselves. This result suggests that these women were marrying men who they saw as having characteristics that they themselves wished to have. Dealing with or compensating for missing elements in oneself is a lifelong task, as Jung has argued. One's partner provides an external source for certain of the missing elements, and functions as a model for the eventual development of these elements within oneself.

Partners encounter difficulties, some therapists believe, when they use a couple relationship to deal with unresolved childhood conflicts; for example, when a woman who felt ignored by a detached and preoccupied father marries a man who is detached and preoccupied. Her purpose, these therapists say, is to obtain her husband's attention and in so doing, in effigy, to win over her father. Such therapists might explain Carol's marriage to Joe in this manner.

I suggest that *solving childhood problems is one of the major positive purposes of marriage.* Carol's childhood-derived problem is her attraction to men who, because they are detached and preoccupied, do not sufficiently provide important things that she wants such as attention and involvement. This factor is the flaw or dilemma at the base of her marriage as it may have been the flaw or dilemma in her childhood relationship with her father. However, she is now a grown woman with more psychological resources than she had as a child. Her present relationship with Joe provides a more favorable setting for dealing with this lifelong issue than did her earlier relationship with her father. In general, the curative potential of relationships is as likely to be underrated as it is to be overrated (Wile, 1981).

Important questions that remain typically unasked are: "Why have a relationship?" "Why bother?" "What is the goal?" The goal, I suggest, is to solve personal problems, resolve childhood conflicts, compensate for personal limitations, and fulfill fantasy-based expectations. These purposes are valid even if they are not always achievable.

INHERENT RELATIONSHIP FLAWS

A point often made by therapists who emphasize the regressive and irrational nature of partners' relationship wishes is that these wishes are often inherently contradictory. An example is a woman who wants a strong husband in order to compensate for her own sense of weakness and inadequacy, but who also wants a weak one because she feels threatened by strong, assertive men. (She was physically abused by her father.) Her attempted solution to this dilemma is to marry a man who *appears* strong (his calm, quiet manner gives the appearance of strength) but who is mild-mannered, nonthreatening, predictable, and eager to please. This woman's contradictory wishes—that her husband be both strong and weak—can be thought of as *a defining problem of the relationship.* Problems will arise when she discovers that her husband's quiet manner is an expression of fearfulness rather than strength.

Mutually incompatible requirements (that one's mate be strong and at the same time weak) would seem to preclude a viable relationship (Bergner, 1977; Sager et al., 1971). I believe that this quandary is simply an extreme form of the dilemma with which perhaps all partners must deal. The wishes that draw one person to another almost always have inherent contradictions. The history of the relationship is then in some sense the working out (or failure to do so) of problems or contradictions inherent in the particular relationship.

In support of the contention that *all* relationships (not just "pathological" ones) have intrinsic flaws and contradictions, I shall discuss three factors. First, associated with the desired characteristics of a particular partner are unavoidable, undesired characteristics. Second, each relationship inevitably has weak spots, points at which the special sensitivities or vulnerabilities of the two partners are simultaneously aroused. Third, unnoticed accusation and defensiveness, almost universal features in relationships, can generate incompatibility even on issues about which partners agree.

Unwanted Side-Products

Associated with the advantages of being married to a particular individual (what one married the person for) are *inevitable disadvantages* (what one married this person in spite of). Joe was attracted by Carol's emotional reactivity—her spontaneity, vitality, and readiness to engage. Being cautious and reserved Joe counted on Carol to provide the spark. He had difficulty, however, when Carol was emotionally reactive toward him; that is, when she complained that he was unresponsive, never initiated anything, and never told her how he felt about her. Carol was attracted by Joe's unflappability, stability, and unemotionality. She had difficulty, however, when he was unemotional about and insufficiently responsive toward her. When conditions are favorable, Guerin (1982) writes, the operating styles of pursuit and distance can "complement each other beautifully and bring out the best in both" (p. 20). When conditions are unfavorable "the very factors that provide the balance and synchrony become the problem" (p. 20). An ongoing relationship task for partners is to come to terms with the undesired side products of the qualities for which they married each other.

I believe that many couple problems typically attributed by analytically oriented authors to regressive functioning can be described instead as unwanted side effects of the qualities that originally attracted the partners to each other.

Whitehouse (1981) reports research findings that "suggest that the initial attracting quality [what draws partners together in the first place] and the most annoying quality at present [what partners like least about each other now] are related in that the latter is an exaggeration, implication, or the opposite of the former" (p. 61). Whitehouse (1982) gives an example: "A person might be attracted to the outgoing and sociable nature of another but subsequently be annoyed that the spouse is too sociable and never spends time around the house, or, alternatively, be disappointed that the spouse is not as outgoing as previously assumed" (p. 62).

Whitehouse (1981) interprets her results as buttressing "Dicks's (1967) idea about unconscious determinants of attraction; that is, that people choose someone as a spouse who possesses a quality about which they are ambivalent. They find the quality initially attractive, but later the other side of their ambivalence surfaces and they find some aspect of the same quality annoying" (Whitehouse, 1981, p. 65). The individuals are ambivalent because these qualities represent unacceptable, warded-off aspects of themselves that they have projected onto their partners.

I prefer what I believe to be a simpler explanation: A person who is attracted to someone who is, for example, dominating or dependent has the problem of dealing with the negative concomitants or undesired side effects of such a characteristic. This individual may enjoy the partner taking command of household chores and weekend plans yet object to the partner making unilateral decisions about important issues such as whether to buy a house or what car to purchase. One's partner may be dominating or assertive in both appealing and unappealing ways and one will understandably like the former and dislike the latter.

Interacting Sensitivities

Partners are often able to compensate for the periodic losses of objectivity by the other. If one has had a bad day and has little patience with relationship difficulties, the other hopefully has had a somewhat better day and can be a resource. Inevitably, however, times occur in which both partners' objectivity is at a low ebb; each may have had a bad day.

The couple interaction itself may generate a mutual loss of objectivity. Each partner behaves in a manner that arouses the historically based, special sensitivities of the other. Early losses in Carol's life caused her to experience a particular disagreement with Joe as an abandonment. Needing to arrive at a quick resolution, she pushed for continued discussion. Her reaction conflicted with Joe's equally desperate need based on his early experiences with engulfment to go off alone in order to reconstitute. The more Carol pushed, the more Joe needed distance. The more he sought distance, the more she pushed. Each partner's solution exacerbated the other's problem.

The potential for interacting sensitivities exists somewhere in the relationship between any two people. These sensitivities are weak points (or sore spots) in the relationship and no matter where these weak points are the course of events is likely to draw them into increasing prominence.

Unrecognized Accusation and Defensiveness

Accusation and defensiveness can produce conflict—even over issues about which partners fundamentally agree. Joe and Carol were equally concerned about a momentary sense of detachment between them on a particular evening. Carol, who is clearly the better observer of such relationship undercurrents, was the first to comment. If she had simply reported her feelings by saying, for example, that she noticed a sense of distance between them and wondered whether Joe noticed it also, Joe might have been grateful that she brought it up. He might have said that he was preoccupied with a problem at work, which he then might have begun to describe. In so doing he would have immediately dispelled the feeling of distance. However, as people often do in such situations, Carol expressed her feeling as an *accusation* ("How come you never talk to me?"). Joe, as people often do in response to accusations, became defensive and withdrew further. Whatever wish he might have had for closer contact was quickly superseded by his more pressing need for self-protection. These partners, who had been having identical desires for intimacy just a moment before, were now polarized.

The problem is not only that partners express feelings as accusations, but also, and even more important, that they do not know that they are doing so. This is common. Occasions inevitably arise in which individuals are provocative or defensive without knowing it. Since these individuals believe they are being reasonable rather than accusatory, they take their partner's defensive reactions as indications of irrationality, childishness, provocativeness, bad faith, and as proof that talking cannot help. Such interchanges give talking a bad name. Since these individuals are unaware of having been accusatory or defensive they think they have made a fair effort to have a discussion.

The persistence with which some partners fight, despite all the obvious counterproductive effects and despite all the therapists' efforts, can lead therapists to conclude that these individuals want to fight, that they have a vested interest in fighting. I believe, instead, that such partners are generally *caught* in the fight. Their fighting becomes understandable once one realizes the situation in which each is operating. Neither is aware of the existence or appreciates the effect of his or her accusations and defensiveness. Each believes that he or she has made strenuous efforts to avoid the fight and that the other has not, that he or she is trying to have a discussion while the other insists on turning it into a fight, and that he or she is making good points, which the other refuses to acknowledge.

The intrinsic flaws or contradictions of the relationship may be apparent from the start. Or these contradictions may be hardly noticeable at first and then gradually come to predominate. Further difficulties occur when people shift in what they want from a partner or when family life-cycle transitions bring attention to new needs. What one sought in one's partner and originally married him or her for may not be what one wants now. A "woman who chose a husband she could easily dominate often feels vulnerable at the time of motherhood and wishes for a man who can take care of her" (Haley, 1973, p. 183).

Ironically, one's partner may be instrumental in bringing about the changes that make him or her no longer desirable. Let us suppose that the woman who wanted a weak husband is at first relatively satisfied with the man she marries. His kindness and attentiveness make her less afraid, more confident, and better able to deal with the world and with men. Her marriage is in some sense an effective correction of her childhood. As a consequence of her relationship with her husband, she becomes less in need of the advantages of being married to a considerate, mild-mannered man (never feeling threatened and always having her needs and wishes attended to) and more preoccupied with the disadvantages (rarely being challenged or stimulated). Because of her husband's success in satisfying her original needs she now wants another type of man.

HAVING FEELINGS ONE THINKS ONE SHOULD NOT BE HAVING

The argument has just been made that relationships have inherent goals and inherent problems. What role do couple or family life-cycle stages play in this? *Each stage provides particular advantages and/or disadvantages in pursuing these goals and in dealing with these problems.* The birth of Joe's and Carol's children provided partial and temporary relief to the couple's pursuer/distancer conflict, the growth of their children into adolescents revived and exacerbated this conflict, and Joe's retirement precipitated a reversal of the conflict.

Two factors appear largely responsible for the ineffectiveness that partners in our society are generally recognized as demonstrating in their efforts to pursue their relationship goals and to resolve their relationship problems. The first—partners' sense of unentitlement to their feelings—will be discussed in this section with special attention given to the feelings of unentitlement associated with specific, family life-cycle stages. The second—partners' subsequent recourse to action-solutions—will be described in the next section. Examples will be presented using the case of Carol and Joe.

Life-cycle transitions become a problem when they exacerbate the underlying conflicts or dilemmas in the relationship and expose partners to feelings that they think they should not be having. A clear example occurred just before Carol's and Joe's wedding. As they approach their wedding day many people fear that their marrying might be a mistake. This problem can often be dealt with by realizing that such worries are common and that one's partner may be having them also. Joe and Carol did not have this advantage. Joe's view of himself as afraid of closeness and as unwilling to make commitments made him think that his sudden doubts about marrying were feelings he should not be having, manifestations of deep-seated character flaws. He feared that these feelings indicated that he might never be able to make a commitment to anyone. Carol was self-critical about her own hesitations regarding marriage. Having worked so hard to convince Joe to marry her, she was unnerved by the presence of doubts within herself.

Joe's and Carol's alarm over these feelings prevented them from confiding in each other about them, so both proceeded as if they were not having them. Joe was worried that Carol would become upset if she knew he was again having doubts. Carol felt a responsibility to appear as if she had no doubts. Having pressed Joe to get married, she felt unentitled to have second thoughts. She worried that any doubts in her might restimulate Joe's ambivalence.

Joe's and Carol's rejection of their own and each other's reactions, their belief that they were having feelings they should not have been having, led to polarization and prevented them from recognizing their underlying commonality. Instead of talking about their feelings Joe and Carol acted on them. Carol's way of dealing with her doubts about marriage was to seek increased contact in an effort to reassure herself that she and Joe really loved each other and that marriage was a good idea. Her reaction was diametrically opposed to Joe's way of dealing with his doubts, which was to seek increased time alone in order to mobilize his resources. Both reacted as they wished the other would react to them. The resulting pursuer/distancer escalation nearly led to a cancellation of the marriage.

There were many other examples of how Joe's and Carol's discomfort with or disqualification of their feelings prevented them from being resources for each other. A major problem in the first several months of their marriage was Joe's interfering mother. (Solomon, 1973, and Barnhill & Longo, 1978, define the initial relationship task as making a commitment to one's partner and breaking away from one's parents.) Here again the problem was Joe's and Carol's inability to confide in and be resources for one another.

If Joe had been able to confide in Carol he would have told her that he was upset about his mother's interfering in their relationship and that he hoped Carol would do what he did and simply ignore his mother's behavior. If this became impossible to do (he knew his mother could be hard to take) he wanted Carol to know that his commitment was to her and that he would always take Carol's side against his mother. Such statements would have been likely to elicit positive responses from Carol and to have led to their working together on the task of dealing with Joe's difficult mother.

However, Joe did not confide in Carol. The reason, paradoxically, was that he felt guilty about exposing Carol to his mother and he believed that dealing with his mother should have been entirely his responsibility. Instead of talking with Carol he sought an immediate solution. He tried to persuade Carol to ignore his mother's offensive behavior. Joe's attempt to save Carol from any part of the burden of dealing with his mother had the effect of placing *all* the burden on her. Carol's response was to feel that Joe did not appreciate her feelings about the matter and was not on her side. The effect was thus the opposite of the one Joe had wanted. Joe now had two women with whom he was having trouble. The situation (or rather, Joe's reaction to the situation) had turned Carol into another difficult person with whom to deal.

The next family life-cycle transition, the birth of a first child, has its own potentialities for arousing feelings that partners think they should not be having. Expectant parents can worry that there is something wrong with them if they find themselves feeling less excited about having a child than they think they should be. Joe's concern expressed itself in indirect ways. In speaking about the expected child Joe occasionally slipped and referred to it as "your" rather than "our" child, which hurt Carol's feelings and led to arguments.

These partners did not recognize that Joe's remark was in part an expression of (or rather, a result of Joe's effort to not express) a common worry. Joe had the concern, which many parents-to-be have, that he might not love the child enough, might not be an adequate parent, and might be unable to meet the demands of having an infant in the house. If Joe had been able to express this worry Carol might have had the opportunity to confess that she had similar concerns about herself. The opportunity to air this worry and the awareness that *both* were apprehensive might have enabled them to realize that they were experiencing a common or even inevitable apprehension.

Philip and Carolyn Cowan (in press) studied the effects of the first child on a couple's relationship. They found that problems occur when partners feel unentitled to their feelings or complaints. A husband who feels left out and jealous because he cannot participate in the major means of relating to a newborn infant—breast-feeding—may be ashamed of such feelings and may try to talk himself out of them. He does not confide in his wife about these feelings but instead withdraws. She is likely to respond to his withdrawal by becoming even more involved in caring for the new baby and by resenting his lack of involvement. The Cowans provided group experiences in which partners were able to express (and to feel justified in having) their previously warded-off feelings and complaints. Preliminary findings showed that partners who participated in these groups had a lower incidence of separation/divorce and reported a higher degree of marital satisfaction in contrast to couples who did not participate in such groups.

Perhaps the most widely discussed family life-cycle transition problem is parents' reputed unwillingness to allow their children to become independent and leave home. Parents are seen as double binding their children and in other ways subtly undermining the childrens' efforts toward independence.

Much of the problem here too may be partners' rejection of their feelings. If parents believe that they should unambivalently support their children's leaving home and that it is not OK to have reservations or mixed feelings, these feelings are likely to emerge in insidious forms. If a mother is unable to say to herself and to her son that she wishes in some ways that he would stay home, even though she knows it's best for him to leave, and that she is a little concerned about how life will be without him, she may be forced to experience and express these feelings in indirect, offensive ways. She might insist on doing his laundry even though he has moved out and lives far away, interfere with the setting up of his apartment, or keep his room at home exactly as it was as if expecting that he will soon return.

The double bind can be understood as a consequence of having feelings one thinks one should not be having. A mother who believes she should not have any negative feelings toward her son may be doomed to act them out; for example, she may call him over to kiss her and then turn away—a classic example of the double bind. A father who feels he should not enjoy his daughter's dependence on him may act out his conflict by telling her she should be independent and then reminding her that since it is raining she should wear her boots. These parents are not necessarily malevolent, controlling, or narcissistic, although their behavior may produce this impression. The major problem is their belief that they should not be having what are essentially ordinary feelings: occasional anger at one's child and occasional enjoyment of the child's dependence. Similarly, Joe's mother's interference in the early stages of his marriage may have been in part a result of her belief that she should not have been feeling as she was—a little jealous and a little left out.

Divorce and/or remarriage have their own potential for generating feelings that partners think they should not be having and with which they do not know how to deal. A man who had been divorced for several years called his eight-year-old daughter who lived with his ex-wife and asked if she wanted to go for ice cream. This behavior was provocative: Taking his daughter for ice cream interfered with his ex-wife's plans and violated his agreement that all visits with his daughter would be prearranged.

The father's invitation to his daughter was his response to a new stage in his relationship with his ex-wife. She had just decided to remarry. Suddenly confronted with this fact, the ex-husband realized that his relationship with his ex-wife was really over, that his half-hoped-for reunion with his wife and daughter was never to take place, and that he was to be cut off permanently from everyday contact with his daughter. Taking his daughter for ice cream was an action-solution, a desperate effort to try to maintain everyday contact with his daughter.

The problem from one point of view was this man's inability to experience his feeling of loss directly or to appeal to his ex-wife as a resource. If he had been able to tell her about these feelings, she later said, she would have been able to tell him that she felt a similar sadness. She too had maintained a fantasy hope that somehow they would all get together again, and she too was unhappy about their daughter losing everyday contact with her father. Since he was unable to verbalize his feelings he had no choice but to act on them. And his manner of doing so alienated his ex-wife. As one might imagine, the inability of these partners to be resources to one another and their subsequent recourse to impulsive actions were in large part what led to their divorce in the first place. Life-cycle transitions become problems then when they expose partners to feelings that they think they should not be having or when, for this or any other reason, they prevent people from confiding in or being resources for one another.

The purpose of this section was to trace couple problems to partners' sense of unentitlement to their feelings. The purpose of the next section is to show how this sense of unentitlement leads to action-solutions that typically make matters worse.

ACTION-SOLUTIONS

Certain relationship flaws or conflicts may be insurmountable. A woman who discovers she wants an assertive, spontaneous, and intellectual husband may be unable to content herself with her inhibited, predictable, and nonverbal one. An individual who comes to the decision that he or she definitely wants children may be unable to make an accommodation to a partner who definitely does not want them.

In the majority of cases that I have seen, however, the major difficulty is not a couple's relationship flaws or conflicts in themselves. The problem is rather how partners deal with these flaws and conflicts and in particular how they do and do not think and talk about them.

I do not mean to imply that couple problems would immediately be resolved if partners would only try to talk to each other about their feelings. If feelings are stated as accusations, as they often are, the accused is likely to become defensive and/or angry. Joe's belief that he was wrong to be jealous of his wife's involvement with their children caused him to withhold this feeling and then to blurt it out as an accusation.

My emphasis on partners' sense of unentitlement suggests that the major problem in couple relationships is self-blame or self-criticism. How does this correspond to the fact that a major, or even *the* major, problem of partners is generally thought to be blaming *each other?* My answer is that sense of unentitlement to one's feelings (i.e., self-blame) typically leads to blaming the other. Joe's discomfort with his feeling of jealousy (or more precisely, his feeling that he should *not* be jealous) prevented him from thinking through and talking about this feeling and led to his sudden accusation of Carol: "You are overinvolved with the children." This accusation was an impulsive and desperate attempt to get her to cease the behavior that had precipitated his jealous feelings.

Carol responded to Joe's accusation with a counteraccusation. She told him that he was like another child demanding mothering from her. Joe had no answer for this and fell silent. He felt she was right about him. Joe's effort to talk thus led not to clarity but to a reaffirmation of the self-critical views that had made him hesitant to talk in the first place.

Stating feelings as accusations is only part of the problem. Even if Joe had expressed his feelings directly and had not turned them into accusations, Carol might still have responded in an invalidating manner. If, for example, Joe were to have said, "I feel ashamed about it, but I'm a little jealous about your closeness with the kids," Carol might have agreed that he should be ashamed and that she thought his feelings were immature, inappropriate, and irrational. Carol's failure to recognize his feelings as ordinary and understandable would thus have reinforced Joe's self-criticism and would have prevented her from being a resource to him on this issue.

The common factor in all these examples is disqualification of feelings (Haley, 1959). Joe disqualifies his feelings (feels unentitled to them) and then, in a sudden outburst, expresses them as accusations. Or Joe states these feelings directly and Carol disqualifies them. The result, in either case, is that one or both partners becomes understandably hesitant to talk in the future.

Disqualification of one's own and/or one's partner's reactions prevents partners from thinking effectively about their problems and from being resources to one another and leads to *action-solutions*, the second major factor responsible for couple problems. Action-solutions (Wile, 1983, in preparation) are strained, desperate, action-oriented, compensatory, and correction-seeking efforts that often compound the difficulty. Watzlawick, Weakland, and Fisch (1974) write about such solution-attempts as the principle cause of clients' symptoms.

The problem is most serious when it interferes with partners' attempts to deal with the central flaws and conflicts in their relationship. Joe's self-criticism about being too withdrawn and Carol's about being too pushy prevented them from thinking and talking effectively about their pursuer/distancer conflict and led to counterproductive solution-attempts.

Consider, for example, the following interaction. Concerned about what he felt to be his fear of closeness, Joe engaged in an action-solution. He tried to force himself to become involved and intimate. His idea of becoming intimate was to listen patiently to Carol without interrupting her, disagreeing with her, appearing disinterested, imposing his own ideas, or leaving the room. Although self-imposed, such restrictions almost guaranteed that Joe would feel trapped in the situation and lose interest in what Carol was saying.

Carol perceived that Joe was losing interest. Her concern about being too critical, however, prevented her from commenting on her perception. Instead, she talked faster and more furiously in a desperate effort to engage Joe's interest. Carol thus responded to Joe's solution (forcing himself to listen to her) with a solution of her own, attempting to engage his interest by furious talking.

Joe responded to Carol's anxious talking by feeling even more bored and trapped. He could not admit that he had such feelings, however, since he saw them not as an understandable response to her anxious talking, but as a manifestation of his fears of closeness. He engaged in another action-solution: sitting down with the evening paper immediately upon coming home in the hope that Carol would see that he preferred to read.

Carol's worry about being too demanding and too critical kept her from commenting on his reading. Instead, she waited until later in the evening when she thought he might feel more like talking and approached him again. When he did not seem to want to talk then or the next morning either, Carol felt frustrated. She accused him of never wanting to talk to her, being afraid of intimacy, being interested only in his own selfish needs, and being unable to have a mature relationship.

Carol's outburst could be thought of as an interruption to the continuous series of action-solutions and as the first direct comment to pass between the partners. Her outburst, however, was in some sense simply another action-solution. It was not so much an expression of feeling as it was a series of accusations. It was an impulsive and desperate effort to force Joe to see the error of his ways and to change. And as was true of the previous action-solutions the results were counterproductive. Joe felt devastated by Carol's accusations. They reinforced his own worries about himself, and he vowed to try harder to force himself to change. Carol felt just as devastated by her accusations. She believed that they proved that she was aggressive and overbearing and that she should try harder to control herself. The scene was set for a new series of counterproductive action-solutions.

These partners' problem was not so much their underlying pursuer/distancer conflict as it was the method by which they tried to deal with this conflict. Their self-criticisms and their belief that they should not be having the reactions they were having prevented them from confiding in and collaborating with each other; their continual disqualification of their own feelings led to unilateral action-solutions that exacerbated the problem. Joe's and Carol's attempts to be respectively less distancing and less pushy led to their becoming respectively more distancing and more pushy.

Whatever inherent flaws or conflicts exist in a relationship are exaggerated by the way partners talk (or do not talk) about them and, even more importantly, by the way partners think (or do not think) about them. In many cases the difficulty is almost entirely in how partners think about and react to issues rather than the issues themselves. They feel that something is seriously wrong with them and/or their partners for having the problem and they engage in desperate action-solutions. Therapy then consists, in a sense, of saving people from their solutions.

HONEYMOON AND DISAPPOINTMENT

The critical factors that produce difficulties in the couple's passage through the family life cycle are, as just described, disqualification of feelings and consequent action-solutions. The same two factors play a major role in the well-known phases of honeymoon, crash, and aftermath that occur early in a relationship.

I view the sequence of honeymoon, crash, and aftermath as a metaphor for and most dramatic example of what may be the major ongoing problem of relationships: how to deal with disappointments. The history of a relationship is in large measure the history of partners' reactions to disappointments, frustrations, and disillusionments. Guerin and Fay (1982) describe a sequential pattern (which they call "Fogarty's litany") in which "idealization leads to expectations lead to disappointment leads to hurt leads to anger leads to resentment leads to bitterness" (p. 4).

The critical underlying psychodynamic factors in this sequence I suggest are disqualification of feelings and resulting action-solutions. Instead of recognizing and confiding in each other about their disappointments and frustrations, partners engage in desperate correction seeking and compensatory efforts that compound the conflicts. Three classic types of partner difficulties—loss of feeling for one another, irresolvable argument, and pursuer/distancer runaway—can be thought of as products of this situation. The sequence is (1) expectation, (2) disappointment, (3) action-solution, (4) situational alienation (mutual withdrawal, mutual accusation, pursuer-distancer interaction), and (5) chronic alienation (loss of feeling, bitterness, polarization).

Expectation

The early phases of an intimate relationship are often described by couples therapists as consisting of honeymoon (romantic fantasy), crash (disappointment), and aftermath (readjustment or exit). This description is admittedly an oversimplification. Romantic love may be absent from the start. Some people are pessimistic about being able to love or be loved and are happy to find someone relatively pleasant who will agree to a relationship. Others enter a relationship not for romantic love, but for the satisfaction of fulfilling the traditional role of wife or husband and later of mother or father. Whether partners seek romantic love, companionship, a traditional role-oriented marriage, or whatever else, they enter the relationship with certain expectations.

Disappointment

While many couples are relatively content with their relationship and some obtain greater overall satisfaction than they had thought possible, a certain amount of disappointment and frustration is inevitable, if not in general expectations, at least in moment to moment interactions. The history of a relationship is in some sense the history of how partners deal with these underlying or recurrent disappointments, frustrations, and disillusionments. Couples react in at least three different ways: mutual withdrawal, mutual accusation, and pursuit/distance.

Action-solutions

As an example of these three reactions, consider a husband and wife who meet at the door at the end of a long day (Wile, 1981). Each has the fantasy hope of being listened to and attended to by a loving, nurturing, concerned spouse. These fantasy hopes are immediately dashed when each discovers that the other is irritable, preoccupied, and worn out.

If this husband and wife are comfortable with their fantasy wishes they might be able to talk about them, sympathize with each other about their mutual disappointment, and find some way of attaining at least partial fulfillment. If the partners are uncomfortable with their wishes, however, they are likely to lose contact with them. Instead of thinking about and confiding in each other about their wishes and disappointments they engage in action-solutions.

One common form of action-solution is withdrawal. The individual abandons the effort to obtain resuscitating fantasy contact with the partner and turns to others or to personal activities (e.g., reading a book or tinkering in the basement). Another type of action-solution is blaming. The individual berates the partner in a desperate effort to force him or her to change. A third form is pursuit. The individual persists in the effort to obtain resuscitating fantasy contact with the partner by initiating sex, for example, or by talking about their next vacation. In none of these three cases does the individual experience, think, or talk about the fantasy wish or feeling of disappointment. Instead he or she simply acts on it.

Situational alienation

The course of the evening depends on the interaction between the partners respective action-solutions. If both partners withdraw the result will be an evening characterized by nonengagement and possibly withheld resentment (*mutual withdrawal*). Both may immerse themselves in independent activities or possibly seek out friends. If there is any contact between the partners it will be in impersonal or ritualized forms such as silently watching television together.

If both partners respond to the frustration of their fantasy hopes with complaints, that is, by expressing their disappointment as anger in a desperate attempt to force the other to "see reason" and change, the result will be an evening of recurring or accelerating argument *(mutual accusation)*. Compared to the subtle and easily overlooked alienation of the mutually withdrawn partners, these individuals are clearly and dramatically at odds with one another. Each feels unacknowledged, misunderstood, or betrayed by an unreasonable, provocative, insensitive, or selfish spouse.

If one partner responds by approaching, either in a renewed appeal for contact or in anger and the other responds by withdrawing, the result is the pursuer/distancer interaction. The wife, let us say, attempts to rescue some element of her plan for an intimate, resuscitating evening by making a desperate effort to engage her husband in "meaningful" conversation. The anxiety underlying her effort, however, causes her to approach him in an awkward, pressuring, or accusatory manner and he withdraws. Later in the evening, the husband may become the pursuer and the wife the distancer. For example, in the hope of reestablishing a sense of intimacy through sex, he goes over and caresses her. This sudden reaching out after his previous cool detachment is felt by her as impersonal and forced and she shrugs him off.

Periods of mutual withdrawal, mutual accusation, and pursuit/distance appear inevitable in couple relationships. Several times each week (or each day or hour) partners withhold comments to avoid hurting one another's feelings or starting an argument (mutual withdrawal). Few couples completely escape this pattern. At some point partners rebel against this withdrawal and have an argument (mutual accusation). Or one partner tries to overcome the withdrawal by a forced attempt to talk, have sex, or go somewhere together, which is felt by the other as a demand rather than as an invitation and precipitates a pursuer/distancer interaction.

Chronic alienation

The patterns of mutual withdrawal, mutual accusation, and pursuer/distancer interaction have been widely discussed. Bach and Wyden (1969), Barnett (1971), Bergner (1977), Cuber and Harroff (1965), Epstein and Santabarbara (1975), Fogarty (1976), Framo (1965), Gehrke and Moxom (1962), Gottman, Markman, and Notarius (1977), Haley, (1963), Hiebert and Stahmann (1977), Jackson (1967), Karpel (1976), Lederer and Jackson (1968), Mace (1972, 1976), Mittelmann (1956), Napier (1978), Rhodes and Wilson (1981), and Satir (1967) have each described one or more of these patterns.

Couples who come for therapy can be viewed as experiencing advanced or chronic forms of one or more of these patterns. Partners who complain of loss of intimacy or vitality in their relationship are generally suffering from ingrained and progressive mutual withdrawal. Those who complain of bitter arguments are suffering from prolonged mutual accusation. Partners who complain of incompatible personalities are often suffering the effects of an escalating pursuer/distancer interaction, generally with one partner trapped in the role of pursuer and the other in that of distancer.

The history of a relationship is in some sense the history of action-solutions engaged in to deal with disappointments, frustrations, and disillusionments. Action-solutions are not always counterproductive. In fact, they constitute major ways in which people successfully solve their problems. Withdrawal often allows useful breathing space. Blaming frequently leads to a productive clearing of the air. Pursuit may bring about the contact that both partners want. However, action-solutions often do have the effect, described in this chapter, of compounding existing problems and producing increased alienation between partners.

RELATIONSHIP DEVELOPMENT

How is the sequence of expectation, disappointment, action-solutions, situational alienation, and chronic alienation related to stages in the family life cycle? My answer is that this sequence may occur regarding any one of the family life-cycle stages as well as regarding issues not connected to these stages.

Each family life-cycle stage (marriage, birth of children, children leaving home, retirement) can be thought of having its own particular fantasy expectations and, consequently, its own potentialities for disappointment. Frank (1977) describes a woman who approached her retirement with "the romantic illusion of spending her remaining years with a totally compatible partner, equally disengaged from the preoccupation of business" (p. 44). Frank discusses how these fantasy hopes were shattered.

For many couples, the sequence of expectation, disappointment, action-solutions, situational alienation, and chronic alienation occur at many or even at every family life-cycle stage. Relationships that have this pattern can more accurately be viewed as stagnating or degenerating rather than as developing.

If transition through the recognized couple or family life-cycle stages is not development, then what is? Development or growth of a relationship occurs when partners experience an increased sense of entitlement to their feelings and as a result are more likely to confide in one another about them rather than to simply employ action-solutions.

If Carol and Joe had felt less self-critical of their anxiety about getting married, they might have been able to discuss these feelings. Such discussion would in itself have constituted an important solution to the problem. In talking directly about important issues, Joe would no longer have been withdrawn and Carol would no longer have felt excluded. Their discussion might have had the additional positive effect of revealing an unsuspected commonality: The actions of each that so offended the other—Carol's pressure for reassurance and Joe's withdrawal—might have been discovered as differing reactions to a common apprehension about getting married. The partners would thus have been using their relationship as a resource for dealing with problems caused by that relationship. Such use of the relationship, even if it occurs at the very beginning of a couple's history, is the mark of a highly developed relationship.

Couples therapy is devoted to facilitating such development; that is, to increasing partners' sense of entitlement to their feelings and rescuing them from their counterproductive action-solutions. The therapist traces the partners' symptomatic reactions (their action-solutions) back to the underlying disappointment or feeling and shows this feeling to be ordinary and understandable (Wile, 1984, in preparation). Carol's and Joe's symptomatic reactions—their escalating pursuer/distancer interaction—would be traced to commonplace feelings: the worries almost everyone has about getting married. The ultimate goal of therapy (and also of couple relationships) is to engage the curative potential of the relationship, to enable partners to use the relationship to deal not only with lifelong problems but also with problems produced *by* the relationship.

Conclusion

A current couples therapy view is that relationship phases—or at least certain relationship phases—cause couple pathology. The honeymoon stage leads to a disillusionment stage. Marriage, birth of children, emergence of children as adolescents, children leaving home, and retirement are viewed as potentially threatening and destabilizing events. In general, partners are seen as suffering from their relationship phases; that is, the family life cycle is seen as the cause of their trouble.

I view the problem as partners' *beliefs that the family life cycle should not cause them trouble.* They think that they should unambivalently welcome whatever new experience or phase unfolds. They may feel something is wrong with them if they find themselves anticipating the birth of their first child with mixed rather than purely joyful feelings, if they sometimes wish that their children would remain small and dependent on them, or if they find themselves not fully enthusiastic about their grown childrens' plans to leave home. Partners' sense of unentitlement to such feelings leads to action-solutions, which often do cause problems.

Some couples therapists might attribute partners' problems to their immaturities (dependency, narcissism, need to control, fear of intimacy), their displacement on each other of unresolved conflicts with parents, their vested interest in remaining symptomatic, and/or their hesitancy in shifting to certain family life-cycle stages. Whether or not any of these explanations is valid, I recommend first considering the possibility that partners' problems are a consequence of their having feelings that they think they should not be having and of their subsequent recourse to action-solutions.

Much of the problem in fact is that individuals themselves incorrectly attribute their conflicts to such immaturities, displacements, vested interests, and so on. Joe and Carol ran into serious difficulties whenever the course of marital life exposed them to relationship conflicts or flaws about which they felt self-critical.

Joe engaged in desperate action-solutions whenever he saw himself as self-centered or afraid of intimacy. Any hesitancy he had about marrying Carol, talking to her, making love, having children, or spending time with the family distressed him because it reinforced his worst fear about himself—that he was afraid of closeness. His jealousy of Carol's intimate relationship with their children when she was nursing them and again when they became adolescent, and his lack of interest in listening to Carol made him worry that he was a self-centered individual concerned only with his own personal needs.

Carol engaged in desperate action-solutions whenever she saw herself as demanding or intrusive. Any complaints she had about Joe's apparent lack of involvement—his hesitancy to get married, talk, have children, or spend time with the family—increased her concern about being too demanding. Her intimate relationship with her children made her worry that she was overinvolved.

This problem, the disqualification of one's own and of one's partner's feelings and the subsequent resort to action-solutions, appears to occur to a lesser or greater degree in everyone's relationships and is my way of understanding the widespread difficulty individuals in our culture have in establishing workable relationships. People are unable to think or talk effectively about their problems because (among other reasons) they are so upset about having them and/or because previous attempts to talk just seemed to make matters worse. They stop being allies at precisely the moment when each is in greatest need of an ally.

A major *purpose of a relationship* is to solve the personal problems, compensate for the individual limitations, correct the childhoods, and gratify the dependent wishes of the partners. The *phases of a relationship* represent alternative, often abortive, attempts to accomplish these general goals and to deal with intrinsic relationship contradictions. *Development or growth of a relationship* occurs when partners feel an increased sense of entitlement to their feelings and as a result are better able to mobilize the curative potential of that relationship.

References

Apfelbaum, B. (1977). A contribution to the development of the behavioral-analytic model. *Journal of Sex and Marital Therapy, 3*, 128–138.

Bach, G. R., & Wyden, P. (1969). *The intimate enemy: How to fight fair in love and marriage.* New York: William Morrow.

Barnett, J. (1971). Narcissism and dependency in the obsessional-hysteric marriage. *Family Process, 10*, 75–83.

Barnhill, L. R., & Longo, D. (1978). Fixation and regression in the family life cycle. *Family Process, 17*, 449–455.

Bergner, R. M. (1977). The marital system of the hysterical individual. *Family Process, 16*, 85–95.

Cowan, C. P., & Cowan, P. A. (in press). In C. F. Z. Boukydis (Ed.), *Research on support for parents and infants in the postnatal period.* New Jersey: Ablex Publishing Co.

Cuber, J. F., & Harroff, P. B. (1965). *Sex and the significant Americans: A study of sexual behavior among the affluent* New York: Penguin Books.

Dicks, H. V. (1967). *Marital tensions.* London: Routledge & Kagan Paul.

Duvall, E. M. (1971). *Family development* (4th ed.). Philadelphia, PA: J. B. Lippincott.

Epstein, N., & Santabarbara, J. (1975). Conflict behavior in clinical couples: Interpersonal perceptions and stable outcomes. *Family Process, 14*, 41–66.

Fogarty, T. F. (1976). Marital crisis. In P. J. Guerin (Ed.), *Family therapy: Theory and practice.* New York: John Wiley & Sons.

Framo, J. L. (1965). Rationale and technique of intensive family therapy. In I. Boszormenyi-Nagy & J. L. Framo (Eds.), *Intensive family therapy: Theoretical and practical aspects.* New York: Harper & Row.

Frank, H. (1977). Retirement: An ego alien view. *International Journal of Family Counseling, 5*(1), 44–47.

Fromm, E. (1956). *The art of loving.* New York: Harper & Row.

Gehrke, S., & Moxom, J. (1962). Diagnostic classification and treatment techniques in marital counseling. *Family Process, 2*, 181–188.

Glenn, N. D. (1975). Psychological well-being in the postparental stage: Some evidence from national surveys. *Journal of Marriage and the Family, 37*, 105–110.

Gottman, J., Markman, H., & Notarius, C. (1977). The topography of marital conflict: A sequential analysis of verbal and nonverbal behavior. *Journal of Marriage and the Family, 39*, 461–477.

Guerin, P. J. (1982). The stages of marital conflict. *The Family, 10*(1), 15–26.

Guerin, P. J., & Fay, L. F. (1982). The envelope of marital conflict: Social context and family factors. *The Family, 10*(1), 3–14.

Haley, J. (1959). The family of the schizophrenic: A model system. *Journal of Nervous and Mental Disease, 129*, 357–374.

Haley, J. (1963). *Strategies of psychotherapy.* New York: Grune & Stratton.

Haley, J. (1973). *Uncommon therapy: The psychiatric techniques of Milton H. Erickson.* New York: W. W. Norton.

Harkins, E. (1978). Effects of the empty nest transition: A self report of psychological well being. *Journal of Marriage and the Family, 40,* 549–556.

Hiebert, W. J., & Stahmann, R. F. (1977). Commonly recurring couple interaction patterns. In R. F. Stahmann & W. J. Hiebert (Eds.), *Klemer's counseling in marital and sexual problems: A clinician's handbook* (2nd ed.). Baltimore, MD: Williams & Wilkins.

Hoffman, L. (1980). The family life cycle and discontinuous change. In E. A. Carter & M. McGoldrick (Eds.), *The Family life cycle: A framework for family therapy.* New York: Gardner Press.

Hughes, S. F., Berger, M., & Wright, L. (1978). The family life cycle and clinical intervention. *Journal of Marriage and Family Counseling, 4*(4), 33–40.

Jackson, D. D. (1967). The individual and the larger context. *Family Process, 6,* 139–154.

Karp, E. S., Jackson, J. H., & Lester, D. (1970). Ideal-self fulfillment in mate selection: A corollary to the complementary need theory of mate selection. *Journal of Marriage and the Family, 32,* 269–272.

Karpel, M. (1976). Individuation: From fusion to dialogue. *Family Process, 14,* 65–82.

Kris, A. O. (1976). On wanting too much: The "exceptions" revisited. *International Journal of Psychoanalysis, 57,* 85–95.

Lederer, W. J., & Jackson, D. D. (1968). *The mirages of marriage.* New York: W. W. Norton.

Lowenthal, M. F., & Chiriboga, D. (1972). Transition to the empty nest: Crisis, challenge, or relief? *Archives of General Psychiatry, 26,* 8–15.

Mace, D. R. (1972). Marriage as relationship-in-depth: Some implications for counseling. In H. L. Silverman (Ed.), *Marital therapy: Psychological, sociological and moral factors.* Springfield, IL: Charles C Thomas.

Mace, D. R. (1976). Marital intimacy and the deadly love-anger cycle. *Journal of Marriage and Family Counseling, 2,* 131–137.

McGoldrick, M. (1980). The joining of families through marriage: The new couple. In E. A. Carter & M. McGoldrick (Eds.), *The family life cycle: A framework for family therapy.* New York: Gardner Press.

Mittelmann, B. (1956). Analysis of reciprocal neurotic patterns in family relationships. In V. W. Eisenstein (Ed.), *Neurotic interaction in marriage.* New York: Basic Books.

Napier, A. Y. (1978). The rejection-intrusion pattern: A central family dynamic. *Journal of Marriage and Family Counseling, 4*(1), 5–12.

Rhodes, S., & Wilson, J. (1981). *Surviving family life: The seven crises of living together.* New York: G. P. Putnam's Sons.

Sager, C. J. (1976). *Marriage contracts and couple therapy: Hidden forces in intimate relationships.* New York: Brunner/Mazel.

Sager, C. J., Kaplan, H. S., Gundlack, R. H., Kremer, M., Lenz, R., & Royce, J. R. (1971). The marriage contract. *Family Process, 10,* 311–326.

Satir, V. (1967). *Conjoint family therapy* (rev. ed.). Palo Alto, CA: Science & Behavior Books.

Solomon, M. (1973). A developmental conceptual premise for family therapy. *Family Process, 12,* 179–188.

Terkelsen, K. G. (1980). Toward a theory of the family life cycle. In E. A. Carter & M. McGoldrick (Eds.), *The family life cycle: A framework for family therapy.* New York: Gardner Press.

Watzlawick, P., Weakland, J. H., & Fisch, R. (1974). *Change: Principles of problem formation and resolution.* New York: W. W. Norton.

Weeks, G. R., & Wright, L. (1979). Dialectics of the family life cycle. *The American Journal of Family Therapy, 7*(1), 85–91.

Whitehouse, J. (1981). The role of the initial attracting quality in marriage: Virtues and vices. *Journal of Marital and Family Therapy, 7*(1), 61–67.

Wile, D. B. (1979). Is a confrontational tone necessary in conjoint therapy? *Journal of Marital and Family Therapy, 5*(4), 11–18.

Wile, D. B. (1981). *Couples Therapy: A nontraditional approach.* New York: John Wiley & Sons.

Wile, D. B. (1983, August) Ego analysis and separation-individuation. Presented as part of the symposium, *Ego analysis and ego psychology,* at the American Psychological Association Convention, Anaheim, CA.

Wile, D. B. (1984). Kohut, Kernberg, and accusatory interpretations. *Psychotherapy: Theory, Research, and Practice, 21*(3), 353–364.

Wile, D. B. (in preparation). A nonadversary approach to couples therapy.

FOUR

The Influence of Gender on Power Dynamics in Relationships

Wendy Stock, Ph.D.
Research Scientist
Department of Psychology
Texas A&M University

In writing about power dynamics in relationships it has become clear that power and intimacy are interlocking issues, issues that are inseparable because the balance of power affects the degree of intimacy in a relationship, and, reciprocally, true emotional intimacy cannot occur without an approximately equal balance of power. This chapter will explore the relationship of these two concepts and the conceptual model to be advanced will attempt to explain their interrelationship. In addition, much research has illuminated the relationship between gender and power, first, in terms of the systematic inequality in access to power which keeps women at a disadvantage vis à vis men, and second, with respect to the manner in which females and males exercise power in their social interactions with others. Gender is not the underlying cause of unequal power dynamics, but gender as associated with differences in access to power is considered an important variable in understanding female-male relationship dynamics. Although contemporary relationships are undergoing change in the relative distribution of power, which implies changes in the manner in which partners will deal with each other, to the extent that power remains distributed asymmetrically within any relationship, there will be disparities in power and control within the relationship.

The conceptual model proposed posits three types of power, which are often but not necessarily related: (1) *Concrete* or external bases of power, the economic, the material, and the physical; (2) *Interactional style power*, the stylistic behavioral and process manifestations of power including direct communication and assertiveness versus indirect, manipulative strategies; and (3) *Intrapersonal and systems power*, the extent to which an individual has resolved intrapsychic conflicts that make her/him capable of intimacy and able to function within a relationship system in an effective and mature manner. The concepts of individuation versus fusion, self-acceptance versus perfectionism, and dependence versus independence are polarities in this category. The latter typology will be used to structure a limited review of the relevant literature. This chapter is not intended as a comprehensive review of the literature on power. For such a treatment refer to Gray-Little and Burks (1983). Gender differences in access to and use of power are omnipresent in our culture. Thus, much of the literature discussed highlights these differences and focuses on their implications for intimate relationships. Although the three categories mentioned above are often interactive, recommendations for therapeutic interventions are made with attention to the specific power typology to be advanced.

CONCRETE POWER

Social scientists have had a long-term aversion to studying actual power usage and instead show a preference for studying perceptions of power. Unger (1982) examined all published articles on power from the years 1967 to 1982 and found that the majority of studies focused on perceived power and interpersonal influence. Unger notes the unwillingness of social psychology to examine the use of overt or covert force in the context of so-called normal relationships. However, studies of marital relationships in which the women could *not* be defined as battered wives reveal that a considerable number of American marriages are characterized by the use of low levels of physical coercion (Frieze & McHugh, 1981). Physical aggression between husbands and wives is often perceived as somewhat normative (Unger, 1982).

The study of sex and gender differences has led to renewed interest in social power, based on a recognition that power, status, and influence are not interchangeable concepts (Unger, 1982). The organization of this chapter reflects this awareness. Carolyn Sherif (1982) proposed that power be defined in terms of the relative control of resources and access to core institutions such as the economy or law, and the use of these institutions in initiating actions, decisions, policy, and effective sanctions. Power use was seen in the past as reflecting either individual personality dynamics or as a response to the situational social context (Unger, 1982). As the major role of the status of women within our society has been recognized, many writers have reconceptualized the nature of power, acknowledging that its basis is in the control of concrete resources.

Johnson (1976) defines concrete power as based on access to tangible or objective resources that are independent of relationships. In our society, males generally control the concrete resources: money, knowledge, position, and physical strength. Millett (1970) noted that men occupy the highest positions of societal institutions, positions that give them strength, wealth, and knowledge. Thus, virtually all the military, scientific, technical, intellectual, and political institutions are male dominated. Men exercise concrete power on both individual and institutional levels, while women even when they possess these resources, are discouraged from using them directly.

Wilhelm Reich (1945) wrote of the effects of economic and power inequality on female-male relationships. Reich claimed that the economic dependence of women on men "forces sexual relationships to take on an entirely different form than that of two independent individuals . . . the permanent sexual relationships, with its biological and psychosexual foundation, thus turns into a compulsive marriage" (p. 129). Reich believed that power inequality, specifically the economic dependence of women, was at the root of most relationship difficulties, including sexual problems. As Reich noted, "It is considered a matter of course that the man 'possesses' the woman, while the woman 'gives' herself. . . . Since possessing signifies honor, while 'giving oneself' has the context of debasing oneself, women have developed a negative attitude toward the sex act . . . and since to most men, the possessing of a woman is a proof of their virility rather than an experience of love, this attitude on the part of women becomes tragically justified" (Reich, 1945, p. 7). Reich argued that eliminating the economic enslavement of women and children would eliminate men's expectation of love as a right and would eliminate such phenomena as spouse abuse and rape of a sexual partner.

Ultimately, Reich's claims may indeed prove to be correct. At this point in history, we are witnessing a power struggle between the sexes over the redistribution of concrete power in intimate relationships. One example in which this struggle is evident is the high frequency of spouse abuse in our culture. The struggle becomes even more clearly delineated when we look at the incidence of spouse abuse among couples in which women are attaining economic parity with their male partners.

According to Walker (1978), violence against women has historically been considered an acceptable resolution to marital disagreements. Brownmiller's (1975) research on the history of rape—another form of violence against women—suggests that from biblical days women have traded freedom for security. Men's physical and economic strength reinforced women's acceptance of their "right to discipline." Societal institutions have facilitated, if not encouraged, the beating of women since police, courts, hospitals, social services, and even psychologists have provided inadequate protection (Walker, 1978).

The frequency of spouse abuse is extremely high. Straus, Steinmetz, and Gelles (1980) conducted a survey of a randomly selected national sample of over 2,100 families which indicated that 1 out of 6 of the couples interviewed had had a physically violent episode during that year—an estimated 7.5 million couples nationally. Violence was defined as any incident in which the spouse went *beyond* throwing things, pushing, grabbing, shoving, and slapping, and included attacking the spouse by kicking, biting, punching, hitting with some object, beating up, threatening with a knife or gun, or using a knife or gun. According to that research, at least 28 percent of all married women will experience violence in their marriage, and 13 percent or 5 million American wives will receive chronic physical abuse from their husbands (Straus, 1978).

Although some men are assaulted by their wives, the injuries to male partners are not generally as serious. Kincaid (1982), in a study of 3,125 cases taken from Canadian court records, found that 54 percent dealt with spousal violence. In 95 percent of these cases the wives were assaulted. Straus, Gelles, and Steinmetz (1980) found high rates of violence by both husbands and wives, but husbands had higher rates of the most injurious forms of violence such as beating up and using a knife or gun. They also repeated their violent acts more than their wives.

Many women remain in battering marital relationships because of economic dependence on the batterer (Gelles, 1977; Walker, 1979) and lack of perceived alternatives, which amounts to an exercise of physical and economic power by the male over the female. In fact, Pagelow (1981) found that wives with the most resources were the first to leave physically abusive husbands. Resources included income, education, and job possibilities. Kalmuss (1981) and Yllo (1981) found that wives with the least earning power were the most likely to be abused.

However, a recent and telling phenomenon is the occurrence of male to female spouse abuse in couples in which the wife's income is higher than the male's. Yllo (1981) found that in marriages where women's status was highest, wife abuse was also high, but these wives were more likely to respond to a husband's violence with violence. Because of the strength and size of men, however, women are still more likely to end up in the hospital. Explaining the batterings of high-status wives, Yllo claimed that husbands were "threatened by the rapid social change and the breakdown of traditional husband-wife roles . . . increased domestic conflict and violence may be short term consequences of women's move toward equality" (p. B–5). Basically, wives are physically abused when they do not have access to concrete power and when they attain or attempt to obtain concrete power. It has often been noted that men beat their wives when their wives initiate some action independently or try to assert themselves (Kincaid, 1982). Beating is the naked use of concrete power. Sometimes all it takes for beatings to occur repeatedly is the establishment of the power of the aggressor (Propper, 1984). Establishment of the aggressor's power can be extremely reinforcing if, as a consequence of a beating, the wife tries to placate her husband by, for example, cleaning the house more, getting meals on time, complying with his sexual requests, or accepting his decisions without question.

In egalitarian marriages, when both husband and wife held professional, typically male jobs, the chance of divorce was twice as high as in dual professional marriages where the wife held a typically female job (33 percent versus 15 percent) (Hiller, 1982). Hiller explains that job segregation is an "ego protector for men" (p. 38). "It's OK for your wife to have a higher-paying or higher-status job, as long as she's a nurse or teacher—because that's what women are *supposed* to be" (p. 38). Hornung (1980) found a high rate of psychological abuse—insults, swearing, sulking, threats to hit or to throw things, actual kicking or smashing of objects—on the part of both partners in marriages where the wife's postgraduate education exceeded her husband's. Moreover, in couples where the wife's occupational status was higher than her husband's, there was an increased risk of violence with a knife or gun. In these marriages we may view in microcosm the societal struggle over redistribution between the sexes of concrete power and its accompanying privileges (including the freedom to choose to remain in a relationship for example). It is clear that a vast amount of energy is required to keep women in a subordinate position, and a high price is paid by many women who somehow have managed to increase their concrete power.

Women as a *class* have not yet achieved economic parity with men or even begun to approach equal political representation. The defeat of the Equal Rights Amendment is indicative of a societal unwillingness to legally grant women freedom from discrimination. Sex as a class or master status is linked to differential opportunities and advantages, as shown in table 1. It should be obvious from women's treatment as an underclass why it is often viewed as being in a woman's best economic interest to affiliate herself with a man who may provide economic support and physical protection (from other men), although we also know from Bernard's (1972) findings that marriage has a deleterious effect on women's psychological health while paradoxically benefiting that of men. These findings are not contradictory when one examines the demands of the structural role of wife and the typical division of labor within a household. For example, it remains the case that even women who work outside of the home also do the bulk of work within the household. Thus, "dual career" couples often have one partner with a dual career—the wife.

In a recent study predicting parental coping styles with the birth of the first baby, Cowan and Cowan (1983) found that a woman's dissatisfaction with her marriage and her role in that marriage usually stemmed not from problems in communication or sex, but from the problems associated with division of household tasks—the "who does what issues." The Cowans found, for example, that at six months postpartum, women were doing many more of the baby related chores than either they or their husbands had predicted, and that 92 percent of the couples reported that they were arguing more than before the baby was born. A recent study by Barnett (1983) found that men do at most one third of the household tasks their wives do, whether or not their wives work outside the home.

It has become increasingly apparent in the field of sex therapy that most sexual problems interact with relationship problems. LoPiccolo (1978), who considers the most important area of assessment to be the couple's interpersonal relationship, has outlined several interpersonal factors that maintain sexual dysfunctions. One such factor is the couple's lifestyle or the general level of mutuality in their relationship. When sex roles are divided strictly along stereotypic lines, that is, where the husband is responsible for the family's financial support while the wife handles the domestic duties, the wife may feel some resentment toward her husband, not only for foregoing a career of her own, but also for having a workday that extends beyond his. LoPiccolo has found this to be a consistent pattern in cases of secondary female orgasmic dysfunction.

In the Frank, Anderson, and Rubinstein (1978) study of the frequency of sexual dysfunction in "normal" couples, 36 percent of the men reported ejaculating too quickly, 9 percent had difficulty maintaining an erection, and 7 percent had difficulty having an erection. Among women, 48 percent reported difficulty getting excited, 33 percent reported difficulty maintaining excitement, and 46 percent reported difficulty reaching orgasm. In terms of sexual difficulties that were *not* labeled dysfunctions, 31 percent of the women compared to 16 percent of the men checked "partner chooses inconvenient time"; 47 percent of the women compared to 12 percent of the men reported "inability to relax"; 35 percent of the women compared to 16 percent of the men reported "disinterest"; and 38 percent of the women compared to 21 percent of the men reported "too little foreplay before intercourse." The higher percentage of sexual difficulties reported by the women supports the notion that women require more emotional sensitivity, or are at least more aware of its absence (Frank, Anderson & Rubenstein, 1978). In addition, the majority of women work the equivalent of two full-time jobs, balancing home and job-related responsibilities. Seidler-Feller (1983) contends that the development of sexual dysfunctions in women may involve "dispute or strike over working conditions" (p. 13). To summarize, it has become clear that the asymme-

TABLE 1 The Myth of Equality *(Compelling Reasons to Support the NOW Legal Defense and Education Fund)*

Nearly 30 percent of female students enrolled in traditionally male vocational programs report being discouraged by teachers, counsellors, parents, and peers from entering those fields.[1]

Within vocational education programs, girls represent 75 percent of students in consumer and homemaking courses, occupational home economics, health and office occupations. In contrast, 75 percent of the students in agriculture, technical, trade, and industrial programs are boys.[2]

"Vocational education" is often a misnomer. 35 percent of the young women enrolled in such courses are taking classes like consumer home economics, which *do not* prepare them for paid employment.[2]

Sixty-five of teenage boys have had enough math to enroll in college calculus—the gateway to science and technology careers—compared to 45 percent of girls so prepared.[3]

Seventy percent of all elementary and secondary school teachers are women, yet for the same job, they make an average of $3,000 a year less than their male counterparts.[4]

Over one third of current MBA candidates are women, but women represent only 5 percent of the executives in America's top 50 companies.[4]

Only 13 percent of public school administrators are women.[5]

Women college graduates are paid $400 a year less than men who have only finished elementary school—$11,609 compared to $12,000.[6]

More than 80 percent of all working women are crowded into clerical, service, sales, and manufacturing jobs, where wages are significantly lower than male dominated manufacturing jobs and skilled trades.[7]

Women earn 98.9 percent of all nursing degrees. They represent 98 percent of all receptionists, 97 percent of all secretaries, 92 percent of all clerical workers.[8]

Even with advances in technology working women are still being hurt. Recent changes have led to most computer programmer, keypunch and microassembly jobs being classified as "women's work," with significant drops in pay[7]

Three out of every five working women earn under $10,000 per year, while half of all working men earn at least $15,000 per year.[7]

Although three out of every four people eligible and registered in Federal work incentive programs are women, a statute requires unemployed fathers to be given priority in placement. When women are placed in jobs through this program, they earn an entry salary of $2.97/hour—less than three-quarters of a man's $4.01/hour.[9]

Whoever is designated as "head of household" takes precedence over others for placement in federal job training programs. However, until the last census, *any* male present in the household, working or not, was classified as the head, thus eliminating female family heads from placement.[7]

About one-half of all families below the poverty level in 1980 were maintained by women with no husband present. The poverty rate for such families was 32.7 percent, as compared to 6.2 percent for married couples.[10]

[1]Laurie Harrison & Peter Dahl, *Vocational Education Equity Study* (1979).
[2]U.S. Dept. of Health, Education & Welfare, Bureau of Occupational And Adult Education, *Summary Data Vocational Education, Program Year 1978*.
[3]National Science Foundation, Directorate for Science Education, *Science Databook*.
[4]*Time*, 7/12/82.
[5]PEER *Back-to-School Line-up* (1979).
[6]U.S. Dept. of Labor: Women's Bureau—*The Earnings Gap Between Women and Men* (1979).
[7]Research Summary Series: #4, Business and Professional Women's Foundation.
[8]*New York Times*, 7/2/82.
[9]U.S. Commission on Civil Rights, Clearinghouse Publication 68.
[10]Census Bureau Report for 1980.

try in concrete power between men and women must be rectified before intimate relationships will be free of these damaging behavioral consequences.

INTERACTIONAL/STYLISTIC POWER

Johnson (1976) has defined interpersonal power as the ability to get another person to do or to believe something he or she would not necessarily have done or believed spontaneously. More generally, power is the amount of resistance to change that one person can bring to bear on another person's "life space" (Cartwright, 1959b). Power is used consciously and unconsciously. Rules about power follow norms, and its use is inherent in most of our interactions with others. High power is usually associated with access to resources, social status, self-confidence, and expertise. High power facilitates obtaining what one wants.

The concept of an interactional power style or strategy developed when it became increasingly clear that power only assumes meaning in social contexts, which encompass a spectrum of social and concrete expectations. Cromwell and Olsen (1975) classified existing research on family power into three domains: power *bases*, power *processes*, and *outcome*. The domain of power bases refers to resources such as knowledge or rewards, possessed by family members, that determine the basis of their control over one another. Power process research involves the direct observation and measurement of family interaction, which can include frequency or duration of a behavior, as well as judging one spouse's compliance with the other's directions. Power outcome studies include those asking who makes decisions on family issues, as well as those comparing the joint responses of couples with previously obtained individual responses to a problem (Gray-Little & Burks, 1983). These authors emphasize the considerable overlap between the three domains: "Whenever one examines power in terms of outcome or process, the issue of power bases is implicit" (p. 530).

The style of power used has been connected to self-image, how others feel about the influencer, and future success in other situations (Raven & Kruglanski, 1970). Johnson (1976) described three dimensions of power styles, pointing out the negative consequences for non-sex role stereotypic uses of power.

Direct versus Indirect Power

Indirect power (or manipulation) is used to avoid personal confrontation and occurs when the influencer acts as if unaware of his/her influence on the other. Recent research has found that women and men *do* differ in the ways they use power. I. Broverman, D. Broverman, F. Clarkson, P. Rosenkrantz, and S. Vogel (1970) have shown that the societal expectation is for women to be less direct and more manipulative. Thus, women might be more likely to use indirect power because of its immediate payoff and its personal and status congruence. When women use direct power they risk being labeled as pushy, overbearing, unfeminine, and castrating. Johnson (1976) also notes that women are explicitly trained to use indirect power. Falbo and Peplau (1980) found that men use direct power more frequently in interpersonal relations while women are more indirect in their use of power. Those people who perceived themselves as and preferred having more power than their partner, usually heterosexual men, were more likely to use bilateral and direct strategies because they expected compliance with their attempts at influence. Women do not expect such compliance; thus, they tend to use unilateral strategies—strategies that are less interactive. Miller (1976) relates the greater use of disguised, indirect, and manipulative strategies by women to a structure of permanent inequality. Falbo and Peplau (1980) and Miller (1976) stress that these differences are not inherent in gender, but are based on power inequality in intimate relations. Men tend to use direct and bilateral strategies because they have more power than women, not because they are men (Cowan, 1981). Empirical support for this hypothesis has been presented by Cowan (1981) who, controlling for status differences in the target of influence, found that both males and females used more indirect power strategies with higher-status objects. Johnson (1976) points out that the use of indirect power, even when effective in the short run, has long-term, negative consequences. Since the source of power is concealed, the use of indirect power keeps its user in a subordinate position. Thus, the user of indirect influence does not usually develop a self-concept as a strong, effective person.

Personal versus Concrete Power

Personal power is based on a personal relationship and includes resources such as loving, liking, or approval, while concrete resources such as money, knowledge, and position are independent of personal relationships. While men tend to exercise concrete power on both individual and institutional levels, women, even when they possess these resources, are discouraged from using them directly.

Women are typically limited to power-based or personal resources, that is, liking, love, affection, and approval. The use of personal resources is consistent with the Broverman et al. (1970) finding that women are stereotyped as being warmer and more affectionate than men. Sexual influence is another interpersonal resource available to women, although it is one which when used may result in negative self-attribution and an alienation of sexuality from self.

Helplessness versus Competence

Because of women's generally subordinate position in American culture, they often have difficulties in attaining feelings of self-esteem and competence. Women also tend to underestimate their successes (Parsons, Ruble, Hodges, & Small, 1976) and by necessity tend to rely on their helplessness to elicit aid from others. While use of helplessness may be effective in the short run, it makes it more difficult to subsequently influence from a position of strength. Raven and Kruglanski (1970) also hypothesized that helplessness leads to a loss of self-esteem. The use of this type of power by women has been demonstrated to contribute to low power status and low self-esteem (Johnson, 1976). Unger (1982) points out that according to Sherif's (1982) definition of power, helpless power becomes especially paradoxical.

Both men and women are punished when they use sex-inappropriate power strategies. Falbo, Hazen, and Linimon (in press) found that those using non-sex role, stereotypic power bases were less liked and were regarded as less competent than those using the types of power more commonly associated with their own sex. Zellman and Connor (1973) found that women were viewed negatively when they transmitted information in a direct rather than in a hesitant and soft-spoken manner. Fear of social disapproval, in addition to prior socialization, may limit the choice of power strategies.

Decision-Making Power

Another framework in which to view interactional power is presented by Frieze (1981). Three approaches to power are considered. In the *decision-making* approach to marital power, *power* is defined as the ability to make decisions of all types. Power is seen as being on a continuum from complete husband dominance to complete wife dominance with egalitarianism being on the midpoint of the continuum. Conflict in this area transcends the bounds of female-male relationships. In a study of interpersonal conflicts in homosexual relationships, the right most frequently perceived as being violated was participation in decision making, and the need most frequently perceived as an issue was power (De Cecco & Shively, 1978).

Most recent studies of decision making are based on the work of Blood and Wolfe (1960), who assessed marital power by asking wives which spouse usually made the final decision in eight areas, ranging from choice of husband's job to purchase of life insurance. Couples were categorized as husband-dominant, wife dominant, or egalitarian in decision making, based on the responses of 909 Michigan wives. A further subdivision was made within the egalitarian category between "syncratic" marriages, in which most decisions are made jointly, and "autonomic" ones, in which equal numbers of separate decisions are made by both partners.

Wives who reported a syncratic decision structure also reported the highest levels of satisfaction; those in the wife-dominant groups were the least satisfied; and the autonomic and husband-dominant groups fell in between. Blood and Wolfe (1960) explained the finding that syncratic wives were more satisfied than autonomic wives by suggesting that equality per se is less important for the wife's satisfaction than being included in the decision-making process. According to Blood and Wolfe (1960) the dominant wife gains her power by virtue of her husband's marginality or abstention from the marriage, neither of which is likely to be conducive to marital satisfaction. These findings provide evidence of a positive relationship between reports of cooperative approaches to decision making and high marital satisfaction, although there are some methodological problems which make their results difficult to interpret (Gray-Little & Burks, 1983). These authors emphasize the difficulty in accurate measurement. For example, Olson and Rabunsky (1972) cite findings to suggest that relative to decision making, husbands tend to overestimate their own power and wives to underestimate theirs, which makes these marriages appear to fit the traditional pattern of male dominance.

A second approach, presented by Frieze (1981), resource theory views power as based on the contributions that each partner makes to the marriage, including education, occupation, income, and social participation. This model has been elaborated by Rodmon (1972, cited in Frieze) who added the factor of cultural or subcultural expectations of who should hold power in the marriage.

Last, marital power can be viewed as one aspect of interaction in a social relationship (Cartwright, 1959a). Using this framework French and Raven (1959) have identified six bases of power

Reward. Power based on explicit or implicit promise of giving the other person something in return for their compliance.

Coercion. Power based on explicit or implicit threats of doing something negative to the other person unless they comply.

Referent. Power based on an appeal to the similarity or liking within a couple.

Legitimate. Power based on socially defined, hierarchical role expectations.

Expert. Power based on the superior knowledge, skills, or credentials of the person seeking compliance.

Informational. Power based on unique information possessed by the person seeking compliance.

Johnson (1976) found that women and men do not have equal access to or success in using the six power bases above. Johnson summarizes a number of studies, demonstrating that reward, coercion, and legitimate, expert, and direct informational power are masculine forms of power, while referent, helplessness, and indirect informational power are associated more with women. Women may also employ false information, nagging (a form of coercion), and sexuality (as reward or coercion) to influence others. Raven, Centers, and Rodrigues (1975) found referent power, based on appeal to similarity and mutual liking, to be the most common form of power used by both spouses in a marriage, and the one most frequently used by wives. Since women are socialized to be more concerned with personal relationships, they may be more comfortable using referent power. However, referent power leaves its users tied to the relationship and, when it is the only base of power available, places the user in a vulnerable position (Johnson, 1976).

Consistent with the findings of Falbo and Peplau (1980) and Cowan (1981), the use of power strategies seems to vary with relative status rather than strictly with gender. Although gender is not inherently linked to differential uses of power strategies, access to power resources is distributed asymmetrically between females and males, and this determines which power strategies are used. Therefore, gender is often predictive of *which* power strategies are used. The female, generally being lower in status in relation to the male, is more often limited to use of indirect power strategies. This pattern can reverse itself when the male perceives himself as having less power with respect to his female partner. The theories presented so far would predict that in a distressed couple, the partner who perceives him/herself as less powerful will be more likely to resort to the use of the traditionally feminine power strategies, those involving personal reward and indirect manipulation.

Power, Intimacy, and Status

The relationship of power to intimacy and status provides the basis for another recently-proposed model that is useful in describing relational dynamics. Peplau and Cochran (1980) found that in love relationships males value power while females value emotional expressiveness. Unger (1980) points out that women behave as lower-status people in heterosexual relationships. While women fear the loss of the relationship (making them more vulnerable emotionally), men fear the loss of power in the relationship. A study by Stone (1973) illustrated this point. A negative correlation was found between the duration of a couple's relationship and the male's willingness to compromise with his mate on the direction of the movement of a pinpoint of light.

Jourard (1971) found that men typically reveal less personal information about themselves to others than do women. Jourard claims that men, who seem to dread being known by others, suffer from more neuromuscular tension than women. In addition, "if a man has something to hide, it must follow that other people will be a threat to him"; thus, by being unguarded, he risks exposing areas of weakness and vulnerability (Jourard, 1971, p. 35). Jourard concludes that since men are reluctant to make themselves known to another person, "men will be difficult to love" (p. 35). As Schaef (1981) has pointed out, when men engage in a committed relationship they feel they have given up something, while women feel they have gained something.

Elizabeth and Stock (1984) have developed a model based on intimacy, status, and power. Males, usually higher in status, derive reinforcement from their external environment—from work-related activities, higher-paying jobs, and so on. Females have traditionally looked to their male partners to confer status, power, and intimacy on them. Using an interactive model based on these issues of intimacy, status, and power, Elizabeth and Stock (1984) argue that true intimacy cannot occur without emotional equality. Thus, males must compromise in relationships, balancing their need for intimacy with their fear of loss of power. Males, therefore, will tend to be more cautious and reluctant to approach intimacy, while females, placing higher value on intimacy, sense that they can only gain from a relationship. This imbalance affects the nature of supply and demand in the relationship; that is, women want more than men want to give.

FIGURE 1 Need for Intimacy versus Loss of Power

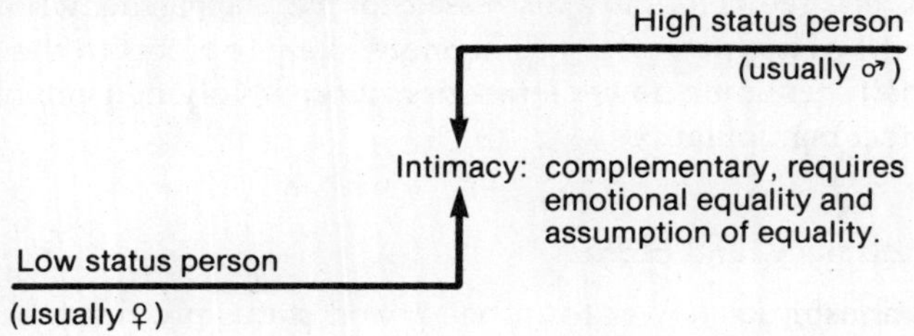

Men who are in relationships have more to lose by engaging in personal or referent uses of power, since this lowers them from their traditionally higher status. It is safer to resort to the male-typed power strategies that are less likely to be matched by female partners. A study on sex differences in comments made during conflict within close heterosexual pairs (Kelly et al., 1978) demonstrated that the female is both expected and reported to cry and to criticize the male for his lack of consideration of her feelings and for his insensitivity, while the male is expected and reported to show anger, to reject the female's tears, to call for a logical and less emotional approach to a problem, and to give reasons for delaying a discussion.

Descent to intimacy is often a frightening and threatening experience for males, while ascent to intimacy is one of transcendence for females. An unusual exception to this formulation is when a female is able to meet her needs for intimacy or status *outside* the relationship through an affair, close family ties, or work related reinforcers. In such cases the male in the relationship is reduced to equal or lower status, and may then resort to lower-status power strategies.

Equity Theory

Equity theory (Walster, Berscheid, & Walster, 1978; Hatfield, Utne, & Traupman, 1979) consists of four, interrelated propositions.

1. Individuals will try to maximize their outcomes.
2. Groups or systems can maximize outcomes by the development of systems of reward and punishment.
3. Individuals involved in inequitable relationships will become distressed.
4. Individuals who discover they are in inequitable relationships will attempt to eliminate their distress by restoring equity. The greater the inequity that exists, the more distress they will feel and the harder they will try to restore equity.

Walster, Traupman, and Walster (1978) found that men and women in inequitable relationships in which they felt "underbenefited" had more extramarital affairs and began their extramarital activities earlier than did men and women in equitable relationships. In applying this theory to sexual relationships, Hatfield, Greenberger, Traupman, and Lambert (1982) hypothesized that men and women who feel underbenefited may find that their anger makes it more difficult for them to respond sexually to their partners. They may begin to respond sadistically or passive-aggressively to sexual advances, while the overbenefited partners may suffer from guilt and find it difficult to receive sexual pleasure. Much of the clinical literature associates such feelings with primary and secondary impotence or orgasmic dysfunction (Barbach, 1975; Heiman, LoPiccolo, & LoPiccolo, 1976; Kaplan, 1974; Masters & Johnson, 1970; Zilbergeld, 1978).

Hatfield et al. (1982) produced some empirical data relating equity theory to sexual satisfaction in recently married couples. Couples in equitable relationships were found to be more content than other couples, not only with their relationships and with their lives in general, but also with their sexual interactions. Overall, equitably treated men and women were more satisfied with their sexual relationship than overenefited and underbenefited men and women. Equitably treated men and women felt more loving and close (versus angry and distant) after sex than did inequitably treated respondents. However, subjects' sexual satisfaction after sex was not exactly as Hatfield et al. had predicted. Both equitably treated and overbenefited men were very satisfied with their sexual relations, while underbenefited men were far less satisfied. Contrary to prediction, overbenefited women were the *most* satisfied with their sexual relations and underbenefited women were the *least* satisfied. Hatfield et al. (1982) note that when emotional aspects of sexuality (how loving and close subjects feel to their partner) are considered, equity theory applies. The results are less clear when only the physical aspects of sexual satisfaction are weighed. It would seem that the more powerful (or the more benefited) an individual is in a relationship, the greater the degree of sexual satisfaction he or she will experience.

An earlier study by Rainwater (1966) supports equity theory. Women's reports of satisfaction with sexual relations were found to vary as a function of social class. Spouses' reports of equal enjoyment of sex varied as a function of class, with the middle-class subjects reporting equality more frequently than the lower-class subjects. Lower-lower-class subjects were more likely to report that the husband enjoyed sex more than the wife. Rainwater (1966) views the relationship between social class and satisfaction as mediated by the variable of conjugal role organization, which also differs with social class. In middle-class couples, joint relationships involving a more egalitarian partnership were the most common. In the lower-lower class, segregated sex role organization is the more predominant pattern.

In another study, Stock and Roberts (1983), attempted to predict the direction of sexual dysfunction based on couples' perceptions of power in their relationship. Two groups of 35 couples each were compared, in which either the male or the female partner in the couple presented for therapy with a sexual dysfunction. Results indicated that one partner's perception of power in the relationship was the best predictor of whether the *other partner* developed a sexual dysfunction. This suggests that power-related marital distress is either recognized consciously as a problem and dealt with through direct conflict resolution, or sublimated unconsciously as sexual dysfunction. Recent support for this hypothesis is provided by Robinson-Metz (1983), who compared couples in sex therapy with couples in marital therapy by observing differences in their styles of handling relationship conflict.

Results suggested that sex therapy couples were more likely to displace general relationship conflict covertly to the sexual area, while marital therapy couples experienced a greater amount and intensity of overall relationship conflict. For example, one means of achieving a degree of bargaining power is through the withdrawal of sexual contact. This may be done consciously, as a manipulative strategy, but often occurs without awareness in the form of a "sexual dysfunction"; that is, low sexual desire, premature ejaculation, vaginismus, or female orgasmic dysfunction. Stock and Roberts's (1983) data indicated that wives who directly contest the balance of power in their relationships may have husbands who oppose that challenge indirectly by developing a sexual dysfunction. An example from the clinical literature speaks directly to this issue. In an article entitled "The Impotent King," Jacobs (1977) writes:

> Secondary impotence occurs within the context of the husband's narcissistic rage, elicited by the wife's unwillingness to pay continued tribute to them. The women react with mounting anger as the men refuse to respond to their increasingly more clearly voiced needs for closeness, equality, and intimacy. . . . The development of impotence often results in a lessening of the wife's challenges to her husband's dominance. . . . She becomes less demanding which naturally reinforces his sexual difficulty which then becomes an interpersonal strategy for him to hold on to his special position with his wife. . . . Treatment of such a form of impotence may be more effective if it moves the couple toward greater equality. (pp. 100–101)

The profile for wives with sexual dysfunctions indicates that they do not want to acknowledge the presence of power conflict, but their husbands consider them overly passive. As Kaplan (1974) notes, "Sexual responsiveness may become a symbol of compliance. It is no wonder that a woman is inorgasmic when for her, orgasm represents submission to her father/husband. Unconsciously, she prefers to give up the pleasure of orgasm rather than give satisfaction to her 'adversary'" (p. 160). Since women generally have only affectional sources of reinforcement at their disposal, sex becomes one of the few areas of reward that is under their control. Sometimes withholding access to sex is not possible, as in the case of the high frequency of marital rape (Gelles, 1977). Women may withhold their enjoyment or active participation in sex either in order to punish their partner or because exchanging sexual pleasure has become totally incomprehensible within the context of their relationship. Seidler-Feller (1983) suggests that female dysfunction may be viewed as a "general status protest" against the power differential between the sexes. In particular, she cites the male's proprietary interest in the female body, his sense of ownership and entitlement. Thus, female sexual dysfunction may represent struggles concerning sexual access and a challenge to the rules regarding male sexual rights (Seidler-Feller, 1983).

Men typically have more objective bases of power in their environments but they pay a high emotional price for maintaining this degree of control, which evidences itself in a performance-oriented attitude toward sexuality and the associated loss of intimacy and emotional contact. Men often develop sexual dysfunctions based on the threat of "female power," or, more precisely, the loss of control in the relationship. They may also be threatened by women's clearly expressed desire for sexual satisfaction. Instead of perceiving their partner's desire as a cooperative goal to be achieved together, they consider it another demand for which they feel totally responsible and by which they may feel intimidated. Men may withhold their sexuality from their partners in ways similar to those of women. They may respond to threats to enactment of their sex role by developing premature ejaculation, erectile dysfunction, or low sexual desire. Sex role issues are certainly not the sole cause of sexual dysfunction, but they do interact with power strategies that enter into the etiology and maintenance of such dysfunction.

To summarize, a power conflict can occur when one partner feels that he or she lacks the means to use direct, problem-solving strategies to resolve difficulties, or that these strategies have been ineffective. The partner who perceives him/herself as having less power will behave as the lower-status person in the relationship, and will probably resort to unilateral, indirect, personal, and referent strategies to maintain some level of influence.

INTRAPERSONAL AND SYSTEMS POWER

Sex Roles and Intimacy

Many people spend their lives feeling constantly off balance, desperately needing acceptance, approval, and love from their family, partners, peers, supervisors, employers, and so on. Many partners in intimate relationships spend their lives passing the responsibility for their psychological well-being from one partner to another in their relationship systems. For many reasons, these individuals have not learned to psychologically nourish themselves, and thus become dependent on others for their nourishment. Consequently, they give a great deal of their power to significant others. This section focuses on patterns in couple systems in which power imbalances derive from deficiencies in self-concept. These dynamics are often related to gender, concrete power, status, and interpersonal power strategies, but they are also fueled by the interplay of individual dynamics.

Herships (1982) relates a prototypical example of a system-related power imbalance that is based on his clinical observation.

> When he initially had entered therapy Jon was depressed and distraught over his wife's total rejection of him. She avoided all physical, sexual, and verbal advances and maintained that she didn't know how she felt and just needed some time. Jon tried everything to please her and win her back. He cooked, cleaned, catered to her every whim. He promised to change every behavior, habit, and piece of his physical being that she objected to. To me, and to her, he pledged his undying devotion and love for his wife. It had taken him five years, but he realized now how much he loved her. The more he pursued, the later she stayed out. The stronger his declaration of love, the greater her expression of ambivalence. He was obsessed. She seemed bored.
>
> With support and some historical reconstruction which allowed him to perceive the situation in terms other than complete rejection, Jon was able to tolerate his wife's withdrawal and achieve a state of emotional stability. He terminated therapy at this point.

"Now, everything is exactly the same," said Jon. "But we reversed roles. Now she says she's sure she loves me, that she wants to make everything work. She's affectionate, keeps the house in perfect shape, buys me little gifts, and even does all those things for me sexually that she said she could never do. But the more she does, the less I seem to care. She's become everything I wanted her to become and now I don't want her at all. I know what I feel but I just don't know what to think about all this." (p. 32)

Waller (1951) proposed an axiom governing dyadic power dynamics—the principle of least interest—which could be used to interpret the clinical example above: The partner who has the least interest in the continuation of the affair is the one who is able to dictate the conditions of association. Waller (1951) believed that most relationships are characterized by a disparity in involvement and that these relationships tend to be exploitative of the one who cares more. Berman and Bennet (1982) tested Waller's principle, using the self-report of 200 couples combined with observational measures of their decision-making process. The individual reporting greater love was judged by the observers to be less dominant in the relationship.

Powers (1964) developed a 14-item scale to measure Waller's principle of least interest. It consisted of 14 Likert-type items such as "I try to like people my partner likes"; "It makes me proud when I know I have pleased my partner"; and "I think marriage places too great a restriction on your freedom." Powers (1964) hypothesized and found differences in relationship interest between college students from entrepreneurial compared to bureaucratic families. Those with entrepreneurial backgrounds were more independent and less interested and less emotionally involved than were those from bureaucratic families, who were more affiliative and more interested in their relationships. However, this association pertained only to males, and was nonsignificant for females. The data did show strikingly significant gender-related differences: The *lowest* female score for emotional involvement and interest was above the *highest* male score. This indicates a greater tendency for females to make more effort to maintain their current dating relationship, while males would generally not object as much as their partners if their present dating arrangements were to "break up." This also indicates that males are in a better bargaining position, and may be able to dominate and possibly exploit women who do not want to risk disfavor and/or loss of the relationship.

Kipnis (1976) explored the consequences of the exercise of power on couples' self- and partner perceptions. Kipnis (1976) found that the very ability to control another's behavior can cause one to be less satisfied with and less attracted to that person. Considering the power act as an independent variable, this investigator found that "control over a target person's behavior is associated with a preference to increased social distance and psychological distance from the target person" (p. 450). In a questionnaire survey of 76 married couples, Kipnis (1976) found that respondents' decision-making power *increased* as their appraisal of partner's worth, their marital satisfaction, and the degree to which they described their spouse in more favorable terms *decreased*. Although these results are only correlational, Kipnis was able to establish directionality in a subsequent industrial simulation study.

As noted earlier, Walster (1978) emphasized the strong tendency of relationship members to restore equity whenever imbalance is perceived. In addition, it was also claimed that unbalanced relations are not viable and will generally be abandoned by one or both partners (Walster, Traupman, & Walster, 1978). In a discussion of the prevalence of exploitation in relationships, Waller (1951) quotes the famous French epigram that "in every love affair there is always one who loves and one who permits himself to be loved" (p. 190).

Partners may enter into and strive to maintain emotionally inequitable and exploitative relationships for many reasons. Recent research has examined gender-related attitudinal differences that might predispose females to behave as lower-status partners in their intimate relationships. Walstedt (1974, 1977) introduced the notion of the Altruistic Other Orientation (AOO) a construct that has been used to explain the lifelong attitude of self-sacrifice of many women involved in male-female relationships. Prior research by social psychologists on prosocial behavior does not pertain to this type of altruism, as the emphasis was previously on situationally specific, transitory, impersonal, or experimental manipulations. The AOO construct and scale reflect a generalized personality disposition that involves women consistently putting men (husbands, lovers, bosses, sons) ahead of themselves and other women. This tendency may be called a "norm of giving" (Bryan & Test, 1967) in which social group standards about how females should relate to men are internalized by individual women.

De Beauvoir (1968) concluded, after reviewing history, literature, psychoanalytic theory, biology, philosophy, and theology, that throughout history women have been regarded as the "Other," the complement to man, rather than as the subject. This custom of defining women as secondary on the basis of gender is a precondition to the altruistic resolution labeled by Anna Freud (1966) as "altruistic surrender," in which the woman transfers her own "unacceptable" ambitions to a man, whose success she then furthers and vicariously enjoys.

A woman with AOO assumes that her secondary position is natural, and "makes altruism the defining characteristic of her lifestyle" (Walstedt, 1977, p. 170). She seeks attachment to a male to fulfill her needs for love and economic well-being, while in return she centers her life on his enhancement. This exchange is based on the expectation of reciprocity in which the altruist, by helping someone else, will eventually receive equally in return. This expectation that "payments" will balance out is seldom met—as many divorced and older women have discovered. Women who are free of this orientation seek control over their own lives. While they may behave in cooperative or altruistic ways, this is not their overriding behavior or preoccupation. Results from Walstedt's (1977) sample of 106 middle-aged women confirmed that women who did not accept the AOO were more likely to be self-supporting in their middle years and to have attained more academic degrees. Walstedt's findings suggest that more high-AOO women lack the education and jobs necessary for independent economic survival.

Included within the AOO is the commonly accepted belief that women should be the primary caretakers and nurturers of children, regardless of their own preferences or abilities, and the assumption that women should follow men wherever men's desires, education, or careers lead them, and put aside their own educational or occupational goals. Walstedt contends that a quid pro quo based on an AOO orientation will rarely be an equitable one, and that altruism will slowly evolve into martyrdom, disillusionment, or rage. She implies that equity in relationships can rarely be achieved by females via a weak, giving position, but rather that it must be attained through the accrual and utilization of typically masculine power resources (education, occupational status, assertiveness, and so on).

Walstedt also found that fathers' socialization practices were significantly correlated with AOO adoption, while mothers' socialization practices were unrelated to AOO. Fathers' socialization practices included the father fostering feminine sex-typing during childhood and adolescence; the father treating the daughter as a subordinate female; and the father reacting in a "sexually defensive" manner, that is, being centrally preoccupied with his daughter as a sex object, objecting to her wearing tight clothing and lipstick, and being overprotective about dating. Walstedt's research suggests that females internalize societal norms and are socialized in large part by their fathers to place themselves in a powerless, vulnerable, one-down position in relationship to males. This pervasive adoption of the AOO by women precludes the possibility of equity being the norm in male-female relations (Herships, 1982).

The training that females receive to focus on the needs of the other, especially in an intimate relationship, has recently been demonstrated to actually affect their perceptual and cognitive processes at a very basic level. Dion, Dion, Khalsa, and Yee (1980) presented a review of the literature on cognition as it is affected by romantic love. They speculated that if love has as potent an effect as is generally assumed, it should influence partner perception. In a perceptual distortion experiment Dion and Dion (1976) found that selective perceptual distortion was positively correlated with the strength of positive cathexis—a pooled index of love, liking, and trust scores. In addition, an interesting sex difference was found. The size judgments of men were sensitive only to the *sequence* in which stimulus persons were observed. In contrast, females showed a tendency toward *selective* perceptual distortion which was instigated *only* by strong positive cathexis for their partners. Thus, only women with a strong emotional attachment to their partners exhibited this tendency, which could be referred to as the "Honi" phenomenon. Dion and Pratt (1977) found sex differences in a memory task. For males there was no relationship between attitudes of love and liking toward the partner and vicarious memory distortion, whereas for females there was a significant relationship. Interestingly, when lesbian couples were tested a strongly significant, positive correlation between positive cathexis and recall of partners' words was obtained, a correlation that was almost significantly stronger than that of the heterosexual female sample.

In a study of the relationship of affective involvement with one's partner with ability to accurately perceive the partner's facial expressions, Khalsa (1980) found a positive relationship between these two variables in females while males showed a trend in the opposite direction.

Finally, in samples of dating couples in high school and college, strength of romantic love was associated with a tendency to distort the partner's perceived attractiveness in a positive direction *only* with female respondents; males did not so enhance their perception of their female partners' beauty (Price, Dabbs, Clower, & Resin, 1974). As Dion et al. (1980) conclude, "to women in love, beauty is in the heart as well as in the eye of the beholder" (p. 4).

To summarize, the review and research by Dion et al. (1980) indicate that the gender of the subject is a key moderator linking affect to cognition and behavior in close relationships with positive interpersonal affect being related to these processes of memory and perceptual distortion only for women. However, these authors emphasize that they do not assume a biological basis for these sex differences. Instead, they view these differences as reflecting the consequences of social and psychological variables. The implication of the research above is that gender socialization affects not only the taking of such roles as the "altruistic other" in relationships, but also affects our very perceptual and cognitive processes.

The research of Kelley et al. (1978) on sex differences in comments made during conflict was discussed earlier. An alternative interpretation of these results in terms of the couple's system and power dynamics is proposed by Herships (1982). Instead of assuming that future resolution of stylistic differences would be affected by personality and behavior change, the results can be seen as a reflection of male-female power differences. Crying, asking for emotional consideration, and *needing* changes are indications of the subordinate power position occupied by females. Males, conversely, are in a *position* to display overt anger, to invalidate the emotional turmoil that results from the female being unfairly or unequally treated, and to postpone the resolution of a problem if they consider the status quo to be acceptable. Herships (1982) notes that these sex-differentiating comments are not only *reflections* of the power imbalance but serve to *maintain* it as well. The implication of this analysis is that even if women were taught assertiveness skills and men were trained to make empathic statements, neither would be likely to employ these skills because men do not *have to* in their relationship systems, and women fear alienating and losing their male partners if they behave assertively or display anger. This analysis has direct applicability to systems theory as applied to relationships. Much of the following summary is drawn from Herships's (1982) excellent review and integration of systems theorists with an acknowledgment of an inherent, asymmetrical power structure in male-female relationships.

Systems Theory and Power

Fogarty's (1977) concept of "fusion" explicates the dimension of distance versus closeness in intimate relationships. As people become closer their emotional attraction and intensity (level of expectation, positive or negative) increases as does the tendency to fuse or unite. In this process self loses differentiation from other, as each partner loses all sense of autonomy and individual responsibility. Fogarty (1977) states that relationship systems are not static, that partners continuously enact a process of overcloseness, fusion, distance, and comfortable balance. In this respect fusion can be said to lead to distance through this alternating process.

Although Fogarty (1977) points out that in a systems approach the individual cannot be understood outside of the relationship system, the predisposing characteristics of individuals as they enter a system are salient to understanding the couple system as well. It has been noted that Waller's (1938) principle of least interest governs the relative emotional investment of each partner, "that movement toward or away from one's partner both defines and creates the balance of power in a relationship" (Herships, 1982, unpublished). Moving closer to the partner physically or emotionally usually translates into a greater time commitment and the expression of liking, loving, and acceptance. Withdrawal is the opposite, movement away in time and space, and is usually experienced by the other as rejection. Fogarty (1977) maintains that partners are in a constant state of movement (i.e., "pursuer") or away from (i.e., "distancer") each other. As Herships points out, "The question becomes whether this loving or rejecting is done in a balanced, shared way or becomes a sequence of scenarios with fixed roles, one of the partners doing most of the loving and the other doing most of the rejecting." Fogarty (1977) claims that fusion is an emotional process; the more emotional and less thoughtful a person becomes, the more he or she becomes highly reactive and susceptible to fusion. The more thoughtful (rational) and structured the individual, the more likely he or she is to resort to emotional distance.

Research (Johnson et al., 1975; Broverman et al., 1970) that demonstrates that females are more likely to assume the emotional or expressive role in relationships and males the instrumental (rational, logical) role suggests that females are therefore predisposed to being emotional pursuers and males are likely to assume the role of emotional distancer (Herships, 1982, unpublished). Theoretically, an inherent power imbalance will exist in most male-female relationship systems. A frequently made clinical observation is the pattern in which the pursuer, seeking closeness, prompts the distancer to withdraw and seek a more comfortable level of closeness. The pursuer panics, and in an effort to restore closeness, pushes the distancer even farther away. In most relationships one partner typically finds him/herself in a one-down position, emotionally pursuing the other.

Napier (1978) also considers polarization of these roles to be the norm, and cites the formation and evolutionary worsening of such skewed distancing dynamics as a major cause of marital disharmony. Partners seek each other out to satisfy mutual needs of "identity definition, intimacy regulation, and defense against covert anxieties (p. 9). Napier proposed two types of persons. Type 1 is a closeness-seeking person who perceives him/herself as warm, loving, and giving. Type 2 is the distance-seeking person who maintains an aura of strength and independence. The behavior of the Type 1 mate masks his/her own fear of rejection and need for closeness. Napier (1978) observes that these patterns seem to be associated with sex role, with women more likely to be Type 1s and men more likely to be Type 2s.

Psychoanalytic Perspectives, Intimacy, and Power

The psychoanalytic approach holds that the emotional dynamics in a marital relationship are determined by early childhood conflicts, the husband or wife serving as a substitute for each partner's opposite-sex parent. Horney (1967) theorized that our cultural model for child rearing (primarily by the mother) creates in almost every man "a recoiling from the forbidding female" (p. 13). Dinnerstein (1977) echoes this theory, considering female-dominated child rearing to be the original cause of male-female relationship problems, as well as a causal factor of societal unrest and war. The mother figure is seen as a source of tremendous ambivalence, being simultaneously the source of warmth, touch, joy, nourishment, and love for the infant and at the same time the source of frustration and prohibition.

According to Dinnerstein (1977), the fact that the mother is the primary focus of such intense positive and negative feelings necessitates that the male child learn to control and cut off his intensity. When the male child becomes verbal and mobile he is able to escape the overwhelming world of emotionality surrounding the mother by allying himself with his father, sports, work, and male camaraderie, which provide methods of distancing from the maternal love-hate dilemma. This dread of female control or power is a tendency that males bring into their adult relationships with women. The equivalent burden that Horney (1967) believed the female carries into relationships is "frigidity." Multiple causes for this include cultural mores, anxiety over being sexually overwhelmed, fear of motherhood, and passive-aggressive retaliation against male dominance.

Although the female child experiences the same ambivalence as the male toward her mother, Dinnerstein (1977) posits that the female develops an idealized love and erotic attachment to her father in order to escape from the dilemma of ambivalence toward her mother. Thus, rather than having to divorce herself from emotionality by identifying with the male (as boys do), she can use and foster emotionality in creating this attachment and pursuit of the father and ultimately of male partners. Unfortunately, many fathers are not warm, nurturing, and involved parents. In fact, fathers often play the role of distancer with respect to their children, as well as with their female partners. Thus, little girls grow up learning to pursue an emotionally distant male, thereby establishing this configuration as the model for their adult heterosexual relationships. The general scheme deriving from these theories is that males are predisposed to be emotionally distant from females in intimate relationships, and females are predisposed to be engaged in endless emotional pursuit of the distancing male (Herships, 1982). With respect to Waller's (1951) principle of least interest, this disparity in emotional involvement creates a decided power advantage for the male in intimate, heterosexual relationships.

Horney's (1967) theory of the etiology of female frigidity, combined with the conceptualization of power dynamics, leads to a common marital scenario. While the male lacks the ability and desire to achieve emotional closeness, he attempts to compensate for this in his desire for sexual closeness. The female compensates for her difficulty in achieving emotional distance by her inability to achieve sexual closeness (frigidity). This sexual distance (experienced by the male as rejection) contributes to the "primary dread" proposed by Horney (1967), giving the female a strong power resource (Herships, 1982). Thus, the sexual arena may become the battlefield in the struggle to balance relationship power when all other emotional dimensions (as well as social and economic ones) favor the male.

Recent clinical literature has described an increase in impotence among younger males in the absence of organic symptomatology. According to Moulton (1977) most women have historically feared male power and have typically acceded to it or developed strategies of indirect manipulation (unilateral power strategies) in order to maintain some control. The recent efforts of women to establish more equality between the sexes is challenging the patriarchal balance of power, and there is more overt struggle between men and women. Many men fear the newly assertive woman. Moulton (1977) and Ginsburg (1972) have cited fear of female power as a cause for the "new impotence" among younger men. Women are becoming more assertive and less accommodating in both sexual and nonsexual spheres, exerting a new type of pressure on men for performance. Virginity is no longer valued or tenaciously preserved; women seek and expect orgasmic release. Moulton (1977) explains the effect of the sexually freer new woman on some men as rooted in the male's deep-seated fear of female power deriving from his early dependency on his mother. The new feminism thus elicits men's deepest fears of being totally controlled by an omnipotent mother figure. As females have in the past reacted with "frigidity" to the fear of male domination, males are now reacting with withdrawal, passive sabotage, excessive criticism of the woman, or with specific sexual symptoms such as impotence or premature ejaculation. They are basically using traditionally "female" power strategies. These observations provide further support for the notion that the roots of sexual and relationship problems may be found in the contest for power in intrapersonal and systems inequalities.

IMPLICATIONS FOR THERAPY: CHANGE STRATEGIES

Changes in Concrete Power

As Johnson (1976) points out, if women limit their use of power to the personal, helpless, and indirect forms, they will be confined to a powerless status in relationships with others and in society. In order to change this system women need to acquire wider access to more forms of power. This requires changing both the societal expectations for women and the actual opportunities women have to use other forms of power.

Shirley Chisholm (1970) proposed two guidelines for promoting these changes. The first is the *taking* of power, for as Chisholm states, "no one is giving it away" (p. 45). This requires attaining power through increased access to concrete resources, to expert knowledge, and to the status systems to which power is linked.

Chisholm's (1970) second guideline is that women's goal in getting power is not to act like the traditional, stereotypic male, but rather to support their positive self-interests (such as welfare and child support reform, child care, and the Equal Rights Amendment) and to promote the acceptance of values now defined as traditionally feminine such as nurturance, gentleness, and empathy—by males as well as by females. If women accrue concrete power and simultaneously share gentler forms with males, everyone will have the opportunity to be both strong and humane (Johnson, 1976).

Critique of the behavioral approach

The behavioral approach to marital therapy assumes an egalitarian model that embraces the role of environmental reinforcers in shaping behavior, is oriented toward action, and includes specific procedures such as goal setting, behavioral exchange, and training in communication and problem-solving skills. Margolin, Talovic, Fernandez, and Cenato (1983) have criticized the lack of research in behavioral marital therapy that focuses on sex role issues and male-female differences in marriage. While there has recently been a growing recognition that the institution of marriage has served as a "principal arena for the exploitation of women," Margolin et al. (1983) assert that even egalitarian marriages have great interpersonal and intrapersonal costs for women and men, which often include ambiguity, conflict, work overload, isolation, and psychological pain.

These authors assert that behavioral marital therapy offers contradictory messages about sex role issues. While there is an underlying assumption that egalitarianism in relationships is a desirable goal (Stuart, 1980; Weiss, 1978), female-male differences and sex role issues are often ignored as factors contributing to marital distress. Thus, typical behavioral interventions generally require spouses to share equally in the planning and accomplishment of therapy related tasks, and to *assume* equality regarding the control of resources, the input into decision making, and the right to relationship benefits. The issue of whether or not the two partners have equal control over the entire range of relationship benefits is often overlooked. Assessment should include the specifics of whether the partners have equal access to the family's financial resources, and whether the relationship is characterized by a democratic decision-making process concerning issues such as how to spend money, how to raise children, how to spend free time, and so on.

Given that few couples actually do experience this egalitarian arrangement, we must consider how most couples respond to egalitarian-based treatment. While it is possible that having the therapist act on false assumptions of egalitarianism may have the outcome of fostering egalitarian actions and attitudes in a couple's relationship, it is more likely (and would be more consistent with behavioral principles) that generalization and maintenance of new behaviors would not be supported if the environmental context is antithetical to equality. In essence, behavioral techniques attempt to equalize the relationship and redistribute privileges but fail to address the underlying power balance. These strategies leave the less powerful partner without the means to enforce the altered system. A power analysis would recognize and attempt to alter the powerlessness of (typically) the female, both within and outside of the relationship, to enable her to bargain more effectively in the relationship system.

Margolin et al. (1983) make several other recommendations for marital therapists. Therapists are urged to look beyond the relationship or family system to the environmental influences including the social, political, and economic determinants of marital satisfaction that affect individuals.

Common interventions directed at equalizing the balance of concrete power include behavioral contracting, negotiation, and the redistribution of work, household responsibilities, and other resources within the relationship. In addition, Walker (1979) recommends that treatment of battered women include an emphasis on attaining economic independence so that the wife has the option of leaving her relationship at any time. Although a single woman, especially with dependent children, will generally have a difficult time due to discriminatory wage practices, legal difficulties in enforcing child support payment, discriminatory credit practices, and so on, it is nevertheless preferable for women to know that they are not bound economically to their battering or abusive spouses.

Because our society does not recognize that the role of housewife involves labor deserving of financial recompense, any person choosing this role is placing herself in a vulnerable and dependent position. Primary prevention might involve educational interventions directed toward women, apprising them that this position is often far from ideal in terms of status, independence, and mental health (Bernard, 1972). As Reich (1945) pointed out, women and men cannot experience true liberation within relationships until women attain equal status and economic power, and are no longer subject to abuses stemming from inequalities in concrete power.

Implications for Change: Interpersonal Power Strategies

Since powerlessness has negative psychological consequences, we might expect sex and marital therapists to be concerned with ways of helping clients gain power. Feminist therapy addresses power conflict in couples by attempting to demythologize the value of sex stereotypic power bases. Of the power bases discussed (French & Raven, 1959) only *referent* power seems inconsistent with the male sex role. For females, however, *expert, legitimate, coercive,* and *informational* power bases are to varying extents inconsistent with the female sex role stereotype. According to Seidler-Feller (1976) power-based interventions address several goals. Women are taught to use power in ways that are congruent with their needs and resources, and not merely congruent with gender role expectations. The advantages for men in learning to use softer modes of influence are expansion of their behavioral repertoires and personal satisfactions.

As therapy progresses it becomes possible to refine the use of these strategies such that partners learn to recognize which mode would be most effective and/or most interpersonally desirable in particular situations. For example, the male may be encouraged to rely on the personal resource of affection when asking his partner for a favor rather than telling her what he wants (legitimate power). The female in turn may learn when a direct statement of feeling will be most effective. Competence in power strategies thus becomes a first step in addressing the role of power in the relationship conflict.

Many behaviorally oriented power strategies address the power conflict issue by teaching different styles of interaction. Training couples to use behavioral contracting and to negotiate quid pro quo agreements is a process oriented intervention which assumes basic equality while attempting to equalize the couple's system of rewards for desirable behavior. The goal is to establish reciprocity. Other interventions seek to increase the use of personal or referent power by assigning each mate a specified number of reinforcing behaviors to perform daily irrespective of the partner's responses.

The behavioral exchange format entails certain problems in light of findings by Margolin, Talovic, and Weinstein (1982) that women desire more overall change than do men in marital therapy. When the husband feels sufficient change has occurred, the wife may continue to experience a number of dissatisfactions. Margolin, Talovic, Fernandez, and Onorato (1983) argue that it must be acceptable to continue working on one person's concerns even if they outnumber the other's, since wives typically experience more relationship strain than husbands.

Assertiveness training clearly falls within the behavioral approach category and is often combined with cognitive restructuring to maximize treatment effectiveness. For example, communication training may require that the therapist give women explicit permission to assert their individual preferences and needs, and give men permission to experience and express their feelings (Margolin et al., 1983). Another example is treatment of the individual who possesses assertive skills but is unable to utilize them because of an inhibiting belief system. As Jakubowski (1977) writes, attempts to use Masters' and Johnson's (1970) sexual shaping therapy are unsuccessful when women cannot be assertive enough to tell the man what they find sexually stimulating or irritating, to refuse sex when they are not sufficiently aroused, or to ask for tenderness after sex. Frequently, the underlying issues involve the woman's sense of her right to refuse sex and her fear of hurting the man if she tells him that she is not being sexually satisfied. The dysfunctional woman often comes to realize in therapy the enormous extent to which her behavior is governed by the fear of losing her husband or his approval. Kaplan (1974) points out that a woman's reluctance to express her needs is not always due to "cultural paranoia." The woman may run a real risk of displeasing her husband if she becomes more sexually assertive.

Assertiveness training is often used as an adjunct to sex and marital therapy and can have some impact on the balance of power in the relationship system. It is important, however, to realize that powerless behavior in women is not simply a matter of faulty socialization and that it is very difficult to counter these effects by teaching assertion (or the use of stronger power strategies) when the external society reinforces and maintains powerlessness and dependence in women while rewarding inexpressiveness, dominance, and control in men. There are inherent limitations in teaching partners to behave as if they are equals, to change their perception of power equilibrium, and to use alternative power strategies. Therapy may introduce an *artificial realignment* of power. If the new behavior is intrinsically more reinforcing for both partners then treatment effects are more likely to maintain. If, however, the new system is not reinforcing enough for the more powerful partner, there is a higher probability of relapse. It has been noted (Margolin et al., 1983) that teaching couples to use more direct forms of communication and reinforcing their right to equal input has *increased* conflict and dissension in many couples. Obviously, these approaches will work most effectively for partners who have both adopted a cooperative and egalitarian model for their relationship. Otherwise, the struggle for control in the relationship may go "underground" and express itself through indirect manifestations of power-seeking behavior. Stylistic change, then, presumes either equal access to concrete resources and/or an agreement between partners to treat each other as equals in their relationship.

Intrapersonal and Systems Change

As the field of marital and sex therapy has realized the limitations of technique-based interventions, a new focus on intimacy has begun to be incorporated. Earlier models of behavioral therapy which involve contracting for change, skills training (assertiveness and direct communication training, problem solving), and reciprocal exchange of positive behavior fell short of addressing intimacy issues. Direct behavioral approaches, even with the inclusion of cognitive intervention strategies intended to modify unrealistic and irrational beliefs and to intercept dysfunctional thought patterns, have not directly addressed priorities involving emotional intimacy, and have not provided effective means to intervene in closeness/distance conflicts or to promote intrapersonal resolution of such conflicts. Therapy that only teaches partners sophisticated bargaining skills is lacking an essential component if it does not also foster communication and sharing on a more fundamental, affective level. The field of sex therapy, for example, has developed an effective technology for treatment of sexual dysfunction (sensate focus, masturbation training, nondemand stimulation, the stop-start method). In essence, sexuality has been reduced to a mere restoration of genital functioning. We have yet to formulate a systematic treatment program which encourages the development of intimacy or proposes a model of sexual fulfillment that goes beyond the mechanical functioning of genitals. Mosher's (1980) model of depth of sexual involvement implies that the sexual experience can occur at different levels of intensity and involvement, and the field eagerly awaits the operationalization of this model in treatment.

Tiefer (1981) has argued that the field of sex therapy has been coopted by institutional forces that have rendered sexuality a marketable commodity, and a product that lends itself more readily to ideological control by medical, state, and professional institutions. This cooptation keeps sexuality within the control of experts who have the power to define its parameters and keeps the field of sexuality both centralized and neutralized as a potentially liberating force. If emotional closeness and true intimacy were recognized as priorities at least equal in importance to genital functioning, this would necessitate fundamental change in the power structure of heterosexual relationships. This formulation is consistent with the Elizabeth and Stock's (1982) intimacy model, which postulates power equality as a *precondition* of true emotional intimacy.

The section above on intrapersonal and systems power conflict began with a review of the literature indicating overwhelming female-male differences both in the desire for intimacy, and in the ability to be intimate. The systems approach suggests interventions and interpretations that make partners conscious of their power conflict. When there is a specific "symptom," for example, a sexual dysfunction, the couple in therapy will explore functional aspects of this problem, its role in displacing conflict into a circumscribed area, and the benefits and liabilities for each partner associated with maintenance of the current system.

Intrapersonal conflicts often determine the form of conflict that is present in a dysfunctional system. Katz (1981) claims that developmental arrests and fixations create chronic relationship conflict; if the individual has not successfully achieved the differentiation of self from object during childhood, this struggle will cause a repetitious pattern of struggle in intimate relationships until "well-developed and internalized psychic structures emerge" (p. 195). The initial therapeutic task, according to Katz, is to promote small degrees of psychic separation by introducing graded interventions which cause minimal anxiety without "producing excessive ego disorganization" (p. 202). For example, when one mate makes a statement, the therapist may interrupt and ask the other partner to (1) paraphrase the content of the statement, (2) ask the client what the partner was referring to, and (3) ask the client why he/she is saying that. The questions and interpretations are directed toward promoting the recognition that "there is another person out there who has a psychic structure which exists independently of their own primitive, internalized object relations system" (page 199).

Fontane (1979) recommends using family of origin material in couples therapy to enhance interaction and aid the process of separation and individuation. Bowen (1978) states that two people who select each other have reached the same developmental level, although they are not necessarily performing at the same functional level. He classifies these marriages as evidencing "overadequate-nonadequate reciprocity," in which one partner makes the decisions and the other is "helpless," but the two are equally immature. Recommendations for therapy include helping clients to recognize the expectations they had for their marriage (often based on family of origin role models), the unconscious elements determining partner choice, and current relationships with parents, which often include overattachment.

Sager (1976) states that culturally determined sex role differences stemming from families of origin often make it difficult for couples to arrive at mutually workable expectations. Fontane (1979) recommends direct examination and interpretation of parental models of the balance of power, their expression of love, affection, and the mode of handling anger, to aid the couple in working through relationship conflicts. According to Fontane, "Bringing to the surface a previously unaccessible pattern renders that pattern amenable to change" (p. 534).

Fogarty (1976b) recommends the direct examination of the emptiness experienced in each individual, the tracking of this emptiness back to the extended family, and in particular, teaching clients the distinction between wanting and needing things from others: "If a want becomes a need and dictates the level of expectation, then the expectation becomes unrealistic and doesnot take the real situation into account" (p. 40). According to Fogarty (1976b), part of the experience of emptiness occurs when individuals realize that self and relationships are confused, and "people continually try to get from others what they can only get from themselves" (p. 39). Because the external environment generally provides more reinforcers for males (which make them less dependent on rewards from their female partners), while paradoxically encouraging females to depend on males for many of their rewards (concrete and interpersonal), we more frequently observe in females the experience of emptiness in heterosexual relationships and unmet needs for intimacy, affection, attention, communication, and so on. Females also are taught to focus their energy on the advancement of their male partners and thus they learn to experience themselves as "selfless," victims of the "altruistic other orientation" described above. Males are unfortunately rewarded for remaining in control, being emotionally reticent. They learn to use this reticence consciously or unconsciously to maintain relationship power, as described above.

While it is generally acknowledged that males would benefit from becoming more emotionally expressive and being able to relinquish control, it is generally the individual who is experiencing the most psychological pain who is most amenable to change. For this reason, Herships (1983) encourages working with the emotional pursuer, usually the female, in systems presenting with the pursuer-distancer pattern. He recommends teaching the female client to distance from her male partner, to learn how to meet her needs independently, and to overcome dependence on her partner. Fogarty (1976a) also advocates teaching the pursuer to distance and to lower their expectation that their partner will be responsible for their happiness. This is often a difficult process, for it is antithetical to the traditional relationship model taught to females in this culture. However, this strategy is functional as it encourages the individual to develop sources of reward independent of the relationship, and it alleviates pressure on the distancing spouse, which often results in less distancing behavior.

This intervention basically utilizes Waller's (1951) principle of least interest on the level of power dynamics. On the level of personal growth it encourages the individual to identify the limitations of his or her relationship system, and spurs the acquisition of personal power resources that can increase the happiness of the individual, and thus effect a change in the balance of power in the relationship. If the relationship remains unsatisfactory, the individual has acquired the means to survive emotionally and perhaps materially without his or her partner, and is thus in a position to exercise more choice concerning whether to continue involvement in the system. Teaching clients to jettison the "altruistic other orientation" and encouraging their personal growth as individuals also has the secondary benefit of affecting the relationship's power balance. The following case example is offered to illustrate intrapersonal and systems interventions:

> Emily and Todd, a young, intelligent, married couple with two children under the age of three, presented for therapy with male premature ejaculation of extremely brief latency. Emily found sexual relations to be unsatisfactory, without emotional passion or excitement. The couple responded well to short-term, behaviorally oriented treatment, and within 10 sessions they were engaging in intercourse with quite an acceptable latency to ejaculation.
>
> However, Emily remained unsatisfied sexually, although she had always been able to attain orgasm. Nothing Todd did seemed to improve things, although communication, as well as specific techniques of massage and other forms of sexual stimulation, had been addressed. Emily noted a "shutting off" reaction when she did begin to experience sexual arousal. In addition, Emily felt "emotionally dead" toward Todd, and claimed to be "no longer in love." Her depressive tone and stance, present from the beginning of therapy, had not changed although all sexual goals had been achieved. Todd was quite successful in his profession, generally received much approval and many incentives from his company, and had recently been promoted. He found his job absorbing and demanding of his intelligence and creativity. Emily had

graduated from college also, but had put any career plans aside to become a housewife, alone daily with two small children except for a part-time sales job at a department store. She looked to Todd as her only source of attention, recognition, stimulation, and emotional intimacy.

Todd attempted to meet these needs, but could not devote (or was unwilling to devote) as much attention to them as Emily required. Todd was encouraged throughout therapy to be more attentive to Emily's emotional needs (conversation, calls from work, flowers occasionally), which he was willing to do, but these attentions did not satisfy Emily's expectations. Emily was encouraged to examine her choice to become the "altruistic other"—to recognize that her role as housewife/mother was isolating, providing privatized, unrecognized labor within the home. In addition, she began to recognize how she was entirely dependent on Todd for praise, contact, and recognition. This insight was supplemented by nonblaming discussion of the situation in joint session, with the understanding that nothing Todd did could likely return her sense of self, and that Emily would likely always feel undervalued and deprived in this role.

Therapy proceeded with exploration of educational and occupational alternatives and long-range career planning for Emily which would utilize her intelligence and expand her bases of power and reward beyond the relationship.

This case history demonstrates intervention strategies at all three levels of power-conflict discussed in this chapter: (1) changes in the concrete power structure of the relationship; (2) stylistic changes in interpersonal power strategies, fostering direct communication and assertiveness in both partners; and (3) systems change in the pursuer/distancer pattern incorporating intrapersonal change through identifying and addressing the altruistic other orientation in the female partner. In addition, by encouraging her emotional independence and the acquisition of concrete power and identification of the role of housewife in this system as unequal, nonrewarding, and depression-inducing, the balance of power in the relationship system was effected without blame being placed on the male partner for his inability to compensate for the deficit created by his wife's role. Behavioral, cognitive, and insight-oriented techniques were utilized at all stages of treatment, which demonstrates that the power-conflict model of relationship dynamics and therapeutic interventions proposed here is not limited to any specific theoretical orientation.

Summary

It is suggested that successful interventions first accurately assess all levels at which asymmetries in power balance are present in the couple system and then tailor treatment to address change at each level, avoiding the assumption that change on one level will "trickle down" to other levels. Clinicians are strongly encouraged to develop a sophisticated understanding of societal, interpersonal, and systemic origins of power inequality in order to be effective agents of change for individuals and couple systems.

References

Barbach, I. (1975). *For yourself: The fulfillment of female sexuality.* Garden City, NY: Doubleday Publishing.

Barnett, R., & Baruch, G. (1983). *Determinants of father participation in child care.* Paper presented at the Annual Meeting of the American Psychological Association, Anaheim, CA.

Berman, J. S., & Bennett, J. B. (1982, August). *Love and power: Testing Waller's principle of least interest.* Paper presented at the meeting of the American Psychological Association, Washington, DC.

Bernard, J. (1972). *The future of marriage.* New York: World.

Blood, R. O., Jr., & Wolfe, D. M. (1960). *Husbands and wives: The dynamics of married living.* Glencoe, IL: Free Press.

Bowen, M. (1978). *Family therapy in clinical practice.* New York: Jason Aronson, 108–109.

Broverman, I., Broverman, D., Clarkson, F., Rosenkrantz, P., & Vogel, S. (1970). Sex-role stereotypes and clinical judgments of mental health. *Journal of Consulting and Clinical Psychology, 34,* 1–7.

Brownmiller, S. (1975). *Against our will: Men, women and rape.* New York: Simon & Schuster.

Bryan, J. H., & Test, M. H. (1967). Models and helping: Naturalistic studies in aiding behavior. *Journal of Personality and Social Psychology, 6,* 400–407.

Cartwright, D. A. (1959a). A field theoretical conception of power. In D. Cartwright (Ed.), *Studies in social power.* Ann Arbor: University of Michigan Press.

Cartwright, D. A. (1959b). Power: A neglected variable in social psychology. In D. Cartwright (Ed.), *Studies in social power.* Ann Arbor: University of Michigan Press.

Chisholm, S. (1970). Black women and politics. *Black Scholar, 1,* 40–45.

Cowan, G. (1981). *The development of gender differences in power strategies.* Paper presented at the Annual Meeting of the American Psychological Association, Los Angeles.

Cowan, C., & Cowan, P. (1983). *Men's involvement in the family affects couples relationships.* Paper presented at the Annual Meeting of the American Psychological Association, Anaheim, CA.

Cromwell, R. E., & Olson, D. H. (1975). *Power in Families.* New York: John Wiley & Sons.

De Beauvior, S. (1968). *The second sex.* New York: Modern Library.

De Cecco, J. P., & Shively, M. G. (1978, Spring). A study of perceptions of rights and needs in interpersonal conflicts in homosexual relationships. *Journal of Homosexuality, 3*(3), 205–216.

Dinnerstein, D. (1977). *The mermaid and the minotaur: Sexual arrangements and human malaise.* New York: Harper & Row.

Dion, K. L., & Dion, D. D. (1976). The Honi phenomenon revisited: Factors underlying the resistance to perceptual distortion of one's partner. *Journal of Personality and Social Psychology, 33,* 170–177.

Dion, K. L., Dion, K. K., Khalsa, K. D., & Yee, P. H. N. (1980, September). *Male-female differences in affect linkages to cognition and behavior.* Paper presented at the Annual Meeting of the American Psychological Association, Montreal.

Dion, K. L., & Pratt, G. (1977). *Selective memory and interpersonal relations.* Unpublished manuscript, University of Toronto.

Elizabeth, P., & Stock, W. (1984). A model of power, intimacy and status. In C. Widom (Ed.), *Sex roles and sexual dysfunction.* New York: Plenum Press.

Falbo, T., Hazen, M. D., & Linimon, D. (in press). The costs of selecting power bases or measures associated with the opposite sex. *Sex Roles.*

Falbo, T., & Peplau, L. A. (1980). Power strategies in intimate relationships. *Journal of Personality and Social Psychology, 38*(4), 618–628.

Fogarty, T. F. (1976a). On Emptiness and closeness, Part I. *The Family, 3*(1).

Fogarty, T. F. (1976b). On Emptiness and closeness, Part II. *The Family, 3*(2).

Fogarty, T. F. (1977). Fusion. *The Family, 4*(2).

Fontane, A. S. (1979, November). Using family of origin material in short-term marital counseling. *Social Casework: The Journal of Contemporary Social Work.* 529–537.

Frank, E., Anderson, C., & Rubenstein, M. (1978). Frequency of sexual dysfunction in "normal" couples. *New England Journal of Medicine, 299,* 111–115.

French, J. R. P., & Raven, B. (1959). The bases of social power. In D. Cartwright (Ed.), *Studies in social power* (pp. 150–167). Ann Arbor, MI: University of Michigan Press.

Freud, A. (1966). *The ego and the mechanism of defense.* New York: International Universities Press.

Frieze, I. H., & McHugh, M. C. (1981). *Violence and other bases of power in marriage.* Presented at the Annual Meeting of the American Psychological Association, Los Angeles.

Gelles, R. J. (1976). Abused wives: Why do they stay? *Journal of Marriage and the Family, 38,* 659–668.

Gelles, R. J. (1971, October). Power, sex and violence: The case of marital rape. *The Family Coordinator,* 339–347.

Ginsberg, G. L., Frasch, W. A., & Shapiro, T. (1972, March). The new impotence. *Archives of General Psychiatry, 26.*

Gray-Little, B., & Burks, N. (1983). Power and satisfaction in marriage: A review and critique. *Psychological Bulletin, 93*(3), 513–538.

Hatfield, E., Utne, M., & Traupman, J. (1979). Equity theory and intimate relationships. In R. Burgess & T. L. Huston (Eds.), *Social Exchange in Developing Relationships.* New York: Academic Press.

Hatfield, E., Greenberger, D., Traupmann, J., & Lambert, P. (1982, February). Equity and sexual satisfaction in recently married couples. *The Journal of Sex Research, 18*(1), 18–32.

Heiman, J., LoPiccolo, L., & LoPiccolo, J. (1976). *Becoming orgasmic: A sexual growth program for women.* New Jersey: Prentice-Hall.

Herships, M. (1982). Emotional equity in couples—it's relation to satisfaction and conflict. Unpublished doctoral proposal, SUNY at Stony Brook, NY.

Hiller, D. (1982, November). Real men don't earn less than their wives. *Psychology Today,* 37–41.

Horney, K. (1967). *Feminine psychology*. New York: W. W. Norton.

Hornung, C. A., McCullough, B. C., & Sugimoto, T. (1980, August). *Status relationships in marriage: Risk factors in spouse abuse*. Paper presented to the American Sociological Association, New York.

Jacobs, L. I. (1977, January). The impotent king: Secondary impotence refractory to brief sex therapy. *American Journal of Psychotherapy, 31*(1), 97–104.

Jacubowski, P. A. (1977). Assertive behavior and clinical problems of women. In E. Rawlings & D. Carter (Eds.), *Psychotherapy for women* (pp. 147–165). Springfield, IL: Charles C. Thomas.

Johnson, P. (1976). Women and power: Toward a theory of effectiveness. *Journal of Social Issues, 32*(3), 99–110.

Jourard, S. M. (1971). *The transparent self*. New York: Litton Educational Publishing.

Kalmuss, D. (1981, August 3). New light on wife beatings. *New York Times,* p. B–5.

Kaplan, H. S. (1974). *The new sex therapy*. New York: Brunner/Mazel.

Katz, B. (1981, Summer). Separation-individuation and marital therapy. *Psychotherapy: Theory, Research, and Practice, 18*(2), 195–203.

Kelley, H., Cunningham, J., Grisham, J., Lefebvre, L., Sink, C., & Yablon, G. (1978). Sex differences in comments made during conflict within close heterosexual pairs. *Sex Roles, 4,* 473–491.

Khalsa, K. K. (1980). *Sex differences in the communication of negative affect and use of manipulative techniques during conflict in couples*. Unpublished doctoral dissertation, University of Toronto.

Kincaid, P. J. (1982). *The omitted reality: Husband-wife violence in Ontario and policy implications for education*. Maple, Ontario: Publishing and Printing Services.

Kipnis, D. (1976). *The powerholders*. Chicago: University of Chicago Press.

Kipnis, D., Schmidt, S. M., & Wilkinson, T. (1980). Interorganizational influence tactics: Explorations in getting one's way. *Journal of Applied Psychology, 65,* 440–452.

LoPiccolo, J., & LoPiccolo, L. (1978). *Handbook of sex therapy*. New York: Plenum Press.

Margolin, G., Talovic, S., Fernandez, V., & Onorato, R. (1983, April). Sex role considerations and behavioral marital therapy: Equal does not mean identical. *Journal of Marital and Family Therapy,* 131–145.

Margolin, G., Talovic, S., & Weinstein, C. (1982). *The areas of change questionnaire: A practical approach to marital assessment*. Manuscript submitted for publication.

Masters, W., & Johnson, V. (1970). *Human sexual inadequacy*. Boston: Little, Brown.

Miller, J. B. (1976). *Toward a new psychology of women*. Boston: Beacon Press.

Millett, K. (1970). *Sexual politics*. New York: Doubleday Publishing.

Mosher, D. L. (1980, February). Three dimensions of depth of involvement in human sexual response. *The Journal of Sex Research, 16*(1), 1–42.

Moulton, R. (1977, October). The fear of female power—a cause of sexual dysfunction. *Journal of the American Academy of Psychoanalysis, 5*(4), 499–519.

Napier, A. Y. (1978, January). The rejection-intrusion pattern: A central family dynamic. *The Journal of Marriage and Family Counseling*, 5–12.

Olson, D. H., & Rubunsky, C. (1972). Validity of four measures of family power. *Journal of Marriage and the Family, 34*, 224–234.

Pagelow, M. D. (1981, August 3). New light on wife beatings. *New York Times*, p. B–5.

Parsons, J. E., Ruble, D. N., Hodges, K. L., & Small, A. W. (1976). Cognitive-developmental factors in emerging sex differences in achievement-related expectancies. *Journal of Social Issues, 32*(3), 47–61.

Peplau, L. A., & Cochran, S. D. (1980). *Sex differences in values concerning love relationships*. Paper presented at the Annual Meeting of the American Psychological Association, Montreal.

Powers, E. C. (1964). *An attempt to develop a scale to measure the principle of least interest*. Unpublished manuscript, Department of Sociology, Ohio State University.

Price, G. H., Dabbs, J. M., Clower, B. J., & Resin, R. P. (1974, April). *At first glance—or, is physical attractiveness more than skin deep*. Paper presented at the meeting of the Eastern Psychological Association, Philadelphia.

Propper, A. M. (1985). The invisible reality: Patterns and power in family violence. In M. Baker (Eds.), *The family: Changing trends in Canada*. Toronto: McGraw-Hill Ryerson.

Rainwater, L. (1966). Some aspects of lower-class sexual behavior. *Journal of Social Issues, 22*, 96–108.

Raven, B. H., Centers, R., & Rodriguez, A. (1975). The bases of conjugal power. In R. E. Cromwell & D. H. Olson (Eds.), *Power in Families*, New York: Sage Publications.

Raven, B. H., & Kruglanski, A. W. (1970). Conflict and power. In P. Swingle (Ed.), *The Structure of Conflict*. New York: Academic Press.

Reich, W. (1945). *The Sexual revolution*. New York: Farrar, Straus and Giroux.

Robinson-Metz, M. (1983, May 22–27). *A multidimensional study of marital and sexual dysfunction couples: The role of conflict management in symptom differentiation*. Paper presented at the 6th World Congress of Sexology, Washington, DC.

Sager, C. (1976). Marriage contracts and couple therapy: Hidden forces. In *Intimate relationships*. New York: Brunner/Mazel.

Seidler-Feller, D. (1983). A feminine critique of sex therapy. In L. B. Rosewater, L. E. Walker, & P. G. Webbick (Eds.), *Feminist therapy: A Coming of Age*. New York: Springer.

Seidler-Feller, D. (1976, Fall). Process and power in couple's psychotherapy: A feminist view. *Voices*, pp. 67–71.

Shaef, A. W. (1981). *Women's reality*. Minneapolis: Winston Press.

Sherif, C. W. (1982). Needed concepts in the study of gender identity. Presidential address to Division 35 of the American Psychological Association. *Psychology of Women Quarterly, 6*, 375–398.

Stock, W., & Roberts, C. W. (1983). Power conflict in sexually dysfunctional couples. [*New Techniques in Sex Therapy*]. Symposium conducted at the meeting of the American Psychological Association, Anaheim, CA.

Stone, W. F. (1973). Patterns of conformity in couples varying in intimacy. *Journal of Personality and Social Psychology, 27*, 413–418.

Straus, M., Gelles, R. J., & Steinmetz, S. K. (1980). *Behind closed doors: Violence in the American family*. New York: Anchor Doubleday.

Straus, M. (1978). Wife beating: How common and why. *Victimology, 2*(3–4), 443–458.

Stuart, R. B. (1980). *Helping couples change: A social learning approach to marital therapy*. New York: Guilford.

Tiefer, L. (1981). The context and consequences of contemporary sex research: A feminist perspective. In S. Cox (Ed.), *Female psychology: The emerging self* (2nd ed.). New York: St. Martin's Press.

Unger, R. K. (1980). Female-male differences in close relationships. Symposium conducted at the Annual Meeting of the American Psychological Association, Montreal.

Unger, R. K. (1982, August). *Controlling out the obvious: Power, status, and social psychology.* Paper presented at the symposium, Gender differences: The effects of status, power, and competence. Annual Meeting of the American Psychology Association, Washington, DC.

Walker, L. E. (1979). *The battered woman*. New York: Harper & Row.

Walker, L. E. (1978, March 4). Feminist psychotherapy with victims of violence. Presented at the American Psychological Association Midwinter Meeting, Scottsdale, AZ.

Waller, W. (1951). *The family: A dynamic interpretation* (rev. ed.). New York: Dryden Press.

Walstedt, J. (1974). Women as marginals. *Psychological Reports, 34*, 639–646.

Walstedt, J. J. (1977, Winter). The altruistic other orientation: An exploration of female powerlessness. *Psychology of Women Quarterly*, 2(2), 162–177.

Walster, E., Traupman, J., & Walster, G. (1978). Equity and extramarital sexuality. *Archives of Sexual Behavior*, 7(2), 127–141.

Walster, E., Berscheid, E., & Walster, G. W. New directions in equity research. (Search for source in progress)

Weiss, R. L. (1978). The conceptualization of marriage from a behavioral perspective. In T. J. Paolino & B. S. McCrady (Eds.), *Marriage and marital therapy: Psychoanalytic, behavioral and systems perspectives*. New York: Brunner/Mazel.

Yllo, K. (1981, August 3). New light on wife beatings, *New York Times*, p. B–5.

Zellman, G. L., & Connor, C. (1973). *Increasing the credibility of women*. Paper presented at the annual meeting of the Women in Psychology Association.

Zilbergeld, B. (1978). *Male sexuality*. Boston: Little, Brown.

SECTION 2

Lifestyle Management

FIVE

Coprofessional Marriage

Lana P. Fishkin, M.D.
Clinical Assistant Professor of Psychiatry and Human Behavior
Jefferson Medical College
Ralph E. Fishkin, D.O.
Clinical Associate Professor of Psychiatry and Human Behavior
Jefferson Medical College

OVERVIEW

As increasing numbers of women are pursuing graduate training and embarking on high-level careers, we are witnessing an increase in the incidence of the coprofessional or dual career marriage. This particular arrangement comes with its advantages but also with its own set of problems. These include special, external difficulties in addition to those that all couples encounter as they progress through the life cycle, as well as interactional and intrapsychic conflicts which interfere with marital, familial, and career satisfactions for the coprofessional couple.

In an earlier work (Fishkin & Fishkin, 1981), we classified the coprofessional marriage according to parental stage and focused upon the special stresses and strains on the relationship coincident with the different phases of child rearing. We would like to review that discussion, enumerate the specific interactional dynamic conflicts that are prevalent in the coprofessional relationship, and show how individual psychodynamics underlie and shape some of these interactional conflicts. Finally, we would like to discuss how, in the treatment of the coprofessional couple, the therapist must take into account issues from external, interactional, and intrapsychic levels of conflict.

First of all, a precise definition is required. After all, current U.S. Census figures indicate that well over 50 percent of married women are employed. Unfortunately, a precise definition is difficult, as Rapoport and Rapoport point out in their comprehensive review of the literature on dual-career families (Rapoport & Rapoport, 1978). Their article cites a number of recent papers, both psychological and sociological in their orientation, that discuss issues pertinent to the coprofessional couple. Many of these issues will be examined later in this chapter. For our purposes, we wish to restrict the concept of coprofessional marriage to one in which both partners are involved in a demanding, graduate-level profession in which an interruption or an extended reduction in their work hours means a sacrifice of career ambitions with respect to faculty advancement, opportunities for research, promotions, partnerships, or outstanding achievements within diverse professional or business fields. For both partners professional obligations and commitments far exceed the limits of the 40-hour workweek.

Thus, the groundwork is laid for potential marital conflict and role strain which are generally avoided in more traditional two-job marriages. In a two-job marriage, as opposed to a coprofessional marriage, the time pressures are greatly reduced since one or both partners can limit their work to the traditional 40-hour week.

In the more conventional marriage, role specifications for husbands and wives (and mothers and fathers) do not permit much latitude. Wives are generally responsible for managing the household and the associated domestic chores. They become the primary caretakers of any children in the household and are responsible for the additional obligations and duties attendant to rearing children. Their feminine self-concept as essentially full-time wives and mothers is satisfied by this arrangement, unless there is some associated, unresolved ambivalence. Their life ambitions generally do not include high-level professional achievement. Husbands in such unions are the primary wage earners, even if their wives supplement their incomes. It falls to the husbands to pursue professions if that is their inclination.

Of particular relevance for the classification of coprofessional marital relationships is Otto Pollak's (1965) categorization according to parental stage. He considers four stages, which will be described in detail: (1) before childbearing, (2) early child rearing, (3) latency and adolescent child rearing, and (4) after the children leave.

Before Childbearing

Sources of potential marital conflict in this marital stage revolve around (1) competition in respective careers, (2) value system clashes, (3) geographical change necessitated by career advancement, and (4) "role reversals" determined by the greater professional and financial success of the wife.

Prior to the arrival of the children the likelihood is that many problems in the relationship will be related to the intense commitment of each partner to his profession. For example, conflicts can occur when both partners are highly competitive, regardless of whether they are in the same or different professions. The disproportionate success of one partner may constitute a narcissistic injury for the other, with subsequent reactions of envy, retaliatory fantasies, or depression. To complicate matters further, the more successful partner may experience guilt. It is generally the case that this reaction occurs more commonly when the wife has the greater professional stature. The shared unhappiness of both husband and wife, or their respective defenses against their feelings, can serve to intensify marital discord, particularly if the relationship is tenuous in the first place.

The following case illustrates some of these issues. A young, childless couple, married since they graduated from college, began to experience substantial marital discord when the wife, a medical student, completed her training and went into practice. The husband had been teaching undergraduate courses at a nearby college and was having difficulty completing his doctoral dissertation. As his wife's professional career flourished, he became markedly more distant, critical, and antagonistic. He spent increasingly more time away from home and became involved in an extramarital affair with one of his former students. It was obvious that he felt threatened by his wife's status as a doctor and by her earning capacity. He was no longer the breadwinner, and the balance of power had shifted to the wife.

It became increasingly difficult for her to accept his ongoing devaluation, which had previously synchronized with her own psychodynamics. The wife initially felt guilty about her obviously greater success including her income, which had doubled. She tried to minimize her professional accomplishments at first, but inevitably felt entitled to them and became aware of her own storehouse of anger and resentment, the accumulation of years of disappointment from her husband. The marital relationship was too troubled to weather this onslaught and the couple separated despite a brief attempt at therapeutic intervention.

This case example illustrates a type of marital conflict syndrome (Berman, Sacks, & Lief, 1975) that is becoming increasingly more common as students marry and subsequently have to confront the rapidly changing situation as they launch their careers. The enhanced professional stature of the wife in this case affected the balance of power between the spouses and contributed to their marital dissatisfaction. The husband, who had married a dependent, subordinate, and self-effacing fellow student, was loathe to acknowledge his wife's growing success. Despite desperate attempts to finish his dissertation, he was unable to complete his graduate work since to do so would have unconsciously meant a submission to his demanding, perfectionistic, sadistic father who expected high-level academic performance of his son. Thus, the son continued to frustrate his father with his failures. Father and son had become locked in an intense power struggle in which the son had to fail in order to defeat his father. The price the son had to pay was high and included the destruction of his marriage. The wife initially tried to support and encourage her husband to finish his graduate studies both for his own sake and the sake of their marriage. However, the husband's unconscious need to fail was greater than his conscious wish to succeed. His behavior became increasingly defensive, regressive, and destructive to their relationship.

There are other considerations in the coprofessional marriage which confront the couple with potential conflicts. Specifically, there are two value systems, goals and commitments, that may not be congruent. Obviously, this is less of a problem in the more traditional marriage, in which the husband generally sets the standards, selects the lifestyle, and determines where the family will live and with whom they will socialize. These decisions are usually made in the service of his professional advancement.

However, in the coprofessional marriage, the clash of value systems can manifest itself in various ways. For instance, one spouse who is a university-based physician or basic scientist might have a very different professional orientation from his or her clinician spouse. To illustrate how this might create a problem for the couple, consider the case of two married psychiatrists. The husband was involved in biological psychiatric research since his interest was in determining biochemical causes of emotional illness. His wife was a practicing clinical psychiatrist, pursuing psychoanalytic training. The husband was contemptuous of his wife's involvement in "Freudian psychiatry," sincerely believing that the whole enterprise was misguided. She, feeling denigrated by her husband's attitude, withdrew from her husband emotionally and became reactively critical of her husband's "cold, unfeeling, scientific" approach to human suffering. Of course, the conflict described above was multiply determined and might not have presented a significant disruption had the relationship been supportive and mutually respectful from the outset. Since it wasn't, the clash of values, which had dictated their respective professional choices, intensified the hostility and contempt in which each held the other. Both partners lost a potential ally and an opportunity to extend the scope of their theoretical and professional understanding.

Another potential source of marital discord unique to the coprofessional marriage arises when a geographical change necessary for the career advancement of one partner creates a career disruption for the other partner. Such a problem arose for a young, childless couple who had married during college and had pursued different graduate training. The husband, upon completing law school, had taken a position in a prestigious law firm and was anticipating an offer of a partnership in the near future. The wife, who had taken several years longer to finish her doctoral training, was now receiving desirable offers of employment in other cities. Since her field was highly specialized she was initially unable to obtain a position in the city where they were currently living. The acute strain which ensued from the untenable situation precipitated the need for marital therapy. Each partner felt that great career sacrifices had already been made on behalf of the other, and wasn't about to deprive him- or herself of important professional opportunities. Both husband and wife could make legitimate cases for expecting the other to now compromise his or her own career goals. Issues concerning competition, power, dominance, and dependency emerged in the treatment of this couple. Fortunately, a happy ending ensued when a local university offered the wife a faculty appointment in her field, providing an external solution to an extremely thorny problem.

On the other hand, being coprofessionals can be mutually advantageous, especially if both partners are in the same profession or at similar levels of training. The potential for empathy, support, and encouragement is enhanced when professional accomplishments are not threatening to one another. The opportunities for sharing ideas, providing discipline, and sustaining enthusiasm can flourish readily in such an environment. For example, a couple who had finished a psychiatric residency within a year of one another was able to take certification boards in psychiatry in the same year. Preparing for this examination together provided an opportunity for professional and personal sharing on an intense level. Although there was occasional trepidation about what might ensue should only one member of the couple pass the examination, the experience was evaluated as positive by both partners. This couple continued to develop together professionally and to share their clinical experiences, as well as psychiatric meetings and conferences. Their mutual toleration for one another's demanding schedules and occasional emotional depletion was enhanced by their similar professional orientation. Each partner was ready to provide a miniconsultation for the other, and their conversations ranged from intimate concerns to theoretical or technical matters. The scope of what they were able to share with each other was far greater than would have been the case had they been in different professions. Since rivalry, competition, and envy had never been of much concern to them, each was pleased to see the other grow professionally.

Keeping the dual career marriage supportive, sustaining, and satisfying is no easy task. Finding relaxed, intimate time for each other is a major challenge to the resources and ingenuity of any couple. It is all too easy to allow the incessant demands of work to encroach upon personal time, with evening meetings, work brought home in briefcases, phone calls waiting to be returned from a busy day, and so forth. It is, therefore, even more essential for the coprofessional couple, who have less flexibility in their schedules than a conventional couple, to set firm priorities with respect to "free" time, and to not erode the boundaries of this space. The commitment of time and emotional availability to one another must be considered as inviolable as any professional obligation would be. While making time for each other is obviously a major task of any marriage, it becomes even more critical for the professional marriage to make this a high priority.

In their recent book on dual career couples, Bryson and Bryson (1978) include a number of papers that address themselves to some of the abovementioned issues. These papers focus on the special problems of the dual career couple, particularly in the areas of job seeking, domestic responsibility, the effects of having children, personal values, and marital adjustment. These papers attempt to provide some statistical and interview data to document many of the points discussed above. One interesting paper by Pingree et al. in this collection examines the extent to which academic administrators hold attitudes that would be prejudicial to the hiring of a couple, thereby preventing a happy solution to the employment problems of academic, dual career couples.

Early Child Rearing

The years of early child rearing present new problems for the coprofessional couple. The dramatically accelerated demands made by the addition of a baby create added pressures for the couple. They must make a consensual, uncoerced decision at the outset that one parent will temporarily reduce his or her professional commitments in order to become the primary caretaker of their child. Generally speaking, it is more appropriate for the wife to assume this responsibility in most marriages, in view of her biological and psychological predisposition to motherhood, as well as the existing social and cultural sanctions for this role. While the above assertion is undoubtedly controversial in some quarters and may seem to be tainted with sexist, discriminatory attitudes, we feel compelled to stand by this premise and will attempt to justify it not politically but psychologically.

The nine months of gestation forge a psychological as well as a physiological bond between the expectant mother and her child. This full-time biological attachment is a unique and unduplicated relationship. It is obvious that the expectant father can participate only vicariously at this time. Delighted observations of the baby's movement in utero add to the excitement and anticipation of *both* expectant parents, but prior to its birth the baby appears to have a more intense psychological reality for the mother. The bonding that occurs between mother and child prenatally is reinforced by neonatal experiences of nursing or bottle-feeding, as well as by other maternal, caretaking behavior. The new father tends to play an auxiliary role at this stage, and is more useful supporting his wife in her attempts to master this onslaught to her psychological and physiological coping mechanisms. Important decisions have to be made concerning when and at what level she will resume her professional activities, as well as what kind of child care arrangements are feasible.

Certain aspects of psychoanalytic theory elaborate the psychological consequences of the biological relationship between mother and child. Johnson & Johnson (1977) describe an "androcentric model" of feminine identification in which the sex of the primary caretaker, the female in all societies, is defensively devalued by children of both sexes, while the sex of the noncaretaker is overvalued. Lerner (1973) discusses the mechanism of this devaluation: The effects of fear, envy, rage, and shame aroused in the child by his helpless dependency on a seemingly all-powerful maternal figure result in a subsequent defensive devaluation of women and corresponding definitions of "masculine" and "feminine" characteristics based upon these values that carry over into adult life. A construct related to this mechanism is "penis envy" in which the male genital and all that it symbolizes is overvalued. Thus, Lerner's conclusion is that "the opprobrious social and cultural depictions of women exist as projections of defensive intrapsychic devaluations, internalized by both males and females during the oedipal resolution" (p. 541). Since the girl's unconscious resolution of the separation from mother consists of her identification with her mother as a devalued object, this dynamic might in part explain the psychological susceptibility of most women to more readily succumb to the demands of others for need satisfaction. This intrapsychic mechanism thus supports the external social expectation that the wife will assume primary executive responsibility for household and child care activities. It also explains the husband's intrapsychic need to devalue maternal roles for himself as an outgrowth of his earlier identification and dependency conflicts with his mother.

Again, we see how intrapsychic mechanisms and sociocultural role expectations within both partners conspire to make the demands of role proliferation more keenly felt by the professional mother. There are both internal and external biological, psychological, and social justifications for her assumption of the primary responsibility for domestic activities. Since she is already heavily invested in her career, she must choose either to temporarily surrender her professional aspirations entirely or to add another role, generally also considered to be full time, to her repertoire. It is not surprising therefore that the concept of "role strain" characterizes the professional mother, who is desperately attempting to do a more than passable job at home and at work—especially if she is continuing to work full time (more than a 40-hour workweek) *and* take care of a new baby. A more viable option might be, if her specialty permits it, a reduced workload. It is even better if both parents are able to reduce their work hours, making more time for accomplishing necessary chores, for caretaking responsibilities concerning the baby, and even for some fun time together.

Johnson and Johnson (1977) have elaborated on the concepts of role proliferation and on role strain in high-commitment career women. Role proliferation refers to an "additive combination of disparate and disassociated roles, each of which requires deep commitment to both role expectations. This constantly poses competitive concerns and demands which are synchronous and continuous in time" (p. 15). They cite an autobiographical case study of 12 successful women recently published in the *Annals of the New York Academy of Sciences*. Virtually all of these women felt that their activities were regarded as deviant by their peers, teachers, and superiors, but that their parents and later their husbands gave them a great deal of encouragement and support with respect to their professional aspirations. It was important that their husbands, in addition to providing support during their training and professional life, chose professions that facilitated reciprocity and the sharing of financial, emotional, and caretaking responsibilities. Such mutual support is as necessary for the attainment of a harmonious coprofessional marriage as it is for the wife to make an uncoerced decision regarding child-rearing responsibilities. Thus, to a greater and lesser extent, both partners are confronted with a degree of role proliferation within the marriage.

Clearly, the years of child rearing make the greatest demands on the coprofessional couple, with maximal role proliferation for both partners. Compromises must be made on professional and domestic fronts to ensure the continuity of these activities for both spouses. It is unlikely that the woman will opt for a full hiatus from her professional involvements and elect to become, even if temporarily, a full-time mother. If she doesn't choose to resume full-time work soon after the birth of her child, she might opt for a somewhat reduced schedule, at least until the child is in school all day. What is important is that the woman feels free to spend a variable number of hours each day with her child when she is unconflicted, unpressured, and undistracted. The actual amount of time spent depends upon the needs of the mother and of the child—and *both* must be considered.

This adjustment in her workload will be advantageous to the professional woman provided that she doesn't suffer in her career advancement. Thus freed, to some extent, of role proliferation and strain, the mother will be more capable of providing a secure, loving environment for her child. Some authors have described this as "quality time," although this view can become a rationalization for shortchanging a child in the pursuit of one's professional ambitions.

It should be pointed out that the above-described dilemma is especially intense for the professional mother involved in the field of mental health because of the following considerations. First, by virtue of her training, this woman is intimately involved with theories of child development that stress the importance of the mother-infant bond and warn of the hazards for the child who is faced with early separation from the mother. Second, if she is a sensitive person, one who readily perceives her own feelings and the feelings of others, she will be much more attuned to the conflict between staying home with her child or returning to work. This conflict is not necessarily neurotic since it is substantially based in an external reality, the resolution of which is complex and difficult if even possible. Thus, the professional mother often feels herself caught between Scylla and Charybdis in her ongoing effort to strike a relatively harmonious balance.

Some women seem to handle this conflict more easily than others. Women whose own mothers worked and women whose mothers were professionals themselves appear to experience less conflict in the pursuit of their professional satisfactions. Or, put another way, they seem less concerned about deviating from a more conventional sociocultural role, and seem able to make whatever arrangements are necessary for the care of their children with minimal anxiety.

The presence of reliable, competent domestic help obviously makes the integration of professional and domestic activities considerably easier. The professional mother who knows that her children are well cared for and that her household is well maintained while she is at work is relieved of a tremendous emotional burden. It has been said only half humorously that the professional mother needs to have a good "wife" at home. While a competent housekeeper can minimize role strain for the professional mother, such a woman is extremely hard to find these days. (Having ourselves witnessed the turnover of four housekeepers in one year, we shake our heads in wonderment at the good fortune of Nadelson and Eisenberg [1977] to have found that elusive but saintly being—the superhousekeeper.)

In fact, coprofessional couples often end up with worse help than their affluent but more conventional married friends. Naively, they begin their search for a highly competent "executive" housekeeper, but lack the luxury, in view of their busy schedules, to carefully screen personnel. Feeling harassed and desperate, and facing tremendous disruption in their work if there is no housekeeper to care for their children and tend to household chores, they often settle for substandard help. Their demanding professional involvements don't permit them to explore community resources and neighbors for baby sitting, home repair, and cleaning services.

In her book *In Defense of Mothering* (Fraiberg, 1977), Selma Fraiberg points out the difficulties for the mother, as well as for the child, inherent in the use of inadequate day care facilities or primitive housekeeping personnel. In fact, the poignant examples in her book are unfortunately not isolated or unusual cases. People who glibly advocate the use of such measures may not have examined the realities closely enough. In view of this somewhat dismal situation, there is a further good argument to be made for the professional mother's reduction in her career activities in order to remain the principal and constant object in her young child's life; that is, she is an ongoing buffer against the inevitable losses and disruptions as hired caretakers come and go.

An alternative to the dismal and frustrating situation with respect to day care and housekeepers might be the greater use of immediate and extended family if they are agreeable and available. For example, a set of coprofessionals blessed with twins found the wife for the first time in her adult life having something in common with her mother, who moved in to help her. Rather than endure a dependent, regressive relationship, she was able to effect a rapprochement with her mother on an adult level, with subsequent enrichment for all concerned. For those lucky enough to have living parents who are healthy and desirous of an active role as grandparents, there is an opportunity to satisfy those obligations of *Invisible Loyalties* (Boszormenyi-Nagy & Spark, 1973) which may not have been fulfilled and, at the same time, to provide children with an opportunity to experience the only unambivalent love relationships that they may ever have.

An obvious way to reduce the extent of role proliferation and disruption for the coprofessional couple is to limit the number of children, or to have children closely spaced in order to get these most difficult but rewarding years behind them before resuming more demanding professional activities.

Role strains for the professional couple with young children are not limited to the allocation of time and energy among career, chores, and children. Husband and wife roles are subjected to acute stress with the advent of a child. Both actual and emotional time and energy must be reapportioned, and those leisurely dinners during which the day's happenings were shared by both partners, become a fond memory as the baby clamors for attention. The intimate relationship may suffer as well, both emotionally and sexually, from the now multiple and intensified demands on both partners. Sexual difficulties such as inhibition of desire (Johnson, Kaplan, & Tusel, 1979; Kaplan, 1977) may occur at this time and represent a situational disturbance. Such difficulties are often related to the level of fatigue engendered in husband and wife as a result of the various activities that lay claim to their days and part of their nights as well. These problems obviously may also represent conscious or unconscious conflicts in the couple which, with the additional stress of new family responsibilities, have now become symptomatic.

Latency and Adolescent Child Rearing

While young children create the most strain on the relationship, raising latency-age and adolescent children can also provide hurdles for the coprofessional marital pair. As children get older they make continued demands for parental attention and compete for precious leisure time, time for the couple to be alone with each other, and time that each spouse might wish to devote to professional activities. After all, a professional motivated to excellence in pursuit of a highly demanding career can be expected to put in substantially more than a 40-hour workweek. Yet one or both must make time for participation with children in their sports, social activities, cultural interests, and education. In fact, in missing out on these activities, the parent loses one of the most satisfying and fulfilling experiences in life—seeing one's own offspring grow and develop. This can be especially poignant and conflictual if the professionals realize that their own intellectual and emotional development was enriched by parents who actively and intensively participated in their own formative years. Conversely, if the professional parents suffered the real or functional absence of either one of their parents, they will inevitably experience guilt as they realize that they are repeating the same process with their children.

Nevertheless, coprofessional parents of latency and adolescent children find themselves with increasingly greater freedom as their children develop more autonomy. Conventions, scientific meetings both in and out of town, and postgraduate professional training become more accessible. Summer vacations, with the children in camp, give a taste of the freedom long ago surrendered. Books can be read and the lost art of unhurried conversation can be rediscovered. The marital relationship can be rejuvenated at this time.

After the Children Leave

After the children leave the coprofessional couple, like all parents, must confront "empty nest" living. A distinct advantage of the coprofessional marriage is that each spouse has continued to remain involved in an absorbing, stimulating, and challenging career, which can more than fill the void of the children's departure. In addition, each has ideally the benefit of a gratifying relationship with an interesting spouse, one who has not stagnated intellectually. There is now even more time for the exploration of separate or shared professional activities and for increased personal involvement with each other. The added income of two, working professionals makes for a luxurious lifestyle, or for the opportunity to pursue expensive hobbies. On the other hand, as is the case at all stages of the marriage, if there are inherent relationship problems that have been masked by the day-to-day involvement with children, it will now be relatively easy for each spouse to withdraw into professional preoccupations. The marital relationship, distant and estranged, might continue to deteriorate but the couple may continue living together out of convenience. Or conditions might become intolerable, with overt hostility being expressed, and the couple might decide to separate since staying together for the children is no longer an issue, and financial arrangements would generally be of small consequence to two, active professionals.

TREATMENT OF THE COPROFESSIONAL COUPLE

Psychotherapy with the coprofessional couple usually presents the same problems and resistances as does therapy with any couple. Some of these problems are accentuated with these particular people and have been extensively discussed by Rice (1979). They include issues of competition, power conflicts, and conflicts associated with the marital support structure. The treatment of coprofessional couples requires particular flexibility, both with respect to the evaluation and the process of data gathering and with respect to the therapist's own personal value system. Coprofessional couples are likely to have an extensive history of alliance (or collusion) and will expect the therapist to work with *their* concept of their problem right from the beginning. In particular, "issues regarding the facilitation of their occupational endeavors and/or problems with the marital support structure have a high salience" (Rice, 1979, p. 93). For example, if one or both patients perceive correctly that the therapist has an obvious bias with regard to the issue of the wife's career versus child rearing that is based upon a conflicting value system, strong resistances will be encountered initially.

Another important issue cited by Rice has to do with the degree of the therapist's activity. Marital therapy in general requires a higher degree of therapist activity than does individual therapy. A nondirective approach by the therapist will often be taken as evidence by the couple that he or she can be rendered ineffective rather easily by their collaboration. "The ideal rhythm of treatment early in therapy involves an active give and take between the therapist and the couple around commonly agreed-upon areas of concern" (Rice, 1979, p. 94).

The therapist who treats dual career couples must honestly examine any biases, positive or negative, regarding alternatives to the traditional concept of marriage. Such biases or unresolved conflicts in the therapist may put him or her in collusion with one spouse with the resulting emotional withdrawal of the other from the therapy, and may produce a therapeutic stalemate. One method of dealing with therapist bias of course is the therapist's own treatment. While it is fortuitous if these issues arise and are resolved in such treatment, this is not always the case. It would be highly unlikely for a therapist to undertake treatment around such values solely to be free of biases that were not a source of conflict in his or her personal life.

An alternative method, although costly, which attempts to circumvent the hazards of value-laden therapeutic biases, is the use of male and female cotherapists. Such a format may provide a useful and stimulating way for the therapists to examine their own values. For example, two psychiatrists treated a coprofessional couple in individual psychotherapy who developed an intense power struggle over whose career advancement would take precedence. The therapists and the couple agreed to work together in conjoint, couples' therapy since this particular issue, while influenced by individual, intrapsychic factors, seemed to be more appropriately investigated in a conjoint format. In their discussions of the content of the therapy sessions, one of the therapists was able to point out to the other (for they were close personal friends) many parallels between the sadomasochistic relationship of the spouses, one of whom she identified with, and her own sadomasochistic marriage. This had far-reaching consequences for the therapist in her own personal life, as well as for the treatment of the patient-couple. In the individual psychotherapy the therapist had used the same mechanisms of reaction formation, idealization of the spouse, and self-devaluation as she had used in her own unhappy marriage, all of which had become incorporated into her own value system. The therapist's gain of insight into this countertransference problem had positive effects on both the individual therapy and the couple sessions, and facilitated further improvements in the couple's marital relationship.

The cotherapy format is also useful as a teaching method for therapists who are learning marital and family therapy, and often provides personal, growth-promoting stimuli in addition to the sharpening of clinical observation and technique. But economic and time considerations often make it unpracticable. Another hazard of the cotherapy format is that the cotherapists may share similar values and may unwittingly collude with one spouse, producing the same disastrous consequences for the therapy as if an individual, couple's therapist had treated the spouses.

In discussing the therapeutic tasks in the early phase of therapy, Rice (1979) recommends helping the couple to become aware of the underlying feelings related to their areas of conflict. This is necessary because professionals often have personality patterns characterized by rigidity, perseverance, and intellectual facility, and they tend to isolate their feelings.

For example, a professional couple in which the husband developed impotence presented for treatment. The symptom started when they decided to have a child after nine years of marriage. He attributed his problem to exhaustion due to overwork. However, initially he had unacknowledged ambivalent feelings about having a child. Many years earlier, he had lived with a woman whom he had loved and who became pregnant. He had wanted to marry her; however, his feelings were unreciprocated. The woman wanted only the child and after requiring his presence at the delivery, she demanded that he cut himself off from her and the child. At first, he was unaware of his fears that having a child would result in some loss of intimacy in his marital relationship as his wife became absorbed in a baby and in her career, thus bringing about a virtual repetition of his wrenching, earlier experience. The wife was intensely interested in her career and tended to deny any anticipation of role proliferation with the advent of a baby. However, their sex life had recently become characterized by a lack of frequency and passion.

Because of their respective isolation and intellectualization, neither partner recognized their underlying feelings and they could not relate their lack of interest in sex to these feelings. However, after confrontation about their failure to carry out the sex therapy exercises, and with an interpretation of their underlying concerns, the couple was able to follow through successfully with treatment.

Rice (1979) recommends the use of the marital contracts concept developed by Sager (1976) in helping to "concretize vague subjective feelings that things are unfair and to show the spouses particular areas that need work in regard to 'rebalancing' the marital system along equitable lines" (p. 105). An important aspect of Sager's concept has to do with the "strong covert aspects which operate out of awareness and yet exert powerful influences on day-to-day behavior" (p. 105). Unlike the behavioral contracting approach (Weiss et al. 1974), the therapist does not help the couple to formulate a fair exchange, but rather to understand the underlying, dynamic reasons for their "pattern of marital bonding" (p. 106). For example, a coprofessional couple who married when the wife was still in training experienced marital difficulties when the wife began to acquire some professional stature after her semiretirement for several years while her children were small. The contract under which they were both operating required that she pursue her profession, the same as her husband's, as an avocation. The husband was unprepared to recognize and accept her marked elevation in professional status, preferring to keep her dependent and therefore nonthreatening. As both partners acknowledged their previously unconscious, contractual expectations, their hostility escalated and their negotiations failed. The couple's longstanding difficulties with communication made a separation inevitable.

Once a couple's resistances to the acknowledgment of the underlying conflicts have been reduced, it is possible for the middle phase of therapy to begin. The core issues mentioned above—competition, power conflicts, and problems in the marital support structure—are worked through in this phase. Dual career couples inevitably compare each other's careers and frequently one has had to sacrifice his or her own career in order to foster the career of the other. Examples of this are given elsewhere in our chapter. Rice states that given the perjorative connotations of the word *competition*, it is best to "encourage the expression of the feelings first, particularly anger, before interpreting the source of the resentment as related to a sense of competition between the spouses" (p. 121). When this interpretation is made the therapist must then buttress it supportively by pointing out how natural such competitiveness is for achievement-oriented people.

Overt use of power by one spouse may result in a stubborn, defiant response by the other which threatens the continuation of the relationship. Or the other may resort to an indirect maneuver in order to "even the score," such as sabotage, criticism, and self-sabotage vis a vis his or her own success. "The therapist's task is first to help bring the underlying power struggle out in the open, then to evaluate each partner's feelings as to their legitimacy and impact on the relationship (in order to) restore a sense of equity" (Rice, 1979, p. 123). "Each partner needs to feel the other will not use power destructively" (p. 124). The reestablishment of trust is often a slow and delicate process. As the partners are able to share sensitive feelings without retaliatory responses, trust begins to build.

> In helping the couple toward an equitable arrangement regarding the marital support structure, the therapist's task is often one of providing advice and information. This does not imply that there are likely to be no underlying psychological conflicts. These are usually addressed in therapy when dealing with more general issues, such as whether the wife will pursue her career after the birth of a child. (Rice, 1979, p. 127)

Rice regards the task here as a "pragmatic" one, and advocates the working out by the couple of a "schedule" for the assignment of domestic and child care activities. Each partner should feel that the type of task and amount of work are distributed fairly. If the couple is unsuccessful the therapist helps them to improve communication and to clarify the underlying issues.

Glick and Borus (1984) describe a similar approach to the treatment of troubled physicians and their families and give several clinical examples, some of which involve coprofessionals. They describe conflicts around issues of role, status, power, and priority, with symptoms such as depression, extramarital affairs, unconscious sabotage by means of illness, and behavioral disturbances in the children. Treatment involved increasing communication between the couple with regard to their anxieties and dissatisfactions about their careers, their relationships, and their concerns about child rearing, followed by role realignment, reordering of priorities, and reduction of familial disruption.

Conjoint treatment of the dual career husband and wife by a single therapist or by cotherapists is the most common form of therapeutic intervention. Another approach might be group treatment for dual career couples. In this format common problem areas are aired, feelings are validated by other group members, and various solutions can be shared. Individual therapy is recommended by Sager, as well as by others for factors that cannot be effectively addressed in couple therapy. These include, specifically, issues of sexual attraction toward others than the mate, severe characterological problems, severe mental illness, significant differences in intelligence between the partners, and conflicts between opposing biological and intrapsychic needs.

Rice disagrees with the point of view expressed above and sees little rationale for individual therapy if the expressed goal of therapy is to improve the marriage. He believes that both spouses should be part of the learning process with regard to the factors underlying characterological problems since they are often similar in both partners. We agree with this except to say that in certain cases neurotic and characterological problems are *so* severe that intensive psychotherapy with a focus on extensive transference interpretations is indicated. In these cases the presence of the spouse would either be unnecessary or an interference. Transference phenomena can also be observed and interpreted in conjoint therapy, and in fact can become an extremely important aspect of the treatment.

For example, the wife in a coprofessional marriage was made more aware of her hostile and condescending treatment of her husband when it was pointed out in their conjoint therapy session that she was treating the male therapist in a similar manner, in contrast to the female therapist who was almost obsequiously overidealized. The origins of the wife's reactions could be discovered in her childhood relationship with her inadequate, unsuccessful father, who was constantly disparaged and criticized by her mother. The patient identified with her mother and treated her father and later her husband in a disparaging, devaluing way. The transference interpretation of her behavior and attitudes toward men, made firsthand and in vivo in the session, provided an opportunity for the wife to step back from her reactions and observe them more objectively than was possible when she was with her husband alone.

One exception to a recommendation for conjoint therapy alone which is endorsed by Rice (1979) occurs when a couple has made a decision to separate. Here, conjoint and individual sessions are interspersed so that practical issues can be resolved and support for the psychological process of separation can be provided.

Summary

As can be seen from the foregoing, the issues facing two professionals who are married to each other can be considerable. This is not to say, however, that all is problem and conflict. There is tremendous satisfaction and fulfillment in both the marital relationship and professional activities that can be achieved by both partners.

What makes some such marriages succeed while others fail? We feel compelled to speculate about this before we close. We hope our guesses will be educated ones.

First of all, flexibility and adaptability are individual character traits important to the success of the coprofessional marriage. While this may be true of any successful marriage, the particular stresses involved in a coprofessional relationship, as noted above, require the ability to adapt to rapidly changing situations. The punches can be multiple, and the capacity to roll with them a real asset. The Group for the Advancement of Psychiatry's monograph (1975) on the educated woman discusses the rapidly changing role conceptions of both sexes. Flexibility is required, both from individuals and from their social environments, in order to accommodate to these new roles.

However, we wonder if these characteristics are merely surface phenomena that are related to a more fundamental, underlying, psychodynamic reality. It seems to us, based on personal observation and clinical experience, that the relative absence of intrapsychic conflict in both partners regarding their multiple roles is a *sine qua non* for the smooth structuring of their lives and activities. Specifically, to the extent that the wife is unambivalent about her desire to undertake several, demanding, concurrent roles, to the extent that her husband can unambivalently support her goals, and to the extent that they are not conflicted about the measures that need to be taken to make their complicated lives workable, coprofessional marriages are viable.

Ultimately, the success of the coprofessional marriage depends on the degree of congruence in the vision of life shared by the marriage partners. Both must have a high commitment to their own and each other's careers, and, at the same time, both must have a strong investment in their family life. They must agree that their personal marital relationship and the relationship they are building with their children are just as valuable parts of their master plan as are their professional goals. With these ideals in common they can encourage each other through smooth or rough waters and provide inspiring, challenging role models for their children. We feel fortunate and privileged to be able to enjoy life to its fullest, both in our professional and in our personal lives. Each aspect of our many involvements has enriched and enhanced the others. We could wish for no better for our children.

References

Berman, E., Sacks, S., & Lief, H. (1975). The two professional marriage: A new conflict syndrome. *Journal of Sex and Marital Therapy, 1*(3), 242–253.

Boszormenyi-Nagy, I., & Spark, G. (1973). *Invisible loyalties*. New York: Harper & Row.

Bryson, J., & Bryson, R. (1978). Dual career couples. New York: Human Sciences Press.

Fishkin, L., & Fishkin, R. (1981). The co-professional marriage. In G. P. Sholevar (Ed.), *The handbook of marriage & marital therapy*. New York: SP Medical & Scientific Books.

Fraiberg, S. (1977). *Every child's birthright: In defense of mothering*. New York: Basic Books.

Glick, I. D., & Borus, J. F. (1984). Marital and family therapy for troubled physicians and their families: A bridge over troubled waters. *Journal of the American Medical Association, 251*(14).

Group for Advancement of Psychiatry. (1975). The educated woman: Prospects and problems. (Report No. 92). New York: GAP.

Johnson, F. A., & Johnson, C. I. (1977). Role strain in high commitment career women. *Journal of the Academy of Psychoanalysis, 4*(1), 13–36.

Johnson, F., Kaplan, E., & Tusel, D. (1979). Sexual dysfunction in the two-career family. *Medical Aspects of Human Sexuality, 13*(1), 7–16.

Kaplan, H. (1977). Hypoactive sexual desire. *Journal of Sex and Marital Therapy, 3*(1).

Lerner, H. (1973). Early origins of envy and evaluation of women: Implications for sex role stereotypes. *Bulletin of the Menninger Clinic, 37*, 538–553.

Nadelson, T., & Eisenberg, L. (1977). The successful professional woman: On being married to one. *American Journal of Psychiatry, 134*(10), 1071–1076.

Pingres, S., Butler, M., Paisley, W., & Hawkins, R. (1978). Antinepotism's ghost: Attitudes of administrators toward hiring professional couples. In J. Bryson & R. Bryson (Eds.), *Dual-Career Couples* (pp. 22–29).

Pollak, O. (1965). Sociological and psychoanalytic concepts in family diagnosis. In B. L. Greene (Ed.). *The psychotherapies of marital disharmony*. pp. 15–26.

Rapoport, R., & Rapoport, R. (1978). Dual career families: Progress and prospects. *Marriage & Family Review, 1*(5).

Rice, D. (1979). *Dual-career marriage*. New York: The Free Press.

Sager, C. J. (1976). *Marriage concepts and couple therapy*. New York: Brunner/Mazel.

Weiss, R. L. (1975). Contracts, cognition and change: A behavioral approach to marriage therapy. *The Counseling Psychologist, 5*, 15–26.

Weiss, R., Birchler, G., & Vincent, J., (1974). Contractual models for negotiation training in marital dyads. *Journal of Marriage and the Family, 36*, 321–330.

SIX

Fertility Management: Infertility, Delayed Childbearing, and Voluntary Childlessness

Marjorie A. Gutman, Ph.D.
Instructor, Department of Obstetrics and Gynecology
Downstate Medical Center

OVERVIEW

Managing fertility is a major task of adult life and of marital relationships. In terms of sheer duration, this task can last for over half of a woman's lifetime, and even longer for a man. More important, parenthood is the arena in which the crucial adult developmental task of generativity (Erikson, 1950) is addressed by most individuals in our society. Whether, when, and how often individuals become parents can greatly influence how successful they are at developing and expressing an "interest in establishing and guiding the next generation or whatever in a given case may become the absorbing object of a parental kind of responsibility" (Erikson, 1950, p. 231).

Managing fertility is an especially important task for couples as well as for individual adults since fertility is by definition an expression of the couple as a unit. Producing and caring for children tends to be the most major task couples undertake after that of forming and maintaining intimacy. This is not to deny that there are couples who treat fertility as largely the province and responsibility of only one partner, but even this pattern is a "joint decision," however implicit.

Tremendous recent changes in the ability and desire to manage fertility make this an increasingly complex task for couples. There is more potential for controlling fertility than ever before. There are also more specific choices to be made as couples move through their lives together, and more options to consider at each decision point.

For all these reasons, managing fertility can be an important source of challenge in marital relationships. It is therefore crucial to consider ways to help couples resolve fertility issues for themselves. This can involve helping couples to identify the various components of the fertility issues they face: physical, psychological, interpersonal, social, and even societal. Couples also often need help in order to assess the extent to which their dilemmas and reactions are part of a "normal" developmental process. Once the issue has been analyzed and put into perspective, couples often need help with the process and content of decision making in order to reach a satisfactory resolution.

In addition to their intrinsic importance, fertility issues can provide a focal point for observing and working through many dynamics in relationships. Crises or decision points such as unplanned (or planned) pregnancy, abortion, sterilization, and the discovery of infertility can be times when the structure and dynamics of relationships are intensified and made clearer. Of necessity, fertility issues often highlight functioning at many levels: each individual's relationship to his or her own body and to the partner's body, individual self-image and needs, the couple's interaction, interaction within the family unit (assuming there are existing children), and the couple's relationship to larger social units such as family of origin, reference groups, and even society.

This chapter will explore how couples manage their fertility. First, a comprehensive overview of the content and process of fertility management will be provided. Next, recent trends in fertility attitudes and behavior are examined, followed by an in-depth view of salient, new issues. Last, current knowledge will be applied to describing treatment approaches for helping couples with fertility concerns.

Interrelationships Among Fertility Issues

A holistic view of the content and process of fertility management is important since the many specific issues and decisions associated with fertility are typically treated separately by researchers, clinicians, and by couples themselves. Researchers and theorists of necessity often focus on specific, identifiable areas of fertility management. Couples often see a current issue, such as when to have their first child or how to resolve an unplanned pregnancy, as an isolated decision in their lives. They fail to see how this immediate issue is part of an ongoing task that runs like a thread through their individual adult lives and through their shared life as a couple.

The flowchart below (Figure 1) describes the global process of fertility management and organizes the many decision points that arise for couples within that process. In this way a specific issue can be seen in relation to many others, a couple can be located in their current process of fertility management, or the process that they have undergone over time can be traced.

The three major components of the fertility management process are goals, means, and outcomes, with specific issues or decisions organized within each component. Major areas of goal setting are identified separately but it should be noted that these types of goals all interrelate. For example, a decision by a couple never to have children precludes the rest of the specific goals. In a less extreme example, a couple's age when they have their first child may greatly affect how many children they ultimately parent and their spacing of those children (Daniels & Weingarten, 1982).

FIGURE 1 The Process of Fertility Management

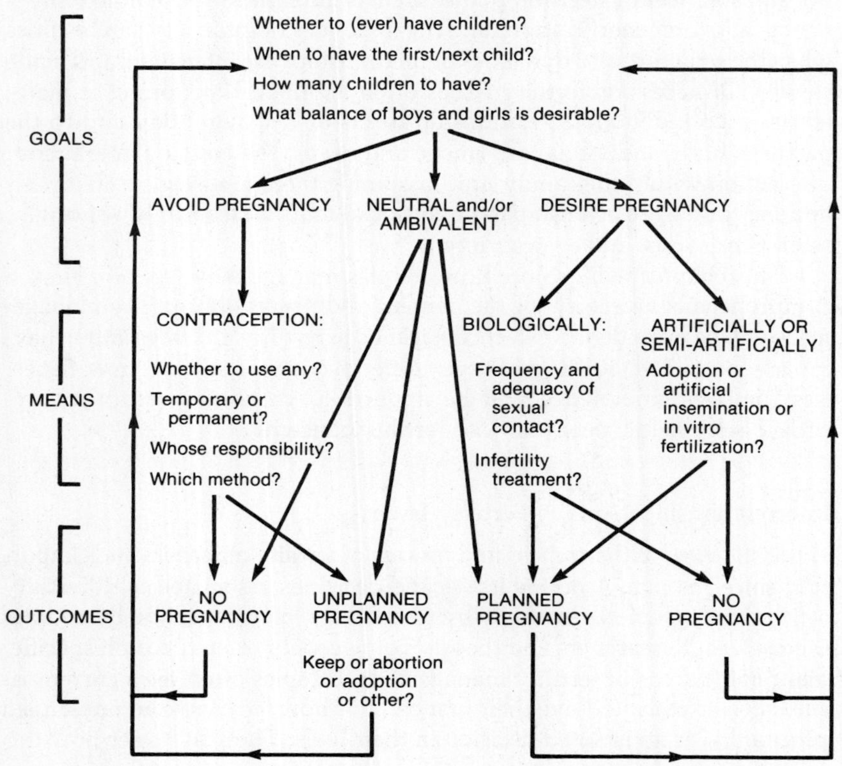

This model can be misleading in that it tends to make the process of fertility management (like the word *management* itself) appear much more goal oriented and deliberate than it often is in "real life." The use of a goal-oriented process model is definitely not meant to imply that all or even most couples treat their fertility in a deliberate, goal-oriented fashion, or that doing so is necessarily desirable. There are many couples and individuals who either are quite passive toward their fertility or who deliberately see it as a "natural" process not to be controlled. Indeed, a crucial and perhaps the most basic underlying dimension of the model is the degree of goal-orientedness or deliberateness that the couple brings to the process. Other latent dimensions of the fertility management process are the degree of mutuality and the degree of consensus within the couple.

Returning to the flowchart, the decisions that the couple makes or avoids about specific goal issues lead to their overall orientation toward pregnancy at a particular time. While this orientation is presented as three, mutually exclusive positions, it is really a continuum from strong desire to avoid pregnancy to strong desire to produce a pregnancy. Active/passive is actually a second overall orientation toward the means of implementing fertility goals which is distinct from but often interacts with the approach/avoidance orientation. A couple can be highly motivated to avoid pregnancy yet very passive about implementing this goal. Conversely, a couple might agree that they want a child very much but persist in taking a passive approach to increasing their fertility, even after a few years have passed. While a passive stance may be symptomatic of ambivalence about the goals by one or both partners, it may also be largely unrelated to the strength and clarity of the goals. Undoubtedly, most often the strength and clarity of goals and the stance toward their implementation are related; that is, couples who tend to be goal oriented and clear about their fertility goals tend to be active in implementing them.

The couple's general orientation toward pregnancy (and toward the means of managing fertility) leads to the particular issues related to the means of promoting or preventing pregnancy. If the couple wishes to avoid pregnancy and is at all active about implementation, they encounter decisions about contraception. If the couple wishes to produce a pregnancy and is not successful, infertility and other issues may become relevant.

The outcome of the fertility management process is either a pregnancy or no pregnancy. However, there is a dimension of "plannedness" that interacts with the biological fact: A pregnancy can be either planned or not planned, just as the lack of a pregnancy can be either planned or not planned. I am avoiding the word *wanted* here since an unplanned pregnancy can become wanted by the time of the birth (or can remain unwanted). Also, a pregnancy resulting from a couple's relatively neutral, ambivalent, and/or passive orientation toward pregnancy can be thought of as either planned or unplanned, depending on where one wishes to put the emphasis.

Last, the flowchart indicates that the outcomes of the "feedback" process over time are additional fertility goals and/or modifications of previous decisions. For example, the experience of an unplanned pregnancy may lead the couple to reassess when they really want to start a family. Parenthetically, many other experiences besides pregnancies can precipitate new or altered goals.

From an heuristic perspective, the model presented serves to guide an examination of recent trends in how couples manage their fertility. Our personal and professional experiences create the impression that there have been enormous and complex changes in this area of adult life since our parents' day. However, the specific nature of these changes are not always clear, nor are their origins, interrelationships, and implications. The model of the fertility management process helps to identify, organize, and interrelate these recent trends.

Recent Trends in Managing Fertility

Dramatic changes have occurred during the past 20 years in fertility management technology, and in the attitudes and behavior of married couples. These global trends include:

1. Greater ability to manage fertility. Advances in contraceptive and sterilization technology have led to improved potential to prevent unplanned pregnancy (Hatcher et al., 1984). Legalization of abortion and improvement in surgical technique have led to greater ability to prevent unplanned births (Hatcher et al., 1984). Advances in medical diagnosis and treatment have increased couples' ability to overcome infertility problems (Corson, 1983; Mazor, 1980; Menning, 1977). Developments in genetic screening, maternal, and neonatal care have decreased the medical risks inherent in giving birth at later maternal ages (Daniels & Weingarten, 1982; Goldberg, Edmonds, & Oakley, 1979).

2. Increased utilization of these recently developed means for managing fertility: temporary contraception (Westhoff, 1976; Westoff & Jones, 1977; Westoff & McCarthy, 1979); permanent sterilization (Westoff & McCarthy, 1979; Nolan, Ory, Layde, Maze & Greenspan, 1982); legal abortion (Henshaw & Reilly, 1983); and amniocentesis (Adams, Finley, & Hansen, 1981).

3. Greater desire (preference) to limit family size and to delay childbearing (O'Connell & Rogers, 1983; Price, 1977; Pebley, 1981; Westoff & Ryder, 1977).

4. Changes in actual fertility behavior. Specifically, couples have fewer children (Westoff & Ryder, 1977), delay the birth of their first child until a later age than did their parents (Bloom & Trussel, 1983; Ventura, 1982;

Adams, Oakley, & Marks, 1982), more couples may be experiencing infertility (Mosher, 1982; National Center for Health Statistics, 1985); and a slightly larger number of couples (though still a very small percentage) may even be opting for permanent voluntary childlessness (Yogev & Vierra, 1983).

Regarding fertility goals, the primary questions now seem to be *when* and even *whether* to have children rather than how many to have. Two decades ago family size seemed to be the most difficult issue for couples. The timing of childbearing tended to vary within a small range from "right away" to "a couple of years from now." Concerning means to manage fertility, there has been a tremendous proliferation of options and decisions.

These trends seem to represent a dramatic example of how technological advances and socioeconomic forces in our society can converge to create changes in marital attitudes and behavior. On the one hand, major advances in medical technology over the past 20 years have increased couples' *ability* to manage their fertility. Simultaneously, social and economic changes in our society seem to have augmented couples' *desire* to manage their fertility. From the economic perspective, the rate of inflation over the past 20 years has made two-income families a necessity for many more couples. From the perspective of social forces, various social movements of the 1960s emphasized greater personal freedom and choice. This often led individuals to question and sometimes to defer traditional life choices such as marriage and children, and to value sexual freedom divorced from reproduction.

The Women's Liberation movement in the 1970s further fostered the questioning of traditional patterns of marriage and childbearing. The emphasis was on women expanding their roles beyond those of wife and mother by adding nontraditional career roles (Friedan, 1963; Russo, 1979; Peck, 1972). Some women even questioned the desirability of assuming traditional roles and/or the feasibility of combining traditional and nontraditional roles in our society. Ideas promulgated by the Women's Liberation movement may also have led to questions about *men's* traditional choices and roles—especially concerning marriage and parenting.

Whatever their origins the recent trends toward increased ability and desire to manage fertility have profound implications for couples today. There is the potential for couples to make a greater number of decisions regarding both fertility goals and especially the means to achieve those goals. A wider range of opinions and options is available at each decision point. This proliferation of decisions and options means greater potential for conflict within couples.

Further, such conflict involves an area central to the individual identity of each partner and yet one which is basic to the couple's life together. For example, a couple may agree about the current need to delay childbearing and about the contraceptive method to use, but they may disagree about what to do when an unplanned pregnancy results despite their best efforts. They may agree to seek help with infertility problems but disagree about how long to continue the process and about what to do if infertility proves conclusive.

Another implication of these recent trends is that couples may have greater needs for information and for decision-making skills. Couples need information in order to understand and assess the many options open to them for managing their fertility. In addition, they may need help in evaluating the social and emotional meaning of the new medical technology that is available to them. For example, a couple may need information about the relative health risks of delaying the birth of their first child beyond a particular age. Once this factual information is obtained, they may still be confused about how they feel concerning the risks involved and how much importance they should attach to these risks relative to the emotional and social risks of "premature" parenthood.

Finally, utilization of new and more complex technology can create or intensify emotional reactions to the process of managing fertility. For example, amniocentesis increases the viability of delaying childbearing without risking certain birth defects. However, if a couple utilizes amniocentesis they tend to be more ambivalent about committing themselves emotionally to the pregnancy prior to the test. They still experience uncertainty about these conditions during the first three to five months of the pregnancy; and then they may have to cope with the emotional sequelae of a late-term abortion should the results be positive (Daniels & Weingarten, 1982). Similarly, current, sophisticated infertility treatment offers many more forms of diagnosis and treatment and a higher success rate than was available even 10 years ago. However, these advances may mean that the couple spends a longer time period (sometimes years) under the pressure of balancing hope for a cure by persisting in undergoing intrusive tests against trying to be "realistic" about the fact that the treatment may not succeed.

In summary, recent advances in medical technology, combined with social and economic changes in our society, have led to an increased ability and desire of couples to manage their fertility. These changes in turn have heightened certain aspects of the fertility management process. Specifically, they have created greater opportunity for conflict between spouses, greater needs for information and decision-making skills, and new or at least intensified emotional reactions to the fertility management process.

The global picture that has been painted of recent changes in fertility management provides a useful overview of the current situation. The summary also serves to pinpoint particular trends worthy of further exploration. The crucial task for those who work with couples is to understand the medical and psychosocial dynamics related to these recent demographic trends in fertility thinking and behavior.

CURRENT KNOWLEDGE ABOUT SELECTED FERTILITY ISSUES: INFERTILITY, DELAYED CHILDBEARING, AND VOLUNTARY CHILDLESSNESS

What are the psychosocial dynamics related to the recent demographic trends in fertility thinking and behavior? This is the crucial question for those who work with couples. What, for example, are the reasons that more couples are delaying the birth of their first child? And how does the degree of delay affect the marital relationship, the individual adults, and the child? Are these "delayers" a monolithic group or are there really several types of situations?

Three issues which seem to be of particular importance and interest right now are delayed childbearing, voluntary childlessness, and infertility. Delayed childbearing and voluntary childlessness are very new concerns for clinicians and couples, concerns that go to the core of fertility decision making, as couples ponder whether or when to start having children. Infertility questions may continue to become a concern for increasing numbers of couples. The increasing difficulties presented by adoption may prompt more couples to seek and pursue infertility treatment. Perhaps most important, recent, dramatic changes in the diagnosis and treatment of infertility have created more widespread awareness of the issue and a greater willingness to seek help. Technological developments have also intensified social and psychological issues surrounding infertility, which suggests an additional role for mental health professionals.

Infertility

The term *infertility* refers to problems in conceiving and/or carrying a pregnancy to term. Typically, infertility refers to any couple not able to conceive or carry a pregnancy to term after one year or more of unprotected sexual intercourse. Note that infertility does not refer to the absolute inability to conceive, which is called sterility, nor to the inability to conceive due to lack of sufficiently frequent sexual contact.

How large a problem is infertility in the United States? Approximately 8–10 percent of married couples in the U.S. between the ages of 15 and 44 are infertile (Mosher, 1982; National Center for Health Statistics, 1985). While the overall proportion of all couples affected by infertility has not changed substantially during the past 20 years, the percentage of young wives (age 20–24) who are infertile soared from 3.6 percent in 1965 to 10.6 percent in 1982. There was also a substantial increase in infertility among wives aged 25–29 and 35–39, with black women exhibiting substantially larger increases and absolute percentages than white women in all age groups (National Center for Health Statistics, 1985).

It has been suggested that the recent increase in infertility among younger couples, and especially among black couples, is mainly due to recent increases in the incidence of sexually transmitted diseases, notably gonorrhea, and that the proliferation of infertility will continue as long as recent trends in venereal and pelvic inflammatory disease persist (Mosher, 1982). Further, it is expected that infertility will become more common among older couples (age 30–40) due to delayed childbearing and the association between age and infertility (Menning, 1977; Daniels & Weingarten, 1979). Infertility has become more problematic for couples as well as numerically more common because of increasingly limited access to adoption as a way to form a family despite inability to conceive children. Thus, infertility seems to be a growing problem for couples in the United States and therefore one that requires an understanding of its related medical and psychosocial aspects.

Medical aspects of infertility

Currently, approximately 90 percent of infertile couples who come for medical help can be definitively diagnosed. Of these, 40 percent are found to have fertility problems that stem from deficiencies in male sperm production and delivery; 40 percent from female structural complications or endocrine deficiencies; and in 20 percent the problem stems from an underlying "immunity" or incompatibility between the woman's ova and the man's sperm (Menning, 1977). Among cases that are definitively diagnosed, approximately 50 percent can be cured—that is, helped to conceive and carry a pregnancy to term (Menning, 1977).

Current knowledge concerning causes, diagnosis, and treatment of infertility will be organized around female, male, and joint contributions. In medical practice all three contributions should be investigated simultaneously until a complete diagnosis is obtained. Unfortunately, infertility investigation and treatment traditionally, and often in contemporary practice, focus primarily or exclusively on the woman. This is partly because for many years infertility was thought of as a female condition, though this is now known to be inaccurate. Another reason may be that women rather than men usually initiate the investigation into the couple's childless state. Men are still sometimes more reluctant than women to investigate their contribution to infertility and their wives sometimes take a complementary attitude; that is, they try to protect their husbands from a potential ego threat. Physicians sometimes augment this overemphasis on the female, perhaps due to their own biases and habits, or perhaps mainly because the investigation of female infertility tends to be more complex and drawn out than that of the male, and successful treatment of female problems is still more common. The following discussion is drawn from two excellent books designed to guide the childless couple (Menning, 1977; Corson, 1983).

The leading causes of female infertility and current techniques to diagnose and treat it are numerous and varied, as shown in Table 1. Infertility problems tend to be of two types: structural or hormonal. Next to each major type of problem are listed its specific manifestations and causes. Diagnostic tests typically used to investigate each type of problem are listed in the third column. The sequence and choice of tests varies, but typically proceeds from less to more invasive. Common treatment strategies for each type of infertility problem are listed in the last column. Treatment of infertility in women, like diagnosis, can be brief or can involve several stages and procedures: It too generally proceeds from less to more invasive. The information presented in Table 1 is by no means exhaustive, but rather is meant to highlight and introduce the reader to the most common medical aspects of female infertility.

The causes, diagnosis, and treatment of infertility in men are less varied than in women, as seen in Table 2. Regarding treatment, there is little consensus among urologists, infertility specialists, and endocrinologists on the feasibility of improving sperm count or motility through medical means. Surgical intervention to remove varicocele exhibits a much higher success rate.

Infertility which directly involves both members of the couple can result from a combination of any of the male and female conditions described. Also, combined infertility can result when both members of the couple have borderline conditions (that is, are subfertile). For example, the woman has mild endometriosis and the man has a borderline sperm count.

In addition, there are two conditions that are uniquely the result of the couple's interaction. Immunologic reaction is one of these interactive conditions and is currently highly controversial. It is clear that some women have immunologic reactions to sperm and some men have similar reactions to their own sperm. The reaction of the woman is nonspecific with respect to a particular man's sperm and it builds every time sexual intercourse takes place.

Coital technique is the other area of interactive infertility problems. Problems of coital techniques which prevent sexual intercourse are not strictly speaking aspects of infertility, which is the inability to conceive *after* sexual intercourse has occurred. However, they will be summarized briefly here since *functionally* they do prevent conception. Severe sexual problems can emanate from the man, the woman, or both partners. A man may experience premature ejaculation or ejaculation that occurs before intromission. The opposite problem, not ejaculating at all (inhibited ejaculation), can also be an issue for men. Perhaps the most prevalent male concern is erectile dysfunction (impotence). In fact, it may be fear of impotence that leads some men to avoid sex and/or rush into sex, with premature ejaculation the result of their compulsiveness. While women may have a number of sexual difficulties, the two most critical areas

TABLE 1 Medical Aspects of Infertility: Women

Problem	*Specifics*	*Diagnostic Tests*	*Treatment*
Structural	Scar tissue within uterus and tubes or around ovaries: typically caused by infection, such as gonorrhea, chlamydia, or other pelvic inflammatory disease (PID).	Tubal insufflation (Rubin's test). CO_2 gas carefully blown into uterus through tube in vagina; done in MD's office; no longer used much.	Correct any underlying health condition such as anemia, obesity, infections of the pelvic region or reproductive organs.
		Hysterosalpingogram (uterotubogram). Radiopaque dye injected into uterus through instrument introduced into vagina; series of X-rays then taken.	Dilatation & curettage (D&C). Gently scrape uterine lining with instrument introduced through vagina. Removes excess lining, adhesions and polyps.
		Laparoscopy. Direct visualization of ovaries, outside of tubes, uterus, and peritoneal cavity; long thin instrument introduced through small incision in curve of navel.	Tuboplasty. Correction of tubal blockage by surgery: success rate depends on location of blockage and whether one or both tubes are affected.
		Hysteroscopy. Direct visualization of *inside* of uterus using a small "telescope."	
	Endometriosis. Normal lining of uterus seeds itself in abnormal places such as tubes, ovaries, peritoneal cavity.	Laparoscopy.	Wait & see. Hormonal therapy to shrink endometrial tissue. Surgery in moderate to severe cases; often followed by hormonal therapy.
	Endometritis. Chronic infection of uterine lining. Severe infection destroys lining and leaves scar tissue.	Cervical culture.	Antibiotics to cure infection. Surgical removal of adhesions, then hormone therapy and an IUD to aid regrowth of lining. Cure rate is about 70 percent.

TABLE 1 (*concluded*)

Problem	*Specifics*	*Diagnostic Tests*	*Treatment*
	Chronic infection of the cervix (opening into the uterus); thick, impassable mucus; or cervical polyps. All can decrease sperm penetration.	Pelvic examination and/or tests of cervical mucus. Culture of cervix to rule out infection. Postcoital test to see how sperm and cervical mucus interact.	Eradication of cervical infection with antibiotics or cautery; hormonal therapy to improve mucus. Husband insemination. Masturbated semen specimen from husband (assuming he is fecund) is introduced by artificial means (tube into the cervix).
	Fibroid (benign) tumors in uterus.	Hysterosalpingogram. Hysteroscopy.	Myomectomy after all other indications are checked.
	Congenital malformation or extreme malposition of uterus.	Hysterosalpingogram. Hysteroscopy. Laparoscopy	Resection or removal of congenital anomaly.
	Weakened or "incompetent" cervix.	Medical history (i.e., multiple miscarriages in advanced stages).	Cervical cerclage (stitch around cervix) at 14th week of pregnancy.
Hormonal	Hormonal imbalance causes irregular ovulation or absence of ovulation.	Basal Body Temperature (BBT) chart. Woman takes and charts her temperature every day, following very precise instructions; chart kept for a few cycles helps to indicate occurrence and timing of ovulation.	Hormonal therapy—biggest recent breakthrough in treatment. Hormones used to stimulate ovulation. Very complex; contraindications and side effects to consider.
	Hormonal imbalance causes inadequate buildup of uterine lining to receive and maintain fertilized egg.	Blood and urine studies to test hormone levels and interactions. Ultrasound. Shows pictures on a screen of mature follicle on ovary (just before ovulation) and of ruptured follicle (after ovulation).	Hormonal therapy with progesterone to stimulate more adequate lining in uterus.

Source: Corson, 1983; Menning, 1977.

TABLE 2 Medical Aspects of Infertility: Male

Problem	*Specifics*	*Diagnostic Tests*	*Treatment*
Sperm	Can be problem of sperm production (spermatogenesis), maturation of sperm, and/or ability of sperm to swim (motility). Leading causes are: Varicocele. Most common cause is a varicose vein usually occurring next to the left testicle. Hydrocele. Small "bag" of fluid within the scrotum. Illness. Adult mumps can cause temporary or permanent damage; acute febrile disease (e.g., hepatitis, mononucleosis) can cause temporary problem. Environmental factors are heat, radiation, diet, extreme emotional and physical stress, drugs, injury, or surgical complications.	History of general health and sexual maturation. Physical examination including examination of the testicles. Semen analysis (sperm count). Ejaculate, produced by man who follows specific instructions, is analyzed regarding several factors: quantity, motility, viability, morphology of sperm cells, total semen volume and viscosity or liquefaction of ejaculate. Culture of semen to check for infection. Blood and urine studies and/or Xray of pituitary to check for hormonal imbalance. "Hamster test" to see if man's sperm can penetrate a hamster's ova; shows problems with sperm that seem normal in other tests; still experimental. Testicular biopsy. If deficiency found in quantity and quality of sperm, this test differentiates permanent sterile or subfecund state from a temporary one.	The man is advised to change his work or personal habits when infertility is thought to be caused by environmental factors. Various hormone therapies have recently been developed and tried. Surgery for removal of varicocele; successful 45 percent to 60 percent of the time.

TABLE 2 (*concluded*)

Problem	*Specifics*	*Diagnostic Tests*	*Treatment*
	Autoimmune reaction to man's sperm.	Blood tests.	Drug therapy.
Blockage	There may be a blockage somewhere in the reproductive tract between where sperm are produced and where they are ejaculated: leading cause is infection such as venereal disease; can cause permanent obstruction of ductal system if untreated.	Fructose test. Absence of fructose from semen means that there is probably a blockage in the ductal system. Testicular biopsy. Vasography. X-ray study of vas deferentia; done if sperm count is *zero and* testicular biopsy shows normal testicular tissue.	Surgery to remove blockages in ductal tracts; success rate is varied.
	Retrograde ejaculation. Sperm are ejaculated into bladder instead of out through urethra; often an adjunct to diabetes mellitis.	Semen analysis and urine analysis.	Artificial insemination after sperm are collected from urine.

Source: Corson, 1983; Menning, 1977.

which might prevent intercourse are vaginismus (involuntary closure of the vaginal muscles) and dyspareunia (painful intercourse). These sexual dysfunctions can be organic and/or psychological in origin. Another sexual dysfunction which can be a fertility issue is low sexual desire. Even in its milder forms, where sexual intercourse occurs perhaps once a month due to the low desire of one or both partners, there simply may not be sufficient contact to provide a chance for conception.

It is important to stress that there are less dramatic aspects of coital technique that can help many couples who do have regular sexual intercourse to increase their fertility. The best position for conception is with the woman lying on her back and the man lying above, with vaginal entry between the woman's flexed thighs. The woman's hips should be slightly elevated and the man should remain motionless inside her for several minutes after ejaculation. The woman should stay in this position for at least one-half hour and ideally longer. The couple should *never* use lubricants, nor should the woman ever wash or douche after sexual intercourse. An article by Masters and Johnson (1978) indicated that one out of eight couples who came to their infertility clinic over the past 25 years conceived within three months of receiving this kind of basic information about coital technique.

If a change in coital technique is not sufficient, diagnosis and treatment of combined infertility can provide additional techniques. A postcoital test (Huhner or "PK" test) indicates the quality and viscosity of the woman's mucus and the presence and activity of sperm cells. Poor results indicate possible cervical infection or immunologic reactions (assuming that the man's sperm have already been tested for quantity and quality). A mucus smear is taken from the woman's cervix shortly after sexual intercourse (2 to 10 hours) and analyzed under a microscope. There is some controversy regarding how to test effectively for immunologic reactions. "Condom therapy" is the usual treatment for the woman's immunologic reactions to the man's sperm. The couple uses a condom for approximately six months or until the woman's immunologic levels have dropped. After that, the couple continues to use condoms, *except* during ovulation.

Psychological aspects of infertility

Traditionally, helping professionals and the public have regarded at least half of all infertility cases as psychogenic (Mazor, 1980). However, we now know that there is little evidence to support the psychogenic basis for infertility in men or women despite an abundance of thinking and research. Summarizing his review of the psychoanalytic literature, Denber (1978) states: "The analytic problem in this review is serious and difficult. It concerns what appears to be generally accepted fact: resolution of psychologic conflict will be followed by pregnancy in infertile women. There is almost complete absence of scientifically valid supporting data" (p. 27).

The earliest and most prevalent view regarding the psychogenesis of infertility is the psychoanalytic one. Psychogenic infertility is thought to be essentially a neurotic manifestation in which inability to conceive is a defensive reaction against pregnancy (Denber, 1978). It occurs with individuals (typically women) for whom pregnancy would make manifest latent, unresolved conflicts. The woman "consciously and obsessively verbalizes the wish for a child but unconsciously rejects pregnancy, childbirth, and motherhood" (Denber, 1978, p. 24).

Sometimes the woman is suffering from a sort of female counterpart to the male castration complex: She views coitus as an attack on her physical well-being, and giving birth is felt to be the ultimate self-destruction. For some women, the conflict relates to their own femininity, often stemming from identification with a hostile mother. Another dynamic is closely related to Freud's notion of penis envy; that is, the woman feels inferior to men and defends against these feelings through resentment.

According to at least one psychoanalytic thinker (Benedek, 1952), the latent conflicts underlying infertility have been exacerbated by recent social developments in our society. Benedek feels that women who incorporate the value system of our modern society may develop personalities with rigid ego defenses against their "biological needs" to mother. Regarding male infertility, apparently no psychoanalytic view has been expounded linking unresolved psychic conflicts to spermatogenesis, a problem that is the chief male contribution to infertility.

Denber (1978) notes that most of the research supporting the psychoanalytic view of infertility is anecdotal. Of studies utilizing psychological testing, 8 out of 12 indicate no difference between women labeled psychogenically infertile and control groups. Those few studies that indicate differences in personality traits are open to conflicting interpretations. Since none of the studies used pre- and posttests and none were prospective, it is just as likely that psychological conflicts and problems are the *effects* of coping with infertility as it is that they are *causes*. Also, the one study that examined patients' histories found that psychological conflict long antedated the infertility and thus was probably not causative.

Two large, longitudinal studies have clearly refuted the notion that pregnancies which occur to infertile couples after adoption support the psychogenic basis of infertility (Weir & Weir, 1966; Tyler, Bonapart, & Grant, 1960). Both studies showed that pregnancy rates over a five-year period were no different for infertile couples who adopted than for infertile couples who did not adopt.

Studies utilizing a more cognitive approach, notably role theory, and measuring overt attitudes provide some support for the psychological basis of infertility (Slade, 1981; Kipper, Zigler-Shani, Serr, & Insler, 1977). However, these studies are quite inconclusive and suffer from severe methodological limitations.

Based on role theory Rossi (1972) offered the following explanation for female infertility. She proposed that social roles always evoke ambivalent feelings but that when a particular role is optional or discretionary, the negative feelings it engenders are permissible. However, since the traditional roles of wife and mother have been required of or ascribed to women, their ambivalence about these roles is unacceptable and heavily sanctioned. Rossi believes that this unexpressed ambivalence has physiological implications for women such as preventing conception.

Expanding on this view, psychogenic infertility is more likely to occur in women who have a traditional, idealized view of motherhood as well as great ambivalence toward it (Allison, 1979). The cognitive view, derived from role theory, differs from the psychoanalytic view because it implies that psychogenic infertility is normal, not pathological, and that it is mainly the result of cultural influences and other social factors.

In support of the role theory view, infertile women with no known physical cause for their problem did hold significantly more traditional sex role values (and also thought that men have more traditional ideals of women) than did married women with no fertility problems (Allison, 1979). The infertile group also reported less role conflict but greater occupational commitment than the control women, thus confirming Rossi's (1972) view that both denial and ambivalence are occurring. Functionally infertile women also exhibited more restrictive sexual attitudes, higher levels of guilt feelings about sex (Slade, 1981), and more conflict than did control groups (Kipper et al., 1977). Further, general research on sex roles has linked role conflict and somatic problems, and has shown that more sex-typed individuals have a narrower range of function, more anxiety, and are sick more often than are androgynous individuals (Bem, 1975; Bem, Myrtna, & Watson, 1976).

While suggestive, these studies all involve small, nonrandom samples (n = 40 to 60) and were not prospective. Greater female role conflict, more traditional sex typing, denial of role conflict, and great occupational commitment could all be *effects* of infertility problems rather than causes. Indeed, clinical observation suggests that there are many psychological reactions to infertility (Bresnick, 1981; Donnis, 1984; Kraft et al., 1980; Mazor, 1978, 1980; Menning, 1977, 1980; Shapiro, 1982). Couples beginning or involved in infertility treatment typically have been trying to conceive for a number of months or years prior to entering treatment and therefore are likely to show the effects of coping with infertility. In fact, the myths that psychological problems cause infertility only seem to add to the pressure that many couples experience while attempting to conceive.

The third view supporting psychogenic infertility is that general, environmental stress affects endocrinological balance (Brand, Roos, & Van der Merwe, 1982). The specific notion is that hormones (LSH, FSH) which govern growth and reproduction are controlled by the pituitary, which in turn is controlled by the hypothalamus, itself influenced by higher centers of the brain.

Little research exists that systematically examines the relationship between stress and infertility. Brand, Roos, & Van der Merwe (1982a) examined the relationship between physiological stress indicators and infertility. No significant differences were found in basal pulse volume, heart rate, skin resistance, and muscle tension among a small group of functionally (psychogenically) infertile women, an organically infertile group, and a fertile group.

To conclude, there is little scientific evidence supporting a psychological basis for infertility. Of course, this does not mean that psychological issues are not at all involved in the etiology of difficulties in conception and pregnancy since such evidence is extremely difficult to find. Much more systematic research is needed on the subject, utilizing a prospective, longitudinal approach, pre- and post-tests, larger samples, and adequate control groups. In the meantime, the findings reviewed mean that curing infertility is a highly questionable goal for individual or marital therapy.

The most significant recent development in thinking on infertility has been to deemphasize the question of the psychological origins of infertility and instead to focus on helping couples manage their immediate reactions to the problem (Bell, 1981; Bresnick, 1981; Menning, 1977; Mazor, 1978; Kraft et al., 1980; Donnis, 1984; Shapiro, 1982). Regardless of etiology, failure to produce a desired conception seems to create varied and intense reactions for couples. Further, diagnosing and treating infertility can and typically does take years, even if the outcome is successful.

This new focus views infertility as an adult developmental life crisis, and sees reactions to this crisis as normal and expected. The therapeutic goals are to help the couple to recognize the problem; to express, understand, and accept their reactions; and ultimately to find a feasible way for them to express their needs to nurture and guide the next generation.

Several major kinds of reactions to infertility, and a global sequence in these reactions, emerge from a synthesis of thinking on this subject (see mainly, Menning, 1977). In the first stage, the couple seems to truly recognize and accept that there is an infertility problem: This stage is initially characterized by surprise and denial.

During the second stage, the couple reacts to the genuine recognition of the infertility problem. Anger, guilt, and anxiety typically characterize these reactions. The anger may overtly focus on the treatment and the care providers, on social pressures from family and friends, and/or on the spouse. Some of the anger may be more rational while other aspects tend to be less so. Family, friends, and care providers may provoke some of these responses by their insensitivity to the couple's dilemma.

Anxiety typically focuses on bodily functions and on the treatment itself, but it also focuses on femininity/masculinity, sexual identity, and the partners' love and commitment to the relationship. Individuals and couples often turn their anger inward and feel that they are being punished for something they have done (an abortion, premarital or extramarital sexual relationships); or they see the infertility as a general manifestation of their unworthiness as potential parents and/or as adults. They often fear a life of never-ending incompleteness and low self-esteem.

It is likely that there will be tension between the partners during the first and second stages of this process. This tension may center around differences in the two individuals' abilities to recognize and cope with the problem. For example, the wife may still be holding onto denial while the husband is moving into accepting the existence of their infertility problem and reacting intensely to it. Tension within the couple may also derive from difficulties in making the many decisions related to infertility; in particular, when to get treatment, which forms of treatment to utilize, and how to proceed if treatment is unsuccessful. Most notably, couples experience tension around systematizing and timing their sexual activity, or "sex on demand." With sex being so divorced from emotion (that is, biology dictating when to have sex), resentment toward this mechanization of sex can build and may be directed toward one's partner.

If the couple experiences loss of the pleasurable aspects of sexual activity during infertility, they may have difficulties readjusting to a satisfying sex life after the infertility is resolved (through childbirth or through terminating further attempts to conceive). Sex has become mechanized for so long that walls to satisfying sexual functioning have been built. Shrednick (1984) used sex therapy techniques of sensate focus and also suggested a ban on intercourse during nonfertile periods to keep the pleasurable, spontaneous aspects of sex alive. The study found significantly higher levels of sexual desire after infertility in the group that used these techniques.

The psychodynamics underlying these intense reactions to infertility are important. From the point of view of ego psychology, infertility may represent a narcissistic injury (Kraft et al., 1980). The body image is the earliest component of self-representation and is always a major one. Body image includes feelings about physical well-being, fantasies about endurance, and one's feelings of intactness versus defectiveness. Indeed, some couples and individuals use infertility as an "organizer" for previous narcissistic injuries—childhood feelings of emptiness, rage, and badness. From a more psychoanalytic viewpoint, infertility may rekindle oedipal wishes to present the parent of the opposite sex with a baby. Infertility may also rekindle feelings of sibling rivalry—if any siblings are fertile (Mazor, 1980).

The last stage of the infertility process and treatment ensues if the diagnosis of infertility becomes conclusive. At this stage grief, with all the attendant feelings and processes proposed by Kubler-Ross (1969) and others, is the major emotion. The couple must mourn for the loss of the child or children which they will never have. Menning (1977) points out that infertility imposes a particularly difficult grieving process because: (1) there is no recognized loss since the loss is of something/someone that never existed; (2) the loss in often uncertain because the infertility may remain inconclusive for years or until the woman reaches menopause; and (3) the loss is often socially unspeakable due to the sexual overtones and guilt associated with it.

The final step in working through reactions engendered by conclusive infertility seems to be for the couple to accept their condition and to move on with their lives. For the clinician, this means helping them to assess the importance of parenthood as a developmental phase in their total life together, and helping them decide how to express their needs for generativity and nurturance. It may also mean helping them to rebuild and re-form their identities as adults, as sexual beings, as male and female; and perhaps to come to a new understanding of the meaning and purpose of their marriage.

Delayed Childbearing

The very term "delayed childbearing" stems from the traditional and still typical view in our society that there is an optimal age for a couple to have their children, especially the first child. This is when they are in their 20s. Having a first child either during adolescence or more toward midlife is generally considered less than optimal. Although there is a trend away from this norm, couples and care providers still have many questions surrounding starting a family after the mother is 30 years old. What are the medical risks for the infant? What are the medical risks for the mother? What are the psychosocial antecedents of delayed childbearing? What is the process of "delaying" that unfolds over time? What are the psychological consequences of starting childbearing and parenthood later—for the parents and for children?

Medical aspects of delayed childbearing

Regarding the medical risks of delaying childbearing, it is only possible to give a very brief summary here. The reader is strongly urged to read further, especially in the Daniels and Weingarten article (1979) summarized here. Before reviewing these medical risks a couple of cautionary notes are essential. First, maternal age rather than paternal age is the factor that has been mainly studied and reported on. The risks attendant to paternal age will be discussed only where relevant research exists. Another limitation is that concern among couples about maternal age in relation to delaying childbirth focuses chiefly on first births. Unfortunately, statistics and research do not usually distinguish age from parity, that is, from the number of previous births. Therefore, regarding many issues it is impossible at this time to distinguish the risks associated with age for first-time mothers and those for multiparous women.

Most important, any nomothetic discussion of the relationship of age to pregnancy and childbearing without considering other factors is to some extent misleading:

> As Dorothy Nortman concludes in her authoritative 1974 report for the Population Council, although there is a biological pattern of reproductive risk—high during the very young childbearing years, decreasing to a minimum in the 20s, and gradually rising again with advancing age—this underlying pattern is subject to tremendous variation in the "rate of risk, in space and time, and across different social classes." A high relative risk at a particular age—that is relative to other ages—does not automatically mean a high absolute risk. Thus, a 35-year-old, educated, middle-class woman, well nourished and in good health, who has access to first-rate medical care, has more reason to expect an uncomplicated pregnancy and delivery than a 20-year-old working class woman who is overweight, prone to hypertension, and without prenatal care because she cannot leave her job during maternity clinic hours. (Daniels & Weingarten, 1979, p. 8).

Equally important, relative degrees of risk across age groups do not necessarily indicate the absolute degree of risk for any group. "Older" women may be slightly more at risk for a particular condition, yet the absolute degree of risk is extremely small.

Risks to the mother associated with pregnancy and childbearing tend to fall into three groupings: maternal mortality; complications of pregnancy related to preexisting disorders such as diabetes, kidney disorders, or hypertension; and obstetrical complications, that is, medical problems that occur only if a woman is pregnant (such as toxemia, hemorrhage, or infection). Maternal mortality is lowest in the late teens and early 20s, then rises: 6.8 (per 100,000 births) at ages 17 to 20; 9.0 at ages 20 to 24; 7.9 at ages 25 to 29; 17.9 at ages 30 to 34; 45.8 at ages 35 to 39; and 65.6 at ages 40 to 44 (National Center for Health Statistics, 1978). Because these data are not classified by parity, we do not know if older, first-time mothers are at greater or lesser risk than older multiparous mothers. Race—or more probably the socioeconomic status it tends to reflect—is an extremely important indicator of maternal risk and modifies these rates considerably. For example, among 35- to 39-year-old women in 1976, the mortality rate for whites was 30.0 while for blacks it was 111.4 (National Center for Health Statistics, 1978).

Complications during pregnancy that derive from aggravation of preexisting disorders or diseases increase to the extent that the likelihood of the relevant diseases increases with age. Major diseases which can complicate pregnancy and which tend to increase in occurrence and/or severity with age are diabetes, fibroid tumors in the uterus, and various cardiovascular conditions such as hypertension. It should be kept in mind that the risk from any of these diseases can be considerably reduced with good medical care during pregnancy and childbirth.

Obstetrical complications include problems likely to occur early in pregnancy, such as ectopic pregnancy and spontaneous abortion; and problems likely to occur later in pregnancy or at the time of delivery, such as toxemia, hemorrhage, infection, and prolonged or dysfunctional labor.

There is no evidence that age is related to the incidence of ectopic pregnancy (where the embryo implants in the fallopian tubes rather than in the uterus, and thus is nonviable and also endangers the life of the mother). The incidence of spontaneous abortion (or miscarriage) does increase with age, especially early miscarriages at less than 12 weeks. One study conducted by a prepaid, comprehensive health insurance plan in New York City indicated that the rate of spontaneous abortion for first pregnancies under 12 weeks was approximately 40 per 1,000 pregnancies for women in their 20s; 75 for women between 30 and 34; and 150 for women aged 35 or older (Shapiro & Abramowitz, 1969). The incidence of toxemia and hemorrhage increases slightly with maternal age, but the incidence of infection does not. Toxemia is a complication that occurs most often in a first pregnancy. It is characterized by high blood pressure and loss of protein in the urine and/or sudden excessive weight gain from retention of fluids. Its cause is still unknown.

Statistics also tend to confirm the widely held clinical impression that older women are more prone to dysfunctional labor. For example, in 1967 a large-scale study on complications of pregnancy and childbirth among older, first-time mothers found that abnormal fetal presentation (a leading cause of dysfunctional labor) was 18 percent among women aged 25 to 29, but 31 percent among women aged 40 to 44 (Kane, 1967).

Infertility is another area of medical risk where health and age are intertwined, and a number of medical problems may occur with the years to jeopardize an older couple's ability to conceive and to bear a child. Basically, human reproductive capacity peaks in the mid-20s and then declines for women after 30 and for men after 40. A woman's stock of oocytes apparently diminishes in quantity and quality as does a man's supply of sperm (although sperm production continues for many more years). The increased risk of early miscarriage among older couples is thought to reflect these changes in reproductive capacity.

There is also a higher incidence of serious, organic pathology which contributes to infertility in women over 35. Such pathology includes injury to reproductive organs through infections, radiation, or surgery; and conditions such as endometriosis (abnormal proliferation of the lining of the uterus) and fibroid tumors. The leading cause of infertility in women, which is a current or previous infection, is only related to age insofar as older women have had more opportunity for its occurrence.

Recently, a controversy has arisen over the degree of increase in infertility with aging. A French study (Schwartz & Mayaux, 1982) suggests that the risk of infertility is far from small at any age and increases sharply starting as early as age 30. In this study, 2,193 women who were found by examination and tests to be normally fecund were artificially inseminated with donor semen (previously frozen) because their husbands were sterile. The generalizability of the startlingly high infertility rates reported in this study has been questioned by at least one researcher. Bongaarts (1982) argues that levels of infertility following artificial insemination which utilizes previously frozen semen are much higher than those resulting from natural insemination. He presents data from national studies in the United States and Britain and from historical populations to support his contention. For example, Mosher's (1982) analysis of data on U.S. women following natural insemination indicates infertility rates that increase with age but at the following rate and levels: 93 percent of women between 20 and 24 become pregnant; 89 percent of those between 25 and 29 years old; 84 percent at age 30 to 34; and 77 percent at age 35 to 39. Further, infertility levels reported in the French study (and indeed in many studies) are misleading in that a substantial proportion of the women who do not conceive after 12 cycles do get pregnant subsequently. In a British study cited by Bongaarts (1982), 80 percent of the women conceived after one year, while 91 percent had conceived after three to four years (Vesey, Wright, McPherson, & Wiggins, 1978).

In summary, infertility does increase with age due to both normal changes in reproductive capacity and the increased incidence of disease and injury. However, the rate of increase of infertility is subject to controversy.

Risks to the infant from delayed childbearing fall into three areas: infant mortality, prematurity, and birth defects. Infant mortality is highest among the offspring of very young mothers, declines and is fairly constant throughout the 20s and 30s, then rises again in the 40s. Further, women aged 35 to 44 are only *slightly* more at risk than those in their 20s or early 30s of having an infant who is born prematurely or with a very low birth weight.

Birth defects pose the greatest risk for infants born to "older" women. It is estimated that 1 in 16 of all babies has a birth defect (Apgar & Beck, 1972). But reports of the incidence of defects depend a great deal on what is being counted as a defect and when. Many birth defects are not apparent at birth or shortly thereafter, and birth defects do not have to be reported on birth certificates. Only 3 percent to 5 percent of serious birth defects are thought to result from chromosomal error (Apgar & Beck, 1972) and it is these defects that are related to maternal age. The relationship between maternal age and birth defects that are *not* chromosomal in origin is statistically insignificant (Nortman, 1974). Thus, 95 percent to 97 percent of serious birth defects appear to have no relationship to maternal (or paternal) age.

Down's syndrome is the most common of these chromosomal error defects that are related to maternal age. While there are no national statistics relating Down's syndrome to maternal age, many local and regional studies have reported such a relationship (Collman & Stoller, 1962; Hook & Chambers, 1977; Mikkelson, Fischer, & Stene, 1976; Miller & Erbe, 1978; Smith & Wilson, 1973). It is estimated that the incidence of Down's syndrome increases from one per 200,000 at age 20 to one per 20 at age 45 or more. Women in their early 30s report one in 750 to one in 870, with one in 300 for women in their late 30s (Miller & Erbe, 1978).

Relationship of paternal age to chromosomal birth defects has been considered, although very little is known about it. Whereas at least one study indicated no positive statistical link between father's age and Down's syndrome, Penrose (1962) found a clear link between paternal age and a special type of the syndrome. Another study (Magenis, Overton, Chamberlin, Brody, & Lourien, 1977) showed that 24 percent of Down's syndrome births result from early chromosomal error in the father (though not necessarily related to age).

The relationship of age to birth defects has been somewhat mitigated by the development of techniques to detect birth defects during pregnancy, notably amniocentesis, which can detect known chromosomal defects such as Down's syndrome. Amniocentesis involves a procedure in which a small sample of amniotic fluid that surrounds the fetus is withdrawn using a hollow needle carefully inserted into the uterus through the abdominal wall. The medical risk of amniocentesis is less than 1 percent based on a four-year national collaborative study and does not increase the risk of fetal loss (Holmes, 1978; Milunsky, 1976). There are no major maternal complications. A drawback of this test is that it cannot be done until approximately the 16th week of pregnancy and it takes about a month for results to be completed. Thus, decision making following a positive test cannot take place until late in the second trimester of pregnancy.

Psychological aspects of delayed childbearing

Very little discussion or research has been published concerning psychological issues related to delayed childbearing, probably due to the recency of the issue. Most of the ideas and data presented here derive from an excellent new study by Daniels and Weingarten (1982). From 1976 to 1979 these researchers conducted lengthy, unstructured interviews with 86 couples all of whom were white and none of whom were selected at random. The couples, however, do represent a range of socioeconomic statuses. The sample was stratified by timing of first birth (early—ages 18 to 22; later—ages 28 to 32); and by current age (30s, 40s, and 50s). A small group of couples who had had their first child in mid-life (37 to 43 years old) were also interviewed, as were most of the sons and daughters of the group of parents now in their 50s. It is important to remember that the results represent only the views of couples who have remained intact and exclude couples who had their first child at the most normative age—in their mid-20s.

Three basic scenarios seem to guide the decision about when to have a first child: natural, brief delay, or programmatic postponement. The "natural" scenario or script is the most traditional one—that love, marriage, and childbearing are all spontaneous events which should follow upon one another naturally. The "brief delay" script holds that it is good for a couple to have a little time after marriage and before children to settle down, to improve their financial situation, and to solidify their relationship. However, any delay after that short time period is undesirable. "Programmatic postponement" typically involves a longer delay between marriage and childbearing in which to pursue educational and career plans and perhaps to solidify the relationship.

The natural and brief delay scenarios occurred most often among the early-timing couples, while programmatic postponement occurred most often among the later parents. The majority of mid-life couples used none of these scenarios: Their "decision" to have their first child after age 37 was not typically a choice so much as a compromise. Childbearing tended to be delayed almost completely because of obstacles in the spheres of intimacy and/or reproductive biology. Specifically, almost all of these couples married in their late 20s or 30s and/or experienced infertility problems. Only one couple reported that career plans had made a major contribution to the delay, although it does not seem clear from the data reported how much career plans may have accounted for the delay in forming a marriage. At least one woman reported that the tempo of individual psychological development was a principal factor in delaying childbearing for her; that is, it took her several years to overcome her ambivalence about her female identity and her fears that parenthood would diminish her as a person.

Concerning overall satisfaction with timing, more early- than late-timing couples would have timed their first birth differently if they had it to do over again. In fact, the couples who waited until their late 20s or early 30s to have their first child were all quite satisfied. Mid-life couples mostly felt that this was not the best time (too late) to start having children but that it was the best they could have done in the circumstances.

More interesting than their overall level of satisfaction are the initial advantages and disadvantages reported by each group. Early-timing couples most often reported financial and personal hardships immediately resulting from the arrival of their first child (often closely followed by a second). Early childrearing was often almost entirely left to the woman, either because her husband intensified his efforts to provide for the family or because her husband was still acting out his needs for some adult freedom. Many of these wives reported that they initially found themselves taking care of their new infants and their husbands as well. Early-timing couples tended to rely more on their families of origin for social, child care, and financial support. In developmental terms, these men and women felt pressures from having highly compressed the phases of adolescent and early adult development. They entered into parenthood before they had had adequate time to form an adult identity or to solidify an intimate relationship.

The late-timing couples mainly reported problems after the birth of their first child in the spheres of household management and child care. They found it difficult to juggle career, marriage, and baby all at once. These couples had more of a sense of marriage and life "before baby" as compared to "after baby" and therefore had more adjustments to make. In terms of advantages, these couples felt that they were ready to take on the challenges of childrearing. Their difficulties in adjusting to a new lifestyle were tempered with the feeling that "I've had my fling," or "We've had our fling" as a couple. There was more reciprocal nurturing of the baby and of each other among these couples, although the woman was the primary caregiver for all but one couple. The advantages and disadvantages reported by these couples are echoed in another study comparing earlier and later childbearing (Frankel & Wise, 1982).

Within the early and late patterns noted, there were also major gender differences in the initial consequences of parental timing. As noted, the woman performed the primary parenting in all cases but one, regardless of timing. All of the women in both groups pulled back at least somewhat from the work force. They either stopped working completely or shifted to part-time work. However, two patterns of managing work and child rearing emerged: sequential and simultaneous. Almost all of the early-timing women exhibited a sequential pattern. First, they devoted themselves to child rearing. Then, when their children were in school or grown, they entered the work force. The later-timing women were evenly divided between following a sequential and a simultaneous pattern, the latter involving juggling work and childrearing all along.

For the men in the sample, fatherhood as an involving "occupation" (rather than just an identity) was optional, and varied in the timing of its onset depending on personal and interpersonal issues. Daniels and Weingarten (1982) called this phenomenon, when a man becomes a "hands-on" parent, the "fatherhood click." For some men hands-on parenting happened immediately after the birth of the child whereas for others it took a few or many years to occur. Presumably, such parenting never happens for some men. Later-timing fathers tended to become more involved, hands-on parents sooner in their child's life, a pattern supported by other research (Nydegger, 1973). There was also a trend toward more involved fathering by younger men regardless of timing.

Turning to the mid-life couples, three different patterns of initial consequences seemed to emerge: the supplemental experience, the new chapter, and the crunch. For all of the men and about one half of the women, becoming parents for the first time was a supplemental experience. There were no radical changes in their lifestyle, life pattern, or sense of self. The baby was basically a positive addition that they fit into their existing lives. The women kept their prebaby jobs and did so at about the same level of involvement by utilizing child care. These women were also very clear about their needs for private and couple time.

For the remaining women, half found that the birth of their first child opened a new and very positive chapter in their lives while the other half found it to be mainly a rather negative, pressured "crunch." In the "new chapter" pattern, the woman's sense of herself and her priorities become reoriented around her child. She tends to find that she is experiencing the nurturing side of herself and enjoying it. The dramatic shift in the structure of these women's lives may not have imposed a crisis because of their willingness to exchange an old script for a new one and because of favorable circumstances such as the husband's involvement with the child.

Motherhood at 40 produced a crisis for a few women because the

> new text differed from what they had anticipated in ways they found difficult to accept. Their fantasies and expectations—of what the baby would be like, of their husbands' responses, or of their own generative capacity—collided with reality, and they were disappointed in the experience and in themselves for not being able to manage and transform it. (Daniels & Weingarten, 1982, p. 213)

For example, one woman, who had had a highly successful career before marriage and motherhood, experienced a sense of crisis after the birth of her first child. The baby was colicky, her husband remained lukewarm and less involved than she had hoped he would be, and she felt she did not match up to her perfectionistic expectations of herself as a mother. Another woman was extremely disappointed that her husband was less pleased and involved after the birth than they had hoped he would be during long years of coping with infertility.

As the children of the couples studied grew older, birth timing remained an important factor in only some areas. Mid-life parents saw two, age-related drawbacks: their present energy level and their future health. When asked about the effect of the varying age gap between parent and child, all couples (early- and late-timing) agreed that timing of childbirth made little difference in terms of interacting with adolescent children: All found it difficult. The couples were also unanimous in their belief that partners should have at least a few years together alone to solidify their relationship before children come on the scene. Couples seemed to experience more mid-life transitions regarding the "empty nest" when they had children early *and* had not given the marriage enough attention initially and throughout childrearing.

In other spheres, early-timing parents felt that there were disadvantages early in child rearing but advantages later, when children are grown. Some felt there was plenty of time left to pursue or begin a career, enjoy grown children, personal freedom, and each other. This is somewhat the opposite situation from that described by mid-life couples, who felt that there were early advantages in child rearing but more disadvantages later. When their children were grown the early timing couples were able to enjoy some of the very freedoms that the mid-life-timing couples had enjoyed before starting a family.

The grown children who were interviewed felt that their parents' age was irrelevant for a long time. Children of later-timing parents saw no disadvantages to themselves or to their parents. By contrast, children of some early-timing parents wondered, once they were grown themselves, if their parents had been ready for them and thought that it would have been nicer for them if their parents had waited longer before starting a family. Of course, these reactions may have been influenced by the current climate of opinion favoring later timing of parenthood.

A small body of research augments our sense of the consequences for children of parental timing. Delayed childbearing seems to have a positive effect on the child. Maternal age and the child's intellectual development show a small, positive, linear relationship across the entire maternal age spectrum (Belmont, Cohen, Dryfoos, Stein, & Zatac, 1981; Neligan, Kolvin, Scott, & Garside, 1976; Zybert, Stein, & Belmont, 1978). Consistent results have been obtained from studies of different countries, races, social classes, and child ages. Significant maternal age effects on children's school readiness (Furstenberg, 1976) and achievement have also been found where offspring of teenage mothers are compared to offspring of "adult" mothers (Broman, 1981; Oppel & Royston, 1971).

Age-related maternal attitudes and behavior which may mediate child outcomes are poorly understood. Some studies have shown that teenage mothers tend to be less responsive to their newborns (Jones, Green, & Krauss, 1980) and to engage in less verbal behavior with infants (Osofsky & Osofsky, 1970). They express less positive childrearing attitudes and have less realistic expectations for infants' development than do older mothers (Field et al., 1980). Other studies, however, have found no significant relationship between maternal age and postpartum behavior (Svedja, Campos, & Emde, 1980) either in early infancy (Field, Widmayer, Stringer, and Ignatoff, 1980), or during the preschool years (Philliber & Graham, 1981).

The problem is that most of these studies focus on the adolescent compared to the adult part of the maternal age spectrum. Ragozin, Bashom, Crnic, Greenberg, and Robinson, (1982) examined the linear relationships between maternal age and behavior along a broad maternal age continuum. Optimal maternal elicitation behavior (that is, trying to get baby to make sounds) increased sharply with age for full-term, first-time mothers aged 16–38 (Ragozin et al., 1982). Parity did interact with age, however, since maternal elicitation behavior was constant for second-time mothers regardless of age, and declined with age for women with three or more children. These results are suggestive of a relationship between maternal age and specific maternal behavior that may promote intellectual growth and achievement, but much more research is needed in this area.

Voluntary Childlessness

Many important questions surround the topic of voluntary childlessness: Why do a small minority of couples choose to remain permanently childless? Are these individuals more maladjusted or neurotic than others in some way? Are there personal characteristics and/or childhood circumstances that are predictive of voluntary childlessness? What are the effects of intentionally remaining childless on individuals and on marriages—especially in middle and old age?

Voluntary childlessness is a particularly distinctive behavior in a society such as ours which is traditionally strongly pronatalist. Studying individuals who choose to remain childless may illuminate the meaning of parenthood and children because these individuals contribute an unusual and extreme perspective. Studying voluntary childlessness may certainly help us to understand how individuals can express and resolve generativity in ways other than parenting. These couples may also help us to understand how children affect marriage by showing what childless marriages are like over time.

It is extremely difficult to estimate the percentage of U.S. couples who are voluntarily and permanently childless because available national data fail to distinguish between voluntary and involuntary (infertility) childlessness and between temporary and permanent childlessness. However, it was estimated that the percentage of married women who remained childless at the end of their reproductive years (that is, by age 45–49) was approximately 10 percent in 1975 (Poston & Gotard, 1977). Note that this percentage includes wives who were permanently childless due to infertility, so that the percentage of voluntary childlessness was probably considerably smaller than 10 percent.

Unfortunately, even this estimate is based only on couples who were already middle-aged by 1975. Any recent trends in voluntary childlessness can not be delineated with complete confidence until couples who started their reproductive years around 1960 reach middle age, that is, around the year 2,000. However, as previously noted, there is clearly a trend toward increased delayed childbearing among recent cohorts of married couples, such as those wives who were 25 to 30 years old in 1980 (Bloom & Trussell, 1983). It is estimated that permanent childlessness will reach 20 to 25 percent among women in these cohorts, a substantial increase over the 10 percent for women 30 to 50 years old in 1980 (Bloom & Trussell, 1983). Again, it is impossible at present to ascertain the proportion of this increase in permanent childlessness that will be voluntary. Many of these couples may remain permanently childless because of infertility problems that they discover only after they have finished delaying the birth of a first child. However, it is thought that much of the recent increase in delayed childbearing and probably some of the estimated increase in permanent childlessness are voluntary; education and labor force participation by the wife are important determinants of delayed childbearing and their influence seems to be increasing across cohorts (Bloom & Trussell, 1983).

Our knowledge about voluntary childlessness derives from a small but growing body of research and thought. When voluntarily childless couples are compared to norms for American couples, some patterns emerge consistently, while data on other patterns are contradictory. Consistent findings are that women who choose to remain permanently childless tend to be urban, white, of middle socioeconomic status, first-born or only children, more educated, more often in the work force (Gustavus & Henley, 1971; Freshnock & Cutright, 1978; Kaltreider & Margolis, 1977; Veevers, 1973, 1980), and are areligious or belong to a liberal religious denomination (Gustavus & Henley, 1971; Feldman, 1981; Veevers, 1973).

There are conflicting data concerning personal adjustment (Centers & Blumberg, 1954; Greenbaum, 1973; Kaltreider & Margolis, 1977; Silka & Keisler, 1977) and childhood happiness (Centers & Blumberg, 1954; Clausen & Clausen, 1973; Veevers, 1973; Kaltreider & Margolis, 1977; Feldman, 1981). Conflicting pictures may arise concerning the level of adjustment of voluntarily childless individuals and couples because of the assumption that all such individuals or couples are homogeneous. Somewhat different antecedents and consequences of voluntary childlessness may be associated with men than with women. Aside from gender, there may be significant subgroups of voluntarily childless people who differ systematically. This appears to be the case.

One typology classifies couples according to their main reason for remaining childless: hedonistic, idealistic, emotional, and practical (Baum, 1983). Hedonistically oriented couples find that they enjoy the freedom and material advantages that a childfree lifestyle affords them. These couples are relatively unconflicted about their choice and are easily able to disregard social pressures. When they married they may have had a vague intention of having children following a brief delay, but they decided that they wanted to maintain their childfree lifestyle after the planned period of delay came to an end.

The "idealistic" couples tended to avoid having children due to their concern about social and environmental problems. Most felt that it was not fair to bring children into today's world. For these couples, avoiding children represents evidence of their commitment to their ideals, which are also typically expressed in egalitarian marriages and in social service-oriented work (often teaching). These couples typically arrive at the decision not to have children after much discussion and time, and they *do* feel some conflicting desires to experience having their own children.

The "emotional" couples are characterized by intense, long-term dislike of children and parenting. They typically made their decision individually before marriage, often in adolescence, and childlessness was part of their marriage "contract."

FIGURE 2 Polarities in the Process of Deciding to be Childless

Timing of decision	Making the decision before marriage	Making the decision after marriage
	Definite point of decision	Drifting into decision
Type of decision	Discursive	Little discussion
	Decision determined by one partner	Equal decision
	Tension	Tension-free

"Practical" is not as pure a type as the other three, and basically serves to cover all other couples. These couples have practical reasons for choosing not to have children: age at marriage, career, health. They usually made their decision before they married, but sometimes they did so afterwards. These couples tend to be highly conflicted, feeling that they would like to have children but are not suited in some way. They also tend to be traditional in their values and in their marriages.

A useful typology of process issues was also derived from the same study and is shown in Figure 2 (Baum, 1983). It can be used to analyze and describe variations among childless couples. One can readily see how this typology guided the descriptive categories of childless couples.

A simpler way of categorizing voluntarily childless individuals has also been proposed (Veevers, 1973, 1980). Three patterns of decision making have been described: early articulators, postponers, and suggestible or indifferent. Early articulators are very similar to the "emotional" subgroup in Baum's (1983) typology: They decided early in life, typically during adolescence, to avoid parenthood due to strong, negative feelings toward children and parenting. They deliberately sought a mate who felt the same way and childlessness was part of the marriage "contract."

By contrast, "postponers" remain childless due to a series of decisions to postpone having children until some future time. At the time of marriage and before, these individuals typically have given little or no thought to children and are rather neutral. They assume that they will have children "some day." Their "decision-making" process tends to proceed in four stages. First, the couple delays having children for a definite time until some practical goals are accomplished such as accumulating a "nest egg," finishing school, traveling, and/or getting adjusted to each other. At this stage they resemble many couples who do eventually become parents. They are similar to the "brief delay" or "programmatic postponement" scenario seen in delayed child bearing. In the second stage having children is postponed again, but this time for an indefinite time and for vaguer reasons such as when "things get better," when they can "afford it," or when they "feel more ready."

At the third stage of this postponement process the couple openly acknowledges for the first time that they may remain permanently childless, and they begin to consider the advantages and disadvantages of this state. By this time they have gotten used to a childfree lifestyle, experienced the advantages of childlessness, and have had a chance to observe friends who are raising children.

In the fourth and last stage the couple reaches a definite conclusion that they will remain permanently child free. However, for many of these couples there is never an explicit decision to remain without children. The process is more one of recognizing an event that has already occurred. It is now "obvious" that they will never have children, just as it was "obvious" when they got married that they someday would. An explicit decision among these couples is usually precipitated by a special event such as an unplanned pregnancy. Adoption can function in an important, symbolic way for couples who never make an explicit decision to remain childless. Even after they seem too old to give birth to a first child, they often hold onto adoption as a vague option.

The "postponers" seem similar to the hedonistic couples in Baum's (1983) typology, but postponers are not as able to openly disparage pronatalist societal norms and pressures. It is also possible that these couples are highly ambivalent toward parenting, and are using avoidance and denial to mask their intense feelings and conflicts. Another possibility is that these are couples in which two individuals who are both rather neutral and passive about parenting have formed a relationship. This last interpretation is supported by a third subgroup of couples Veevers (1973, 1980) found in which the women were indifferent or even vaguely positive about having children before meeting their future husbands, but by the time of marriage had converted to a childless perspective. It is possible that when both husband and wife are this neutral *and* passive they can either drift into parenting or drift into childlessness depending on circumstances.

The existence of early articulators and postponers has been confirmed by other research, and some additional characteristics of these subgroups have been identified (Houseknecht, 1979b; Kaltreider & Margolis, 1977; Callan, 1983). Early articulators report less warmth in the family of origin, especially from their mothers; more achievement pressure, especially from their mothers; more distance between themselves and their parents in adolescence or more general autonomy; more divorce and/or death and mental illness in their families (Kaltreider & Margolis, 1977; Houseknecht, 1979b). Single childless women between the ages of 19 and 30 who were applying for sterilization also tended to have been tomboys or "their father's daughter" in childhood, feared being a bad mother or being destroyed by a child, and/or becoming like their own (bad) mother. They also had had no or few long-term relationships with either men or women, and they tended to see career and motherhood as "either/or" (Kaltreider & Margolis, 1977). This study concluded that remaining childless was a functional, wise decision for these women.

Characteristics of voluntarily childless men suggest that the dynamics of childlessness may vary by gender. Two studies have compared vasectomized, childless men to fathers. No differences were found in childhood happiness and background, marital satisfaction, and maturity or psychological adjustment (Silka & Keisler, 1977; Magarick & Brown, 1981). Concerning specific personality characteristics of childless men, one study found no difference in independence and self-esteem between childless men and fathers (Silka & Keisler, 1977), while another found childless men to be more independent thinkers and more willing to experiment (Magarick & Brown, 1981). It is possible that maladjustment is more prevalent among childless women (or some subgroups thereof) than among childless men because parenting is less central to the male self-concept in our society than it is to that of the female.

Two principal consequences of voluntary childlessness have been investigated: marital satisfaction and well-being in old age. Overall, voluntarily childless couples seem to be more satisfied in their marriages than couples with children but this difference is mitigated by many other factors. Duration of marriage seems to modify the relationship between childlessness and satisfaction. From 10 to 19 years of marriage, the same level of satisfaction was reported by childless couples, by active parents, and by former parents. However, after 20 years of marriage, childless couples were happier than either active parents or former parents (Renne, 1976). This finding coincides with the pattern found in the timing of childbearing, where couples who had solidified their relationship before having children and maintained it during childbearing were more able to have satisfying marriages in later years when children departed. It seems logical that childless couples who stay together have much energy and motivation to put into maintaining their marital relationship. Moreover, many dissatisfied couples stay together for the presumed benefit of their children, whereas childless couples who are dissatisfied more readily separate.

Intentionality may be the issue rather than childlessness *per se*. The one study (Feldman, 1981) that found similar levels of marital satisfaction among voluntarily childless couples and parents tried to establish a homogeneous parent group by including only couples who had *wanted* and *planned* their first child.

Examining specific components of marital satisfaction may be more important and helpful than comparing one, global index. When four components of satisfaction were measured, childless couples were higher on "cohesion" but similar to parents on affection, consensus, and satisfaction (Houseknecht, 1979a). Cohesion refers to engaging in more outside interests and more frequent exchange of ideas. The tasks associated with child-rearing may mitigate against opportunities for "togetherness," but overall marital satisfaction may be quite similar for these two groups.

Well-being in old age is the second major consequence of voluntary childlessness which needs to be considered. The common traditional assumption is that elderly people who are parents are better off because children provide emotional and practical support when their parents reach old age. Childless elderly individuals are assumed to be more isolated, lonelier, and to have fewer resources. This assumption is still widespread despite the growing discussion concerning the breakdown in family supports for the elderly. More recently, a counterargument has been proposed; namely, that voluntarily (and even involuntarily) childless elderly people may in fact be as well off as are parents because they have become more self-sufficient and autonomous. The childless elderly may be more autonomous in two ways. First, they are *emotionally* more independent and self-reliant, and therefore are able to feel satisfied with fewer ties (Gubrium, 1975). Second, they are socially adaptive in that they may compensate for their lack of offspring by developing relationships and supports with family members other than offspring and/or with nonfamilial sources such as friends, formal organizations, and volunteer helpers (Cumming & Schneider, 1961; Keller, 1968).

Results concerning the effects of childlessness on well-being during old age are only suggestive because of the small number of studies completed. Further, studies vary regarding the aspects of well-being examined and the nature of the elderly group studied. What is especially problematic is the fact that most studies focus on elderly subjects who are "currently childless" and do not distinguish between members of subgroups within this group such as individuals who are childless because they have never married, those who have been married but are voluntarily childless, and those who have been married and had a child or children who died.

Granting these limitations, some support has emerged for the recent argument that childless, elderly people experience the same or a similar level of well-being as that of elderly parents. Concerning their emotional state, elderly childless individuals were found by most studies to be no more lonely or unhappy than elderly parents. This finding was the same for the never married (childless) elderly (Gubrium, 1975; Clark & Anderson, 1967), for currently childless individuals who were 50 years old or more (Glenn & McClanahan, 1981), and for the very old (72 years old or more) (Keith, 1983). Further, a similar level of subjective well-being seems to exist despite some objective differences between the childless elderly and elderly parents—in particular, fewer social contacts for the former.

However, marital status may be a powerful modifier of the relationship between parental status and subjective well-being in old age, at least for women. Among married elderly women, those with no children had the same feeling of well-being as those who were parents but childless widows had a slightly lower feeling of well-being than widows who were parents (Beckman & Houser, 1982). Further, poor health and less religiosity also contributed to lower feelings of well-being among widows.

There are mixed findings concerning the belief that childless elderly people have similar objective levels of well-being (i.e., social contact) as do elderly parents because the childless elderly compensate by developing stronger relationships with extended family and with nonfamily. Concerning family relationships, the childless do seem to have more contact with family other than children than do elderly parents (Shanas et al., 1968; Clark & Anderson, 1967; Townsend, 1957; Cicirelli, 1981) but the total amount of familial contact, when children are included, is still less than for elderly parents (Keith, 1983; Bachrach, 1980). It is important to recognize that these studies do not report on the subjective importance which the childless elderly place on family as an important resource in their lives; they only look at behavior, that is, number of social contacts.

In terms of nonfamilial relationships, there are also mixed findings. Two studies indicate no increase in nonfamilial contacts among the childless elderly (Rosenberg, 1970; Keith, 1983), although one study shows that the childless elderly used more services from neighbors, volunteer organizations, and paid help (Cicirelli, 1981). Perhaps these inconsistencies are the result of crucial modifiers of nonfamilial contacts such as health. When in good health, the childless elderly saw more of friends and neighbors than did elderly parents and this contact seemed to compensate for their lack of offspring. However, the childless who were in poor health had fewer social contacts than the elderly parents who were also in poor health (Bachrach, 1980). Elderly childless who had engaged in higher status occupations also made more contacts with friends and neighbors than elderly childless people from lower status occupations, regardless of health (Bachrach, 1980).

One study (Keith, 1983) found that gender was much more significantly related to resources than was parental status. Women tended to have more friends and belong to more organizations, but to have less money than men regardless of their parental status.

In summary, it is not at all clear whether childless elderly people have less satisfactory lives than elderly parents. Clearly, objective measures of well-being by themselves can be misleading since the elderly person's subjective experience may not fit objective criteria. Specifically, an elderly person can be more isolated in objective terms (fewer visits, fewer phone calls, fewer people to call) but still feel no more lonely, upset, or pessimistic. It also seems clear that other more immediate factors, such as marital status, health, and gender are equally or more important for objective and subjective well-being during old age than is parental status.

Perhaps most important, the research to date underscores the need to study married, voluntarily childless elderly as a separate group from other childless elderly or at least to determine the extent to which the various subgroups of the childless elderly are heterogeneous.

PERSPECTIVES ON TREATMENT

Given the many issues facing contemporary couples, it is helpful to have a conceptual framework that can guide the treatment of couples experiencing problems in managing their fertility. Some ideas concerning interventions emerged from the preceding discussion, especially that on infertility, but a more comprehensive and widely applicable framework is needed. The emphasis here will be on couples who come into treatment presenting a fertility issue as the main (or only) problem, rather than on situations where fertility issues are introduced in the course of long-term, intensive therapy.

The PLISSIT model proposed by Annon and Robinson (1978) seems useful as a global framework for guiding interventions with couples who present fertility issues. PLISSIT is an acronym standing for: Permission, Limited Information, Specific Suggestions, and Intensive Therapy. This model was originally developed to guide treatment of sexual difficulties but it applies equally well to fertility issues. The model proposes a treatment process in which four types of interventions are sequenced from less to more intensive. The treatment process stops at any stage, whenever the issues are resolved to the couple's satisfaction and only proceeds if more intensive measures are required.

It is assumed that this treatment process begins only after the care provider has made an initial evaluation of the couple and determined that no severe pathology exists. For couples with infertility problems, the evaluation process should include a careful sexual history since untreated sexual dysfunctions (or unacknowledged ones) may be preventing conception. Some couples tend to gloss over those sexual issues involved in the infertility process which may or may not have predated their attempts to conceive a child. Therefore, a detailed discussion of their sexual life and their past sexual interactions needs to occur before the actual treatment can be planned.

In the first type of intervention, giving *permission*, the care provider makes statements designed to reassure the couple that they have a right to their concerns and reactions and (if appropriate) that these are "normal." The couple is thus given permission to be themselves and to communicate their thoughts openly. Merely airing a problem and/or feeling more "normal" may be a tension-reducing release for some couples and provide a sufficient level of treatment. If not, the tension reduction may at least help the couple to be more receptive to further interventions.

For example, a couple may be seriously at odds over whether to delay childbearing any longer. It may be reassuring for them if the therapist puts their concerns into a developmental context and explains that inevitably individuals develop at somewhat different rates. Most husbands and wives do not feel equally ready to have their first child at exactly the same time. Additionally, the couple may need permission to drop the idea that they *must* have their first child by a particular age to be normal, or even to drop the idea that they *must* have children at all.

For couples with infertility problems, it may be important to give them permission *not* to be passionate when they are having sexual intercourse at prescribed times. Couples often feel pressure to be romantic even when having sex "on demand" makes them feel just the opposite way. Another crucial intervention when there are infertility problems may be to give the couple permission to have the intense reactions they are experiencing. Many individuals need reassurance that intense feelings of anger, fear, guilt, and self-doubt are normal adjuncts to infertility problems. As these examples illustrate, theories of adult development like Erikson's (1950), and of irrational cognitive beliefs such as that of Ellis and Grieger (1977), are particularly useful for guiding permission-giving interventions.

Providing *limited information* is the next stage in the model. The couple may feel less tense and more reassured that neither of them is "crazy," but still have concerns regarding factual issues. This will typically mean providing relatively simple facts about the medical aspects of childbearing issues. For a couple concerned about whether to continue delaying childbearing, information about the health risks to mother and child and the relationship of infertility to age might be useful. For couples facing infertility problems, information regarding when and how to have sexual intercourse in order to maximize the chances of conception could be especially pertinent. It is important at this stage that the care provider not overstep the boundary of his or her own expertise. Providing limited information may resolve disagreements and/or confusion for the couple to such a degree that further interventions are not needed.

If providing limited information does not resolve the fertility issues presented, then treatment focuses next on *specific suggestions.* These could be relatively simple interventions such as giving the couple a referral so that they can obtain more complex medical information or suggesting a book or article that will help them to further explore the issues at hand.

However, specific suggestions can involve more complex interventions such as increasing the couple's problem-solving and communication skills. For the couple at odds over whether to further delay childbearing, the therapist may need to guide them through the process of making a decision. One part of the problem may be that one or both members of the couple are not clear enough about their own priorities and preferences, are having difficulty openly communicating their thoughts to their spouse, and/or are having difficulty hearing and respecting the other's thoughts. When it is relevant, decision-making help or training needs to occur in two stages. First, the members of the couple go through the process separately in order to achieve clarity about their own individual views. Next, the decision-making process is repeated with both spouses in order to enable them to arrive at a joint decision.

Theories or models of decision making, such as that proposed by Janis and Mann (1977), can be used to guide first individual, then joint decision making. The steps in the process they propose are (1) appraising the challenge, (2) surveying the alternatives, (3) weighing the alternatives, (4) deliberating about commitment, (5) planning implementation, and (6) adhering to the decision despite *limited* negative feedback (after the action is taken or in anticipation of taking the action). The fifth step does not appear in the Janis and Mann model (1977); it has been added here. Each step in the process requires specific skills; for example, surveying and weighing the alternatives often require utilizing resources in order to obtain additional information. An especially crucial skill in individual decision making is the ability to *imagine* future consequences of each alternative, which is similar to Lazarus's (1981) concept. Here it may be important that each individual be able to imagine in some detail life with a baby now, life with a baby a given number of years from now, and/or a whole life without a child.

During the second, dyadic stage of decision making, the couple may also need help with many specific communicating and negotiating skills. Ideas about constructive communication such as Stewart's (1980) can be applied here to help the couple learn how to negotiate a mutually satisfying decision. These include: (1) making "I" statements (that is, talking about oneself instead of about the spouse); (2) focusing on the present (rather than reviewing past grievances); (3) listening; (4) making positive rather than negative statements ("I want" rather than "I do not want"); and (5) making behaviorally specific statements to and/or requests of the partner.

Similar training and guidance in decision making might also be useful for the couple coping with infertility problems. Depending on their stage in the infertility investigation, the couple may be at an impasse over decisions such as whether to proceed with the investigation and/or treatment; what tests and/or forms of treatment to pursue next; or whether to pursue alternatives other than further infertility treatment (that is, "wait and see," adoption, voluntary childlessness).

If the couple reaches an impasse at any step along the way, for example, they are not able to reach a mutually satisfying decision, then *intensive therapy* may be indicated. A decision would also have to be made about whether intensive therapy should be individual and/or joint.

For example, the impasse over when to have a first child may occur because one or both spouses have not adequately resolved developmental tasks prior to generativity, notably identity formation and creating intimacy. Parenthood may function as an attempt to avoid these unfinished developmental tasks or as a misguided attempt to complete them. Ambivalence about becoming a parent may be related to lack of resolution at even earlier stages of development. Individuals who never adequately separated from their own parent(s) may have a deep-seated fear of being psychologically overwhelmed by the needs of a totally dependent baby. This fear is often complicated by the wish or compulsion to fuse with love objects, in this case the child.

Ambivalence toward parenthood may also result from a dim recognition that the *couple* is fused to such a degree that bringing a child into the situation would threaten their pseudo intimacy. Again, this fear may be complicated by the wish to have a child in order to diminish the couple's degree of fusion. One or both spouses may need intensive therapy in order to help them see and resolve these deeper problems. These examples illustrate how Erikson's (1950) theory of the human life cycle, and ego psychology conceptualizations such as Kohut's (1971), can facilitate diagnosis and treatment of issues requiring intensive therapy.

The PLISSIT model thus provides a useful framework for intervening with couples who present fertility related issues. Various more specific models drawn from adult developmental, psychoanalytic, cognitive, and interpersonal perspectives, can be used to guide specific interventions within the four stages of the PLISSIT model.

Summary

Certain themes emerge from examining fertility-related issues such as infertility, delayed childbearing, and voluntary childlessness. First, the high degree of relatedness among issues (as depicted in Figure 1) becomes clear when one "steps back" from each issue and looks at them *in toto*. For example, some couples who delay childbearing for several years seem to eventually "slide" or "fall into" voluntary childlessness. One explanation for this phenomenon is that by delaying, these couples discover such an enjoyable lifestyle, they become reluctant to give it up. Other couples may delay childbearing for some years, then decide to have a child only to discover that age-related infertility problems have arisen. Even if the infertility problem is not related to age, the couple has less time to investigate and treat it if they start their childbearing efforts later in life.

Another theme that emerges from examining these issues is the far-reaching effects of fertility decisions and events upon the individual spouses and upon the couple's life together. For example, couples who have their first child rather early seem to have more difficulty forming adult identities and building an intimate relationship than do couples who delay childbearing. Second, it seems clear that childless couples (whether voluntary or involuntary) pursue their relationship in quite a different setting than do couples with children. Spousal relations among childless couples may be better or worse than spousal relations among couples with children, but they do seem to be different in some interesting ways.

Last, fertility related situations which engender immediate and intense reactions for couples can become "crises." It is important that the mental health professional be able to distinguish a couple's chronic personal and interpersonal problems from reactions engendered by one of these crises.

The preceding review of fertility related issues also highlights areas that need further examination. On the broadest level, studies are needed which explore the relationships among various, fertility related decisions and events as these unfold over time. An ideal study would follow couples over their entire reproductive lives together, either retrospectively or, ideally, prospectively. The model of the fertility management process (see Figure 1) could guide such an inquiry.

Another area in which an inquiry is needed are the alternatives to parenthood that couples can use to express generativity. Do voluntarily or involuntarily childless couples find alternative ways to express generativity, and if so, what are some of these ways? Do some people instead forego this stage in adult development?

Finally, it is important to devote more attention to the effects of delayed childbearing on parenting. How do mid-life parents differ in their relationships to their infants, young children, and adolescents from the parenting styles and skills of couples who start their families when they are in their 20s and early 30s?

References

Adams, M. M., Finley, S., Hansen, H. (1981). Utilization of prenatal genetic diagnosis in women 35 years of age and older in the United States, 1977 to 1978. *American Journal of Obstetrics & Gynecology, 139*, 673–677.

Adams, M. M., Oakley, G. P., & Marks, J. S. (1982). Maternal age and births in the 1980s. *Journal of the American Medical Association, 247*, 493.

Allison, J. R. (1979). Roles and role conflict of women in infertile couples. *Psychology of Women Quarterly, 4*(1), 97–113.

Annon, J. S., & Robinson, C. H. (1978). The use of vicarious learning in the treatment of sexual concerns. In J. LoPiccolo & L. LoPiccolo (Eds.), *The handbook of sex therapy.* New York: Plenum Press.

Apgar, V., & Beck, J. (1972). *Is my baby all right? A guide to birth defects.* New York: Trident Press.

Bachrach, C. A. (1980). Childlessness and social isolation among the elderly. *Journal of Marriage and Family, 42*(3), 627–637.

Baum, F. E. (1983). Orientations toward voluntary childlessness. *Journal of Biosocial Science, 15*(2), 153–164.

Beckman, L. J., & Houser, B. B. (1982). The consequences of childlessness on the social-psychological well-being of older women. *Journal of Gerontology, 37*(2), 243–250.

Bell, S. J. (1981). Psychological problems among patients attending an infertility clinic. *Journal of Psychosomatic Research, 25*(1), 1–3.

Belmont, L., Cohen, P., Dryfoos, J., Stein, Z., & Zayac, S. (1981). Maternal age and children's intelligence. In K. G. Scott, T. Field, & E. Robertson (Eds.), *Teenage parents and their offspring.* New York: Grune & Stratton.

Bem, S. L. (1975). Sex-role adaptability: One consequence of psychological androgyny. *Journal of Personality and Social Psychology, 31*, 634–643.

Bem, S. L., Martyna, W., & Watson, C. (1976). Sex typing and androgyny: Further explorations of the expressive domain. *Journal of Personality and Social Psychology, 34*, 1016–1023.

Benedek, T. (1952). Infertility as a psychosomatic defense. *Fertility & Sterility, 3*, 527.

Bloom, D. E., & Trussell, J. (1983). *What are the determinants of delayed childbearing and voluntary childlessness in the United States?* (Working Paper No. 1140). Cambridge, MA: National Bureau of Economic Research.

Bongaarts, T. (1982). Infertility after age 30: A false alarm. *Family Planning Perspectives, 14*(2) 75–78.

Brand, H. J., Roos, S., & Van der Merwe, A. B. (1982a). Psychological stress and infertility: I. Psychophysiological reaction patterns. *British Journal of Medical Psychology, 55*(4) 379–384.

Brand, H. J., Roos, S., & Van der Merwe, A. B. (1982b). Psychological stress and infertility: II. Psychometric test data. *British Journal of Medical Psychology, 55*(4) 385–388.

Bresnick, E. R. (1981). A holistic approach to treatment of the crisis of infertility. *Journal of Marital & Family Therapy, 7*(2), 181–188.

Broman, S. (1981). Longterm development of children born to teenagers. In K. G. Scott, T. Field, & E. Robertson (Eds.), *Teenage parents and their offspring.* New York: Grune & Stratton, 1981.

Callan, Victor J. (1983). Childlessness and partner selection. *Journal of Marriage and Family, 45*(1), 181–186.

Centers, R., & Blumberg, G. H. (1954). Social and psychological factors in human procreation. *Journal of Social Psychology, 40*, 245.

Cicirelli, Victor G. (1981). Kin relationships of childless and one-child elderly in relation to social services. *Journal of Gerontological Social Work, 4*(1), 19–33.

Clark, M., & Anderson, B. (1967). *Culture and aging.* Springfield, IL: Charles C Thomas.

Clausen, J. A. & Clausen, S. R. (1973). The effects of family size on parents and children. In T. T. Fawcett (Ed.), *Psychological aspects of population.* New York: Basic Books.

Collman, R. D. & Stoller, A. (1962). A survey of mongoloid births in Victoria, Australia, 1942–1957. *American Journal of Public Health, 52,* 813–829.

Corson, S. L. (1983). *Conquering infertility.* Norwalk, CN: Appleton-Century-Crofts.

Cumming, E., & Schneider, D. (1961). Sibling solidarity: A property of American kinship. *American Anthropologist, 63,* 498–507.

Daniels, P., & Weingarten, K. (1979). A new look at the medical risks in late childbearing. *Women and Health, 4,* 5–35.

Daniels, P., & Weingarten, K. (1982). *Sooner or later: The timing of parenthood in adult lives.* New York: W. W. Norton.

Denber, H. L. (1978). Psychiatric aspects of infertility. *Journal of Reproductive Medicine, 20*(1), 23–29.

Donnis, S. (1984). Common themes of infertility: A counseling model. *Journal of Sex Education and Therapy, 10*(1), 11–15.

Ellis, A., & Grieger, R. (1977). *Handbook of rational-emotive therapy.* New York: Springer Publishing.

Erikson, E. H. (1950). *Childhood and society.* New York: W. W. Norton.

Feldman, H. (1981). A comparison of intentional parents and intentionally childless couples. *Journal of Marriage and the Family, 43*(3), 593–600.

Field, T. M., Widmayer, S. M., Stringer, S., & Ignatoff, E. (1980). Teenage, lower-class, black mothers and their pre-term infants: An intervention and developmental follow-up. *Child Development, 51,* 426–436.

Frankel, S. A., & Wise, M. J. (1982). A view of delayed parenting: Some implications of a new trend. *Psychiatry, 45*(3), 220–225.

Freshnock, L., & Cutright, P. (1978). Structural determinants of childlessness: Non-recursive analysis of 1970 U.S. rates. *Social Biology, 25*(3), 169–178.

Friedan, B. (1963). *The feminine mystique.* New York: W. W. Norton.

Furstenberg, F. F. (1976). *Unplanned parenthood: The social consequences of teenage childbearing.* New York: The Free Press.

Glenn, N., & McLanahan, S. (1981). The effects of offspring on the psychological well-being of older adults. *Journal of Marriage and the Family, 43,* 409–421.

Goldberg, M. F., Edmonds, L. D., & Oakley, G. P. (1979). Reducing birth defect risk in advanced maternal age. *Journal of the American Medical Association, 242*(21), 2292–2294.

Greenbaum, H. (1973). Marriage, family, and parenthood. *American Journal of Psychiatry, 130,* 1262.

Gubrium, J. (1975). Being single in old age. *International Journal of Aging and Human Development, 6,* 29–41.

Gustavus, S., & Henley, J., Jr. (1971). Correlates of voluntary childlessness—a select population. *Social Biology, 18,* 277–284.

Hatcher, R. A., Guest, F., Stewart, F., Stewart, G. K., Trussell, J., & Frank, E. (1984). *Contraceptive technology, 1984–1985* (12th ed.). New York: Irvington Publishers.

Henshaw, S. K., & Reilly, K. (1983). Characteristics of abortion patients in the United States, 1979 and 1980. *Family Planning Perspectives, 15*(1), 5–15.

Holmes, L. B. (1978). Genetic counseling for the older pregnant woman: New data and questions. *New England Journal of Medicine, 298*(25), 1419–1421.

Hook, E. B., & Chambers, G. M. (1977). Estimated rates of Down syndrome in live births by one year maternal age intervals for mothers aged 20–49 in a New York State study—Implications of risk figures for genetic counseling and cost-benefit analysis of prenatal diagnosis programs. *Birth Defects: Original Articles Series, 13*(13A), 123–141.

Houseknecht, S. K. (1977). Reference group support for voluntary childlessness. *Journal of Marriage and the Family, 39*(2), 285–292.

Houseknecht, S. K. (1979a). Childlessness and marital adjustment. *Journal of Marriage & Family, 41*(2), 259–265.

Houseknecht, S. K. (1979b). Timing of the decision to remain voluntarily childless: Evidence for continuous socialization. *Psychology of Women Quarterly, 4*(1), 81–96.

Janis, I. L., & Mann, L. (1977). *Decision-making: A psychological analysis of conflict, choice, and commitment*. New York: The Free Press.

Jones, F. A., Green, V., & Krauss, D. R. (1980). Maternal responsiveness of primiparous mothers during the postpartum period: Age differences. *Pediatrics, 65*, 579–583;.

Kaltreider, N. B., & Margolis, A. G. (1977). Childlessness by choice: A clinical study. *American Journal of Psychiatry, 134*(2), 179–182.

Kane, S. (1967). Advancing age and the primigravida. *Obstetrics and Gynecology, 29*, 409–414.

Keith, P. M. (1983). A comparison of the resources of parents and childless men and women in very old age. *Family Relations: Journal of Applied Family and Child Studies, 32*(3), 403–409.

Keller, S. (1968). *The urban neighborhood: A sociological perspective*. New York: Random House.

Kipper, D. A., Zigler-Shani, Z., Serr, D. M., & Insler, V. (1977). Psychogenic infertility, neuroticism and the feminine role: A methodological inquiry. *Journal of Psychosomatic Research, 21*, 353–358.

Kohut, H. (1971). The analysis of self: A systematic approach to the psychoanalytic treatment of narcissistic personality disorders. *Psychoanalytic Study of the Child Monographs*, (No. 4). New York: International University Press.

Kraft, A., Palombo, J., Mitchell, D., Dean, C., Meyers, S., & Schmidt, B. W. (1980). The psychological dimensions of infertility. *American Journal of Orthopsychiatry, 50*(4), 618–628.

Kubler-Ross, E. (1969). *On death and dying*. New York: McMillan.

Lazarus, A. (1981). *The practice of multi-modal therapy*. New York: McGraw-Hill.

Magarick, R. H., & Brown, R. A. (1981). Social and emotional aspects of voluntary childlessness in vasectomized childless men. *Journal of Biosocial Science, 13*(2), 157–167.

Magenis, R. E., Overton, K. M., Chamberlin, J., Brody, T., & Lourien, F. (1977). Parental origin of the extra chromosome in Down's syndrome. *Human Genetics, 37,* 7–16.

Masters, W. H., & Johnson, V. E. (1978). Advice for women who want to have a baby. *Redbook, 70.*

Mazor, M. (1978). The problem of infertility. In C. Nadelson & N. Jones (Eds.), *The woman patient: Vol. I.* New York: Plenum Press, p. 137–160.

Mazor, M. D. (1980). *Emotional reactions to infertility.* Paper presented at 133rd annual meeting of American Psychiatric Association, San Francisco, CA.

Menning, B. (1977). *Infertility: A guide for the childless couple.* Englewood Cliffs, NJ: Prentice-Hall.

Menning, B. (1980). The emotional needs of infertile couples. *Fertility and Sterility, 34*(4), 313–319.

Mikkelson, M., Fischer, G., & Stene, J. (1976). Incidence study of Down's syndrome in Copenhagen, 1960–1971. With chromosome investigation. *Annals of Human Genetics, 40,* 177–182.

Miller, W. A., & Erbe, R. W. (1978). Prenatal diagnosis of genetic disorders. *Southern Medical Journal, 71,* 202–209.

Milunsky, A. (1976). Prenatal diagnosis and genetic disorders. *New England Journal of Medicine, 295*(7), 377–380.

Mosher, W. D. (1982). Infertility trends among U.S. couples: 1965–1976. *Family Planning Perspectives, 14*(22), 22–27.

National Center for Health Statistics (1978). Advance report—final mortality statistics, 1976. *Monthly Vital Statistics Report,* March 30, *26*(12, Supp.2) (a).

National Center for Health Statistics (1973). *Mortality from linked records by age of mother, total birth order, and other variables* (Series 20, No. 14). Rockville, MD: U.S. DHHS Public Health Service.

National Center for Health Statistics (1985). Fecundity and infertility in the United States, 1965–1982. *NCHS Advance Data,* February 11 (no. 104).

Neligan, G. A., Kolvin, I., Scott, D. M., & Garside, R. F. (1976). Born too soon or born too small. *Clinics in developmental medicine, No. 61.* London: Spastics International Medical Publications.

Nolan, T. F., Ory, H. W., Layde, P. M., Maze, J., & Greenspan, J. R. (1982). Cumulative prevalence rates and corrected incidence rates of surgical sterilization among American women, 1971–1978. *American Journal of Epidemiology, 116,* 776.

Nortman, D. (1974). Parental age as a factor in pregnancy outcome and child development. *Reports on Population and Family Planning, 16,* 1–52.

Nydegger, C. (1973 November). Paper presented at Gerontological Society Annual Meeting, Miami Beach, FL.

O'Connell, M., & Rogers, C. C. (1983). Assessing cohort birth expectation data from the Current Population Survey, 1971–1981. *Demography, 20*(3), 369–383.

Oppel, W. C., & Rayston, A. B. (1971). Teenage births: Some social, psychological, and physical sequelae. *American Journal of Public Health, 61,* 751–756.

Osofsky, H. J., & Osofsky, J. D. (1970). Adolescents as mothers: Results of a program for low-income pregnant teenagers with some emphasis upon infants' development. *American Journal of Orthopsychiatry, 40,* 825–834.

Pebley, A. R. (1981). Changing attitudes toward the timing of first births. *Family Planning Perspectives, 13*(4), 171–180.

Peck, E. (1972). *The baby trap.* New York: Pinnacle Books.

Penrose, L. S. (1962). Paternal age and mongolism. *Lancet, 1,* 1101.

Philliber, S. G., & Graham, E. H. (1981). The impact of age of mother on mother-child interaction patterns. *Journal of Marriage and the Family, 43,* 109–115.

Poston, D. L., & Gotard, E. (1977). Trends in childlessness in the United States, 1910–1975. *Social Biology, 24*(3), 212–224.

Price, J. (1977). *You're not too old to have a baby.* New York: Penguin Books.

Ragozin, A. S., Basham, R. B., Crnic, K. A., Greenberg, M. T., & Robinson, N. M., (1982). Effects of maternal age on parenting role. *Developmental Psychology, 18*(4), 627–634.

Renne, S. (1976). Childlessness, health, and marital satisfaction. *Social Biology, 23*(3), 183–197.

Rosenberg, G. S. (1970). *The Worker Grows Old.* San Francisco, Jossey-Bass.

Rossi, A. S. (1972). The roots of ambivalence in American women. In J. M. Bardwick (Ed.), *Readings on the Psychology of Women.* New York: Harper & Row.

Russo, N. F. *The motherhood mandate.* New York: Human Sciences Press, 1979.

Schwartz, D., & Mayaux, M. J. (1982). Federation des centres d'etude et de conservation due sperme humain [Female fecundity as a function of age.] *The New England Journal of Medicine, 307,* 404.

Shanas, E., Townsend, P., Wedderbarn, D., Friis, H., Nilhaj, P., & Stehoirwer, J. (1968). *Old people in three industrial societies.* New York: Atherton Press.

Shapiro, C. H. (1982). The impact of infertility on the marital relationship. *Social Casework, 63*(7), 387–393.

Shapiro, S., & Abramowicz, M. (1969). Pregnancy outcome correlates identified through medical record-based information. *American Journal of Public Health, 59,* 1629–1650.

Shrednick, A. (1984, June). *Infertility and sexual problems.* Paper presented at the combined annual conference of the American Association of Sex Educators, Counselors, & Therapists and the Society for the Scientific Study of Sex. Boston, MA.

Silka, L., & Kiesler, S. (1977). Couples who chose to remain childless. *Family Planning Perspectives, 9,* 16.

Slade, P. (1981). Sexual attitudes and social role orientations in infertile women. *Journal of Psychosomatic Research, 25*(3), 183–186.

Smith, D. W., & Wilson, A. A. (1973). *The child with down's syndrome.* Philadelphia: W. B. Saunders.

Stewart, R. (1980). *Helping couples change.* New York: The Guilford Press.

Svedja, M. J., Campos, J. J., & Emde, R. N. (1980). Mother-infant "bonding": Failure to generalize. *Child Development, 51,* 775–779.

Townsend, P. (1957). *The family life of old people.* London: Routledge & Kegan Paul.

Tyler, E. T., Bonapart, J., & Grant, J. (1960). Occurrence of pregnancy following adoption. *Fertility and Sterility, 11*, 581.

Veevers, J. E. (1973). Voluntarily childless wives: An exploratory study. *Sociology and Social Research, 57*(3), 356–366.

Veevers, J. E. (1980). *Childless by Choice.* Toronto: Butterworths.

Ventura, S. J. (1982). Trends in first births to older mothers 1970–79. *Monthly Vital Statistics Report, 31*(2), May. National Center for Health Statistics, Washington, DC: DHHS, PHS.

Vesey, M. P., Wright, N. H., McPherson, K., & Wiggins, P. (1978). Fertility after stopping different methods of contraception. *British Medical Journal, 2*, 265.

Weir, W. C., & Weir, D. R. (1966). Adoption and subsequent conceptions. *Fertility & Sterility, 17*, 283.

Westoff, C. F. (1976). Trends in contraceptive practice: 1965–1973. *Family Planning Perspectives, 8*, 54.

Westoff, C. F., & Jones, E. F. (1977). Contraception and sterilization in the United States, 1965–1975. *Family Planning Perspectives, 9*, 153.

Westoff, C. F., & McCarthy, J. (1979). Sterilization in the United States. *Family Planning Perspectives, 11*, 147–152.

Westoff, C. F., & Ryder, N. B. (1977). *The contraceptive revolution.* Princeton: Princeton University Press.

Yogev, S., & Vierra, A. (1983). The state of motherhood among professional women. *Sex Roles, 9*(3), 391–396.

Zybert, P., Stein, Z., & Belmont, L. (1978). Maternal age and children's ability. *Perceptual and Motor Skills, 47*, 815–818.

SEVEN

The Developmental World of Children in Divorced Families: Research Findings and Clinical Implications*

John W. Santrock, Ph.D.
Professor of Psychology
University of Texas at Dallas
Karen Sitterle, Ph.D.
Psychologist
Timberlawn Psychiatric Hospital

Divorce has become epidemic in our society. It is now estimated that nearly half of the marriages begun in the mid-1970s will end in divorce (Cherlin, 1981); and that as many as one out of every three children will experience the divorce of their parents before they reach the age of 18 (Glick, 1979). This chapter critically reviews the nature of the research on children of divorce and then provides suggestions for the clinical treatment of members of divorced families.

RESEARCH ON THE CHILDREN OF DIVORCE

For many years we lamented the fact that there was far too little research on the effects of divorce on children. However, the rate of research on di-

*We would like to express our appreciation to Nancy Bray for her constructive feedback on an earlier draft of this chapter.

vorce has accelerated tremendously in the 1970s and 1980s. A thorough review of the divorce literature is beyond the scope of this chapter. However, several comprehensive reviews of divorce are available for the interested reader (Camara, Baker, & Dayton, 1980; Hetherington, 1979, 1981; Hetherington, Camara, & Featherman, 1982; Levinger & Moles, 1979; Shinn, 1978). While the amount of research on divorce has increased dramatically, the quality of much of that research lacks empirical rigor. Hence, part of our task will be to provide a framework for evaluating the quality of the massive divorce literature that has now accumulated. We will describe three traditions in divorce research and in the process we will highlight methodological problems inherent in many studies of divorce. We will then use a developmental perspective to discuss the social worlds of children of divorced families. Included is information about the social worlds of adults and parents of divorced families, as well as some important aspects of relationships and the divorce setting that mediate the effects of divorce on children.

The Three Research Traditions

Conducting research studies of children of divorce is not the domain of psychology alone. Sociologists, as well as psychologists, have shown an increased interest in studying divorce, and within psychology, both clinical and developmental psychologists have published extensively on the topic. These three disciplines have spawned three approaches to the study of divorced families: (1) the family sociological, (2) the clinical, and (3) the quasi experimental, developmental. Our discussion of these three approaches focuses on the nature of their sampling techniques, concern about the presence of a control group, methods of measurement, amount of time spent with subjects, degree of interest in directly studying the child with respect to developmental orientation, control for or investigation of demographic variables, and statistical analysis.

Family sociological. Research by family sociologists on divorced families has increased considerably in recent years. For the most part this research, in keeping with sociological tradition, attempts to generate a large sample of divorced families. This sample is usually highly heterogeneous with families of varying socioeconomic status (SES); children of varying ages; families of different sizes and with different sibling configurations; children who have experienced the onset of divorce at very different ages; and in many cases subjects who have experienced multiple divorce, different custodial arrangements, or who are now part of a step family. Rarely is a control group of intact families included in this approach. Questionnaires, and sometimes structured interviews, are the measures chosen by family sociologists to study divorced families. In most instances, there is no face-to-face interaction with the child during the assessment process. The major orientation is toward uncovering information about the embeddedness of the family in a larger social context or on a detailed analysis of adult relationships and circumstances. When information about the child *is* obtained it is usually secondary to the latter interests and is assessed indirectly through the parent. Rarely do family sociologists control for demographic variables such as SES, age of the child, family size, sibling status, and so forth. Rather, such variables are free to fluctuate in the effort to obtain a heterogeneous sample. In many instances, however, particularly in more recent investigations, such variables are statistically analyzed through multiple regression techniques. Sophisticated statistical analyses have characterized many of the sociological studies of divorced families.

An excellent example of the family sociological tradition, which provides valuable information about divorced families, is the research of Frank Furstenberg and his colleagues (Furstenberg, Nord, Peterson, & Zill, 1983). Unlike most family sociological studies this investigation obtained information directly from children. A sample of 1,377 children from 48 states and their custodial parent, was studied with respect to: (1) the incidence of marital disruption in the children's lives; (2) the type of living arrangements that children encounter after a marital disruption; and (3) the amount of contact that children maintain with an outside parent. The Furstenberg et al. (1983) analysis revealed large racial differences in both the incidence and the aftermath of disruption. Blacks were one and one-half times as likely as whites to undergo a disruption by early adolescence. However, only one of eight black children, compared to four of seven white children, were in a step family five years after the disruption. Frequent contact with the outside parent (defined as an average of at least once a week for the past year) occurred in only 17 percent of the disrupted families, regardless of race. The provision of child support, the residential propinquity of the outside parent, and the length of time since separation occurred were the most likely predictors of the amount of contact between the outside parent and the child. From this study we can see the family sociological orientation toward a large, heterogeneous sample, investigation of demographic variables, such as race, and the use of the questionnaire/structured interview approach. What sets the Furstenberg et al. (1983) investigation apart from many family sociological approaches is the actual collection of data from children and the concern about children's developmental status.

A developmental orientation has begun to appear in a limited number of other family sociological studies of divorce as well. One particular study deserves mention because of its effort to investigate divorced families from a life-span developmental perspective. David Chiriboga (1982) drew names at random from an area in the city of San Francisco and was able to interview 310 adults, ranging in age from 20 to 79, about their divorce and its subsequent impact on their lives. A positive feature of the investigation was the use of multiple measures which assessed such factors as morale, psychiatric symptoms, time perspective, self-reported physical health, social disruption, personal disruption, and divorce induced upset. The older respondents showed more stress and disruption in their lives than their younger counterparts; those 50 and older consistently showed depressed emotional patterns. Interest in this investigation focused on the adults who had experienced divorce. Indeed, one of the negative features was the study's failure to investigate or control whether these adults were or were not parents.

In sum, the family sociological perspective is providing valuable information about divorced families. The strengths of this approach include a large sample size, investigation of demographic trends, development of detailed questionnaires about the embeddedness of the family in their social context, (e.g., the availability and use of support systems), and the use of sophisticated statistical analysis. Its weaknesses lie in the failure to study control groups of intact families, a limited choice of measures, and the amount of time spent with subjects, particularly children.

The clinical approach. Clinical psychologists, counseling psychologists, psychiatrists, and psychiatric social workers have also shown an increased interest in divorced families as their practices have become heavily populated with both children and adults who have experienced the disruption and stress of divorce. The clinical tradition in divorce research is characterized by small, heterogeneous samples that usually do not include a control group of intact families. The choice of methods of measurement typically is an unstructured to somewhat structured interview and/or clinical judgments. Compared to the other two traditions discussed here, the clinical approach is based on many more hours of actual face-to-face interaction with the subjects in which detailed, in-depth information is obtained about the lives of divorced adults and children. Often there is concern about the age and developmental status of children, but rarely are such demographic variables as SES, family size, and the like controlled for or investigated, and frequently there is a less sophisticated use of statistical analysis than exists in the other two traditions.

The prototypical investigation of the effects of divorce on children in the clinical tradition is the well-known research of Judith Wallerstein and Joan Kelly (Kelly & Wallerstein, 1976; Wallerstein, 1982, 1984; Wallerstein & Kelly, 1974, 1975, 1976, 1980). They are the only investigators to have conducted a longitudinal study of the effects of divorce on children of different ages. In their Children of Divorce project, Wallerstein and Kelly (1979) interviewed 131 children, adolescents, and their parents about their reactions to divorce. The participating children were interviewed at the time their parents were taking action for the divorce, at 1 year following the divorce, and more recently, at 5 and 10 years after the divorce. The sample consisted of white, middle-class families who responded to an invitation for free preventive counseling. While this sample is larger than many clinical samples, when it is broken down into children of various age groups the sample size for a child of a particular age is not very large. In addition, the sample is heterogeneous. Such factors as the child's age at the time of divorce, sex of the custodial parent, family size, sibling status, remarriage, and the like were not controlled for and were not sufficiently investigated. Further, no control group of intact families was included in this investigation. And, statistical analysis of the data rarely has gone beyond the reporting of percentages. However, as clinical data, the Wallerstein and Kelly research is a marvelous example of the importance of detailed, extensive examination of the lives of divorced parents and their children over an extended time. The clinical interviews, although of unknown reliability, provide rich knowledge of children's feelings about the divorce experience. And of particular importance, Wallerstein and Kelly (1980) have provided a developmental picture of how children and adolescents of different ages may have different vulnerabilities as they face divorce and its aftermath. More recently, this research has spawned information about the long-term effects of divorce, information suggesting that 10 years later, as adolescents and adults look back on their childhoods and adolescences, their mood is somewhat sad and contains feelings of unfulfilled wishes of having lived in an intact family as they grew up (Wallerstein, 1982). Much more about the results of this investigation appear later, particularly as we discuss the role of developmental status in divorced families.

In sum, the strengths of the clinical tradition in divorce research lie in the detailed, in-depth examination of children's and parents' lives that come from many hours of face-to-face interaction with subjects, as well as concern about the child's developmental status. Among the methodological problems encountered in the clinical tradition are the somewhat small samples, the absence of an intact family control group, the reliance on clinical judgment of unknown credibility, the failure to control for or investigative demographic variables, and the absence in some cases of robust statistical procedures.

The quasi-experimental, developmental tradition. A third tradition in the study of divorced families is housed in developmental psychology. The topography of this approach has changed considerably over the last several decades as more developmental psychologists have become interested in the effects of divorce on children. For many years the quasi-experimental, developmental tradition focused heavily on the role of the father's absence in the child's development. This father absence tradition, heavily influenced by psychoanalytic theory and its emphasis on the identification process and sex role behavior in children (e.g., Biller, 1969; Hetherington, 1966; Santrock, 1970a; Sears, 1951), has fallen out of favor among developmental psychologists in recent years. It became apparent that while family structure and the father's absence are important considerations in studying the effects of divorce on children, such an approach represents an extremely global and limiting strategy. Thus, the father absence tradition has been replaced by an orientation that studies the effects of divorce on children in a more fine-grained manner and focuses more extensively on the factors that mediate the effects of divorce on children such as the nature of postdivorce family functioning.

The current version of the quasi-experimental, developmental tradition in divorce research includes samples of small to moderate size that emphasize more homogeneity than do the other two traditions. A control group of intact families is carefully matched to the divorced family group. This matching process is likely to include such variables as sex of the child, age of the child, the child's age at the time of separation or divorce, family size, sibling status, SES, and sex of the custodial parent. In many instances one or more of these demographic variables, particularly sex of the child, will be investigated rather than controlled. Further, the use of behavioral observation has come to characterize the measures selected. It is also believed that a multimethod approach to studying the effects of divorce on children is beneficial, so it is not unusual to find investigators including behavioral observation, standardized tests, child and parent interviews, and trait ratings by individuals with differing relationships to the subject (such as mother, father, and teacher). Further, the behavioral observations may include parent-child interaction as well as peer interaction. Statistical analysis is usually a strong feature of such investigations.

The prototypical quasi-experimental, developmental investigation of the effects of divorce on children has been conducted by Mavis Hetherington and her colleagues (Hetherington, Cox, & Cox, 1978, 1979, 1982). Ninety-six preschool children and their parents were studied. Half of the children lived in a family in which the parents were getting divorced, while the other half lived in intact families. The families were carefully matched on most of the criteria mentioned earlier. Half of the children were girls and half were boys. The measures included behavioral observations of the child, interviews with the parents and the child, and standardized tests. In addition, the families were evaluated over a period of two years so that, like the Wallerstein and Kelly investigation, the unfolding of the aftermath of divorce could be observed. Unlike the Wallerstein and Kelly investigation the subjects in Hetherington's study initially were the same age. Among the many important findings of this investigation, a number of which will be discussed later, was the significant disequilibrium and disorganization in the family during the first year after separation and divorce. This first year was observed to be a period when family members were experimenting with a number of coping mechanisms—some successful, others unsuccessful—in dealing with the new life circumstances. By the end of the second year after the divorce, however, a reorganization and new pattern of equilibrium seemed to be established in the divorced family. Nonetheless, the effects of divorce seemed to still be damaging to boys, even though the divorced mother-custody families were coping much more effectively at that time. The patterning of both the Hetherington, Cox, and Cox (1978) and Wallerstein and Kelly (1980) investigations suggests that divorce is best conceptualized as a sequence of experiences involving a transition in the lives of parents and children, rather than as a single event (the approach that characterizes the father absence tradition).

In summary, the strengths of the current version of the quasi-experimental, developmental tradition in divorce research lie in its careful matching of demographic variables, use of a control group of intact families, and use of a multimethod approach including behavioral observation and extensive use of statistical analysis. Its weaknesses include the difficulty in generalizing to a population from a somewhat limited homogeneous sample produced by the concern for control of demographic variables, and the somewhat limited amount of time spent with the subjects. Ironically, another negative feature of much of the research on divorce conducted by developmental psychologists has been a lack of concern for studying the developmental status of the child. As was noted earlier, in the Hetherington, Cox, and Cox (1978) investigation age was controlled for rather than investigated. Perhaps the greatest deficit in our knowledge of the effects of divorce on children rests in the virtual absence of studies that compare children of different ages along the lines of the Wallerstein and Kelly (1980) research.

Conclusions about the three traditions of divorce research. As we have noted there are both strengths and weaknesses inherent in each of the three traditions of divorce research. All three disciplines are contributing considerably to the knowledge base about the effects of divorce on children. However, there still are far too many investigations that are cast within the father absence tradition, a tradition that has not been as effective as other orientations in generating sound information about the effects of divorce on children. Further, it is hoped that more researchers from a particular discipline will consider including the strengths of other traditions in their own research strategies. Thus, developmental psychologists could benefit considerably from the clinical tradition by spending more time with subjects and by collecting more detailed, in-depth information about children and their parents, particularly in terms of how the divorce process is carried forward over time in relationships. Developmental psychologists could benefit from the family sociology tradition by studying more varied socioeconomic and racial groupings. Virtually all of the research on divorce conducted by developmental psychologists focuses on middle class, white families, yet the research conducted by Furstenberg, Nord, Peterson, and Zill (1983) suggests that black children are more likely to experience divorce than white children. Researchers in the clinical tradition also could benefit from studying individuals from more varied demographic backgrounds, and their research would be enhanced by the inclusion of a control group of intact families, control for or investigation of demographic variables, and more attention to statistical analyses that have become commonplace in the quasi-experimental, developmental tradition. The family sociological tradition could be enhanced by following Furstenberg's lead in showing a concern for collecting data from children, an approach that has characterized both the developmental and clinical traditions, and by following the clinical tradition of obtaining detailed, in-depth information about children and parents. A summary of the characteristics of the three major traditions in divorce research is presented in Table 1.

THE DEVELOPMENT OF CHILDREN IN DIVORCED FAMILIES

We begin this section by describing several important themes for the reader to keep in mind when studying children's responses to divorce. Then we review what is known about children of divorce from a developmental perspective, focusing extensively on the age of the child. Where appropriate, information about such important factors as the sex of the child, the sex of the custodial parent, and changes in the parent-child relationship are interwoven into our discussion of the age differences in children's responses to divorce.

Adjustment Phases and Individual Variation

Two important themes that characterize the nature of children's reactions to divorce are the adjustment of children over time in the postdivorce family and the fact that children's responses to divorce vary a great deal.

It is important to distinguish between children's early responses to divorce and those involving long-term adjustment. Hetherington (1981) suggests that divorce is best viewed as a two-phase process, the first phase a short-term or crisis phase involving temporary emotional reactions, and the second a long-term phase associated with the child's postdivorce adjustment in a single-parent family. Hetherington, Cox, and Cox (1982) comment that the time at which we tap into the course of divorce will to some degree influence our evaluation of the effects of divorce on children. As noted earlier, these researchers have found the first year following di-

TABLE 1 The Three Traditions in Divorce Research: Family Sociological, Clinical, and Quasi-Experimental, Developmental

Strategy	*Family Sociological*	*Clinical*	*Quasi-Experimental, Developmental*
Sampling	Large to very large samples; a major goal is generalization.	Small samples characterized by heterogeneity.	Small to moderately sized samples; greater homogeneity of samples.
Inclusion of control group of intact families	No	No	Yes
Nature of measures	Questionnaire, structured interview.	Unstructured to somewhat structured interview; clinical judgments.	Multiple measures including questionnaires, interviews, observations, standardized tests, and trait ratings.
Amount of time spent with subjects	Little. Not unusual for individual interaction with a subject to be absent.	Considerable. Data often based on many hours of contact with subjects.	Varies, but usually more than family sociological and much less than clinical; 15 minutes to several hours.
Degree of interest in child and child's developmental status	Usually very low, but recently several life-span studies have appeared. Rarely is information obtained directly from child.	High	Moderate to high, although age comparisons are rare.
Control for or investigation of demographic variables such as SES, family size, sibling status, and so on.	Rarely control for but often investigate.	Rarely control for but sometimes investigate.	Often control for.
Nature of statistical analysis	Extensive, use of multivariate strategies such as factor analysis and multiple regression	Limited use.	Considerable use; heavy reliance on analysis of variance.

vorce to be the most difficult for the child, but after two years considerable improvement in the child's adjustment appears, particularly for girls.

A second consideration is that there is tremendous variability in children's responses to divorce. While all children initially experience divorce as highly stressful, some children emerge as competent, well-functioning individuals, while others exhibit severe or enduring disruptions in development. As we will see next, the child's developmental status also has a profound influence on his or her reactions to divorce.

The child's developmental status

The child's reactions to his/her parent's divorce will to a certain extent vary with his or her developmental status. Each developmental stage is characterized by different levels of competence in the child's cognitive, emotional, and social functioning. In addition, children are attempting to master different developmental tasks at different stages. It is our belief that children's reactions, their needs, and their individual coping strategies will differ depending upon their age at the time of parental separation and divorce. A developmental perspective provides not only an important conceptual tool for understanding children's reactions to the stressful event of divorce, but also has important clinical implications for designing age-appropriate prevention and intervention approaches.

The following discussion is organized by age groups that are consistently used by developmental psychologists: infancy (0 to 2 years), early childhood (3 to 5 years), middle childhood (6 to 8 years), late childhood (9 to 12 years), and adolescence (13 to 18 years).

Infancy (0 to 2 years). During this developmental stage, the healthy infant actively attempts to establish a relationship with a responsive care giver. Attachment to the child's primary care givers develops during the first six to nine months of life. When parents provide responsive care the child develops a secure base or trust in the environment from which to move out and explore the world. At 18 months of age, most infants are at the height of the attachment process and show marked behavioral changes if their parents leave them, even for brief periods of time (Robson, 1982).

We know very little about the effects of divorce on infants. Although there has been considerable research interest in the development of the attachment process during infancy (Ainsworth, 1979; Bowlby, 1969; Sroufe & Waters, 1977), how divorce might interfere with that process remains virtually unexplored. However, it can be speculated that the stress associated with the trauma of divorce might disrupt the child's development of a secure attachment relationship with the custodial parent. While infants are not cognitively aware of the divorce process, the task overload that is coupled with being a single-parent mother may produce added vulnerabilities for infants. For example, the infant's mother who is overwhelmed may be tense or inattentive toward her child. Such maternal behavior may, in turn, result in reduced responsiveness, hyperactivity, or insecurity on the part of the infant.

Also, it is a well-established fact that many divorced mothers are faced with drastic reductions in their income and are pushed into a wage-earning position whether they wish to work or not. Many infants of divorce must therefore spend a considerable portion of their day in some form of day care—either at home with relatives or at day-care centers. Research examining the link between day care and infant behavior consistently reveals that competent day care is associated with competent infant behavior (Belsky & Steinberg, 1978). However, studies which demonstrate such competency are typically conducted at university-based day-care centers where there are extremely low care giver-infant ratios and where there are extraordinarily rich environments (e.g., Kagan, Kearsley, & Zelazo, 1978). Unfortunately, the day care received by most infants from divorced homes does not approach the quality of the university-based day-care center. The concern is that infants from divorced families may be receiving care from poorly educated, under qualified personnel for up to 9 to 11 hours per day. As Selma Fraiberg (1977) comments, there is a great deal to worry about when infants and small children are delivered like packages to neighbors, strangers, and "storage houses." For example, Vaughn, Gove, and Egeland (1980) studied the effects of routine daily separations of mother and child in day care on the formation and maintenance of infant-mother attachment in economically disadvantaged families. The out-of-home care arrangements were varied and changes in the routine of care were common. Many of the infants were cared for by an adult female in a nonrelative's home. Significant disruption in the infant-mother attachment relationship was found in the day-care group. Significantly, they found that by eighteen months of age, insecurely attached (both anxious-avoidant and anxious-resistant) infants were more likely to come from nonintact families than from intact families. Interestingly, many of the nonintact families were families of divorce.

While there has been little research that directly assesses the infant's reactions to divorce, it has been found that the experience of divorce during infancy is associated with less competent social and intellectual behavior at later ages. Most of these investigations have been conducted in the father absence tradition mentioned earlier. For example, in one study (Santrock, 1970b), lower-class, fifth-grade boys who became father absent (half divorced, half widowed) before the age of two showed more disruption in personality development than their counterparts who experienced father absence when they were older. For instance, boys who became father absent before the age of two were less trusting, less industrious, and felt more inferior than boys who became father absent between the ages of three to five years. Other findings support the conclusion that divorce during infancy may have detrimental effects on subsequent personality development (Biller, 1971, 1974). Similarly, lower-class junior high and high school students who experienced the divorce of their parents before the age of two, or who were deserted by their fathers had lower IQ and achievement test scores than children whose parents were divorced at a later point in the child's development (Santrock, 1972).

The processes that explain the early divorce findings have yet to be delineated. Disruption of the attachment process may be one possibility. Another may be that when the child experiences father absence early in his development, he has less contact with his father than when the father's absence occurs later. Also, evidence obtained from families in which the father deserted the family, often during pregnancy, suggests that these families may experience more severe economic difficulties than those who decide to separate or divorce when the child is older. Clearly, we need more information about the effects of divorce on infants and the factors that mediate these effects.

Early childhood (3 to 5 years). During the preschool years, children continue to depend heavily upon their parents for having their needs met. Their relationships with parents and their home life are often the center of their psychological and social worlds. Children at this age are confronted with the challenge of developing trusting interpersonal relationships, and they need a secure and predictable home environment. Cognitively, these children are egocentric in their reasoning and their explanations for the events around them are likely to center on themselves.

In their study, Wallerstein and Kelly (1975) found that preschoolers' reactions to divorce included regressive behavior, increased irritability, confusion, and anger. These children also displayed ambivalence in their interpersonal relationships characterized by an excessive dependency on adults, general neediness, and clinging. This ambivalence was sometimes acted out in indiscriminate demands for attention and affection from adults, especially older men. A pervasive reaction of self-blame for their parents' divorce was striking among the children of this age group. Wallerstein and Kelly (1979) also reported that young boys who had highly involved, positive relationships with their fathers showed intense initial anguish in response to their parents' divorce.

Similar to Wallerstein and Kelly's findings, Hetherington, Cox, and Cox (1978, 1979, 1982) found that the preschool child's initial reactions to divorce were characterized by pervasive sadness, fear, anger, feelings of guilt, helplessness, and anxiety. However, even after the initial stress of divorce subsided, disruptions in the child's adjustment at home and at school continued to linger. For example, dramatic changes in the parent-child relationship were prominent, with mothers having difficulties controlling their children, particularly their sons. The divorced mother often tried to control her children by resorting to negative commands that were often resisted or ignored. Boys and girls differed, however, in the way they expressed their negative behavior. Boys tended to be more oppositional and aggressive, while girls were more likely to whine, complain, or sulk. The difficulties exhibited by the girls gradually disappeared, but they persisted for the boys.

The Hetherington et. al., study (1978, 1979) also indicated that preschool-aged children of divorced families have difficulty at school and with their peers. At two months following divorce, both boys and girls were more attention seeking, more oppositional, and more dependent upon their teachers than children living with both parents in intact families. The children from divorced homes often refused to share with their classmates, and their interactions with peers were often characterized by pouting, whining, and complaining.

These findings on preschool aged children's responses to divorce are understandable in light of the young child's limited cognitive and psychological skills. Preschool children are not as accurate as older children in evaluating the cause of divorce, their own role in the divorce, and the possible outcomes. Consequently, young children may blame themselves for the divorce. They may also distort the feelings and behavior of their parents, fostering hopes for their parents' reconciliation. Children at this age may reason that the divorce was a result of their *own* wrongdoing. Longfellow (1979) cites the example in which a child concluded that "Daddy left home because I was a bad boy—I didn't put away my toys that day" (p. 300). At this age, a child relies extensively on fantasy play and denial as ways of coping with stress. Such defensive maneuvers serve to maintain a safe psychological distance from the unbearable feelings of rejection and grief, and allow the child to cling to the idea that someday his/her parents will be reunited.

In addition, parental separation and divorce threaten the security of the most important and basic relationship the child has—the child's attachment to the parents. The child's concept of the dependability of relationships has been abruptly and severely shaken. The preschool child is at a developmental point in which secure and trusting interpersonal relationships are critical. Children of divorce, having already experienced the loss of one parent, may also fear abandonment by the custodial parent. These children are painfully bewildered and anxious about the stability of their present and future lives. Not surprisingly, the child may respond with regressive behavior, a common reaction in young children to stress, major change, or loss. For example, the child may show increased dependency, enuresis, or difficulties with eating. Such behavior is an expression of the child's wish to be an infant again, to return to the times before the stress of divorce set in. The child moves backward from the painful present to a time when he/she was loved and the parents were together. Unfortunately, in these circumstances, many parents become angry with the child's behavior rather than responding with reassurance, firm limits, and the affection so important to the child's adjustment.

In the 10-year follow-up of preschool children who had experienced parental divorce, Wallerstein (1984) found that these children as adolescents, had few memories of the intact family or of family disruption. A substantial number of adolescents, while they had spent much of their lives in either a single parent divorced family or a step family, felt that they would have been happier if they had grown up with both biological parents in the home. In fact, more than half of these adolescents continued to express reconciliation fantasies. In comparing individuals who experienced divorce in their early childhoods with those whose parents divorced while they were adolescents, Wallerstein (1984) concluded that when divorce occurs very early, children are less burdened and may carry fewer bad memories. In this comparison of early and late onset of divorce, it seems that later divorce appears to be more detrimental than earlier divorce. Such findings do not necessarily contradict the results suggesting that divorce or desertion during the child's first few years has a more negative impact than does divorce or desertion when the child is older. The latter conclusion was drawn from studies comparing primarily the first two years of life with the early childhood years, while in the Wallerstein investigation, disruption in early childhood was compared to disruption in adolescence.

Middle childhood (6 to 8 years). In middle childhood, children continue to become more independent and to move out into a world away from home. Although parents are still the most important adults in the child's life, they are less likely to be the only significant social agents in the child's world. School and peers are two important and inviting social worlds which are prominent at this point in the child's development. Emotionally, however, these children still tend to rely on somewhat immature strategies for coping with uncomfortable feelings and situations: Their thinking tends to be magical and they rely heavily on denial. However, at this age children may also express their stress through disruptive behavior, such as being difficult to control or disobedient.

Kelly and Wallerstein (1976) report that six to eight-year-old children suffered the most intense reactions to divorce. Their responses included intense, immobilizing sadness and grief. Most of the children were frightened by the family instability and felt that their entire world had been profoundly shaken. While acutely aware of their suffering, these children seemed unable to obtain relief. Most of them continued to harbor open and intense fantasies of parental reconciliation and of the reunion of their family. At one year following divorce, Kelly and Wallerstein (1976) noted that the intensity of the child's initial reactions had gradually diminished, that the children had sadly resigned themselves to their parents' divorce and had reluctantly accepted it as final.

In addition, the six to eight-year-old children, particularly the younger boys, expressed a great sense of loss and rejection with regard to their departed father. In fact, even when the father had been unavailable or rather distant prior to the divorce, many of these boys continued to fantasize about their fathers' return and to retain a strong sense of loyalty to their male parent. Most of the children, both boys and girls, wished for more frequent visits with their fathers and felt that the current visitation schedule (e.g., two weekends per month) was inadequate.

Although these children were unable to express their anger toward their fathers, they had no difficulty expressing their anger openly and directly toward their mothers. They often blamed their mothers for the divorce and were not reluctant to say so. The child's anger was also directed at other "safe" targets such as teachers, friends, or siblings, resulting in problems in the classroom and with peers. Wallerstein and Kelly (1975, 1980) report that almost half of the seven to nine-year-olds they interviewed showed a decline in their academic performance, had peer problems, and exhibited behavioral difficulties at school. These early difficulties, unfortunately, foreshadowed later ones. The follow-up data at five years postdivorce indicated that children who had experienced problems in their play and with peers continued to have social problems four years later (Wallerstein & Kelly, 1980).

How can we make sense of the intense reactions of six to eight-year-old children to divorce? At this point in life, the child's new cognitive and emotional strides result in an increased awareness of his or her feelings. Consequently, these children have a greater capacity to understand the meaning of divorce and some of its implications for them. In addition, they are better able to experience and openly express their sadness and grief than the younger child. Unfortunately, however, these children have yet to develop the emotional resources necessary for coping with the trauma of divorce. Denial no longer serves them as well as it has in the past. And, these children are not able to channel their feelings into organized and group activities as much as are older children.

Moreover, we must remember that six-to-eight year olds are at a special developmental juncture in their lives. They are concerned with taking the giant step from their secure home base into the outside world of school and friends. These children are in the midst of both a cognitive and psychological transition between these two worlds. Wallerstein and Kelly (1980) observe that children at this age have a "precarious sense of being in transition between home and community, and their fear of retreating from their most recently acquired and still shaky gains in independence are increased by the family rupture and particularly by the father's departure from the family" (p. 65). It would seem that the developmental pressures confronting the six to eight-year-old child, coupled with the impact of divorce, are more than the child can cope with both cognitively and emotionally.

Late childhood (9 to 12 years). During the late childhood years, social agents outside the child's family take on even greater importance. Peers, teachers, and other adults play increasingly important roles in the child's life. This developmental stage also marks a cognitive step forward. Children at this age show a decrease in egocentrism and are more capable of understanding another person's perspective. They are also able to maintain conflicting feelings toward the same person. Changes are occurring in the social arena as well. These children are confronted with the formation of close relationships with same-sex peers or "chums" as Sullivan called them (1953). Academic achievement and mastery of intellectual activities assume even greater importance for this age child.

Wallerstein and Kelly (1976) found that the 9 to 12-year-old children in their study looked surprisingly different from the younger children. Although experiencing underlying feelings of loss, rejection, and helplessness, the older children were not as immobilized by their feelings as the six to eight year olds had been. In contrast, the older children were more poised and were actively struggling to master their painful feelings through a variety of coping strategies. For example, these children were trying to understand the divorce by soliciting support from others, becoming involved in organized activities, keeping in constant motion, and/ or exhibiting courage. One similarity between the middle and late childhood groups was that few children from either group expressed feeling responsible for their parents' divorce.

Wallerstein and Kelly (1976) found that children in the 9 to 12-year-old group were highly susceptible to certain changes in their relationships with their parents. This group of children was likely to form particularly strong alignments with one parent. Alignment in this context means a relationship in which the child allies him- or herself with one parent in an attack against the other parent. These older children seemed to serve as the most useful allies in divorce related fighting. It seems that at this age, the child's natural tendency and capacity to be a loyal, steadfast, and reliable friend and team member is easily co-opted in the service of his/her parents' postmarital power struggles. Interestingly, differences between boys and girls apparently exist. Mothers find sons to be more successful in abetting them when they battle with their ex-husbands, whereas fathers fare better with their daughters. Moreover, children at this age have a propensity to split their parents into the "good parent" and the "bad parent."

So far, our discussion of the effects of divorce on children has documented the fact that divorce seems to have a more disruptive influence on boys than on girls. However, it is important to note that this conclusion pertains to families in which the mother receives custody of the children. Does this same pattern hold true if the father is the custodial parent? One investigation (Santrock & Warshak, 1979; Santrock, Warshak, & Elliott, 1982; Warshak & Santrock, 1983a, 1983b) addressed this question by comparing children living in father custody, mother custody, and intact families. Sixty-four children between the ages of 6 and 11 were studied using a multimethod approach including videotaped observations of the child with the custodial parent, videotaped observations of the child with an adult stranger, teacher ratings, and standardized personality tests. The families were matched for a number of demographic variables such as sociometric status, family size, age of children at time of divorce, and the like. The findings consistently revealed that boys showed more socially competent behavior in father custody families, and girls were more socially competent in mother custody homes.

Specifically, boys whose fathers had custody were less demanding than girls in this family constellation, whereas girls were less demanding than boys in mother custody families. A similar, significantly positive, same-sex child and parent effect was shown in the children's maturity, sociability, and independence. The quality of the ongoing relationship between the custodial parent and the child was related to the child's behavior. Three observed parenting styles (Baumrind, 1971)—authoritarian, authoritative, and laissez-faire—were correlated with the child's observed behavior. These three categories were chosen because they represent Baumrind's widely adopted set of parenting strategies. Regardless of whether the child lived with the mother or the father, authoritative parenting (warmth, clear setting of rules and regulations, and extensive verbal give and take) was significantly related to increased self-esteem, maturity, sociability, social conformity, less anger, and fewer demands on the part of the child.

To cope with the demands of single parenting, divorced parents were enlisting the aid of additional caretakers. These included the noncustodial parent and nonparental adults such as babysitters, relatives, day-care centers, and friends. Overall, these support systems were being used twice as much by fathers with custody of their children than by mothers with custody (24 hours per week versus 11 hours per week). When examining how much support single parents were receiving from their ex-spouses alone, it seems that custodial fathers were more likely to solicit help from their ex-wives than were custodial mothers from their ex-husbands. Thus, father custody children had more frequent contact with their noncustodial mothers than mother custody children had with their fathers. Interestingly, in both mother custody and father custody families, the amount of contact the child had with either the noncustodial parent or with other nonparental caretakers was positively related to the child's warmth, sociability, and social conformity as observed in the laboratory.

Information about children's reactions to divorce and the custodial parent's perception of the impact of divorce on his/her child was also obtained. Mothers with custody reported that the child's relationship with the father began to deteriorate in the weeks and months following the divorce. In contrast, half of the custodial fathers detected changes in the child's relationship with the mother and felt that these changes were for the best. This pattern of results also appeared when parents were asked about how things were now compared to how they had been before the divorce. Mothers with custody reported a deterioration in the father-child relationship, whereas fathers with custody reported an improvement in the mother-child relationship.

There were some interesting differences in what parents said about their children's perception of the divorce and what the children themselves reported. A large majority (80 percent) of the parents stated that their child initially wanted the parents to get back together, but only 40 percent indicated that at two years after the divorce their children still voiced this wish. However, 85 percent of the children interviewed said that they still would like their parents to get back together again. More than two thirds of the children said that overall things were better than before the divorce. The children from divorced homes enjoyed visiting with the noncustodial parent, but a majority reported that they would like to have more frequent visits. And a majority of these children also said they would like their custodial parent to get married again. It seems that children continue to want to live in two-parent families rather than single-parent homes long after the initial distress of divorce has abated.

In conclusion, the results of this investigation indicate that there may be systematic effects of divorce on children that favor the same-sex child with the same-sex custodial parent. There may be a number of reasons for these effects. While custodial fathers have many responsibilities as single parents, their sons may feel more comfortable with them; and the fathers themselves may be more accepting or even encouraging of traditional masculine behavior, such as aggressive, rough-and-tumble play. A father is more likely than a mother to play football or other sports with his son, and he often feels more comfortable in discussing sex-related issues with his son. Conversely, because he lacks female role experiences, a father may be less sensitive to his daughter's needs and less capable of fulfilling those needs even if he senses them.

Sometimes, the opposite-sex child in a single-parent family may serve as a substitute for the ex-spouse. In such cases, the relationship between the custodial parent and the opposite-sex child may become more intense than is psychologically healthy. Such a relationship may inhibit the child from engaging in peer interaction to the extent that he or she normally would and may keep the child from developing independence. In this vein, boys in father custody homes show more independence than girls, while in mother custody homes girls show more independence than boys (Santrock & Warshak, 1979; Santrock, Warshak, & Elliott, 1982).

The second conclusion these data support is that the effects of father and mother custody on children are influenced by many factors other than gender. Although we have strong evidence supporting the importance of the same-sex child with the same-sex custodial parent, we clearly do not recommend that in custody decisions the girls should always be given to the mother and the boys to the father. In the past, custody decisions have been based on cultural stereotypes and historical biases that give mothers preferential claim to children. Clearly, we have found that some children, particularly boys, function in socially competent ways in father custody families, suggesting that an a priori decision to award the child to the mother is not a wise one. The impact of a custody disposition is influenced by a host of factors in addition to the sex of the child. We have found that the child-rearing practices of the custodial parent show important linkages to the child's social competence, and that the availability of support systems to the custodial parent are important to consider as well.

Adolescence (13 to 18 years). Along with infancy, adolescence has been the least productive period in terms of divorce research (Santrock & Madison, in press). There is an increasing tendency to consider adolescence in terms of early and late periods. Early adolescence (10 to 15 years) is more likely to coincide with the process of puberty and is a time of considerable physical change. By late adolescence (16 to 18 years) physical changes have slowed down considerably and individuals are much further along the path to the development of independence and identity. During early adolescence, individuals become increasingly interested in members of the opposite sex and matters of sexuality occupy a great part of their thoughts. At a time when sexuality has become a preoccupation, it may be particularly difficult for the adolescent to deal with his/her parent's dating patterns and sexual activity. At this point, the adolescent from a divorced family may be confused and may try to deny that his/her parents are sexual beings.

Adolescents are also undergoing cognitive and social changes. Cognitively, the adolescent can reason in more logical ways, but such logic is still often flawed in early adolescence. Early adolescence is also characterized by a curious sort of egocentrism (Elkind, 1976) in which the individual shows a heightened self-preoccupation. Indeed, adolescents often see themselves as the center of the world. Coupled with their increased ability to think abstractly, this egocentrism may result in the adolescent looking at his/her parents in terms of an idealized standard. In relation to such an ideal, divorced parents often do not measure up very well, and they may become easy targets for an adolescent's hostility. At the same time, early adolescence is associated with an increase in parent-adolescent conflict (Montemayor, 1982). Divorce may well escalate the nature of this conflict. While this moderate increase in conflict between parents and their adolescents serves the positive developmental function of promoting independence and identity formation (Blos, 1962), divorce may lead to a premature or false independence and identity on the part of the adolescent. Or it may delay the formation of such important developmental milestones. And it is during adolescence that the individual often moves even more deeply into a world of peers, school, and other social agents—and away from home. Such settings and social agents may serve to buffer the effects of divorce or they may serve as an arena in which the stress of divorce is expressed.

Mavis Hetherington (1972) has conducted a study of the effects of divorce on adolescents which provides a model of methodological rigor in the study of divorce. For example, 13 to 17-year-old girls from divorced, widowed, and intact families were matched carefully for age, sociometric status, and family size. The multimethod approach revealed that it may be important to observe children's and adolescents' behavior in natural settings. For instance, Hetherington (1972) did not find differences among the girls on standardized personality tests, but did find significant differences when the girls were observed at a recreational center and when they were interacting with an adult stranger. The daughters of divorces showed early heterosexual behavior, openness and responsiveness around males, and attention seeking from males. These behaviors were not characteristic of the daughters of widowed or intact families. Also, separation at an early age had more pronounced effects on the girls than did separation when they were older.

Hetherington (1977) reported a follow-up of the adolescent girls as they moved into late adolescence and early adulthood. The daughters of the divorcées were marrying earlier and tended to select marital partners who were more likely to have drug problems and erratic work histories. In contrast, daughters of widows were marrying men with more puritanical values. In addition, the daughters of the divorced and widowed families reported more sexual adjustment problems than their intact family counterparts. The daughters from intact families, on the other hand, reported fewer sexual and marital adjustment problems. They seemed to be more relaxed and were more competent as wives, suggesting that they had worked through their relationship issues with their fathers and may have been more psychologically free to be successful in their relationships with other men. The daughters of divorcées and widows, however, appeared to more frequently marry men who resembled their fathers.

In the Wallerstein and Kelly (1974) investigation, 21 of the participants were 13 or older at the time of the divorce decision. Almost without exception, these adolescents perceived their parents' divorce as a painful family event. A profound sense of loss and anger were common responses. Although some of the anger exhibited by adolescents was age-related, their tantrums and embittered threats were also attempts to disguise their intense feelings of helplessness and vulnerability. For some adolescents the divorce triggered concerns about their future in marriage and their competence as sexual partners, as well as loyalty conflicts. One to two years later, however, Wallerstein and Kelly (1974) found that most of the adolescents were able to restabilize their lives and to proceed toward young adulthood at a reasonable pace. In fact, for some adolescents the divorce catalyzed emotional and intellectual growth. Unfortunately, however, some youngsters experienced a major setback, often resulting in regressive or immature behavior. For example, some adolescents responded with delinquent behavior, sexual promiscuity, or severe depression (Wallerstein & Kelly, 1980). By far, the adolescents who had the most difficulty in coping with their parents' divorce were those who had had long-standing difficulties in their families. These problems were, in turn, further exacerbated by their parents' problems after the divorce.

In contrast, the adolescents who were able to cope most effectively with the trauma of divorce were those who kept a psychological distance from the parental crisis. In many cases, their parents did not involve them in the divorce proceedings. The parents of these adolescents had also permitted these youth to maintain strong ties with their friends and their outside interests. At first, these youth had appeared insensitive and even somewhat self-centered in their reaction to their parents' divorce. But over time, they were better able to adjust, the be empathic, and to realistically assess their family situation.

In a 10-year follow-up, Wallerstein (1982) states that these individuals, who are now young adults, continue to report that the divorce of their parents years ago has had a lasting effect on their lives. Many of the young adults feel that the divorce of their parents during their childhood and adolescence burdened them in their efforts to grow up and become mature adults. As these young adults look back, they recall feelings of sadness and a lingering wish to have grown up in an intact family. They also express considerable concern about their own marriages ending in divorce, and are anxious to avoid having their own children grow up in divorced circumstances.

Virtually all of our information about children of divorce has been collected *after* the separation or divorce of their parents. It is usually assumed that divorce is a critical life event that induces stress and leads to changes in the interaction between individuals in the family system. However, it is possible that family members may have been interacting with each other in a maladaptive way long before the divorce occurred. If this is the case, then postdivorce family functioning is not necessarily discontinuous with family functioning prior to the divorce. In one recent investigation (Morrison, Gjerde, & Block, 1983), the home environment of families was studied as long as six years before the divorce. Those families that were eventually disrupted by divorce were observed to be less stable, less peaceful, and less child centered than those families that remained intact. In particular, mothers of boys from divorced families employed strict discipline and control while deemphasizing warm and intimate interaction with their sons. Thus, parental functioning in some families may decline in important ways even before the separation or divorce occurs.

How can we understand the adolescent's response to his or her parents' separation and divorce? The answer to this question seems to involve the continuing importance of parents as secure attachment figures, a base from which the adolescent can explore and achieve without fear of abandonment and continued support. While the concept of attachment has been reserved primarily for infancy, attachment can be understood as a lifelong process. A secure base of attachment to parents is important during adolescence, just as it is in infancy. During adolescence, the family functions as a safe retreat, a place for the individual to replenish emotional security, receive support and guidance, bolster waivering self-esteem, and restore courage to venture back out into the world of risk and opportunity. Disruption of the family during this developmental period—when the individual is making the transition between the dependency of childhood and the independence of adulthood—may interfere with the process of developing autonomy and a secure identity. Adolescents may come to feel that the family can no longer provide a safe haven in divorced circumstances. They may feel that their parents, now preoccupied with their own distress and needs, are less available for support and guidance than are parents in intact families. Other functions normally carried out by the family may also be disrupted. For example, the provision of firm limits, discipline, and external controls may slacken or disappear. The adolescent, who still lacks consolidated inner controls, may have difficulty exercising independent decisions and effectively coping with the increased freedom and the atmosphere of relaxed discipline.

Another reason that divorced parents of adolescents may provide less support and guidance is that the adolescent and the parent are going in opposite directions in their development (Steinberg, 1980). For example, while the adolescent is approaching the peak of strength and virility as glorified in the popular culture, the divorced parent often faces a mid-life crisis and is worried about his/her appearance, health, and sexual attractiveness. The adolescent is coming to view life as having endless opportunities and possibilities, whereas the mid-life parent is undergoing a shift in perspective toward boundaries and limits, and may feel that time is running out. And just as the adolescent is preparing to enter adult society and is considering issues of work and career, the mid-life parent is looking back—for better or worse—on his/her occupational history and may be facing an occupational plateau. Although society recognizes that the adolescent is just starting out, it labels mid-life parents as having already had their chance.

THE SOCIAL WORLD OF ADULTS IN DIVORCED FAMILIES

Separation and divorce are disruptive and traumatic for the adults involved. Up to now we have been describing the child's response to divorce and how children's reactions differ depending upon their age at the time of parental separation and divorce. But how do the adults involved experience the dissolution of their marriage and cope with the chain of reactions, demands, and stresses involved in making the transition from a two-parent to a one-parent family? And how do these changes and experiences affect the parent-child relationship?

We will now examine the research findings on the adult's reactions to divorce and the effects of divorce on the parent-child relationship. The research indicates that the newly divorced adult experiences problems in three major areas: the practical matters of living day to day in an organized fashion; the emotional stress and changes in self-concept produced by the divorce; and the stresses and changes occasioned by new interpersonal relations, as well as those involving relations with ex-spouses and children (Hetherington, Cox, & Cox, 1977a).

Practical matters of daily living are especially difficult for divorced adults, particularly custodial mothers. Single parent mothers complain of "task overload" (Hetherington, Cox, & Cox, 1982). As you might expect, when one parent takes on the roles and responsibilities that were once shared by both parents, the job becomes overwhelming. According to Hetherington et al. (1982), this task overload, in turn, results in greater chaos and disorganization within the family, particularly during the first year after the divorce. By family disorganization, we are referring to the initial inability to provide a predictable and consistent household routine; the lack of well-defined family roles and responsibilities; and the failure to get many household chores accomplished. Hetherington (1981) reports that the households of both divorced mothers and divorced fathers were more disorganized than those of intact families. For example, divorced mothers and their children were likely to have erratic mealtimes and bedtimes, and the children were often late for school. In addition, the playful interactions during caretaker activities, such as reading a story before bedtime, were greatly reduced (Hetherington, Cox, & Cox, 1982). Children may precociously assume more responsibility and adultlike roles in an attempt to help their mothers cope with task overload (Weiss, 1978). Hetherington (1981) sums up the dilemma facing many single-parent mothers: "the challenge of mothers seems to be how to relieve themselves of some of the household responsibilities by assigning manageable, age-appropriate tasks to children, without making the children feel grossly overburdened or incompetent" (p. 45).

Divorced mothers were not the only ones having difficulty adjusting to their new marital status. Divorced fathers were having problems of their own. Hetherington (1981) reports that divorced men were sleeping less and picking up meals on the run. These men also fumbled along in trying to maintain their households and in managing routine chores such as laundry, cooking, and cleaning. However, many of these men received help either from female friends or by hiring a cleaning person (Hetherington, Cox, & Cox, 1977b). Interestingly, Hetherington et al. (1982) found that the men who had the most difficulty were those who had relied extensively on their ex-wives to perform the household duties prior to the divorce. In contrast, the men who were coping well with this aspect of single life were those who had been active participants in the domestic activities before they were separated.

Money and finances were also a source of stress for divorced adults. For divorced mothers, the divorce dealt out some harsh economic realities. Most divorced women suffered a substantial reduction in their standard of living. If not working already, many of these women were forced to obtain a job for which they were often inadequately prepared. Moreover, four out of five divorced women have school-aged children and are therefore faced with the additional task of arranging adequate child care (U.S. Bureau of the Census, 1979). Divorced women were often worried about making ends meet and were frustrated that their salaries did not contribute to an increased sense of financial security (Wallerstein & Kelly, 1980).

The term *displaced homemaker* describes the dilemma of many divorced women. These women have always assumed that their work will be in the home. Although their expertise at managing a home may be considerable, future employers may not recognize or value this experience as "work" experience. Wanda is typical of this type of woman. She married young and at age 18 she had her first child. Her work experience consisted of being a part-time waitress while in high school. Now Wanda is 32 and has three children, ages 14, 12, and 6. Her husband divorced her and remarried. The child support payments are enough for food, but little is left for rent, clothing, and other necessities. With limited education and vocational skills, Wanda now works as a sales clerk in a local department store. She cannot afford a housekeeper and she worries about the children being unsupervised while she works, particularly on Saturdays and during summer vacations. Creating a positive single identity is essential for these divorced adults so that they can come to grips with their loneliness, lack of autonomy, and financial hardship (Carter, 1977; Hancock, 1980).

Hetherington (1981) reports that the woman's decision to work at the time of the divorce can also have repercussions in terms of children having a higher incidence of behavior problems. In contrast, the children of mothers who waited a few years after the divorce before returning to work appeared to be coping better. It seems that the mother leaving the home to work means yet another loss at a time when children are already struggling with the loss of their father. Unfortunately, most divorced mothers do not enjoy the luxury of waiting several years before seeking employment.

Although maternal employment was associated with ill-effects for the child, there do appear to be certain advantages for the parent. Many divorced women reported positive feelings associated with working. Their jobs bolstered failing self-esteem and restored feelings of competence and satisfaction. In addition, work also provided a source of social contacts and friends for these women (Hetherington, Cox, & Cox, 1982; Wallerstein & Kelly, 1980).

The difficulty of trying to juggle the varying demands of home and work takes its toll on the single parent's capacity to parent. This results in what Hetherington (1976) calls a "coercive cycle" between divorced mothers and their children, particularly their sons. During the first year after divorce, mothers are depressed, under considerable pressure, and absorbed with their own needs. These factors are often reflected in their attitudes toward their children and result in erratic, unaffectionate behavior and a dictatorial style of parenting. Reliance on more restrictive, power-assertive disciplinary practices (Coletta, 1979; Kriesberg, 1970; Phelps, 1969) and negative sanctions (Burgess, 1978) have been reported in a number of studies on single-parent mothers. These women may feel they are at the end of their emotional rope: They bark out negative commands to their children, have difficulty being warm and supportive, and feel helpless about controlling the events and others around them. Consequently, these feelings are reverberated in their relationship with their children, particularly their sons. The ineffective parenting practices of these mothers, in turn, escalates their sons' aversive, oppositional, and aggressive behavior. Her child's (and particularly her son's) behavior subsequently contributes to the mother's growing feelings of incompetence, helplessness, and mounting depression. This in turn leads to more coercive parenting and the vicious cycle continues (Hetherington, 1976). Fortunately, as we noted earlier, the second year after divorce is characterized by the mother's use of more effective parenting practices and an improvement in her overall ability to cope with the pressures and demands of single parenthood. Hopefully, this change breaks the coercive cycle.

Another area in which divorced adults report difficulties is in terms of their emotional adjustment and self-concept. Divorced adults, both mothers and fathers, report feeling more anxious, depressed, angry, rejected, and incompetent. As we mentioned previously, custodial mothers, particularly those with sons, feel the worst. This group of women feel more helpless, and feel that they have lost control over their lives compared to married mothers or divorced mothers with girls (Hetherington, Cox, & Cox, 1982). Divorced women are caught in the midst of an identity crisis. They are confused about their role, they feel unattractive, and having lost their identity as both wife and mother appears to make them particularly vulnerable after the divorce (Santrock, 1983).

One year following the divorce marks the beginning of a gradual emotional upswing, however, for both divorced men and women. Divorced mothers and fathers begin to date, socialize with friends, and attend more parties and social gatherings. Hetherington et al. (1982) also found that divorced mothers and fathers become increasingly concerned with self-improvement. These adults signed up for art classes, physical fitness programs, and many returned to school for advanced education. They seemed to be searching for a new identity and experimenting with their newfound freedom. Men and women alike became concerned with their physical appearance. Women were losing weight, trying out new hairstyles, and buying less conventional clothes. Similarly, men were growing beards and moustaches, wearing mod clothes such as leather jackets and boots, and buying sportscars. At the two-year mark, this frenzy of social activity and self-improvement gradually began to wind down (Heatherington, Cox, & Cox, 1982). These activities appeared to serve as healthy outlets where divorced individuals could channel their emotional distress and to also provide a source of competence and an opportunity for social contact.

The third major area of difficulty for divorced adults is their social life and the establishment of intimate interpersonal relationships. Divorced people bemoan the difficulties inherent in being a single adult—particularly one with children. They point out that in our society many social activities are couples oriented. They feel pinned in, lonely, and limited in their ability to meet available men and women who are their age. As might be expected, divorced mothers with children, in particular, feel trapped in their child's world and estranged from other adults including their married friends (Hetherington, Cox, & Cox, 1982; Wallerstein & Kelly, 1980).

During the first year after the divorce, noncustodial fathers are more socially and sexually active than their female counterparts. Divorced men report more frequent dating and involvement in more casual affairs than do divorced women. However, by the end of the first year, these fathers report that they are tiring of casual affairs, that they want more meaningful and lasting relationships. Divorced women voice a similar complaint. They too are tired of brief sexual encounters and describe feeling depressed, desperate, and bad about themselves afterwards. By the end of the second year, Hetherington et al. (1982) found that most of the divorced adults they had followed had entered a close relationship. Interestingly, the formation of an intimate relationship and remarriage often signaled an important turning point in the lives of divorced adults. For the first time since the divorce, these adults reported feeling happy and satisfied with their lives.

Noncustodial or visiting fathers are confronted with some different problems (problems not encountered by divorced mothers) because of the unique nature of their relationship with their children following the divorce. It is important to remember that this new relationship between father and child—of "part-time parent and part-time child"—is extremely awkward (Wallerstein & Kelly, 1980). This relationship has no counterpart: It is no longer defined by the daily routines and responsibilities as it had been before the family rupture. Visiting fathers and their children are suddenly confronted with the task of trying to express all their feelings and needs, which were once shared daily, within the narrow confines of their visit. Both child and adult are unsure of their roles and are no longer privy to the full life of the other. Fathers may wonder about how much discipline they should provide or whether they should ensure that the child's homework is completed. All of these complexities combine to keep the father's sense of who he is now unsettled and unsettling (Wallerstein & Kelly, 1980).

Not surprisingly, the noncustodial father was beset with many problems and intense feelings regarding his changed relationship with his child. While the divorced mothers complained of feeling "trapped in," the noncustodial fathers complained of feeling "shut out" (Hetherington, Cox, & Cox, 1977a). They reported suffering an intense feeling of loss regarding their children. Surprisingly, the predivorce relationship between the father and the child was discontinuous with his relationship following the divorce (Hetherington, Cox, & Cox, 1978; Kelly, 1978). Right after the divorce, many fathers saw their children frequently, some more than they had when they were married. This group of fathers reported a dramatic improvement in their relationship with their children and reported enjoying the time they spent with them. In contrast, another group of fathers saw their children less frequently as time passed. Ironically, these fathers had been deeply attached to their children before the divorce, and could not now tolerate the pain of being on the sideline of their child's life. Their solution was to psychologically pull away from their children and to reduce the frequency of their visits. Unfortunately, the child was deeply disappointed and angry when his or her father did not arrive for his visits or canceled them (Wallerstein & Kelly, 1980). Tragically, children feel that visitation is a measure of their fathers' love, and his absence confirms their worst suspicions and fears—that their father no longer loves them.

Another phenomenon also characterized many of the children's visits with their noncustodial fathers: the Santa Claus syndrome. Many divorced fathers wanted their limited time with their children to be as happy and as much fun as possible. They were extremely afraid of rejection by their children. Consequently, they tended to be permissive and indulgent with their children during visits, to shower them with gifts and special treats, and to keep them constantly entertained. Not surprisingly, this generosity often enraged their ex-wives, who felt stuck with the mundane and practical functions of parenting and missed these fun times with their children.

Another problem that worried some divorced men was how to handle their children and their new relationships with women. For example, many fathers were concerned about what to do with their lovers when their children came to visit, and how this new relationship would affect the child. At other times, however, the father was insensitive to the child's need to spend time alone with him—without the new woman around.

Visits also became a second battleground for divorced spouses. They could be times of considerable conflict and were filled with acrimony, resentment, and anger. In the group of families they interviewed, Hetherington et al. (1982) found that 66 percent of the verbal exchanges between ex-spouses during the period immediately following the divorce involved conflict. Yet, despite such emotional turmoil, attachment to the ex-spouse continues to persist in many cases. For example, Hetherington (Hetherington, Cox, & Cox, 1978) reported that of 48 couples observed, 6 had sexual intercourse during the first two months after separation. She also reported that many of the divorced women continued to rely on their ex-husbands for support and that he was the first one they would call during a time of crisis. Some divorced fathers also continued to help their ex-wives with household maintenance or would baby sit while the mother was out on a date (Hetherington, Cox, & Cox, 1982). It seems that prior attachments and patterns of interaction are hard to break. Weiss (1975) suggests that although the divorce is a marker event in the relationship between the spouses, it often does not signal the end of the relationship. He believes that the attachment between the divorced couple lingers on, whether the couple likes it or not much as the research would have us believe otherwise.

Further information about the separation and divorce process suggests that former spouses often alternate between feelings of seductiveness and hostility (Hunt & Hunt, 1977). They may have thoughts of reconciliation and wonder if the divorce was a mistake. However, by two years after the divorce, the intensity of the anger and resentment between divorced people has subsided considerably and few express any regrets about the divorce. In addition, the formation of a new intimate relationship or remarriage of one of the divorced adults is particularly powerful in mitigating the intensity of feelings and attachment between the divorced couple (Hetherington, Cox, & Cox, 1982). Divorce then is a complex emotional process for adults as well as for children.

SOME IMPORTANT FAMILY PROCESSES IN THE DEVELOPMENT OF CHILDREN IN DIVORCED FAMILIES

So far we have been discussing the stresses and negative effects of divorce on children and adult adjustment. Woven through this overview have been comments about processes that might possibly explain or ameliorate the effects of divorce on children. It is important to point out that despite the stress of divorce, some children manage to come through the experience relatively unscathed. In the following section we will look more closely at three family process factors that appear to mediate the effects of divorce. These include (1) conflict and stress, (2) the family as a system of interacting individuals, and (3) attachment and carrying forward relationships.

Conflict and Stress

Conflict and acrimony precede and accompany most divorces, and often continue or escalate following divorce (Hess & Camara, 1979; Hetherington, Cox, & Cox, 1982; Wallerstein & Kelly, 1980). In general, family conflict is a factor that has been found to have profound adverse effects on children's adjustment and to lead to the development of behavior disorders. That is, children who are exposed to families in which there is a high degree of conflict between parents and children or in which there is marital discord are more maladjusted, experience more peer difficulties, are more aggressive and dependent, and display higher levels of stress and disruption in academic and intellectual functioning than children in low-conflict families (Hess & Camara, 1979; Hetherington, Cox, & Cox, 1982; Rutter, 1971; Wallerstein & Kelly, 1980).

This relationship between conflict and maladjustment in children holds true irrespective of whether children are from divorced or nondivorced families. However, the effects of conflict are more harmful for children living in divorced families than for children who live in nondivorced families (Hetherington & Camara, 1983). The point is often made that children function better in single-parent families than children living in conflict ridden, two-parent families. The picture, however, is more complicated than this statement implies. When children from divorced families are compared with children from nondivorced families that are characterized by a high degree of marital discord, two patterns emerge. First, the differences between the two groups change markedly over the course of the two-year period following divorce. Second, boys appear to be more vulnerable to the effects of both marital conflict and divorce than girls (Hetherington, Cox, & Cox, 1982). In the first year following divorce, children from divorced families are less well adjusted than children from high-conflict nondivorced families. During this period, children from both high- and low-conflict divorced families are more oppositional, aggressive, lacking in self-control, distractible, and more attention-seeking at home and at school than are children living in conflict ridden families with both biological parents. However, two years following divorce this pattern of differences is reversed. At this point, children from conflictual nuclear families, particularly boys, are experiencing greater difficulties (e.g., show more acting-out, aggressive behavior and less prosocial behavior such as helping, sharing, and cooperation) than children from low-conflict divorced families.

These findings suggest that the old adage of staying together for the sake of the children may be ill-advised—if the alternative is a stable, conflict free single-parent home. As Hetherington et al. (1982) point out, in the long run marital discord may be associated with more adverse outcomes for children than the divorce itself. However, the picture in the short run appears to be quite different. During the period of family disequilibrium and reorganization in the first year following divorce, children's problems may be exacerbated before they begin to subside. The question that many parents ask about whether it is better to stay together or to get a divorce often assumes that marital conflict and dissension cease at the time of divorce. This is clearly not the case for many families. In both the Hetherington et al. (1982) and the Wallerstein and Kelly (1980) investigations, a substantial number of the families remained as conflicted following the divorce as they had been during the marriage. Unfortunately, in the year immediately following divorce, conflict does not decline but rather, it escalates (Hetherington, Cox, & Cox, 1978). Children are often exposed to open conflict, quarreling, put-downs by one parent of the other, or they may even be asked to choose sides. It is the presence of continued conflict rather than conflict from the past that appears to be associated with most emotional and behavioral problems in children. Children residing in stable, conflict free, single-parent families are able to recover within about two years from the hostility and dissension associated with the separation and divorce of their parents. However, if intense conflict continues following divorce, particularly for boys, the effects are more deleterious than they are for children living in a confict ridden family with both biological parents (Hetherington, Cox, & Cox, 1982).

Why should this be the case? Hetherington (1981) suggests that the explanation for these findings regarding conflict may lie in the role of protective parental buffering. It seems that a very good relationship with either parent can buffer or attenuate the adverse effects of conflict and disharmony in nondivorced families, whereas only an exceptionally good relationship with the custodial parent can serve this function in the divorced family (Hetherington, Cox, & Cox, 1982). The noncustodial parent is not available to mediate in the day-to-day battles and quarrels and, therefore, cannot be an effective buffer. However, highly involved and available noncustodial parents can have more impact as a buffer than those who are unavailable and less involved (Hess & Camara, 1979; Hetherington, 1981).

An organized and predictable home environment with clearly defined and consistently enforced rules, responsibilities, and a responsive, nurturant atmosphere can also have an ameliorative influence on the child's adjustment in the single-parent family (Hetherington, Cox, & Cox, 1978). Structure, organization, enforcement of rules, and assignment of responsibilities are more important for children from divorced families than for children living in intact families (Hetherington, Cox, & Cox, 1978). Similarly, these characteristics in the school are associated with greater self-control in children from nondivorced families with high levels of conflict. It seems likely that young children who have undergone the stress, inconsistency, and multiple changes associated with divorce or intense family conflict may need a more predictable environment than children who have not experienced such difficulties. Under stress, young children may have particular difficulty structuring their own world and exerting self-control. Therefore, external controls and a stable environment, both at home and in the classroom, may become more important for these children than for children who are not undergoing stressful life events. Such an environment may be a way of reassuring children that their world is not going to fall apart.

The Family as a System

As suggested earlier, it is important to look at the interaction of the family members and the social context in which they live, rather than just to look at the type of family structure, such as whether the father is present or absent, or whether the family is divorced or separated. It is equally important to continue observing the family in this manner following the separation and divorce. For example, it has been found that the child's relationship with both parents after the divorce influences his or her ability to cope with stress (Hetherington, Cox, & Cox, 1978; Kelly, 1978). Children do best with continued involvement of *both* parents following divorce. The continued involvement of the father in mother custody families has been found to be an important factor in alleviating some of the adverse effects of divorce on children. Several studies have demonstrated that frequent availability and contact with the noncustodial father is associated with positive adjustment and peer relations (Hess & Camara, 1979; Hetherington, Cox, & Cox, 1978; Wallerstein & Kelly, 1979). Although the availability of the noncustodial father is important for both sons and daughters, it appears to be particularly critical for sons living in mother custody families (Hetherington, Cox, & Cox, 1978).

The majority of information we have about divorced families emphasizes the absent father or the relationship between the custodial parent and the child. But child psychologists have become increasingly interested in the role of the support systems that are available to the child and to the family. Our research (e.g., Santrock, Warshak, & Elliott, 1982), as well as that of others, suggests that the availability and use of support systems play an important role in the child's development and subsequent adjustment to divorce. With the increased task overload placed on the divorced parent, it is not surprising that divorced parents need to rely on support from friends, family, and community resources. Often a divorced parent needs help handling practical problems such as emergencies, transportation, finances, and child care. Hetherington et al. (1978) found that support from parents, siblings, close friends, or a competent housekeeper were all related to the mother's effectiveness in interacting with her children after divorce. In addition, support systems for divorced families have been found to be more important for low-income families than for middle-income families (Colletta, 1978; Spicer & Hampe, 1975). The extended family and community services played a more crucial role in family functioning in the low-income families in both of these investigations. In addition, competent support systems may be particularly important for divorced parents with infants and preschool children since the majority of these single parents must work full time.

Unfortunately, it has been found that divorced parents tend to be more socially isolated than parents in nuclear families (Weinraub & Wolf, 1983). These divorced parents work longer hours and receive less emotional support from friends and from their own parents. In general, their support systems tend to be less stable. Interestingly, it has been found that increased support in parenting was an important factor in predicting optimal interaction between the mother and the preschool child in the divorced single-parent family.

Attachment and Carrying Forward Relationships

Surprisingly, little has been written about the role of secure attachment in understanding the effects of divorce on children. Although attachment has been a concept reserved almost exclusively for the relationship between the infant and the care giver (e.g., Ainsworth, 1979; Bowlby, 1969), we believe the concept has merit for understanding relationships throughout the life span, and specifically as a context for understanding the effects of divorce on infants, children, and adolescents.

Mary Ainsworth (1979) argues that infants can be classified as being either securely or insecurely attached to the care giver. A securely attached infant is one who uses the care giver as a secure base from which to explore the environment. Although the securely attached infant may move away from the care giver, he/she is generally cognizant of the care giver's location and continually glances in her direction. This infant responds positively to being picked up, and when put down, he/she moves away freely to play. In contrast, infants who do not use the care giver as a base for exploration and who are not easily comforted by contact from the care giver are labeled as anxious/resistant infants, while those who withhold contact and avoid the care giver following separation are said to be anxious/avoidant infants. The resistant and avoidant infants both represent subclasses of insecurely attached infants.

Relationships are not only internalized by the individual, but are carried forward into new relationships (Sroufe & Fleeson, in press). As the infant moves forward to new relationships, his/her behavior reflects expectations and feelings that have built up over time in the course of the attachment relationship. Thus, a secure attachment reflecting a history of sensitive, responsive care is predictive of more socially competent behavior in preschool (Waters, Wippman, & Sroufe, 1979). These children have more friends, are better able to engage in reciprocity, are more socially oriented, more empathic, and more popular. They also approach and respond to others with more positive affect and fewer negative feelings (Sroufe, Schork, Motti, Lawroski, & LaFreniere, in press).

In contrast, anxious/resistant infants become easily frustrated, whiney, and negativistic even when faced with simple problems (Gove, 1982; Matas, Arend, & Sroufe, 1978). These children have highly dependent relationships with teachers and ineffective relationships with peers. This is presumably due to inconsistent care and the child's expectation that in times of stress the care giver will be emotionally unavailable (Sroufe & Fleeson, 1983). An ambivalent child thus seems to have internalized an ambivalent relationship, whereas an empathic child appears to have internalized a responsive relationship.

The behavioral and emotional portrayal of divorced children provided by Wallerstein and Kelly (1980) and Hetherington, Cox, and Cox (1982) fit all too well the above description of insecurely attached children. That is, children of divorce display anxiety about the security of their relationships with their parents that is more pronounced than that of children from intact families. This anxiety is also carried forward into the child's new relationships with his/her agemates. Children of divorce have more peer difficulties and dependent relationships with their teachers than children from intact families. We are suggesting that the divorce experience may be carried forward to influence the child's relationships not only within the family but also with others outside the family. This experience can either prevent the child from developing a secure attachment in the first place, or undermine a secure attachment relationship which had characterized earlier development. Thus, the child of divorce may come to internalize a relationship with the care giver that is characterized by a lack of nurturance, unresponsiveness, instability, coercion, or conflict which is later carried forward and created in the context of interactions with peers and teachers. Moreover, our knowledge of the importance of a secure attachment relationship for the child's future interpersonal competence provides further support for the child's maintaining positive, ongoing interaction with the noncustodial parent as well as with the custodial parent. A secure relationship with one parent may help to insulate or buffer the child from later difficulties and from the anxiety associated with an insecure attachment to the other parent.

CLINICAL IMPLICATIONS FROM THE DIVORCE RESEARCH

Following divorce families are faced with the difficult task of putting their lives back together and constructively reorganizing their family. Many of these families will require assistance from helping professionals with this reorganization process. Parents may need help regarding how to tell their children about the divorce. They may need help concerning how to give their children support during the transition period, as well as how they too can cope with the onslaught of economic, social, and emotional changes that occur in the wake of divorce. Parents are especially concerned about ways in which they can provide joint care for their children from two separate households and about how to cope with the changes in their relationships with their children. In addition, many of these families may need help later when they decide to remarry and another family reorganization occurs.

Until now, we have been discussing the research findings on child and adult reactions to the divorce process, as well as important factors that influence postdivorce adjustment. From this body of information it is possible to derive a model of expectable responses or "norms" for children who are experiencing the stress of divorce and undergoing family reorganization. It is possible to formulate a realistic timetable for the duration of this process and for the time required for most children and adults to recover from the initial stress of divorce and to go through the period of transition, changing roles, and new challenges associated with family reorganization. In the absence of this type of normative information about the nature and duration of divorce related reactions, professionals have had difficulty identifying children who might be at risk for psychological problems and who require professional attention.

We believe that the research on divorce provides a framework for sensitive and informed parenting and professional advice. Information about the changes in parent-child relationships and the identification of factors that mitigate the adverse effects of divorce can also serve as important building blocks for enlightened parenting and clinical intervention. In this section we will provide an overview of the range of community services that are currently available to families of divorce. We will also discuss the implications of the divorce literature and outline specific guidelines for parents and clinicians who are working with divorced parents and their children. Finally, we will address the issue of how to determine the child who is in need of therapeutic intervention.

Service Programs for Divorced Families

A network of supportive services has emerged in recent years in response to the growing needs of children and adults experiencing divorce and family transition. These programs are directed toward helping family members learn more adaptive coping strategies and helping them to build a new life after divorce. Other goals include helping parents and children to reduce the initial feelings of distress following divorce, improving parenting skills, helping adapt family members to adapt to the changes in their roles and responsibilities, and helping them to cope with specific divorce related issues and problem areas. In addition, these programs provide families with a network of resources for continued support as they make the transition to life in a single-parent home (Camara, Baker, & Dayton, 1980; Hetherington & Camara, in press).

Our current mental health system provides three major types of community services: primary prevention, crisis intervention, and intensive therapeutic intervention. Primary prevention is concerned with identifying target groups of individuals and families who run a special risk of incurring psychiatric disorders. The goal of this type of intervention is to provide individuals in high-risk groups with information, education, and resources before symptoms occur or a crisis results. Children of divorce are considered to be one such high-risk group (Rutter, 1978). Crisis intervention provides short-term, focused help to people in crisis states and has been conceived as an important way of averting later, more damaging mental disorders. As was previously mentioned, the period during and immediately following divorce is best conceptualized as the crisis phase. The third type of service involves more intensive treatment efforts for individuals with identified psychological problems that interfere with adaptive functioning. Most of the programs designed to assist families of divorce fall into the first two categories—primary prevention and crisis intervention.

There is tremendous diversity in the programs that are offered to families of divorce, and these programs vary dramatically from community to community. Traditionally, most of the services have been sponsored by local mental health agencies, child guidance clinics, or family service agencies. Recently, however, programs designed to deal more specifically with the problems of divorced family members have become increasingly available. These services include self-help groups such as Parents without Partners, church support groups, single mother groups, hotline phone services, and educational workshops sponsored by churches, school districts, or community colleges (for a review see Baker et al., 1980).

Parents without Partners is the most extensive program of its kind and has hundreds of chapters all over the United States and Canada.[1] This organization provides opportunities for single parents to meet other single adults and for children to become involved with opposite-sex adult role models. In addition, the organization hosts various family activities, outings, and picnics. Discussion groups and lectures also provide members with valuable information about the divorce process and adjustment in a single-parent home. Recreational and discussion groups for children and adolescents help these youngsters to feel less stigmatized and offer opportunities for dealing with the special problems that confront the children of divorce.

Most of the programs we have been describing tend to be brief and time-limited, usually lasting between six and eight weeks. These programs tend to be preventive or crisis oriented, and the emphasis is on assisting families through the initial crisis phase during and immediately following divorce and before more serious problems develop. The services include a variety of approaches, ranging from individual sessions to groups formats to programs that include all family members. Some programs focus on the child, while others concentrate on helping parents to help their children.

In addition to the programs described above, a number of centers specializing in the problems of divorced families have sprung up all over the country. We will describe a few of these programs and the methods they use to help families reorganize their lives. The Marin County Divorce and Mourning Project in northern California provides counseling to family members of divorce. This project was established by Judith Wallerstein and Joan Kelly and is based on many of the findings, which were discussed earlier, from their longitudinal investigation of divorce. This project is designed to assist family members through the divorce process before more serious problems develop, and to help family members make a smoother and more effective transition to life in a single-parent home. Family members are usually seen on an individual basis, although they are occasionally seen in groups.

Another example is the Children of Divorce Group in South Orange, New Jersey. This project is based in the schools and provides support groups for children of divorce who are between the ages of 7 and 12. These groups are led by a trained, group facilitator and they use an open-

[1]Headquarters for Parents without Partners: 7910 Woodmont Avenue, Washington, D.C. 20014.

ended, discussion format that encourages children to share their concerns and feelings. In addition, the groups use books that are divorce related, and role-playing techniques to enable children to talk about family events. Support from peers is also encouraged as a means of helping children to solve problems related to their parents' divorce.

The Center for Children in Family Crisis is another such project, and is located in Pittsburgh, Pennsylvania. This project offers a program for divorced parents and its emphasis is on helping parents in their caretaker role. In contrast, the Family Change Project in Minneapolis, Minnesota, focuses on the children of divorce. Staff members from this project conduct children's groups using such structured activities as reading books on divorce and remarriage. Other therapeutic activities include role playing problematic family situations, group games, and family sculpturing exercises.

As can be seen, there is a wide variety in the types of services offered to parents and children of divorce. While these programs may serve as useful models for professionals and other individuals who are trying to help members of divorced families, little is known about their effectiveness. Few programs include evaluations of their own interventions but rather, tend to rely upon client reports regarding their services. It is, therefore, difficult to assess the relative effectiveness of these various approaches and techniques. However, important content areas for intervention and preventive efforts can be extrapolated from the research findings on divorce. These findings can serve as guideposts for professionals working with families of divorce, and can highlight critical issues that should be addressed to facilitate a constructive adjustment to the divorce process. In addition, the findings can serve to alert professionals to the special needs and problem areas facing individuals from divorced families.

Therapeutic Guidelines for Working with Parents

The actions of parents can make a real difference to their children. We believe that parents are in need of information and education about the divorce process in order to assist their children and themselves with the task of family reorganization. The goal of such parent education is prevention: Educating parents of the children of divorce may facilitate adjustment and preclude the development of serious problems.

A starting point in educating parents is to provide them with information about the course of divorce and the responses they can expect to see from their children along the way. Parents can be informed of current research regarding the different stages of the divorce process, and warned that this process may last two to three years (Hetherington, Cox, & Cox, 1982; Wallerstein & Kelly, 1980). Parents also need to be educated about the impact of divorce on their children and instructed about the types of responses and behavior to expect from their children at different points during the divorce process. For example, parents can be told about the range of children's acute responses to the initial stress of divorce and to expect the worst during the first year. This kind of information allows parents to establish reasonable expectations regarding their children's behavior following divorce and it often helps to allay parents' fears and feelings of guilt. Many parents are relieved to discover that their children's reactions are part of a normal continuum of responses, and that although children experience initial difficulty, most recover from the trauma of divorce. Many parents are also relieved to learn that their children are not going to sustain serious psychological problems as a result of their divorce.

As we mentioned in our discussion of the research literature, there are several factors that can have a positive or ameliorative influence on children's postdivorce adjustment. These factors can substantially reduce the stress and trauma of divorce, as well as contribute to a positive, long-term outcome for the child. Thus, a second step in working with parents is to educate them about the importance of these factors and to encourage them to take constructive steps to safeguard their children. That is, parents can be instructed about the specific steps they can take to actively contribute to the successful reorganization of their family. Such instruction often gives direction to parents' aimless energy and diminishes their feelings of helplessness. Below is an outline of several important steps that parents can be encouraged to follow. As will become clear, these steps have been derived from the research findings presented earlier.

1. *The Coparenting Relationship.* A constructive coparenting relationship is essential for positive postdivorce adjustment of children. Recall from our earlier discussion that a continued, cooperative, and mutually supportive relationship between divorced parents was found to be a critical factor in the child's adjustment to divorce (Hetherington, Cox, & Cox, 1982). By coparenting relationship, we are referring to "the relationship between both parents that permits them to continue their child-rearing obligations and responsibilities after divorce" (Ahrons & Perlmutter, 1982, p. 37). To achieve this relationship divorced partners must separate their parental roles from their marital roles, redefining the first while terminating the latter. This is not an easy task!

Often there is continued hostility and animosity between former spouses, particularly during the period immediately following the separation. Generally, hurt feelings and resentment color every negotiation and transaction, many of which revolve around parenting. It is important for parents to appreciate that the longer the hostilities continue, the greater the likelihood that their children will suffer harmful reactions to the divorce. Not surprisingly, parents often require special help with this difficult task of redefining their relationship with their former spouse. One priority is to help divorced parents to separate their remaining marital conflicts from parental issues (Greif, 1982). In addition, divorced parents need to understand that each of them has parental rights and responsibilities and that to carry these out usually requires some sort of continuing relationship between them. Parents need to be advised of the importance of working together, particularly regarding child-rearing issues and matters of discipline, so as to provide a united and consistent front to their children. In working with parents on this task the focus of the professional should always be on the task of parenting and on what relationships are necessary for healthy parenting to occur (Ahrons & Perlmutter, 1982).

Unfortunately, some divorced parents are unable to establish a constructive relationship with their former spouses. Long after their marriage is legally terminated, these individuals allow their animosity toward each other to interfere with their parental obligations. Often the children are enmeshed in the parental warfare with the result that they later develop more serious psychological difficulties (Wallerstein & Kelly, 1980). These divorced parents can be extremely difficult to work with and they *and* their children may require treatment.

2. *Continued Availability of the Noncustodial Parent.* Continued contact with the noncustodial parent is another important factor contributing to children's successful adjustment following divorce. For most children of divorce, the noncustodial parent is the father. Recall from our earlier discussion that continued involvement of the father, characterized by frequent access and contact between the father and the child, was found to result in better psychological adjustment of the child (Hess & Camara, 1979; Hetherington, Cox, & Cox, 1978). In fact, those children who had the least amount of contact with their fathers were the ones who suffered the most severe emotional distress and developmental disruptions (Wallerstein & Kelly, 1980). However, a continued relationship with the father is dependent, in part, on a constructive, coparenting relationship between the divorced parents (Ahrons, 1979, 1981).

Greif (1982) offers some suggestions to professionals working with divorced parents on how to foster the relationship between the child and the noncustodial father. She suggests that fathers may need to be advised about the importance of their remaining actively involved with their children, and of how this involvement can mitigate against their own feelings of depression, their feelings of loss regarding their parental role, and their alienation. In addition, both parents need to be instructed about the importance of ensuring that visits occur with regularity. Visiting parents should be reliable and punctual, and inform the child well in advance if a visit must be canceled. Gardner (1977) points out that many noncustodial parents "seem to be oblivious to the fact that building up the children's hopes and then disappointing them at the last minute can be devastating" (p. 289). On the other hand, the custodial parent needs to be responsible for making sure that children are ready and prepared for the noncustodial parent's visits.

In addition, parents need to appreciate that stipulated visitation times do not always coincide with the needs and desires of parents and children. Parents may need to be helped to be flexible about visitation schedules and to consider custodial arrangements that best protect and encourage the attachment between the child and *both* of them. Obviously, such flexibility requires a certain amount of trust and cooperation between former spouses. Professionals may also need to caution parents against using visits as a weapon in their battles with one another. For example, the custodial mother may deprive the father of his visit with his children in an attempt to punish him for not paying child support on time. Using the child in this kind of parental conflict can result in psychological difficulties for that child which may eventually require treatment.

Greif (1982) suggests that fathers may require special assistance and considerable support to remain actively involved with their children. She recommends support groups for noncustodial fathers to address this issue, as well as helping fathers with some of the unique problems inherent in being a part-time parent. Fathers may also need practical education about child care and the help in planning meaningful activities with their children.

These research findings have implications for the legal system as well. Current custody laws and visitation regulations do not always work to encourage the continued involvement of fathers. It is important not to burden the relationship between the noncustodial parent and the child with cumbersome legal restrictions that do not serve the individual needs of either person. Often innovative custody arrangements and the flexibility of both parents are called upon to foster this important relationship.

3. *Providing a Predictable and Stable Home Environment.* Children who are experiencing family disruption are in special need of a predictable and stable home environment. Earlier, we presented findings indicating that children from divorced families who lived in predictable home environments where there were clearly defined schedules, explicit rules and regulations, and consistent but warm discipline made a more rapid and satisfactory recovery (Hetherington, Cox, & Cox, 1978). During times of stress children have difficulty structuring their own world and need the safety of a stable environment.

Parents may need to be educated about the particular importance of providing such an environment, a task that requires heroic efforts on the part of most single parents since they are trying to juggle a full-time job, parenting, and the maintenance of a household. Thus, parents may benefit from assistance in establishing a reasonable daily schedule in which meals and bedtimes occur at predictable hours. Parents may need help formulating clearly defined rules and regulations in the house, and encouragement to enforce these rules when they are broken. Also, professionals can help parents to obtain relief from task overload by assisting them in the process of assigning manageable and age-appropriate responsibilities to their children.

Most importantly, parents may need instruction on how to improve their parenting skills, particularly custodial mothers with sons. Remember how a cycle of coercion develops between single-parent mothers who relied excessively on the use of negative commands to control their sons. Single parents might benefit from instruction about how the coercive cycle develops and how their behavior escalates the noncompliance of their children. It is important to point out to these parents that they can break this cycle by adopting a more effective parenting style. Behaviorally oriented parenting programs can be particularly helpful in this regard and can lead to rapid improvement in the children's behavior (Hetherington, Cox, & Cox, 1982). Parents should be advised to use abundant reinforcement for positive behavior, to provide reassurance and warm attention to these children, and to combine this positive support with their attempts to control their children's behavior. There needs to be extensive verbal give-and-take between parent and child. This type of parenting can result in increased self-confidence and feelings of competence on the part of the parent, and a positive outcome for the child.

Recognizing Children in Need of Treatment

Children's responses to divorce run the full gamut of emotional and behavioral disturbances—denial, sadness, fear, anxiety, depression, lowered self-esteem, and behavior problems with peers and teachers. How then does the clinician determine the child who needs therapy from those who are making a normal adjustment to the stress of divorce? When evaluating divorced parents and their children, clinicians need to first consider the chronicity or the duration of the child's difficulties and symptomatic behavior (Gardner, 1976). Generally speaking, children who exhibit symptomatic behavior beyond the expected time limits that are normally required to recover from the trauma of divorce are in need of therapeutic intervention. As was pointed out earlier, the course of adjustment to and recovery from divorce usually spans a two-year period. Children's behavior reaches an all-time low around the end of the first year after divorce, with a gradual improvement following in the second year. Therefore, it would seem that when children's symptomatic behavior persists unabated beyond the one and one-half to two-year mark, therapy or at least parental counseling may be necessary. It should also be pointed out that a child's initial reaction to his/her parents' divorce may be so severe (e.g., a suicide attempt, or running away from home) that therapy and consultation with parents is immediately warranted.

Another important factor to consider in determining whether a child is in need of treatment is the onset of the child's difficulties. Children who exhibit behavioral or emotional problems prior to the separation and divorce of their parents are more at risk than children who develop symptomatic behavior following the divorce. For this high-risk group of children, the divorce often exacerbates and intensifies their problems. Another group of children who appear to be at risk for more serious emotional problems are those who are exposed to continued parental conflict. With these children the onset of problems often dates from the time of parental separation, but their symptoms persist and intensify without abatement. Parents often enmesh children in their battles with one another by forming alignments with their children against their ex-spouses or by enlisting the children as spies against the other parent. Both children and parents in these situations may require treatment. In all of the above-mentioned situations, the key factor to consider in determining whether treatment is necessary is the *duration* of the difficulties.

Children who manifest longstanding problems either at home or in the classroom may also need to consult a therapist. Those children who show a serious deterioration in their academic performance or classroom behavior would fall into this group. Children with severe peer problems may also be suffering from psychological difficulties and may need treatment. It is important to find out whether the child has friends, and to determine the quality of the child's interactions. A child with significant difficulties in peer relationships usually needs therapy.

Treatment strategies for children and parents from divorced families range from play therapy with children to individual and group psychotherapy with adults. Recently, the field has witnessed a shift in focus from the individual to the entire family system as the target for intervention. A variety of family therapy approaches, often embodying a systems model, are based on the assumption that the functioning of any family member is dependent upon the entire context of family life, which includes the system of interactions among all the members of the family.

Although there is no research on the comparative effectiveness of each of these approaches with divorced families, we believe that treatment should be oriented to the developmental phase of the child. In our previous discussion of children's responses to divorce, we emphasized that the child's developmental status governs the level of understanding of the divorce process, individual styles for coping, and defensive strategies for dealing with the stress of divorce. We also believe that intervention approaches should be rooted in a developmental context. The age of the child should be carefully considered in determining treatment interventions, goals, and in dealing with special problem areas.

As an example, we will briefly discuss a treatment approach that might be taken with the preschool child and his/her family. Because of the child's extreme dependence and limited inner resources at this early age, it is paramount to involve and work with parents. As a starting point professionals often need to educate the parents (which usually means the custodial parent) about the special needs of their preschooler and the range of expectable behaviors they might see following the divorce. Recall that following divorce, the preschool child is likely to regress behaviorally and to be worried about who will continue to provide care for him/her. According to Wallerstein and Kelly (1980) the preschool child is "likely to worry about being abandoned by both parents; is more likely than his or her older siblings to feel responsible for causing the divorce and driving one parent away; is likely to be troubled at the many separations of day and bedtime and to find these threatening and distressing; is likely to be tearful, irritable, and more aggressive; and is likely to suffer an inhibition in play" (pp. 312–313).

In working with parents about the issue of how to address their child's fears and concerns, many of the therapeutic guidelines that were outlined earlier can be useful. For example, parents should be reminded of their child's need for a predictable and consistent home environment and for increased love and security. During this period of tremendous upheaval and instability children need to be reassured that the basic necessities will be taken care of. Children can be told, for example, that they will still have enough to eat, clothes to wear, and a roof over their heads (Gardner, 1977). They may also need to be reassured that their custodial parent is not going to leave them, and parents may need to be sensitive to the importance of letting the child know where they are going and when they will return. Moreover, because of their limited cognitive ability, children at this age need explanations about what is happening, and they particularly need to be reassured that the divorce is not their fault. Parents can be warned that their child may regress and helped to understand that their child's behavior is a response to feelings of instability and an inner sense of chaos. Even though parents may have insight into the causes of this regression they should be encouraged to maintain consistent discipline. It is important to explain to parents that discipline in itself offers the children a sense of security by conveying the message that their parents *are* concerned. In general, preschool children's fears are more easily allayed by concerned parents, and their symptoms dissipate more rapidly when they receive appropriate reassurance and continued contact with both parents (Wallerstein & Kelly, 1980).

The therapist can also work conjointly with the child. At this age play and fantasy are the primary media for the child to express his/her thoughts and feelings and thereby resolve emotional conflicts. Thus, play therapy can often be an effective treatment intervention for this age group. Wallerstein and Kelly (1975) observed that preschool children were unable to obtain relief or mastery of the impact of their parents' divorce through play. However, with the special expertise of the clinician, the child can come through this difficult experience successfully via the therapeutic use of play.

Adolescents, on the other hand, appear to accept advice and direction not only from adults but also from peers. For example, they tend to seek the advice of friends who have also experienced parental divorce. This observation has led to the development of peer counseling groups as a treatment of choice for adolescents. These groups are moderately structured and are often time limited. The groups must be confidential and free from parental influence, and there is often a counterindication to siblings being in the same group. Certain topics are common in these groups, as well as in individual therapy sessions with these youngsters. They include strongly charged feelings about marital infidelity, parental dating, and sexual activity. Discussion of loyalties is predominant in group sessions when holidays are imminent, especially summer and Christmas. Adolescents also become concerned if their parents are not socially active, and they express an increased sense of responsibility and guilt.

A dominant theme throughout this chapter has been that children's reactions to divorce are governed by their developmental status. It is important that professionals, such as teachers, counselors, lawyers, and mental health professionals, who come in contact with the children of divorce be attuned to the developmental needs and age-related responses of these children. As was noted earlier, parent education can often facilitate the child's adjustment and prevent more serious problems from developing. However, when treatment is necessary, intervention approaches should be tailored to the developmental needs and symptoms of the child.

Summary

In this chapter we have attempted to critically review the available research on the effects of divorce on children and to provide suggestions for preventive approaches and treatment for members of divorced families. We first examined three research traditions: family sociological, clinical, and quasi-experimental, developmental. These research traditions were evaluated based on seven research criteria, examples of each tradition were presented, and suggestions were made for improving the quality of research within each tradition. Our discussion of children's reactions to divorce was organized from a developmental perspective. Emphasis was placed on the possible differential effects of divorce in infancy, early childhood, middle and late childhood, and adolescence. It was argued that children's responses, needs, and individual coping strategies differ depending upon their age at the time of parental separation and divorce. A developmental perspective provides not only a conceptual framework for understanding children's reactions to divorce, but also has implications for designing age-appropriate preventive and intervention approaches. Then, three important processes that help to explain the effects of divorce on children were highlighted: conflict and stress, the family as a system of interacting individuals, and attachment and carrying forward relationships. To conclude, we presented an overview of the clinical services that are available to members of divorced families and we outlined the clinical implications of the divorce research. Specific therapeutic guidelines for working with divorced parents and their children were also provided.

References

Ahrons, C. R. (1979). The binuclear family: Two households, one family. *Alternative Lifestyles, 2,* 499–515.

Ahrons, C. R. (1981). The continuing coparental relationship between divorced spouses. *American Journal of Orthopsychiatry, 5,* 415–428.

Ahrons, C. R., & Perlmutter, M. S. (1982). The relationship between former spouses: A fundamental subsystem in the remarriage family. In J. Hansen & L. Messinger (Eds.), *Therapy with remarriage families* (pp. 31–46). Rockville, MD: Aspen Systems Corporation.

Ainsworth, M. D. S. (1979). Infant-mother attachment. *American Psychologist, 34,* 932–937.

Baker, O. V., Druckman, J., Flagle, J., Camara, K., Dayton, C., Egan, J., & Cohen, A. (1980, February). *The identification and development of community-based approaches for meeting the social and emotional needs of youth and families in variant family configurations.* Final Report, American Institutes for Research, Palo Alto, CA.

Baumrind, D. (1971). Current patterns of parental authority. *Developmental Psychology Monographs,* (Pt. 2) *4*(1).

Belsky, J., & Steinberg, L. D. (1978). The effects of day care: A critical review. *Child Development, 49,* 929–949.

Biller, H. B. (1971). The mother-child relationship and the father-absent boy's personality development. *Merrill-Palmer Quarterly, 17,* 227–241.

Biller, H. B. (1969). Father dominance and sex-role development in kindergarten-age boys. *Developmental Psychology, 1,* 87–94.

Biller, H. B. (1974). *Paternal deprivation: Family, school, sexuality, and society.* Lexington, MA: D.C. Heath.

Blos, P. (1962). *On adolescence.* New York: Free Press.

Bowlby, J. *Attachment and loss,* (Vol. 1) (1969). New York: Basic Books.

Burgess, R. L. (1978). *Project interact: A study of patterns of interaction in abusive neglectful and control families.* Final report, National Center on Child Abuse and Neglect.

Camara, K. A., Baker, O., & Dayton, C. (1980). Impact of separation and divorce on youths and families. In P. M. Insel (Ed.), *Environmental variables and the prevention of mental illness.* Lexington, MA: D. C. Heath.

Carter, D. K. (1977). Counseling divorced women. *The Personnel and Guidance Journal, 55,* 537–541.

Cherlin, A. J. (1981). *Marriage, divorce and remarriage.* Cambridge, MA: Harvard Univ. Press.

Chiriboga, D. A. (1982). Adaptation to marital separation in late and earlier life. *Journal of Gerontology, 37,* 109–114.

Coletta, N. D. (1978). *Divorced mothers at two income levels: Stress, support, and child-rearing practices.* Unpublished doctoral dissertation, Cornell University.

Coletta, N. D. (1979). Support systems after divorce: Incidence and impact. *Journal of Marriage and the Family, 41,* 837–846.

Elkind, D. (1976). *Child development and education: A Piagetian perspective.* New York: Oxford University Press.

Fraiberg, S. (1977). *Every child's birthright: In defense of mothering.* New York: Basic Books.

Furstenberg, F. F., Nord, C. W., Peterson, J. L., & Zill, N. (1983). The life course of children of divorce: Marital disruption and parental contact. *American Sociological Review, 48,* 656–668.

Gardner, R. A. (1976). *Psychotherapy with children of divorce.* New York: Jason Aronson.

Gardner, R. A. (1979). *The parents book about divorce.* New York: Bantam Books.

Glick, P. C. (1979). Children of divorced parents in demographic perspective. *Journal of Social Issues, 35,* 170–182.

Gove, F. (1983). *Patterns and organizations of behavior and affective expression during the second year of life.* Unpublished doctoral dissertation, University of Minnesota.

Greif, J. B. (1982). The father-child relationship subsequent to divorce. In J. Hanson & L. Messinger (Eds.), *Therapy with remarriage families* (pp. 47–57). Rockville, MD: Aspen Systems Corporation.

Hancock, E. (1980). The dimensions of meaning and belonging in the process of divorce. *American Journal of Orthopsychiatry, 59,* 18–27.

Hess, R. D., & Camara, K. A. (1979). Post-divorce family relationships as mediating factors in the consequences of divorce for children. *Journal of Social Issues, 35,* 79–96.

Hetherington, E. M. (1966). Effects of paternal absence on sex-typed behaviors in Negro and white preadolescent males. *Journal of Personality and Social Psychology, 4,* 87–91.

Hetherington, E. M. (1972). Effects of father-absence on personality development in adolescent daughters. *Developmental Psychology, 7,* 313–326.

Hetherington, E. M. (1977). *My heart belongs to daddy: A study of the remarriages of daughters of divorcees and widows.* Unpublished manuscript, University of Virginia.

Hetherington, E. M. (1979). Divorce: A child's perspective. *American Psychologist, 34,* 851–858.

Hetherington, E. M. (1981). Children and divorce. In R. Henderson (Ed.), *Parent-child interaction: Theory, research and prospect* (pp. 33–58). New York: Academic Press.

Hetherington, E. M., & Camara, K. A. (in press). Families in transition: The processes of dissolution and reconstitution. In R. Parke (Ed.), *Review of child development research,* (Vol. 7).

Hetherington, E. M., Camara, K. A., & Featherman, D. L. (1982). *Cognitive performance, school behavior and achievement of children from one-parent households.* Report prepared for the National Institute of Education, Washington, D.C.

Hetherington, E. M., Cox, M., & Cox. R. (1977a). Beyond father absence: Conceptualization of effects of divorce. In E. M. Hetherington & R. D. Parke (Eds.), *Contemporary readings in child psychology.* New York: McGraw-Hill.

Hetherington, E. M., Cox, M., & Cox. R. (1977b, April). Divorced fathers, *Psychology Today,* pp. 42–46.

Hetherington, E. M., Cox, M., & Cox, R. (1978). The aftermath of divorce. In J. H. Stevens & M. Mathews (Eds.), *Mother-child/father-child relations.* Washington, DC: National Association for the Education of Young Children.

Hetherington, E. M., Cox, M., & Cox, R. (1979). Play and social interaction in children following divorce. *Journal of Social Issues, 35,* 26–49.

Hetherington, E. M., Cox, M., & Cox. R. (1982). The effects of divorce on parents and children. In M. E. Lamb (Ed.), *Nontraditional families* (pp. 233–288). Hillsdale, NJ: Erlbaum.

Hunt, M., & Hunt, B. (1977). *The divorce experience.* New York: McGraw-Hill.

Kagan, J., Kearsley, R. B., & Zelazo, P. R. (1978). *Infancy.* Cambridge, MA: Harvard Univ. Press.

Kelly, J. B. (1978, February). *Children and parents in the midst of divorce: Major factors contributing to differential response.* Paper presented at the National Institute of Mental Health Conference on Divorce, Washington, DC.

Kelly, J. B., & Wallerstein, J. (1976). The effects of parental divorce: Experiences of the child in early latency. *American Journal of Orthopsychiatry, 46*(1), 20–32.

Kriesberg, L. (1970). *Mothers in poverty: A study of fatherless families.* Chicago: Aldine Publishing.

Levinger, G., & Moles, O. C. (1979). *Divorce and separation: Context, causes, and consequences.* New York: Basic Books.

Longfellow, C. (1979). Divorce in context: Its impact on children. In G. Levinger & O. C. Moles (Eds.), *Divorce and separation: Context, causes, and consequences* (pp. 287–306). New York: Basic Books.

Matas, L., Arend, R., & Sroufe, L. A (1978). Continuity of adaptation in the second year: The relationship between quality of attachment and later competence. *Child Development, 49,* 547–556.

Montemayor, R. (1982, October). *Parent-adolescent conflict: A critical review of the literature.* Paper presented at the first Biennial Conference on Adolescent Research, Tucson, AZ.

Morrison, A., Gjerde, P., & Block, J. H. (1983, April). *A prospective study of divorce and its relation to family functioning.* Paper presented at the biennial meeting of the Society for Research in Child Development, Detroit, MI.

Phelps, D. W. (1969). Parental attitudes toward family life and child behavior of mothers in two-parent families. *Journal of School Health, 89,* 413–416.

Robson, B. (1982). A developmental approach to the treatment of children of divorcing parents. In J. Hansen & L. Messinger (Eds.), *Therapy with remarriage families* (pp. 59–78). Rockville, MD: Aspen Systems Corporation.

Rutter, M. (1971). Parent-child separation: Psychological effects on the children. *Journal of Child Psychology and Psychiatry, 12,* 233–256.

Rutter, M. (1978). Protective factors in children's responses to stress and disadvantage. In M. W. Kent & J. E. Rolf (Eds), *Primary prevention of psychopathology,* (Vol. 3). *Promoting social competence and coping in children.* Hanover, NJ: University Press of New England.

Santrock, J. W. (1970a). Paternal absence, sex-typing, and identification. *Developmental Psychology, 2,* 262–274.

Santrock, J. W. (1970b). Influence of onset and type of paternal absence on the first four Eriksonian developmental crises. *Developmental Psychology, 3,* 273–274.

Santrock, J. W. (1972). The relation of onset and type of father absence to cognitive development. *Child Development, 43,* 455–469.

Santrock, J. W. (1983). *Life-Span development.* Dubuque, IA: Wm. C. Brown.

Santrock, J. W. (1984). *Adolescence* (2nd ed). Dubuque, IA: Wm. C. Brown.

Santrock, J. W., & Madison, T. (in press). The social worlds of adolescents in divorced families. *Journal of Early Adolescence.*

Santrock, J. W., & Warshak, R. A. (1979). Father custody and social development in boys and girls. *Journal of Social Issues, 35,* 112–135.

Santrock, J. W., Warshak, R. A., & Elliott, G. W. (1982). Social development and parent-child interaction in father custody and stepmother families. In M. E. Lamb (Ed.), *Nontraditional families.* Hillsdale, NJ: Erlbaum.

Sears, P. S. (1951). Doll-play aggression in normal young children: Influences of sex, age, sibling status, father's absence. *Pscyhological Monographs, 65* (Whole No. 323).

Shinn, M. (1978). Father absence and children's cognitive development. *Psychological Bulletin, 85,* 295–324.

Spicer, J., & Hampe, G. (1975). Kinship interaction after divorce. *Journal of Marriage and the Family, 28,* 113–119.

Sroufe, L. A., & Fleeson, J. (1983). Attachment and the construction of relationships. Unpublished manuscript, University of Minnesota.

Sroufe, L. A., Schork, E., Motti, E., Lawroski, N., & LaFrenier, P. (in press). The role of affect in social competence. In C. Izard, J. Kagan & R. Zajonc (Eds.), *Affect, cognition, and behavior.* New York: Plenum Press.

Sroufe, L. A., & Waters, E. (1977). Attachment as an organizational construct. *Child Development, 48,* 1184–1199.

Steinberg, L. (1980). *Understanding families with young adolescents.* Carrboro, NC: Center for Early Adolescence.

Sullivan, H. S. (1953). *The interpersonal theory of psychiatry.* New York: W. W. Norton.

U.S. Department of Commerce, Bureau of the Census (1979, April). Population profile of the United States: 1978, population characteristics (Current Population Reports, Series P–20, No. 336). Washington, DC: U.S. Government Printing Office.

Vaughn, B. E., Gove, B. L., & Egeland, B. (1980). The relationship between out-of-home care and the quality of infant-mother attachment in an economically disadvantaged population. *Child Development, 51,* 1203–1214.

Wallerstein, J. S. (1982, July). *Children of divorce: Preliminary report of a ten-year follow-up.* Paper presented at the 10th International Congress of the International Association for Child and Adolescent Psychiatry and Allied Professions, Dublin, Ireland.

Wallerstein, J. S. (1984, April). *Children of divorce: Preliminary report of a ten-year follow-up of young children.* Paper presented at the annual meeting of the American Orthopsychiatry Association, Toronto.

Wallerstein, J. S., & Kelly, J. B. (1974). The effects of parental divorce: The adolescent experience. In E. J. Anthony & C. Koupernik (Eds.), *The child in his family: Children of psychiatric risk,* (Vol. 3). NY: John Wiley & Sons.

Wallerstein, J. S., & Kelly, J. B. (1975). The effects of parental divorce: Experiences of the preschool child. *Journal of the American Academy of Child Psychiatry, 14,* 600–616.

Wallerstein, J. S., & Kelly, J. B. (1976). The effects of parental divorce: Experiences of the child in later latency. *American Journal of Orthopsychiatry, 46,* 256–269.

Wallerstein, J. S., & Kelly, J. B. (1979). Children and divorce: A review. *Social Work,* 468–475.

Wallerstein, J. S., & Kelly, J. B. (1980). *Surviving the breakup: How children and parents cope with divorce.* New York: Basic Books.

Waters, E., Wippman, J., & Sroufe, L. A. (1979). Attachment, positive affect, and competence in the peer group: Two studies in construct validation. *Child Development, 50,* 821–829.

Weinraub, M., & Wolf, B. M. (1983). Effects of stress and social supports on mother-child interactions in single- and two-parent families. *Child Development, 54,* 1297–1311.

Weiss, R. (1975). *Marital separation.* New York: Basic Books.

Weiss, R. (1978, February). *Single-parent households as settings for growing up.* Paper presented at the National Institute of Mental Health on Divorce, Washington, DC.

EIGHT

The Other Woman: Phenomenological, Psychodynamic, and Therapeutic Considerations

Salman Akhtar, M.D.
Professor of Psychiatry and Human Behavior
Jefferson Medical College

For reasons that remain unclear little attention has been paid to the specific dilemmas and conflicts of the woman who becomes romantically involved with a married man. The omission is a curious one since professional literature on contemporary marriage deals with almost all other aspects of the extramarital affair in considerable detail. There exist studies of the variety of extramarital involvements (Cuber & Harroff, 1965; Beltz, 1969), their frequency (Bell & Peltz, 1974; Pietropinto & Simenauer, 1976), their conscious reasons (Ellis, 1969; Whitehurst, 1969), their unconscious motivations (Christensen, 1958; Neubeck & Schletzer, 1969), their effects upon the marriage (Spotnitz & Freeman, 1964; Hunt, 1969; Ziskin & Ziskin, 1973), and the moral and ethical questions that beleaguer such relationships (Neubeck, 1969; Ellis, 1969). What is not to be found in this literature or in monographs exclusively dedicated to the study of long-term, extramarital affairs (Block, 1978; Strean, 1980) is an in-depth account of "the other woman," that is, the woman who is having an affair with a married man.[1]

The striking paucity of literature on this topic is evident in the fact that a Medlar computer search extending over the past 10 years and surveying multiple language resource materials retrieved only two relevant citations. The first of these was a study (Hollander, 1976) which compared 10 single women who had been repeatedly involved with married men with 11 women who had never had an affair or a casual sexual encounter with a married man. The instruments used were a personal interview, the Roe-Siegelman Parent-Child Relations Questionnaire II, the MMPI, and the Thematic Apperception Test. The study revealed an excessively close or intense father-daughter relationship and a poorer mother-daughter relationship among "the other women" and no significant differences in hysterical and masochistic character traits between the two groups. The second citation referred to a study (Richardson, 1979) of the "management styles" used by 26 single women involved in long-term, intimate relationships with married men and the correlation of these styles with the manner in which the liaison was finally terminated. It was found that women who employed "submissive management styles" felt powerless and emotionally devastated at the end of the affair. They had difficulty letting go of the affair and continued to be distressed for long periods afterwards. On the other hand, women "who adopt a dominance management style are more likely to initiate the sudden termination, choose to opt out in a slow, sustained withdrawal, and avoid the drag outs" (Richardson, 1979, p. 412). In either case, the study pointed out, such relationships are difficult to mourn and are often not successfully given up by these women.

While both these studies shed light on important aspects of the lives of "the other women," their data may have limited clinical applicability. The emphasis of these studies is on overt behavior, with relatively little acknowledgment given to the intrapsychic forces at work. Their data are solely based upon conscious recall with little attention paid to the possibility of potential distortion by unconscious factors. Their backdrop is social rather than clinical. The other women in these studies were volunteer subjects and not patients seeking professional help. All of the above tends to restrict the usefulness of these studies for clinical purposes. The same can perhaps be said of the portraits of the other women in literature and

---

[1]The same can be said of the literature's disregard of the man who repeatedly and exclusively gets involved with married women. Block (1978), in an informal, sociological study of extramarital relationships, does briefly comment upon such men. The somewhat clumsy but insistently nonsexist title of his book *The Other Woman, The Other Man* is a testimony to his having paid attention to this matter. My own decision to restrict this chapter to "the other woman" is based upon a simple clinical reality. I have never been consulted by a man who was intimately involved with a married woman and who sought psychiatric help for problems leading to and/or emanating from such involvement.

movies.[2] One is therefore left with little clinically based information in this area. This is puzzling since such women often seek professional advice and their anguish may be quite familiar to most practicing psychotherapists.

The purpose of this chapter is to highlight the psychodynamic factors that lead a woman to select a married man as her romantic partner. It will also attempt to describe certain specific issues in the psychotherapy of such women. However, before embarking on these topics let me describe the other women I have seen in my clinical practice and explain their reasons for seeking psychiatric consultation.

DESCRIPTIVE AND PHENOMENOLOGICAL CHARACTERISTICS

My impressions are based upon a clinical sample of eight other women seen in brief consultations and upon an additional two such patients treated in psychoanalytic psychotherapy. In developing a descriptive profile of the other woman I have attempted to stay away from two major sources of distortion: the description of such individuals by either a male patient who is having an extramarital affair or a female patient whose husband is involved with another woman. Such descriptions—and I have heard plenty of them—tend to be affectively charged, simplistic, and one-sided. Men who are having affairs describe the other woman in unrealistically glowing terms. Among the adjectives and phrases they frequently use are *wonderful, kind, warmhearted, unique, deeply human, really compassionate, a beautiful person,* and so on. Wives of such men on the other hand portray the other woman as basically a self-centered, immature, and manipulative individual with dubious moral standards. Both husbands and wives may add a few qualifying statements to make their descriptions appear well rounded. However, the depth of perception thus conveyed has never failed to impress me as largely intellectual and not genuinely felt. It is for these reasons that I decided to restrict my phenomenological data base to

---

[2] The portrayal of the mistress and the other woman in Western literature is a topic worthy of independent study. My own impression (admittedly based on limited knowledge of both fields) is that the topic has constantly fascinated writers and moviemakers. While the classics and even the contemporary, serious literature may fare better, current popular fiction, television, and movies fail to rise above stereotypes in their depiction of the other woman. One frequent stereotype is that of the other woman being a sensually charged, glamorous, and hence primitively idealized part-object (e.g., screen movies *Just Tell Me What You Want,* 1979; *Midlife Crazy,* 1983; television movie *His Mistress,* 1984; popular Joy Fielding novel *The Other Woman,* 1983). Other depictions include those of a confused but well-meaning rescuer of a troubled and unhappily married man (e.g., television movie *The Other Woman,* 1983), a deeply conflicted masochist (e.g., screen movie *A Touch of Class,* 1973), and finally, a symbol of the plight of contemporary women in a male-dominated world (e.g., Marilyn French's novel *The Bleeding Heart,* 1980). Obviously these are only individual facets of the same, multidetermined and highly complex phenomenon: a woman's involvement with an unavailable man.

actual and direct clinical contact with women who were repeatedly and/or chronically involved with married men.

Demographic Profile

The age range for the other women in my clinical sample was from 27 to 40, the mean age being 32.5 years. Nine of the 10 other women were white and one was black. Five were divorced and the remaining five had never been married. Being divorced or single did not seem correlated with the age factor. Almost all these individuals had had some education beyond high school, with three of them holding college or postgraduate degrees. All were employed. Their jobs included secretary, schoolteacher, nurse, air hostess, buyer for a large department store, clinical psychologist, and professional journalist. All these women were financially secure and independent and most lived by themselves.

It is difficult to assess the significance of these demographic features in view of the small size of the clinical sample and in the absence of a reasonable control group. Indeed, it is possible that no difference on numerous demographic variables will be found should a statistical comparison be made between this sample of the other women and the remaining female patients whom I have evaluated or treated over the same period of time. Somewhat impressionistically however I am struck by the fact that none of these women were currently married, a fact that appears significant when contrasted with the marital status of other female patients I have seen over the same time period. This finding can have many meanings. For instance, it may be taken as evidence of these women's inherent inability to establish or maintain a deep and full relationship with a man, or it may be interpreted simply as a referral artifact. In other words, it can be argued (Sands, 1978) that there are in reality equal numbers of both married and unattached other women, but that only the single and divorced ones seek psychiatric help. This line of thinking would suggest that married other women have better support systems and greater social taboos to contend with and that both of these factors minimize the appearance of these women at the professional's doorstep.

Yet another explanation for the preponderance of unattached women who are chronically involved with married men would invoke the "natural selection" hypothesis; that is, there are more single and divorced other women because married men are more attracted to unattached women since it is logistically easier for these men to have affairs with them than to have affairs with married women (Block, 1978). While this explanation has the advantage of appealing to common sense, it does tend to underestimate the complexity of human relationships and the extent to which people will go in order to appease their inner demons. Clearly, these three hypotheses do not exhaust the possibilities. The purpose of this brief digression is therefore not to provide conclusive answers but to point toward a potentially interesting clinical finding and to raise questions about it. Are there really more single and divorced persons among the other woman group? Why?

Clinical Features

The most common presenting clinical feature in this group of patients was depression. The dysthymic complaints however were not associated with impairment of job related abilities or with significant vegetative disturbance. Even the mood disturbance was ill-sustained, with periods of relative relief interspersed with periods of guilt, impotent rage, bleak despondency, and aching loneliness. The depressive feelings were most marked around holidays that these women often had to spend without their lovers. Feelings of anxiety, personal insecurity, and low self-esteem were frequent in the group. Most had sought help following a crisis with their lovers, though only one third of the patients revealed their involvement with a married man in the very first interview. Others, somewhat better defended individuals, indicated that they were troubled by their relationships with men and only in later sessions elaborated upon the turmoil of being involved with a married man. Sooner or later almost of them displayed painful, conflicted, and deeply ambivalent relationships with their lovers, though the mechanisms they employed in dealing with such ambivalence varied considerably. It became apparent that underneath their seemingly well-adapted, poised, and purposive social existences, most of these women were quite distressed and were preoccupied with this particular relationship in their lives.

The way these women described their lovers caught my attention and I began to suspect that perhaps there were two distinct subgroups in the clinical sample. The first group were women who seemed capable of consciously experiencing deep ambivalence toward their lovers. They described their lovers as unhappily married men who were nonetheless charming, handsome, sophisticated, and efficient in their work. However, at the same time they also felt that these men were weak, childlike, potentially callous, afraid of genuine intimacy, selfish, and unreliable. These women appeared constantly puzzled by what they recognized to be contradictory aspects of their lovers' characters.

They were also disturbed by their own ambivalence toward these men. While the painful ambivalence came readily to the surface in the clinical situation, careful scrutiny revealed that these women had, in their day-to-day lives, handled this ambivalence differently. They compartmentalized their minds, thus keeping the two contradictory attitudes separate from each other. This compartmentalization was akin to what Freud (1927/1957), in one of the many ways he used the term, described as the *splitting* of the ego. In describing this mechanism Freud specifically referred to the fetishist, whom he saw as simultaneously acknowledging and disavowing the absence of penis in women by his use of the fetish. Freud saw the ego as effecting a cleavage or division of itself so that it could contain two contradictory psychic configurations. It should be parenthetically noted here that the currently popular use of the term *splitting* occurs in a considerably different context (Akhtar & Byrne, 1983). However, the current way in which the term is used has relevance for how the remaining other women viewed their lovers.

While the other women in the second group also had mixed feelings toward their lovers, they seemed unable to experience the two sets of feelings simultaneously. As a result they failed to hold onto an in-depth, composite picture of him in their minds. At times they experienced him as loving, witty, empathic, and sexually gratifying. At other times, usually following a canceled date or some other disappointment, they viewed him as petty, cruel, dishonest, and fundamentally untrustworthy. The two descriptions carried comparable conviction, and alternately each appeared to these patients as valid and truly representative of the "real" nature of the men with whom they were involved. The disregard they showed toward the discrepancy in their two accounts was striking. Upon being confronted with this discrepancy during diagnostic or psychotherapeutic sessions, most of these patients *intellectually* recognized the inconsistency but *affectively* dismissed it as irrelevant. Some however felt anxiety and annoyance at being confronted. In either case it became apparent that the two images of their lovers existed independently of each other in their minds. When one of these internal images—object representations, to be precise—was affectively, cognitively, and behaviorally active the other was blandly "forgotten," and vice versa.

This propensity toward "forgetting" was obviously a manifestation of defensive splitting. However, unlike the first group of other women, the use of splitting in this group did not seem restricted to the internal image of their lovers. It was pervasive and included almost all their significant object relations. It also affected their view of themselves. Their knowledge of the real objects was, in general, dim as it was determined by the need-satisfying potential of the external objects rather than by the objects' autonomous existence and inherent qualities. In addition, their selves were not solidly established; hence, these patients were vulnerable to extreme oscillations of their self-esteem. All this was reminiscent of the primitive splitting that is associated with a borderline personality organization (Kernberg, 1967).

The two groups of other women were distinct, though admittedly with some phenomenological overlap in regard to other clinical features as well. The first group had few overt symptoms besides the occasional dysthymic complaints associated with the relationships with their lovers.

They constantly attempted to "figure out" their men and frequently ruminated about the moral correctness of their involvements. Sexually they were reasonably comfortable, though at times they did experience anxiety and guilt about having sexual relations with a married man. Romantic love appeared to be of greater significance to them rather than actual sexual intimacy. They valued friendships in general and most had maintained other deep friendships of many years' duration.

These women had solid ethnic, vocational, and sociocultural identities; and their future plans, though inevitably colored by their troubled relationships with the married men, were reasonably realistic and quite clear to them. Finally, though unconscious masochistic strivings were evident in their involvement with less than optimally available men, these other women did not display overt self-destructive behaviors.

The second group on the other hand was comprised of women who had many diffuse symptoms besides their involvements with married men. They had had many other frustrating and futile relationships with men in the past, they had fewer friends, and they had experimented with drugs more often than the women in the first group. They were sexually less inhibited. (One of them had been quite promiscuous in past.) They drank more and all of them had attempted suicide at one or more occasions in their lives. The other women in this group showed confusion about their identities, experienced feelings of emptiness, and had lived their lives in a fragmented fashion over the years. One of them, for instance, described her life as "floating in the air, wanting to put an anchor somewhere but not knowing where or in what." Another displayed contradictory character traits and "as if" (Deutsch, 1942) qualities, in addition to feeling compelled to put on makeup and her business clothes—even on weekends—since she felt empty and directionless without such external manifestations of her identity.

All of this suggested the presence in these women of the "syndrome of identity diffusion" (Erikson, 1959; Kernberg, 1980; Akhtar, 1984). This suspicion was further strengthened by the fact that they also showed many of the cardinal manifestations of primitive splitting (Akhtar & Byrne, 1983): inability to experience ambivalence, impaired decision making, intensification of affects, ego-syntonic impulsivity, and oscillations of self-esteem.

Developmental Backgrounds

It should be mentioned at the outset that most of the data on the developmental backgrounds of these patients were gathered in brief consultations. Hence, to what extent the recollections of childhood and early family life by these women were defensively altered in the manner of a "personal myth" (Kris, 1956) is difficult to determine. One can of course be more certain about the background of the two patients who were seen in psychoanalytic psychotherapy. The brief accounts that follow should therefore be taken as trends in certain directions, and not as pathognomonic developmental antecedents of a person becoming an "other woman." Human psychopathology is far too complex for such linear determinism.

The two groups of other women had both similarities and differences in their developmental backgrounds. With respect to their similarities, both groups seemed to have come from small, nuclear families with few extended relations, a factor that tends to maximize the impact of parental psychopathology on growing children (Modell, 1983). Also, women in both groups recalled experiencing feelings of inferiority while growing up. Some related these feelings to rivalry with an older sibling, usually a brother, who they felt had been better treated by the parents. Others more directly related their sense of inferiority to being a girl. Finally, almost all the women in both groups complained about having been unfairly treated, inadequately appreciated, and harshly judged by their fathers.

There were many differences however in the developmental backgrounds of the two groups. The three women who recalled themselves as having been happy as children all belonged to the first group. None in the second group remembered herself as having been a happy child. All four women in the second group recalled having been beaten—two rather frequently and badly—by their fathers, while none of the women in the first group were beaten as children. Moreover, while the women in the first group considered their mothers as generally affectionate though a little strict, the women in the second group reported their mothers to be rejecting, critical, and unempathic. Their portrayals of their mothers were regarded as reasonably valid in light of what was learned through the psychotherapy of one other woman from the first group and another from the second. The mother of the first type of other women was comfortable with her own femininity but the mother of the more troubled, second type was not at ease with her own womanliness.[3]

Finally, the two groups differed in their accounts of the latency and adolescent phases of their lives. Women in the first group had had reasonably pleasant, energetic school lives, many friends, and painful but not disastrous adolescences. Women in the second group however had been chronically unhappy during latency, had day-dreamed a lot, and were generally withdrawn and shy. During their adolescences they had had greater difficulties with their parents, indulged in more sexual experimen-

---

[3]Bernstein (1983) suggests that important among the factors that predispose a girl to future masochistic tendencies is an "early identification with a mother who has a negative or depreciatory attitude toward her body, genitals, and femininity" (p. 483). This factor seemed to be one basis for the considerable masochism that was evident in the second group of other women.

tation, and seem to have needed tighter external controls over their behavior than the women in the first group.

One curious finding referring to the entire sample was that the fathers of 4 of the 10 other women had themselves had extramarital affairs about which their daughters had had at least a vague knowledge. Since neither of the two women seen over a protracted length of time had such fathers, it is difficult to hypothesize that the fathers' extramarital affairs played a role in the daughters' subsequent involvement with married men. Clearly however factors of continued and prolonged oedipal titillation, identification with the fortunate rival, and identification with the aggressor may all be at work here.

Diagnostic Categories

Seven of the 10 other women in this sample belonged to the first group mentioned above. These women appeared to be deeply feminine, mildly seductive individuals who were prone to affectualization of their relationships with older, unavailable men. They had solidly established ego identities and fairly strict and internalized superego systems. Their capabilities for experiencing genuine guilt, sadness, mourning, empathy, and concern, though somewhat compromised in the specific area of their romantic involvements, were generally intact. They were also capable of peaceful aloneness. Almost all of them displayed intact "autonomous functions of the ego" (Hartmann, 1958). Despite frequent emotional crises in their romantic affairs, they were remarkably stable and appropriate at their jobs. Their object relations appeared to be of the "total" type insofar as these permitted ambivalence, separateness, and the ability to maintain libidinal ties despite temporary frustrations. Their intrapsychic conflicts were of the "structural" type (Arlow & Brenner, 1964), and their defenses centered around repression. These patients therefore displayed evidence of a "higher level" (Kernberg, 1970) character organization. The descriptive nosological label appropriate for most of them was "hysterical personality disorder," though obsessional, depressive, and masochistic features existed in them as well. Within the hysterical personality range (Zetzel, 1968) itself, there was some variation regarding the level of integration and functioning, though none of these women appeared to be what Lazare (1971) has labeled the "sick hysteric."

The second group, comprising three other women, displayed considerably different characteristics. Self-destructiveness was pronounced in these women. Their emotional lability was generalized and diffuse. There were few, if any, conflict free areas in their lives. They experienced much confusion about their identities. "Non-specific manifestations of ego weakness" (Kernberg, 1967, p. 660) were evident in some of them. These included lack of anxiety tolerance, lack of impulse control, and lack of developed sublimatory channels. These women had limited capacity for empathy, concern, and mourning. This was most evident in their response to disappointments with their lovers. Under such circumstances they either used flat denial or were filled with consciously experienced impotent rage. Thus, not only was their capacity for mourning and sadness limited, but their ability to experience inner guilt was also compromised. Their superego functions, though archaic and sadistic, were vulnerable to reprojections and externalizations. They frequently experienced fear and shame rather than genuine guilt. Their intrapsychic dilemmas were of the nature of "object-relations conflicts" (Dorpat, 1976), rather than intersystemic, structural conflicts and their defensive operations revolved around splitting, denial, and projective identification. These patients therefore seemed to display from "intermediate level" to "lower level" (Kernberg, 1970) character pathology. The nosological labels that seemed most appropriate to this group included "narcissistic" and "schizoid personality disorders." A borderline personality organization (Kernberg, 1967) was clearly discernable beneath these women's overt narcissistic level of functioning. One other woman in this group however was more overtly borderline, and seemed to have experienced occasional psychotic breaks of brief duration in the past.

PSYCHODYNAMICS

Why does a woman who is unattached and has other options open to her get involved with a man who is married to someone else? What internal forces compel her to have a relationship so encumbered by societal taboos, logistical nightmares, and personal torment? What anxieties prevent her from making a different choice? What profound joy helps her to overlook the deep frustrations of such an entanglement? Where is the wellspring of her adamant hope, and what pain makes it unspeakably difficult for her to let go of this relationship? These and many other similar questions demand answers when one encounters an other woman in the course of clinical work. Clearly, there are no simple answers. Being or becoming an other woman seems, like any other neurotic symptom or character trait, overdetermined and subject to the "principle of multiple function" (Waelder, 1930).

The involvement with a married man may have many different meanings, some of which may exist simultaneously. Such a relationship may thus be an enactment of certain infantile instinctual wishes and at the same time an execution of superego induced punishments over these wishes. It may have its ontogenetic origins in the oedipal and/or the preoedipal period of development and its multifaceted phenomenology may contain important unconscious fantasies about oneself, others, or both. It should also be pointed out that while many different psychodynamic explanations underlie the syndrome of the other woman some constellations were more frequent in the first group mentioned above while others were seen more often in the second group. Which constellations were present seemed predominantly determined by the level of character organization. In general, the "higher" (Kernberg, 1970) the level of character organization, the more being an other woman seemed to have oedipal underpinnings. Similarly, in the other woman with an overt or covert borderline personality organization, the more frequent mechanism appeared to be the search for an "all-good" object as a defense against a paranoid and cynical distortion of all other relationships. These are however generalizations and should be taken as such.

Caution is also required in consideration of the psychodynamic explanations of a woman's involvement with a married man since the categories that follow are neither intended to be exhaustive nor are the various factors necessarily mutually exclusive. Only certain themes, repeatedly encountered either clinically or in the literature, are highlighted with a tacit acknowledgment of etiological heterogeneity and hitherto undetected mechanisms. Needless to add that the focus here is on the intrapsychic, since the external realities can only facilitate and not cause such involvements.[4]

Unresolved Oedipal Longings

In one of his papers on the psychology of love, Freud (1910/1957) described a special type of love object chosen by certain men. This object is characterized by two "necessary conditions for loving." The first of these preconditions is

> that there should be an "injured third party"; it stipulates that the person in question shall never choose as his love-object a woman who is disengaged—that is, an unmarried girl or an unattached married woman—but only to whom another man can claim right of possession as a husband, fiance, or friend. . . . The second precondition is. . . . that a woman who is chaste and whose reputation is irreproachable never exercises an attraction. . . . but only a woman who is in some way or other of bad repute sexually, whose fidelity and reliability are open to some doubt. (p. 166)

In addition to these two preconditions, Freud described two characteristics of the man's behavior towards his love object: (1) the consuming nature of this involvement, and (2) the powerful urge to rescue the woman he loves. Freud suggested that these four features, present to a variable

[4]This is not to deny that most lay writers (e.g., Sands, 1978), as well as certain professionals (e.g., Ellis, 1969), hold the contemporary social realities (e.g., relaxed sexual mores) responsible for involvements between married men and single women. In my view external reality can merely facilitate the expression of intrapsychic tendencies. Its etiological role in extramarital liaisons is contributory, not causative.

extent in each individual case, emanated from a growing boy's sensuous longings toward his mother and were defensively disguised expressions of those longings. The precondition of the woman belonging to someone else and the attitude of overvaluation seem quite directly derived from the mother image. The "injured third party" of course is none other than the father. Freud saw the precondition of sexual ill-repute as a cynical exaggeration by a child of his newly acquired knowledge of his mother's sexual activity with his father. Finally, the rescue motif, consciously rationalized as an attempt to protect the supposedly weak woman, has a meaning and history of its own that is related to certain other aspects of the oedipus complex.

The reason for mentioning all this in some detail is that the other women reported here showed a similar proclivity when it came to choosing a love-object.[5] They fell in love with men who were already attached and whose sexual reputation carried at least a "faint breath of scandal" (Freud, 1910/1957); a few of these men were openly promiscuous. All these other women were deeply and intensely involved with their lovers. Most of them thought that they were giving these men the love and understanding that their allegedly cold and unempathic wives had failed to give them. This appeared to be a variant of the rescue fantasy described by Freud. There was thus considerable phenomenological evidence of oedipal underpinnings to these womens' involvements with married men.

In the case of one such woman seen in psychoanalytic psychotherapy this was amply confirmed. Intense, romantic, and guilt ridden attachment to the father and hostile rivalry with the mother—frequently appearing in the patient's associations as the current lover's wife—emerged as the main dynamic theme in this particular case. Interestingly, this woman's initial description of the father as harsh and critical came to be understood in different terms during her treatment. He had appeared harsher to her than perhaps he was in reality because he had failed to appreciate the depth of her love for him. Also, viewing her father in this manner served a defensive purpose vis-à-vis her erotic longings for him, in addition to assuaging her guilt over such longings.

Masochism

Almost all the other women complained of the chronic suffering that resulted from being involved with married men. They felt constantly deprived of their lovers' affections. They felt treated as second-class citizens every time they were excluded from an important social function, a reli-

---

[5]It was almost 10 years after his description of such object choices in men that Freud (1920/1957) demonstrated the occurrence of precisely the same type of object choice in women. However, the case was one of a homosexual girl and not of an "other woman."

gious festival, an anniversary, and so on in which they would have participated had they been married to their lovers. They experienced sadness, humiliation, and resentment at having to keep their romances secret. The assertions of some other women that a secret liaison was somehow more romantic than one publicly acknowledged often proved to be a defensive rationalization. Despite all this torment these women clung to their married lovers. Or was it *because* of this torment? In instances where consultations went beyond one or two interviews and especially in the two cases seen in psychoanalytic psychotherapy, it did appear that one of the many needs being gratified by such a relationship was that of suffering.

The sources of this masochism[6] were however quite varied. In the case briefly mentioned above, a prominent motive for seeking pain and suffering was an "unconscious sense of guilt" (Freud, 1924/1957, p.166) related to unresolved oedipal longings. This woman felt that she was not allowed a painless relationship. For her, the involvement with a married man was both a near actualization of an oedipal wish, and a punishment for having this desire. In the other case seen in-depth however there existed additional and perhaps more significant origins of the need to suffer. This particular woman had had a very traumatic childhood. She was the fourth and youngest daughter of her parents and she felt that she had been a burden to them. She remembered frequently being ridiculed by her parents for her large build and for her "unfeminine" behavior (which *they* perhaps unconsciously encouraged). At the same time her mother constantly bemoaned the plight of women and repeatedly told the patient that she was unfortunate to have been born a girl in this male dominated world. The patient had grown up feeling unworthy of making demands, secretly ashamed of being a woman, and with a self-representation of being a burden to others. The progression from such an internal state of affairs to masochism is expectable (Reich, 1954; Blum, 1976; Bernstein, 1983), though it may take varying routes. A degraded and ugly self-representation may lower what one may confidently seek and result in a phenomenological masochism. Such a self-representation may itself result from the turning inward of the anger directed at frustrating objects of childhood, a "secondary masochism" (Freud, 1924/1957). This particular kind of interpersonal relationship may be unconsciously recreated again and again (Bergler, 1969) in order to achieve belated mastery and/or to maintain a semblance of object relationships, since it has now become seemingly the only way of object contact (Berliner, 1958).

In view of all of the above, it was not surprising that for this patient her lover not only stood for the prohibited oedipal father but more importantly for the disappointing father who failed to help her extricate herself

---

[6]The term *masochism*, frequently employed "with little consistency and at varied levels of abstraction" (Maleson, 1984), is being used here in its purely descriptive sense.

from the mother during the separation-individuation process (Mahler, Pine, & Bergman, 1975). Beyond that of course, her lover represented the deeply conflicted and frustrating image(s) of her preoedipal mother from whom a satisfactory separation had not been achieved. The involvement with a married man and the associated masochism here were more a result of preoedipal than of oedipal conflicts. Seemingly genital strivings for the father were being used as a substitute gratification of the oral-dependent needs that were frustrated by the mother. However, the traumatic experiences—I prefer the term *experiences* since it encompasses both the actual events and their internal processing by the child—of childhood mentioned above may result in additional dynamics that underlie such object choices.

The Continued Need for an Omnipotent External Object

Individuals who have successfully resolved the separation-individuation process (Mahler, 1974; Mahler et al., 1975) no longer demand absolute perfection from their love objects. They come to accept the reality that "all-good" external objects—derivatives of the mother of the symbiotic phase—do not exist. Hence, these individuals can accept limitations in others and experience ambivalence toward them. Individuals who have failed in resolving the separation-individuation process however continue to demand perfection from themselves and from others. They keep searching for blissful union with bountiful others, a sort of "symbiotic omnipotence" (Khan, 1969) in which all aggression is split off and denied.

The three other women with a borderline personality organization displayed a tendency to use such primitive idealization toward others. This mechanism, according to Kernberg refers to

> the tendency to see external objects as totally good, in order to make sure that they can protect one against the "bad" objects, that they cannot be contaminated, spoiled, or destroyed by one's own aggression or by that projected onto other objects. . . . One other function of such an ideal object is to serve as a recipient for omnipotent identification, for sharing in the greatness of the idealized object as a protection against aggression, and as a direct gratification of narcissistic needs. (Kernberg, 1967)

The use of primitive idealization, generally alongside the defensive mechanism of splitting, creates powerful, unrealistic, and "all-good" objects. Reliance upon such objects is badly needed by individuals with borderline personality organization since they lack a sustained, internal feeling of safety and optimism. In the absence of such "emotional object constancy" (Mahler et al., 1975, p. 166) they are vulnerable to the dreadful, subjective experience of inner emptiness (Kernberg, 1975; Singer, 1977a, 1977b), as well as to the lure of potentially ecstatic encounters. Their need and search for all-good objects is further heightened by their weak ego's inability to contain ambivalence, a necessary condition of all deep human relationships. All these features of borderline personality organization, along with the deficient superego integration, predispose such individuals to a peculiar kind of interpersonal relationship. This relationship invites idealization, limits actual knowledge of the love object, discourages genuine intimacy, and conspires to discharge aggression exclusively outside the boundaries of the relationship. Obviously, however "loving" such a relationship may overtly appear, its internal psychological structure runs counter to the prerequisites of mature love (Bergman, 1971; Kernberg, 1976a). Although devotion to cult leaders more graphically illustrates a relationship born out of primitive idealization, the attachment of the three other women with borderline character organization to their lovers was not much different. These women knew little about their lovers. Especially striking was their lack of curiosity about how their men came to be married to such allegedly cold wives in the first place. It is this aspect that most clearly distinguishes primitive idealization from mature forms of idealization. In the latter the knowledge of the external object is deep and despite idealization some ambivalence is permissible.

Other Psychodynamic Factors

The three dynamic factors commented upon so far, (1) oedipal strivings, (2) masochism, and (3) a continued need for omnipotent external objects, are neither totally mutually exclusive nor do they exhaust the list. I do however regard them as the more frequent and thus the more important psychodynamics to consider. Among other factors is the formation of a "negative identity" (Erikson, 1959) with the resultant desire to live in a drastically different fashion from the one dictated by parental mores. Often however the need for such deviation emanates from the deep-seated awareness of one's lack of internal separation from the parental introjects of childhood. Another factor which may facilitate such relationships among women with low self-esteem is the manner in which their lovers treat them, especially in the beginning phases of their relationship. These men pour out their complicated and often tragic life histories during hours and hours of intense conversation with these women. They seek warmth, empathy, and understanding. While this kind of self-disclosure seems phenomenologically real, what these men are often seeking is absolution for guilt, mutual denial of their aggression, and encouragement to further project and split off their hostile introjects.

All this leads to a sort of transference idealization of the other woman in which she is viewed as a savior, friend, mother, therapist, and lover—in essence, someone badly needed to depend upon. It is this feeling of being needed that may be intoxicatingly pleasurable to women with low self-esteem and cause them to get more and more deeply involved in such relationships. Yet another common factor which may facilitate such relationships is a fear of intimacy (Berdy, 1984). This fear is frequently an outgrowth of childhood disappointments in parental responses to one's needs, and is especially true in the case of schizoid individuals. The self of such an individual, having felt unsupported in its once vigorous needs for attachment and interaction, has undergone a split between a superficially compliant, social, false self, and an inwardly withdrawn, trapped, inexperienced true self (Winnicott, 1976; Guntrip, 1968). To such individuals, the semirelationship with a man who is already attached and hence is not available for a fuller relationship may offer a desirable compromise between their deep longings to love and their reflexive but powerful tendency to retreat into interpersonal indifference.

Finally, it should be kept in mind that the manifest content of a character trait or a symptom is not a very reliable guide to its childhood origins or its current psychodynamic meanings. In order to understand the nature of a symptom—in this case involvement of women with married men—it is necessary to take a deeper look at the entire character organization. This would mean taking into account the developmental history, the nature of intrapsychic conflicts, the defensive organization, the state of the ego and its identity, the degree of superego integration, and the depth of internal object relationships. The initial formulations about a patient may thus serve only as guidelines since a deeper understanding of this sort is often not possible unless the patient is involved in ongoing, in-depth psychotherapeutic work.

SPECIFIC ISSUES IN THE PSYCHOTHERAPY OF "THE OTHER WOMAN"

One may treat an other woman with supportive psychotherapy, psychoanalytic psychotherapy, or psychoanalysis. The choice of treatment modality would depend upon the treatment goals,[7] the nature of present-

---

[7]It should not be automatically assumed that the other woman seeks psychotherapy to become able to relinquish her painful romantic involvement. Though this is frequently the case, there are other conscious and unconscious motives for entering treatment. Prominent among these are seeking moral absolution and searching for more adaptive skills in the face of a puzzling relationship. All these have to be taken into account while deciding upon therapeutic strategies and goals. One especially difficult situation is when the other woman is quite schizoid. Therapeutic zeal based upon naive theoretical purity may dissolve this "pathological" relationship only to leave her in a bleak and potentially dangerous, object-less despair. Yet another unusual clinical situation (A. Goldman, personal communication) is when the other woman becomes overtly symptomatic and seeks help only after learning that her married lover has finally decided to leave his wife and to marry her. She thus acts in a manner reminiscent of "those wrecked by success" (Freud, 1916/1957, p. 316). All this suggests that there is considerable variation in clinical phenomenology, psychodynamics, character organization, and the realistic situations of various other women, a variation that affects the objectives of her treatment.

ing complaints, the urgency with which symptomatic relief is required, the level of character organization, the degree of analyzability, the reality situations as these affect the overall quality of the patient's life, and the feasibility of an ongoing treatment process. Before such a choice can be made a careful diagnostic assessment is required. In addition to the conventional aspects of anamnesis, a detailed description of the affair should be obtained. Attention should be paid not only to what is being said but also to how it is being said, as well as to what is not being said and why is it being withheld. Most important however is the assessment of the level of character organization.

In general, if the other woman presents with a higher level character organization, displays other evidences of analyzability (e.g., Glover, 1954; Joseph, 1967; Tyson & Sandler, 1971; Lower, Escoll, & Huxster, 1972) and the affair is not presenting acute and dramatic distress but is a source of mild albeit lingering and chronic difficulty, the treatment of choice should be psychoanalysis. If however there are more pressing needs to resolve matters relating to the affair and/or there is doubt about the level of character organization and analyzability, then face-to-face psychoanalytic psychotherapy on a twice (preferably thrice) weekly basis should be recommended. Finally, if the affair is on the end and/or the patient shows marked ego weakness and/or presents in a crisis situation, a more reality oriented, supportive approach should be undertaken.

Since it is my impression that the majority of other women seeking psychotherapeutic help belong to the second of the three categories outlined above, I will restrict my comments to this group. Even in this realm of psychoanalytic psychotherapy I am aware that each individual other woman will pose unique dilemmas and challenges. It is therefore not possible to generalize regarding the problems one might expect and the therapeutic strategies one might choose. One can only say that like any other psychoanalytic psychotherapy, such tratment will not involve the development of a full-blown, transference neurosis nor will it lead to the resolution of transference by interpretation alone. Also, there will be only an incomplete genetic reconstruction of various transference developments and the treatment will include supportive and ego-strengthening elements. While these comments are valid in a general way, there are three specific aspects of psychoanalytic psychotherapy with the other woman that need further comment. These are: (1) the patient's use of external reality, in this case the involvement with a married man as a massive resistance to revealing, experiencing, learning, and changing; (2) the effect of carrying a secret upon the patient's overall life and specifically upon her engagement in the psychotherapeutic work; and (3) the potential countertransference difficulties in the treatment of a woman involved with a married man.

Reality as a Resistance

One major problem in doing psychoanalytic psychotherapy with the other woman is the continued presence of a painful external reality in her life. To a much greater extent than women with more conventional relationships, she has to contend with social taboos, logistical difficulties, broken promises, and lonely holidays in the context of a romantic relationship. Not only does she have to constantly mourn her own unmet yearnings but she also has to repeatedly digest and "metabolize" the more than usually traumatic aspects of this relationship. Moreover, she is not the only one who has mixed feelings about the relationship. Her married lover too has conflicting and contradictory stances toward their liaison. He is usually a troubled, narcissistic individual who idealizes her but cannot provide her with sustained empathy and concern. All this leads the other woman to seek help with dysthymic suffering which has both intrapsychic and interpersonal determinants.

It is this interpersonal component that causes difficulties in an insight oriented work. The patient tends to focus on it and to avoid exploring potential intrapsychic contributions to her malady. She yields to the temptation to view her distress as largely related to and at times even as being caused by her lover's attitude. She presents "evidences" of *his* indecision, *his* ambivalence, *his* cruelty in some sessions, and of *his* kindness and *his* wanting a deeper relationship during other sessions. She sees the "push and pull" of their relationship as largely coming from him and not as representing two sides of her own intrapsychic conflict. This externalization is a major resistance in the therapy of the other woman.

Three things need to be kept in mind about this matter. First, a head-on confrontation with this externalization propensity is generally not very productive. Such an approach may enhance resistance causing the psychotherapeutic sessions to become quasi-legal battles where the patient and the therapist both present contrary "evidences" to prove their points. Indeed, the patient may soon drop out of the treatment. It is therefore more tactful and productive (and perhaps even more truthful) to acknowledge in a straightforward manner the real difficulties of the relationship and not to dismiss the patient's elaboration of the affair as "only a resistance." Indeed, it is through listening to the detailed description of this relationship that the therapist can begin to discern the unfulfilled needs and hence various potential transference paradigms of the patient. Paradoxically, it is paying attention to the affair (though clearly more at the beginning of the treatment than during its more advanced stages) that leads to a minimization of the resistance use of this material. On the other hand, it should be emphasized that this listening should not be *too* focused merely on the reality of the affair; rather, it should use the affair as important, but only one manifestation of the patient's unresolved intrapsychic conflicts.[8]

Second, it should be remembered that patients who have a marked tendency toward the use of primitive defenses of projection, splitting, denial, and externalization will sooner or later bring these up in their relationship to the therapist. Thus, the push and pull and the contradictory expectations attributed by the patient to her lover may soon become the characteristics of the therapist in the patient's mind. Despite its seemingly chaotic effects on the treatment situation this is a welcome development since it provides the therapist with an opportunity to clarify and interpret the distorting effects of these mechanisms in the here and now of their relationship (Kernberg, 1975).

Third, it is also useful to keep in mind that patients whose use of externalization borders on what Winnicott (1935) labeled the "manic defence"; that is, almost complete negation of their inner reality as a result of the emphasis on external reality, may not be suited for psychoanalytic psychotherapy and may have to be treated with only a supportive approach.

Secret Aspects of Being "The Other Woman"

A secret is an intrapsychic cul-de-sac. It not only disrupts life's experiential continuity but it also sets in motion defensive processes to guard its own existence. It may defensively contain significant contemporary and/or past experiences and fantasies which are symbolic stand-ins for each other. Or the very fact of a secret may itself serve symbolic purposes irrespective of its contents. Thus hidden omnipotent, obstinate, retentive, teasing, seductive needs (and associated fantasies) from different levels of psychosexual development may all find expression in an individual's keeping a secret. On the other hand, a "secret life" may imply the existence of a defensively split off sector of psychic organization with quasi-independent self and object representations. Keeping a secret may also serve narcissistic purposes and help to allay fears of humiliation and shame. All these matters clearly have significant effects upon the day-to-day life of the individual. Moreover, by getting surrounded by more and more material, rather like a gallstone, a secret effects a psychotherapeutic dialogue adversely.

The other woman is brought to the psychotherapist by her secret agony. The immediate temptation for the therapist therefore is to assume the

---

[8]In a similar vein though different context, the eminent British photographer Lord Snowdown said "a background has to be just this side of being something, and just the other side of being nothing" (quoted in *Time*, August 27, 1984).

role of sympathetic confidante and to overlook the foregoing issues, as well as the possibility that concerns which led to the birth of a secret pocket of social and psychic existence may be active in the here and now of the treatment situation. It is important to keep in mind that the patient's bringing in a secret story as the centerpiece of her suffering may serve as both a major impetus for psychological inquiry as well as a built-in resistance that can be easily overlooked.

Countertransference Difficulties

The other woman's therapist encounters two sets of countertransference difficulties. The first of these involves the countertransference hatred characteristically generated by patients with self-destructive tendencies and self-defeating behaviors (Winnicott, 1949; Maltsberger & Buie, unpublished; Kernberg, 1976b). As a rule the greater the self-destructiveness in the patient, the stronger is the intensity with which these countertransference feelings are experienced by the therapist. Thus, the group two other woman induces more such feelings than the group one other woman. These patients' therapist finds his efforts repeatedly thwarted, his professional self-esteem chronically lowered, and his interventions invariably falling as if on deaf ears. The patient's contradictory versions of her lover make it difficult for the therapist to develop a composite picture of him or of their relationship. He feels pulled in one direction by the patient during some sessions and in a totally opposite direction in other sessions. He may feel confused and impotent. All this in and of itself may not be a source of any difficulty in the therapy. Indeed, such feelings in the therapist if carefully "diagnosed" by him may lead to a deeper understanding of the disowned, dissociated, and externalized aspects of the patient's psychic structure (Kernberg, 1976b). The situation is thus one of "concordant identification" (Racker, 1957) with the patient's sadistic parental introjects. However, such understanding and its potential technical usefulness depends upon the therapist's ability to recognize in himself the existence of such strong feelings without acting upon them. The therapist's anxiety about his own aggression on the other hand may lead to a premature defensive warding off of such affects in him. This would necessitate defensive operations such as reaction formation (e.g., being excessively concerned and worried about the patient), turning against the self (e.g., excessively doubting one's therapeutic abilities), displacement (e.g., irritability with others), and may predispose the therapist to subtly act out his hostility toward the patient (e.g., forgetting an appointment or being late for sessions). Therefore, it is the "absence" of the negative feelings in the therapist that are more problematic than in the situation where such feelings and accompanying hostile fantasies can be permitted conscious awareness. In the latter situation a therapist can derive hypotheses from such fantasies regarding the aspects of the patient that have undergone projective identification.

The second set of countertransference difficulties involves the stirring up in the therapist of a moralistic stance that insists that a woman *not* be romantically or sexually involved with someone who is married. This may propel the therapist to subtly or overtly disparage the woman's lover and to overlook the depth and complexity of the patient's need for such a relationship. Very often however such a moralistic stance is an unconscious disguise for strong oedipal wishes that are being stirred up in the therapist. The patient has put herself in between a couple (her lover and his wife) and has put the therapist in a "complimentary identification" (Racker, 1957); that is, an identification with the infantile in the patient that compels him to put himself in between another couple (the patient and her lover). The wish to rescue a woman from an unsatisfactory lover (Freud, 1910/1957) and the attraction of the other woman (Feldman, 1964) get powerfully mobilized in the therapist and may impinge upon his work ego.

In view of the foregoing it is obvious that the therapist of the other woman should be prepared to handle in himself the development of strong aggressive and libidinal wishes toward his patient. His knowledge of his own childhood wishes and conflicts, gained from personal analysis whether therapeutic, didactic, or self-conducted, should help him in this regard.

Summary

Women who have sustained intimate relationships with married men are generally of two types. The first type is a deeply feminine, affectualized, and histrionic one whose involvement with a married man represents unresolved oedipal wishes as well as punishment over those wishes. This type of other woman led a relatively peaceful life until her entanglement with a married man began. She is socially well adapted and is capable of mourning, sadness, empathy, love, and concern. Her superego is strict and well internalized; she experiences guilt regarding her sexuality and intimacy with a married man. The second type had a troubled childhood, a searing adolescence, and an adult life characterized by overt self-destructive acts, inner uncertainty, cynicism, and chronic boredom. Her object relations are shallow and she displays a continued need for omnipotent external objects. This need finds expression in her relationship with a married man. A pseudo relationship of occasional intoxicating pleasure is established at the cost of sacrificing knowledge and ambivalence, two prerequisites for genuine intimacy.

Both types of the other women present to the mental health professional with dsythymic complaints centering around their romantic entanglements. They are distressed and puzzled by these relationships. The first type of other woman feels this anguish on a more sustained basis than the second type who at most times splits off and denies such concerns only to suffer libidinally unmitigated agony and doubt at other times. However, some defensive splitting and denial of the painfully ambivalent nature of the relationship is seen in both types of the other woman. These mechanisms either cause (in the first type) or result from (in the second type) a cleavage of the ego which has its own deleterious effects upon affect integration and decision-making processes. It is with these problems and a generalized, low-grade dysthymia that the other women seek psychotherapy.

One can help the other woman by recommending psychoanalysis, psychoanalytic psychotherapy, or supportive psychotherapy. The choice of treatment modality depends upon the nature of conflicts, the level of character organization, the degree of analyzability, the realistic feasibility of establishing and maintaining a treatment situation, the urgency with which symptom relief is required, and the degree to which one suspects that involvement with the married man will continue to foster externalization and negation of intrapsychic conflict. In most instances however psychoanalytic psychotherapy seems to be the treatment of choice. This treatment, while following the general rules and expected developments of any psychoanalytic psychotherapy, may pose certain specific dilemmas. These include a built-in reality resistance, exploring the effect of keeping a secret upon an overall life situation and the treatment alliance, and a greater than usual risk of countertransference difficulties. With careful attention however these problems should generally be manageable.

Finally, it should be remembered that these descriptions, hypotheses, and recommendations regarding the other women are based upon a relatively modest clinical experience. Methodologically sounder studies with larger samples of women who are involved with married men on the one hand, and deeper, more detailed psychoanalytic data on the other, are required to shed further light on the nature of the various phenomena involved. Meanwhile, I can conclude this basically clinical contribution by saying to the inquisitive reader what Freud (1957/1933) said to his audience at the end of his lecture on femininity: "If you want to know more . . . enquire from your own experiences of life, or turn to the poets, or wait until science can give you deeper and more coherent information" (p. 135).

References

Akhtar, S. (1984). The syndrome of identity diffusion. *American Journal of Psychiatry, 141*, 1381–1385.

Akhtar, S., & Byrne, J. P. (1983). The concept of splitting and its clinical relevance. *American Journal of Psychiatry, 140*, 1013–1016.

Arlow, J., & Brenner, C. (1964). *Psychoanalytic concepts and the structural theory.* New York: International Universities Press.

Bell, R., & Peltz, D. (1974). Extramarital sex among women. *Medical Aspects of Human Sexuality, 8.*

Beltz, S. (1969). Five year effects of altered marital contracts. In G. Neubeck (Ed.), *Extramarital Relations.* Englewood Cliffs, NJ: Prentice-Hall.

Berdy, M. D. (1984). Women who are drawn to unavailable men. *Medical Aspects of Human Sexuality, 18,* 138–146.

Bergler, E. (1969). *Selected papers of Edmund Bergler.* New York: Grune & Stratton.

Bergman, M. S. (1971). Psychoanalytic observations on the capacity to love. In J. B. McDevitt & C. F. Settlage (Eds.), *Separation-Individuation.* New York: International Universities Press.

Berliner, B. (1958). The role of object relations in moral masochism. *Psychoanalytic Quarterly, 27,* 38–56.

Bernstein, J. (1983). Masochistic pathology and feminine development. *Journal of the American Psychoanalytic Association, 31,* 467–486.

Block, J. (1978). *The other man/The other woman.* New York: Grosset & Dunlap.

Blum, H. P. (1976). Masochism, the ego ideal, and the psychology of women. *Journal of the American Psychoanalytic Association, 24,* 157–191.

Christensen, H. T. (1958). *Marriage analysis* (2nd ed.). New York: The Ronald Press.

Cuber, J. F., & Harroff, P. B. (1965). *The significant Americans.* New York: Appleton-Century-Crofts.

Deutsch, H. (1942). Some forms of emotional disturbance and their relationship to schizophrenia. *Psychoanalytic Quarterly, 11,* 301–321.

Dorpat, T. L. (1976). Structural conflict and object relations conflict. *Journal of the American Psychoanalytic Association, 24,* 885–874.

Ellis, A. (1969). Healthy and disturbed reasons for having extramarital relations. In G. Neubeck (Ed.), *Extramarital relations.* Englewood Cliffs, NJ: Prentice-Hall.

Erikson, E. H. (1959). *Identity and the life cycle* (Psychological Issues Monograph 1). New York: International Universities Press.

Feldman, S. (1964). The attraction of "the other woman." *Journal of the Hillside Hospital, 13,* 3–17.

Fielding, J. (1983). *The other woman.* New York: Signet Books.

French, M. (1980). *The Bleeding Heart.* New York: Ballentine Books.

Freud, S. (1957). A special type of choice of object made by men. In *The standard edition of the complete psychological works of Sigmund Freud.* (Vol. 11). London: Hogarth Press. (Original work published in 1910)

Freud, S. (1957). Some character types met with in psychoanalytic work. In *The standard edition of the complete psychological works of Sigmund Freud* (Vol. 14). London: Hogarth Press. (Original work published 1916)

Freud, S. (1957). The psychogenesis of a case of homosexuality in a woman. In *The standard edition of the complete psychological works of Sigmund Freud* (Vol. 18). London: Hogarth Press. (Original work published in 1920)

Freud, S. (1957). The economic problem of masochism. In *The standard edition of the complete psychological works of Sigmund Freud* (Vol. 19). London: Hogarth Press. (Original work published in 1924)

Freud, S. (1957). Fetishism. In *The standard edition of the complete psychological works of Sigmund Freud* (Vol. 21). London: Hogarth Press. (Original work published in 1927)

Freud, S. (1957). Femininity. In *The standard edition of the complete psychological works of Sigmund Freud* (Vol. 22). London: Hogarth Press. (Original work published in 1933)

Glover, E. (1954). The indications for psychoanalysis. *Journal of Mental Science, 100,* 393–401.

Goldman, A. (1984). Personal communication.

Guntrip, H. (1968). *Schizoid phenomena, object relations, and the self.* New York: International Universities Press.

Hartmann, H. (1958). *Ego psychology and the problem of adaptation.* (D. Rapaport, Trans.). New York: International Universities Press.

Hollander, L. S. (1976). The other woman: Personality characteristics and parent-child relationships of single women repeatedly involved with married men. *Dissertation Abstracts International, 12,* 6383–B (University Microfilms No. 76–13880)

Hunt, J. (1969). *The affair.* Bergenfield, NJ: The New American Library.

Joseph, E. D. (Ed.). (1967). *Indications for psychoanalysis.* (In Kris's Study Group of the New York Psychoanalytic Institute, Monograph 2). New York: International Universities Press.

Kernberg, O. F. (1967). Borderline personality organization. *Journal of the American Psychoanalytic Association, 15,* 641–685.

Kernberg, O. F. (1970). A psychoanalytic classification of character pathology. *Journal of the American Psychoanalytic Association, 18,* 800–822.

Kernberg, O. F. (1975). The subjective experience of emptiness. In *Borderline conditions and pathological narcissism* (pp. 213–229). New York: Jason Aronson.

Kernberg, O. F. (1976a). Mature love: prerequisites and characteristics. In *Object relations theory and clinical psychoanalysis* (pp. 215–239). New York: Jason Aronson.

Kernberg, O. F. (1976b). Transference and countertransference in borderline patients. In *Object relations theory and clinical psychoanalysis* (pp. 161–184). New York: Jason Aronson.

Kernberg, O. F. (1980). The conceptualization of intrapsychic structures: An overview. In *Internal world and external reality.* New York: Jason Aronson.

Khan, M. M. R. (1974). On symbiotic omnipotence. In *The Privacy of the Self.* New York: International Universities Press.

Kris, E. (1956). The personal myth: A problem in psychoanalytic techniques. *Journal of the American Psychoanalytic Association, 4,* 653–681.

Lazare, A. (1971). The hysterical character in psychoanalytic theory. *Archives of General Psychiatry, 15,* 131–137.

Lower, R., Escoll, P., & Huxster, H. (1972). Bases for judgments of analyzability. *Journal of the American Psychoanalytic Association, 20,* 610–621.

Mahler, M. S. (1974). Symbiosis and individuation: The psychological birth of the human infant. In *The selected papers of Margaret S. Mahler, M.D.,* (Vol. 2). New York: Jason Aronson.

Mahler, M. S., Pine, F., & Bergman, A. (1975). *The psychological birth of the human infant.* New York: Basic Books.

Maleson, F. G. (1984). The multiple meanings of masochism in psychoanalytic discourse. *Journal of the American Psychoanalytic Association, 32,* 325–356.

Maltsberger, J. T., & Buie, D. H. (Unpublished manuscript). *Countertransference hate in the treatment of suicidal patients.*

Meeting of two masters. *Time,* (1984, August) 27 pp. 54–55.

Modell, A. H. (1983). Comments on the rise of narcissism. In A. Goldberg (Ed.), *The future of psychoanalysis.* New York: International Universities Press.

Neubeck, G. (1969). *Extramarital relations.* Englewood Cliffs, NJ: Prentice-Hall.

Neubeck, G., & Schletzer, V. (1969). A study of extramarital relationships. In G. Neubeck (Ed.), *Extramarital relations.* Englewood Cliffs, NJ: Prentice-Hall.

Pietropinto, A., & Simenauer, J. (1976). *Beyond the male myth: What women want to know about men's sexuality.* New York: Times Books.

Racker, H. (1957). The meanings and uses of countertransference. *Psychoanalytic Quarterly, 26,* 313–357.

Reich, A. (1954). Early identifications as archaic elements in the superego. *Journal of the American Psychoanalytic Association, 2,* 218–238.

Richardson, L. W. (1979). The other women: The end of the long affair. *Alternative Styles, 2,* 397–414.

Sands, M. (1978). *The mistress manual.* New York: Berkley Books.

Singer, M. (1977a). The experience of emptiness in narcissistic and borderline states, I: Deficiency and ego defect versus dynamic-defensive models. *International Review of Psychoanalysis, 4,* 459–470.

Singer, M. (1977b). The experience of emptiness in narcissistic and borderline states, II: The struggle for a sense of self and the potential for suicide. *International Review of Psychoanalysis, 4,* 471–479.

Spotnitz, H., & Freeman, L. (1964). *The wandering husband.* Englewood Cliffs, NJ: Prentice-Hall.

Strean, H. S. (1980). *The extramarital affair.* New York: Free Press.

Tyson, R. H., & Sandler, J. (1971). Problems in the selection of patients for psychoanalysis: Comments on the application of the concepts of 'indication,' 'suitability' and 'analyzability.' *British Journal of Medical Psychology, 44,* 211–227.

Waelder, R. (1930). The principle of multiple function: Observation on overdetermination. *Psychoanalytic Quarterly, 5,* 45–62.

Whitehurst, R. (1969). Extramarital sex: Alienation or extension of normal behavior. In G. Neubeck (Ed.), *Extramarital relations.* Englewood Cliffs, NJ: Prentice-Hall.

Winnicott, D. W. (1949). Hate in the countertransference. *International Journal of Psychoanalysis, 39,* 69–75.

Winnicott, D. W. (1958). The manic defense. In *Collected papers: Through paediatrics to psychoanalysis.* London: Tavistock. (Original work published in 1935)

Winnicott, D. W. (1976). *The maturational process and the facilitating environment.* New York: International Universities Press.

Zetzel, E. R. (1968). The so-called good hysteric. *International Journal of Psychoanalysis, 49,* 256–268.

Ziskin, J., & Ziskin, M. (1973). *The extramarital arrangement.* London: Abelard-Schuman.

NINE

Alternative Lifestyles: Marital Options

William R. Stayton, Th. D. (Psychology)
Assistant Professor of Psychiatry and Human Behavior
Jefferson Medical College

OVERVIEW

Thirty years ago there were few sexual lifestyle choices that were considered valid. Either you got married, or if it was your vocation, you became a priest or nun. Anything other than marriage was considered as going against home, family, and religious and national heritage. Certainly, if you never married, you could expect to be pitied. Today it is a different world. Our children and indeed even we ourselves have many lifestyle choices, any one of which is considered legitimate by some section of our society, and it is a fact that in this latter part of the 20th century a large proportion of Americans are feeling free to choose from this wide variety.

Sexual lifestyle, for the purposes of this chapter, refers to the relational patterns around which individuals organize their living arrangements, and shall henceforth be termed simply as *lifestyle*. (Sometimes the term *lifestyle* is confused with the term *sexual orientation*. The latter refers to a person's individual preference in erotic patterns—what "turns a person on.") These lifestyles can be heterosexually, homosexually, or bisexually oriented. Many contemporary women, men, gay persons, young people, married couples, single adults, and older people are pioneering by living in nontraditional ways.

Unfortunately, most clinicians are not trained to work with persons living alternative family lifestyles. Most training in marital and family therapy is based upon a traditional monogamous nuclear lifestyle. It is the experience of many if not most clinicians that the traditional monogamous nuclear marriage is now a minority lifestyle. What about other marital and family styles? How can the clinician be better informed and better trained for more creative therapeutic interventions? In this chapter the concepts behind some of these choices will be explored, as well as the types of lifestyles that Americans are choosing today, and special consideration will be given to the clients and the therapists who are dealing with these choices.

PSYCHOPATHOLOGY AND ALTERNATIVE LIFESTYLES

There are those professionals who will read this chapter and immediately come to the conclusion that what is being discussed is a manifestation of neurotic conflicts regarding intimacy issues and disturbed object relations. They may or may not be correct. There are also those professionals who are such advocates of alternative lifestyles that they will read this chapter and proclaim how healthy it is that more and more people are breaking the bonds of traditional lifestyles and developing relational patterns that are more fulfilling to them. The latter group too may or may not be correct. Speaking to both of these groups of professionals, I would make the following observations.

First, the lifestyles mentioned in this chapter are neither being advocated nor disavowed. They are all lifestyles that are being chosen by large numbers of people. What *is* being offered is a description of the various lifestyles, some statistics if they are available, and occasional examples from my own private practice as a marital and family therapist. Second, there is certainly no unanimity among the various professionals in education, therapy, or research as to what is or is not a healthy lifestyle. If each lifestyle could be dissected there would still be diverse opinions as to whether it is healthy or not.

Third, there can be healthy or pathological aspects in any of the lifestyles. Each person or system has to be evaluated individually. Although there are no statistics available, there is probably no more pathology, proportionately, among the alternative lifestyles as in the more traditional lifestyle of the monogamous nuclear family.

MONOGAMY

One of the most important issues that arises in the process of analyzing and understanding the various choices is that of monogamy. Prior to the 16th century most Western philosophical and religious thinkers were not interested in lifestyle choices, especially within marriage. Today however such choices are a matter of major importance and concern. Pickett (1978) found that practically all cultures have had alternatives to monogamy which were usually reserved for the elite or upper-class citizens. Monogamy was usually prescribed for the lower and slave classes as a way of controlling them. It may be that monogamy is not natural for all people, which could account for the fact that so many people are not monogamous. My purpose is not to challenge monogamy nor to make a value judgment regarding it, but rather to point out that for many people in our society monogamy is not an important issue. Certainly our divorce statistics today indicate commitment to marriage as an institution but not to "lifelong" monogamy.

Most couples marry with the expectation and hope that each will be able to meet the other's needs as a partner, friend, and lover. Each goes into marriage wanting and making a commitment to fidelity. Since the terms *fidelity* and *infidelity* can be defined in many ways and can include many facets of a relationship other than sexuality, for our purposes we will limit this discussion to sexual fidelity and infidelity and we will assume that maintaining a healthy sexual relationship is of primary concern to most couples entering marriage.

It is likely that many who make the commitment to sexual fidelity (monogamy) will not adhere to that commitment throughout their marriage. Couples react differently to changes in commitment; thus, it becomes important to define when a couple is involved in sexual infidelity.

First, there are couples who for various reasons change their commitment to sexual fidelity. They may decide that they want a sexually "open marriage." Thus, the commitment changes so that when one or both spouses become involved sexually with another person, they are not involved in sexual infidelity because they are not violating a commitment to each other. New agreements had been made *before* new behaviors began.

Second, there are couples who make allowances for certain types of sexual expression outside of marriage. For example, one spouse may want his or her partner to remain sexually exclusive while at home, but will make allowances for the partner to experiment sexually while at a conference or business meeting away from home. Or one or both partners may want certain agreements such as "just don't tell me about it." As long as the partners hold to that agreement, it cannot be said that the couple is engaging in infidelity (even if they have "one-night stands" while away from home) because they are being faithful to their mutually agreed upon commitment.

Third, there are couples who through the years place a high value on sexual exclusivity and who do not want or intend to break their commitment to sexual fidelity. Many couples have the expectation when they marry that they will always completely satisfy one another's needs and will never be attracted to any other person. However, sexual attraction to other persons probably occurs no matter how much in love one is with one's spouse. If couples believe that sexual attraction is akin to sexual infidelity, then just the feeling of attraction can be a real threat to the marriage even though neither partner acts upon that feeling.

Persons and relationships inevitably change. Thus, it is important for couples to understand that their relationship will most likely change over time. The most critical changes occur in a couple's communication patterns, their sexual relationship, and in their experiences of feelings of closeness and intimacy with one another.

REPRESENTATIVE VALUE SYSTEMS

As a clinician, the most important issue that I uncover while working with persons regarding lifestyle choices is that of values. It is important then for clinicians to be able to listen, hear, and know the people we are serving since our clients represent a variety of value systems and, for them, their values make rational what may appear irrational or even inappropriate to others. As a therapist it has been helpful for me to begin to understand these value stances, to appreciate them, and to know that they are sacred to the people holding them. By outlining the various value stances, one can more easily understand some of the underlying motives for behavior choices. Working with people from various value stances has also confronted me, both as a person and as a clinician, with my own prejudices and values.

A client, struggling with an alternative lifestyle issue, has at least five major concerns to consider. It is best if the client can sort these through before entering therapy. However, this is not the way it usually happens.

1. If therapy is a choice, a major consideration is finding a therapist who can be trusted to not be judgmental about lifestyle desires or choices. All too often people enter therapy not sure of what the therapist believes and thus they may or may not divulge real information about their lifestyles. A large number of clients have come to me after having had one or more therapists whom they could not trust with their lifestyle information. After talking with the therapist for a few sessions they knew the therapist's values and probable judgments.

   It is a sad commentary that a person or couple can be in therapy—perhaps for years—and not feel free to tell the therapist about their lifestyle. I have also had clients who told their former therapists about their lifestyle choice and had the therapists spend many sessions trying to no avail to help them change their values regarding that choice.

   My own approach has been to accept almost all lifestyle choices as valid. My criteria for validity include choices that are freely made, among consenting adults, without any form of coercion, and that are within the value systems of those involved. I have found that if there are strong, neurotic reasons behind the lifestyle choice, these come out in the normal course of therapy, and I handle them as therapeutic issues, much the same as if the person has a traditional lifestyle. The end result *could* be a change in lifestyle choice—but not necessarily.

2. The client needs to be aware of his or her own value stance regarding lifestyle choice.
3. There is a need to explore the value stances of others, both directly and indirectly, involved in the lifestyle choice.
4. The psychodynamics of all the persons involved in the lifestyle need to be understood and dealt with as part of the problem-solving process.
5. The values of society and the impact of those societal values on the lifestyle choice need to be understood and appreciated.

Therefore, the values of therapist, client, others involved in lifestyle choice, and society must all be taken into consideration in helping persons with lifestyle issues.

In America, we basically have three types of value stances (Stayton, 1981). These are important for clinicians to understand so that they can know where both therapist and client are coming from when working on lifestyle choices. Two outstanding pioneers in the field of human sexuality have influenced my thinking in this area: Lester A. Kirkendall (1977) and James Schulte (1981). I have tried to integrate their concepts regarding values and have created a paradigm that has been useful for me both in teaching and in therapeutic sessions with persons in alternative family forms (see table 1). Because the subject of values is so emotionally loaded, I am going to use Systems A, B, and C to designate the categories in order to be as fair as possible to each one.

TABLE 1 Representative Value Systems

Value System	*A*	*B*	*C*
Focus of concern	Acts		Relationships: Motives and consequences
Location of authority	External		Internal
Moral responsibility	Detached/aloof		All involved
Purpose	Tradition		Promote growth
Reward	Divine favor		Meaningful life

Source: Adapted from Lester A. Kirkendall (1977) and William Stayton (1981).

System A is the value stance with which most Americans are probably familiar. It could be considered a traditional view because it is the "official" stance of most religious groups and even of our society today. It is "act" centered. There is something inherently good or bad, moral or immoral, healthy or unhealthy about any act including the various forms of sexual expression involved in lifestyle choice. Thus, in System A any nonmarital sexual act would be considered wrong, immoral, or unhealthy because the act itself is at issue.

On the opposite end of the value continuum would be System C, which is "relationship" centered. Here, good and bad, moral and immoral, healthy and unhealthy are seen in connection with the motives and consequences of the act rather than in the act itself.

This value stance is exemplified by a couple I saw who had been married for more than 40 years. The wife was diagnosed as having multiple sclerosis (MS) shortly after their marriage. In obtaining information on the disease the couple discovered that sexual apathy would be a symptom as the illness progressed. They discussed this in depth over many months and even though they were very religious, they decided that a way they could combat the apathy and its effect on their relationship would be to open their marriage to include other sexual partners. For over 35 years they have had an open marriage and each has had a number of significant partners. Interestingly, the wife has been free of MS symptoms for that same amount of time. They both attribute her symptom free years, their good sex life, and their strong marriage to the openness they share. Becoming active in a liberal church tradition has helped them to work through their own values regarding their lifestyle choice. Forty years ago their pastor helped them to look at their motives and consequences and to develop criteria for making their decisions based on what would build love and trust, enhance communication, and encourage cooperation and mutuality. After weighing all the above factors they chose an open marriage.

A second dimension in regard to values is the location of the authority for those values. Under System A the location of authority has been external; for example, "God says" or the "Bible says" or the "law says" or "Freud says" or "such and such authority says" are quoted to give credibility to the stance. Under System C it is believed that the location of authority really has to be internal—one's own sense of authority.

As psychotherapists, part of our task in working with individuals, couples, and families is to help them to sort out all the issues around their value concerns and to come to their own decision—their own internal sense of authority. They will take the responsibility for what is right or wrong for them after examining their motives and the consequences of their decision. Regarding nonmarital sex, there are many authorities who represent the spectrum of viewpoints about this issue. There are the precepts and concepts of a particular faith group or religious denomination the perspectives of experts in the field of individual psychodynamics, marriage, and the family, the official positions of organizations such as the Sex Information and Education Council of the United States (SIECUS), the laws of the various states and the nation, and the personal authorities from each person's background. Based upon the information these resources offer, persons are urged to come to their own conclusions and to make up their own minds concerning what is right and responsible for them. Thus persons from System A or System C can be guided through this process and both will feel more secure about their decisions regarding lifestyle.

The third dimension to consider regarding values is where moral responsibility for a person's actions lies. Moral responsibility under System A derives from a detached and aloof position. Usually, a person who is in authority tells a person who is not in authority what is right or wrong, healthy or unhealthy. The detached, aloof authority figure may never have had to struggle with the issue on a personal level. Those in System C proclaim that moral responsibility is something that involves all of us. The moral climate of a family, a couple relationship, or the alliance between therapist and client are processes that all share equally. Moral responsibility, according to System C, is not something one can remain detached from while proclaiming the moral irresponsibility of others who make lifestyle decisions that do not agree with the external authority's preferred choice.

A couple came in to see a therapist. The husband turned to the therapist and said, "My wife has been having an affair with our neighbor for five years. I have been a good husband. I have never gone outside our marriage for sex. I get up early every morning and after jogging a few miles, I go to work and work hard trying to make enough to keep this family in a comfortable lifestyle. I get home at about 10 P.M. every night and now I find out that she has been sleeping with our neighbor all these years. Fix her up!" This husband is a good example of a System A person. If the therapist is also from System A, he or she might be judgmental about the affair. A therapist from System C would regard the husband as being just as responsible for the affair as the wife herself. The latter therapist might even view the affair as understandable because the husband was never around and he was detached and aloof from the wife's need for companionship.

The fourth dimension of a value is its purpose. Under System A the purpose of a value is to maintain a tradition. If that tradition is to revere monogamy, then the purpose in helping couples to develop their marriage potential is to maintain that tradition. Persons in System C say that the purpose of values is whatever will promote their own personal growth as individuals, couples, or family. They say that values should help us to be better people. In fact, this group contends that the only reason we have values is to promote growth and not to maintain a tradition which may be obsolete. An example might be a couple who find no meaning in maintaining a monogamous relationship, but who find both their individual and joint lives enriched through sexual sharing with other individuals or couples.

Finally, when looking at values, it is also important to consider the reward for holding a particular value. Some say the only reward for holding a particular value is Divine favor, or that a particular value is the "only" psychologically healthy alternative. Those in System C believe that the reward for holding particular values is that life can be lived more meaningfully in the here and now. Further, many believe that living a meaningful life now is fostering their health—even though their choice is a nontraditional lifestyle—because they have taken motives and consequences into account and they are continuing to grow to be better persons.

We will now turn to System B. This value stance probably represents the majority of persons in our society. Most often people in this group were brought up under System A and believe that it is important to maintain and teach this system of values, but when it comes to their own personal and very private decisions, they make these based on System C. They rationalize in some way that System A is just not relevant to them for a particular issue. An example of this occurred recently when a clergyman and his wife came to talk to me about their open marriage. He continued to preach and teach about monogamy as the only "right" value for members of his congregation, but privately felt that monogamy was not an appropriate choice for his marriage. Another example is the number of Roman Catholics who practice birth control, which is against official church doctrine, yet continue to attend the mass and partake of the sacraments. They believe that somehow the church doctrine regarding birth control is just not relevant to them personally. Persons in System B often move back and forth on different issues between Systems A and C.

People who seek a psychotherapist because of lifestyle choice and who are having difficulty with that choice are usually persons in System B, people caught between two opposing, incompatible systems. These are the persons who can benefit from therapy that helps them to sort out the issues and to make decisions regarding the marital style that will best foster individual and couple growth and fulfillment.

It is important therefore for the client to choose a therapist who can be helpful in sorting out the value issues. A therapist whose own values come from System A will probably not be helpful to many clients because most representatives from this value stance have difficulty tolerating other value positions. The therapist from System A who can tolerate other value stances and not be judgmental can be very helpful to persons who are struggling with Systems A and B. The therapist from System C, unless a crusader for that system, is usually able to be more nonjudgmental and tolerant of all the value systems.

LIFESTYLE OPTIONS

When considering the types of lifestyles people are choosing today, at least 14 possible lifestyles have been identified, although there is no consensus on the total number and variation. Those discussed in this section are to a great extent taken from a listing in *The New Intimacy* (Mazur, 1973), and have been observed in my own clinical practice.

Traditional monogamy. It is interesting that this traditional and societally upheld lifestyle is no longer the strongly predominant lifestyle in American culture. In fact, even the traditional family, composed of father, mother, and children "accounts for only about a third of all U.S. households" (Nass, Libby, & Fisher, 1981, p. 288). From various studies it is estimated that only approximately 30 percent to 40 percent of married couples in America continue in one monogamous relationship for life without having any secret affairs or one-night stands and with sexual fidelity as one of the most valued parts of the relationship (Kinsey, Pomeroy, & Martin, 1948; Kinsey, Pomeroy, Martin, & Gebhard, 1953, Athanasiou, Shaver, & Tavris, 1970; Hunt, 1974; Tavris & Sadd, 1975).

Most couples who marry do so believing that they will be faithfully married "until death do us part." The most serious threat to this lifestyle is not from without but from within, given the high rate of divorce and separation and the number of couples who turn to an alternative lifestyle later in marriage. But certainly we should not consider traditional monogamy on its way out as a viable lifestyle, as there are many who will continue to choose this pattern as a fulfilling and valued way of life.

As therapists we need to be careful that we do not make the judgment that sexual fidelity is the only healthy, correct marital lifestyle, or conversely, that sexual fidelity is an unhealthy marital lifestyle. There are therapists who will condone extramarital or comarital relationships when they and the couple believe that such relationships would be healthy for the marriage and/or one of the spouses. Criteria for condoning extramarital relationships might include such factors as a couple who does not experience jealousy or a sense of genital possessiveness, and who have a good and meaningful sexual relationship with each other. With these criteria met, if the couple desires to expand their marriage to include other sexual partners, the therapist might not be opposed. Another circumstance where a therapist might condone or even recommend an extramarital relationship is where the illness of one partner would preclude a meaningful sexual relationship such as mental illness or coma. (It seems to me that it would also be necessary that such actions be within the client's value system.) Therapists may also recommend that an extramarital relationship cease or not begin for the health of the marriage and individuals.

Child-free relationships. It is very difficult for most people who have children to understand those who decide against parenthood. There are a growing number of couples today who want to be in a long-term relationship but who feel that their lives will be more meaningfully fulfilled if they remain childless (Francoeur, 1982). Not many years ago, this decision would have been unthinkable. It was traditional that couples who did not have children were to be pitied and encouraged to adopt so that their "marriage could be complete." Marriage and parenthood have been synonymous in our culture. But those who choose a child free lifestyle today are making the choice with valid and justifiable reasons. With the growing world population and nuclear warfare as real threats, couples do not feel guilty for not procreating. Other, more personal factors that can affect this decision are dual careers, the influence of divorce on the couple's own childhood, and interracial and interfaith considerations. There are even materials available today to help a couple decide whether or not they would make good parents (Granzig & Peck, 1978).

Single parenthood. This lifestyle is very different from the "unwed" or "illegitimate" motherhood that I heard about so often as a young person. There are a good number of responsible members of our community today who are saying that, although they do not want to be bound in a permanent relationship, they *do* want the benefits of parenthood. Both women *and* men are choosing to raise a child or children without a partner in marriage. It is also true that single parenthood is a transitional lifestyle for many persons such as divorced persons. Many hope that they will remarry at some point in the future.

Today, at least one in every five children is living with just one parent. Interestingly, between 1960 and 1978 "children living with a separated parent doubled, those living with a divorced parent tripled, and those living with a never married parent were seven times the number they were in 1960" (Francoeur, 1982, p. 709).

No definite statistics on the number of never married men choosing single parenthood are available. However, it is not unusual to find ads in the personal columns of magazines or underground newspapers through which a man is seeking a woman to bear his child. Many fertility clinics have made their services available to single women who are seeking artificial insemination, a procedure that is safe and involves few legal complications. Some singles use terms like "elective parent" and "single parent by choice" to describe their lifestyle.

The fact that up to 50 percent of our school children come from couples who are divorced and live with one parent has contributed to removing the stigma of illegitimacy once associated with out-of-wedlock births.

Singlehood. Persons who do not marry are no longer considered second-class citizens. Words like *spinster,* with its negative overtones have virtually disappeared from our vocabulary. At least 10 percent of our population will never marry. One third of all adults in America are single (Francoeur, 1982). This figure includes divorced, widowed, and never married singles. Marriage is not something many of these single persons avoid "as the plague," but is rather a state they choose not to enter for many valid reasons from career choices to being mobile and without family responsibilities. The Bureau of Census has reported that in the last dozen years the number of Americans aged 25 to 34 who have not married has doubled. While it is true that many of these persons will later marry, there is a definite trend toward staying single longer. In 1978, 22 percent of all households were made up of single persons. This represented an 8 percent increase over the preceding year (Nass et al., 1981).

Cohabitation. In this lifestyle two or more people live together in a relationship that is similar to marriage but lacks the legal ties. It has often been identified with college students. Indeed, several studies indicate that between 50 percent and 80 percent of college students would elect cohabitation arrangements if permissible on their campus, while probably up to 35 percent of college students are already in such a lifestyle (Nass, et al., 1981). Problems can occur when the commitment to this lifestyle is different for each person in the relationship. For example, one partner may see the commitment as one for the duration of the year or until graduation while the other partner considers it a part of the engagement period and expects that it will eventuate in marriage.

But students are not the only ones who choose this lifestyle. More and more couples in their middle and later years are now choosing cohabitation. In 1970, the Census Bureau reported one million couples living together; by 1977 this figure had grown to two million (Francoeur, 1982). Many gay couples set up cohabitation agreements and contracts, representing for them the pattern closest to a legal marriage. Also, many senior citizens—widowed or divorced—opt for this lifestyle because of the financial disadvantages of marriage with respect to social security payments, and so on, and in order to avoid inheritance problems for the children.

As a college teacher and a clinician, I have noted two interesting phenomena. One is in the number of parents who are actually encouraging their youngsters to live together for a while before getting married. A reason often given is that marriage is meant to last for a long time and these parents want their children to be absolutely sure of the decision. There are parents who do not want their children to repeat their own mistakes by entering into a bad marriage or getting married for the wrong reasons, and they think cohabitation may be helpful. The other phenomenon is the increasing number of persons who are cohabiting before entering into a second (or later) marriage. A reason often given is that they want the choice to be right and responsible.

Serial monogamy. Most people who become divorced may want to remarry and many do. The trend however is that fewer are remarrying, and those who are take longer to make that decision (Glick & Norton, 1977). If they have been receiving marital therapy for the first marriage, they may have a better chance that the second marriage will be a happier and more satisfying experience although at present 60 percent of second marriages also end in divorce (Francoeur, 1982). The majority of those who go from one monogamous relationship to another are however looking for one that is more mature and fulfilling than the previous one. While married, these persons are monogamous, and during their adult lives there may be a number of such marriages, thus, the term serial monogamy. As mentioned previously a sizable number of this group will live together before remarriage.

Communes. Considering the kinds of ecological and economic crises we are facing today, one can understand the appeal of a communal setting. Thousands of communes have sprung up across the country during the last two decades or so. While we have tended to think of communes as a phenomenon of youth, today this lifestyle is more and more being identified with older people—middle-aged and up. An entire book could be written on the different types of communes. People live together for many and varied reasons: professional, philosophical, political, therapeutic, religious, economic, or some combination of these. Participants can be single, married, divorced, or widowed. Communes are found at every level of society, economically and educationally. In the foreseeable future many people, in order to maintain the economic style of living to which they have become accustomed, may find the solution in communal living.

In the mid-1970s, a group of American Baptists, with encouragement from their denomination, lived communally near Philadelphia in a Roman Catholic abbey which was no longer in use. As a consultant to this group I felt involved in the life of this community. There were eight family units, from a one-person unit to married couples without children to married couples with children. The age range of the group was from 3 to the mid 50s. The community was interested in ecology as well as in building relational support systems among its members. They found that among them they had 12 automobiles; they needed only eight. Instead of eight refrigerators, washers, dryers and other appliances, they needed less than half that number when they began living together. They shared household chores which meant that each had less work than in their single-unit houses. Each family unit had its own private space as well as community space: a common kitchen, dining room, living room, playroom, and library. They ate one meal a day together, usually dinner; the other meals were fixed individually. (What amazed me was that in 1978, with their own garden produce and through buying in bulk, they fed their community for $7.50 per person per week, and they ate well. We could not feed our family of six on twice that amount.)

While there are some communes that include the sharing of sexual intimacies, this particular one did not. The community remained together until the Catholic order took the abbey over again. All of the members felt that the five-year experience had been a very valuable and significant part of their lives and, although the majority returned to their single-unit lifestyle, those I have talked to would live communally again under the right circumstances.

Swinging and/or group sex. Most men and women have probably fantasized about a sexual relationship with someone other than their spouse. Today a growing number of couples are making this fantasy a reality. There are estimated to be 10 million so-called swinging couples today, with national, state, and local organizations for them to join (Nass, et al., 1981).

Swingers are couples who meet other couples with the intention of pairing off for sexual and/or sensual experiences with someone new. Individuals and couples who do not belong to an organized swingers' group may join together as friends for sexual purposes. People who enjoy this lifestyle come from every economic, educational, religious, and racial group in our society. Most often these people lead conventional lives in every other respect. They consider sex a healthy, recreational pastime rather than a sin, vice, or indulgence in perversion (Francoeur, 1982).

Contrary to popular myths, some research studies have found that swingers often rate their marriages as happier and more fulfilling than do those couples who have no other intimate relationships (Gilmartin, 1975). I have known several swinger couples, none of whom fit our society's stereotyped "far out" picture of such people, including a 70-year-old couple who have been married for 43 years.

While this sexual lifestyle may meet with disapproval in the population at large, it is important to remember that this is a mutually agreed upon lifestyle between the partners and it does receive support from other swingers. Swingers then have the advantage of an internalized ideology that considers their behavior both moral and desirable. The swinger couples with whom I have talked insist that they strongly value fidelity in their marriages, but they discuss fidelity in terms of an open, honest, and trusting relationship.

There seem to be at least three types of swingers: those who desire only sex with an outside partner, with no social or emotional expectations; the recreational swingers who see the social aspects of swinging as being as important as the sexual aspects and who often belong to private clubs with rather stable memberships; and finally, those who are seeking close and lasting relationships or friendships with their outside partners.

Group marriage. While heterosexual monogamy is the only legally accepted marriage, there are those in our society who are choosing to live in a marriage-type relationship involving three or more committed adults. Some group marriages are closed, in that sexual intimacy is kept within the bounds of the relationship. Others have an open contract that allows members of the marriage to have other outside sexual contacts. My first experience with group marriage clients—two men and one woman who came to my office—was very helpful to my understanding of some of the dynamics and pressures involved in this lifestyle. The woman and one of the men, legally married, met and subsequently became close friends with the second man—close on almost every level: intellectual, emotional, social, and spiritual. And, as they described it, "it was a logical and smooth transition for our feelings of intimacy to be expressed on a physical/sexual level." They had their three-person union solemnized by a member of the clergy. Their purchase of a home together precipitated the twofold problem that brought them to me. First, because of their lifestyle, the neighbors had signed a petition against their living in that neighborhood. Second, one of the men was in danger of losing his job because his employer felt that his lifestyle would be offensive to the public his company served. The threesome wanted my help in learning how to build a greater understanding between themselves and those who were against them. They were very sincere about wanting to be creative in educating their critics.

As we worked together on their problem, I developed a real appreciation of their love and commitment to one another. They had no other outside sexual relationships but were committed to the idea of fidelity in their "marriage."

Synergamous relationship. I first read about this lifestyle concept in the book *Thursday, My Love* (Rimmer, 1972). The idea is that a couple involved in a primary relationship go on to develop a committed secondary relationship. The resulting secondary couple may even set up another residence where they spend time, which could be one day a week (as in *Thursday, My Love*) or one weekend a month, or one month a year. Ideally, the primary partner knows about and approves of the secondary relationship. Indeed, I have met several couples who have a synergamous marriage and find it to be a very meaningful arrangement. I have also known several couples where one or both of the partners is bisexual. These people have found a synergamous relationship to be ideal for their marriage since it allows the bisexual partner an opportunity to have a committed same-sex arrangement. In two of these situations the secondary relationship of one of the partners has been ongoing for several years and in each case the spouse knows and approves.

Open-ended relationship in marriage. Some couples, although they want to be married, just cannot adjust to and be happy with a monogamous relationship. If both partners agree they may decide to enter into an open-ended marriage. In this arrangement both are free to establish other, independent, significant relationships. Sexual exclusiveness may or may not be part of the open contract. Open-ended marriage can be growth producing and successful for some couples, especially if they already have a strong and rewarding sexual and emotional relationship with one another. However, I have never known an open relationship to save a troubled marriage. This lifestyle has no place in a relationship that is characterized by jealousy and possessiveness.

McGinnis (1981) gives extensive data on extramarital relations. He has identified different personality and marital types and, based on given combinations, can predict whether or not a particular couple can have a successful, open marriage contract.

Celibate marriage. It is difficult to know how many couples are living in a celibate relationship, but from my own clinical practice I know that it does exist. There are couples who have an otherwise excellent relationship but have no sexual desire or activity. A phenomenon often seen by the clinician is the madonna/whore syndrome. In this syndrome women are divided into two types. The madonna represents the woman who, held up and adored, is the person one marries and cares for but for whom one has no sexual desire or need (other than to have children) and whose model is the Virgin Mary. The other type of woman is whore, representing the woman of passion and sexual appetite, the woman who is sensual, sexual and seductive. If both partners view the married woman as "madonna" they are likely to develop a fulfilling celibate marriage after procreational needs are met. If only one partner exemplifies the syndrome, a celibate marriage may exist but without fulfillment for both partners.

Celibate marriages may occur among couples whose high level of sexual activity in the beginning quickly deteriorates after marriage or after the birth of children. Negative reasons for a relationship becoming celibate are hostility, boredom, apathy, and depression. Such celibate couples would benefit from therapy unless both partners are happy with their arrangement.

Some persons choose a lifestyle of lifelong celibacy. Their reasons may be based on religious vows, as in the case of priests and nuns, or simply on the fact that they have never found a partner with whom they want to develop a sexual and emotional relationship. Other reasons for choosing celibacy include a fear of sexual intimacy or a lack of need for and/or interest in a sexual relationship.

Family network system. In this lifestyle, also known as the voluntary extended family, two or more family units join together as a way of sharing life's experiences (e.g., meals, vacations, special events), and as an emotional support system. In a world too often filled with loneliness and isolation, the family network system can fill a real need. Sharing sexual intimacy with other members of the network may or may not be part of the system.

It seems to me that fulfilling a supportive role was an original intention, sociologically, of our religious institutions. At one time the church or synagogue was the center of family life. It provided a support system for family members and was the center of social, cultural, educational, and recreational activities for the family. Today, in our highly mobile and compartmentalized culture, the church and synagogue have too often lost the feeling of the family network system. Thus, many families are reaching out on their own to establish and become a part of an expanded network that will help them to feel less isolated and alienated from others.

If I were to describe my own family's present lifestyle it would fit best under this category. Several years ago we joined with two other families, both of whom, like ourselves had no relatives in the area. We established a family network system by having three evening meals together each week. On a rotating basis the host family prepared the meal and cleaned up afterward. We also share tools, help each other with some home repairs or maintenance, and often socialize together. Our particular network pattern does not include sharing sexually intimate relationships. It has been a rewarding experience and all of us have received a valuable support system in times of stress and crisis through the years.

The secret extramarital relationship. Finally, I add to the above list the seemingly monogamous relationship in which one or both of the partners carry on a secret affair. Several studies estimate that 65 percent to 70 percent of married men and 45 percent to 65 percent of married women engage in extramarital relationships at some time during their marriage (Nass et al., 1981). The majority of these are secret and in general they are not helpful to the primary relationship. The amount of energy used to nourish the relationship and maintain its secrecy can rob the primary relationship of the kind of energy needed to keep it alive and healthy. This type of lifestyle is usually a forced choice and not a person's preferred pattern. Having chosen to participate in a secondary relationship, the person would prefer to be able to be open with her/his spouse. More than in other lifestyles discussed, the person involved here is often filled with guilt and remorse and is not interested in dissolving the primary relationship. Secret affairs can consist of anything from a one-time experience to an ongoing and committed sexual relationship.

It is important to note however that in some cases the extramarital relationship is a possible outlet for a partner who may have a greater sexual need or capacity than his/her spouse or in cases where physical disability in one's partner precludes sexual activity. In a situation where the partners' sexual relationship is unsatisfactory, an extramarital relationship may give the involved partner important new insights into sexual communication and make possible an improved primary relationship.

As a therapist I would not ever advocate the secret affair lifestyle to a client because of the secrecy factor. First, I have never known an affair to remain a secret. When the information does become known, the spouse sooner or later admits that she/he either knew, suspected, or at least was not surprised. It is very difficult, I believe, to live in an intimate relationship and keep an extramarital relationship a secret unless the communication between partners has totally broken down and they are virtually living separate lives anyway. Second, it is very difficult if not impossible to help a couple strengthen and grow in their relationship while one partner is maintaining an outside affair. Since many couples that I see are involved in a secret affair, one of the primary goals of therapy is to resolve how the issue of that affair will be dealt with in the context of marital therapy. If the affair is to remain a secret then the goals of increased intimacy and communication will need to be compromised. The therapist will have to decide in each case whether he/she will be able to work with that client system.

With the exception of this last lifestyle, I have tried to put forth the above alternatives without making judgments about them. There are moral and socially responsible persons to be found in all of them and, if we were to analyze the lifestyles of people we associate with in our everyday life, we would no doubt discover that many of these individuals have, at one time or another, been involved in more than one of these patterns. Thus, the lifestyles I have described are not mutually exclusive. One final thought. As a society we need to be more accepting of and open to the various alternatives that fit people's emotional, social, and sexual needs or desires. If these alternatives involve no inherent physical or emotional harm and no infringement on the rights of others, then it is my judgment that a chosen lifestyle has the right to exist—as an individual's "typical way of life."

CONSIDERATIONS OF THE THERAPIST

Just as I mentioned in the beginning of this chapter that a client struggling with an alternative lifestyle issue has major concerns to deal with, so too, in order to be helpful to a client, does the therapist.

First, the therapist needs to be clear about his/her own value orientation. If the therapist comes from System A, then it is very important for that therapist to be honest with the client about his/her value stance from the beginning. This therapist will generally not be accepting of any nontraditional sexual lifestyle. This person will believe that either for psychological or theological reasons nature intended human beings to live together in prescribed ways such as in a monogamous bonded relationship. Anything else would be considered either sick or sinful (or both). A couple coming from System B or C will be in conflict from the beginning with the therapist from System A.

If the therapist comes from System C, there is a better chance that the client will feel more comfortable in discussing lifestyle issues, even though the therapist may also believe that a monogamous nuclear marriage is the best of the options. Usually a person in System C will have considered the options and made a decision that for him/her a particular lifestyle was the best option. It would be just as important for a therapist from System C not to force any particular alternative on that client.

Second, in working with persons in alternative lifestyles, it is important that the therapist be nonjudgmental about lifestyles that may be nontraditional. This means that the therapist must work through his/her own belief system regarding monogamy. Therapy training programs have often espoused monogamy and marriage as the only truly healthy option. However, as many of the books in the references at the end of this chapter state, many people are capable of and successfully develop deep and intimate relationships with more than one other person. Contemporary lifestyle choices do not support monogamy as the only lifestyle suitable for humans, even though it may be the desired choice of the majority within a community.

Third, the therapist will need to clarify the value stances of those within the client system and try, in some way, to reconcile the differences. Sometimes I have found that by presenting the various value stances, the clients have gained a better appreciation of each other. They may find that their different value systems are irreconcilable. Thus, the therapeutic issue will be how the clients are to resolve those differences. The therapist's task is to clearly point out the differences and the values they represent. Hopefully the clients will be able to grow with the insights gained and then move toward a creative resolution of their conflict.

Fourth, the therapist needs to be at least academically familiar with the various lifestyle options. It is important to be able to point out the positive as well as the negative aspects of that lifestyle for each client system. The positive and negative factors will be different for each client. Part of this task includes putting societal values in perspective in terms of each client system. I have worked with several group marriages and two cases will suffice to illustrate this point. One group marriage consisted entirely of professional people who were involved in academia. There were four adults and three children. They were able to develop an acceptable living arrangement within their community because it was located in a large university section of the city where there were many known alternative lifestyle arrangements. Traditional societal values had little effect on their lives because of the particular community they lived in. Another group marriage, comprised of four adults and four children, broke down largely because the four adults were blue collar, lower-middle-class people trying to live in a suburban and highly conservative community. The societal and family pressures were too great for this lifestyle to survive in its surroundings, yet none of the adults were willing to move out of that type of environment. Part of the therapeutic task was to clarify the societal impact on their lifestyle choice.

In obtaining professional help for a lifestyle choice, a client needs to find a therapist who is aware, comfortable with, and informed about the various options. There are training and educational opportunities available. The American Association of Sex Educators, Counselors, and Therapists (AASECT) requires professionals seeking certification to participate in a sexual attitude reassessment (SAR) where attitudes and values are confronted and discussed through the viewing of explicit films regarding sexuality and sexual lifestyles. This is an important process for all who are working with persons and their sexual lifestyles. SARs are now available throughout the country through professional organizations, some graduate schools, and continuing education programs (see AASECT in References). The various professional organizations in the field of human sexuality also provide workshops and professional opportunities to learn more about the various lifestyle options that people are choosing (see addresses in References). Many universities and graduate schools are also introducing courses on alternative lifestyles.

With the majority of Americans living at one point or another in an alternative sexual lifestyle, it is becoming increasingly important for the marital therapist to be informed, trained, and comfortable regarding lifestyle options.

References

Athanasiou, R., Shaver, P., & Tavris, C. (1970, January). Sex. *Psychology Today*, pp. 37–52.

Francoeur, R. T. *Becoming a sexual person*. (1982). New York: John Wiley & Sons.

Gilmartin, B. G. (1975, February). That swinging couple down the block. *Psychology Today*, pp. 55–58.

Glick, P. C., & Norton, A. J. (1977, October). *Marrying, divorcing, and living together in the U.S. today.* Washington, DC: Population Reference Bureau (32, No. 5).

Granzig, W., & Peck, E. (1978). *The parent test: How to measure and develop your talent for parenthood.* New York: G. P. Putnam's Sons.

Hunt, M. (1974). *Sexual behavior in the 1970s.* Chicago: Playboy Press.

Kinsey, A. C., Pomeroy, W. .B., Martin, C. E., & Gebhard, P. H. (1953). *Sexual behavior in the human female.* Philadelphia: Saunders.

Kinsey, A. C., Pomeroy, W. B., & Martin, C. E. (1948). *Sexual behavior in the human male.* Philadelphia: Saunders.

Kirkendall, L. A. (1977, October 6). *Sex education and the citizen: A transition in values*. Paper presented at University of Delaware, Newark, DE.

Mazur, R. (1973). *The new intimacy: Open-Ended marriage and alternative lifestyles*. Boston: Beacon Press.

McGinnis, T. (1981). *More than just a friend: The joys and disappointments of extramarital affairs.* Englewood Cliffs, NJ: Prentice-Hall.

Nass, G. D., Libby, R. W., & Fisher, M. P. (1981). *Sexual choices: An introduction to human sexuality*. Belmont, CA: Wadsworth.

Pickett, R. S. (1978). Monogamy on trial. *Alternative Lifestyles, 1,* 157.

Rimmer, R. H. (1972). *Thursday, my love.* New York: New American Library.

Schulte, J. H. (1981). Roman Catholic views of sexuality. In John M. Holland (Ed.), *Religion and Sexuality*. San Francisco: Association of Sexologists.

Stayton, W. R. (1981) Testimony of Dr. William R. Stayton. *Constitutional Amendments Relating to Abortion*. (Vol. 1). Hearings before the Subcommittee on the Constitution of the Committee on the Judiciary United States Senate.

Tavris, C. & Sadd, S. (1975). *The redbook report on female sexuality*. New York: Dell.

Professional Organizations

AASECT (The American Association of Sex Educators, Counselors and Therapists)
Eleven Dupont Circle, N. W., Suite 220
Washington, DC 20036

The Association of Sexologists
1523 Franklin Street
San Francisco, CA 94109

SIECUS (Sex Information and Education Council of the U.S.)
80 Fifth Avenue, Suite 801–2
New York, NY 10011

The Society for the Scientific Study of Sex, Inc.
P.O. Box 29795
Philadelphia, PA 19117

TEN

*Sexual Messages: Parental Influences on Children's Sexual Development**

Janet R. Kahn, Ed. M.
Research Associate
American Institute for Research

OVERVIEW

As a nation we are in a great state of transition concerning our sexual behaviors, attitudes, and beliefs. In the focus of our social research and commentary and in the fabric of our daily lives, we see a great interest in both sexual functioning and in the feelings associated with our sexuality. The signs of this process are all about us. In the not too distant past women's erotic pleasure was at best a low priority and at worst something shameful. The clitoris was rarely mentioned in anatomy classes, let alone in conversations between friends, lovers, or parents and children. Now, at least in some circles, women's erotic pleasure is a high priority; researchers and clinicians state that it is an essential component of a successful marriage. Couples work hard to achieve expanded forms of pleasure, for

*The gender-specific nature of English pronouns has been increasingly recognized by authors wishing to reduce the sexism in our writings. However, this increased awareness has not yet led to the general adoption of any nonsexist conventions. Since I find that "he or she" and the contractions "s/he" or "he/she" disrupt the flow of the reading, I have elected an alternative solution. Where gender is irrelevant to the content I have simply alternated my use of masculine and feminine terms.

example, in multiple orgasms and in attempting to locate the treasured and perhaps mythical "G-spot." Whereas once the rugged man of few words was virtually unchallenged as the model of masculinity, now the media present us with a variety of male images. Many of our male heroes talk now; some of them even talk about feelings. A few of them cry or hug their children. When today's adults were in their adolescence, most teenage girls who became pregnant either married immediately or delivered their babies (often away from home) and surrendered them for adoption. Now, many more pregnant teenagers remain unmarried. The vast majority of these youngsters proudly keep their babies and raise them either alone or in their familial home.

Although some of these changes in our sexual mores have an immediately liberating effect for some people, and many more may ultimately be of benefit to most of us, it is also true that for many people they create painful confusion in the present. For instance, husbands interviewed in a 1976 study about family life and sexuality expressed more uncertainty about the statement "women prefer strong masculine men" than about any other attitudinal item (Roberts, Klein & Gagnon, 1978). They no longer know what is appealing, what is wanted of them. And understandably, they find not knowing uncomfortable.

It is in this context of confusion and mixed messages that contemporary parents attempt to fulfill their responsibility to guide their children's sexual development—both a formidable and an essential task and an inevitable process. Even those parents who wish to avoid the topic and the task will still have an indelible effect on the formation of their children's beliefs and feelings about all sexual aspects of life.

SEXUAL DEVELOPMENT THROUGH SEXUAL LEARNING

In our culture when one mentions the words *sex* or *sexuality*, people most often think about those physical activities between two people that are erotic or reproductive in nature. In this chapter, when I discuss parents' impact on their children's sexual development I mean much more than erotic or reproductive behavior. I mean all those ways in which parents play a role in a child's learning about what it means to be a male or a female, what are appropriate ways to express intimacy, affection, and other interpersonal or individual emotions, how a child feels about his or her body both in terms of its appearance and its capacities for pleasure and accomplishment, the ideas the child forms about family roles and other aspects of lifestyle, as well as all of the issues related to reproductive and erotic behavior and their social consequences. In recent years there has been much support for such an expanded view of sexuality. Some of the strongest voices urging us in this direction have come from the feminist movement. In addition, organizations such as the American Medical Association (AMA), the Sex Information and Education Council of the United States (SIECUS), and the World Health Organization (WHO) have all issued statements affirming that human sexuality is more than what we do; it is also a basic part of one's identity, an essential expression of the self.

The term *sexual learning* is used here to refer to the entire process (or the many processes) by which an individual, in childhood and throughout life, gathers information, both factual and impressionistic, about all aspects of sexuality and makes meaning of that information. Despite the tremendous and largely warranted concern about the mass media as a major transmitter of sexual messages, and despite much research documenting the fact that for teens and young adults peers may be the dominant source of sexual information (Ramsey, 1943; Thornburg, 1972; Gebhard, 1977), there can be no doubt that parents play a critical role in their children's sexual learning. Children learn from their parents in many ways. From the first moments of life the ways a child is touched or not touched, the toys that are offered or denied, the conversations that are initiated or avoided, and the behaviors that are rewarded or punished all are a part of sexual learning. Through all of these actions or inactions, parents send messages about how boys and girls should behave, about the experiences of the body, about topics that may be discussed with anyone, only with family members, or not at all. All of the channels of communication just mentioned involve the child directly. Yet, much childhood learning takes place through observation. Children watch and imitate the ways in which parents interact with one another, the motions and emotions of their daily lives. They notice, for instance, not only what is said to them about their own nudity, but also who in the family is naked in front of whom, and how they seem to feel about it. As the child grows up other message sources will enter her sphere of awareness. Some of the new messages will reinforce the parental perspective while others will broaden or conflict with it. But all of these messages will be interpreted within a framework created through early interactions with and observation of the parents.

At this point I want to state that this discussion will virtually ignore the role of biology and physiology in sexual development. This is not because the latter are unimportant. On the contrary, as our research grows more sophisticated we will acquire a much deeper understanding of hormonal, chromosomal, and other influences. For instance, one recent study found that among males homosexuality runs in the family; that is, the brothers of gay men are more likely to be gay than are the brothers of heterosexual men. While the research presents no conclusive evidence for biological versus sociological causation, the authors suggest that certain events in prenatal life may exert strong influences on sexual orientation in adulthood (Pillard & Weinrich, 1984). Other work has found a correlation between an adolescent's rate of physiological maturation and his pace of sexual initiation, including age at first intercourse (Teddlie et al., 1979). This was true for both males and females. Yet, again it is unclear to what extent the tendency to be sexually active at an earlier age is a response to the colloquial "raging hormones," or a response to differential expectations on the part of both peers and adults to an adolescent who looks and sounds more like an adult than like a child. Hence, there are two reasons why this chapter will focus on the social learning aspects of parental influences on children's sexual development. First, the data on biological influences appear to be quite inconclusive at this time. Second and more important, there may be more practical benefits to discussing those aspects of sexual development that a parent can consciously address.

THE RESEARCH

Although some sex research was being conducted in this country even before Kinsey's landmark studies, the last two decades have seen a significant increase in the volume of work produced annually on various aspects of human sexuality. In part, this expansion of the research has been made possible by a general relaxation about sexuality which allows researchers to ask many questions that might previously have been considered off limits. Both positive and negative motivations have prompted new research. On the one hand our goals for greater sexual comfort and reduced gender role restrictions have led to closer examination of the factors involved in sexual pleasure and the formation of our attitudes about gender. Simultaneously, parents and policymakers alike have become concerned about the increased rates of coital activity among teenagers and the concomitant problems of adolescent pregnancy, parenthood, and sexually transmitted diseases.

Although much of the literature generated by this research has strongly influenced the perspective presented in this chapter, our discussion will rely most heavily on two related studies concerning parent-child communication regarding sexuality. These studies were conducted in Cuyahoga County, Ohio, which encompasses the greater Cleveland area. The site was selected because its population includes members of many racial and ethnic minorities, and it enabled the researchers to avoid the greater liberalness of residents of major East and West Coast cities. Despite this care it should be remembered that people who agree to be interviewed about sexuality are likely to be more comfortable with this aspect of life than people who refuse to be interviewed. So the picture which is painted by the results of this research is likely to be rosier than the national reality.

The first of these studies was conducted in 1976 by the Project on Human Sexual Development (Roberts, Klein & Gagnon, 1978). It involved interviews with over 1,400 parents, both mothers and fathers and members of both dual and single parent households. Each of these parents had at least one child between the ages of 3 and 11. The study was an unprecedented major effort at gathering information on how parents feel and function in their role as the primary sex educators of their young children. Questions were asked about respondents' values and behavior concerning many aspects of sexuality. Some examples are how often they had sex, who did the family cooking, whether they cried in front of their friends, kissed in front of their children, and what they believed about abortion. Many questions concerned verbal communication with their children such as what sexual topics they had or had not discussed and what topics they planned to discuss by the time the children reached their teen years.

The second study was a follow-up to this original work. It was conducted by the author and her colleagues in 1983 (Kahn & Pierson, 1984). The principal informants in this study were the children of the 1976 parents. Interviews were completed with 215 children who had reached the ages of 12 through 19. Interviews were also conducted with 111 additional teens whose parents had not taken part in the 1976 study. The supplemental respondents were added for two reasons. The first was to increase the sample size. Although there were roughly 700 eligible families from the 1976 study, and we were able to relocate 70 percent of them after seven years, fewer than half of the parents (48 percent) consented to have their children interviewed. This low parental consent rate is not unusual for studies that involve lengthy, personal interviews with children, especially when the interviews deal with the topic of sexuality. It is one manifestation of the extent to which old assumptions about sexuality—that it is private, too revealing, upsetting to children, and so on—still linger.

In the end interviews were completed with a total of 326 adolescent males and females. Following the interviews the parents of these teens were sent questionnaires to provide us with an update from their perspective. Many identical questions were asked of both teens and parents so that their responses could be compared. In addition, both the 1976 and 1983 studies involved the use of focus groups (e.g., face-to-face group interviews) so that some matters could be explored in more depth than is possible in the interview and questionnaire formats.

This chapter, then, deals with what we have learned about the process of parent-child communication about sexual issues and its effects on the sexual behavior and attitudes of those children during their adolescent years. A few major themes emerge repeatedly from our own and other people's data. One is that there is plenty of room for improvement. Although parents firmly believe that they should be their children's primary sex educators (80 percent of them said so in 1976 and in other studies), they are doing an inadequate job. While this statement may seem somewhat harsh, it can be upheld whether measured in terms of parents' own assessment of their success at this job, the many areas of sexuality which are neglected in most parent-child communication, or the high rates of unplanned and unwanted pregnancy among adolescent women.

The second theme is the extent to which fathers are absent from conversations about sexuality—whether by design or by default. This is certainly not to imply that fathers are absent from their children's sexual socialization, since their lack of participation in discussions and activities in itself constitutes a strong message about gender roles. In addition, we will see much evidence of a lingering double standard as parents, often in spite of their best intentions, continue to raise their sons and their daughters differently. Finally, we will hear of parents' troubling confusion in their role as sex educators. Caught between the sexual standards of the past (which many of them reject) and of the future (which they can barely imagine), many parents truly do not know what they want to communicate to their children today. In all likelihood, this confusion plays a large part in their silence.

TOPICS OF SEXUAL COMMUNICATION

Parents indicate repeatedly that although they support sex education in the schools, they would still like to be their children's primary sex educators. Therefore, one would hope that they would talk to their children about a variety of sexual issues. Sadly, most parents find this a very difficult task.

In the 1976 study parents were presented with a list of 20 sexual topics and asked which of these they had discussed with their children. At the time of the questioning, the children ranged in age from 3 to 11. The list included topics that touched on most aspects of human sexuality. The emotional aspect was included via questions concerning love, marriage, and divorce. The physical or biological dimension of sexuality was represented by such topics as the physical differences between males and females, menstruation, and wet dreams. Parents were asked whether they had discussed issues related to gender roles such as situations in which boys and girls should not be together, or warning a child not to act like a sissy or a tomboy. In addition, the list included erotic topics such as masturbation and intercourse; social issues such as abortion, prostitution, premarital sex; and topics related to reproduction. These categorizations, of course, are not rigid. Depending on the content, a discussion of premarital sex, for instance, could be used to communicate many different messages. Such a discussion could focus on the biological reality that people do not need to be married in order to have sex and/or get pregnant; it could deal with the emotional or erotic aspects of why unmarried people would want to make love with each other; or it could be used to emphasize the social dimension of the parents' values about premarital sex.

Setting aside for a moment the issue of conversational content, Table 1 presents the percentage of parents who, in whatever way, had discussed each of these topics with their children *at any point in time*. Perhaps the clearest message to emerge from this table is how few topics most parents had discussed with their children. In fact, there are only four topics that more than half of the mothers had discussed with either their sons or their daughters: pregnancy and birth, love, the physical differences between men and women, and marriage or divorce. The investigators labeled these the "easy topics" because they are issues that most young children will raise themselves, and they are topics that most parents can discuss with relative ease.

One will notice, however, that only one of even these easy topics had been discussed by the majority of fathers. Far fewer fathers than mothers had discussed all but one of the topics with either their sons or their daughters. In fact, many fathers were not even aware of a number of the sexual conversations that had taken place in their families. They were

TABLE 1 Percentage of Parents Reporting Having Ever Discussed Sexual Topics with 3- to 11-Year-Old Children (1976)

	Mothers With		*Fathers With*	
Topics	*Sons*	*Daughters*	*Sons*	*Daughters*
Marriage and/or divorce	53.0%	52.0%	36.0%	34.0%
Love	73.0	74.0	40.0	46.0
Pregnancy and birth	76.0	71.0	46.0	39.0
Abortion	17.0	20.0	8.0	13.0
Rape or sexual abuse	38.0	53.0	21.0	24.0
Intercourse	14.0	16.0	9.0	6.0
Premarital sex or sex before marriage	9.0	14.0	2.0	3.0
Homosexuality or lesbianism	17.0	13.0	10.0	8.0
Prostitution (having sex for money)	9.0	13.0	7.0	6.0
Situations in which boys and girls shouldn't be together	25.0	32.0	16.0	17.0
The physical differences between men and women	73.0	66.0	54.0	57.0
Contraception or birth control	7.0	9.0	2.0	2.0
Venereal disease	8.0	12.0	7.0	6.0
Nudity (being naked)	49.0	43.0	38.0	38.0
Wet dreams	1.0	1.0	2.0	1.0
Menstruation	16.0	38.0	3.0	5.0
Masturbation or playing with your genitals	20.0	13.0	13.0	7.0
Sex play	26.0	28.0	36.0	34.0

missing out on an important part of their children's socialization, and perhaps more importantly, the children were not benefiting from the male's perspective on sexual issues. Fathers do seem to share more in the sexual education of their sons than of their daughters (Koblinsky & Atkinson, 1982).

Parents gave a number of reasons for not talking more with their young children about sexual matters. In part, they were confused about what to say. Sometimes they weren't certain what they believed, given all the changes in society's sexual mores. Unsure of what they wanted to communicate to their children they lapsed into silence. Sometimes they weren't sure what a young child needs to know or will be able to comprehend. Viewing sexuality as confusing or complex, these parents seemed to decide that "the less said the better it will be." Observations of and conversations with young children, however, indicate that they are most likely to absorb what is salient to them, fit it into their current knowledge of the world, and dismiss the rest. A child's capacity for forgetting sexual (and other) details is quite impressive, a situation that is one of the strongest arguments for encouraging parents to discuss all aspects of sexuality with their children—not once, but repeatedly at various stages of their children's development. It is likely that each discussion will have new meaning for the child.

However, the most frequent response given by parents to the question of why they had not discussed more sexual topics was that the child was not old enough, or that the child had not asked. Often these reasons were contained in the statement, "When he is ready, he will ask." Unfortunately, this is often not the case. One of the truisms about human communication between people of any age is that it is an imperfect process. The message one person meant to send often fits only partially at best with the message received. One of the clearest messages received by many children from their parents' silence about or discomfort with discussing sexuality is that the issue should not be raised. It is taboo, it is dirty, it is dangerous, it makes mom and dad upset or angry. "No one is talking about this; therefore, I better not either." Thus, in all too many American households discussion of sexuality is skirted in the early years, and by the time the child is old enough for the parent to be willing to talk about sexuality, the child has learned not to raise the subject.

Even in households where young children are willing to ask sexual questions, verbal communication is hindered by at least two factors. The first is that in some cases a child would almost have to know the answer in order to properly formulate the question. For instance, the information that many parents convey about how a woman becomes pregnant provides the child with little sense that there are ways to avoid pregnancy. Some children emerge from these discussions with the sense that pregnancy is a direct result of love or marriage or wanting a child. Far fewer have been told that heterosexual intercourse is required. What then would ever prompt these children to ask a question about birth control? Now on the one hand we might say that a 3- to 11-year-old child has no need to know about birth control. This is true. These children are not, for the most part, going to experience an unwanted pregnancy in the immediate future. It is worth noting, however, that it is the youngest teens, those aged 11 to 14, whose birthrate is rising, while for all other women, including older teens, the birthrate has leveled off or is on the decline. In fact, it is my years of work with teenage mothers that makes me wish that discussions of birth control would begin in early childhood. In the absence of any evidence to support my case, I can only wonder whether adolescents would be more willing and able to contracept effectively if they had, from their earliest introduction to reproduction and sexuality, learned that pregnancy is a process we can control; that most times people make love it is for pleasure rather than to become pregnant; and that when pregnancy is not wanted, there are things we can do.

Thus, in households where sexual conversations occur only in response to the child's initiative, many topics are left untouched due to the child's ignorance or learned reluctance to ask questions. Given how important and pervasive sexuality is in our lives, it is quite remarkable that parents, acting as sex educators, are willing to leave curriculum development almost entirely up to the students.

One of the areas in which parents do take some initiative is in emphasizing gender roles. Almost half of the mothers and almost one third of the fathers had spoken to their children about not acting like a sissy or a tomboy. In general, apart from the "easy topics" the issues most likely to be discussed were those dubbed by the researchers as "the control topics." These are aspects of sexuality about which the parents tended to caution their children regarding their behavior. In the early years parents seem more concerned about "gender appropriate behavior" with their sons than with their daughters.

Although girls were more often cautioned about situations in which boys and girls should not be together, parents were more troubled by the possibility of a boy acting like a sissy than by a girl acting like a tomboy. Not only did they mention it more often, but they began the warnings at an earlier age. These parental patterns are in keeping with our current social norms which have incorporated a sense of the advantage to females of various, previously "masculine" traits and privileges, but which do not yet appreciate the benefits that may be experienced by males of including "feminized" behaviors and perspectives in their repertoire. This tendency to caution boys also reflects parents' greater fear of male homosexuality than of lesbianism. Many parents in the 1976 study voiced the concern that their boys not grow up "sissified" or gay. I believe such homophobia has serious consequences for male development, particularly for father-son relationships. This is more clear in the realm of behavior than in oral communication.

The pattern of frequent communication about sexuality with words of caution is not what parents desire. Many of them remember getting the same messages from their own parents when they were young and they express a strong desire to break the cycle. However, when they try a different approach they often meet with limited success. The issue of masturbation is a good case in point. The following two quotes are from mothers who believe that most children masturbate and that masturbation is acceptable. One of them reported, "I just said that I thought if she had to do it, to please do it in the privacy of her own room." The other said, "I told her as long as she does it in bed and doesn't overdo it or get sick, it's fine." These messages are certainly not all bad. Neither mother told the child not to masturbate and the behavior was acknowledged and discussed. For this they are to be commended. Inadvertently, however, they also may have communicated that the behavior is not fully acceptable. "You can do it if you *have* to, but you may get sick." And, "please do it in private." The results of such communication are evident among the adolescent subjects of the 1983 study. Over 50 percent of the girls and 40 percent of the boys said that they would feel guilty if they masturbated. Fewer than 25 percent of either sex disagreed with that statement. The task of communicating positive sexual messages is a difficult one for parents who did not receive them in their own childhood.

In summary we see that verbal communication about sexuality in early childhood is sparse. Mothers play a larger role than fathers in the sexual socialization of both girls and boys. It is the children, however, who are most responsible for initiating discussions because many parents talk about sexuality only when they are asked a direct question, or when the child's behavior prompts them to issue some warning. Given that most of the parents interviewed in 1976 expected to discuss most sexual issues by the time their child had reached adolescence, it is interesting to look at which patterns had changed and which had remained the same after the passage of seven years.

THE INFLUENCE OF GENDER ON SEXUAL COMMUNICATION

In the 1983 study both parents and teens were given a slightly revised list of 19 sexual topics and asked which of the 19 they had ever discussed and which ones they had discussed during the past year. Some patterns had clearly remained intact. By everyone's report mothers were still talking to their children more than fathers. Table 2 presents the percentage of parents who had discussed each topic with their sons and daughters; it is the

TABLE 2 Percentage of Parents Reporting Having Ever Discussed Sexual Topics with Their Teens (1983)

	Mothers With		*Fathers With*	
Topic	*Sons*	*Daughters*	*Sons*	*Daughters*
Marriage and/or divorce	83.9%	87.7%	69.9%	66.3%
Love	83.9	86.1	63.9	61.4
Pregnancy and birth	86.5	93.9	68.3	54.2
Abortion	56 3	73.0	42.2	44.6
Rape or sexual abuse	65 2	78.3	47.0	45.8
Intercourse	58.0	64.3	50.6	34.9
Premarital sex or sex before marriage	75.0	83.5	55.4	53.0
Homosexuality or lesbianism	69.6	71.3	45.8	48.2
Prostitution (having sex for money)	61.6	72.2	47.0	42.2
Situations in which boys and girls shouldn't be together	57.7	68.4	44.6	46.3
Religious teachings about sexuality	43.2	53.0	39.0	41.0
The physical differences between men and women	64.3	72.2	51.8	42.7
Contraception or birth control	46.4	63.5	43.4	39.8
Venereal disease	60.7	70.4	51.8	44.6
Nudity (being naked)	56.3	62.6	51.8	34.9
Wet dreams	25.0	19.3	19.3	2.4
Menstruation	47.7	93.0	22.0	28.0
Masturbation or playing with your genitals	25.7	20.9	28.0	9.6
Orgasm	15.2	17.5	18.3	6.0
Average Number of Topics Discussed	10.9	12.5	8.4	7.3

parents' report. The teens' report is presented in Table 3. In general, parents and children had similar assessments of which topics had been discussed. Overall, however, teens reported lower levels of communication than did parents. The average number of topics fathers reported having discussed was about eight with their sons and seven with their daughters. That is, they had discussed fewer than half of the topics listed. The children did not recall having had even this many discussions with their dads. Both boys and girls reported an average of five topics. Mothers' scores were of course higher. They said they had discussed an average of 12 topics with their daughters and 11 with their sons. The daughters pretty nearly agreed, saying that they had talked about 11 of these topics with their

TABLE 3 Percentage of Teens Reporting Having Ever Discussed Sexual Topics with Parents (1983)

	Boys With		*Girls With*	
Topic	*Mother*	*Father*	*Mother*	*Father*
Marriage and/or divorce	65.0%	57.6%	87.9%	62.9%
Love	60.6	38.0	76.4	47.8
Pregnancy and birth	61.3	40.5	86.1	30.2
Abortion	40.6	25.9	66.1	28.9
Rape or sexual abuse	38.8	29.1	70.3	42.1
Intercourse	40.6	36.1	59.4	20.8
Premarital sex or sex before marriage	38.8	34.8	64.8	28.3
Homosexuality or lesbianism	36.3	27.2	52.1	29.6
Prostitution (having sex for money)	35.0	35.4	51.5	32.7
Situations in which boys and girls shouldn't be together	40.6	30.4	71.5	44.0
Religious teachings about sexuality	31.9	25.3	44.2	22.6
The physical differences between men and women	46.3	34.2	70.9	29.6
Contraception or birth control	32.5	20.9	52.7	17.0
Venereal disease	25.6	22.2	50.9	18.2
Nudity (being naked)	26.9	21.5	37.6	20.1
Wet dreams	20.0	12.0	9.7	3.1
Menstruation	17.5	11.4	93.3	20.1
Masturbation or playing with your genitals	12.5	9.5	14.5	3.8
Orgasm	8.8	9.5	11.5	3.1
Average Number of Topics Discussed	6.8	5.2	10.7	5.1

mothers. The sons on the other hand reported having talked about an average of eight.

Many inferences can be drawn from these figures. In most American households, for instance, talking about sexuality is largely a female activity. Since mothers talk to daughters more than to sons while fathers, according to teen reports, talk to all children about the same, the net result is that sons receive less verbal input about sexuality from their parents. This is true even about topics of special salience to one sex or the other. For instance, over 80 percent of the girls said that a parent had discussed menstruation with them before their first period. By contrast, only 20 percent of the boys said that a parent had told them about wet dreams before they experienced one.

In response to a question about how ready they felt when they had their first period or wet dream in terms of knowing what might happen and feeling ready twice as many girls (33 percent) as boys (16 percent) reported feeling very ready. In terms of preparing their children for their own biological development, American parents could be doing better. There is more room for improvement in terms of educating our children about the physical development of the other sex. Fewer than one out of five of the boys recalled having been told about menstruation by a parent, and wet dreams had been discussed with less than 10 percent of the girls. I believe this is but one manifestation of viewing males and females as "opposite" sexes, wholly different and mysterious in their bodily and emotional functioning. Lack of information about the other sex during childhood and adolescence helps to keep alive destructive myths such as the "uncontrollable male sex drive" which is still believed by many teenage girls and which may prevent them from responding to their own desires to engage in or abstain from erotic activity. Simultaneously, the perpetuation of this myth gives young (and old) males great license to apply pressure on young (and older) women.

THE EVAPORATION OF SEXUAL COMMUNICATION

The gap between teens' and parents' recall of discussions is even more striking than tables 2 and 3 reveal when one compares the responses of members of the same household. Concerning every topic, and across every type of parent-child dyad (mother-daughter, mother-son, father-daughter, father-son) there are substantial numbers of individuals who do not recall a conversation that the other person said took place. This does not mean that they disagree about the specific timing or content of a conversation. Rather, it means that someone does not even believe that the topic was ever discussed. Although disagreements do occur in both directions, it is by far more frequent that the teen does not recall a topic that the parent says had been discussed.

To give you some sense of the magnitude of the potential problem, we will look more closely at a topic of great importance to most contemporary parents of teenagers—premarital sex. Almost half of the fathers and three quarters of the mothers said they had discussed this topic with their teen at some point. When their children's responses were examined, however, fewer than half recalled any conversation on this subject. The only exception to this pattern was the mother-daughter dyad. Yet even among the females (who overall seem to have the best-shared recall), over a quarter of the daughters whose mothers said they had discussed premarital sex reported having had no such discussion. With respect to mothers and sons it could be said that for every 100 mothers walking around feeling that she has covered premarital sex with her adolescent son, 55 of them are mistaken. Whether they have actually discussed the topic or not, they have sons who say they have not. The picture for fathers is even slightly worse.

The pattern of adolescent amnesia (or parent-child disagreement) is neither uniform nor apparently random. Following the lead of the 1976 investigators, we grouped most of the 19 topics into three broad categorizations. The "easy" topics, which continued to be most frequently discussed, were the least likely sources of disagreement. In the middle range were the control topics (premarital sex, venereal disease, abortion, rape, homosexuality, and prostitution). On the average in every dyad other than mothers and daughters, over 55 percent of the teens disagreed with their parents who thought the topic had been discussed. The greatest discrepancies, however, concerned the more erotically related topics of intercourse, birth control, and orgasm. Here even mothers and daughters approached a 50 percent disagreement rate, while over 75 percent of the fathers who thought they had discussed any one of these topics had daughters who did not concur.

How shall we interpret these impressive discrepancies in recall? Do parents overreport the number of topics they have discussed because they believe they should have talked more to their kids and they want to look good to the researchers? That is certainly one possibility. It is also possible that some parents think so much about talking to their kids about venereal disease, premarital sex, and so on, planning in their minds, perhaps with their spouses, exactly how to say it, that they come to feel they really have had a conversation with the child when in fact they have not. It is also possible that the kids forget. They may have learned about a particular topic first from some other source such as a book, a friend, an older sibling, or a sex education class. Under this circumstance they may not recall a conversation with a parent because the conversation was of little consequence. They already had another place from which they could get information or sort out their values. They may also be more likely than their parents to forget a conversation that took place in early childhood. Parents are apt to remember how cute or upsetting it was when at the age of three Sarah wanted big breasts or Johnny asked to take a bath with Grandma. Children, however, tend to remember these events only when they are recounted to them repeatedly as they grow up.

Alternatively, discomfort on the part of both parties may make any sexual conversation so charged that the child absorbs little other than the sense of anxiety and later blocks any memory of the event. This explanation would certainly make sense of the finding that the greatest discrepancies in memory are related to the most erotic topics, and are greatest for dyads with one member of each sex. Both parents and children have difficulty seeing each other as erotic, sexual people. Thus, anxiety is likely to be highest when these topics are discussed. A frequent response to anxiety, of course, is to avoid it. Thus, even the anticipated anxiety of discussing a sexual topic may be enough to deter many parents, even when they believe the topic should be covered. Alternatively, if parents were able to accept their own anxiety and that of their children, they could compensate for this dynamic by trying to discuss anxiety-producing topics more often. Such acceptance would increase the likelihood of the content sinking in and would probably reduce the associated anxiety as well.

In addition to all of the reasons given above, I suspect that parents and children have different estimations of what interactions are worthy of recognition as conversations. For example, as mentioned earlier, parents, particularly when the children are young, tend to leave intercourse out of explanations of pregnancy. When the child gets a few years older and learns about intercourse he may feel that his parents did not really discuss pregnancy with him.

Children of all ages are trying to figure out their role in the world, their feelings, their code of conduct. These goals, often unacknowledged, influence the child's focus during much parent-child interaction. While school-based sex education may be an excellent source of factual information about many aspects of human sexuality, there is reason to believe that directly or indirectly both young children and adolescents attend to conversations with their parents on the level of values. Almost 60 percent of the daughters and over 33 percent of the sons named their mother as their most important source of help in terms of sorting out their values. Fathers were in second place for sons (14 percent) just ahead of teachers (12 percent). For daughters, fathers were in a third-place tie with sisters (5 percent), both of whom were cited less frequently than female friends (11 percent). Almost no one consciously uses the media as their primary source of help with sexual values. The combined scores of print and broadcast media amounted to less than 4 percent for either sex. In contrast, there is noticeably more variation in who teens cite as their most helpful source of sexual information. Mothers are still first for daughters (42 percent) but second for sons (20 percent), teachers being their primary source (28 percent). Fathers are further down on the list. Thus, children may be most apt to recall those parental conversations that were directly helpful in addressing their value-based concerns.

A somewhat distinct, but closely related issue is the extent to which parental comments are personal or general in nature. Fathers in particular have been seen as discussing sexual issues most often on a social, sometimes platitudinous level (Hepburn, 1981). If parents make general comments about sexual conduct at a time when teens want more personal conversations to help them with the sexual dilemmas of adolescent life, it is reasonable that the two groups would disagree about whether an issue had been discussed.

TABLE 4 The Percentage of Teens Reporting They Would Like to Talk More with Their Parents about Various Sexual Topics (1983)

Topics	*Females*	*Males*
Dating	53.0	46.0
Love	51.0	40.0
Marriage and/or divorce	48.0	37.0
My parents' own experiences	39.0	24.0
Pregnancy and childbirth	33.0	15.0
Birth control	27.0	11.0
Sexual intercourse	25.0	14.0
The ways my body is changing	13.0	16.0
Menstruation	9.0	2.0
Homosexuality	4.0	3.0
Masturbation	2.0	2.0

That adolescents look to their parents less for information than for guidance with the emotional dimension of sexuality is made very clear by the topics they say they would like to talk with them about more. As Table 4 illustrates, there was tremendous agreement between the sexes on this matter. Dating, love, marriage and divorce, and their parents' own experiences are the issues that both male and female adolescents would most like to discuss more with their mothers and fathers. These were mentioned much more frequently than the biological or physical aspects of sexuality. Another recent study found that preadolescents are most concerned with their bodies and the biological dimension of sexuality while adolescents are most concerned with the interpersonal aspect (Riddle 1984). Surprisingly, marriage, divorce, and love were the topics that the greatest proportion of parents said they had discussed with their children of all ages. Yet, children want more communication in these areas. Nothing could argue more strongly for encouraging parents to discard the "innoculation theory" of sex education which holds that a topic once discussed can be considered taken care of. Sexuality, in all its dimensions, is a vital part of life. Children, both young and old, should be provided multiple opportunities for discussing it with their parents and with others.

Hopefully, parents will take heart from the fact that it is the emotional aspects of sexuality that their teenagers would like to discuss more. For if they are willing, they will certainly be able to share their perspectives on these issues. Having such discussions does require parents' willingness to engage on a more personal level, particularly in sharing their own experiences. Fathers especially may require help with this task. The task does not require mastery of high-level anatomy or other facts of which a parent may be unsure. It does, however, require that parents be open to their children, that they reach some clarity about their own sexual values, and/or that they be willing to share their uncertainties.

Those service providers who work directly with parents should, of course, not neglect their concerns. Parents report that the topics they would most like to discuss more easily with their teens are those related to eroticism (intercourse, orgasm, and masturbation), physical issues (wet dreams, venereal disease), and of course, premarital sex. It is certainly possible that one reason adolescents rarely say they want to discuss these issues more with their parents is that they feel it would be impossible since such discussions have not yet occurred, or they do not appear to be worth the tension they create. In addition to discussing erotic topics, parents have expressed the desire for help in dealing with adolescent rebellion, peer pressure, and the art of single parenting a child of the other sex as these issues relate to their children's sexual development (Riddle, 1984).

A RATIONALE FOR INCREASING SEXUAL COMMUNICATION

Talking about sex begets talking about sex. Parents who report that sexuality was discussed frequently in their own childhood homes had, on the average, discussed significantly more sexual topics with their own children both when they were young and when they were adolescents. Parents who had discussed more with their children in the past also had teens who more frequently initiated conversations about sexuality during the last year. Hence, just as a parent's silence can lead to a child's learning not to ask sexual questions, a parent's willingness to talk about sex leads to a child's comfort in raising issues herself. Essentially, anxiety about sexual communication seems to be desensitized by more frequent discussions.

Having spoken with a young child about sex also makes it more likely that she (or he) will be able to come to the parents in the event of sexual abuse. It may increase the child's chances of resisting sexual coercion as well. In the 1976 study just over half of the daughters and one third of the sons had been spoken to about the possibility of sexual molestation or abuse. Now that we as a nation are discovering how frequent incest and other forms of child sexual abuse are it seems imperative that we speak to our children about the subject and encourage them to report any abusive events to their parents. I am not arguing for this topic to be discussed above all others. On the contrary, warnings about molestation in the absence of any discussion of the positive aspects of sexuality could be harmful. I am recommending that the topic be included, and that in general helping a child to feel good about her body and at ease talking about bodies and touching is likely to help her prevent sexual abuse or to limit its ill effects because she will not have to carry it around as a secret. The rape of adult women too remains a drastically underreported crime. If, as we change the practices of our police departments and courts, we also change the nature of early childhood sexual education, perhaps future generations of women will suffer less.

This tendency for "talking to lead to talking" extends beyond the family boundary as well. Teens who reported more conversations with their parents were more likely to believe that it is OK to talk about sex with people outside the family. This opens up new sources of help and information to them and is likely to be of great benefit in their own present and later intimate relationships. This belief is already manifest in the positive relationship between the number of sexual topics teens had discussed with their parents and the number of nonparental sources of help with sexual information and values they had already used. In addition, the more topics they had already discussed and the more sources of information they had, the more likely they were to want to talk more. So the communication channels must be opened and kept greased if they are to be used most beneficially.

In addition, we found that the more both mothers and fathers talked with the children, the greater was the likelihood that the children, as adolescents, would remember the conversations. For mothers, who do the bulk of the talking, this also led to a greater number of shared sexual values between them and their children. Certainly, one of the reasons that parents would want to talk with their children about sexuality is that they, the parents, have a set of values, a perspective on sexuality, which they would like to transmit. Given all the data indicating that as children grow older their parents become a less important reference group and are supplanted by peers, parents should know that if they talk to their children enough they can still have a profound effect on the development of their children's values concerning abortion, homosexuality, premarital sex, nudity, sex roles, and so on.

It is all well and good that talking leads to talking but is it good for anything else? Or does it carry any potential danger? Some opponents of sex education in the schools, for instance, have asserted that too much talk amounts to temptation and is directly related to teenage sexual activity. Parents have sometimes worried that by talking about sex with their children they will be putting ideas into their heads. The research literature, however, overwhelmingly contradicts this concern. The only studies which have shown a positive relationship between parent-child communication and adolescent sexual activity are those that measured very recent communication. In these cases the investigators have tended to conclude that it was the teen's sexual activity that prompted the communication, rather than vice versa (Inazu & Fox, 1980). There is also some indication that mothers talk more with their daughters when they believe that premarital sex is the norm in their community, whether or not they think their daughters are sexually active (Herceg-Baron & Shea, 1983).

There is much more evidence that parent-child communication may have the effect of delaying a child's first experience of intercourse. In particular, when sexuality is learned about first in the home, intercourse is likely to be delayed (Lewis, 1973; Spanier, 1977). Conversely, others have found that where there is poor parent-child communication, the child is more likely to become sexually active at a young age (Jessor & Jessor, 1975; Kantner & Zelnik, 1972; Chilman, 1978). Lewis has said, "Specifically, the greater the number of sexual topics discussed by parents, the less likely were the children in their adolescent and young adult years to have had a coital experience and to have been promiscuous" (Lewis, 1973, p. 162). Our own data support this most strongly for the mother-son relationship.

There are, of course, many reasons for encouraging teens to delay sexual activity, especially sexual intercourse. The high rates of pregnancy and sexually transmitted diseases have received much attention from policymakers and researchers. Parents certainly share these concerns, as well as their own concerns about morality, bad reputations, broken hearts, distractions from schoolwork, and coercive sex to name a few. One of the most surprising reasons I have found for slowing the pace of adolescent sexual experience emerged from our own 1983 study. Simply stated, we found that the higher the teens' level of sexual activity, the less satisfied they were with their sex lives. This was true for both males and females. Furthermore, it did not relate only to a teen's status as virgin or nonvirgin. Teens were asked about eight specific sexual behaviors which were then condensed into a five-point scale of no experience, kissing, petting, nonintercourse orgasm (petting to orgasm and/or oral-genital sex), and intercourse. The higher their score on this scale, the lower their reported level of sexual satisfaction. In the absence of detailed information on the basis of their discontent, we can only speculate on the dynamics of this finding. There are two basic plausible scenarios. The first is that erotic contact between teenagers is in itself unpleasant, tense, emotionally difficult, guilt inducing, or otherwise somehow unsatisfying. The alternative is that these experiences are quite pleasant and that the dissatisfaction comes from wanting more, whether it be more frequent contact, more varied activity, or more control over their sex lives.

Closely related to this was our finding that, particularly in the father-son relationship, higher levels of communication are related to greater sexual comfort for the sons. Sexual comfort was measured by the teens' level of agreement or disagreement with the following statements: I enjoy the feeling of being a little bit turned on; I enjoy how my body changes as I get older; I often feel guilty after making out or having sex with someone; It is easy for me to talk with my friends about sexual things; and I would feel comfortable looking at myself naked in the mirror when no one else is there. So there is some indication that talking with one's children about sexuality makes them more comfortable as sexual beings and is likely to lead to a delay in the onset of their own sexual activity, especially intercourse, which may lead to greater satisfaction with their sex lives.

So there are many positive reasons for parents to assume an active role in the sexual education of their children at all ages. However, it should be recognized that sexual communication might have some negative effects in that parents could pass on their own misinformation (Roberts, Klein, & Gagnon, 1978; Herceg-Baron & Shea, 1983) or their own problematic attitudes. For instance, interviews with a sample of mothers with sexually active teenage daughters revealed that "Over half the mothers agreed that using birth control was a bother and that if girls were prepared with a birth control method it meant they were looking to have sex" (Herceg-Baron & Shea, 1983, p. 21). It is to be expected, of course, that generations of sexual timidity and ambivalence are part of what will be communicated when parents and children talk about sexuality. How could it be otherwise? These dangers, however, are certainly less harmful to a child's sexual development than silence. For as we have documented, the major message conveyed by talking about sex is that it is not a closed or private subject. It can be talked about. This opens the possibility that the parents may communicate new messages as their values change and as new issues become more salient in the child's life. And it increases the chances that the child, throughout his life, will turn to other people and to the media for more information and new ideas on all aspects of sexuality.

NONVERBAL COMMUNICATION

During a child's early years the parents' nonverbal communication—their facial expressions, gestures, and behaviors—are likely to have at least as much impact on the child's sexual learning as anything the parents say. Through the social influence of modeling, children absorb many messages by watching their parents, their siblings, and others. Some of the behavior they imitate immediately and directly. Some of it they just notice and store away for later in their lives. At this stage in their lives much of their sexual learning is related to their bodies and their gender roles, that is, their understanding of what it means to be a girl or a boy. Many of the messages that parents communicate in these areas are inadvertent; they are simply embedded in the very structure of the household. For instance, are bedroom doors kept open or closed? How about bathroom doors? Who cooks dinner? Who earns money? Many messages are gleaned from observing the parents' own habits. Are they affectionate with each other? With the children? Do they cry? Do they exercise?

Parents' behavior is sometimes at odds with their stated values. For instance, in the 1976 study 90 percent of the fathers said they wanted to communicate to their children that it is good for men to cry. Yet most of these men also reported that they themselves rarely or never cry. Given that in most American households children at all ages are far more likely to see their mothers than their fathers cry, it seems reasonable to expect that future generations will grow up with the sense that crying is a feminine and not a masculine behavior. Does it matter that the majority of parents no longer think this should be the case even though they were raised with these stereotypes? Will fathers have to learn to cry in order to get across the message that it is OK for men to cry? It is hard to say. Modeling certainly is a potent form of communication. Also important, however, is how parents, both mothers and fathers, respond to their children's tears. In many instances girls are "rewarded" for their tears with lots of attention and concern for their physical or emotional hurts. Boys on the other hand are less likely to receive holding or comforting words. At very young ages, many American males are told not to cry, told that things "aren't that bad," or otherwise distracted from their expression of hurt or sorrow. Perhaps an easier first step for parents would be to try to change their responses to their children's emotional expression since their own emotional patterns will be very difficult to dislodge.

Crying is only one example of the countless ways in which parents every day act out the social norm that males and females are very different. From the moment of their birth boys are handled more roughly than girls. Girls are spoken to more gently than boys. Their worlds are different. They are given sex-stereotyped toys and encouraged in different forms of play. Girls, for instance, from their early years are encouraged to play in small groups. From this experience they tend to form a few, special friendships in which they learn among other things the art of intimate disclosure, the habit of confiding. They are provided few opportunities to learn teamsmanship and comfort in a large group. These early lessons become lifetime patterns. Boys on the other hand are encouraged to and do tend to play in larger groups. If their young son has a very special friend, many parents become concerned that this is inappropriate, or may be an early sign of homosexuality. Thus, boys are steered away from developing close friendships in their childhood. The skills of intimacy are thwarted and another generation of men who have trouble sharing their emotions—especially with other men—is created.

Similarly, girls are typically given many opportunities to develop their caring and nurturant skills. Dolls and stuffed animals are the first recipients of this care taking. Later they graduate to babysitting. Too often these opportunities are not available to boys. Thus, boys have little practice in tending to the needs of others, developing their nurturant capacities, and preparing for parenthood. This dichotomization of sex roles most often is simultaneously being modeled by their parents via their own division of household labor.

Sex role behavior is another way in which parents' own patterns often do not reflect their stated values. Approximately 50 percent of the fathers interviewed in 1976 agreed with the statement that "It is the woman's responsibility to run the house and care for the children." The remaining 50 percent of the fathers and well over half of the mothers disagreed with this statement. Yet when asked who in their own households took care of the cooking, routine child care, and discipline of the children, between 85 and 90 percent of all parents reported that the woman handled each of these tasks most or all of the time. This pattern held true in 1983 as well. Among the three activities, men were far more likely to share responsibility for discipline than for either cooking or routine care of the children. The investigators conclude that this is unfortunate because "the only activity in which fathers and mothers agree the father takes a more active role in the family is an area that may cast him in a negative or punitive light before his child" (Roberts, Kline & Gagnon, 1978, p. 36).

This uneven distribution of household responsibilities has many ramifications. The first, as we have said, is that it presents for the children a strongly sex-differentiated view of family life. Fathers simply are not involved in the daily maintenance of the household and the lives of its members. This is reflected in the 1983 findings that both male and female teenagers were far more likely to say that the family member to whom they felt closest was their mother (47 percent of the boys and 57 percent of the girls) rather than their father (21 percent of the boys and 9 percent of the girls). Both sexes also said that their mother knew more about what was going on in their lives than did their father.

Most important, perhaps, by not taking part in the routine aspects of family life fathers miss out on many opportunities for casual contact and conversation with their children. It is in just these casual contexts that most of the home-based conversations about many aspects of sexuality take place. When asked (during parent group discussions) when they talk to their children about sexual issues, mothers often answered that it was in the course of some regular activity. Frequently, a child would start an informal conversation after school while the mother was cooking dinner. Or a question would come up during bedtime preparation. One mother reported that when she had something she wanted to discuss with her teenage son she sometimes waited until she was giving him a haircut. This situation had many advantages in her eyes. It was informal and friendly. He couldn't get up and leave. They had the closeness of being in physical contact because of the haircut, but they were not looking directly at each other which allowed them to ask and say some things that otherwise might have been too hard. By not taking part in such routines fathers are not able to participate in these discussions. This connection is not pure speculation on our part. The 1976 study found that fathers who shared more of the household labor were more likely to be approached by their children concerning sexual matters.

Physical affection as an expression of intimacy and love is another important part of children's sexual learning in the home. Again children may learn from all dimensions of parents' touching behavior. How often or how rarely do they hug or kiss each other? Their children? Their same-sex and other-sex friends? Wives have expressed concern about the lessons their children might be gleaning from parental habits concerning affection. Some mentioned their fear that their children saw more bickering between the spouses than affectionate exchanges. Some worried about what the children thought when they saw a husband recoil from his wife's kisses when he returned home from work. A number of wives told us that their husbands were only affectionate as a prelude to lovemaking and that this behavior took place in the bedroom, away from the children's eyes. Many men expressed their counterpart to these statements. They said touching was difficult for them since it had not been part of how they were raised. They talked of having to remind themselves to show their affection for their wives or children. They knew it was something their family members liked, but not something they felt a need for or did easily.

Children learn these lessons early on. Among the 3- to 11-year-olds, parents observed that 60 percent of the boys did not hug their friends much while 60 percent of the girls did. By adolescence over 80 percent of the boys reported that they *never* hugged or kissed their male friends. An additional 15 percent did this only rarely. Girls are far more likely to engage in affectionate behavior with their girlfriends. These figures do not add much to our understanding. They simply illustrate how universal this code of behavior is among American males, and how early it is learned. The home certainly is not the only learning environment that reinforces the notion that male-to-male affection is not to be expressed physically. Clint Eastwood is more likely to hug his horse or his rifle than his buddy.

However, a different message could be communicated in the home and all too often it is not. Fathers are less affectionate with all of their children than are mothers; and far less affectionate with their sons than with their daughters. By watching this behavior it would be quite reasonable for children to assume that while women are generally pretty affectionate, males do not express affection often and when they do it is only toward women, and then often as a way of initiating lovemaking. Whatever needs boys may have to feel close without feeling "sexual" or to engage in passive and receptive touching are met within the family largely by their mothers, sometimes by their sisters, and rarely by the other males.

Daughters of course also gather lessons from their parents' affectionate behavior. Probably, they learn that in couple relationships women give more physical affection than they receive. It has been found that parental displays of spousal affection have implications for daughters' later erotic behavior. College women who had more often observed their mothers acting or speaking affectionately to their spouses were more likely in their own couple relationship to be open to a variety of erotic behaviors and to be more comfortable talking to their partners (Koblinsky & Palmeter, 1984).

The mothers who voiced concern that their children saw more conflict than tenderness between parents are reinforced by our 1983 findings. Teens were asked to rate (on a five-point scale) how in love they thought their parents were. Then they were asked why they had given their parents that rating. No matter how in love teens thought their parents were, how the parents handled conflict was a central aspect of their evaluation. Some adolescents thought their parents were not in love because they fought frequently. Others noticed that their parents rarely argued, handled disagreements well, or always made up quickly. The point is that more teens mentioned their parents' conflict behavior than any other aspect of the relationship when deciding how in love they were. Every aspect of the marital relationship, of course, comes under scrutiny as children watch and wonder what their own adult married lives will be like. This is typically the closest view they will get of an ongoing, intimate relationship, and many lessons are drawn from it.

In summary, parental behavior toward children, spouse, and friends is an important source of children's sexual learning. From every aspect of home life children glean lessons about their bodies, emotions, abilities, and potentials as males and females in contemporary America.

THE SPOUSAL CONNECTION

Children's emerging sexuality may have many ramifications for the spousal relationship. At times it will undoubtedly be the source of much pride and closeness as together husbands and wives watch their offspring mature and embrace life. It may also be a source of conflict, highlighting their own sexual discomforts or differences in values. Children's sexuality may trigger their parents' concerns about their own sexiness, their continuing appeal to their spouse. While it happens for both genders, there is evidence that men, more often than women, respond to their young daughters' "feminine" traits. They appreciate what they view as the girls' coy or flirtatious behavior. They prefer to see them in frills more often than their wives would choose. This is true even when the girl is under the age of five. In response, wives may feel angry or jealous (Maccoby & Jacklin, 1974). Such tension may emerge or reemerge during a daughter's adolescence. Although comparable scenarios could occur in which husbands compare themselves to their sons, this seems to be less frequent. Although sometimes such tensions may be temporary or only "skin deep," this sexualized attention to a child is often a result of conflict between the two parents. In essence, one parent may feel that the child offers gratification of needs for attention or affection which are not being met in the marriage. Turning to the child is a way of adapting to the underlying conflicts with the spouse. Such triangulation has serious potential for a young woman's or man's emerging sense of self as a sexual being. The clinical considerations of this are beyond the scope of this chapter.

Undoubtedly, one of the best antidotes to any such tensions would be for spouses to maintain an open channel of communication with each other—to share their own reactions to their children's emerging sexuality and keep each other informed of sex-related discussions with the children. In many households such spousal exchanges are infrequent and may be inhibited by underlying marital discord. When asked how often they talked to their spouse (or live-in partner) about what they had said or planned to say to their children about sexual matters, over half of the parents replied that they did this rarely or never. This lack of communication affects not only the marital relationship. It may also mean that the child receives very different messages from his two parents. Divorce is likely to exacerbate this situation. Nearly three quarters of the divorced parents reported that they had not talked to each other about their children's sexual education even once during the prior 12 months. Although there may be benefits for a young person in experiencing different approaches to sexuality, some communication between parents seems desirable.

Interestingly, mothers who talk frequently with their daughters about sexuality seem to be no more likely than nontalkers to discuss parent-child sexual communication with their husbands (Herceg-Baron & Shea, 1983). They are, however, more likely to discuss the sexual aspects of child rearing with friends and relatives. Husbands, it appears, are not considered a primary source of support in this area by many of their wives. In fact, women are much more likely than men to prefer discussing sexual matters with their children by themselves. Husbands prefer to have their wives present. Women find this pattern most problematic in terms of handling sexual issues with their sons. Many wives had expected their husbands to take more responsibility for the sexual guidance of male children. Instead, they find that with sons as well as with daughters they are more in touch with the goings on in their children's lives, more often approached with questions or concerns, and more often worried. They serve as information conduits for fathers, passing along information to them that the children do not share directly. While for some this division of responsibilities is comfortable, for others it is disappointing.

Many men with whom we spoke seemed baffled by this state of affairs. They are still waiting for their children to come to them. They attribute the lack of such approaches to shyness, ignoring the fact that the children talk more openly with their mothers. In fact, some men are truly unaware of the discussions and interactions that take place between their family members. Mothers and children come to regard them in a sense as outsiders. In these families, the men are denied some of the richness of family life; the children do not benefit from an adult male's perspective on sexuality; and many married women find themselves functioning as partnerless parents.

Summary

In summary, parents influence their children's sexual development both directly and indirectly. Through what they say and what they do parents communicate messages about all aspects of sexuality and its role in life: what it means to be female or male; with whom and when it is acceptable to touch or not; to be naked, or not; to talk about sex, bodies, and relationships or not.

Many adults feel that their own parents handled sexual learning inadequately and they would like to do better by their own children. Yet they find their attempts hindered by long-standing embarrassments, by their confusion about changing social norms, and by workplace policies and traditions that leave many fathers with too little time to spend with their children.

Parents need encouragement in their roles as sex educators. They must be encouraged to talk more openly with their children, even when this means revealing their uncertainties about sexual facts or values. Above all, mothers and fathers must be encouraged to take more initiative in raising sexual issues. For while parents wait for children to become older or to ask specific questions, the children learn that mom and dad are not the right people to talk to about sex. When sexual discussion and exploration cannot take place in the home then sexuality becomes an extrafamilial affair.

Resources

There are literally hundreds of books available to help parents open up discussions with their children about sexuality. Some books are designed for parents to use to educate and prepare themselves. Others are designed to be read aloud to young children. Still others could be used appropriately with or by teenagers or preteens. Some books have many helpful pictures while others have none. Some books present a religious perspective on sexuality, while others do not. I encourage all parents to review the selections available at their local libraries, bookstores, clinics, and religious centers. I include here a few books that I think are very good.

1. *What is a Girl? What is a Boy?*
   by Stephanie Waxman
   Peace Press, Inc.
   3828 Willat Avenue, Culver City, CA 90230

With few words and many pictures this book beautifully addresses the young child's curiosity about bodies and physical development while it broadens our understanding of sex roles.

2. *Sex Education: The Parents' Role*
   by Sol Gorden and Irving R. Dickman
   This 28-page booklet is available inexpensively from:
   National Clearinghouse for Family Planning Information
   P.O. Box 2225
   Rockville, MD 20852

This booklet encourages parents to discuss sexuality openly with their children and includes questions often asked by both children and parents.

3. *Sex: The Facts, The Acts, and Your Feelings*
   by Michael Carrera
   Crown Publishers, Inc.
   One Park Avenue
   New York, NY 10016

For parents or teens, this book covers most aspects of human sexuality simply and thoroughly. It includes clear drawings and the answers to many frequently asked questions.

4. *Parents: Yes You Can*
   by Sally McCormick & Maggi Boyer
   Planned Parenthood Association of Bucks County
   721 New Rodgers Road
   Bristol, PA 19007

This 12-page pamphlet is designed to aid parents in discussing sexuality with their children. Topics include sexuality education, values sharing, and ways to communicate effectively.

5. *Changes and Choices—Your Children and Sex* (for parents)
   Changes—Sex and You (for preteens)
   Changes—You and Sex (for teenagers)
   National Clearinghouse for Family Planning Information
   P.O. Box 2225
   Rockville, MD 20852

These three companion booklets (each 16 pages) discuss both the facts and value issues related to physical development, pregnancy, birth control, and responsible sexual decision making.

References

Chilman, C. S. (1978). *Adolescent sexuality in a changing American society.* Washington, DC: U.S. Government Printing Office.

Gebhard, Paul H. (1977). The acquisition of basic sex information. *The Journal of Sex Research*, 13(3), 148–169.

Hepburn, E. H. (1981, Spring). The father's role in the sexual socialization of adolescent females in an upper and upper-middle class population. *Journal of Early Adolescence*, 7(1), 53–59.

Herceg-Baron, R., & Shea, Judy. (1983). *Sex-related communications in families with adolescent children: Implications for family planning providers.* Report prepared for the Bureau of Community Health Services, Office of Adolescent Pregnancy Programs, Washington, DC.

Inazu, J. K., & Fox, G. L. (1980, March). Maternal influence on the sexual behavior of teenage daughter. *Journal of Family Issues, 1*(1), 81–102.

Jessor, S. L., & J., R. (1975). Transition from virginity to non-virginity among youth: A social-psychological study over time. *Developmental Psychology, 11*(4), 473–484.

Kahn, J., & Pierson, J. (1984, June 9). *The effectiveness of parent- child communication about sexuality.* Paper presented at the Joint Annual Meetings of The Society for the Scientific Study of Sex and The American Association of Sex Educators, Counselors, and Therapists, Boston.

Kantner, J. F., & Zelnik, M. (1972). Sexual experience of young unmarried women in the United States. *Family Planning Perspectives, 4,* 9–18.

Koblinsky, S., & Atkinson, J. (1982, January). Parental plans for children's sexual education. *Family Relations, 31,* 29–35.

Koblinsky, S., & Palmeter, J. G. (1984, February). Sex-role orientation, mother's expression of affection toward spouse, and college women's attitudes toward sexual behaviors. *The Journal of Sex Research, 20*(1), 32–43.

Lewis, R. A. (1973). Parents and peers: Socialization agents in the coital behavior of young adults. *The Journal of Sex Research, 9*(2), 156–170.

Maccoby, E. E., & Jacklin, C. N. (1974). *The psychology of sex differences.* Stanford, CA: Stanford University Press.

Pillard, R. C., & Weinrich, J. D. (1984). *Male homosexuality runs in families.* Paper presented at the Annual Meeting of the Society for the Scientific Study of Sex, Boston.

Ramsey, G. V. (1943). The sex information of younger boys. *American Journal of Orthopsychiatry, 13,* 347–352.

Riddle, P. K. (1984, February). Helping parents become sex educators. *Children Today,* pp. 9–11

Roberts, E. J., Kline, D., & Gagnon, J. (1978). *Family life and sexual learning.* Cambridge, MA: Population Education.

Spanier, G. B. (1977). Sources of sex information and premarital sex behavior. *The Journal of Sex Research, 13*(2), 73–88.

Teddlie, C., N., S., Udry, J. R., Bauman, K. E., Smith, M. C., & Gilbert, M. *Determinants of adolescent sexual behavior: Biological, social, and psychological factors.* Paper presented at the Annual Meeting of the American Psychological Association, New York.

Thornburg, H. D. (1972, February). Comparative study of sex information sources. *The Journal of School Health. 42*(2), 88–91.

SECTION 3

Treatment

ELEVEN

Assessment of Marital Disorders

G. Pirooz Sholevar, M.D.
Clinical Professor of Psychiatry and Human Behavior
Jefferson Medical College

INTRODUCTION

The essential components in the assessment of a marital relationship consist of the description of marital problems in objective and observable terms, the identification of the psychodynamic forces and situational variables that control the problematic behaviors, and the evaluation of both assets and weaknesses in the marital relationship. The goal of comprehensive assessment is to establish guideposts to treatment outcome and to enable the clinician to consider a range of treatment methods and select the most appropriate and effective one for a particular couple. In a manner of speaking, such a process should provide the clinician with a "road map" to assist troubled couples, rather than a uniform, empirical approach to all couples seeking treatment.

The goal of marital assessment and the initial interview are intimately interwoven. In the initial interview, the clinician attempts to orient the couple to the assessment process, as well as to gather information about the presenting problem and the dysfunctional and functional areas in the marriage. However, the additional crucial task of the initial interview is to serve as the first treatment session where not only the couples' distress and hopelessness are addressed but positive expectations about treatment and marriage are raised. Therefore, it is essential that the therapeutic goals of the initial interview be given parity with its assessment function.

The type of clinical data gathered during the assessment process is determined largely by the theoretical orientation of the clinician. Although one can imagine the optimal clinical assessment as a clinical and behavioral treasure chest where any clinician can find the type of behavioral and clinical information essential to his intervention, we are far from such a comprehensive approach to human behavior. Thus, clinicians with different theoretical orientations seek divergent types of information to aid them with their therapeutic task.

All marital therapists have the common goal of helping the couple to describe their marital problems in objective, observable, and quantifiable terms. Furthermore, knowing the situational context of the behavior is crucial to an understanding of the genesis and maintenance of the problem behavior. Clear communication of the needs and expectations is subscribed to as the cornerstone of a healthy marital relationship by all marital therapists. However, basic differences lead clinicians to stress different types of clinical data. Behavioral marital therapists are keenly interested in the identification of the situational variables that control the symptoms—the antecedents and consequences of the behavior. The first set of variables sets the stage for the target behavior and the consequent variables are the environmental changes that follow the responses and affect their frequency. For the psychodynamically oriented marital therapists, the identification of the interacting personality traits, the conscious and unconscious needs, and the defensive organization of each spouse's personality assume a significant position. The subjective feelings, ideas, and experiences of each spouse are the keys that lead the clinician to recognize the derivations of the unconscious conflicts of each spouse which are projected onto the marital relationship and give rise to symptomatic interactions. The followers of marital contract theory attempt to discover incongruency between the marital contracts of the two spouses. A clinician with a family systems orientation will examine the multiple levels of communications and the concealed, covert messages within the family system, all of which maintain symptomatic interactions through multiple feedback mechanisms in order to reestablish homeostasis within the (nuclear or extended) family unit.

Regardless of orientation, assessment of the marital relationship should be considered as an ongoing process beginning with the first contact between the clinician and the troubled couple and continuing throughout the course of treatment. Such a continuous course will allow the clinician to address the areas of optimal functioning and dysfunction in married couples during the course of treatment. For nonbehavioral marital therapists, the task of assessment is achieved through joint and individual interviews. Behavioral marital therapists rely differentially on the utilization of a variety of behavioral instruments for the assessment of marital disorders. This chapter begins with the description of the initial interview as it serves as a significant assessment tool, particularly for nonbehavioral marital therapists.

INITIAL INTERVIEW

The goals of an initial interview are twofold: (1) To gather assessment information, and (2) To set the stage for the therapeutic change by building positive expectations in the couples about treatment and about their marriage.

To begin the interview, it is helpful to provide the couples with an orientation to the assessment process by reviewing the entire evaluation phase. This helps to reduce confusion and apprehension in the spouses. The orientation should indicate the clinician's interest in obtaining some detailed information about the presenting problems, the situations that give rise to the target symptoms, different areas of marital satisfaction and dissatisfaction, including relationships with children and other relatives, the history of the marital relationship, and the spouses as separate people and their communication patterns. The overview should be presented in a relaxed and conversational manner while warmth and interest in the couple is communicated through eye contact and nonverbal behavior.

The assessment process in the interview commonly begins by asking the couple to define their marital problems in specific, objective, and discrete terms. The troubled couple generally arrives at the clinician's office describing their difficulties in condensed or general terms. Such broad generalizations serve as a vehicle for the couple to attack each other's personalities rather than provide them with guidelines for behavioral change. Therefore, the clinician should patiently ask the couple to define the specific behavioral manifestations of statements such as "my husband is inconsiderate or unappreciative."

The description of the antecedents and consequences of problem behavior are crucial to both understanding the nature of the problem and providing the means for change. The goal of bringing about change is usually achieved by asking the couples to describe the events that precede and follow the target behavior. Direct attack on the target behavior is generally unsuccessful and has been attempted by the couple for a long time. However, by addressing the antecedent and consequent variables of the same behavior, the clinician can succeed in bringing about change.

The examination of the situational characteristics of problem areas can naturally lead to the exploration of the role of each partner in generating the problem behavior. Although it is obvious that the interacting couple contributes to the genesis of any behavior, this view is adamantly opposed by the couple, each of whom tends to see him/herself as a victim of the other. The description of the setting and the sequences leading to the problem behavior can generally clarify the role of each spouse in the genesis of symptomatic interaction. For example, the concrete symptom of the physical abuse of a wife by a husband can lead to a broader picture of the husband entering the home preoccupied and tense, the wife nagging him for failure to carry out a task, and escalation of negative verbal exchanges into a physical fight where the wife gets the worst of it. Thus, the description of the situational sequences is essential to clarify each spouse's role. This awareness puts the spouses in a position of control and reduces both guilt and lack of cooperation between a married couple.

When inquiring about the presenting problems, the clinician should explore the first signs of significant problems after marriage. Such early problems are frequently related to the subsequent difficulties and presenting problems. Furthermore, one spouse's initial attempt at changing the behavior of the other spouse is generally part of the current problem. Faulty behavior-change techniques such as remaining silent or utilizing punitive strategies can generally lead to an exacerbation of the problems. The problem-solving deficits are therefore associated with the development and exacerbation of marital conflicts.

A detailed description of the problem areas should not occupy the major part of the initial interview. Although the limited expression of anger and frustration may help to reduce a couple's feelings of hopelessness and despair, prolonged blaming and "negative tracking" can produce the opposite results and undermine the couple's positive expectations regarding treatment and their marriage.

Assessment of the marital relationship should address multiple aspects of marital functioning such as communication and need satisfaction, rather than dwelling on the problematic areas described by the couple. Examination of a wide range of couple interactions should provide a detailed analysis of both the strengths and weaknesses of a particular couple. The latter will serve as a vehicle for broadening the perspective of the couple on the totality of their relationship. Identification of the behaviors that would enhance the relationship quality can be of great help particularly after the initial presenting problems are altered in the treatment or have lost their sense of immediacy and urgency. Therefore, the identification of desirable behaviors should be made at the outset of the treatment.

The assessment of marital behavior should not be based strictly on a couple's overt behavior. The beliefs of the spouses about themselves, their mates, and the quality of their relationship are important variables which are intimately related to their overt behavior. The clinician should attempt to unearth the spouses' self-dialogue prior to unearthing their overt behaviors. In addition to searching for irrational, cognitive concepts about self and others which can mediate unadaptive responses in the couple, the clinician should make a note of the couple's lack of knowledge of key concepts or the couple's failure to produce such cognitions under certain circumstances which may interfere with adequate performance and adjustment. For example, the couple may fail to recognize the crisis situations that can overwhelm their problem-solving capacity and instead may attack each other for being unavailable, unhelpful, or inconsiderate.

The therapist should explore the reason the couple has requested consultation. It is simplistic to assume that couples seek consultation solely for the purpose of improving their relationship, for it may be that the couple is seeking consultation to reach an amicable separation. At times, the couple may be truly undecided about whether to remain together or to separate and seek consultation to arrive at such a decision. Commonly, the inevitability of separation may be clear to one or both spouses. They may arrive at the clinician's doorstep with one spouse acting cooperative and thoughtful and the other acting panicky. It may be some time before the clinician recognizes the inevitability of divorce. Therefore, a separate interview with each spouse is essential in order to learn about their hidden agendas and to obtain other information such as the presence of extramarital involvement. Many clinicians insist on routine individual sessions in the assessment phase in order to gather such information in an open fashion. Other clinicians may conduct individual assessment interviews only when the course of treatment is moving contrary to their expectations and there is deterioration in the marital relationship in spite of treatment.

Following the exploration of the presenting problems the clinician can obtain the developmental history of the marriage.

DEVELOPMENTAL HISTORY OF THE RELATIONSHIP

The developmental history of the marriage, or the marital chronology, is an essential part of the assessment and has significant diagnostic and prognostic value. Its therapeutic function is also significant in that it helps the couple to gain a perspective on their relationship by refocusing their attention on their strengths and on the happier days in their marriage when they viewed each other positively. The history helps the therapist to understand the nature of the marital relationship and disorder while providing him with the opportunity to actively structure family sessions.

The family life history is one of the most effective ways of concretizing the relationship for the couple. Through this device the couple can recognize that the relationship has, in fact, a history similar to the developmental history of a person. In addition, taking the history helps the couple to gain a broad perspective on the nature of the therapeutic process, rather than promoting the expectation that the therapist will take the side of one spouse against the other. The recognition of the therapist's comprehensive approach is a potent factor in relieving the couple's fear about the therapeutic situation and in decreasing their despair about their marriage.

Taking a marital history should be a dynamic process rather than simply a dry, fact-collecting exercise. The therapist should join the family and help them to paint a dynamic picture of their past by moving back and forth between the past and present in an atmosphere of hopeful discovery, while simultaneously trying to explain their family situation.

Taking the family history should logically start with when the couple met and the circumstances of their meeting. The exploration of the early phase of the relationship will immediately refocus the couple's attention away from the current problem and on happier times, as the beginning of a relationship is usually an exciting and exhilarating experience. This should be followed by a description of the early relationship and lead to the couple's decision to marry. The spouses should be asked to describe their reasons for being attracted to each other, their expectations from the marriage, and how they communicated their wishes to each other. The discrepancies in the pictures described by the spouses should be underlined as they may be early indicators of later communication problems. The therapist should note that discrepancies in perceptions are common, everyday phenomena rather than leave the couple with the impression that the marriage took place based on the wrong assumptions.

The inquiry into what attracted the spouses to each other should be structured as a positive experience, and the therapist should interrupt any attempt on the part of the couple to transform their recollections into criticisms of each other. The characteristics of the early phase of courtship have prognostic significance too because couples who can give a long list of "positive" reasons for having chosen their partners are usually more capable of forming positive relationships than are those who were depressed, lonely, or rebounding from a prior, traumatic relationship.

The inquiry should continue into the early stages of courtship and the early interaction patterns. Again, those courtship periods that were characterized by intense and positive interactions are generally prognostic of a better marital relationship than those courtship periods that were mixed and lacked any real passion or positive exchanges. Also, one can differentiate between courtships that were based on actual shared positive exchanges and those that were based on the anticipation of such experiences.

The examination of the circumstances surrounding the decision to marry should attempt to differentiate between and delineate the expectation of direct relationship benefits from marriage rather than other factors such as the expectation of financial help, pregnancy, and so on. The characteristics of courtship and the wedding ceremony can be indicators of the intensity of the relationship, as well as indicators of other interferences such as disagreement from parents, conflict ridden wedding ceremonies, or the need to elope in order to get married.

The description of the relationship between the time of marriage and the birth of children demonstrates the couple's interest in and capacity to form an intimate relationship. Each mate's relationship with his or her own parents is an important factor in this period, as a conflictual relationship with families of origin can interfere with the formation of the new family and lead to early marital conflicts. This can logically lead the therapist to concentrate on each mate's life in the family of origin, the premarital life of each spouse, and the gratification and conflicts of such early times. Such inquiries can be followed by the exploration of each couple's relationship with their in-laws in the beginning days of marriage as well as later on.

The exploration of each spouse's genogram should describe the relationships and the cast of characters in the family of origin, which should include each mate's parents, brothers, sisters, and other members of the extended families. The ordinal position of the spouse in the family of origin can reveal special family role assignments such as parentification of the oldest children, infantilization and overprotection of the younger children, and isolation of the middle children.

Inquiring about the marital status of siblings can be a sensitive indicator of the nature and quality of the marriage in the family of origin. For example, multiple divorces and separations among the siblings of one spouse can reveal the presence of overt or covert marital problems in the parents which may have left continuing conflicts or skill deficits that are contributing to the current marital difficulties. The exploration of the current relationship of each mate with his or her siblings can often reveal sources of extramarital support as well as conflict. Total isolation from one's siblings can characterize the phenomenon of "emotional cutoff" with its hidden conflict which can be projected readily onto the spouse.

The exploration of the premarital environment of each spouse should include how food, nurturance, money, sex, discussion of children, disagreements, and fun were handled in each family of origin.

The therapist should be prepared to deal with the extensive premarital history of one or both spouses. At times, the premarital history of a spouse can be extensive in terms of multiple events in the family of origin such as multiple deaths, recurrent illnesses, multiple financial reverses, or psychiatric illness in a mate or other members of his or her family. The therapist will be well served to take his time in collecting such information.

The early marital history should clarify what the expectations were of each spouse from their marriage, including expectations in terms of desire for children, continued schooling, level of financial security, place of living, type of work, and so on. The discrepancy between the spouses' expectations should be clarified. One spouse may have been looking primarily for a roof over his or her head or comfort, while the other spouse had much more extensive and ambitious expectations of the marriage.

The therapist should concentrate on the traits that each spouse particularly liked in the other and find out if expectations were clearly expressed from one to the other. A couple is initially attracted to complementary traits in each other. However, the failure to negotiate differences in expectations can become the source of disagreement and irritation later in the marriage. The discrepancies in the spouses' perception and communication should again be pointed out at this point as they may be significant contributors to the present marital problems, and the differences in expectations should again be cross-referenced to the determinants of their behavior from each mate's past family models.

The plans for the arrival of the children and the circumstances at the times of birth should be carefully explored. Exploration of the timing of each spouse's decision to become a parent can point out the subtle differences in expectations which precede the universal change in marital relationships after the birth of each baby. The circumstances of the birth and the raising of each child can reveal traumatic experiences such as congenital or repeated childhood illnesses that required multiple surgical procedures which may have resulted in one spouse being overwhelmed, particularly if the other spouse was relatively unavailable and unsupportive.

Traumatic events in the life of the family should be explored actively as the family tends to exclude these events due to their painful nature. Such events may include loss or death in the extended or nuclear family, severe, chronic, or protracted illnesses, miscarriages, stillbirths, abortions, financial reverses, business failures, bankruptcy, and educational and career failures.

A developmental history of the marriage should conclude with an exploration of experiences in the early relationship that resembled or hinted at the present problems. This history will help the clinician to determine whether the couple had been able to develop and consummate a strong relationship but later found themselves unable to expand on it for internal and external reasons. The latter should be differentiated from those instances where the emotional marriage was never consummated due to internal and external factors, including interferences from in-laws or a succession of crisis situations.

THE BEHAVIORAL INTERVIEW

In behavioral interviews the therapist teaches the couple to impart information in a systematic way, prepares the couple for further data collection at home, and makes detailed observations about the couple's interaction which include an actual sample of their problem-solving behavior. The couple is asked to report verbally on their activities, thoughts, and feelings. The data gathered during the behavioral interview tend to be more subjective than the data collected by questionnaires. The couple is asked to provide observational data on their interactions with each other and on how they present themselves to a third party. One source of the observation is to note how a spouse responds to a therapist versus the other spouse. The spouses are asked to state the behaviors they wish to accelerate rather than to focus only on decreasing undesirable behaviors. A request to accelerate certain behaviors tends to present a more optimistic picture and is less punitive for the recipient.

Then the couple is asked to describe the environmental conditions that surround both the pleasing and displeasing behaviors. This information will provide a detailed analysis of all related factors. The couple is asked to describe the scene and the set, what would lead up to the situation, who would be present, what each participant would be doing, and how the scene might end. In addition, the couple is asked to state their feelings in regard to each other's expectations. This helps the couple to concentrate on their perceptions of the nature of their disagreements rather than having them attempt to "get to the truth of the matter." Attempts at resolving differing impressions are counterproductive and foster competition and blaming.

During the behavioral interview, the therapist should pursue information that portrays the spouses' lives together in a more global context. This would include a description of typical weekdays and weekend days and how they spend their shared and alone time. In addition to conflicts the areas of skills deficit in different relational areas should be noted.

The behavioral interview sessions tend to be flexible and the information gathered can lead readily to specific behavioral interventions. The interview should maintain a positive focus on the totality of the spouses' interaction including enjoyable tasks rather than just on changing the problem behaviors.

The behavioral interview sessions allow for accurate paraphrasing of each spouse's position in a way that will demonstrate how both partners have contributed to the problems and how they both suffer as a result of these problems. Maintaining a focus on the chain of events demonstrates each person's participation in the escalation of conflicts and suggests alternative ways of viewing problems and handling situations. At times, the recognition of skill deficits in one spouse can be reassuring to the other by reducing the feeling of victimization.

ADDITIONAL ASSESSMENT OPTIONS: OBSERVATIONAL METHODS

A variety of behavioral instruments can provide the clinician with additional options for collecting data about the areas of strength and weakness in the marital relationship. The instruments address one or more of the following aspects of the marital relationship:

The beliefs of spouses about their relationship.

The nature of the day-to-day interaction of the couple.

The factors contributing to the central relationship problems.

The techniques utilized by the couple to bring about change.

The most commonly used marital instruments are reviewed below.

The Locke–Wallace Marital Adjustment Scale (MAS) (Locke & Wallace, 1959). This widely used instrument is an inventory of global marital satisfaction.

The short form contains 15 items to rate

1. The level of overall satisfaction.
2. The amount of disagreement between the spouses in eight subareas of marriage such as recreation and finances.
3. The extent of spouses' mutual activity and mutual decision making.
4. The nature of each spouse's personal retrospections about the decision to marry.

MAS scores range from 2 (high marital distress) to 161 (high marital adjustment) with 100 as the accepted cutoff score between the distressed and nondistressed couples. Reliability and validity studies on MAS have shown this instrument to be internally consistent and to be an accurate discriminator of distressed and nondistressed couples.

A related instrument, *Dyadic Adjustment Scale (DAS)* (Spanier, 1976) assesses the relationship of unmarried, cohabitating couples as well as married couples.

Areas of Change Questionnaire (A–C) (Patterson, 1976). This widely used instrument assesses marital satisfaction in terms of the amount of change a couple desires to bring about in their relationship. It helps the couple to clarify the behaviors they wish to increase or decrease.

Marital Precounseling Inventory (MPI) (Stuart & Stuart, 1972). This is a comprehensive questionnaire to assess the strengths and weaknesses of marital partners. It directs the couple's observation to positive elements of their spouse's behavior, provides highly organized, comprehensive data relevant to therapeutic goals, and provides the therapist and the couple with a periodic evaluation of the therapeutic progress.

The nature of the day-to-day interaction of the couple can be assessed through a variety of instruments. *The Spouse Observation Check List (SOC)* (Patterson, Weiss, & Hopps, 1976) addresses a comprehensive list of specific behaviors which are the source of pleasure or displeasure in the relationship. It spans the range of instrumental-expressive-companionship dimensions of the interaction and includes a variety of behaviors such as meals, shopping, child care, finances, housekeeping, family recreation, and affection.

Another commonly used instrument for marital assessment, *Behavior Coding Systems (BCS)* (Patterson, Ray, Shaw, & Cobb, 1969), is a 29-category coding system used to label family interactions. The *Behavioral Diary* is the procedure most commonly used to obtain information about the environmental variables that control a specific behavior in addition to providing data on the strength of that particular behavior. It focuses particularly on the events immediately preceding the target behavior.

The spouses' attempt to bring about changes in their relationship can be assessed through the *Marital Interactional Coding Systems (MICS)* (Hopps, Wills, Patterson, & Weiss, 1972). This instrument provides an analysis of the couple's problem-solving discussions. Different aspects of problem-solving behavior such as acceptance of responsibility, negotiation, compromise, and positive and negative verbal and nonverbal behavior are measured through this instrument. It has been applied primarily to 10-minute, videotaped samples in which each spouse strives to come to a resolution of problem areas.

THE EXPLORATION OF MARITAL FUNCTIONING

The multiple dimensions of marital functioning should be examined systematically and routinely as the couple may function well in one or several areas while failing dramatically in others. The different functional areas include:

1. Marital Role: The adequacy of the marital relationship in terms of two adults who can provide each other with companionship, support, sexual gratification, and intellectual stimulation.
2. Parental Role: The adequacy of the couple in providing for the everyday and developmental needs of their children.
3. Chores: The adequacy of the management of the everyday activities and the equity in the assignment of household and family chores.
4. Finances: The adequacy and equity of handling finances in a way that optimally satisfies the competing needs of the family members in terms of nurturance, education, recreation, and future security needs.
5. Sex: Satisfactory sexual relationship between the parents and the provision of age-appropriate sex education for the children.
6. Communication: The adequacy of the communication system in making each spouse aware of the other's needs.
7. Boundaries: The existence of clear and flexible boundaries between the nuclear family, extended family, and the community. Functional

boundaries are also essential within the family subgroups—spouses, children, and so on.

The family's capacity for enjoyment, fun, and commitment to recreation are important aspects of family health. Dysfunctional families are equally committed to the avoidance of intense pleasure and pain and tend to submerge themselves in routine and tedious activities.

Disagreement between spouses in handling food, nurturance, money, sex, discussion of children, disagreements, and fun are usually related to differences originating in the extended families of each spouse. The spouses' loyalty ties to the old "model" from their own families may give rise to disagreement between them.

Rigid loyalty ties to the families of origin also result in the faulty management of differentness. In dysfunctional families the differentness is considered undesirable and each spouse tries to force the other to comply with his or her ways of handling situations. The recognition of the origin of their differing ideologies as the products of their families of origin leads the couple to explore ways of accepting, negotiating, and working out the differences in their approaches. Couples observe that the lessons learned from their parents may not fit their own current families and that they should forge their own ways of dealing with different issues and circumstances.

One major area of difficulty is the style of handling disagreements in the two families of origin. Spouses who were raised in families where disagreements were denied find it difficult to accept the approaches of mates who came from families where disagreements were fought out openly.

ASSESSMENT OF COMMUNICATION PATTERNS

Communication problems are the most common presenting problem in marital therapy. This generally means that the couple does not like the messages they receive or that the messages they send out are misinterpreted. Here, the couple commonly reports that their needs are not being met.

Communication skills are subtle. Thus, failure to acquire effective communication skills or the acquisition of dysfunctional techniques that produce interpersonal problems are common. In dysfunctional relationships spouses do not receive or send sufficient positive messages to their partners to counterbalance the negative ones.

In assessing the communication patterns between spouses, the clinician should explore the following common reasons which usually prevent the occurrence of positive exchanges:

1. A spouse does not clearly send information to the partner about the positives he or she would like to receive.
2. A spouse does not perceive information about his/her partner's needs accurately.

3. Information about desired positives are sent and received accurately, but the sender uses punitive means (demands) for requesting positive responses and thus decreases the receiver's tendency to comply.
4. A spouse tends to give a partner positives but does not do so in a clear enough manner for the partner to perceive them as such.
5. A spouse intends to give a partner positives, but what he or she uses is not a reward for the partner.
6. A spouse fails to perceive the positives given by his/her partner.
7. A spouse perceives the positives from the partner but fails to acknowledge them, thus extinguishing the partner's positive responses.
8. Partners are unable to engage in problem-solving communications that would produce a positive outcome for each of them.

The process of improving communication includes clarification of the messages, increasing their positive quality, and reducing their negative impact. The emphasis on positive exchanges counters the tendency of each partner to become involved in "cross complaining" and in summarizing one's own complaints rather than trying to understand the other's point of view. The negative exchanges can result in a "summarizing self syndrome"; that is, a pattern of escalating negative exchanges that ends in quarrels and periods of withdrawal. The spouses can be helped to recognize such destructive patterns and the impact of their messages through feedback during the assessment and treatment period. Discrepancies between the intent and impact of messages are to be noted and discussed in order to clarify misunderstandings. This process helps the spouses to find out about their mutual subjective experiences. A useful practice is to encourage one partner to paraphrase the messages he or she is receiving regarding the other partner's thoughts and feelings in order to enhance accurate perception. The speaker should also be held responsible for making clear, direct, but nonattacking statements of his thoughts and feelings.

The couple should be encouraged to increase their feeling expression and their self-disclosure. The expression of negative feelings should occur according to certain ground rules, such as limiting them to conditions that can be changed, pinpointing behavior rather than attacking character, and commenting favorably on the positive aspects.

Additional rules for the expression of the negative feelings are that:

1. Reports of perceptions and judgments should be acknowledged to be subjective rather than statements of fact.
2. Feelings associated with ideas should be expressed separately and directly.
3. Negative expression should include an acknowledgment of the positive side of the issues.

4. Descriptions of thoughts, feelings, and perceptions of events should be specific.
5. Any request by the expressor for an action should be made explicitly and clearly.
6. A statement of the expressor's feeling or personal request also should convey empathy for the listener's position.
7. "The feeling talks," where the goal is the expression of feelings, should be differentiated from the "executive talks," where the goal is brainstorming in preparation for problem solving.

Assessment of Skills in Assertion and Problem Solving

Need satisfaction, the essential element of a satisfactory marriage, is dependent on having the skills necessary to express one's expectations to one's spouse and to gain compliance and cooperation between the marital partners. Among the skills necessary to achieve this goal are assertiveness and problem solving. The latter skills are frequently lacking in dysfunctional couples. Assertiveness refers to direct but noncoercive expression of thoughts, feelings, and preferences. Problem solving refers to searching for a solution to a problem that is acknowledged by both spouses. A major step in problem solving is the generation of alternative solutions.

BOUNDARIES BETWEEN NUCLEAR AND EXTENDED FAMILIES

The boundary formation between the nuclear and extended families occurs within a developmental framework. A marriage, like an individual, goes through different developmental stages before it is emotionally consummated. The process of disengaging from the families of origin and shifting loyalties to the marital partner is a major task in marriage. This process is sabotaged frequently and unwittingly by all parties involved. For example, the newlywed may not recognize that extensive dependency on and loyalty to the family of origin occurs at the expense of the marital partner. In the process of marriage one needs to disengage from one's parents and demand that one's spouse do the same. Parents should accept the necessity of loosening their grip on their children so that those children can have a meaningful marriage. The process of freeing the children to invest in a new person is emphasized concretely in marital ceremonies when the bride's father gives her away. Symbolically, the father gives up the claims of the family on the daughter so she can invest emotionally in a new individual. This step is in keeping with folk wisdom and with our knowledge of child development which tells us that women tend to maintain stronger loyalty ties with their families of origin than do men.

The boundaries between the family units tend to blur at a time of marital crisis. In such situations the marital stress and conflict can result in the retreat and regression of each partner toward his or her parents. This is partly due to the fact that extended families with unresolved dependency issues produce long-standing relational distortions that fail to prepare the children for coping effectively with stress when they marry.

The blurring of the boundary is facilitated by the following circumstances: (1) financial dependence on one or both parents, (2) immaturity in newlywed couples who cannot negotiate a need-satisfying relationship with each other, and (3) an emotional void in the marriage of the parents that is filled by overinvolvement between one parent and one child.

The emotional dependence of a child on a parent is usually a byproduct of relational distortions in the families of origin. Here, the unsatisfactory marital relationship between the parents has resulted in one of them being emotionally overinvolved with a child. When that child has grown up, the unrealistic expectations of such a parent make him or her unable to negotiate a satisfactory give and take relationship. Such grown children, after a brief but heated argument with their spouse, run to their family of origin which readily showers them with emotional or financial support. In this case the old tie with families of origin is continuously strengthened.

The formation of adequate boundaries is synonymous with the establishment of the primacy of the marital bond between the new couple over their bonds with their families of origin. This does not mean the abandonment of loyalty ties to the families of origin once one is married. However, one cannot have two equally strong sets of loyalties to two groups whose interests may at times conflict. It should be clear to each partner that at the time of intergenerational conflict, one's primary loyalty is to one's spouse. Here, the clinician needs to help newlywed couples to establish a united front against incursions by their in-laws. Once they have successfully established the new family rules, the relationship with in-laws becomes manageable and the new and old generations can enjoy each other.

EXTRAMARITAL RELATIONSHIPS

The current and past involvement in extramarital relationships will be revealed frequently during the initial interviews or has been part of the immediate reason for seeking consultation. However, the reluctance of a spouse to disclose extramarital relationships can frequently result in what has been described as "illicit contracts" (Weiss 1975) which will impede the progress of treatment. Therefore, an individual interview with each spouse should be used on the occasion when such relationships are suspected or the progress of treatment is unsatisfactory. The spouse will require an assurance of confidentiality from the therapist before disclosing such information. Although the opinions of different marital therapists vary widely as to the maintenance of confidentiality about such information, it may be more prudent not to disclose the information until the spouses feel confident enough to discuss it in joint sessions or decide to terminate their extramarital relationships.

MARITAL ASSESSMENT IN THE COURSE OF CHILD THERAPY

Covert marital problems can commonly exhibit themselves by symptomatic behavior in a child who is referred for psychiatric evaluation and treatment. The selection of a child as a "symptom bearer" is multiply determined, and the reasons include reluctance of the couple to recognize marital problems because of the fear of divorce, lack of a deep interest in the mate or the marriage, or masochistic gratification. However, the marital pain and distress assumes a higher level of salience once the child's symptoms are improved through individual or family treatment. Therefore, the clinician should keep a watchful eye on the quality of the marriage while evaluating a symptomatic child in family or individual sessions. The clinician should make a mental note to himself about the quality of the marriage but refrain from forcing the couple to deal with their marital difficulties prematurely. And the clinician should continue to make mental notes about different aspects of marital problems, as well as the areas of optimal functioning and dysfunctioning in the marriage.

The appropriate time to address the marital problems is when the symptomatic improvement in the child allows the parents to broaden their expectations and request help with their marital relationship. Frequently, improvement in the child encourages the couple to seek help for their marital disorders. The ongoing acknowledgment of the areas of marital strengths by the clinician also helps the couple to gain perspective on their marriage and alleviates their fear of divorce.

In the course of family therapy symptomatic improvement of the children results in a shifting of the focus onto the marital relationship and problems. Such a shift of focus may occur rapidly in the course of any family therapy session, thereby requiring immediate attention. If the children need to be excluded from the family therapy session precipitously to allow the open discussion of an urgent marital issue, the situation should be explained to the children thoroughly in order to reduce their confusion while underlining the couple's right to privacy.

A frequent pitfall in addressing marital disorders while working psychotherapeutically with symptomatic children is the general tendency of clinicians to limit the scope of the assessment and to move into a therapeutic posture prematurely. This can generally weaken the therapeutic alliance with the couple and limit the treatment outcome. The clinician can remedy the situation by making a conscious effort to counter this general tendency.

EVALUATION OF MARITAL CONTRACTS

The marital contract (Sager, 1976) is a useful concept in helping the therapist to organize the mass of data about marital relationship and disorder, determine the basic areas of marital disagreement, and clarify his intuitive responses to the couple. Marital contracts are categorized on three levels: (1) conscious and verbalized, (2) conscious and unverbalized, and (3) beyond awareness.

The contract is a notation of the range of conscious and unconscious feelings, expectations, and fantasies the couple maintains in regard to each other and to their marriage. Couples have two separate contracts which may be congruent, complementary, or conflicting and incongruent. The incongruence between the contracts is the underlying factor giving rise to the range of complaints and countercomplaints expressed by the couple.

Data on the first (conscious and verbalized) and second (conscious and unverbalized) levels of contracts can be supplied by the couple during the marital therapy sessions, as well as by their written, individual statements. The data on the third level of contract, which deals with information that is beyond awareness, are more difficult to obtain and more controversial as they depend on theoretical constructs. The greatest aid in bringing the unconscious material into awareness is each spouse's understanding of the other spouse's deepest needs. Thus, using the couple's perceptions of each other's psychological needs is a vehicle for understanding their unconscious life. Such insight may include the partners' deep conflicts over dependency, power, gender identity, passivity, or activity. The couple can use the clues they receive from each other to recognize each other's thoughts, fears and wishes. Other helpful steps in the reconstruction of the third level contract consist of obtaining the history of each spouse, observing the verbal and nonverbal interaction of the spouses, dream material, the individuals' description of their parents' relationship, and the individuals' impressions of their own parents' contracts. Recognition of the factors and incidents that arouse feelings of conflict and disharmony or, on the other hand, love and tenderness, give additional clues to the nature of the marital contract. Each spouse's view and observation of the mate's current relationship with his own parents is often illuminating.

The therapist should attempt initially to speculate to himself about each partner's contract and the level of the spouses' congruence, complementarity, or mutual exclusiveness. For example, a partner may feel deeply embarrassed to reveal his wish to be totally taken care of by his spouse without reciprocation. However, his daily behavior and interactions with the spouse may reveal his one-sided expectations both to his mate and to the therapist. Once the therapist forms a tentative hypothesis about the third level of the couple's contract, it should be presented to them for confirmation or negation. With the progression of treatment, the therapist should attempt to refine his understanding of the couple's multiple level contracts.

The concept of a marital contract should be presented to a couple after the therapist hears their presenting problems and once the therapist has determined that the couple intends to change their relationship. It should not be presented to a couple routinely on the first or subsequent visits. The proper timing would be after the pressure of their immediate complaints is relieved and the spouses intend to work on changing their relationship.

The concept of contracts is introduced following observations of the level of lovingness between the spouses, their interactional, communicative, and cognitive styles and values. In addition, the sources of reality based stress should be considered.

It would be most helpful to introduce the concept after the couple's initial self-rightousness and self-justifications are overcome in treatment. The therapist can then introduce the concept of the marital contract by explaining that the couple consists of two interdependent persons who have expectations of each other, themselves, and the marriage which have somehow turned into something unanticipated and have therefore given rise to marital problems. The marital contracts can help the couple to get a grasp on their contractual understandings and misunderstandings, the latter giving rise to disappointment, anger, and depression.

The data on marital contracts are gathered during the individual or conjoint sessions with the therapist as a part of the general assessment process. The therapist poses a series of questions, exploring each couple's wishes, needs, expectations, or fantasies about various aspects of their marital relationship. The questions are then reversed by asking each spouse about the other spouse's expectations.

In the initial sessions the couple can be provided with a "reminder list" of their contractual parameters to help them clarify their current marital contract. The reminder list is used by the couple at home where they tend to be more forthright than they are apt to be during the sessions, and it helps them to identify their present contracts. The written contract can then be supplemented by the data collected during the sessions. The therapist determines the nature of the interactional contract by observing the couple's interactions in the sessions, their reporting of their transactions, and the way they carry out their marital responsibilities.

The process of assessment of marital contracts begins with the couple and the therapist noting the areas of congruence, complementarity, and conflict between the contracts, all of which disclose the needs underlying the couple's behavioral patterns. The lack of a written response to a particular item on the reminder list is usually indicative of a troublesome area. The reluctance of the couple to bring in the written contract is generally indicative of the couples' reluctance to examine their marital relationship. The connections among complaints, interactions, and contract terms have to be made by the therapist. The therapist then starts negotiation or arbitration of difficult areas at once in order to test the flexibility and motivation of each spouse. The resistance of the couple to simple, quid pro quo solutions is usually indicative of intrapsychic conflicts or a basic distrust of self and/or others. In addition, the use of contracts is counterproductive when the marital problems are confined to one specific area or when one spouse has a secret of major proportion.

Reminder List for Marriage Contract

The reminder list can be used by the therapist or the couple. It describes the concept of the marital contract and the three levels of verbalized, conscious but unverbalized, and beyond awareness or unconscious contracts. One spouse is asked to use the three different categories to list in writing his expectations of his spouse and his belief about the failure of the spouse to live up to the bargain. The responses should emphasize feelings and disregard the issue of fairness. The couple is instructed not to compare their written contracts with each other until they have completed the process.

The *first category* in the reminder list is related to the expectations from marriage. It states the most common expectations in marriage such as expectations of loyalty, support, companionship, sexual availability, provision of a home-refuge, provision of status in the society, economic unit, and so on. The couple is asked to summarize their expectations of each other and to state what they are willing to give in exchange for those expectations.

The *second category* is based on the internal psychological and biological needs of the person. It addresses areas such as independence-dependence, activity-passivity, closeness-distance, the use of power, submission and domination, level of anxiety, and ability for love and acceptance. The couple again summarizes their expectations and states what they wish to give in exchange.

In the *third category* the derivatives or externalized sources of the problems are described. This area is the symptomatic and manifest cause of marital distress but it is considered secondary to categories one or two. This category includes communication, intellectual style, energy level, interests, relations with families of origin, children and child rearing, sexual values, and so on. The couple is again asked to summarize their expectations and what they wish to provide in exchange.

ASSESSMENT OF REMARRIED FAMILIES

Remarried families require special evaluation along structural and dynamic lines in addition to the general marital assessment issues (Sager et al., 1983). The previous failed marriages of remarried families make such families very fearful of additional failures. The low level of cohesiveness, cooperation, and trust in the multiple subsystems of a remarried family tend to undermine the consolidation of the new marriage into a viable functioning unit. Therefore, the vulnerability of remarried families and the level of their cohesiveness have to be specifically assessed.

Competing alliances with children from the previous marriage who may be living in the house, living out, or visiting are frequent points of stress in the new marital relationship. Therefore, the "suprasystem" of remarried families has to be examined carefully in order to determine the points of loyalty, friction, and stress. A genogram may be particularly useful in addressing such dimensions in a remarried family. A genogram would allow the clinician to organize the large sum of data about the complicated history and the structure of the family into a manageable form. The genogram should address the different structural characteristics and properties of each subsystem, exhibiting their differences. Furthermore, it should characterize the intergenerational patterns of behavior, separations, divorces, illnesses, losses, and timing of deaths. In terms of the history, one should examine how the present remarried unit was formed. The data obtained should include the couple's meeting and courtship, a chronology of the relationship to the ending of the previous marriage, the level of preparedness of the children from the previous marriage for the remarriage, and so on. The genogram should also include the information on when, where, why, and how the original nuclear family systems were dissolved, as well as each person's perception of the dissolution.

In regard to the issue of the choice of a mate, the unconscious and conscious factors for the selection should be determined. Furthermore, one should determine to what degree the present marriage is one of convenience; that is, a marriage whose purpose is taking care of children and obligations.

The following dimensions in a remarried family unit should be examined:

1. The consolidation of the remarried couple into a functioning unit and the establishment of its position within the larger suprasystem.
2. The consolidation of the parental authority in the remarried subsystem.
3. The degree of completion of the task of mourning for the previous nuclear family, partners, neighborhoods, friends, and way of life.
4. The acceptance and tolerance of the difference of a remarried family from an idealized, intact nuclear family model and its attendant limitations in terms of the lack of complete control over money or children, and so on.

A particular structural property of the remarried family is the couple's attempt to scapegoat onto an ex-spouse in order to consolidate or maintain their romantic, short-term bonding and to avoid the inevitable disillusionment that is inherent in the transition to long-term bonding. Another common characteristic—particularly for men—is the abdication of parenting responsibility in the new household to the new wife who often moves in prematurely to accept such responsibility before she has developed a relationship with the children and prior to the transfer of the parental authority. Premature parenting of the children puts the new spouse in the role of the "wicked stepparent" (with the aid of the children's displaced anger from their biological parent to their new stepparent).

From the dynamic point of view the lack of a psychic and emotional divorce is a frequent phenomenon in remarried families, and will interfere with the emotional investment in the new partner, contribute to reluctance to assume and form a new parental coalition, and facilitate the continuation of anger toward the former spouse.

The discrepancy in the life cycle is an important characteristic of a newly remarried couple as people must parent the children prior to enjoying a sustained marriage or even a honeymoon. The honeymoon period in remarried families may be postponed for a long time because the new couple is burdened by the reality demands and is unable to find enough time to invest in each other.

Summary

The comprehensive assessment of marital disorders should be broad based and address the multiple aspects of the marital relationship. It should address both marital assets and distress rather than concentrate only on problematic behaviors. The motivation of the couple to utilize treatment to improve the quality of their marital relationship is an important aspect of the assessment. A thorough assessment of the marital relationship will enable the therapist to select the most promising and effective treatment modality for the specific disorders of distressed couples. Furthermore, it helps the couple to see their problems objectively and within the context of their total relationship. Such a perspective enables the couple to develop working plans for improving their relationship in terms of increasing the level of pleasure while decreasing the level of distress and frustration. A sensitive assessment also can enable the couple and the therapist to prognosticate accurately about the outcome of treatment and marriage. One important guide for assessment of a marriage's potential is the level of emotional consummation of the marital relationship prior to the onset of the presenting problems.

References

Hopps, H., Wills, T., Patterson, G. R., & Weiss, R. L. (1972). *Marital interaction coding system*. University of Oregon and Oregon Research Institute, Eugene, OR.

Locke, H. J., & Wallace, K. M. (1959). Short marital adjustment and prediction tests: Reliability and validity. *Marriage and Family Living, 21*, 251–255.

Patterson, G. R., Ray, R. S., Shaw, D. D., & Cobb, J. A. (1969). *Manual for coding of family interactions*. Oregon Research Institute, Eugene, OR.

Patterson, D. R. (1976). Some procedures for assessing changes in marital interaction patterns. *Oregon Research Institute Bulletin, 16*(7).

Patterson, G. R., Weiss, R. L., & Hopps, H. (1976). Training of marital skills: Some problems and concepts. In H. Leitenberg (Ed.), *Handbook of behavior modification*. New York: Appleton-Century-Crofts.

Sager, C. (1976). *Marriage contracts and couple therapy*. New York: Brunner/Mazel.

Sager, C. J., Brown, H. S., Crohn, H., Engle, T., Radstein, E., & Walker, L. (1983). *Treating the remarried family*. New York: Brunner/Mazel.

Sholevar, G. P. (Ed.). (1981). *The Handbook of marriage and marital therapy*. New York: SP Medical and Scientific Books.

Spanier, G. B. (1976). Measuring dyadic adjustment: New scales for assessing the quality of marriage and similar dyads. *Journal of Marriage and the Family, 38*, 15–28.

Stuart, R. B., & Stuart, F. (1973). *Marital pre-counseling inventory*. Champaign, IL: Research Press.

Weiss, R. (1975). *Marital separation*. New York: Basic Books.

TWELVE

Therapist Reactivity in Couples Therapy

Daniel C. Goldberg, Ph.D.
Assistant Professor of Psychiatry and Human Behavior
Jefferson Medical College

INTRODUCTION

To state that the conduct of psychotherapy is an extremely difficult endeavor is to reaffirm the obvious. Reactions of clinicians to the therapeutic process can be intense and, depending on one's theoretical orientation, a very important predictor of the therapy's effectiveness. The focus of this chapter is on what therapists go through in working with couples and the special forces that are unleashed in this particular context.

Most existing literature on therapists' reactions to patients examines therapist-patient interactions in the limited context of individual treatment. Yet it is readily apparent to therapists that working with couples (and families) is quite different than working in a one to one format. In fact, it is not rare to hear skilled clinicians acknowledge that they have enough to deal with when there is just one person in the room and to hear them wonder how therapists manage all their own emotionality while working with couples. Therapists who are brave (or foolish) enough to venture into therapy with couples often describe how their "insides" are working overtime and how they often seem to spend more effort during a therapy hour with a couple than they do with an individual. This effort seems to occur even when therapists attempt to remain affectively neutral (as Dr. William Masters says to couples who are in sex therapy with him, "I am neither for you nor against you.")

It is striking how little literature exists on this subject despite the experiential magnitude of these reactions. This trend may be due to the assumption that discussing such issues may reflect a lack of skill and experience on the therapist's part, and that once clinicians are fully trained they cease to react so much to their patients (Napier & Whitaker, 1973). Moreover, the golden rule of couples therapy is not to take sides and become aligned with one person. If therapists indicate, for example, that they are drawn toward one partner and/or away from another, have they really learned the basics of working with couples?

One of the central goals of this chapter is to defuse the negative associations toward therapists' reactions to couples. As opposed to considering these strong emotions a reflection of a therapist's incompetence or neurotic tendencies, they need to be seen as a natural by-product of the therapeutic process. Yet the issue cannot be simply smoothed over with such rationalizations as, "Well, it's just tough working with couples, and you have to expect it to be an emotional roller-coaster." The more complex question involves an analysis of what we bring as therapists to the therapy session. How do we increase or decrease our emotional reactivity so that we can be in "control of self" during therapy?

At the outset, describing the ideal role of the therapist in couples therapy may clarify the problem of reactivity. It is important to keep in mind throughout this chapter that we are mainly discussing the internal life of the therapist. A behavioral prescription for how therapists *should* behave with patients is not intended and would in fact be antithetical to the objectives of this chapter. Essentially, the goal can be described as freedom of movement (Bowen, 1976). Therapists can take in the couple's emotional field, have that field interact with their own thus identifying with either member of the couple, and then detach from the patient(s) (Willi, 1982). The therapist can thus know what it's like to "sit in their shoes," can truly be with each person. Through such temporary identifications, the therapist can shuttle back and forth as needed between the two people. Likewise, the therapist can stay at the periphery, can remain "an outsider" who comments on the process occurring between the couple and thus keeps from becoming drawn into the couple's system of emotional turmoil. The issue is that the therapist is not caught in any one position—either of being too close or of being too distant. The therapist has an emotional choice.

In order to accomplish this goal therapists must have an accurate view of what they bring to the clinical situation. Guerin (1980) describes the task facing therapists by noting that "if the therapist can avoid becoming judgmental of the family and keep from adding his or her emotional reactivity to the stew, he will be fulfilling his responsibility to the family as an agent of change and his responsibility to himself to be himself" (p. 5).

The therapist's goal (dealing with one's own reactivity) parallels early developmental issues. The therapist attempts to develop an optimal level of intimacy within the therapy setting while avoiding the pull toward fusion with the couple (Bowen, 1976). Early symbiotic ties to parents can be linked to the possibility of becoming fused with the couple's emotional system. As Bowen notes the therapist's ability to experience differentiation of self will help to avoid fusion. Of course, the therapist's task here mirrors issues around early attempts to separate/individuate. In short, the therapist attempts to balance involvement with the couple while remaining a separate individual.

Easier said than done. The difficulty rests at a very basic level. Perhaps the one emotional reaction that builds therapeutic trust and thus a climate for change is empathy, and empathy is based on the ability to develop concordant identification (Racker, 1957). This connection with the patient stems from "the resonance of the exterior in the interior, on recognition of what belongs to another as one's own ('this part of you is I') and on the equation of what is one's own with what belongs to another ('this part of me is you')" (Racker, 1957, p. 312). The task of being empathetic while not becoming fused and overinvolved with the couple is the key to understanding the importance of therapist reactivity.

HISTORICAL CONTEXT AND DEFINITIONS

In considering therapists' responses to their clients the notion of countertransference is useful. However, the problem here is that the lack of a consistent and coherent description of countertransferential phenomena has led to much confusion. Two major positions around countertransference can be identified (Lakovics, 1983): the *classical* position and the *total* position.

Typically, the classical position tends to regard therapists' reactions to patients as negative and as reflecting the therapists' unconscious issues which reside in the therapists' past, thus limiting therapist's effectiveness (Freud, 1959/1910). These problems, which are a manifestation of the therapist's still unresolved neurotic conflicts, become mobilized during therapy. Freud (1959/1912) provides a picture of the appropriate affective response to patients. "I cannot recommend my colleagues emphatically enough to take as a model in psycho-analytic treatment the surgeon who puts aside all his own feelings, including that of human sympathy, and concentrates his mind on one single purpose, that of performing the operation as skillfully as possible" (p. 327). Classicists tend to regard these therapist reactions as episodic and not that useful in the therapeutic process.

The total position takes a broader view of how clinicians respond to their patients. Here countertransference can be conscious as well as unconscious and thus can be elicited by the immediate interactions with patients. The total position therefore does not regard all reactions to clients as a reflection of the therapist's psychopathology. It emphasizes the patient-therapist interaction as the critical arena for understanding countertransferential material and not as residing within the therapist alone. Feelings within the therapist such as liking, fear, and frustration are normal and are continuous aspects of psychotherapy. Countertransference is only a problem when it goes unrecognized by the therapist. Often, patients can elicit responses within the therapist that say much about which of the patient's conflicts are predominant. Such therapist reactions are thus useful clues to knowing the internal life of the patient. For example, the patient may express a great deal of distress to the therapist about his marital relationship. He may describe many examples of his wife's disinterest in him, her preoccupation with the children, and his inability to talk to his wife about any of this. Dependency on others is a recurring pattern for this fellow, who finds many examples throughout his life of instances where he is not appreciated and is overlooked by others. He continually seeks the approval of others, but his aggressive style makes it difficult for others to respond positively to him.

The therapist notices his growing irritation with his patient who keeps seeking the therapist's opinions only to challenge them. The therapist begins to notice that he is saying less and less to the patient and that his irritation remains unchecked. The therapist might share his frustration and associated decreased energy during therapy with the patient and point out the man's pattern of needing approval but continually challenging the therapist. A discussion could then follow as to what might be going on for the patient and whether this parallels patterns found outside the therapy situation.

The title of this chapter, "Therapist Reactivity," reflects the view that neither position—classical or total—is adequate for examining therapists' reactions to helping couples change. While the former is too pathological, inaccessible to conscious analysis, and narrow in scope, the latter is too broad and is overly geared toward the contemporary aspects of the therapy session. The difference between countertransferential reactions and simply *any* reaction to a patient is obscure in the total position. Another critical problem with these two definitions is that they concentrate on the patient-therapist relationship as the organizing focus for therapy. Typically, clinicians who work with couples deemphasize this relationship and concentrate instead on the couples' transactions.

Bowen, Guerin, Fogarty, and others of the extended family systems "school" use the phrase *therapist reactivity* partly in order to avoid some of the problems associated with the two positions on countertransference described above. They have not offered a precise definition of what they mean by this phrase, so my explication of it here may not exactly reflect what they have in mind—but it is at least based on their thinking. (The notion of reactivity can apply to any interaction and does not have to refer to therapist-couple interactions alone. For example, some couples tend to criticize each other in front of their children but when alone they tend to be much more supportive. Moreover, people can feel highly reactive to others only in certain situations: A person might have a high degree of reactivity when others become angry with him/her and might subsequently withdraw to cope with the perceived injury to self.)

Therapist reactivity can be seen as the therapist's emotional response that is elicited by particular types of clients or by certain kinds of situations during therapy. These emotional responses are usually out of the therapist's voluntary control and indeed often occur despite the therapist's efforts to not get "caught" by the couple. The reactivity results from clearly unresolved (yet not pathological) issues and the therapy situation mirrors difficult issues that therapists faced (or face) in their own families.

In essence, while reactivity is elicited by the current therapist-couple relationship, one can actually view it as the therapist's own transference onto the couple. Whitaker, Felder, and Warkentin (1965) describe this phenomenon as a situation in which the therapist may be reliving early life experiences with a particular couple. Imagine a 33-year-old therapist who always believed that her parents might have been better off divorced. She is referred a couple in their mid-60s, the same age as her parents. They begin therapy by immediately blaming each other for their problems, which is similar to the way the therapist's parents behaved in the past. Moreover, the husband resembles her father in some important ways. There is a good chance that this therapist's reactivity will be high in the face of a couple such as this. Is her infantile wish about to come true?

PATTERNS OF THERAPIST REACTIVITY

Therapist reactivity to patients can take various forms. Highlighted below are a number of behaviors, thoughts, and feelings that demonstrate how a therapist can be caught in the web of emotional reactivity to the patient.

Two themes seem to characterize these patterns: overinvolvement and underinvolvement. One could argue that any form of therapist reactivity represents an overinvolvement with the patients, but this premise does not capture the different styles and manifestations of therapist reactivity that illustrate the quality of the therapist's phenomenological experience with a particular couple. These two themes seem to closely parallel the complementary patterns described so well by Fogarty (1984a) in his descriptions of pursuers and distancers. Fogarty uses these labels to describe people who are in a close relationship, one that is often formalized through marriage, although marriage is not a necessary precondition for the dynamics to operate. These labels describe emotional (and often physical movement) in relationships whereby one person, the pursuer, tends to seek out the partner, to search for closeness, to want immediate results, to be responsible for the couple's "dream," and to notice problems threatening the relationship. The distancer tends to focus more on boundaries, on individual space, to assume that problems will work themselves out, to be realistic, and to minimize his or her emotions.

We could construct a chart that describes emotional reactivity along a continuum. Emotional reactivity in the therapist can be seen as a description of the depth of involvement occurring within therapy. The chart below (see Figure 1) helps to illustrate the association between the notion of pursuer-distancer and the tendency to become over- or underinvolved with clients. Therapists can use this chart to determine whether they have a general tendency to get caught in either end of the continuum. The chart can also be used to make an assessment of trends in reactivity around particular issues and/or with particular clients. For example, a couple may be questioning in the first session whether to really pursue therapy. This situation may prompt a "pursuer's response" from the therapist who attempts to "hook" the patients into the therapy relationship. Then, overeager to pursue the relationship, the therapist takes responsibility for the couple's struggle with that decision. He makes a summary statement attesting to the couple's strengths and telling them that they are clearly not headed for a divorce, but adding that he has some sense that they want to work on improving their relationship. The therapist thus misses the extent of this couple's distress by trying to essentially minimize their problems and flatter them into engaging in therapy. The next session is spent learning that the wife is ready for a separation and wonders whether seeing a lawyer would be better than seeing a psychologist.

The following are some of the major examples of therapist reactivity taking the form of *overinvolvement*. Many of the examples are based on Napier and Whitaker's (1973) analysis of problems that beginning therapists often have. While experience plays an important role in the emergence of therapist reactivity, my own sense is that therapist reactivity is an ongoing issue that needs to be repeatedly assessed by all therapists who work with couples.

Overfocus on content. Many couples target certain issues around which they can focus their distress. Money, sex, work, and household chores are just some of these issues. In addressing these topics couples of-

FIGURE 1 Depth of Involvement

0	1	2	3	4	5	6	7	8	9	10
underinvolvement (distancer)					flexible involvement					overinvolvement (pursuer)

ten perceive the therapist as an expert or an impartial referee who will be able to determine "right and wrong." This is a terribly seductive role for the therapist, but it may represent a pattern of the therapist getting overinvolved in the manifest content of the arguments and thus missing the latent process issues around this couple's sense of connectedness which lie at the heart of the matter.

Questions about normalcy often elicit a therapist's tendency to become overfocused on content. For example, a couple might be arguing over their sex life and in particular the husband's masturbatory behavior. The wife sees his autoerotic activities as a sign of his indifference toward her and says that this is not normal for a married man if he truly cares for his wife. She turns to the therapist and asks, "Am I right? Is that normal?" The therapist might get caught at that moment and attempt to deal with the content by citing Kinsey's cogent remarks on masturbation. Typically, this only adds fuel to the couple's dissension since it misses the mark in terms of what is really bothering this couple.

Overeagerness to help. Usually, this pattern can be seen in the communication network occurring within the therapy sessions. The therapist is drawn into a very active role and does much of the talking. The therapist tends to dominate the interactions with feedback and/or interpretations about what is going on between the couple and as this happens the couple talks to each other less and less. Often, the couple lapses into silence and the intensity of their affect tends to decrease. This silence (or lessened activity level) might be due to the fact that the couple is overwhelmed by so much input from the therapist. In addition, the therapist's overeagerness to help might decrease the couple's sense of responsibility for their own change.

Overidentification with the couple. Sometimes, the therapist's mood and behavior are determined by the couple. If the clients are depressed the therapist tends to be depressed. If the couple is angry and engages in mutual blaming, the therapist gets caught up in this behavior and blames the couple (or one partner) for blaming. Essentially, the problem for the therapist is fusion and the inability to relate on a different emotional plane such as with humor.

Acting out on sexual feelings toward one partner. The whole issue of sexual thought, feelings, and behaviors with patients is complex yet needs to be examined as a potential manifestation of overinvolvement. Working with couples or individuals who are distressed over a relationship with a significant other is the breeding ground for sexual feelings. Sexual energy is a given in therapeutic work with couples (Edelwich, 1982). However, therapists often feel quite conflicted either when they recognize their own attraction to a patient or when seductive behavior from the patient is noted. Dickes and Strauss (1979) note that therapists may prematurely terminate patients, particularly in short-term forms of treatment such as when working with patients on sexual problems. Focusing on erotic material can foster the patient's eroticized transference and this in turn can produce heightened reactivity within the therapist. Early termination helps to alleviate the therapist's discomfort (perhaps unconscious sexual feelings) but leaves the therapeutic work in an unfinished state.

Guilt often prevents therapists from dealing directly with their own sexual feelings toward patients. Sometimes, such guilt can lead the therapist to become underinvolved with the couple and thus to become colder, more detached, and/or more aloof during therapy sessions as a way of controlling his anxiety. Acting out can take the form of smiles, hugging patients, identifying with the position of the partner to whom the therapist is attracted, considering seeing one partner in individual therapy to work on "underlying" issues, switching of topics, and ending the therapy session later than is scheduled. These behaviors often are not the result of the sexual fantasies toward the patient. The acting out occurs because of how we feel about having such fantasies.

Taking sides. Manifestations of this form of overinvolvement are self-evident. The therapist tends to deal with one member of the couple more extensively than the other. This attention can take the form of focusing on one partner's responsibility for a problem or being overly empathetic to one partner's position. For example, the husband may tend to pursue individual activities at night when returning home from work. He enjoys gardening, reading, and occasionally watching television. His wife, on the other hand, needs more togetherness and feels that he does not communicate with her. She too works hard and wishes at night to feel close to her husband. "The popular choice" is often with the pursuer, while distancers tend to be unpopular and may be regarded as unfeeling souls. A therapist might also reflect this bias and unwittingly side with the wife by trying to get the husband to reach out to her more and to work on initiating discussions about his feelings.

Investment in saving the marriage. Often therapists attempt to avoid this form of reactivity as much as they try to stay away from taking sides. Yet therapists can tend to become invested in keeping the couple together and examining the question of staying together can be viewed as a therapist's failure to really help the couple. Moreover, research into therapy effectiveness contributes to a focus on the goal of increased "togetherness" (however togetherness is operationally defined), since much research would find a couple's decision to separate a sign that therapy had no beneficial effect.

On the other side of the coin additional patterns of therapist reactivity can be described which reflect *underinvolvement* with the couple.

Withdrawal. The reasons can be as numerous as the stars, but the net result is that the therapist needs to withdraw in order to manage his or her emotions in the therapy setting. In couples where either one or both members can be diagnosed as having a borderline personality disorder, a great deal of reaction can be elicited within the therapist. Such couples may present a special situation that fosters therapist withdrawal. The patient keeps communicating "save me," and when the therapist fails in doing so, anger at the therapist is unleashed. Often, the therapist's withdrawal can be manifested as a lack of leadership within therapy. Couples are often in some form of crisis when they decide to enter therapy. The volatile nature of the couple's emotional atmosphere combined with patient neediness at such times can arouse anxiety within the therapist. While some therapists might get caught in this system through overinvolvement, others might emotionally retreat. The couple then runs the session through such behaviors as arguing endlessly or dictating the terms of how the therapy should be conducted.

Feelings of helplessness. This form of underinvolvement is similar to the description above but often represents the aftermath of an unspoken contract with one member of the couple. Masterson (1983) discusses therapist countertransference in individual psychotherapy and notes how patients stipulate certain conditions for therapy. "I will love you if you don't criticize me." The therapist in some way agrees to this so that he can avoid his fear of anger toward the patient and assure himself of continued admiration. Thus, a therapeutic impasse develops and the therapist feels helpless. Masterson's formulation can be applied to couples therapy in that an agreement is reached with either the couple or perhaps one member. In the latter case the dynamics are more inventive. Essentially, an alliance is reached with one partner to either side with him or to avoid certain issues. The other partner picks up on this and increases her resistance to change and thus a stalemate is reached.

Emotional disconnection to the couple. This category is a catchall for the general inability to connect with a particular couple. The issues which they are struggling over are unclear or the therapist cannot relate to them for some reason. The concerns of the couple may conflict with one's value system as a therapist or may represent issues that are yet to be worked through by the therapist such as extramarital affairs or death. Certain therapist behaviors might go along with this disconnection such as patterns of rescheduling, lateness, and clockwatching and boredom during therapy.

THEORETICAL FORMULATIONS OF THERAPIST REACTIVITY

Therapist reactivity implies that clinicians are vulnerable to becoming fused with the couple and thus struggle to maintain clear and secure boundaries. Certain theoretical concepts might help to guide our understanding of what takes place in the process of a therapist developing a reactive stance with a particular couple.

The social context of conducting therapy with couples is quite different from that of working with one patient. There are now three people in the room and the potential for issues being aroused within the therapist may be even greater in this context than in individual treatment. With two people before her, the therapist can be reminded of her own marriage or of her family of origin. As Bowen (1976) notes the therapist's own family is the framework for how he or she responds to patients. If therapists remain caught in the web of their own family dynamics, they will be less free to flexibly move in and out of a couple's emotional system. In addition to issues with the therapist's family of origin, his own, immediate marital status creates a cognitive set that can be threatened by particular couples.

Let us, for example, take a therapist who is a pursuer in his own marriage and whose wife is a distancer. His wife is going back to school while holding down a full-time job and he feels left out. He tends to deal with his feelings by reaching out for her sexually and his wife often responds with less enthusiasm than he would like. He takes her distance personally and sees her outside activities as being more important to her than he is. Now this therapist is referred a couple who has been married for two years and shortly after the marriage the husband began to distance himself sexually and otherwise. The extent of the husband's involvement in work, his interest in watching sports on television and in playing golf were never apparent during their courtship. His sexual desire has dropped dramatically as he tries to convince his wife that no marriage could sustain the activity level that they had before marriage. He feels that no matter what he does he cannot satisfy her. The therapist might sense parallels between this marriage and his own. Thus, he might tend to get overinvolved with the wife's position by focusing more energy on the husband's emotional retreat and feeling more empathy for the wife.

Social learning theory is the most obvious set of concepts that would explain the dynamics described in the example above. We learn to play certain roles (i.e., a conditioned set of responses) in our family of origin and in our own marriages. When similar stimuli appear in therapy, we respond in patterned ways. For example, uncommunicative and passive patients may tend to remind us of one of our parents and if we are highly reactive to that parent, we might tend to become overly involved with that patient by trying to get him/her to change. Or we might become distanced as a way to cope with the aggression we feel toward this patient. The problem with social learning theory is that it tends to be static and does not capture the richness of the interactive forces occurring within couples therapy.

Another explanation could come from a psychoanalytic perspective. Certain oedipal wishes in the therapist might become activated in couples therapy. These wishes might be the result of the therapist's fantasies or they might be activated by helpless and seductive patients who communicate how terrific the therapist is in contrast to their partner. Whatever the horse and the cart are, the net effect is that oedipal wishes are activated by the therapist's reactivity to the opposite gender patient. A triangular relationship develops whereby the therapist bonds more with the opposite gender patient. The therapist feels superior, strong, and courageous as a model for what the patient is seeking is presented to the patient's partner. A form of collusion (Willi, 1982) ensues between patient and therapist perhaps motivated by the therapist's unconscious fantasies so that "in this triangular relationship he is seeking revenge for his oedipal wound" (p. 227). The collusion might also stem from the wish for an oedipal victory and thus finally receiving that special attention longed for from mom (or dad for female therapists).

Willi (1982) describes how patterns of collusion between therapist and patient are even more prevalent when the patient is undergoing individual therapy. The partner who is not in therapy feels left out and will sabotage the individual treatment on some level. Thus, a power struggle between the therapist and the patient's partner ensues. The collusion between therapist and patient can result in fostering the patient's autonomy and this collusion can be focused around the theme of "fear of divorce versus fear of independence." The therapist might project his aggressive and negative feelings onto the patient's family, yet all that has really happened is that a new triangle has formed with the patient now becoming dependent on the therapist as the third leg of the triangle.

The notion of triangular forces has emerged in this discussion as a theme. Hence, it may be that systems theory offers the most fruitful explication of the dynamics within couples therapy for explaining therapist reactivity. The therapist becomes the third leg of the triangle and thus can be used by couples to stabilize the conflict between them. Therapists thus either get caught in playing such a role for clients or, in refusing to do so, get paralyzed by their own reluctance to be drawn into the couple's system.

Fogarty (1980b) describes how trangles function and how triangles take different shapes. The tensions that cause marital distress are often too uncomfortable and/or too unmanageable for couples to be able to deal directly with one another to resolve their problems. The inability to reach problem resolution makes a person seek another means of stabilizing the tension. Forming a triangle with another person or another activity helps to form an adaptation to the tension. For example, if a couple's sex life is unsatisfactory, a sexual affair might help to alleviate the anxiety aroused by one partner's lack of sexual interest. Focusing on the "bad" behavior of one's children allows the couple to find some common ground for their relationship and thus their dissatisfaction with each can be avoided. Another instance of a triangle can be seen in the person who gets involved with work as a way to avoid confronting the partner with some important sources of distress in the relationship. In short, triangles form because the family system cannot manage emotional distress and cannot find solutions to problems that are satisfactory to its members.

The same dynamics that apply to the family group can be used to describe how therapists become a leg of a triangle. Sometimes, a member of the couple tries to bring this about and at other times the therapist might move into the couple's emotional system in such a way that he initiates the formation of the triangle. An example of the former situation is when a patient calls crying over the phone and expressing a great deal of strain. She requests a special session with the therapist (outside of their normal couples therapy time). Agreeing to this, the therapist sees her individually. She then reveals that she has had an ongoing affair with a man for quite some time and has not been able to tell anyone about this. She was sure that the therapist would understand but the therapist must promise not to reveal this in couples therapy. The patient has attempted to form a "special" alliance with the therapist as a means of not confronting her husband directly with the affair. The obvious example of a therapist being the initiator of a triangle is when he experiences much more compassion for one member of the couple or the family. A therapist might identify for instance with the child and form an alliance against the parents. In aother example, the therapist might unwittingly ridicule the patient who is the pursuer in the relationship out of his frustration with the patient's constant complaining about his wife's overconcern for everyone else but him.

Fogarty describes three major triangles. The first is an *equilateral* triangle (see Figure 2). In this formulation the sides of the triangle are of equal length.

FIGURE 2 Fogarty's Equilateral Triangle

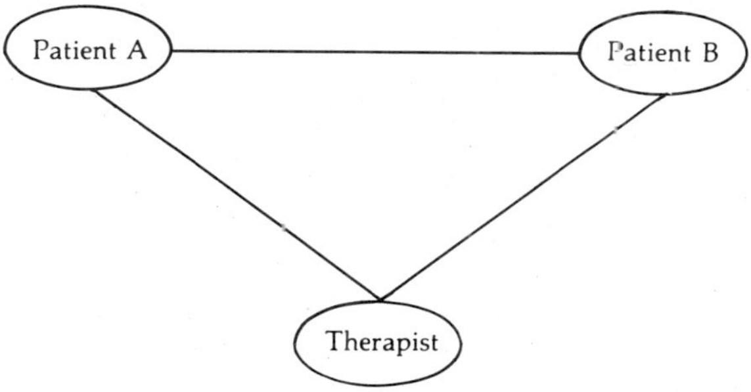

This is quite difficult to see in couples therapy because everyone is managing to keep a measured amount of distance between them. It is as if a rubber band is wrapped around the three people (i.e., the couple and the therapist with the rubber band being constantly taut). Any movement toward one member of the couple will be resisted by the other member. Tension therefore increases in therapy when, for example, the therapist spends too much time focusing on the feelings of the wife. The husband tends to resist this behavior by the therapist. Sometimes, the husband becomes silent and withdrawn, feeling left out. At other times he changes the topic to himself or to another issue altogether, feeling threatened by the therapist's discussions with his wife. The same dynamic would occur if the therapist spent time focusing on the husband's feelings.

The therapist might contribute to the triangle by inadvertantly communicating negative feelings about whichever partner he is not focusing on. The therapist may also wish to maintain much distance within therapy as a way of keeping things safe. He might be highly reactive to the negative responses that occur when he makes a move in therapy. Thus, the therapist needs to keep his involvement minimized because either her own conflicts become aroused in therapy or those that get activated between the patients are too unsettling.

The second triangle (see Figure 3) can be labeled the *isosceles* triangle wherein the therapist has formed an overly close alliance with one member of the couple with the partner being a distant leg of the triangle. For this to occur, the therapist tends to better understand the insides of one member of the couple and covertly blames the partner for the couple's problems. It should be noted that the distant member may even prefer to remain distant. For example, couples therapy might begin with one member indicating her lack of interest in changing and communicating her belief that it is due to her husband that they are having such problems. She indicates that the therapist should work with her husband, but that she wants to be present in therapy because her husband will throw it up to her if she does not attend.

FIGURE 3 Fogarty's Isosceles Triangle One

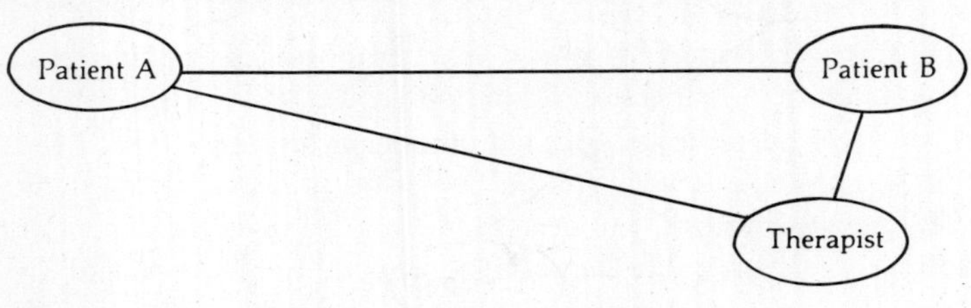

FIGURE 4 Fogarty's Isosceles Triangle Two

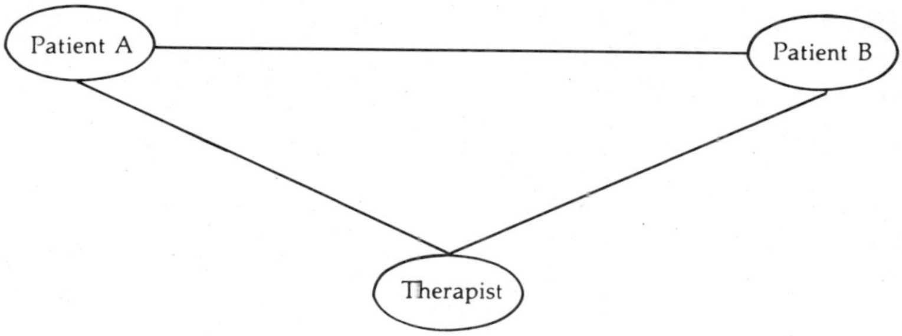

The final triangle (see Figure 4) can be viewed as another form of the *isosceles* since it also has two sides equal in length with a longer third side. In this triangle the two members of the couple are quite distant and the therapist gets drawn in as a go-between. The therapist tries to fill the void between the couple, tries to set their agenda, tries to be overactive in building a bridge between the two partners.

The question is: What is the therapist attempting to avoid by engaging in such triangles with couples? Again, systems theory indicates that successful attempts to triangulate decrease tension and are thus an adaptation to not directly addressing the real issues associated with therapists' own reactivity. Therapists (as with all mortals) have a great deal of difficulty being sufficiently involved yet distant enough to keep from getting too close to "the action." Therapists can tend to feel anxious and guilty about their impulses in therapy and to not want to look at their aggressive feelings or their feelings of attraction to their patients (Racker, 1957). Couples therapy often stimulates in the therapist feelings of impotence, uncertainty, fear, anger, and love. Triangles help to cut down the uneasiness associated with such feelings.

STRATEGIES TO COPE WITH THERAPIST REACTIVITY

The overriding path for the management of therapist reactivity is fairly clear: Self-awareness of these emotional experiences toward patients is an ongoing effort. Tolerance for uncertainty, impotence, and ambiguity will aid in this attempt to understand and be in control of one's insides.

Beyond this need for self-focus, a number of strategies have been noted by a number of leaders in the field of marital and family therapy. Bowen's (1976) emphasis on the therapist's own family stems from the belief that a therapist will be vulnerable to fused therapy relationships if that therapist has not gone back to his own extended family and dealt with the triangles that pull him toward fusion with that family. It becomes critical for the therapist to increase his differentiation within his own family as a blueprint for being able to be differentiated from couples in a therapeutic context.

Another strategy involves the therapist's ability and willingness to take an "I" position (Fogarty, 1984b). This ability to directly communicate, to say what one sees, to reveal feelings, models for the couple a differentiated self.

Fogarty (1984b) offers yet another avenue for the therapist to reduce her reactivity. He suggests that the therapist examine her expectations and how invested she is in the couple changing. Typically, high expectations are met with little success since her frustration is communicated and the couple then forms an alliance against her effort. Focusing on the process helps to decrease such expectations. In fact, Fogarty (1984b) argues for therapists to imagine what it would be like for no change at all to be expected. How would the patient feel then? The patient would most likely feel a significant gap, a sense of emptiness, and it is this emptiness that needs to be explored in therapy.

Whitaker, Felder, and Warkentin (1965) point to a few additional thoughts to help the therapist deal with reactivity. The use of cotherapy will help the therapist monitor his response to couples. The dynamics within couples therapy are too complex for one person alone and a cotherapist will help identify the "blind spots." Taped records are another source of information which can be analyzed to identify sources of therapist reactivity. These authors also urge the therapist to attempt to identify with each member of the couple. Imagine how you would feel if you were in their position. They also encourage therapists to share their feelings with the couple so that therapists will not indirectly act out those feelings. However, they offer few guidelines for such self-revelations. It is clear that not all thoughts and feelings within the therapist can or need to be communicated to the couple. A useful rule of thumb might be that when the feelings are based on the therapist's own reactivity, these reactions need to be worked through outside of therapy. When these reactions are truly elicited by the couple and are not a reflection of the therapist's own issues, sharing these feelings with the couple might indeed be useful. Quite often, making such determinations is very difficult.

Summary

This chapter has attempted to describe those forces that shape the internal life of therapists who work with couples. It is striking how much attention therapist's reactions to clients receives when having an informal lunch with a friend or colleague, but how much shame seems to be associated with these responses when analyzed in a more systematic way such as through a case conference or through a paper presented at a conference.

Therapists bring their own history of family roles, expectations, and ongoing conflicts into the therapeutic environment. This fact is not necessarily a sign of immaturity, personality deficiency, or lack of competence, but a recognition that therapists take their life space with them wherever they go. The difficult issue for therapists is to deal with their anxiety and guilt over certain responses to couples. Somehow, therapists tend to forget that there is both a connection among as well as differences between thoughts, feelings, and behaviors. We cannot assume that if we do not act on our feelings they will not influence our work with couples. Neither can we be vulnerable to fusing these three notions so that the mere thought of certain feelings toward our patients makes us feel guilty and inept.

References

Bowen, M. (1976). Theory in the practice of psychotherapy. In P. J. Guerin (Ed.), *Family therapy: Theory and practice*. New York: Gardner Press.

Dickes, R., & Strauss, D. (1979). Countertransference as a factor in premature termination of apparently successful cases. *Journal of Sex & Marital Therapy, 5*(1), 22–27.

Edelwich, J. (1982). *Sexual dilemmas for the helping professional.* New York: Brunner/Mazel.

Fogarty, T. F. (1980a). On emptiness and closeness: Part 2. In E. G. Pendagast (Ed.), *The family: compendium I.* New Rochelle, NY: Center for Family Learning.

Fogarty, T. F. (1980b). Triangles. In E. G. Pendagast (Ed.), *The family: compendium I.* New Rochelle, NY: Center for Family Learning.

Fogarty, T. F. (1984a). The distancer and the pursuer. In E. G. Pendagast (Ed.), *The family: compendium II.* New Rochelle, NY: Center for Family Learning.

Fogarty, T. F. (1984b). Operating principles. In E. G. Pendagast (Ed.), *The family: compendium II.* New Rochelle, NY: Center for Family Learning.

Freud, S. (1959a). The future prospects of psycho-analytic therapy. In E. Jones (Ed.), *Collected papers, Volume 2.* New York: Basic Books. (Original work published 1910)

Freud, S. (1959b). Recommendations for physicians on the psychoanalytic method of treatment. In E. Jones (Ed.), *Collected papers, Volume 2.* New York: Basic Books. (Original work published 1912)

Guerin, P. J. (1980). Family therapy: Style, art, and theory. In E. G. Pendagast (Ed.), *The family: compendium I.* New Rochelle, NY: Center for Family Learning.

Lackovics, M. (1983). Classification of countertransference for utilization in supervision. *American Journal of Psychotherapy, 37*(2), 245–257.

Masters, W. (1983, November). Lecture delivered at the Postgraduate Workshop, Masters & Johnson Institute. St. Louis, MO.

Masterson, J. F. (1983). *Countertransference and psychotherapeutic technique*. New York: Brunner/Mazel.

Napier, A. Y., & Whitaker, C. (1973). Problems of the beginning family therapist. In D. Bloch (Ed.), *Seminars in psychiatry: Techniques in family psychotherapy*. 5, 2, 229–241.

Racker, H. (1957). Meanings and uses of countertransference. *Psychoanalytic Quarterly, 26*(3), 303–357.

Whitaker, C. A., Felder, R. E., & Warkentin, J. (1965). Countertransference in the family treatment of schizophrenia. In I. Boszormenyi-Najy & J. L. Framo (Eds.), *Intensive family therapy*. Hagerstown, MD: Harper & Row.

Willi, J. (1982). *Couples in collusion*. New York: Aronson.

THIRTEEN

*Experiential Psychotherapy with Couples**

Marlene Schneider, M.S.W.
Director of Family Services
Addiction Treatment Program
Mt. Sinai Hospital

Experiences are the essential phenomena of existence. Experiences in which *we interact with other people called encounters are the most powerful of all experiences for the* development of skills *which we can use to cope with future experiences. The encounters which we have within our families, past and current, are the most significant in generating and influencing our capabilities.*

Walter Kempler, "Experiential Therapy Within Families"

"He doesn't give a damn what I feel, I've told him time and again not to look at women that way and he keeps doing it. I can't go anywhere with him without being humiliated. The women he letches after can't stand it either, I think it's disgusting. No matter what I say he keeps doing it. He just doesn't care."

She is sitting with folded arms, narrow eyes, and accusing voice, angry yet frightened. Her husband is sitting on the same couch but he has retreated as far as possible into the opposite end. He is staring out a nearby window. Finally he responds in a controlled tone.

"She's crazy. She's crazy with jealousy. I m just friendly. I smile a lot. I like people. She thinks I want to get into bed with every woman I say hello to. I'm just friendly, that's all."

*I wish to acknowledge the help and support of Lincoln Potter, M. D. in the preparation of this chapter.

"He says he's just being friendly! You should have seen the look on the waitress's face when he was just being "friendly" last week. I thought she was going to slap him. Instead, she just walked off shaking her head."

"That was not last week, it was several months ago. And she just misunderstood my friendliness, that's all."

It was not several months ago. It was just last week. Don't you remember, we were coming home from . . . ."

Arguing of this type is often a symptom of a couple's inability to effectively communicate their needs to each other. The cycle of accusations and defensiveness can go on and on. Each attempts a rational defense of his or her position. Each analyzes and reanalyzes the partner's position in an effort to discredit it and thereby get his/her own needs met. Most often this cognitive, pseudo-logical dance is a dead end. Issues are not resolved, there is no negotiation, and both partners may resort to power plays involving sex, money, or physical and emotional abuse in order to get their own way. The resulting frustration is shared by both therapist and clients.

Experiential couples therapy provides an alternative to this cycle. With its focus on individual responsibility and free choice, it helps clients to feel in control of their own lives.

Through the use of role playing, behavioral rehearsal, and various other forms of in vivo experience, couples learn how to identify their needs and feelings and to directly communicate and negotiate with their partners.

The major focus of experiential couples therapy, as with any other experiential therapy, is in its emphasis of the present, both in the linguistic sense and in the action sense. It is what is happening *now* that is important.

Gerald Cory writes:

> For so many people the power of the present is lost; instead of being in the present moment, "they invest their energies in bemoaning what was or anxiously anticipating what will be." (1982, p. 115)

For the experiential therapist change is made possible by becoming fully aware of what is happening now.

The next focus comes from its emphasis on experience. The early learning theorists were aware of the importance of involving as many senses as possible to facilitate learning (Hergenhahn, 1982). When we analyze with a client, we appeal primarily to his cognitive understanding through his sense of hearing. The value of experiential therapy lies in its ability to dramatically affect all senses simultaneously. This ensures that the client is learning from the modality that suits him best. The learning is then congruent with his mode of perceiving his world. This is especially important in conjoint couples therapy because the partners frequently differ in their styles of perception. They each need an approach that is meaningful to them.

Fear is always an issue in conjoint therapy. Each partner is afraid of being exposed, rejected, or overwhelmed by the other. Because experiential therapy pays attention to the experience of what is happening in the present, that fear and the defensiveness it engenders can be dealt with directly in the session.

Technically, the term *experiential therapy* is used to describe an approach where the therapy session itself is used as a laboratory in which clients have new experiences. It is an action therapy (Kempler, 1981).

Gerald Cory writes:

> I am impressed with the action approach, which brings conflicts and human struggles to life. Through such techniques, I have found people actually experience their struggles, as opposed to merely talking about problems endlessly. (1982, p. 99)

There are many forms of experiential psychotherapy, each presenting its own mixture of experiential and cognitive focus.

Gestalt, psychodrama, psychosynthesis, music, art, and dance therapies tend to be more orthodox in their approach to experiential therapy, whereas Systemic Family Therapy, Neurolinguistic Programing, and sometimes even Behavior Therapy would lean more toward the cognitive end of this continuum.

I tend not to be a "true believer" in any one method of therapy, but work hard to pick from the rich garden of techniques and opportunities which is available.

I present you now with a short overview of my understanding of what works with hope that you may find something that works for you. Please keep in mind that reading and writing are linear activities while therapy goes on at many levels simultaneously. I will present these levels in a linear fashion, but ask you to integrate them with your understanding so that they occur simultaneously.

In this chapter I will discuss how to use the experiential couples therapy to diagnose problem areas and remediate these problems with new learnings.[1] This will be followed by a sample of illustrated "experiments" that can be used for diagnosis and/or learning.

---

[1]The more orthodox experiential therapists would take issue with my statement regarding diagnosis. For them, experiential therapy is a means of helping the client to become aware of his own process and that is all. Any attempt by the therapist at remediating the problem would be regarded as an intrusion on the client's process. They assume that that would create resistance and thereby interfere with the client's ability to generate his own solutions to his problems.

DIAGNOSIS

In my use of experiential couples therapy I encourage the couple to encounter each other during the therapeutic session. This provides an opportunity for me to observe the couple's interaction directly. The process of diagnosis is a continual one, allowing me the chance to hypothesize, evaluate, and revise treatment procedures throughout therapy.

In contrast to more traditional forms of therapy, experiential diagnosis is an ongoing process which focuses more on the dynamics of the present interaction than on each client's history or internal psychodynamics. History becomes important only when it is clear that it is affecting the present situation. By observing the couple's interactions in the present, I am given an opportunity to see the behavioral process, not just to hear about it. The amount of information couples present to the therapist is staggering. For example:

Nonverbal:

- How is each client holding his/her body, head, arms?
- Which muscle groups are tense?
- Does the couple sit close together or far apart?
- Do they make movements toward or away from each other, and when?
- Do they look at each other, do they look down, do they look up, and when?
- How is each client breathing; is it rapid or shallow? When does it change?
- Are their cheeks flushed or pale, tense or flat?
- Are their jaws clenched, and when?
- What do you see in their eyes; do they seem frightened or sad; are there tears?
- Is what you see in their eyes or body congruent with what they are saying?

Verbal:

- What is their tone of voice: high, low, whiney, complaining, domineering, seductive? When?
- Does either client use excessive drama or generalizations in trying to get his/her point across?
- Is either client verbally withdrawn?
- Does either client withdraw from a confrontation?
- What methods does each use to get control in a situation?
- Do they let each other speak?

- Does one talk for the other?
- Do both partners have an equal chance to talk?
- Are statements or phrases completed?
- Is logic used to invalidate partner's feelings?
- Are they able to hear what the other is saying without changing the content?
- Can they validate each other's feelings or do they become defensive?

From behavioral observations like these, I formulate a hypothesis of how and why this couple interacts as they do. These hypotheses can then be tested. If found accurate behavioral remediation can start. As an example, consider the case of Judy and Bill.

BILL AND JUDY

Bill keeps talking at Judy. He does not give her a chance to respond to his questions. Bill's face is flushed. He is talking with a lot of animation. He is trying to convince Judy that his fear that she will leave him if he took more time for himself is justified. Judy sits patiently waiting for him to finish. She is keeping her eyes on him the whole time.

As therapist I ask myself, "What is happening NOW?" "What is their process?"

Bill seems to have Judy's total attention. The content of his talk seems irrelevant. Judy keeps looking at Bill's mouth. Her jaws are clenched and her breathing is very shallow.

I begin to form a hypothesis: Bill appears to be thriving on Judy's attention and seems to be working hard to maintain it. Judy appears stressed but manages to continue giving attention anyway. To test my hypothesis I will use what J. Zinker has termed, an *Experiment* (Zinker, 1977). I ask Judy to look away from Bill for 30 seconds while he is talking to her. Bill is asked to note any physiological responses he has to Judy's looking away. I watch Bill's face as Judy follows instructions. His eyes dilate, his shoulders tense, his voice grows in volume and then begins to trail off. I ask what he is experiencing at the moment. He tells me he feels even more upset when she looks away. He doesn't like it. I ask Judy to look at him again. The tension in Bill's body eases. I ask them to repeat the whole process. Again there is the appearance of tension when she looks away and a return to comfort when she is looking at him.

Bill's response generates many questions Is this a common experience for Bill? Does it happen with anyone besides Judy? Does it happen all the time with Judy? Does it reflect a fear of being alone or a need for attention? Observing the answer to these questions and others that are generated by the experience allows the therapist to decide what skills the client would have to learn in order to function more successfully.

LEARNING

The goals of learning within the session are to help the couple

1. To become aware of and name their own process, (how they interact with the environment and others).
2. To identify their own needs and wants.
3. To establish boundaries.
4. To learn how to negotiate in order to get those needs and wants met.
5. To learn to meet their own needs if their partners are not available.

All of these goals are generally applicable to most couples. However, the continual diagnostic process helps me focus on which goal is most relevant at any specific time and place. For example, a client may function very well when his spouse is continually available to meet his needs for nurturance, but he may become severely regressed and abusive when she is ill. He experiences her withdrawal as an abandonment which frightens him because he has not learned to meet his own nurturance needs. The goals of therapy at that particular time might be to teach him to meet his own needs and to help his wife learn how to give him more opportunities to be independent even when she is well. This may mean that a goal for her would be to identify and validate her own needs and wants instead of her husband's. And so it goes. When working with a couple, each goal in the process is intricately interwoven with the others. Their use is dictated by the situation.

Awareness of Process

Awareness exists in the present. It is the experience of each NOW. It can focus on the internal environment.

What am I feeling NOW (emotionally or kinesthetically)?
What am I thinking NOW?
What am I fantasizing NOW?

It can focus on the external environment.

What am I seeing?
What am I hearing?
What am I touching?

Awareness usually shuttles between both internal and external awareness. There is a famous Gestalt exercise that helps a client bring his/her awareness into the present. It calls for the client to complete the sentence: "Now

I am aware of" over and over again so that the client has the experience of following his/her own process. For example:

Now I am aware of the sound of the pencil on the paper.

Now I am aware of someone yelling outside my office.

Now I am aware of the excitement I feel at coming close to finishing this section of the chapter.

Now I am aware that I'm saying things to myself.

Now I am aware of my hand holding the paper.

Now I am aware of my next idea.

And so it goes. The client learns to identify what is figure and what is ground, to notice any patterns in his selection of figure.

For example, if a client becomes aware that he frequently notices what he doesn't like in a person (figure) rather than what he likes (ground), he can decide whether this pattern is useful or whether he would rather learn another way to focus his attention. The awareness allows choice.

Identifying Needs and Wants

When a client is aware of his own process and is able to name it, he can then identify what he needs and wants by noticing what is figure for him most frequently. For example:

Now, I am aware of being hungry = NEED food.
Now, I am aware of being cold = NEED warmth.
Now, I am aware of being tired = NEED sleep.

He can also learn to distinguish between needs and wants. Needs have an immediacy that is associated with survival while wants allow for more choice.
For example:

Now, I am aware of being bored = WANT an interest.
Now, I am aware of being sad = WANT comfort.

The identification of needs and wants is vital to having an intact boundary.

Recognizing Boundaries

Gestalt theory proposes that unless boundaries are intact people cannot have close contact. It is my experience that clients who do not have an intact boundary usually put physical or emotional distance between themselves and their partners because they have no other way of getting their needs met. For example:

Ann, an attractive 46-year-old housewife, was raised with a mandate to forget her own needs and to care for her family. She is married to John, who has learned to commit himself mainly to his work.

In the course of their marriage Ann gave up her art career to raise the children. She moved away from family and friends because of her husband's job. In several ways she says no to her own needs. Even little things like wanting to watch public television stations give way to her husband's need for football.

As might be expected, Ann whines and complains a lot. She is often too tired to make love to her husband. In a secret place in her heart she is beginning to think she does not love him. John of course feels rejected by Ann. He is tired of her complaining and feels rejected by her sexually. His secretary is beginning to look very good to him. But he doesn't know how to talk about how upset he is. He doesn't like to talk about such things and he doesn't want to hurt Ann. He may even be more aware of his attraction to his secretary than he is of his own upset.

If Ann had been able to identify and validate her own needs for a career, for contact with family and friends, and for all the little things like watching public television, she could have negotiated with her husband and at least had them partially met. Identifying her own needs and making them clear to her mate is what comprises her boundary. This identification takes courage. Ann was too frightened so instead she *pushed her husband away* with her complaining and withdrew from him sexually.

John too never stated his need for closeness. He ignored his own needs and as a result went looking elsewhere to get his needs met.

There are two major reasons for the inability to establish boundaries and thus create distance in an intimate relationship: safety, lack of skill.

Safety

The boundary problem described in the story of Ann and John was called *confluence* by Fritz Perls. Ann does not ask for what she wants; she does not set limits in order to get her needs satisfied. She does not negotiate or even allow conflict. John does the same thing. Confluence is the loss of differentiation between the self and the other. "It is an agreement not to disagree (Perls, 1973, p. 85). It is the beginning of the end of the relationship.

Too often the seeds of confluence are sewn at the beginning of a relationship when love is new and physical attractions are strong. Each is afraid to lose the other. Each is afraid to say something that will incur disapproval. Each is afraid that exploration of their differences will hurt or upset the other, perhaps to the point of losing the other. Differences are denied or glossed over in order to keep the other person physically close. The example I often use is as follows.

Man meets woman. There is instant chemistry. The man risks asking the woman for a date. She accepts. They go to dinner and have a wonderful time. He likes the way she looks, her femininity, her accomplishments. He feels good being with her. She gives him a lot of what he has been missing: warmth, excitement, education, and sociability.

She feels lucky just to be with him. He seems so strong and competent. He too is accomplished and looks good. Best of all he's available and she hasn't been dating much lately. She's delighted that he returns her feelings. But she's afraid it won't last.

This then is the setting, the fertile soil, for a confluent beginning—and a confluent end.

As the relationship continues she begins to notice a large pimple on his face. She finds the pimple repulsive, but is afraid to say anything lest he get angry and withdraw. Each time they are together she becomes more and more aware of the pimple. She uses a great deal of energy and attention in order to *not* to say something. Soon *all* she sees is the pimple. She can think of nothing else. If she had just said "That is a bad pimple, does it hurt?" she would be able to use the energy she is now using to withhold her spontaneous response, to enjoy her time with her new man.

We all experience this withholding when we first see someone who is badly disfigured. It is hard to notice anything but the disfigurement, but we usually don't say anything for fear of hurting the other person. As a result we have a hard time saying anything at all. Our spontaneity is gone.

This happened to me once while driving in New England. I stopped to ask directions of a man who was walking by the side of the road. As I drove up behind him I could not see his face. When he turned toward me I could see that he had *no nose.* He had put a regular BAND-AID over the hole where his nose should have been. I was startled to say the least and could not bring myself to respond to what was going on inside of me. I was aware of the voice inside. It was saying, "What happened to your nose? Is it cancer? Does it hurt?" and more. I did not have the courage to say it and as a result I squeezed out my original question and paid no attention at all to the answer he gave me. There was no contact between what was going on inside of me and in the outside world. As a result I drove away as ignorant about my whereabouts as I had been before.

When spontaneous responding stops, when each partner stops acknowledging the inner voice, it is the beginning of the incomplete boundary.

Lack of skill

Often one or both members of a couple have had very poor models either in an overly close or fragmented family. They have not learned the specific skills of identifying needs and setting boundaries with appropriate assertiveness.

It may be useful to think of a complete boundary as a complete circle. Everything within the circle would then be the self. Behaviorally, a complete boundary is represented by the following skills:

1. The ability to be aware of what the self wants and needs.
2. The ability to be aware of subvocalizations (inner voice).
3. The ability to be able to risk making them appropriately audible in situations where emotional intimacy or real contact is desired.
4. The ability to be able to be assertive in asking for what the self wants and needs.
5. The ability to negotiate with another to have needs met.

I'd like to be clear here that I don't advocate clients communicating this way all the time. They could get fired from a job or punched by a stranger. What I do suggest is that this skill be developed and used when closeness and real contact is desired.

Perls said that contact of closeness is "the appreciation of differences" (1973, p. 85). Closeness is enhanced by identifying those differences and negotiating the attainment of different expectations and goals with one's partner. Put another way, contact is enhanced by having intact boundaries.

Negotiating Needs and Wants

Negotiation is a skill with two parts: assertiveness and negotiation.

Assertiveness

Once the boundaries have been identified they must be protected. Assertiveness can be defined as a method of protecting boundaries. Bakker and Bakker-Rabdau (1976) developed a territorial model of assertiveness training which complements Perls's model of boundaries.

The model is based on the notion that each of us is born with certain "rights" or territories. These include: (1) our bodies, (2) our geographic space, (3) our emotions, (4) our labor, and (5) our action territory.[2] Defending these territories comprises assertion. Trying to get someone else's territory is aggression. Which is it when one partner tells the other to stop laughing or crying?

The Bakker and Bakker model indicates that aggression is often accomplished by means of weapons such as guilt, helplessness, and rapid

---

[2]How we do, what we do, that is, cook, clean, dress, walk, and so on.

takeover. They stress the importance of being able to identify those weapons in order to defend against them.

Negotiation

Many books have been written on negotiation skills (Cohen, 1980; Fischer, 1981; Gottman, Notarius, Gonso, & Markman, 1976; Ilich, 1980; Karrasor, 1974; Morley, 1977) and I do not want to go into detail here. I do want to say that I find that *negotiation is one of the most important skills I can teach my clients.* If they can negotiate they have an effective way of dealing with differences, and they will not be afraid to differ. If they are not afraid to differ, they can have boundary. If they have boundaries, they can have closeness.

I use two major forms of negotiation and one technique which I'd like to mention because it is unusually effective.

1. *Compromise.* Each partner gives a little on the same issue. For example, one partner wants to go out to dinner every week while the other wants to go out to dinner once a month. A compromise would be to go every two weeks.
2. *Trade-off.* One partner has his way on one issue and the other partner gets her way on the next. For example, one partner wants to go out to eat every week, and her partner agrees—if they can go bowling every week also.

If there is a disagreement about an issue, and compromise or trade-off is difficult, there is a third alternative. Ask each partner to rate (on a scale of 1 to 10) how much he or she wants what he or she wants. For example, if he rates Movie A at 8.5, and she rates Movie B at 6, they both go and see Movie A. There is an obvious danger in this technique insofar as one partner could take advantage of the situation by overrating his/her choices. But it has been my experience that couples are very happy to have this additional tool to help them set priorities. If one member does take advantage, the other is usually quick to feel resentment and this becomes a therapeutic issue.

Learning How to Meet One's Own Needs

Teaching clients to uncouple and meet their own needs for themselves when necessary can be the most difficult part of couples therapy. Yet without this ability, dependency becomes too great for healthy functioning.

The method I use for teaching this skill is derived from Eric Berne's (1961) *Transactional Analysis.* I call it the "Metaphor of the Child." Berne divided the personality into three functional parts: parent, adult, and child. The parent part is further divided into the nurturing parent and the critical parent. The adult part functions like a computer. It is objective and appraises reality without distortion. The child part is divided between the frightened child and the playful child.[3]

Clients learn that the playful child is creative, happy, centered, has fun, and generally is glad to be alive. The frightened child, on the other hand, experiences a lot of fear, is unhappy, and may be self-destructive and impulsive. Many people resort to drugs, alcohol, affairs, or workaholism to get away from the experience of chronically being in the frightened child ego state.

Clients also learn that stress creates regression from adult level perceptions and functioning to functioning as a frightened child. Regression can be so complete as to produce the uncontrolled survival rage of the two-year-old or the preverbal muteness of the six-month-old.

We can all learn that by reducing stress and nurturing our child, we can avoid severe regression, or if we become regressed we can learn to reduce regression with self-nurturance. Often the nurturing parent part of us is skilled at nurturing others rather than the self. Frequently, the critical parent (internal, negative, self-statements) is what is given to the self.

Clients learn to quiet the critical parent and begin to nurture the child within them. I often ask clients to recall a picture of themselves as a child so that there is a visual image on which to focus their nurturing energy.

Sometimes clients respond very well to the metaphor of the child but can't seem to identify what their child part needs or how to nurture it. In that case a technique called "I want" exercise helps clients to focus on the needs of the child.

Clients are told to ask the question, "What do you want, Suzie?" over and over again. (They are asked to use whatever name they were called as a child.) They give their first internal response. If an answer does not come right away, they respond with the word *blank*. They are asked to write down all responses. It is very important to make responses specific and behavioral. For example, "I want to be happy" is too general, but "I want to sit in the sun for half an hour" is very specific.

When a client can identify his child's needs, he is then taught to mediate those needs by accessing his internal adult. As mentioned above, the client uses the assertiveness and negotiation skills he has learned in order to get his needs met within the relationship.

EXPERIMENTS

Joseph Zinker (1977) devised the term *experiment* to mean the specific learning strategies that were set up within a therapeutic session. The goals

---

[3]I realize this is a simplication of Berne's work. However, this breakdown is usually sufficient to help most clients identify the process of self-nurturing. The imagery is often powerful enough to effect a change in behavior.

of these strategies are threefold: (1) diagnosis, (2) facilitating awareness, and (3) facilitating learning.

The sample of experiments listed below are some that work particularly well for me. I would like to remind readers, however, that experiments are designed to suit each couple and each situation. The therapist is limited only by his creativity.

Note in the design of most of these experiments the qualities of simplicity, present tense, drama, and the focus on the use of language.

Language

There are a number of experiments involving the way couples use language which can dramatically affect their ability to communicate. Defensiveness is a major problem. Having a couple make some minor linguistic changes during a session will effectively demonstrate how they can reduce defensiveness with their partners at home.

There are four major linguistic changes that I have found to be particularly important.

- Ask clients to start sentences with *I* instead of *you*. "*You* didn't do the dishes" becomes "*I* am very busy, would you do the dishes?" The use of *you* as the subject increases defensiveness. The use of *I* as the subject increases the likelihood of expressing feelings and helps to reduce the intrusion into the other person's territory that comes with *you* statements.

  In addition, using the word *I* helps clients to take responsibility for their own feelings. There is less blaming.
- Ask clients not to use general qualifiers such as *always, never, nothing,* or *everything*. For example, "You're *always* late" becomes "I am upset that you are late tonight." "You *never* do *anything* I ask" becomes "I'd be happy if you helped me wash my car." "*Nothing* I do is good enough for you" becomes "I'm sad that you are not pleased with my efforts." "*Everything* you do is a disaster" becomes "I'm upset that you lost your job."

  Generalizations bring up defensive objections in the listener. These objections get in the way of the speaker's ability to negotiate for what he wants.
- Ask clients to be *specific* about what they ask for.

  A general statement like "I want you to make me feel special" can be overwhelming to a mate. This is a statement without limits. A person is more likely to get what he wants if he asks for specifics such as "I want you to bring me coffee on Sunday morning," or "I want you to take the children for three hours one day a week so I can have some free time."
- Ask clients to speak in the present tense.

When clients insist on referring to past incidents they increase defensiveness and present a situation for which there is no remediation. For example, "You drank so much at that party last week you made a complete fool of yourself. I was totally embarrassed." They need to ask for what they want now. "I would like you to stay sober at the next party we go to together."

This allows the partner to save face and to change future behavior rather than to defend previous behavior.

Back to back

Have partners sit back to back and take turns saying what each wants from the other. *I* statements come more easily in this position and reduce the minimal cues which may trigger aggressive responses.

For example, consider Dina and John. They are a couple in their early 30s who have been living together for five years and are now contemplating marriage. They came in for therapy because of recurrent bickering. They both lead highly stressed lives: He is an attorney, she is a physician. Neither has been married.

[They come in bickering about the "stupid" way he drove the car.]

Therapist: Would you be willing to continue this back to back? *[They turn their chairs so that they face away from each other. For a moment each is at a loss for words.]*

Dina: *[Starts again to tell John how terrible his driving is but begins to lose energy half way through her sentence.]* You scare me when you drive so fast. I want you to drive more slowly.

John: I'm sorry. If you say it like that I can hear you. When you scream at me, I just get angrier and angrier. Then I want to drive faster and faster.

Dina: It's hard for me to show you this side of me. I feel vulnerable.

Look at the eyes

This is another exercise to reduce the minimal cues that trigger aggressive responses.

Have each partner sit facing the other looking into the eyes of his/her mate, and describe what he or she sees. While defensiveness usually comes out verbally, the hurt behind defensiveness can often be seen in the eyes. This exercise is especially good when one partner is verbal and the other is not. Have a verbal partner begin. A very important feature of this experiment is for the describer to check out the accuracy of his/her perceptions with the mate.

For example, let us consider another couple. Tom and Ellen are a couple in their early 40s and have two children, ages 9 and 11. They have been married for 17 years. Tom is a scientist; Ellen is in public relations. They come to therapy feeling ready for a divorce. Each has excellent professional skills but communication and negotiation within their relationship is mediocre. She came from a home where anger was freely expressed. In fact, it was the only emotion freely expressed. Tom's father died when he was a boy. He and his mother were very close and rarely fought. Tom deals with Ellen's anger by withdrawing, by working at his profession day and night, and by forgetting to do chores he had agreed to do. Ellen deals with her resentment by picking on Tom whenever he is around. Neither feels their needs are being met in the relationship.

[Ellen is sitting with her lips pursed and her arms folded over her chest. She has just finished telling Tom coldly how angry she gets when he is away all the time. Tom is sitting with his head down, a pillow in his lap.]

Tom: Well, if you weren't so damned critical all the time then I . . .

Therapist: Just a minute, Tom. I'd like you to look at Ellen's eyes. Tell her what you see.
[Pause.]

Tom: They're red and the lower rim seems full. *[Ellen's face softens, her lips relax, her cheeks flatten. She drops her hands to her lap.]*

Tom: She seems frightened.

Therapist: Tom would you please check out your perception?

Tom: Is it true? Are you feeling frightened?

Ellen: No . . . not so much frightened as sad. I'm sad. I feel alone.

Therapist: Tom, if you look at Ellen's eyes you will know more of what she's really feeling than if you look at her mouth.

Ellen's mouth would tighten when she felt upset. She looked angry. Tom's response to only seeing her mouth was to distance himself further. By looking at her eyes he could see her loneliness and respond to it more positively.

Closeness indicator

Have each partner stand at opposite ends of a room. One (A) walks toward the other (B) taking slow, small steps. Partner B stands still and tells partner A to stop the approach when the closeness feels uncomfortable. The process is then reversed. I have found that the resulting geographic space often reflects need for *emotional* space. This exercise provides both clients and therapist with a dramatic indication of different needs for and ability to tolerate closeness.

Empty chair

This well-known Gestalt technique helps each partner explore his or her relationship to other family members, as well as to each other. The client is asked to visualize the person he wants to encounter sitting in an empty chair. The encounter then unfolds with the client taking both roles.

This technique (Zinker, 1977) has been written about extensively, and details of its use will be found elsewhere. For couples it is especially useful because the partner of the client using the technique can observe the process. This technique can provide an experience of one partner's pain which talking about could never equal.

Marsha and Lenny are a couple in their late 40s. This is a second marriage for each of them. Both have children from previous marriages. They came to therapy because their fighting was escalating in intensity and frequency.

Lenny: I don't want you to tell me what to do.

Marsha: *[Defensively.]* I'm not telling you what to do. I'm letting you know what my needs are.

Lenny: I hate it when you do that. I try so hard to give you what you need. It feels like it's not good enough. It's never good enough.

Therapist: Is that a familiar feeling?

Lenny: *[Pause.]* Yes. I often feel that what I do is not good enough.

Therapist: Who said that to you?

Lenny: *[Pause. Dramatic shift in tone to an angry and intense voice.]* My father. He was always letting me know that what I did wasn't good enough.

Therapist: Would you be willing to imagine your father sitting in this empty chair?

Lenny: I suppose so.

Therapist: Fine. When you are ready, I'd like you to tell him how he taught you that you are not good enough.

Lenny: *[Focusing on the empty space in the chair.]* You never praised me. When I came home from school with 95s, you wanted to know why they weren't 100s. When I cleaned the yard, you wanted to know why I didn't clean the garage too. When I finished my potatoes, you were disappointed that I didn't finish my carrots. It was never good enough.

Therapist: Try saying, "I was never good enough."

Lenny: *[His eyes welling up with tears.]* I was never good enough. It's true, it's true. *[Pause.]* [Marsha is sitting quietly observing. She appears visibly upset by Lenny's tears.]

Lenny: *[Still to father.]* I wanted your approval just once, I wanted you to recognize what I was doing right. I need to know the good things I do too.

[Marsha appears to have heard the message even though and perhaps especially because it was not directed at her.]

Communication without words

Ask a couple who has difficulty speaking with each other to stop using words to communicate. If they have to demonstrate a feeling or desire they are less likely to trigger defensiveness in their partners.

Michael and Linda are a couple in their early 40s, married for 15 years. The presenting problem was Linda's recurrent bouts of manic behavior. They have daughters ages seven and nine. They both come from homes where they were dominated by the parent of their own sex. Linda deals with Michael's attempts to dominate her by repressing her responses for months and then acting out. Michael keeps Linda from dominating him by compulsive talking. He rarely lets her get a word in.

Michael: I don't like the way you act at parties. You're just entirely too friendly.

Linda: But that's the way I . . .

Michael: But it bothers me. You should stop it because it bothers me.
[To the therapist.] Don't you think she should stop it because it bothers me? You know what the trouble is, I don't trust her.

Therapist: Tell Linda.

Michael: I don't trust you. The way you get when you go into your episodes.

Linda: I like being friendly.

Therapist: Tell her specifically what your concern is.

Michael: She'll . . . you'll get manic again.

Therapist: What does that mean specifically?

Michael: She'll lose control?

Therapist: Tell her what that feels like—only I want you to tell her without words.

Michael: What do you mean?

Therapist: Communicate how her loss of control feels to you *without* words. [Michael sits bewildered for a moment. He doesn't know what to do. He tries to talk again but is again stopped by the therapist. His frustration is apparent. He begins to tremble. His eyes dart from Linda to the therapist and back again. Soon tears begin to well up in his eyes. He begins to cry quietly but it then becomes deep sobs as he pulls Linda toward him.]

Linda: *[Holding Michael tenderly she looks up at the therapist and says]* I've never seen him like this. He's always the strong one. I've always been the one who was needy.

Too many words block communication rather than facilitate it.

One sentence each

Another way to help a couple focus on expressing their needs rather than on trying to use words to justify themselves or manipulate their partners is to limit their statements (in the office) to one sentence. For example: "I want help with the children." "Please talk to my family when they visit." "Please don't look at other women that way."

Role reversal

An experiment that can help partners to gain understanding and experience what their mates are feeling is the role reversal technique developed by J. L. Moreno. Ask one or both partners to take the other's role in a disagreement or negotiation.[4]

Sherry and Bob originally came because their 15-year-old son was failing in school and their two younger sons, 5, and 6-1/2, were out of control. Bob was an ex-hippie and is now a salesman working 60-plus hours per week. His salary is high and he wants it to be higher. He sees himself on his way to a six-figure salary. Sherry, on the other hand, is not interested in so much money. She met Bob in his hippie days and wants him to stay that way. She wants him to stay home more and help with the kids. She also wants a chance to do her art work. She resents being the only one taking care of the children. When Bob is home he loses his temper with the children easily and often hits them. The couple finds it impossible to set up a management program to get the younger boys under control. Sherry and Bob's resentment is picked up by the older child who is acting out in school.

Sherry: He just doesn't seem to understand that I've had it with raising kids.

Therapist: Tell Bob, Sherry.

Sherry: I'm raising kids since I'm 18. I don't want to do it any more.

Bob: *[Defensively.]* Well, what do you want me to do? I'm trying to make a living. I can't work full time and take care of the kids too.

Therapist: If you are willing I'd like to try an experiment. Sherry, would you be willing to role-play Bob and continue from where he's left off? Bob, I'd like you to take Sherry's role.

Sherry: *[Pause]* I'm not sure I can do it right.

Therapist: You don't have to be right, just play the role from your own perceptions.

---

[4]A note of caution: This will not work when either partner's only affect is anger.

Sherry: *[As Bob.]* I really want to make a lot of money. I want nice things. I don't want to be hassled with the house or the kids. Nothing can stop me now. I'm on my way up.

Bob: *[As Sherry.]* I love you as you are. I don't need so much money. I want you, and I want you to be part of our family.

[Bob appears to have heard his wife for the first time. Taking her role allowed him to understand her without defending his own position.]

Sherry: I don't know what to say now. He really seems to understand how I feel.

Bob: You don't have to say anything. I guess I just never heard you until I stepped into your shoes. It just seemed like you were getting in my way.

Therapist: Does this change something for you, Bob?

Bob: No, I still feel the need to keep going, but I'm very touched by Sherry's love. I don't know how I'll work this out; I'm very confused.

Say it soon after you feel it

Often when one partner wants the other to change something she or he will withhold saying it until there is so much anger that a statement comes out with a great deal of negative affect. For example, consider the difference between "I wish you would lose five pounds," and "You're too fat; you don't turn me on any more." If a partner can avoid withholding, what needs to be said can be said in a much less hurtful way.

Say the whole thing

Encourage clients to say *all* of what they are experiencing when asking their mates to change something. It is important to include the positive with the negative. Like: "It's very hard for me to ask you this because I'm afraid you'll be angry with me and I'd like you to help me clean the house." This reduces fear and defensiveness in the partner.

Reinforcing positives

The office is an excellent place to teach clients to reinforce the other's desired actions with words, touch, and/or actions. Clients need to be taught what responses are the most meaningful reinforcement for their mate. They can also learn to reward successive approximations of an eventual, desired behavior. Doing it experientially allows the therapist to guide reinforcement so that it is effective.

Listen-touch dichotomy

Teaching clients that different people choose different ways of communicating helps them be more effective with their mates. For example, some people want to talk, while others want to be touched or to be noticed. We usually give to others what we want for ourselves. The people who want words will give words, and those who want touch will often give touch. This can become a real problem if a toucher and a talker are in a couple relationship, as they usually are. Touchers need to learn to actively listen to their mates, and talkers need to learn to touch when they want to reach and comfort their mates. Practice in the office is of inestimable value.

Active listening

Another skill of major importance for helping couples to feel close is active listening. Thomas Gordon (1975) discusses the technique in his book *Parent Effectiveness Training.* Most therapists are familiar with the technique. However, I mention it here to emphasize its importance. With this skill couples can learn to validate each other's feelings. In this way individual boundaries are not violated. Defensiveness disappears, partners feel safe and therefore willing to risk more closeness.

Barbara and Mike are a couple in their early 30s. They have two children, ages three and four. Mike is an ambitious salesman. He recently left a major company to go into business for himself. Barbara's sole career interest was in playing the flute. She gave up playing when she had her children. She is an attractive woman who is very much a perfectionist. She feels protected by Mike and respects his personal power in the outside world. On the other hand, she often feels his dependency on her at home. He seems to want endless attention. "He's always trying to please me." "It's too much pressure." "He gets upset if I'm not happy."

Mike does get anxious and resentful if Barbara's not happy. He also takes responsibility for making her happy. Put that together with her perfectionist standards regarding her own happiness and we have a very difficult situation.

Mike comes home from work very tired. He is too depleted himself to "make her happy," yet he experiences her unhappiness as a threat to his survival. His answer is to shut her out.

Barbara: He just won't listen to me. I'm just so turned off to him. *[Her face is tight, her eyes are filled with tears.]* Maybe there's something wrong with me. I just don't want him to touch me. Sometimes I feel sorry for him and go along with it, but then I want to stop in the middle.

Mike: She's driving me crazy.

Therapist: Barbara, you said you wanted Mike to listen to you, will you tell him more specifically what you mean?

Barbara: Sometimes I just get so frustrated when I'm telling you something that's important to me and you don't respond.

Mike: I'm just tired when I get home from work. I can't fix everything.

Barbara: I don't want you to fix it. I just want you to hear it.

Therapist: Mike, see if you can just listen to Barbara, and tell her what you hear.

Mike: I'm not sure I know what you mean.

Therapist: You're confused by my instructions?

Mike: Yeah, that's it, I'm confused.

Therapist: I've just modeled it for you, Mike. I just restated what I heard you saying.

Mike: I'll try it, but what about helping her?

Barbara: *[Frustrated.]* I don't want help, I want you to hear me.

Therapist: Go for it Mike. Try it with what she just said.

Mike: *[Pause.]* You don't want any help, you just want to know that I hear you?
[Barbara's shoulders relax.]

Therapist: Did you notice any feeling in her voice when you said it?

Mike: Yeah. She sounded disgusted.

Therapist: Now add that to your sentence.

Mike: You feel disgusted because all you want is for me to hear you.

Barbara: Yes. Yes. Yes! Oh thank you. That's it. That's what I mean. *[Her eyes are sparkling. She reaches over to Mike who visibly reacts to her touch.]*

Appreciations and resentments

Giving partners a chance to express all resentments and appreciations to each other allows the opportunity to express pain over past hurts without allowing those hurts to interfere with the process of therapy. Each client is asked to list every resentment that can be dredged up in order to let go of it. The resentment is expressed with the help of the therapist. Appreciations are difficult to express before the resentments are complete. Then they flow more freely and help the couple to reexperience some of their positive feelings for one another.

Sally and Fred are a couple in their early 40s. He is an engineer and she is a nurse. They have two children, ages 2½ and 5. They have been married for 12 years. Although they were deeply in love when they were first married, their relationship has deteriorated to the point of considering divorce. Sally and Fred are very angry about real and imagined hurts. They haven't learned how to deal with their differences. They do not know how to fight. Each is harboring intense resentment that is interfering with their learning how to deal with their differences.

[Sally and Fred are seated with their hands in their laps. They both stare at the walls in opposite directions in silence.]

Therapist: What is happening with you, Sally?

Sally: Nothing. I'm sort of numb I guess.

Therapist: Fred, what is happening with you? *[Fred squirms in his seat and doesn't answer.]*

[Pause.]

Therapist: We've been meeting for a while now, and it seems to me that old hurts are getting in the way of what we can do here. So, I'm going to ask each of you to focus your attention on your inner voice and to begin to make some statements about all your past resentments toward each other. When you are ready I would like you to make those statements to me rather than each other.

[I want to make it clear that these hurts are as much a result of their lack of negotiating their needs as they are a product of the mates doing. So I ask them to speak to me. The partner will still get the message but again it allows him to save face.]

It may be difficult to begin. It becomes easier once you start. Please continue until there are no more resentments left. You can listen to each other's resentments or not as you wish. The purpose is to express feeling and not to accuse. Accuracy is not necessary. After you complete your list of resentments I will ask for a similar list of appreciations. They will come more easily than the resentments. I'm going to suggest you begin, Sally, because I think it's easier for you to talk. Sally, begin with the words *I resent* for each resentment.

Sally: *[Pause.]* I resent all the hours you spend working at your business. *[Pause.]* I resent you for yelling at me, making me feel stupid. I resent you for not touching me. I resent you for being so cold to me. I resent you for wanting me to clean the house your way. I resent that you hate the dogs. I resent . . . .

[Fred is still looking away.]

I resent that you wanted your mother to come live with us. I resent that you don't like to dance.

[Her resentments flow quite easily.]

I resent that you don't discipline the children. I resent that you don't smile. I resent that you don't give me your approval.
[After awhile she begins to slow down.]

Therapist: What else is there? This is your opportunity. Please see if there is any more.

Sally: I resent you for leaving the toilet seat up. *[She begins to smile at the relative silliness of this one. She may be getting close to the bottom of her list.]*

Therapist: Please continue.

Sally: I resent you for forgetting my birthday. *[She goes on for a few more and then stops.]*

Therapist: Is that it?

Sally: That's it!
[She appears refreshed. She does not look at Fred, but she appears much more relaxed.]

Therapist: Now is the time for appreciations. These will be easier now, Sally. Start with "I appreciate"

Sally: I appreciate the way you have supported me financially. I appreciate that you've been faithful to me. I appreciate your intelligence. I appreciate your good looks. I mean, I really like your good looks.
[Pause. For the first time Fred begins to look at Sally.] I appreciate the way you have fixed up our home.
[She is looking at him now.] I appreciate the way you fixed the red chair. *[Pause.]*

Therapist: What else is there?

Sally: I appreciate the way you loved me when we were first married.
[Her eyes are beginning to tear.] I appreciate the way you love the children. *[Sally continues for several more statements. The muscles in Fred's face soften, his shoulders relax. His eyes are bright.]*

Therapist: Are you finished?

Sally: *[Pause.]* Yes. I'm pretty tired too.

Therapist: It's your turn Fred.
[It takes Fred a little longer to get started, but he completes the experiment with a similar result.]

A list of the experiments I use could go on and on. They evolve continually from the creativity of each therapist and are limited only by his or her imagination. Some of these experiments are quite short, some can take up a whole session or more. Sometimes the results are dramatic; often they just move the client along just one more step. Whatever the variations though, they are all designed to help clients become more aware and effective at getting his needs met in the present.

Summary

Couples today are demanding more of their relationships. With women gaining increasing economic independence, many unhappy couples have refused to stay together purely for economic reasons. Add to this the additional emotional stress of two career couples with multiple role expectations (most of which have not been clearly defined). The result is an increasingly complex situation that places extraordinary stress on the individual as well as on the relationship.

Few of us have been taught to successfully cope with those stresses. We have not learned to identify and meet our own needs in the context of these new demands. We have not learned the negotiating skills and creativity necessary to have our needs met within our relationships. We want so much to experience the promised happiness that we are turning more and more toward divorce as an answer, with the hope that it will be different with a new partner. Imagine the dismay when each partner experiences similar stresses and patterns of unhappiness in their next relationship.

Experiential couples therapy is certainly not a cure-all for the woes of these transitional times, but it does teach us to be real with ourselves and with those we love, it teaches us more about who we are and what we need to be happy, and it provides us with some groundrules to help us meet our needs with someone we love.

References

Bakker, C. B., & Bakker-Rabdau, M. K. (1976). *The territory model of assertiveness training.* Unpublished manuscript.

Berne, E. (1961). *Transactional analysis in psychotherapy.* New York: Grove Press.

Cohen, H. (1980). *You can negotiate anything.* Secausus, NJ: Lyle Stuart.

Cory, G. (1982). *Theory and practice of counseling and psychotherapy.* Monterey, CA: Brooks/Cole Publishing.

Fisher, R. (1981). *Getting to yes.* Boston, MA: Houghton Mifflin.

Gordon, T. (1975). *Parent effectiveness training.* New York: New American Library.

Gottman, J., Notarius, C., Gonso, J., & Markman, H. (1976). *A couples guide to communication.* Champaign, IL: Research Press.

Hergenhahn, B. R. (1982). *An introduction to theories of learning.* Englewood Cliffs, NJ: Prentice-Hall.

Ilich, J. (1980). *Power negotiations: Strategies for winning in life and business.* Reading, MA: Addison-Wesley Publishers.

Karraso, C. L. (1974). *Give and take.* New York: Crowell.

Kempler, W. (1981). *Experiential psychotherapy with families.* New York: Brunner/Mazel.

Morley, I. (1977). *Social psychology of Bargaining.* London: G. Allen and Unwin.

Perls, F. (1973). *The gestalt approach and eyewitness to therapy.* Ben Lomond, CA: Science and Behavior Books.

Zinker, J. (1977). *The creative process in gestalt therapy.* New York: Vintage Books.

FOURTEEN

Multimodal Marital Therapy

Lillian F. Brunell, Psy.D.

APPROACHES TO MARITAL THERAPY

Therapists have called upon every therapy system in seeking useful approaches to marital therapy. These have run the gamut from identifying and treating one partner as the "patient" responsible for the malfunctioning marriage to approaches that focus on the marriage as a "system" in need of remediation. While in some cases the particular theoretical orientation of the therapist is quite clear from the formulations and strategies employed in treatment, frequently that is not the case. It would be difficult to determine the orientation of the therapist from a sample marital therapy session.

As practiced by many therapists, marital therapy draws heavily on behavioral and cognitive strategies. A wide range of techniques has been adapted for use in marital therapy including contingency contracting, behavioral rehearsal, problem solving, assertiveness training, and many others. Some therapists refuse to see either partner individually after the initial assessment interviews have been concluded and focus exclusively on conjoint sessions with both partners, requiring that neither see another therapist during this time. Others have relied mainly on concurrent therapy with both partners rather than conjoint therapy (Lazarus, 1981). Whatever the approach or system of therapy employed, there are basic issues in marital therapy that are determined by the marital relationship itself and that must be addressed during the course of therapy.

MULTIMODAL MARITAL THERAPY

Multimodal therapy is a systematic, comprehensive, psychotherapeutic approach developed by Arnold Lazarus (1976, 1981, 1984). Multimodal marital therapy uses a conjoint approach to therapy, both in its assessment structure and in its treatment strategies. It identifies problems across seven personality modalities and employs a wide array of interventions that are entirely determined by the nature of the problems that have been identified. The treatments selected are not derived from a particular theoretical orientation, nor are they restricted by those boundaries, but are tailored to meet the specific needs of the distressed marital partners without concern for theoretical constraints. Multimodal marital therapy is a systematic, integrated approach, a synthesis of strategies and treatment interventions selected on the basis of their utility in the remediation of identified problems. It is *not* a system limited to the parameters of a particular theoretical orientation.

Multimodal Overview

> The multimodal orientation transcends the behavioral tradition by adding unique assessment procedures, and by dealing in great depth and detail with sensory, imagery, cognitive, and interpersonal factors and their interactive effects. A basic premise is that patients (or clients) are usually troubled by a multitude of specific problems that should be dealt with by a similar multitude of specific treatments. A multimodal assessment examines each area of a person's BASIC I.D. (B = Behavior, A = Affect, S = Sensation, I = Imagery, C = Cognition, I = Interpersonal relationships, D = Drugs/Biology). It provides an operational way of answering the question—what works, for whom, and under which conditions?
>
> Multimodal therapy is personalistic and individualistic. A diligent scrutiny for individual exceptions to general rules characterizes the approach; the search is for appropriate interventions for each person. Clinical effectiveness is predicated on the therapist's flexibility, versatility, and *technical* eclecticism. The *theoretical* eclectic tends to draw from diverse systems that may be epistemologically incompatible, whereas the technical eclectic uses procedures drawn from different sources without necessarily subscribing to the theories or disciplines that spawned them. The upshot is a consistent, systematic, and testable set of beliefs and assumptions about human beings and their problems, and an armamentarium of effective therapeutic strategies for remedying their afflictions. (Lazarus, 1984, p. 491.)

Multimodal therapy employs an educational, social-learning, cognitive, and a communications or systems model to account for the acquisition of maladaptive response patterns and therapeutic change. However, multimodal therapists also recognize that the current state of psychological knowledge does not permit the development of an accurate theory of human functioning. Accordingly, theory in Multimodal Therapy concentrates largely on determining *what* interventions are effective rather than explaining *why* they are effective.

The principle of "technical eclecticism" permits the multimodal therapist to develop a wide range of interventions. A technical eclectic adopts techniques on the basis of their demonstrated effectiveness without necessarily subscribing to the theoretical explanations their originators propound. (Lazarus, Kreitzberg, & Sasserath, 1981, pp. 504–505)

Multimodal therapy is an open system. The principle of technical eclecticism encourages the constant introduction of new techniques and refinement or elimination of existing ones. Multimodal therapists subscribe to no dogma other than the principles of theoretical parsimony and therapeutic effectiveness. (Lazarus, et al., 1981, p. 513)

Methodology

Multimodal therapy is a flexible approach that allows for individual differences among therapists and clients. Generally, Multimodal Therapy is organized around four processes:

1. *Assessment* of problems according to the BASIC I.D. framework.
2. *Development* of an individually tailored intervention plan based on each problem across the BASIC I.D. (modality profile).
3. *Implementation* of the intervention plan as a cooperative client/therapist enterprise.
4. *Refinement* of the intervention plan (and of the modality profile) through ongoing evaluation and feedback.

All four processes are employed during the course of therapy, but the emphasis given to each varies. Early in therapy, the therapist concentrates on assessment and the development of an intervention plan. As therapy progresses, the intervention process receives increasing emphasis. Feedback and refinement are ongoing processes during the course of therapy. (Lazarus, et al., 1981, pp. 507–508)

ABOUT MARITAL THERAPY

Marital therapy is different from other kinds of therapy in that the agenda is frequently more complex and sometimes more obscure. ("Couple therapy" can be substituted for "marital therapy" in this chapter.) To begin with, the marital partners may not share the same level of discomfort: One may be perfectly content with the relationship (or say that he or she is) while the other may be miserable. Acknowledging unhappiness in a marriage usually is seen by the other partner as a rejection by the one person whose approval is needed more than any other. This unacceptable rejection may initially trigger blanket denial of all of the partner's complaints, and synergistically, may cause the complaining partner to overemphasize and solidify his or her position. The need to maintain some level of privacy about events or feelings that may never have been exposed before may also complicate matters.

The fact that the therapy involves three people rather than two is another problem. Each partner is particularly concerned that the therapist understand his or her point of view. Each may go to some lengths to determine what the therapist's views of a good marital partner may be in order to demonstrate his or her conformance to those perceived standards and thereby win the therapist's approval. This may cause an overstatement of issues and feelings about the other person's flaws and an unwillingness to discuss one's own contributing problems. This effort to enlist the support of the therapist can produce an atmosphere of rivalry which can be very destructive and effectively block progress if not dealt with appropriately. Thus, the triadic nature of marital therapy itself can create problems.

The most important single factor necessary for successful marital therapy is *goodwill.* Each partner must have an attitude of goodwill toward the other, must perceive his or her partner's goodwill, and must believe that the therapist feels acceptance and goodwill for both. Without these ingredients successful marital therapy is impossible.

THE NEED FOR ASSESSMENT

In working with a couple the therapist encounters two sets of expectations, which may differ drastically, as well as the effect of their interaction. All of these need to be dealt with in therapy. Strupp said, "It is a clinical reality that a patient's character is thoroughly intertwined with the nature of the difficulties he presents to the therapist, the manner in which he views himself and others (including the therapist) and the manner in which he pursues the therapeutic task" (Strupp, 1979, p. 130). This is particularly true in marital therapy where the two partners may have experienced the same events during their married life together but view them entirely differently, and have totally different perceptions about how to go about remedying their problems. In addition, their ideas about what is important in life may have changed considerably over the years and may have emerged now as diametrically opposed to one another's. Thus, each partner's value system and plans for the future may now be radically different from those at the beginning of their marriage.

More than in any other type of therapy, marital therapy has the potential for a hidden agenda. Establishing the necessary trust for the therapeutic alliance is essential for the success of any therapy. In marital therapy such trust is particularly important since the therapy frequently starts with an atmosphere of uneasiness about the therapist's potential alliance with *one* spouse. In such an atmosphere the real problems and concerns of each partner may not emerge immediately and in fact may not emerge at all—unless the therapist establishes an appropriate climate of support and trust. In short, the therapist must be seen as an ally of each partner and as an objective participant in the therapeutic process.

The first obligation of the therapist is to focus on the presenting symptoms. This is the issue that the couple agreed on as their reason for seeking therapy. The therapist may recognize that the particular discomfort in the marriage as stated by the couple is not an accurate presentation of the situation or that another problem must be dealt with first, but it is important to acknowledge the presenting problem, identify its components, and discuss how it can be remedied. The therapist can use the discussion of this problem to demonstrate understanding and support for both partners and to establish an atmosphere of trust and hope. Lazarus has referred to this procedure as *bridging*: The therapist deliberately tunes into the client's preferred modality (problem) before branching off into other dimensions that seem likely to be more productive (Lazarus, 1984a).

Sometimes the wife (or husband) comes to the therapist expressing anger at the partner and states that she wants a separation or divorce. There is nothing left to do; she is only there because of the insistence of the mate. She may have complained bitterly to friends and relatives about the mate, sometimes exaggerating the situation to justify herself, and she may now find it impossible and potentially embarrassing to turn back from a much advertised course of action. What is really wanted is for the therapist to keep them together, to say it is not necessary to break up the marriage, that the problems can be worked out, and that what has been said to others does not need to be a determining factor in such an important decision. At other times, the reverse may be true: The couple may state that they have come to marital therapy because they want to keep their marriage going, but in fact what they really want from the therapist is permission to end a destructive relationship.

In order to deal with the marital problems, an assessment is essential. Often, through the evaluation process the problems are restated and defined in such a way that they then can be dealt with effectively. The assessment process itself can be highly therapeutic for the couple since it enables them to participate in a cooperative identifying and labeling procedure that is much different from what they had experienced previously. This process itself may provide the beginning of remediation of commonly seen communication problems. Without the therapist's participation previous efforts to determine what was wrong may have revolved wholly around each partner's need to identify the other as the culprit responsible for all of their problems. The agreed upon symptom(s) of distress which brought them to the therapist can be used to provide the springboard for a more comprehensive and realistic assessment of the basic marital discord.

Before attempting assessment it is important to recognize that the presenting problem may be a smokescreen to cover the real issues, which may be too difficult to deal with or are simply unrecognized. All of the clinician's training needs to be employed to identify accurately the significant problems in the always complex marital relationship. However, it is not necessary that the entire assessment be completed immediately; it can be an ongoing process where problems are recorded as they emerge during the therapy.

STRUCTURE OF MULTIMODAL MARITAL THERAPY

1. Initial contact with one or both partners.
2. Establishing participation of both partners for conjoint therapy.
3. Multimodal assessment to produce parallel BASIC I.D.s for both partners. Problems are identified across all seven modalities: behavior, affect, sensation, imagery, cognition, interpersonal relationships, drugs/biology. (The same problem may occur under one or more modalities but is expressed differently according to the modality.) Therapist guides and assists couple to produce a comprehensive, mutually agreed upon problem list.
4. Treatment interventions are selected by the therapist (with the agreement of the couple) to remediate each problem.
5. Problems are grouped to facilitate treatment planning and to establish priorities. Problems that affect more than one modality will be evident in this grouping process, and several problems may be alleviated with one treatment. Sometimes, a particular problem must be dealt with before approaching another: Communication problems, for example, must be dealt with before identified issues can be discussed for problem solving.
6. The planned treatments are discussed to demonstrate what can be anticipated. The need for both partners' active participation in their therapy is emphasized. The use of "homework assignments" will be included in this discussion: completing assigned tasks at home as instructed.
7. Treatment proceeds with the first group of problems.
8. Periodic review of progress takes place as therapy proceeds. Sometimes new problems are uncovered and additional treatments are planned and implemented as required. Thus, the BASIC I.D. is not a static document but an assessment process continuously open to adjustment and refinement.
9. Therapy continues with the stated problems listed in all seven BASIC I.D. modalities until sufficient remediation has occurred

to bring the marital relationship to a mutually acceptable state of harmony.

10. Multimodal marital therapy requires comprehensive, integrated treatment across all seven BASIC I.D. modalities in order to obtain effective remediation and durable results.

INITIATING THERAPY

Couples who come to therapy have generally taken this step after much unhappiness and pressure from at least one of the partners. They arrive at the therapist's office not knowing what to expect, with considerable apprehension about what may be revealed about themselves and what the outcome will be, and with a great deal of anxiety. It is important that the therapist gives the couple "permission" to be anxious. Identifying the anxiety and the feelings it produces and conveying to the couple that it is normal under these circumstances can help it to subside sufficiently to allow the couple to proceed with the task at hand. Later, the effects of anxiety on the relationship may emerge as an issue to be dealt with during the course of the therapy.

The first session of marital therapy is used to begin to identify the problems in the relationship but probably more important, it is used to help the couple to develop a therapeutic alliance and to feel that they can accomplish something constructive in therapy. Just having the opportunity to ventilate their feelings to someone who will listen in a nonthreatening manner and who they perceive as accepting and objective will help to accomplish that. They have each undoubtedly reviewed many times what it is they want to say, and both need an opportunity to do that in the presence of someone who will not be judgmental. Sometimes only one partner seems able to express himself, but it is essential that the other partner be eased into the discussion as well. It is just as important not to cause the "nonverbal" partner to feel threatened and "exposed." If the first session is successful, the couple will leave with a sense that they have been listened to, that the therapist will be objective and can be trusted, and—if that determination has been made—that their problems can be approached constructively.

At the end of the first session the therapist can introduce the assessment by explaining to the couple that the cornerstone of successful therapy is assessment, the process by which the problems are identified and defined, and remedies are planned. Questionnaires to start this process may be given to the couple to complete at home. There are a number of good questionnaires for this purpose. One of these is the "Marital Satisfaction Questionnaire." (Lazarus, 1981.) Another is the "Reminder List for Marriage Contract." (Sager, 1976.) The main function of the questionnaire is simply to start the process of thinking about the relationship in more constructive terms, cutting through the anger and acrimony, in order to focus on specific issues which can then be incorporated into the assessment. This session can be used to explain something to the couple about the purpose and structure of the BASIC I.D. assessment, and how it will be utilized in multimodal marital therapy. (Lazarus, 1981.) This will increase the likelihood of attaining the couple's full cooperation and participation.

The BASIC I.D. Assessment

The BASIC I.D. Assessment is the cornerstone of multimodal therapy. It uses seven major personality modalities: Behavior, Affect, Sensory, Imagery, Cognition, Interpersonal relationships, and Drugs/Biology (physical). Problems are identified in each of these areas, their interrelationship across the various categories is evaluated, and treatment interventions are planned for each problem. The therapist interviews the marital partners and identifies and defines the problems in terms of the seven stated BASIC I.D. modalities. Excesses, deficits, and strengths are noted. Antecedents that may trigger certain behaviors, affects, sensations, imagery, cognitions, interpersonal activities, and physical problems are noted. Identifying the antecedents and consequences of the stated problems and determining the reinforcing agents are part of this assessment process.

It is important to examine the "firing order" of the different modalities. A client may dwell first on negative imagery, seeing him- or herself in the unpleasant situation. This may then be followed by a physical sensation such as an unpleasant feeling in the pit of the stomach, then by a rush of anger, and finally by a verbal outburst. The sequence here would be I (Imagery), S (Sensation, A (Affect), B (Behavior). Lazarus refers to this as *tracking* (Lazarus, 1984). Tracking is an essential aspect of the assessment process since it gives information about which interventions may be required to avert a particularly disruptive problem.

In multimodal marital therapy it is essential that there be an evaluation by each partner of all of the BASIC I.D. modalities as they apply to the functioning of the marriage. Individual assessments are undertaken to identify the problems as seen by each one, and then a parallel assessment is completed to clarify the problems and conflicts in each category and their corresponding remedies. The case presented below will demonstrate this process and the resulting BASIC I.D. assessments which were used as the framework for this therapy, thus providing both the structure for the therapy and the foundation for the planned treatment interventions. (For further information about multimodal assessment, see Lazarus, 1976, 1981; Brunell & Young, 1982.)

MARITAL THERAPY AND DEPRESSION

Frequently, marital therapy is initiated after one of the partners seeks therapy for depression. This partner is often the woman. The statistics indicate that women have a greater incidence of diagnosed affective disorders than men. Whether these are merely "unmasked" disorders that derive from a similar number of affective disorders as those experienced by men has been a question open for much discussion and opinion. Monroe and Bellack have identified stressful life events as significant precursors of depression in women. (Monroe, Bellack, Hersen, & Himmelhoch, 1983.) Beck has pointed out that "women, by virtue of sex role definitions, face a daily routine that is more repetitious, frustrating, emotionally exhausting, and narrow in scope than that of their masculine counterparts . . . the social roles allotted women . . . are inherently depressing" (Beck & Greenberg, 1974, p. 113). It may also be more socially acceptable for a woman to seek treatment for depression than a man. Whatever the reason, it is generally agreed that women seek help for depression more frequently than men, and frequently the depression is closely related to marital dissatisfaction.

When the woman arrives in the therapist's office for assistance she may describe herself as unhappy, unable to function as she has in the past, and lacking in motivation to do anything constructive. After discussing herself and her feelings of depression, she may then talk about her marriage and indicate that she feels it is a major factor in her unhappiness. The therapist may decide to deal directly with the depression first and then later request that the partner join the therapy so that the marital situation can be improved. Although this is not always the way marital therappy is initiated, it does occur in this manner often enough to be mentioned. The case I have selected began in this way.

THE CASE OF MRS. D

Mrs. D. arranged to see the therapist after her psychology professor suggested that she might want to discuss her problems with someone. Mrs. D. was a married woman, aged 38, with two teenage sons, ages 16 and 13. She was pursuing a master's degree in psychology at the time therapy was initiated. During her exams she had felt a great deal of distress and was compelled to leave the room midway, unable to continue. Her professor, whom she admired a great deal, encouraged her to continue in another room where she completed her exam successfully. He then met with her to discuss the problem. When he perceived that she was suffering from anxiety and depression he suggested that therapy might be helpful.

Mrs. D. arrived for her first session looking extremely distressed. She required much reassurance by the therapist about the process of therapy and what effect it might have on her life. Her husband had been opposed to her seeking help, and they had argued heatedly about it. He thought there was nothing wrong, that she just needed to get back into the old routines she had followed before starting graduate school. He felt that she had always been a good wife and mother and that everything was OK. He was unable to understand her feelings of dissatisfaction and depression or even willing to accept that they existed. However, since he loved his wife he acknowledged her distress and agreed to support her therapy as well as he could.

Mrs. D. started by talking of her feelings of helplessness and hopelessness. She saw herself as an "unworthy" person who was capable of little more than running a household under her husband's explicit instructions. When she followed his orders about what was to be accomplished on the schedule he provided, all was peaceful and everything ran smoothly. When she digressed from this schedule, he became angry and very upset. Her husband was a top executive for a very large and prestigious international company. He worked long hours under a great deal of stress and traveled abroad frequently. At those times she was left alone to manage the household, sometimes for a period of several weeks. Interestingly, she described herself as most relaxed and happy when she was left alone during his many trips.

For some time she had felt that her life was lacking in interest: She was bored and dissatisfied with her household role and with her intellectual isolation. Her two boys were now teenagers, and she felt that they no longer required the same amount of supervision as they had previously. She therefore had decided to go back to school to pursue graduate studies that might hopefully lead to a career. She had enrolled in a master's program in psychology since she was interested in a "people helping" occupation and was perhaps motivated to find out more about what was troubling her.

Mrs. D. was apparently very anxious about what might occur in therapy. She was unable to verbalize what that might be, but dreaded it nonetheless. As therapy proceeded one source of her anxiety was revealed to be her fear that she would discover that she wanted to leave her marriage. This was terrifying to her. Despite their difficulties she had always viewed her husband as exceptionally loving and caring, willing to do almost anything for her. She thought she no longer reciprocated his feelings but recognized that she was very dependent on him for the very comfortable living he provided. She was accustomed to their lifestyle, and she had no financial resources to cope with life on her own. She was certain that her husband would not provide her with any funds if she were to leave. She did not express any concerns about living alone. The idea seemed to intrigue her.

The problems that Mrs. D. described initially were:

1. Feelings of depression, helplessness, and hopelessness.
2. Extreme feelings of tension and anxiety.
3. Difficulty with people who she saw as authoritarian.
4. Feeling both indecisive and opinionated simultaneously.
5. Dread of parents-in-laws' impending, annual, six-week visit.

As therapy progressed additional problems surfaced, a great many of which were directly related to the marital situation. During the early sessions serious difficulties with both children emerged. The younger child had been classified "Neurologically Impaired" from the time he entered school; he was a hyperactive child with serious impulse control problems. This had caused great difficulties at home, particularly since the father was unable to accept the situation and was continuously in conflict with this child whose behavior he could not tolerate. Mrs. D.'s views about how to handle the child were very different from her husband's. Mr. D. assumed a strong disciplinarian stance, and his wife took a more accepting, tolerant position. Mrs. D. greatly resented her husband's approach to the situation and was very distressed and hurt by it. The inconsistent parental positions further complicated matters, and much acrimony ensued.

Although the elder son had always done well in school, he changed when he entered high school. During the first week of therapy the school authorities advised Mrs. D. that her son was suspected of selling marijuana in the school. In checking at home, she found that he was growing marijuana in his closet with a "grow-lite." In view of the many problems that centered on the family and the marriage, it was decided to ask her husband to participate in marital therapy. After much hesitation he agreed.

Marital Therapy with Mr. and Mrs. D.

During the first sessions of individual therapy Mrs. D. had talked a great deal about herself and her relationship with her children. She saw herself as being on "their side" and attempted to accept and deal with their adolescent problems by identifying with them. When they rebelled against assigned duties at home, she tended to see things from their point of view and to accept their transgressions. When they become enamored of a particular "rock" group, she too became enthusiastic about the same group and bought tickets for their concerts. The result was that her behavior emerged as out of step with and oppositional to her husband's. He was portrayed in an unsympathetic, "different generation" role. She expressed an interest in and generally approved of most of her children's adolescent behavior, relegating her husband to the role of unsympathetic disciplinarian. Thus, she was in constant conflict with her husband via the medium of the children's behavior. When the evidence of her son's involvement with marijuana trafficking emerged, she became very upset and her depression increased. She felt personally betrayed and worthless as a parent, taking Mr. D's behavior as a personal rejection of her values and parenting efforts.

In order to avoid the constant conflict at home Mrs. D. spent more and more time away, as did her husband. She spent a great deal of extra time at school working and with newly made friends. As a result the boys and her husband saw less and less of her. As she spent fewer evenings at home her husband's work regimen at his office increased so that they spent very little time together. Resentments and confusion over this situation caused their time together to be unpleasant and tense. This carried over into their sex life, which changed from a gratifying aspect of their marriage to another source of tension and unhappiness. In addition, they were both angry and in disagreement about how to handle the problems with their children. Each felt the other could do more to deal with the situation by assuming a different approach: Their ideas about how to handle matters were diametrically opposed. She thought her husband should be more understanding; he wanted her to exercise more discipline. It was unclear how much of this conflict was communicated verbally and how much of it was perceived through their behavior toward one another.

The First Session of Marital Therapy

Mr. and Mrs. D. arrived for the first session both clearly apprehensive. Mrs. D. immediately lapsed into silence. She allowed her husband to talk, saying very little, but expressing a great deal nonverbally. She pulled her chair back so that she was not in his direct line of vision and demonstrated disagreement with him through various physical signs of discomfort and annoyance. She would not express her disagreement directly. He spent the early part of the session conveying to the therapist that he was a good husband, totally committed to making his wife happy. She had consistently reiterated the same idea to the therapist during her own sessions and found it difficult to reconcile her husband's expressed loving feelings with the fact that she was not happy. She disagreed with him on many issues and objected to much of his behavior. Mrs. D. behaved as if it would be disloyal to voice her disagreement with her husband openly—that there might be serious consequences. In fact, that seemed to be the message her husband was conveying to her.

The therapist encouraged Mrs. D. to participate in the discussion, helping her to phrase some of her concerns and wishes in a nonthreatening manner. Haley (1976) has suggested that the therapist avoid forcing the couple to ask explicitly for what is wanted: "I want you to ask your husband for what you want in a way that it takes him a while to understand what you mean" (p. 166). A similar approach was helpful in this case. In the same manner the husband was encouraged to explore some of the issues that concerned him. The therapist was supportive of each partner's participation. The rest of the session was devoted to a discussion of the assessment process and how their combined input would be used to plan an effective therapy approach. Both partners were asked to fill in a "Marital Satisfaction Questionnaire" (Lazarus, 1981). Since Mrs. D. had discussed her perceptions of the marriage previously in her individual sessions, the therapist asked if Mr. D. would like to come in for an individual session. He agreed. The next session planned then was with the husband individually, and the session after that was to include both partners.

Prior to the first joint session the therapist had used the individual session with Mrs. D. to begin a BASIC I.D. of the marital problems. When Mr. D. came in for his individual session it was used to prepare a corresponding BASIC I.D. assessment that would parallel his wife's. Mr. D.'s perceptions of the issues Mrs. D. had identified as problems were obtained, as well as his added insights into other problems that she might not have mentioned.

Some of the problems each partner brought up during their separate sessions were individual issues that were not actually derivatives of the marital relationship but impacted directly on it. For example, Mrs. D. perceived herself as "fat and unattractive." In fact, she was just moderately overweight and of pleasant appearance. Her husband found her attractive and her weight was not a particular concern for him, although he had on occasion teased her about putting on a few pounds. However, Mrs. D. felt that her perception of herself as "fat and unattractive" affected her sexual responsiveness and behavior. This perception was therefore included in the Imagery modality as a problem. Similarly, Mr. D. often arrived home tense and anxious from the great pressure he experienced at work. This was not directly related to the marital issues but influenced his behavior toward his wife and children. This was therefore included in the Affect modality. Under the D (Physical) modality, the fact that both partners expressed the need for more exercise was included, since it served the purpose of giving them something they might do together as well as a way of helping each other to feel better.

Some issues that arose were not seen by one partner as affecting the relationship with the other. For example, Mrs. D. felt very disturbed by her husband's frequent shouting behavior at home. He insisted that he never shouted directly at her but at the children for their misbehavior. He was not really aware of how upsetting this behavior was to his wife, although she had made many efforts to convey this to him.

Other issues were not seen by either partner as a problem but were included because they were important to the relationship. For example, they had very few couples as friends. They had no other couple their own age with whom they could socialize regularly, have fun, compare notes, ventilate, and so forth. Yet neither expressed a real interest in expanding their social life to include other couples. Some issues were seen as a problem by one partner and not by the other. For example, Mr. D. saw his efforts to protect and shelter his wife from all "worldly" concerns as loving. She saw these efforts as smothering and restrictive. They also encouraged her childlike stance in the marriage and hindered her moves toward independence and maturity. Mr. D. felt that his wife had no appreciation for his hard-won business success and his resultant ability to provide a high standard of living for his family. Mrs. D. rarely, if ever, discussed their standard of living nor did she express recognition of his efforts. Partially, this was due to her ambivalence about her own reliance on his earnings, the fact that she felt locked her into her dependent role. Partially, it was due to a kind of adolescent rebellion against "the establishment" and its rewards. Both felt that the other did not appreciate or acknowledge his or her contribution to the family sufficiently.

The resulting parallel BASIC I.D. ASSESSMENTS are shown below.

Mrs. D.

B—(Behavior)

1. Does not reinforce husband's efforts to please her.
2. Does not acknowledge husband's desire to succeed for family.
3. Does not set aside time for husband.
4. Does not discuss issues that cause friction openly.

Mr. D.

B—(Behavior)

1. Too much shouting.
2. Does not compliment wife's appearance.
3. Does not acknowledge her efforts to please him.
4. Insufficient pleasant and relaxed time with wife.

5. Too dependent upon husband.
6. Behaves like another child in the family.

A—(Affect)

7. Depressed.
8. Anger at husband and son.
9. Anxiety and tension.

S—(Sensory)

10. Decreased sexual responsiveness.

I—(Imagery)

11. Sees self as "unworthy."
12. Sees self as "fat and unattractive."
13. Romantic fantasies to escape boredom.

C—(Cognition)

14. Poor opinion of self.
15. Difficulty dealing with authority figures.
16. Confuses husband and father roles.
17. Does not use good intellectual resources.
18. Has difficulty making decisions.

I—(Interpersonal)

19. Few couples as friends.
20. Excessive dependence on husband and others.
21. Communicates poorly with husband.

D—(Physical)

22. Needs more exercise.
23. Would like to lose weight.

5. Insufficient recreational activities with wife.
6. Does not consult wife about parents' extended visits.

A—(Affect)

7. Anxiety over feared loss of wife.
8. Anger at both sons.
9. Work-related tension and anxiety.

S—(Sensory)

10. Limited sensual and sexual awareness.

I—(Imagery)

11. Sees self in strong authoritarian role in family.

C—(Cognition)

12. Stereotyped thinking about family role models.
13. Feels need to be strong authority figure in family.
14. Lacks understanding of wife's needs.

I—(Interpersonal)

15. Unable to communicate effectively with wife and children.
16. Issues "orders" to family.
17. Plays role of disciplinarian.
18. Relies excessively on wife for all personal needs and wishes.
19. Few couples as friends.

D—(Physical)

20. Needs more relaxed time.
21. Needs more exercise.

The BASIC I.D. assessments were started during the individual sessions with both partners and then continued during the joint sessions. The assessment process itself was a valuable part of the therapy. It required joint and active participation. In this way problems that emerged could be clearly identified and elaborated with the cooperation of both partners; they could also be tracked across the interrelated modalities. Mutual agreement that an issue that one brought up was indeed a problem in their relationship served as a starting point for successful resolution. The assessment also provided the material needed for marital contracting, which took place during later sessions.

During the assessment process the tendency of one partner to maximize a problem and the other to minimize the same problem was seen clearly (Haley, 1976). In the case of Mr. and Mrs. D., this occurred repeatedly. Mrs. D. would discuss her distress over Mr. D.'s shouting, and Mr. D. would say that he shouted only at the children—and infrequently. Mrs. D. complained of the in-laws' protracted and unpleasant visits, whereas Mr. D. would say that the visits caused no dissension and that his parents helped to supervise the boys while his wife was at school. In fact, he felt that their presence was beneficial to the family, and so forth.

The two, resulting BASIC I.D. assessments incorporated what each partner perceived as the problems in the relationship, assigning the particular problem, or some aspect of it, to its source. Thus, by mutual agreement, difficulties reported by both spouses appeared on each one's BASIC I.D. Many problems were identified on both BASIC I.D.s.

Since over 20 problems appear on each BASIC I.D. (some appearing on both), the combined assessments could be seen as a comprehensive overview of the marital relationship. By reviewing the assessments the overriding issues became clear. The most pressing problem was poor communication. In order for progress to take place in therapy improving the communication system was essential. Communication training and modeling, therefore, became a first priority.

Communication

Improved communication is undoubtedly a first priority for most marital therapy. Self-disclosure is an important aspect of communication in the marital relationship. The significance of self-disclosure and its relationship to marital satisfaction has been discussed by Waterman (1979). The advantage of the BASIC I.D. assessment in multimodal marital therapy is that it provides a wealth of material for the communication training process that has been identified as crucial to the relationship by both partners. Its structure permits self-disclosure in a safe and neutral setting. It then becomes possible to zero in efficiently and effectively on the significant issues that the couple was probably unable to acknowledge or discuss previously. Having reached joint agreement about what the problems are through this process, the groundwork for good communication has been prepared.

Grouping Problems and Planning Treatment

Since there are a total of 44 problems identified for both Mr. and Mrs. D., it is necessary to group them for efficient management. Many of these problems are closely interrelated and reflected across more than one modality, and the same problem may be stated on each partner's BASIC I.D. Therefore, it is particularly important to review and group the problems for planned treatment. Some may be issues that can be resolved simply by improving the system of communication, some may be handled through special activities and treatments, and some may be dealt with through marital contracting. Many of the problems listed on Mr. and Mrs. D.'s assessments were problems that related to a nonfunctional family structure that required revamping. Mrs. D. felt that she could no longer tolerate the authoritarian family system that she had previously accepted. The problems that emerged as a result of Mr. and Mrs. D.'s changing views about how to conduct their relationship were grouped together to be used in communication training and discussion. Since Mrs. D. was experiencing anger and depression due to this situation, as well as decreased sexual responsiveness, it was felt that these problems, listed under Affect and Sensory, might also be influenced by a structural change in the relationship. Later, the remaining problems could be dealt with individually through discussion, planning, and in some cases, instruction and exercises.

Planned Treatments

The main treatment approaches indicated by the problems identified on the BASIC I.D. assessment were communication skills training, assertiveness training for Mrs. D., labeling and identifying feelings for Mr. D., demonstrating to both partners constructive ways of dealing with anger, teaching constructive "fighting" techniques, anxiety and tension reduction training for both, and planned social and recreational activities for both. The communication training process would focus on their interpersonal difficulties. It would include discussion and problem solving related to their nonfunctional family structure and their conflicts over the handling of their children. Plans were made for Mrs. D. to work on a weight loss program individually (Brunell, 1985) and for both to develop a program for the physical exercise they required. Further identification and remediation of their sexual problems would take place after some of the other problems that were maintaining the anger and the impasse were remedied.

Progress of Therapy

The problems on the assessments were used to initiate the process of discussion and to help Mr. and Mrs. D. to develop effective communication skills. The grouping of problems for treatment planning uncovered how one problem sometimes affected several modalities. Similarly, treatment of a problem in one modality often helped alleviate a related problem (the "ripple effect" as discussed by Lazarus, 1976). Although a problem that appears under several modalities may be related and even sound quite similar, it can affect the individual's functioning in very different ways under each modality. It is important to investigate how each problem affects *all* modalities for the planning of effective, integrated remediation. This is the crux of comprehensive, multimodal treatment and is an important factor in providing durable treatment.

Frequently, resolution of a problem occurred simply because each partner displayed concern about the other and demonstrated a willingness to listen and to make a small requested change. Sometimes, individual treatment for a particular problem was given to increase the ability of the partner to make the requested change. For example, Mrs. D. complained of Mr. D.'s shouting which he seemed unable to control and did not fully acknowledge initially. Mr. D. met separately with the therapist for a session during which he was given training to identify the situations that caused him to lose control and was taught how to recognize and label the feelings he was experiencing. He was then taught how to maintain control and to deal with his feelings more appropriately and constructively. Afterwards, the procedures were discussed during a joint session so that both could participate and be helpful to each other. The BASIC I.D. was used frequently as a reference point.

Being Assertive and Fighting Constructively

Another problem that emerged was that Mr. and Mrs. D. did not know how to "fight" constructively. Mrs. D. would retreat into silence and sulking when she was upset, sometimes leaving the house rather than confronting her husband on an issue. This avoidance behavior fed her depression, and she became correspondingly less able to communicate effectively. It was felt that in order for this situation to be remedied, it was necessary to teach Mrs. D. how to be more assertive and to teach both how to "fight" effectively in their marriage. Assertive training was provided during Mrs. D.'s individual sessions and she was asked to read *Don't Say Yes When You Want to Say No* (Fensterheim & Baer, 1975) and *The Assertive Woman* (Phelps & Austin, 1975). Both partners were asked to read *Intimate Enemy: How to Fight Fair in Love and Marriage* (Bach & Wyden, 1970). The issues raised in this book were discussed during their sessions. They were also asked to keep notes during the week preceding each session of upsetting incidents about which they disagreed. These issues were then used to teach and model effective communication and effective "fighting" techniques.

Outcome of Therapy, Mr. and Mrs. D.

In Mr. and Mrs. D.'s therapy, their communication difficulties were extremely important, an urgent issue in most marital therapy cases. The BASIC I.D. assessment process provided the first breakdown of communication barriers. This progress then had a synergistic effect on the entire therapy process. As they talked more openly they were able to work on solutions to problems identified on their BASIC I.D.s and to engage constructively in the process of remediation.

The outcome of this multimodal, marital therapy case was excellent. Therapy was terminated when the family moved to a distant state in an important career change for Mr. D. Mrs. D. stayed behind for several months and was faced with many difficult tasks which she had to accomplish alone including difficulties with the children, selling their house, and major surgery. She remained in therapy during this time. The couple has written that they were able to deal well with a stressful move and that their improved relationship has benefited all members of the family. They stated that their therapy has enabled them to reach a level of gratification in their relationship that they had not thought possible.

GENERAL ISSUES IN MULTIMODAL MARITAL THERAPY

Dealing in the Here and Now: Breaking the Impasse

It was particularly important to remind the couple to deal in the here and now. The temptation in a long-term relationship is often to focus on past history rather than on present events, each blaming the other for their difficulties based on that past behavior. Focusing on the past is frequently less threatening since the past is familiar territory and it enables couples to quickly reach an anticipated impasse which they may welcome. When dealing with the here and now, neither partner is certain what the outcome might be. Thus, a far greater challenge is presented to the status quo of the relationship. Intrinsic to their avoidance of confronting current issues directly may be their concealed wish to preserve the marriage at all costs, even if it means continuing with the same familiar unhappiness.

A method of breaking through the impasse is to ask each partner to keep a brief set of notes: one small piece of paper for the entire week. One or two words are recorded each day in one column to remind the person of one event that occurred that day, and in the parallel column, the associated feeling(s). It is important to explain to the couple that the events can be very ordinary. They merely need to demonstrate the regular sources of conflict and distress. They do not have to be dramatic. This is a very effective method to help couples focus on the actual situations which occur day by day in the marriage that are symptomatic of the problems in the relationship. It is also helpful to see how differently each perceives the same events. When these situations are presented the therapist is then able to engage the couple in constructive, assertive communication which can lead the way to effective remediation. Again, the multimodal structure is of great value here since it can be used to demonstrate how the daily events are reflected in the problems identified across all of the modalities. (A problem in the Behavior category can be reflected in problems identified in other categories: for example, anxiety or anger in Affect, and decrease in sexual responsiveness in the Sensory modality.)

Sexual Issues

The most sensitive area in a marital relationship is the sexual relationship. It is essential to wait until a good communication system has been established before attempting to deal with this delicate area. Each may have totally different perceptions about the level of sexual gratification. One may see the sexual relationship as dull and boring, while the other may feel that it is working fine. It is important to discuss this area delicately since the intrusion of a third party into this very sensitive area may cause iatrogenic problems. The very fact that the process is taking place may cause difficulties since it is an invasion of accustomed privacy. The couple must be guided gently into an open but sensitive discussion. Such a discussion can then serve as a model for their own open discussion about how to improve their sexual relationship. Frequently, this openness is exactly what is needed to increase the level of gratification that each partner can experience since each may have been withholding his or her true feelings and wishes in the sexual relationship. If special problems are uncovered, such as premature ejaculation or a gap in sexual knowledge that is causing problems, these issues must be dealt with fully.

Contracting

In order to make some changes it is important to teach each partner how to ask specifically for what is wanted in a way that will be acceptable to the other, and how to give something in return. This can be done in the general discussion or in a specific contracting situation. Sometimes, the idea of contracting may be resented by some couples, but the importance of give and take and of reinforcing desired behavior in a relationship must be conveyed and is usually accepted.

Summary

The structure of multimodal marital therapy provides a sound framework for identifying and clarifying the problems that require remediation. Accurate identification of the issues is crucial in marital therapy where the complexity of the situation can lead to obfuscation (sometimes intentional) or confusion. Since there is joint participation in identifying their problems, the resulting BASIC I.D. assessment provides a mutually agreed upon, comprehensive overview of the relationship and a foundation for constructive communication. It deals with all aspects of the marriage rather than one or two issues that may emerge initially as important but do not reflect the true complexity of the marital relationship. By properly viewing the relationship across all seven modalities and by planning comprehensive, integrated treatment for the broad array of problems that can then emerge, it is possible for effective, durable remediation to take place.

The BASIC I.D. assessment structure of multimodal marital therapy permits and encourages an examination of the efficacy of treatment, an essential and frequently overlooked issue. The comprehensive approach to treatment offered by multimodal marital therapy and its emphasis on treating the problems of the marital partners rather than adhering to a particular theoretical orientation, provide a flexibility and range of treatments that are especially suited to dealing with the broad complexities of marital therapy.

References

Bach, G. R., & Wyden, P. (1970). *The intimate enemy.* New York: Avon.

Beck, A. T., & Greenberg, R. L. (1974). Cognitive therapy with depressed women. In V. Franks & V. Burtle (Eds.), *Women in therapy.* New York: Brunner/Mazel.

Brunell, L. F. (1985). Treatment of depression and obesity: The case of Single Susan. In A. A. Lazarus (Ed.), *A multimodal therapy casebook.* New York: Guilford Press.

Brunell, L. F., & Young, W. T. (1982). *Multimodal handbook for a mental hospital: Designing specific treatments for specific problems.* New York: Springer.

Fensterheim, H., & Baer, J. (1975). *Don't say yes when you want to say no.* New York: Dell Publishing.

Haley, J. (1976). *Problem solving therapy.* San Francisco: Jossey-Bass.

Lazarus, A. A. (1976). *Multimodal behavior therapy.* New York: Springer.

Lazarus, A. A. (1981). *The practice of multimodal therapy.* New York: McGraw-Hill.

Lazarus, A. A., Kreitzberg, C. B., & Sasserath, V. J. (1981). Multimodal therapy. In R. Corsini, (Ed.), *Handbook of innovative psychotherapies* (pp. 502–514). New York: John Wiley & Sons.

Lazarus, A. A. (1984). In R. Corsini (Ed.), Multimodal therapy. *Current psychotherapies* (pp. 491–529). Itasca, IL: F. E. Peacock Publishers.

Lazarus, A. A. (1985). *A Multimodal Therapy Casebook.* New York: Guilford Press.

Monroe, S., Bellack, A., Hersen, M., & Himmelhoch, J. (1983). Life events, symptom course, and treatment outcome in unipolar depressed women. *Journal of Consulting and Clinical Psychology, 51*(4), 604–615.

Phelps, S., & Austin, N. (1975). *The assertive woman.* St. Louis Obispo, CA: Impact.

Sager, C. J. (1976). *Marriage contracts and couple therapy.* New York: Brunner/Mazel.

Strupp, H. H. (1979). Psychotherapy: Theory, research and practice. *Modern Behavior Therapy, 16*(2), 130.

Waterman, J. (1979). Family patterns of self-disclosure. In G. J. Chelune and associates, (Eds.), *Self-disclosure* (pp. 225–242). San Francisco: Jossey-Bass.

FIFTEEN

A Group Is a Group Is a Group: Working with Couples in Groups

Matti K. Gershenfeld, Ed.D.
Temple University

INTRODUCTION

Contemporary society not only puts strains on a couple's relationship, but at every level couples feel overwhelmed. The rules have changed in marriage from a traditional relationship, where men were the financial providers and women nurtured and had primary responsibility for children, the house, and of course being the sexual partner. *Functional* roles were the basis for relationship: If he was a good provider and she did a good job with the children and as a cook and homemaker, there were no problems.

In what area are there problems now? A prime reason for relationship is no longer sex. Women as well as men work full time in the labor force. Women and men may both have career aspirations. Couples opt to have children or not to have children. There will be job transfers, geographic moves. There are constant hassles about money and values. Further, the impact of religion with its strong moral code has greatly diminished. Children, who should be growing up and leaving, often cannot find jobs and return home to their parents. They do this not by choice but as a way to save money as they pursue different careers—which they hope will produce a job. Middle-aged couples report that what is even worse is a daughter returning home divorced with her two-year-old child.

In a different era it was rare for people to live to be over 65. There are now couples who live well into their 80s. This has resulted in middle-aged couples referring to themselves as the "squeeze generation." They are constantly feeling pressure from the responsibilities of their children. And just as their children grow up, they are ensnared in the responsibilities for their aging parents. A common cry is, "When does it get to be my turn?" Middle-aged couples feel entitled to be selfish, to use their time and financial resources for their own pleasures. Confusion abounds as couples feel as if they are searching for stability in "quicksand." Stability seems impossible.

All the while there are factors of individual aspirations, goals, needs, and wants. How do you parent and still have a career? Is there enough time? How do you spend time together as a couple when there are constant pressures? How does a relationship continue to have pleasure and enjoyment rather than becoming routine and boring? With whom do you raise these questions and get answers in a world where everybody is doing "their own thing"?

The world of groups for couples has emerged, not so much in relation to therapy, but out of a need to create, build or sustain a relationship amidst confusion and chaos. There is a search on to find answers to what seem like impossible questions. This search is a response to people feeling alone and adrift. There is a second aspect—that marriage is part of a different era. The skills that were once needed were skills in earning a living, being a good cook, rearing children—those skills. The concept of relationship skills (how does a couple talk, listen, or understand each other) was considered trivial and unnecessary.

Of course people got along. All they had to do was love each other and try. The rest followed inevitably, like a river flowing to the sea. In recent years, and increasingly, there has been an emergence of groups to help people deal with the anxieties and difficulties of being a couple in a time of tremendous change and concomitant confusion.

There are three broad categories of couple's groups, none of which are categorized as therapy groups. One type is called mutual help, self-help, or sometimes mutual support groups. Typically, these do not have a professional leader. Their basis for membership is a common situation or problem; usually there is no payment. Another category is what is often called marriage enrichment or marriage enrichment groups. These groups may have a professional leader or people trained in the method of that program. They will meet for a limited time—typically a weekend or four sessions with an objective of building the marital relationship. These are frequently community or church sponsored, and there is usually a nominal fee. (The fee here will be considerably less than the fee for marital therapy.) Announcements for marital and enrichment groups will typically include a statement to the effect that the object of this program is "to make good marriages better." The program is not a substitute for marriage therapy.

Finally, the third and newest category, referred to as educational workshops for couples or microlabs, consists of programs designed by their leader to meet the objectives that he/she sees as being needed. For example, in the 1980s, when the major issue reported by couples as being an area of difficulty is money, there might be a workshop, a microlab, or a course specifically focusing on couples' issues relating to money. These programs are professionally led and are designed to help the couples who participate to gain an understanding about how their relationships are affected by money. This newest category involves a leader whose skills include being able to design and conduct such a program. The cost is considerably less than that of marital therapy, but more than church-sponsored enrichment programs. What will follow is an explanation of each type of group, a brief rationale for each form, the theoretical base, and some examples. In addition, there are some guidelines and references for learning more about such groups.

A RATIONALE FOR COUPLES GROUPS

Working with groups is very different from working with individuals or with individual couples. Working with groups involves a diagnostic mentality in determining what a group needs, planning a training design derived from that diagnosis, reviewing the design, and making changes prior to implementation. It involves creating group norms for trust, nonjudgmentalism, empathy, and expression of personal feelings.

Groups today are the ultimate analogue to being in a relationship. Immediate, clear information exists that the leader cannot control the group process as much as she would like. Participants will not only have their input, but everything that is done will basically derive from the participants' expression of their needs. And the group leader who does not understand what the couples are saying will be in big trouble if he does not ask what happened, modify his design, and be flexible. The group process is also more complicated than it used to be back in the early days of the 1960s. Then participants were enamored of the sensitivity group experience with its emotional high at an end of a weekend which "lasted all the way 'til Wednesday."

Today there needs to be a greater understanding of the dynamics of groups and what is to be accomplished. The autocratic leader is no more effective today in a group than is the dominant member in a hierarchical marriage. To be successful, today's group leader needs more skills, more alternatives, more options, greater flexibility, and more willingness to focus on the desired outcomes.

Couples groups, designed as programs that allow couples to understand the myriad, successful patterns they can create, can be tremendously stimulating. A richness, a variety, and an excitement emerges in such groups. There is laughter and teasing and a closeness that builds. An intimacy develops which makes it possible at the end of a first session for couples to say, "These people who were strangers 2 hours ago know me better than people who have known me for 20 years." Conflict and anger are expressed, and couples learn ways to resolve their conflicts rather than allowing them to escalate into relationship-eroding experiences. There is a line from Carl Rogers (1961): "I stand in awe of a human being unfolding." I would modify that to: I am always amazed at the changes a relatively few hours make in helping a couple to understand each other differently and to build a closeness that they desire but do not know how to attain. While I do couples therapy I am most excited by the outcomes, the effectiveness, and the changes that occur in couples through a course or workshop.

I see couples groups as one of the major methods of prevention of relationship difficulties. As couples learn skills in defining themselves and what they want from a marriage in a situation with other couples, they lift the mask of privacy. To clarify their values and their expectations of their partners, they come to experience themselves in the present. The skills they learn have only recently come to consciousness as being "needed." They learn skills in speaking authentically, in listening to the other (it is fascinating that sometimes a person cannot hear his own wife say something, but when another woman says the same thing suddenly he hears it), they learn skills in problem solving, in nurturing, and in joint decision making. They come to understand that the boundaries of an individual are different from those of a couple. There is a kind of learning that takes place in these groups that I believe is the cutting edge of how to render preventive services to couples. This will sound very strong, but I believe that if there was some way we could create ongoing groups with couples on a fairly regular basis, there would be a markedly increased ability for couples to relate positively and enhance their relationships.

MUTUAL HELP GROUPS

Once there was not a formal category of mutual help or mutual support groups. Each of us belonged to a mutual support group: It was called our family or our extended family. Too often today, the familial bond is not there because of geographic distance or more often, emotional distance. Hence, we have the phenomena of mutual support groups. These may also be called mutual help groups or self-help groups.

There are a wide variety of mutual help groups ranging from the classic Alcoholics Anonymous to women's consciousness-raising groups. In a mutual help group professional credentials are irrelevant. Sharing of experience is the fundamental concept that distinguishes the mutual help experience from other helping exchanges. Mutual help occurs when the helper and the person being helped share a history of the same problem. The essence of the process is "mutuality" and "reciprocity."

The people attracted to a mutual help experience are often suffering from conditions that dramatically changed their worlds. They may have been struck by a life-threatening experience, a physical handicap, or the recent loss of a spouse or a loved one. They may be new immigrants, battered women who can no longer tolerate living with violence, children whose parents have recently been divorced, or couples who have married a second time. Although the people close to them may be able to meet some of their physical and emotional needs, many find they have additional needs, needs that can be appreciated only by someone who has had the same problems. They join a mutual support group to help them make the changes that are needed in their view of themselves and in the ways that relate to their changed worlds. Through a mutual help group, participants acquire new information and new role models. In summary, mutual help groups provide people with:

- Information on how to cope with their problems.
- Information on resources, if necessary.
- A feeling of being cared about and being supported.

This type of help is often very effective because:

- Participants find other people, "just like me."
- They learn that other people have similar feelings and that these feelings can be normal in their circumstances.
- They are encouraged that they too can learn how to deal with the problems successfully.

Examples of couples mutual support groups are:

- Newly marrieds.
- Interfaith couples.
- Childbirth groups (couples expecting a child).
- Couples groups with children who have Down's Syndrome.
- Parenting groups with children in their first year (or first child).
- Parenting groups as children enter school.
- Parenting groups for adolescence (teaching about sex, dating, hours, friends).
- Parenting groups for coping with adolescents.
- Step-family groups.
- Coping with aging parents groups.
- Preretirement groups.
- Retirement groups.

The focus here has been specifically on couples' self-help groups. Each meets to deal with an ongoing problem or situation. The group serves as a tremendous support at an emotional and cognitive level.

ORGANIZATIONAL STRUCTURES

The organizational structures adopted by mutual help groups vary widely. Some choose to remain small and relatively informal. Others choose to incorporate. There are two major models. One is the corporate hierarchical, where there is a main organization and branches as in the Childbirth Education Association with its early parenting groups after the childbirth classes. There is also a less traditional, nonhierarchical "consensus structure." In the second model the group is run with shared responsibility, each member having equal authority and perhaps even the chair being rotated among members. Whatever their form of structure, however, most mutual help groups are flexible and informal in both practice and function.

The following characteristics may be said to apply to most formal mutual help groups:

- They develop an organizational structure with officers, a governing body, and procedures for continuity of the group.
- The members determine all policy and control all resources.
- The members are both the providers and recipients of the services.
- Membership is limited to people who have the particular problem or problems with which the group is concerned.
- There is an assistance program which has evolved from members' experiences in dealing with the shared problem.

The assistance offered by mutual help groups can take many forms such as one-to-one exchanges, group discussions, educational seminars, or sharing of personal experiences.

Mutual help groups can aid participants in adding a new supportive community of associates to existing social networks. They can satisfy a need to be connected with others in similar situations and to learn how to deal with potentially frightening new experiences. Such assistance allows people to not feel dependent, problematic, or overwhelmed. The very structure creates an environment of not being alone, of being with other people who are also coping with the tensions of their common situation. Mutual help can be regarded as a supplement to professional help.

Further, mutual help groups enhance couples' abilities to cope with change and through them it is possible that considerable emotional stress will be prevented. During periods of dramatic transition and change people who are not adept at coping are particularly vulnerable to the development of emotional problems. In a mutual help exchange (as in a couples retirement group), learning how to accept change calmly and to make orderly transitions is facilitated, and the possibility of developing more serious and lasting problems is lessened. It would seem that an interest in mutual help groups can strengthen a professional's effectiveness through working in a preventive context where people help each other to problem solve.

TENSION BETWEEN THE PROFESSIONAL AND THE MUTUAL HELP GROUPS

Relationships between mutual help groups and the professional community are not without strain. There are a number of factors that make collaboration between professionals and mutual help groups difficult.

Professionals are trained and have gone through a formal process of education, practice, and supervision leading to appropriate licensure. Services are exchanged for money. Mutual help groups on the other hand stress experiential rather than professional knowledge. Experiential knowledge is derived from direct experience and mutuality and reciprocity are the key elements in the helping process. There is confusion about these two kinds of knowledge. Mutual help groups focus on *experiential* as distinguished from *professional* knowledge. The latter factor has to do with autonomy. Since many experts are intimidating, people are often fearful of sharing their experiences in the presence of such an eminent "judge." They may sit mutely listening to the expert and being passive. In their own group—without experts—couples feel freer to express their experiences and what worked.

Another factor has to do with involvement and commitment versus objectivity. Professionals sometimes talk of the involvement of participants in mutual help groups as being fanatic. In their view there is too much personal concern and perhaps too much taking over of others' problems. However, these very elements of devotion and obligation are essential to effective caring and help in many situations. There are those who would say that a mutual help group does not really solve the problem, that "ultimately people must deal with their own problems." However, as people who are feeling at a loss find that they can help others solve problems, and as they take on a role of being a helper, they often have renewed energy to cope with their own problems.

The Role of the Professional in Mutual Help Groups

Human service professionals can work effectively with mutual help groups in at least four ways.

1. By making referrals.
2. By serving on professional advisory boards.

3. By serving as consultants to existing groups.
4. By initiating or helping to develop new mutual help groups.

A professional renders a real service appropriate to a client when he or she can identify a self-help group that might be helpful. Of course, such identification involves the professional knowing some of the self-help groups in the area or those convenient for the client. The therapist (professional) would also need to know either the name of a contact person or a telephone number where the client can get further information. As a general principle it is advisable that, with the information given, the client contacts the self-help group. The issue of privacy becomes somewhat sticky if the therapist calls and says he/she will be referring a client and then the client calls. It is then obvious that the client is seeing that therapist.

Involvement in a mutual help group does not mean that a couple may not be in other helping modalities. In making such a referral, the professional provides clients with an opportunity to expand their resources for help. Clients can decide whether at that moment they would like to be in the mutual support group, in therapy, in both—or what kind of help they think they need.

Many mutual support groups have a professional advisory board that serves as a link between the group and community institutions and professionals with expertise in their problem area. Professionals are typically invited to serve on such boards because of their expert knowledge, and as an expression of support of the mutual help groups. For the professional, serving on such a board can be viewed as a function of that person being a community psychologist who is helping the group to deal with some of the problems that may occur. Professionals may be helpful with ideas for how to obtain space for meeting, how to create community linkages, how to deal with problems of leadership, or even with dissemination of information about new research. It is important that they not view themselves as the watchdog of how a mutual help group should function. Nor should they see their role as that of promoting their services or their institution. Serving on an advisory board may produce referrals to the professional, but the purpose of sitting on an advisory board is not to enlarge a practice or promote an organization.

Usually, the mutual help group invites professionals to sit on their advisory board. Often, because it is a voluntary position, members of mutual help groups are reluctant to ask professionals to donate their time. It can be appropriate for a professional in a particular area to indicate an interest in that self-help group and to indicate that he/she is available to serve on its advisory board. My experience has been that the groups are usually very pleased to receive such offers.

Mutual help groups may have a consultant whom they call upon when they have a need for professional knowledge, yet the consultant does not interfere with their ongoing, regular activities. The role of consultant can be a paid one, but usually it is done at a volunteer level. There are certain givens. The consultant becomes involved only by invitation. As in any consultation, the consultant recognizes that the consultees' value system may be different from his own and the consultees will determine if they want to continue with that consultant. The consultant cannot dictate how the consultees will use his contribution or how they will integrate it into their group; and the consultant is in no way involved in the implementation of his ideas or recommendations. The latter task is up to the group. The consultant then must realize that she can give information and advice, but does not have the power to act in or control the system. Being a consultant to a mutual help group can also be arranged on a contractual basis, with a fee for services. By and large, however the consultant is used, the same guidelines prevail.

Finally, the professional can be an initiator of a mutual help group. Historically, a number of groups which have developed have been originated by professionals.

One such effort is in St. Paul, Minnesota, where there is a network of groups for separated and divorced persons and for married couples called Fellowship for Renewed Living. The Fellowship began as a mutual help and support group at the Wilder Foundation, a community mental health center. Initially, the professional staff convened the group, acted as facilitators, and provided training for the members. As members became able to take on the responsibility, the professional's role changed to a consultative one, and the Fellowship now trains the facilitators of individual groups. In the above illustrations, the professionals who initiated the programs were eventually able to step back and let the members take control. Serving as an initiator of a mutual help group can be a significant follow-up activity for a workshop or training program as couples receive more than a casual exhortation to get together afterwards, or to keep in touch. A mutual help group provides a structure for couples who have already come together, who know and trust each other, who can continue their help and support in an ongoing way, and in the process build confidence.

A CASE ILLUSTRATION

In the fall of 1983 the Couples Learning Center, a nonprofit, educational organization near Philadelphia, received a grant to conduct a program for step-families. It was to be a five-session course in which the requirements were that one of each couple had to be the custodial parent of their under 18-year-old children. Our goal was to help newly constituted families cope with some of the pressures of remarriage with children living at home. Research indicates that the divorce rate is especially high for couples who experience the complications of two families, visitations with former partners, and all kinds of related issues. The program was advertised in a brochure, in press releases, and in the newspapers. Better than 90 people registered to attend.

The program was especially designed to examine the areas of difficulty with such families, and an educational course model (to be described in the third session) was created. Units were developed on creating a new family as an entity, on celebrations, on discipline, on money, and on problem solving. A variety of group methods was used so that at the end participants felt very close to each other. The participants were grouped in myriad ways—in women's groups, in men's groups, by the age of their oldest child, by decades of chronological age, and by selection of special problem areas.

They interacted with many people at various stages of the life cycle. While a part of the course was lecture, the majority of the program was interactive and experiential. The skills built in the course were many that could be utilized in a mutual help group. Participants learned to interact with people they had not known previously. A trusting, nonjudgmental environment was established. There was an understanding that their feelings and experiences were the prime data of the program. It was exciting to see how each week there was an anticipation of what would happen at that session. People found each other very attractive. They felt they had permission to be authentic and hence it was safe to express their feelings. By the next to the last session, panic was setting in. Participants were saying, "Can't the program continue?" They did not want it to end, and they felt they had been greatly helped. It was evident that the participants really meant that the program had been highly beneficial. Attendance was almost perfect; even a snowstorm one night was not a deterrent.

At the closing session we distributed an evaluation of the program but added a new section. We asked if people would like a continuance and offered them three choices. The first was for individual couples therapy; we would recommend a therapist. A second alternative was an additional, five-unit program. The third alternative was to help them create a mutual help group. There were participants who checked all three alternatives. But the largest group, while indicating that they were not quite clear about what a mutual support group was, thought that they would like one. We then proceeded to get them started.

We thought that the age of the children might be the prime basis for dividing participants into mutual help groups. We set the date for the first session about a month after the program formally ended, inviting those interested in a step-families mutual help group to attend. One group was to be for couples with preschool children, one for those with children in elementary school, and one for those whose children were in high school. We found people most inexperienced with their oldest child, so if there were children who fell in several categories we encouraged couples to attend the group appropriate for the age of their oldest child.

Those who were interested came to a meeting of their designated group. There were a sufficient number to establish each group (between 10 and 20). For support groups to be effective there need to be a large enough number of participants to represent a variety of experiences, and also a group large enough to function regularly so that if someone is absent the group can still function. At this initial session, the project director gave a short lecture on mutual help groups, something of their theory and rationale, especially emphasizing that *they* (the members) *are* the group's leaders; that they will be both givers and receivers of the help. She further explained that while she would help them get started, they would now be operating on their own. She was not abandoning them. She would return after they had had several sessions to check on how they were doing and to be helpful. The project director's role was designed to get them started. A few people were visibly apprehensive about what it would be like to be in a group without a professional leader. However, the majority were enthusiastic about the challenge and relieved to know that there would be a structure through which they could stay in contact with these people to whom they felt so close.

After this overview each of those present was asked to briefly introduce him/herself and say something about his/her situation ("I am 26, divorced with two children, 14 months and four years. I have recently remarried. My new husband does not have children and is very impatient with two little ones. How do I include my present husband in child rearing when he does not especially want to be?") Each participant briefly told of his/her situation and then indicated what he/she wanted from a mutual support group.

In the course of this "go-around" couples got to know each other in this setting, and they developed a vague agenda of what their support group might talk about. At times, after one person had described what he/she wanted, one of the listeners would interject, "That is a problem I have, too. Let me give you an incident of what happened to me." After relating the incident, the speaker could see clear signs in others of recognition of the issues that had been related. While it seemed a meandering process, members were actually gathering data on whether there were in fact common areas which would be the basis for an ongoing support group.

Then the project director asked the group, since Christmas was coming, to respond to the question, "What is one concern about celebrating Christmas this year?" Again each person was asked to respond. (There are those who reject the formal structure of a go-around, that is, asking each person to speak in order. However, I have found it a very effective method to ensure norms that each person is expected to participate, that all will be active and not passive in the group, and that everyone's feelings and experiences are important.) Each person responded to the question, and again members responded with their similar experiences, how they had solved those problems, or what they had learned over time. There was now sufficient information to move on to the administrative aspects of actually forming a support group. Participants were given time to talk to each other privately as couples and then to respond to the ultimate question: Would they want to be part of this support group? Rather than being pressured to affirm, during the first part of the course people experienced in microcosm what being in a support group would be like. It was indeed what they wanted. Every person in each of the three groups indicated a desire to be in such a group.

There was then a period for questions and answers, and the project director served as an expert resource. For example, they asked, "How often do such groups meet?" She explained that it would be most beneficial if the groups met at the same time on a regular basis that might be for 1½ to 3 hours on the same night of the week—either weekly, twice monthly, or once a month. The group then negotiated finding a mutually agreeable night, the length of a session, and the frequency with which the group would meet. It is interesting to note that the groups selected different lengths of time for sessions and different frequencies. It was agreed that what was decided that night would be a first approximation to be modified after the group had some experience meeting.

Then the question arose as to where to meet. The project director explained that it was her experience that such groups went better in one person's house which was reasonably convenient for all the members. Rotation to different houses proved difficult; there was a tendency for the hosts to feel more like they were giving a party than providing the physical setting for a group. She suggested that, if possible, sessions be held in one house and that there might be a rotation to another house after six months or a year. That system worked well. Each of the groups had a number of people who volunteered their homes or offices, and one home was selected based on accessibility.

Another question was asked: "Could other people be invited to be members of the group?" The project director suggested that for now, since this group had had a prior experience and a degree of working together in the previous sessions, it would build a more cohesive base if only those present were included in the group at this time. However, later, after the group had been meeting for a time, they could themselves decide if they wanted to admit additional couples and what the criteria for such admissions would be.

What about leadership and structure of the sessions? It was suggested that one way to start was to have a different member of the group volunteer to chair or facilitate each session—at least to get the group started. Further, it was decided:

- That each session would begin promptly at the designated time.
- That the chairs or furniture should be arranged so that people sat in a circle and could face each other.
- That the couple who are leaders would welcome everyone. They would then put out a question to which each person was to respond. For example, "What happened this week of which you were proud?"
- Then the leader couple would select a topic representing an area in which they wanted help and have that topic be the basis for discussion in the group. For example, one couple wanted to discuss "How do you handle it when the former husband does not pay child support and is often late in picking up the child for visitation? What do you do?" This might be dealt with by the lead couple telling their experience and inviting others to recount theirs. Or the lead couple might raise the topic as a hypothetical situation and ask the group to divide into thirds and demonstrate the problem through role playing. Or the lead couple might talk about their experience and then ask each person to fantasize what they would do, and tell that fantasy to the group, as a means of getting in touch with anger and frustration.

- Finally, about 20 minutes before the end of the session there is a closing go-around in which each person again responds to a question like, "Where are you at the end of tonight?" or "What have you learned tonight that will be helpful to you?" Then the leaders would remind the group of when the next session is and who the leaders will be.

The participants that first night felt relieved to hear that there was a definite structure and that the meetings would be more than a diffuse "bull session." The idea of shared responsibility, while a bit intimidating, was also exciting. Each group agreed to hold their first meeting and decided on a location. One member circulated a sheet requesting each person's name, address, and telephone number and volunteered to copy it and send it to each of the participants. One couple agreed to be the leaders of the first session.

There is a rapidly evolving literature on self-help groups. One of the best is by Silverman (1980) on mutual help groups. This book describes in detail aspects of mutual help groups, from recruiting members to letters of invitation to what happens at typical meetings to problems that mutual help groups face. Another book (Maguire, 1983) focuses on the concept of networking at many levels. Two books by Napier and Gershenfeld (1981, 1983) focus on understanding aspects of group dynamics and factors involved in leading groups.

MARRIAGE ENRICHMENT

Yet another kind of couples group is called "marriage enrichment." *Marriage enrichment* is a term that refers to a philosophy of marriage and the functions it serves for persons; to an educational model of couple and group services offered by mental health professionals or trained group leaders; and to a number of specific programs that provide these services. The major focus is the improvement of married life. While there may be differences in how the improvement of married life is defined, most commonly this improvement is described as enabling partners to "create a climate between them which will enable them to increase self—and other—awareness of the growth potential of their marriage; to explore and express their thoughts and feelings with honesty and empathy; and to develop and use the skills needed to relate effectively, solve their problems, and resolve their conflicts. In such a climate it is believed that the individual and the couple are best able to maximize their potential for relationship satisfaction, and personal and couple growth" (Hof & Miller, 1980, p. 5).

Although marriage enrichment is frequently conceptualized as a preventive service, it really moves beyond the dichotomy between prevention and treatment and subscribes to the belief that is is essential to give persons the knowledge, attitudes, and skills they can use to develop relationships that are unique to their needs. This learning enhances and enriches the lives of many who are not at risk or in need of preventive or therapeutic services.

Marriage enrichment has emerged from two quite different sources. One source is humanistic psychology and the research in group dynamics. That work gave rise to the human potential movement which emerged in the 1960s and was a forerunner to marriage enrichment. The human potential movement encouraged criticism of the medical model of "illness" in human relations and stressed strengths and assets rather than limitations. Developments in the fields of human sexuality and family life education provided an additional understanding of marital relationships and the variables that influenced interpersonal satisfaction. Finally, the need for marriage enrichment services has been increased due to the sociological changes in our culture. The move from traditional to "companionship marriage," with its desire for intimacy, reexamination of roles, and flexible interaction between partners, has changed the requirements for feeling effective in marriage. What has been called "the failure of marriage" has rather been the failure of large numbers of couples to make the transitions that the present culture requires.

The result of all of these changes has been a whole world of new, nontraditional educational services for married couples. Organizations exist that train and certify marriage enrichment leaders, university courses offer marriage enrichment programs and train professionals to provide these services, and practitioners specialize in leading marriage enrichment groups. All of these programs share a common goal—to teach spouses interpersonal skills that will enable them to continue to relate to their partners over time. It is through this kind of continuing change that the growth of both spouses is enhanced throughout the marriage. These models emphasize an educational and not a therapeutic approach that is designed to "make good marriages better" (Otto, 1976).

The other branch which led to the development of marriage enrichment developed in church settings. The church has always supported the family as an institution. Marriage enrichment, as it comes from the church, represents the concerned response of religious groups and their leaders to changes in modern family life and especially to the rising divorce rate. It is important to distinguish between secular and church-related approaches to marriage enrichment, not only because they have different institutional origins, but also because their goals differ in several respects.

Secular marriage enrichment programs are designed to enhance people's ability to communicate within and derive satisfaction from marriages. These services strive for effects that can be described in terms of the skills couples learn and the happiness they report in their marriages. The church's approach is also concerned with strengthening the couple's belief in the validity of the institution of marriage. Its goals may include a demonstration of Christian love in action, a return to the church, and the development and growth of Christian communities.

In recent years the lines of separation beyond origins are becoming obscure as secular marriage enrichment services are taking place under church sponsorship and as there is increasing recognition that a spiritual belief system may be a significant aspect of a couple's relationship.

Marriage Enrichment Services and Marriage Therapy

A question arises as to which is appropriate. Should a given couple be encouraged to enter a marriage enrichment program or marital therapy? To begin, it is important to define the key difference between the two kinds of treatment.

Ordinarily, it is considered inappropriate to offer marriage enrichment services to couples who are considering separation or divorce. It is assumed that these couples need help in determining whether to continue their marital relationship, not help in enhancing it. Generally, marriage enrichment services are considered most appropriate for couples who are committed to their marriage and who are not in a midst of a marital crisis. However, a case can be built for both kinds of services. Sometimes, when a couple enters therapy they may be encouraged to attend a basic communications, four-session marriage enrichment program that builds communication skills. The idea here is that in acquiring these skills, couples will have some of the basic tools to increase the possibility of changing in therapy. The reverse rationale also exists; that is, once couples have completed their work in therapy, a marriage enrichment program serves as an effective follow-up for having them maintain awarenesses they have acquired. Moreover, they can build on their skills through the marriage enrichment experience.

Advantages of an educational model

There is an increasing understanding that an educational approach has a number of advantages. One of these advantages is that in marriage enrichment programs couples learn interpersonal skills that are applicable not only to various aspects of their current relationship but also to changes that may take place over months and years. Such skills include empathizing, defining and resolving problems, managing conflict, being supportive, and developing intimacy. Another advantage of an educational model is that participants can take part in programs that correspond with their needs at various times in the developmental life cycle. Participation, if not at a time of crisis, can be designed to address the needs of a couple at a particular stage of their lives. Thus, enrichment services can be designed for couples with young children when marital satisfaction is typically low, as well as for couples approaching retirement or facing the crises associated with aging. Yet another advantage is that marriage enrichment has the potential for reaching the general population. Educational services are deemed accessible, and couples are more likely to participate in a program offered by their church or a university than they are a program sponsored by a hospital or community mental health agency.

There are those who suggest that change occurs at a faster rate with multiple rather than individual family units. The group engenders a sense of normalcy about conflict and developmental crises. Couples gain new perspectives on world problems, and the group gives members opportunities to learn and practice various interactional skills with each other. Finally, because trained leaders rather than helping professionals provide educational services, enrichment programs are less costly than marital therapy. It is considerably less expensive for trained nonprofessionals to learn a particular program and to present it, using training films and tapes, than it is for professionals to develop and present such programs.

The major limitation of educational programs is that they are not designed to provide remediation for a couple's specific problems. Further, there is not the same emphasis or time lavished on a couple and the resolution of their areas of difficulty or crises.

The role of a professional helper in marriage enrichment

Coordinators of marriage enrichment programs are nonprofessionals, although trained leaders. In the ACME model developed by David and Vera Mace (1978), leaders are couples trained to conduct that model. The pattern is that persons can be trained to conduct specifically designed enrichment programs. The question then arises: What is the role of a professional in marriage enrichment groups? Should they be rendering a service that can be obtained less expensively elsewhere? Is it a misuse of the professional's time to duplicate services available from other sources? And, in fact, if professionals do conduct marriage enrichment programs, are they expected to provide services beyond those provided by trained lay leaders? There are any number of other interesting questions.

Professionals can serve numerous functions. First, professionals can train group leaders who will then be conducting marital enrichment programs. Next, professionals can lead an initial program. Potential lay leaders can learn by observing the professionals and can build increased skills through such observation and supervision. This leaves professional leaders freer to take on more "at risk groups" and to conduct and train with them. Since professionals have greater skills they may be able to successfully conduct an enrichment program with such groups. Yet another role for professionals is work as a consultant to organizations of the marriage enrichment movement. Finally, some professionals have enjoyed taking the training with their spouses and developing yet another relationship in their own lives. They can enhance the skills within their own marriages as they work on this special relationship in this model with their own partners.

Theoretical Bases for Marriage Enrichment

The major approaches to marriage enrichment have been based on General Systems theory, Rogerian theory, behavioral and learning theories, and the philosophies of church related marriage enrichment programs.

General Systems theory

General Systems theory has become the dominant theoretical framework in the treatment of marital and family relationships and therefore the basis for the development of a variety of marriage enrichment programs (Olson & Sprenkle, 1976). General Systems theory has as its basic concern processes and structure of relationships rather than specific problems that couples want to resolve. In other words, it deals with relationship variables rather than personality variables. And, in fact, some research indicates that process variables are more important than attribute variables (personality variables) in discriminating between disturbed and healthy couples. Quick and Jacobs (1973) found that empathy, genuineness, openness of communication, and unconditional positive regard were process variables associated with marital satisfaction. These variables can be translated into skills and taught to couples who can then use them to modify their relationships.

The marital relationship is defined in General Systems theory as a social system, or "a consistent network of interacting relationships between persons, with the persons considered as units of the system above and beyond their individual characteristics" (Murrell, 1973, p. 9). A central concept in this theory is that the system functions to develop patterns of coping with and relating to changing input from within the system (developmental, affective, and other changes in each partner) and from the environment (changes in employment, relationships to extended family). The system uses information from both sources to understand how it is functioning for its members and for its environment. If these data indicate some disparity between the actual effects and the intended effects, the marital relationship or system must change in some way. In conceptualizing the marital relationship as a system, spouses' roles are defined as processes requiring adaptation and change in both the individual and the system. The system thus involves interaction and adjustments between its components.

For couples to make adjustments, they must go through three processes of communication. First, new information about the components, spouses, and the system (the marital relationship) must be transmitted. Second, spouses must receive this information. Finally, the partners must react to and act upon the information. If the goal of marriage enrichment is to increase marital adjustment, the adjustment process should be designed to increase the information available to the spouses about themselves and the environment.

The Minnesota Couples Communication Program (MCCP) (Miller, Corrales, & Wackman, 1975; Miller, Nunnally, & Wackman 1975, 1976) is one of the most highly structured and well-researched programs. It is based on family development theories, symbolic interactionism, and modern systems theory. In this program couples are taught two sets of skills: awareness skills, enabling them to understand their interaction patterns; and communication skills, enabling them to make changes in those patterns. The program consists of four, 3-hour sessions, typically presented once a week by trained, certified instructors. Each session focuses on one of four conceptual frameworks. The first, the awareness wheel, helps participants to identify information themselves and is made up of five components: sensing, thinking, feeling, wanting, and doing. Participants learn skills to express this information. The second framework is the shared meaning process, designed to increase information about the spouse. Spouses learn listening/interaction skills so that they receive messages as their partners intended them to be received. The third framework, communication styles, is designed to help spouses identify the kinds of communication styles they use and the effects of these styles on their partners. The final framework, a kind of *I'm OK—You're OK*, emphasizes each person's responsibility for his/her own self-esteem and his/her partner's self-esteem. Research on MCCP has shown positive results consistently. Participants in the program significantly increased their interactional awareness and communication skills. Wampler (1982) summarized 19 research studies and concludes that there is strong evidence based on behavioral measures that MCCP increases the use of the desired skills in married couples' interaction. Other programs, based on General Systems approach, are Workshop in Couples Communication and Negotiation Skills (Garland, 1978) and the Systems Marriage Enrichment Program (Elliott & Saunders, 1982).

Rogerian theory

The client-centered therapy developed by Carl Rogers (1961) has been the basis for another major group of marriage enrichment programs. Rogers' central hypothesis is that "the growthful potential of any individual will tend to be realized in a relationship in which the helping person is experiencing and communicating realness, caring, and deeply sensitive nonjudgmental understanding" (Meador & Rogers, 1973). Therefore, the theory can be applied to a marital relationship in which understanding and individual growth are desired. In a helping relationship the attitudes considered necessary and sufficient for one partner to effect change in the other are genuineness, congruence, empathy, and unpossessive caring, and confirmation of the other. Genuineness and congruence incorporate reliance on one's immediate experiencing in the relationship with the other. One person is able to imagine, and in this way experience, what the other reports. Empathy involves understanding the world of the other as the others sees it. Unpossessive caring and confirmation of the other (or positive regard) require a caring that avoids any overtly or covertly judgmental behavior, whether it is approving or disapproving.

If one is successful in communicating these attitudes, the therapist can expect certain things of the client. Rather than remoteness from inner experiencing, he expects that there will be more immediate awareness and expression of those inner experiences; that there will be movement from disapproving of parts of the self to greater self-acceptance; from a fear of relating to a willingness to relate more directly; from holding rigid black and white constructs of reality to holding more tentative constructs; and from seeing the locus of evaluation outside of the self to finding the locus of evaluation in one's own inner experiencing. These expectations, which the therapist holds for the client, are equally applicable to a relationship in which partners want to understand each other and themselves and are willing to reveal themselves to one another (Meader & Rogers, 1973).

Utilizing the Rogerian approach to communicate effectively with one another, spouses must avoid being judgmental. The expressed thoughts and feelings of one partner must be understood and felt from the other's point of view so that the other's frame of reference can be achieved. To improve communication it is useful for the listener, before making a statement in conversation, to first restate the thoughts and feelings communicated by the speaker. The speaker can then indicate if the listener has correctly understood the message and, if not, can clarify any misinterpretation; that is, before presenting one's own point of view an understanding of the other's frame of reference is achieved.

Rogerian client-centered therapy is the basis for a comprehensive skills training program known as Conjugal Relationship Enhancement (Guerney, 1977). The Rogerian principles of acceptance, respect, and empathy are integrated into an instructional program to teach the desired skills to participants. The skills are designed to develop greater sharing and psychological intimacy between spouses.

In the Relationship Enhancement Therapy (RET) program, spouses learn four sets of skills: speaker, listener, mode switching, and facilitator skills. Speaker skills are designed to help speakers communicate their own feelings to their spouses openly and honestly, without generating unnecessary defensiveness. As listeners, spouses are taught to convey acceptance of the other's communication and to understand and empathize with the other's perceptions, thoughts, and feelings. The third set, mode switching, helps to identify the appropriate time and technique to switch from speaker skills to listener skills. Finally, the facilitator's skills enable couples, in a group, to help others learn the three sets of skills. The Relationship Enhancement Therapy program has produced significantly positive results in a number of studies summarized by Gurman and Kniskern (1977).

Behavioral theory

Behavioral therapy is based on theory derived from experimental research and underscores such concepts as positive and negative reinforcement, conditioning, and shaping. An empirical approach views each intervention as an experiment to test and refine the principles of learning. The theory emphasizes behavior that can be explained by learning processes. "Behavior is composed of cognitive, motor, and . . . emotional responses. Behavior is seen as responses to stimulation, external and internal. Therefore, the goal of therapy is to modify unadaptive stimulus-response (S.R) connections and the methods insofar as possible, are analogs from experimental psychology. Behavior therapy is marked by its adherence to scientific method in evaluating its results and designating process variables" (Goldstein, 1973, p. 207).

Behavioral marital therapy intervenes in coercive, interactional patterns in three ways: (1) to reduce the rate of aversive behaviors when spouses attempt to negotiate behavior change (Patterson & Hopps, 1972); (2) to develop the power of each partner to mediate rewards for the other by increasing the frequency and intensity of mutual, positive reinforcement (Stuart, 1974); and (3) to help the couple to develop a system that provides for continuous readjustment to the reinforcers from their partner (Azrin, Naster, & Jones, 1973). While behavioral theory has been applied less often than systems theory or Rogerian client-centered therapy to educational programs for nonclinical programs, several smaller scale behavioral programs have developed. One program by Fisher (1973) taught couples the principles of positive reinforcement. Spouses functioned as observers while their partners discussed marital problems in a small group. Following the discussion, spouses awarded points to one another for changed behavior. The three couples who accumulated the most points each week and who were most accurate in predicting their spouses' responses on an attitude inventory were reinforced by group applause weekly and a financial reward at the end of the program.

Harrell and Guerney (1976) designed the Behavioral-Exchange Program to teach groups of married couples cooperative negotiation skills, thereby enabling them to deal more successfully with their marital conflicts. In this program didactic presentations and skill practice exercises train couples to employ a problem-solving sequence. The problem-solving skills are: listening carefully, locating a relationship issue, identifying one's own contributions to the issue, identifying alternative solutions, evaluating alternative solutions, making an exchange, determining conditions of the exchange, implementing the behavioral exchange contract, and renegotiating the behavioral exchange contract.

Researching the behavioral exchange program, Harrell and Guerney (1976) found that while couples showed significant improvement in conflict management, they showed no significant improvement in marital satisfaction. Fisher (1973) similarly found that spouses in behavioral groups had more accurate perceptions of their partners, although there were no significant changes on measures of empathic behavior. Gurman and Kniskern (1977) report that "behavioral exchange programs have not fared especially well, showing no difference from control groups in two-thirds of the studies reviewed" (p. 8).

Marriage enrichment in the church

Although group procedures vary widely, they can be broadly characterized by three particular religious bodies that originated them—the Roman Catholics, the Methodists, and Quakers (Mace & Mace, 1978). The Roman Catholic marriage enrichment program, known as Marriage Encounter, is usually a weekend retreat program held for couples in a residential facility. The encounter weekend, beginning in 1948, was the first marriage enrichment program. Otto estimated in 1975 that over 180,000 couples had participated in this program (Otto, 1975). The weekend retreat is lead by a team of three couples who have attended encounter programs and a minister, usually a priest. The three couples give 12 presentations on various marriage topics based on a sequence of themes: self-examination, examination of the couple relationship, examination of the couple's relationship to God, and finally, examination of the couple's ministry in the world. (Materials are available through National Marriage Encounter, 1978.) Following the presentations leaders ask open-ended questions that participants meditate on and then write about. Usually, the men will write in the conference room of the residential facility, and the women will write in their motel rooms for 10 minutes. Each couple shares their written statements in private and discusses them so that spouses can better understand each other (again for 10 minutes). This is generally referred to "in shorthand" as "10 on 10." The weekend culminates with a religious service and a final 90 on 90, which frequently concludes not only with shared emotional intimacy but frequently with physical intimacy.

The program emphasizes learning about one another and sharing feelings, not learning communication skills. The group only interacts socially and during religious observances of the weekend. The marriage encounter is designed to give married couples the opportunity to examine their lives together. It is not designed for learning or practicing communication skills, negotiation skills, or problem-solving skills. From Marriage Encounter, there has developed National Marriage Encounter, an ecumenical organization that includes Jewish and Protestant leaders.

The Methodists began the Marriage Communication Labs, a carefully constructed program which has been used by other denominations. Unlike the Catholic model, the labs consider group sharing an important component. In addition to sharing thoughts and feelings with one another, couples receive training in communication such as the use of active listening skills and "I"-messages from Gordon's *Parent Effectiveness Training* (1975). The emphasis is on helping couples to know how to deal with issues rather than on tackling specific problems. The training is experiential and inductive. Frequently, the way an issue is examined is by asking couples to do a specific exercise, to reflect on that experience in terms of what it says to them about their relationship, and then to determine what changes they want to make, if any. In the experiences and discussions derived from the exercises, as well as in the skills training, partners share with other couples as well as with each other.

Because church-related marriage enrichment is a more philosophical approach than an application of theory and because many of its leaders are lay couples who have participated in the research, little research has been done on its effects. Reports on program results frequently rely on testimonies from participating couples rather than on a controlled examination of specific variables. This is not viewed as a serious obstacle since marriage enrichment has as its prime benefit a program to instill hope and to enhance for the couples a vision of their relationships' potential. Whether marriage enrichment provides the skills to make dreams a reality has not been researched. Follow-up contacts suggest that couples need additional help if they are to achieve their goals. Many couples report the Marriage Encounter weekend as resulting in a closeness, a special intimacy, an increase in trust, and an increase in marital satisfaction. Doherty and Lester (1982) reported on a 10-year, retrospective study of 129 randomly selected couples who had participated in Marriage Encounter. They found that while the majority of couples reported positive outcomes as a result of their marriage encounter weekend, 19 percent of the couples reported more frustration because of the awareness of unmet needs, 14 percent reported conflict over marriage encounter itself, and 9 percent reported greater discomfort in discussing feelings with their spouses.

Summary of Marriage Enrichment

In summary, a professional offering a marital educational program can choose from an increasing variety of models and theories. Even from the limited amount of available research, any of the approaches is potentially effective in meeting specific goals. The key to making the selection is deciding on the purpose of the intervention and the desired outcome. For a fuller description of marriage enrichment with couples, an excellent source and the basis for the present discussion can be found in *Working with Couples for Marriage Enrichment* by Diana S. R. Garland (1978). To date there is limited evaluation and research on marriage enrichment programs. Whether evaluation is described for formal research or for feedback on effectiveness of the program presented, it is important that professionals know instruments available for conducting such feedback activities. The book also includes an extensive array of such resources.

COUPLES BY DESIGN

Marriage enrichment involves having a particular design typically based upon some theory and then implementing that design with each group.

Another form of group work with couples occurs when there is a goal to be achieved. For example, with an aging population an emergent area of couples' concern is how to deal with their aging parents. The question that arises then becomes: How could middle-aged couples understand how to relate to their aging parents in an ongoing couples group or in some form of couples program?

Another question for other couples is: How do couples who are over 65 or 70 in age develop confidence in their own lifestyle? How can they be a support system for each other and develop confidence in their style? Can this subject be approached?

Women between 30 and 50 are under special stress. One of the areas of that stress has to do with their relationships with their husbands. A question that arises here is: Can a training program be developed that focuses on the specific issues of women between 30 to 50 and their husbands? What we are talking about is taking an emergent issue which is defined by a population of couples and creating a training design to meet the needs of those couples. This is very different from the "standardized" marriage enrichment programs which may have certain defined objectives like enhancing communication and giving couples an awareness of their communication style (i.e., the more generalized aspects of their relationship). What I am talking about here is a couples group that meets in the structure of a specific training design created for that population. This training design is created and may only be used once for that population.

This kind of program involves a different kind of trainer skill. What is needed is a person who is well trained, not only in couples' issues, but in group dynamics, laboratory training, and techniques in design. The theoretical base for this kind of couples group is derived from work of the great social psychologist Kurt Lewin (Lewin, 1948, 1951). Lewin used a few simple concepts to develop his action research. These concepts were amplified in the work of the National Training Laboratories at Bethel, Maine, and were further expanded into the process of laboratory training. The prime element is the concept of training design. How do you create a program to meet particular objectives? For many who are training in working with couples, training design and the laboratory approach are all but unknown. It would seem that the major, emerging work with couples groups is the ability of the professional to be a group trainer who knows how to understand the goals of a particular group and to design a program for them. These programs may range from a microlab to a one-day workshop, from a course that may be conducted over a period of 4 weeks to a 16-week course.

The microlab is a two- to-three-hour training design which uses time as a dynamic variable to help participants get in touch with their feelings, assumptions, and experiences on a particular topic. In a microlab, there is a series of short experiences (7 to 10 minutes) on a question about which the participant talks to one or more people in a small group. And in the sequencing of these questions a participant may come much further in a couple of hours on a subject than he may come in weeks or even months of therapy. A workshop is a one-day (or even a five-day) experience on a theme, again designed to help a participant understand his/her feelings, attitudes, expectations, and desired outcomes, and may even include creation of an action plan. In a course a subject is defined. There are specific aspects of the subject to be examined and the trainer/facilitator designs the program to meet those objectives over a series of weeks.

The key concept is "design," Too often there is a grab-bag mentality. Effective design involves much more than "painting by numbers." It is much more than simply reshuffling a number of pat events, games, simulations, or activities in the guise of meeting the needs of a particular group. In fact, many trainers could easily be labeled "bag people." A bag person is someone who always has at hand a group of activities or events that somehow seem to "work" in virtually any group meeting for virtually any reason. When in doubt the bag person simply pulls from the bag of events or activities one of the tried and true designs and applies it to any group. While the event or activity is often interesting, fun, or challenging, it may have little value for the stated goals of the program. We have carried and relied too heavily on the manuals—the training bibles, the sure things. The problem is that few situations are in fact replicable, and it is a rare design that has the staying power to be used from one situation to another.

We realize that we attempt to go to "our bag," or to rely on the designs of others when we are fearful, confused, or unsure. We reach for something that "worked" previously for others and for ourselves—something that will pull us through, that it is not exactly what the doctor ordered. Thus, as bag people, we squeeze an event or activity into a situation because it generates interest or because the "surefire" experience relieves our own anxieties and uncertainties, and psychologically takes us off the spot of having to create or design for the needs of the group. As we mature as trainers, we find that although we will always carry the "bag" there are fewer and fewer times when we need to reach inside. We begin to see designs as unique to each situation, literally to each moment, and the "old reliable" designs tend to have less and less appeal as we become more demanding of ourselves and of the outcomes we desire for the group.

Quite simply, when we talk about "design" we are talking about the core of the training and facilitating process. We are talking about the development of creative and sequentially appropriate activities or events to provide a satisfactory experience for the couple. Perhaps one way to demonstrate this concept of training designs further is to briefly present two illustrations.

Example: Training design on marriage questionnaire

The following training design was created as a program for organizations who might want an evening's educational program on the subject of marriage. Doctoral students were trained in the design which was conducted in response to requests. They presented this training design to couples groups at churches, PTAs, and husband and wife special sessions at philanthropic and community organizations. It represents an example of a formal training design "written up."

Training Design on Marriage Questionnaire

Introduction

Welcome participants. Indicate that there is a renewed interest on the subject of male-female relations. What is it and what is expected? There seem to be many questions on marriage. There is concern with the increasing divorce rate. There is concern about how we raise our children so that they may lead satisfying adult lives. There is our concern about intimacy and relationships.

The Objectives of This Program Are:

- To help participants become aware of their own attitudes.
- To begin to understand some of the dilemmas of our society; hopefully, to understand some of the issues and to have an opportunity to share yours and discuss them.

It Involves:

- Your being a participant.
- Your being willing to share your understandings.
- Your understanding that THERE WILL BE NO ADVICE GIVEN OR MAGIC ANSWERS AT THE END, although *you* may have developed some answers for yourself in the course of the session.

I hope all of you will participate. I think you will be stimulated by the discussion—and learn much.

Materials Needed:

- Marriage questionnaires, one for each person; preferably, one extra per group to be used for group tallying.
- Extra pencils—possibly even enough for the audience if you have reason to believe they won't have them.
- A couple of sheets of newsprint (for posting summary tallies), a piece of masking tape, one or two magic markers.

Program, following introduction

1. Begin with Introduction (above).
2. Ask people to group themselves, five or six to a group but not with people sitting on either side of each other. Encourage people to sit with people they don't know well or with people of different age groups. (Explain that we have a tendency to sit with the people who are our friends and with whom we are most comfortable making asides. However, in this instance there is a real opportunity for understanding other perspectives by sitting with relative strangers.) Allow time for this.
3. Distribute questionnaires. Either have one of the panel members distribute them, giving one more than the number of people in each group (one for each member, one extra for summary), or put questionnaires on table and ask a representative from each group to come and "get one more than there are members of your group."
4. Check that people have pencils. If not, distribute.
5. Ask that all look at questionnaire. Note that there is no room for a name because questionnaires will not be collected. The data are important. Answer each question honestly as you feel (stress as *you feel*). "Would you answer these questions, please." (Allow time for replies.)
6. Ask group to sum (or tally their group replies on the extra sheet). Be sure participants understand they are not to convince each other or attempt to change answers. "We simply need a tally of the data." (Allow time for replies.)
7. Record data on newsprint on wall. Basically, write shortened version of questionnaire on newsprint sheets (this could be prepared in advance), and post in prominent place on wall where readily visible. Write big. Use a color that is easy to read.

   Examples:

   a. Marriage is "forever."
   _____ Yes _____ No

   b. Marriage is the same at 25 as at 55.
   _____ Yes _____ No

   c. Prime reasons women marry.
   _____ Security
   _____ To have children (could be abbreviated, i.e., "Children")
   _____ Sex
8. Tallies can be recorded by the leader from the tally sheets of each group. Or a member may be asked to record the tallies on newsprint.

Question 1. Read back data. Expectation is that most will reply yes. You might ask some of the participants why that is (culture, that's the way it has always been, first commandment is be fruitful and multiply, we all have that fantasy, and so on). Incidentally, we all believe it. Marriage is the most common voluntary institution known. Better than 90 percent of the people in the United States will be married at least once by age 40. Actually, marriage is so important that everyone does it. We believe about 10 percent of people are homosexual. When we consider the number of people in our society who married at least once, the number is 95 percent, it would seem we have even convinced homosexuals to marry.

Question 2. Report out data on this question. The anticipated reply is no. (This sets up the basic dilemma. How can marriage be forever if people change?)

Ask some members to tell why they felt the statement was wrong. (We all change, we have different experiences, we know more of the world. The man has his career, the wife has her house and children, they develop different interests, they acquire and cultivate hobbies, we read differently. Life's experiences leave their mark—fighting in a war, losing a child, the long illness or death of a parent, moving to another part of the country, different friends, and so on.)

Now, ask them, how they would reconcile (make sense out of) a yes reply to question 1 and a no reply to question 2. Ask them to talk about it in their groups. (allow 10 minutes.)

Just before the end of the time indicate "one more minute." Ask, "What happened? How did you reconcile those replies?" Let a few people report out—but be sure to hit the dilemmas. (What if people don't grow the same way? What if they grow differently? What are the odds of their being the same people at 25 and 55? What might have been fascinating at one time becomes boring, or silly, or not so attractive at another time. What are the implications?)

If someone gives a lead into divorce, go into Question 5 next. (It becomes more interesting than reading replies in routine order.)

Question 5. Report out data. (It should always be done verbally because some can't see newsprint.) The expected reply is no. (There can be a variety of answers: It shouldn't cost much to marry or divorce; people should take it seriously. If it's a bad marriage and they make an adequate financial arrangement, why shouldn't it be easy to terminate? Women fear that a man can remarry quickly; a woman could not, and so on.) Ask some people to reply with their reasons.

Some issues to consider:

- Who gets divorced? Poor can't afford it. For the rich money is no problem. Expense of divorce is primarily a middle-class phenomenon.

- The statement (is just an often-spoken quip), but what does it really say about marriage and divorce—and how do you feel about it?
- Do women have special fears about divorce (opportunities to remarry—bad. Care of children: problems of being a single parent; financial burden)?

(If there is time, ask participants to discuss question 5 in relation to their replies to questions 1 and 2. What would that mean?) "Now, let's look at some myths."

Question 3. Expected reply: no. Ask some people to report out their reasons. (Once this was the reason: Good girls held out when the petting got heavy and said, "If you want to go any further, you'll have to marry me." There is the white bridal gown and the tradition of the bride being a virgin.) *But it is a myth*—and we all know it. In 1948 and 1953 when Kinsey did his studies, he found that over 60 percent of the men and over 40 percent of the women had had intercourse prior to marriage. The more recent Masters and Johnson (1975) studies indicate that over 50 precent of women and over 80 percent of men have had intercourse prior to marriage (most typically for women with the person who will become their husbands, i.e., women have only had sex with one partner). But we view these statistics as conservative. Overwhelmingly, people do not marry to have sex.

Question 4. Expected reply: no. Ask some people to report out their reasons. (*Another myth* that we know is not true. Who you marry depends on who asks you, who you meet. Clearly, if you had lived in another city, had gone to a different college, had lived in a different neighborhood, you would have met and perhaps married someone else. And we have no way of knowing or measuring whether that would have been a better or worse relationship. We know also that widows and widowers who loved their spouses remarry and report happiness.) So, if we don't marry for the reasons in questions 3 and 4, why do we marry? Let's look for replies in question 6.

Question 6. Read back the data. What were the items most scored (largest number of tallies next to them)? What item got most number 1s? (The dilemma is, do people marry for companionship [personality, and presumably could change over time and so could partner] or for institutional reasons [to have children, security, and so on])? This dilemma represents the problems of marriage today. In the 1960s marriage was primarily for institutional reasons and for many women it continues to be that way. Now emphasis is on companionship marriage. What are problems, hazards, difficulties? In group ask them to talk about what this dilemma means. What are the problems they see *themselves* having with the institution of marriage—for their marriages, their children, their friends, the future?

Ask if there are any conclusions or comments any of the groups have to make. Conclude by saying you hope they better understand some of the questions of marriage today. There are no easy answers; it is a very different situation; it should become clearer why there is so much discussion and concern. "We hope you have learned more about marriage, about you, and perhaps what you need to do next."

Marriage Questionnaire

There are a number of questions listed below. Read the question, then answer it in terms of what *you think*.

1. Do you believe marriage is "forever" (until death do us part)?
   _____ Yes _____ No

2. Do you believe people are pretty much the same at 25 as at 55?
   _____ Yes _____ No

3. Do you believe the prime reason people marry is to have sex?
   _____ Yes _____ No

4. Do you believe there is one man for every woman?
   _____ Yes _____ No

5. Do you believe "It should cost $500 to marry and $3 to get a divorce?"
   _____ Yes _____ No

6. The prime reasons women marry are (put 1 next to the most important reason and checks next to the following two next most important reasons):
   _____ Security
   _____ To have children
   _____ To have sex
   _____ To have a place in society
   _____ For companionship
   _____ To please their parents
   _____ To be fulfilled

Example: Training design on a course: being supportive in a marriage

At the Couples Learning Center, courses are designed to meet special needs of the population we are addressing. This course evolved because so many couples report that they don't feel that their partners are supportive of them. We need to understand that marriage has changed. Formerly, it was an institution with set roles and functions. Now it is first and foremost a relationship. It involves two people coming together, intent on staying together, and yet frequently not knowing how to create a supportive relationship. Marriage is the most complex process of all.

As with conflict, we are never taught how to be supportive. We learn to deal with conflict by understanding how we have related to significant others in the past and how we relate to significant others in the present around conflictual issues. The same is true of being supportive. We watch how our parents or significant others have been supportive and we try to copy them. We establish a pattern of what we think supportive behavior is and we stay with it. It may be wrong and inappropriate. It may even be ineffective in terms of what our partner wants.

This is a five-session course conducted for six couples (or an even number). Each session is 2½ to 3 hours, conducted weekly. The course is designed to help partners understand what is meant by being supportive in a relationship. It is meant to give them a wide variety of information about their early experiences of what being supported meant, their early ideas of what being supportive meant, and to help them learn what their partner expects of them in order to feel supported. The course will also stress understanding individual differences regarding what being supported and giving support means. In the course participants will practice both being supportive and understanding what being in a supportive relationship means. It will further involve really understanding what a partner says about being in a supportive relationship., (This is a summary of what is explained as part of an introduction to the first session.)

A Course: Being Supportive in a Marriage*

Session 1

Objectives

- To create participative norms.
- To build skills in speaking and listening.
- To recognize individual differences.
- To build a supportive relationship through an "advocate."

Overview

- How marriage has changed.
- Marriage is a relationship.
- Couples find it essential to feel supported in that relationship.

---

*Note: What is marked in quotes are the instructions the leader actually gives the group.

Introduction

Chairs will be in a circle. All people will introduce themselves.
"In the course of these weeks, we will be doing much to know each other and also to understand what being supportive in a relationship would be. Let's begin by getting to know each other in a somewhat different way. Tell us your first name. So that we can really understand you, describe yourself with three (3) adjectives, and with each adjective explain what that means to you. Then, will you introduce your partner. Introduce your partner with his/her name and then explaining briefly what is special about her or him." (Go around the group.)

A microlab

In this next experience couple partners will not be together but people will be in pairs. A simple method is to have women move to the left and pair with the first person (not their husbands). On the next round continue by having the women pair with the next man on their left, and so on.

1. "What follows is a brief microlab to understand what has happened to you and your partner over time. Pair with someone, not your husband or wife. Will you take 10 minutes to talk to each other? Discuss how you met your partner (husband or wife), what you were like then, what he or she was like then." (10 minutes)

   "Shift partners."
2. "When did things start to change? How did you change? How did he or she change?" (10 minutes)

   "Shift partners."
3. "How have things been lately—for you, for your partner? What upsets you? What frightens you? What did you want to happen?"(10 minutes)

   "Shift partners."
4. "Each person should now have a piece of paper and a pencil. Will you write the answers to three questions. What do you want from these five (5) weeks for

   Yourself?
   Your partner?
   The two of you (for us)?

   Will you write your answers. Then, you and your partner (hereafter called your 'advocate') go to a separate place where there is privacy. Will you discuss what is on your sheet so that it is clear to the other person. If it is not, then ask questions so that it is clear. Each of you should have on your own pieces of paper what you want to have happen in the next five weeks that would make you feel supported. The person with you should be helping you clarify your ideas so you can express them clearly. (20 minutes)

Remember who your advocate is because you will be continuing this next week."

(Whole group comes together in a circle, and each person responds to the question, "How are you at the end of tonight"? They reply with any feeling, thought, comment.)

Session 2

Objectives

- Expressing personal perspectives to partner.
- Receiving support through an advocate.
- Giving support as an advocate.
- Practicing.
- Observing.
  Building skills.
- Giving feedback.

Introduction

(Bridge from first week.) Chairs in circle. Each person responds to question, "What happened since last week?"

Me, you, us

1. "Take five minutes with your advocate from last week to remember what was on your sheets. Take one or at most two items from each category. What is one thing I want for me, for my partner, for the two of us? Each person should talk." (10 minutes)

   (Partners will speak with each other away from the group. Return to circle and the total group.)
2. "Now we will begin a process. A couple will agree to go. They will sit facing each other. Next to each of them will sit their advocates so that a husband and wife will sit facing each other. Next to the husband will sit the woman who was his advocate. Next to the wife will sit the man who was her advocate." (See Figure 1.)

Step 1. One person (the husband or wife) will begin by explaining one thing from his sheet that he wants for himself, one thing he wants for her, and one thing he wants for the two of them. She will listen and then she will reply to what has been said. She can agree, disagree.

Step 2. The other person reads from their list. The partner listens and replies.

FIGURE 1 Support Exercise

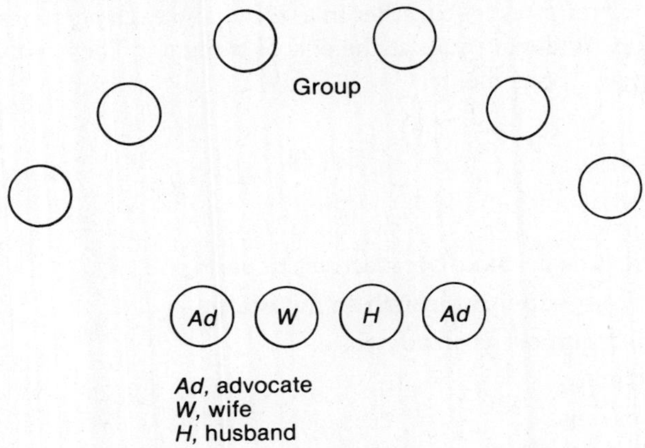

Step 3. If a person has difficulty explaining to their spouse what they mean, they can ask their advocate for help. And the advocate helps.

Step 4. The facilitator asks each advocate how the person was different talking to them than they were with their spouse just now.

Step 5. Then each person in the group is invited to feed back what they observed with that couple. Observing means to report on what was seen, heard, or felt. It is not intellectual or judgmental. It is experiential. If a person wants to, he/she can pass, that is, not comment with an observation. This process should take approximately 20 minutes per couple: 10 to 15 minutes in the interchange and 5 to 7 minutes in the feedback. Then the couple responds to a few of the comments. (They get "the last word.") Someone might keep time to make sure the time constraints are adhered to. Then the group continues the same process with the next couple who volunteers.

Closing

About 15 minutes before the end of the session, but not in the middle of a couple speaking, stop and explain that the end of the session is coming. Ask each couple to respond to the question: "What got to you tonight? It might be an observation, or how you felt at a certain time, or what you understood about you and your partner." (Let each person respond.) "This week there is a homework assignment. Practice doing one of the things you said you wanted or that your partner wanted. Next week you will report on how it went."

Session 3

Objectives

- To complete the objectives of session 2.
- To understand what it means being supported in a personal, specific way.
- For a woman to practice interviewing a man.
- To understand what being supportive means to him.
- To understand what men need to feel supported.

Opening

In a six-couple group, some of the couples will not have had a chance to have taken their turn the previous week. Complete having the couples—with their advocates—explain what they want. For example: "Pat and Dick are suffering. They have had a whole week to review what they were going to say. Let us end that. Will they face each other. Will their advocates sit next to each of them."

Each of them goes. Their advocates respond. The group feeds back their observation.

Getting started: Reporting on the homework

"How did things go since last week? It was a high-risk experience—talking about what you want for yourself, your partner, and for the two of you. Then there was the group feedback—thinking of what was said or what you learned watching the other couples and relating that to you. How was it going home? Finally, remember your assignment was to actively do one of the things you wanted. How did it go? You can

Brag.
Get an E for effort—and try again.
Feel you bombed—and explore why.

Will you tell us how it went? What did you try? How did it go?" (Each person reports out.)

Being supportive

1. "Let's talk about being supportive. It involves:
   - Being *known*, understood.
   - Caring and wanting to please the other person.
   - Not wanting to induce pain on the other.
   - Intimacy (knowing and being sensitive to the other in the present)."

2. "Now there will be another experience in learning what being supportive means. This week we will focus on what being supported means to a man. We will be doing this in two ways. The first way is by learning about your partner. You may think you know, but then again you may not. The second aspect will deal with what men need to feel supported."

Ask two couples to group together, but they should not be the same persons who were the couples' advocates in the previous session. They will group so that a woman will face a man (the husband of the other couple). Her husband will be behind that man and that man's wife will be behind her. (See Figure 2.) The woman is instructed to interview that man and to try to understand him. Some of the questions she will ask are:

- What is important to him?
- How has he changed in the last three years?
- What does work mean?
- What does family mean?
- What makes him feel understood and supported?

Other questions might be:

- How does he feel when he is misunderstood?
- What makes him angry?
- What is an ideal day?
- Give an example of how it would be if he really felt supported.

She can ask other questions. She might want to know the other man's opinions (which may be different from her husband's) about, for example,

FIGURE 2 Support Interview: Man One, Woman Two

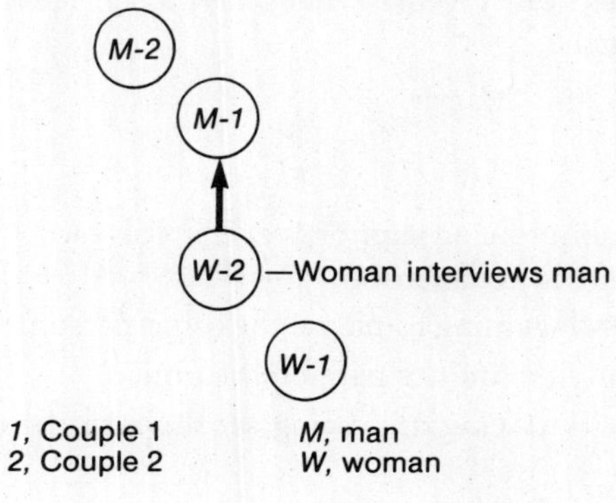

money, vacations, sex, free time. She is to use this interview to her advantage. She should not back off. She should use this as an opportunity to find out what she wants to know.

The woman next to her can prod her and whisper to her to ask about any questions to which she might want to hear her husband's answers. The interviewer then incorporates those questions.

The man behind the interviewee is basically to listen and to hear the interviewer's responses, also noting his wife's questions and style. After 15 minutes the facilitator stops the interview.

All four are then invited to respond to how they felt in the interview process:

- How did the man being interviewed feel about being interviewed and about what he said?
- How did the interviewer feel about asking the questions and about the responses?
- What did his wife learn about him in the course of the interview?
- How did she feel it went?
- How did the husband feel listening to his wife conduct the interview?
- How did he feel about his wife?

And then, a question to all of them: "What did you learn"? (The debriefing should go about 10 minutes.)

Now switch. The other man will now be interviewed by the wife from the other couple. (See Figure 3) Continue the process as described above.

Now switch so that the other man in the two couples is interviewed. There is a 15-minute interview. There are 10 minutes of debriefing.

FIGURE 3 Support Interview: Man Two, Woman One

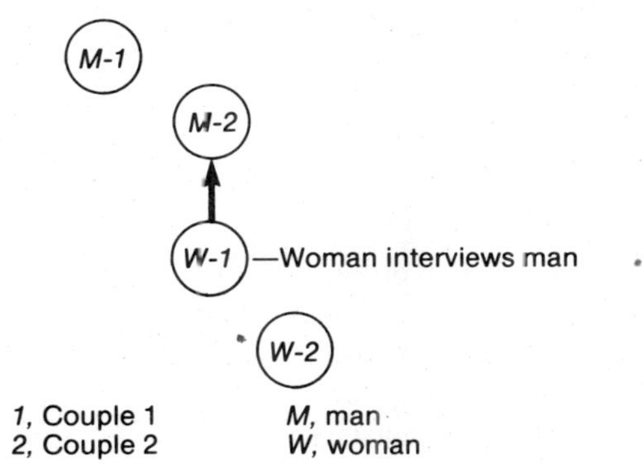

Closure

"Stay with your group of four. Will the women respond to this question: From this process, what do you understand of your husbands' needs to be supported?"
(Women speak and men listen.) (10 minutes)

"Now will the men respond: What do you hear yourself saying that is important to you?"
(The men speak and the women listen.) (10 minutes)

"This coming week—especially the women—will you practice being supportive, translating into behavior what you learned.

Next week, our focus will be on what women want to feel supported."

Session 4

Objectives

- For women to practice being supportive and to report on how it went.
- For men to understand what women want to feel supported.
- To understand what your wife wants from you to feel supported.
- For a man to practice interviewing a woman and to understand what being supportive means to her.
- To understand when the communication process does not go well and the person feels unsupported.

Opening: reporting of homework assignment

"Go into the groups you were in at the end of last week when women did the interviewing of being supportive to a man. (They go.)

Last week there was a homework assignment—for the women to decide to do something that demonstrates that they are supportive. Tell your group what you did and how you feel it went. Then let your husband report on his experience." (10 minutes)

Being supportive

(The group comes together as a circle.) "Another aspect of being supportive means talking and hearing each other. I will distribute some sheets on what *not* to do. (Distribute handout)

Each couple will take one communication process which does not go well. Will you as a couple do a role play of it? One person will do a "bad thing." After the role play explain it. Describe how you feel when that happens. What can you do about it?"

Each couple is asked to take one or two items from the list. They are given 10 minutes to prepare. They then do a role play, demonstrating their item. For example, a couple might choose number 1: "Do not listen." At the end of a few minutes the facilitator stops the role play and the person at the receiving end of the bad process explains how he/she feels. Then the person who feels not listened to, not supported, can discuss what his/her partner might do to remedy the situation. If the person gets stuck, other members can suggest alternatives. Then the next couple does a quick role play, and the next, until all have demonstrated a communication process that did not go well. (30 minutes for entire sequence)

Interviews

"Last week we talked about how men feel supported. Of course today we will focus on how women feel supported—again through interviews finding out what each woman wants and needs.

Will you pair with a couple you did not work with last week. Again line up your chairs so that a man will interview a woman, not his wife. Again, a woman will sit behind the woman being interviewed and a man will sit behind the man doing the interview. They will act as advocates. The goal is for the interviewer to understand this woman. Interview her on questions like

- What's important in her life?
- How important is a career?
- What does she need from her husband?
- How has life changed for her in the last three years?
- How does she feel about decision making in her family?
- How does she feel about free time, leisure?
- How does she feel about household responsibilities?
- What gets her angry?
- If there was one thing she wished she had from her partner, what would it be?"

Her husband listens. He can ask the interviewer to ask his wife specific questions. (Begin the interviews.) (15 minutes)

Call time for the debriefing. The woman explains how she felt being interviewed, whether she felt understood. The man doing the interviewing reports on how he felt the interview went. The two spouses discuss what they learned from the interviewing process. (10 minutes)

"Let us shift now. Let us do the other set of interviews. The other man in the group will now interview the other woman, continuing the same process." (15 minutes)

(The debriefing, 10 minutes)

Closure

Will the four of you come together. The men will speak, the women will listen. "What did men hear women want to feel supported? What did your wife want? How would she feel supported?" (10 minutes)

Women comment on what was said or their feelings about being supported. Men listen. (10 minutes)

Homework assignment

"Will men practice being supportive of their wives. Decide on what you will do that your wife indicated would represent being supportive. Will you practice it, and next week you will report on how it went.

Next week is the last week. Let's be supportive of each other and have a celebration. Each person bring something for dessert."

Session 5

Objectives

- To report on men's experience of being supportive of their wives.
- To discuss changes in self, being supportive.
- To discuss changes in spouse, in being supportive.
- To define future goals on being supportive.

Opening: reporting on homework

"Will each man report how he was supportive of his wife during the last week. And will each woman respond with how it went."

Putting it all together

Pair with another couple.

"Talk to each other about what you learned in the last four weeks. Again, let us find out in a series of interviews. One person interviews another, not his/her spouse.

How do you think you are different?
Are you more supportive? How?
Give examples of illustrations."

The spouse then replies. She might say that she agrees with what was said. She might add more or she might disagree.

Then there is another series of interviews where the same questions are asked. Afterwards, the spouse replies. This will occur four times. The spouse will reply in terms of what changes have been observed and how she/he feels about what has happened. (30 minutes)

Finally, will each of you finish this sentence, "One thing I would like still is. . . ." Each person will state one thing she/he still wants in order to feel supported. A partner or a member of the group of four may comment or respond to what is said.

Closure

Let's come together as a group. Let's be in a circle as when we started. "We have talked a lot about being supportive and feeling supported. What is one thing you will remember from these five weeks? And, most important, what is one thing you will do for your partner after this course ends? Because, while the course is ending, being supportive does not end. Learning and being supportive, like growing and being, is a lifetime process."

(Each person answers those two questions.) "Will you now as we break for the celebration take a few minutes to tell the people with whom you have worked and whom you found supportive how in this program they have been supportive of you. That feedback is helpful to them and again gives you practice in affirming support."

(The course has been so effective that there has been a five-week, "advanced" program as the couples continue.)

Being Supportive Handout

Being supportive in a marriage means listening to each other. There are two aspects to the message of what is said. One part is the content, the other is the feelings. Listen for both.

The communication process doesn't go well when you

1. Don't listen (as in continuing to read the newspaper).
2. Mind read.
3. "Yes, but."
4. Cross complain.
5. Drift off beam (kitchen sink).
6. Interrupt.
7. Do a standoff.
8. Do heavy silence or escalate quarrels.
9. Don't ever call "stop action" (feeling; check impacts and intents).
10. Insult each other.
11. Don't validate. For example, you say, "That's ridiculous. Now what I'm saying is. . . ."

The communication process generally goes well when you

1. Use stop action.
2. Ask for feedback.

3. Give good feedback.
4. Listen to both content and feeling.
5. Summarize and validate.
6. Check impact with intent.

Example: Training design on a microlab—being supportive in a marriage

A microlab is a two- to three-hour experience in which time is used as a dynamic variable to help people understand their feelings on a subject. The brief time units and different partners encourage participants to respond to questions spontaneously. They are often surprised at what they said and become aware of previously unconscious feelings. A microlab may be used with a church group, at a public presentation for couples, or at an introductory session.

A Microlab: Being Supportive in a Marriage

Overview

The importance of being supportive in a marriage

We do not formally learn how to be supportive. We observe and make sense of what we see.

1. Pair with someone (not your partner) of the opposite gender.
   "When you hear the word *support*, what does it mean to you?
   Does it mean being submissive?
   Does it mean always going places together?"
   (7 minutes)
   "Does it mean always agreeing with the other, that is, about politics, and so on.
   or
   Does it mean always discussing and negotiating?"
   (7 minutes)
2. Switch partners. Continue the discussion.
   "Does being supportive mean
   Providing the money for the other to live well. That is enough?
   or
   Cooking, cleaning, and taking care of the house and the children. That is enough?" (7 minutes)
   Continue the discussion.
   "Does being supportive mean
   Not rocking the boat (not upsetting him or her)?
   or

Always holding someone up who is falling down (like a tomato plant)?
or
Taking care of them when they are sick (like being a nurse)?"
(7 minutes)

3. Pair with your partner (husband/wife).
"Which of these do you feel strongly about—either positively or negatively. Explain." (10 minutes)
(If participants are *not in couples*, omit this.)
4. Pair with someone with whom you have not paired before.
"Name a time in your life (as a child) that you felt supported. What was special about that? Explain." (10 minutes)
"Name a time in your life that you definitely did not feel supported, and it hurt you. Why did you feel hurt? Explain." (10 minutes)
5. Pair with someone else.
"Will you discuss this question. When you as a child looked at other families, what did you see and want for yourself?" (7 minutes)
"When you as a child looked at other families, what did you see, and what were you sure you did not want?" (7 minutes)
6. Join two other groups. Become a group of six.
"As you begin to define being supportive, will each of you discuss what it means to you." (15 minutes)
7. Join your partner (husband/wife).
"Express to your partner what you learned from this discussion. What does being supportive mean to you. Let your partner explain what he/she has learned and what being supportive means to him/her." (10 minutes)
(If not in couples, *omit* this unit.)
8. Stay with your partner. Join one or two other groups.
"As you reflect on this experience, what are other words that express what being supportive means? Some examples are: being flexible, feeling special, feeling cared for, not feeling alone. What words do you use? What does being supportive mean to you, and how can you be supporting? Discuss." (10 minutes)

Summary

Couples groups are an emerging area. In this chapter we have discussed three main types of couples groups beyond marital therapy groups. They are:

1. The mutual support group typically consists of people with a common problem who are working together in a mutually supportive rela-

tionship. Usually, such groups are participant led. While a professional marriage therapist or other helping professional may be involved with the group that involvement will not be as the group leader. It may be as a consultant, as someone who may be involved in organizing the group, or as a member of the advisory board.

2. Marriage enrichment groups are that broad category of groups with a primarily educational focus which are designed to help couples build certain skills. Their theoretical bases are General Systems theory, Rogerian theory, and to some extent behavioral therapy. There are a large number of such programs. Some of the most famous are the Minnesota Couples Communication Program (MCCP) and the Guerney, Conjugal Relationship Enhancement (CRE) Program. Many marriage enrichment programs are conducted through the church, the most famous being Marriage Encounter. Typically, these groups are conducted by people who are specially trained as leaders to conduct a specific program. These leaders may be lay persons or professionals.

3. The third kind of couples group is one in which an expert professional creates a training design for that population. The training which emerges is created from the particular goals developed for that program. It often involves an understanding of the current research in that area, participation of the eventual participants in determining many of the foci of the training design, and an expert in training design. It is conducted by the professional who designed the program or, if the designer is also the consultant, by someone trained by the consultant to conduct the design. It involves creating training designs for couples on a wide variety of subjects determined by the needs expressed by that population. Training design represents the forefront of emerging work with couples groups in an educational mode.

References and Additional Readings

General readings on group dynamics and leading groups

Bertcher, H. J. (1979). *Group participation: Techniques for leaders and members.* Beverly Hills: Sage.

Cathcart, R. S., & Samovar, L. A. (1979). Small Group Communication. Dubuque, IA: Wm. C. Brown.

Corey J., & Corey, M. S. (1982). *Groups: Process and practice.* Belmont, CA: Brooks/Cole Publishing.

Lieberman, M. A. (1979). Analyzing change mechanisms in groups. In M. A. Lieberman & L. Borman (Eds.), Self-help groups for coping with crisis. San Francisco: Jossey-Bass.

Napier, R., & Gershenfeld, M. (1981). *Groups: Theory and experience.* Boston: Houghton Mifflin.

Napier, R., & Gershenfeld, M. (1983). *Making groups work: A guide for group leaders.* Boston: Houghton Mifflin.

Mutual help groups

Bertcher, H., & Maple, F. F. (1977). Creating Groups. Beverly Hills: Sage.

Egan, G. (1976). *The skilled helper.* Monterey, CA: Brooks/Cole Publishing.

Gartner, F., & Riessman, A. (1981). *Help: A working guide to self-help groups.* New York: New Viewpoint Books.

Gottlieb, B. H. (1976). Lay influences on the utilization and provision of health services: a review. *Canadian Psychological Review, 17*(2), 1176–1199.

Lauffer, A. (1978). Natural and extra-professional helping systems. In A. Lauffer (Ed.), *Social planning at the community level.* Englewood Cliffs, NJ: Prentice-Hall.

Lieberman, M. A. (1979). Help seeking and self help groups. In M. Lieberman & L. Borman (Eds.), *Self-help groups for coping with crisis.* San Francisco: Jossey-Bass.

Low, A. A. (1950). *Mental health through will-training.* Boston: Christopher.

Maguire, L. (1983). *Understanding social networks.* Beverly Hills: Sage.

Pearson, R. E. (1983). Support groups: A conceptualization. *Personnel & Guidance Journal, 61,* 361–364.

Raiff, N. R. (1978). *Recovery, Inc.: a study of a self-help organization in mental health.* (Unpublished doctoral dissertation), University of Pittsburgh.

Silverman, P. R. (1980). *Mutual help groups: Organization and development.* Beverly Hills: Sage.

Marriage enrichment

Azrin, N. H., Naster, B. J., & Jones, R. (1973). Reciprocity counseling: A rapid learning-based procedure for marital counseling. *Behavior Research and Therapy, 11,* 365–382.

Doherty, W. J., & Lester, M. E. (1982). Casualties of marriage encounter weekends. *Family Therapy News, 13,* pp. 4, 9.

Elliot, S., & Saunders, B. (1982). The Systems Marriage Enrichment Program: An alternative model based on systems theory. *Family Relations, 31,* 53–60.

Fisher, R. (1973). *The effect of two group counseling methods perceptual congruence in married pairs.* Unpublished doctoral dissertation, Department of Educational Psychology, University of Hawaii.

Garland, D. R. (1978). *Couples communication and negotiation skills.* New York: Family Service Association of America.

Goldstein, A. (1973). A behavior therapy. In R. Corsini (Ed.), *Current psychotherapies.* Itasca, IL: Peacock.

Gordon, T. (1975). *P.E.T.: Parent effectiveness training.* New York: New American Library.

Guerney, B. G., Jr. (1977). *Relationship enhancement: Skill-training programs for therapy, problem prevention and enrichment.* San Francisco: Jossey-Bass.

Gurman, A. S., & Kniskern, D. P. (1977). Enriching research on marital enrichment programs. *Journal of Marriage and Family Counseling, 3,* 3–9.

Harrell, J, & Guerney, B. (1976). Training married couples in conflict negotiation skills. In D. H. Olson (Ed.), *Treating relationships.* Lake Mills, IA: Graphic.

Hof, L., & Miller, W. R. (1980). Marriage enrichment. *Marriage and Family Review, 3,* 1–27.

Hof, L., & Miller, W. R. (1981). *Marriage enrichment: Philosophy, process, and program.* Bowie, MD: Brady.

Hopkins, L., & others. (Eds.). (1978). *Toward better marriages: The handbook of the association of couples for marriage enrichment (ACME).* Winston-Salem, NC: Association of Couples for Marriage Enrichment.

Hopkins, P., & Hopkins, L. (1976). The marriage communication labs. In H. A. Otto (Ed.), *Marriage and family enrichment: New perspectives and programs.* Nashville: Abingdon Press.

Knox, D. (1971). *Marriage happiness: A behavioral approach to counseling.*; Champaign, IL: Research Press.

Mace, D. R. (1975). We call it ACME. *Small Group Behavior, 6,* 31–44.

Mace, D. R., & Mace, V. (1978). The marriage enrichment movement: Its history, its rationale, and its future prospects. In L. Hopkins and others (Eds.), *Toward better marriages: The handbook of the association of couples for marriage enrichment (ACME).* Winston-Salem, NC: Association of Couples for Marriage Enrichment.

Maxwell, J. W. (1979). A rational-emotive approach to strengthening marriage. In N. Stinnett, B. Chesser, & J. DeFrain (Eds.), *Building family strengths: Blueprints for action.* Lincoln: University of Nebraska Press.

Meader, B. D., & Rogers, C. R. (1973). Client-centered therapy. In R. Corsini (Ed.), *Current psychotherapies.* Itasca, IL: Peacock.

Miller, S., Corrales, R., & Wackman, D. B. (1975). Recent progress in understanding and facilitating marital communication. *The Family Coordinator, 24,* 143–152.

Miller, S., Nunnally, E. W., & Wackman, D. B. (1975). *Alive and aware.* Minneapolis: Interpersonal Communication Programs.

Miller, S., Nunnally, E. W., & Wackman, D. B. (1976). Minnesota couples communication program [MCCP]: Premarital and marital groups. In D.H. Olson (Ed.), *Treating Relationships.* Lake Mills, IA: Graphic.

Murrell, S. (1973). *Community psychology and social systems: A conceptual framework and intervention guide.* New York: Behavioral Publications.

National Marriage Encounter. (1978). *Marriage enrichment resource manual.* St. Paul, MN: National Marriage Encounter.

Olson, D. H., & Sprenkle, D. H. (1976). Emerging trends in treating relationships. *Journal of Marriage and Family Counseling, 2,* 317–329.

Otto, H. A. (1975). Marriage and family enrichment programs in North America—report and analysis. *The Family Coordinator, 24,* 137–142.

Otto, H. A. (Ed.). (1976). *Marriage and family enrichment: New perspectives and programs.* Nashville: Abingdon Press.

Patterson, G. R., & Hopps, H. (1972). Coercion, a game for two: Intervention techniques for marital conflict. In R. E. Ulrich & P. T. Mountjoy (Eds.), *The experimental analysis of social behavior.* New York: Appleton-Century-Crofts.

Quick, E., & Jacobs, T. (1973). Marital disturbance in relation to role theory and relationship theory. *Journal of Abnormal Psychology, 82,* 309–316.

Rogers, C. (1961). *On becoming a person.* Boston: Houghton Mifflin.

Schutz, W. C. (1976). *The FIRO scales: Manual.* Palo Alto, CA: Consulting Psychologists Press.

Stuart, R. B. (1974). *Marital pre-counseling inventory: Counselors guide.* (rev. ed.). Champaign, IL: Research Press.

Travis, R. P., & Travis, P. Y. (1975). The pairing enrichment program: Actualizing the marriage. *The Family Coordinator, 24,* 161–165.

Wampler, H. S. (1982). The effectiveness of the Minnesota couple communication program: A review of research. *Journal of Marital and Family Therapy, 8,* 345–355.

Couples by Design

Agazarian, Y., & Peters, R. (1981). *The visible and invisible group.* London: Routledge & Kegan Paul.

Benne, K. D., Bradford, L. P., Gibb, J. R., & Lippitt, R. O. (Eds.). (1975). *The laboratory method of changing and learning.* Palo Alto, CA: Science and Behavior Books.

Galembiewski, R. T., & Blumberg, A. (Eds.). (1978). *Sensitivity training and the laboratory approach.* Itasca, IL: F. E. Peacock.

Kanter, R. M., & Zurther, L. A., Jr. (Eds.). (1973). *The Journal of Applied Behavioral Science,* (Vol. 9). Washington, DC: NTL Institute.

Kinsey, A. C., & Gebhard, P. H. (1953). *Sexual behavior in the human female.* Philadelphia: W. B. Saunders.

Kinsey, A. C., Pomeroy, W. B., & Martin, C. E. (1948). *Sexual behavior in the human male.* Philadelphia: W. B. Saunders.

Lewin, K. (1951). Cartwright. D. (Ed.). *Field theory in social science: Selected theoretical papers.* New York: Harper & Row.

Lewin, K. (1948). Lewin, G. W. (Ed.). *Resolving social conflicts: Selected papers on group dynamics.* New York: Harper & Row.

Marrow, A. J. (1969). *The practical theorist: The life and work of Kurt Lewin.* New York: Basic Books.

Masters, W. H., & Johnson, V. E. (1975). *The pleasure bond.* Boston: Little, Brown.

Miles, M. B. (1981). *Learning to work in groups.* New York: Teachers College Press.

Napier, R., & Gershenfeld, M. (1981). *Groups: theory and experience.* Boston: Houghton Mifflin.

Napier, R., & Gershenfeld, M. (1983). *Making groups work: A guide for group leaders.* Boston: Houghton Mifflin.

Smith, P. B. (1980). *Group processes and personal change.* London: Harper & Row.

SIXTEEN

Jealousy: Its Etiology and Treatment

Albert Ellis, Ph.D.
Institute for Rational-Emotive Therapy

Jealousy in love and marital relationships is so ubiquitous that it is almost synonymous with the human condition. Almost all the great writers, from Euripedes, Homer, Petronius, and Lucian, through Shakespeare and Milton, to Nabakov have used it as a central theme (Ellis, 1954/1962a). Innumerable psychologists and social thinkers have stressed its importance, including Alder (1928), Arnold (1960), Barrell and Richards (1982), Bergler (1952), Berscheid and Fei (1977), Bohm (1961), Bringle (1981), (Buunk (1981, 1982), Clanton and Smith (1977), Ellis (1949a, 1949b), Francis (1977), Freud (1922/1950), Fromm (1947), Hibbard (1975), Hupka (1981), James (1890/1951), Jones (1937), Jung (1928), Klein and Rivière (1964), Pines & Aronson (1981), Reik (1944), Robbé-Grillet (1959), Schoenfeld (1980), Sokoloff (1947), Stekel (1938), Wagner (1976), Walster and Walster (1977), and White (1981a, 1981b).

DEFINITION OF JEALOUSY

As Clanton and Smith (1977) state, jealousy is a Rorschach word that evokes a rich variety of images and associations and that means different things to different people. For the purpose of this chapter, we shall use Ewald Bohm's (1961) definition:

> Jealousy may be defined as a feeling of displeasure accompanied by an urge for release which expresses itself either as fear of imminent loss of the love-object or as displeasure over a real or imagined erotic union that

> the love-object has with someone else. The feeling can be directed toward the love-object, toward the rival, or toward both. (p. 567)

RATIONAL AND IRRATIONAL JEALOUSY

Is jealousy ever rational, or is it usually or always irrational and therefore a disturbed feeling? Authorities significantly disagree on their answers to this question. After giving this matter serious consideration, I came up with a dualistic answer (Ellis, 1972). Normal or healthy jealousy consists of one's caring for a sex-love partner and strongly *wanting* or *preferring* this partner to refrain from becoming too emotionally involved with others and thereby being deprived of companionship and/or sex temporarily or permanently. Irrational jealousy consists of *demanding* or *commanding* that because one cares for a partner, that partner *must* not, under any condition, become emotionally involved with others and thereby deprive one of interest, love, or sex. Rational jealousy sometimes leads to mating problems (because one partner may dislike even the slightest manisfestation of the other's feeling and experiencing the green-eyed monster). But irrational jealousy almost always creates self-defeating feelings of anxiety and hostility in the jealous partner and frequently leads to poor relationships (Bernard, 1971; Ellis, 1954/1962a, 1962b, 1971; Ellis & Harper, 1975; Hibbard, 1975).

IS JEALOUSY INNATE OR SOCIALLY LEARNED?

William James (1890/1951), Alfred Adler (1928), and Havelock Ellis (1936), among many other authorities, have insisted that jealousy is an innate part of the human condition. But James G. Frazer (1910), William Graham Sumner (1940), and Bronislaw Malinowsky (1913), as well as scores of other anthropologists and sociologists, have just as stoutly insisted that sex-love jealousy is largely a product of cultural learning and is almost entirely absent among several peoples, such as the Eskimo, the Singhalese, the Lobi of West Africa, the Marquesans, and various other groups. After reviewing the literature on this question in detail, I concluded in *The American Sexual Tragedy* (Ellis, 1954/1962a) that:

> Sexual jealousy is not a completely innate emotion, since it varies among different peoples of the earth, and is far less prevalent in some cultures than in others. It is largely rooted in human cravings for socioeconomic and sexual monopoly and possessiveness, and in the insecurities, anxieties, and feelings of inadequacy that are engendered when the fulfillment of these cravings is threatened. But desires for sexual monopoly, even though they may possibly have an innate or unlearned element, are closely related to attitudes developed through social learning. Such attitudes appear to be particularly pronounced in cultures which favor romantic and monogamic philosophies of sex, love, and marriage, and to be less pronounced in cultures which favor less romantic and less monogamic philosophies. (p. 152)

The Causes of Rational Jealousy

Rational jealousy seems to be a natural part of the human condition and is a complex feeling with a multiplicity of causes (Arnold, 1960).

Feelings of frustration and loss. Desires and preferences, when thwarted, lead to normal feelings of loss, frustration, and annoyance. If people love others and desire companionship, sexual favors, love, or help, and if their partners give some of these favors instead to another partner they will almost always feel frustrated and annoyed, will be rationally concerned about this, and will (depending on the degree of desire and conception of their loss) feel more or less jealous (Barrell & Richards, 1982; Constantine, 1976; Ellis, 1972; Farber, 1973; Francis, 1977; Seeman, 1981).

Feelings of rejection. Love, when diluted or refused, usually leads to some feelings of rejection and consequently jealousy. When people love and want reciprocation but instead receive neglect, they tend to feel they are lacking in certain desirable qualities, and they feel sad about this. Even though they may be rejected for other reasons (e.g., their partners think they have fine qualities and are too good for them), they easily tend to feel deficient (Clanton & Smith, 1977; Ellis, 1972).

Exclusivity. Where exclusive, sex-love arrangements are agreed upon between partners and monogamic ideals prevail, people tend to feel more threatened by loss of relationships than when exclusivity is not the rule. In the former situations people tend to make themselves more jealous than when they agree on nonmonogamous relations (Daher & Cohen, 1979; Davis, 1936; Ellis, 1954/1962a, 1972; Mazur, 1973).

Ego involvement. Most lovers to some degree involve their ego or self-rating in their choice of and acceptance by their partners. Consequently, when they are neglected or rejected they feel that they have lost *themselves* and not merely their *lover,* and therefore they may become quite jealous. Self-downing, according to Rational-Emotive Therapy (RET), is irrational. When jealousy includes a large element of self-denigration it too is irrational. But ego involvement or vanity is so common in jealousy that I include it here as a semirational cause (Buunk, 1982; Ellis, 1972). As La Rochefoucauld aptly noted, "Jealousy springs more from love of self than from love of another" (*Maximes,* No. 324, 1665).

Cultural learning. Some cultures (such as our own) deliberately foster jealousy by depicting it as a valid sign of intense or "true" love, and many individuals in these cultures adopt these views and deliberately or unconsciously make themselves jealous by following them (Adams, 1980; Ellis, 1954/1962a; Hansen, 1982; Hupka, 1981).

Economic and domestic possessiveness. Most societies (including our own) make marriage and even living together arrangements, (LTAs) economic partnerships and consequently provide financial and domestic penalties for people who break up their relationships. This encourages jealousy (Clanton & Smith, 1977).

Unavailability of new partners. When the availability of new partners is restricted—for example, women are older or men are unprepossessing—jealousy is likely to arise more frequently and more intently than when substitute partners are more easily found.

Dearth of other vital interests. When people have vital, absorbing interests such as work, art, science, or sports, in addition to sex-love affairs, they tend to be less jealous than when their one and only interest in life is their relationship with their beloved (Bringle & Evenbeck, 1979).

Lack of self-sufficiency. Independent, self-sufficient, and resourceful people tend to be less needy of a particular love relationship and hence are less often and less intensely jealous when that relationship may possibly be jeopardized (Ellis, 1972; Hawkins, 1976). People who are healthy and successful tend to be less jealous than those who are physically weak and "unsuccessful" (Schoenfeld, 1980).

History of significant loss of love. People who see themselves as having lost out on significant love relationships in the past (either as children or as adults) and as having suffered keenly because of such losses are wary of present love deprivation and tend to be more jealous than those who have not experienced keen feelings of loss.

External locus of control. Lovers who are field oriented and who view their lives as being particularly affected by external events are prone to feel more jealous than those who have more of an internal locus of control and who feel more in command of their emotional destiny.

Importance of relationship. People who feel that love is a very important part of their lives and that their present relationship is an extremely valuable one tend to feel more jealous than those who give love itself and/or their present relationship less importance (Adams, 1980; Pines & Aronson, 1981; Clanton, 1981; Veereshwar, 1983).

Romantic involvement. Partners who are passionately or romantically in love tend to ask for exclusivity and reciprocal intensity of feeling from their lovers and therefore often make themselves quite jealous (Berscheid & Fei, 1977; Clanton & Smith, 1977; Ellis, 1954/1962a).

Perception of partner as very desirable. People who view their partners as very desirable—particularly those who see their partners as exceptionally attractive physically—frequently are more jealous than those who do not have this perception (White, 1981a).

Causes of Irrational Jealousy

As is true of feelings of rational jealousy, feelings and expressions of irrational jealousy also arise for many different reasons.

Extreme ego insecurity. Irrationally jealous indiviudals often rate themselves as "good" or "worthy" or "acceptable" only when they are strongly loved by their beloveds. They thereby jeopardize their feelings of self-acceptance enormously if they are not loved as much as they *must* be—and they make themselves insensately jealous (Adler, 1928; Bringle & Evenbeck, 1979; Ellis, 1962b, 1972; Hansen, 1982; Klein & Rivière, 1964; Mathes, 1983; Pines & Aronson, 1981; Westheimer, 1983; White, 1981b).

Serious hostility. People who demand that others *always* treat them considerately and fairly, and who make themselves very hostile when others do not act as well as they *must*, frequently work themselves into rages against their love rivals and in some instances become obsessed with harming or killing them (Ellis, 1972, 1977a; Ellis & Gullo, 1972).

Extreme low frustration tolerance. While possible frustration of love and sex desires leads people to feel rational jealousy, the whining attitude that they *must* not be frustrated and that they *can't stand it* if they are constitutes low frustration tolerance (LFT) which, I hypothesize, is significantly correlated with strong feelings of irrational jealousy (Ellis, 1962b, 1972; Ellis & Becker, 1982; Ellis & Harper, 1975).

Dire love need and dependency. People who have a dire need (rather than a strong desire) for their partner's attention and love and who make their happy existence utterly *dependent* on reciprocation tend to be much more jealous than nondependent lovers (Buunk, 1982; Ellis, 1954/1962a, 1972, 1985; White, 1981a, 1981b).

Obsessive-compulsive attachments. Some people are obsessive-compulsively disturbed and may become addicted to many things, including love (Ellis, 1985; Peele, 1975). Such individuals sometimes are insensately jealous of their mates and can act quite self-defeatingly in this respect (Pao, 1982).

Projection. Jealousy often stems from a lover's desire for new or additional partners. Consequently, he or she assumes that the mate is equally interested in others, greatly fears that the mate has such interests, and paranoically "finds" it (Fenichel, 1955).

Misdiagnosing a partner's unloving or provocative behavior. When a partner seems to lose interest or to act unlovingly, many lovers (rightly or wrongly) conclude that he or she is quite interested in someone else and become irrationally jealous. When partners are seen to be unusually interested in another person, jealousy frequently escalates and sometimes becomes enormous (Bernard, 1971; White, 1981a).

CURRENT FORCES IN OUR SOCIETY THAT CONTRIBUTE TO JEALOUSY PROBLEMS

Jealousy has always been something of a problem in Western society because its insistence on monogamous mating and on the linking of romantic love with marriage have encouraged a possessive or property oriented view of mating. Such a view makes husbands and wives (and partners in LTAs) feel particularly aggrieved when their mates show interest in or act amorously toward other eligible individuals. Current forces in our society—both fictional and nonfictional—have exacerbated this problem by often taking a liberal attitude toward open marriage, adultery, prostitution, bisexuality, and other kinds of nonmonogamous relationships. Although, according to some theorists sexual pluralism will ultimately minimize jealousy, in the short run it has not done so. Even the young people of the 1980s have been reared with (to say the least!) conflicting views about the desirability of monogamous mating. And the older (and usually already legally married) members of our culture were reared to be quite monogamous and were later encouraged to throw off strict ties to sex-love exclusivity and to embrace more liberal views. Both groups are now more sexually conflicted than perhaps they have ever been before. And our soaring divorce rates, as well as the large numbers of both single and married people who are far from sexually satisfied, probably mirror and partially stem from this confusion.

Reflecting current inconsistencies in this regard is the fact that sexual and marital conservatism is still highly influential in Western society, as evidenced by the popularity of such institutions and organizations as the Moral Majority, the Right to Life movement, the Vatican under Pope John Paul II, "Born Again" Christianity, and many other sexually conservative groups. On the other hand, innumerable sociological and psychological writers during the last two decades have frankly and openly espoused alternative lifestyles of sex and mating that are quite nonmonogamous. In an effort to prevent the references to this chapter from being impossibly long, let me cite just a few of these sexually liberal authorities: Beecher and Beecher (1971), Boylan (1971), Clanton and Downing (1975), Clanton and Smith (1977), Constantine and Constantine (1973), Ellis (1965a,

1965b, 1971, 1972, 1976a, 1979), English (1968), Garrity (1969), Kerista Village (1979), Libby and Whitehurst, 1977), Mazur (1973), Myers and Leggett (1975), Neubeck (1969), O'Neill and O'Neill (1972), Otto (1970), Ramey (1975), Rimmer (1966, 1972), Rogers (1972), Stayton (1984), Vaughan and Vaughan (1980), and Wagner (1976).

As a result of this conflicting espousal of monogamic and nonmonogamic ideals, and as a result of the unprecedented sexual experimentation that has been taking place among both mated and unmated Westerners for the last two decades, problems of jealousy have probably increased today and seem at the present time to be far from disappearing.

THE TREATMENT OF RATIONAL JEALOUSY IN MATING RELATIONSHIPS

Usually, rational jealousy causes few serious mating problems and even serves in many instances to enhance relationships. For the rationally jealous person overtly or implicity says to his or her partner, "I distinctly prefer you to give me your main sex-love interest, to refrain from being away from me too much, to always (or almost always) have sex only with me, and not to leave me for another partner. But if you don't act the way I prefer, it's inconvenient but not horrible. I can tolerate it and you are still a lovable, undamnable person." If rationally jealous people consistently think, feel, and act this way they rarely make themselves self-defeatingly anxious, depressed, or enraged; and their partners tend to feel loved and flattered and rarely disappointed or upset.

Marriage and family therapists and psychotherapists can help to rationally minimize feelings of jealousy in many ways. They can teach their clients how to take the following attitudes and stances:

1. Recognize and accept the fact that rational jealousy is almost always a concomitant of love and mating and to some extent even "proves" that you truly care for someone.
2. Rational jealousy actually has advantages (e.g., it keeps you on your toes and encourages you to act and express yourself in a loving manner rather than to take your partner for granted.)
3. If you are only rationally jealous, you will feel sorry and disappointed when your partner is not sufficiently companionable or leaves you for someone else, but these are appropriate negative feelings that may help you to do something effective to see more of your partner or to win him or her back. If you have *no* such negative feelings you will tend to have little incentive to get more of what you want, and you will have less of what you don't want from your partner.
4. Because jealousy is often encouraged and exacerbated by lack of communication, you can work at becoming more open and com-

municative with your partner. You can practice expressing your distress assertively but *un*angrily, and you can ask your mate to set limits for his or her outside involvements. You can also encourage your mate to be more candid about his or her feelings for others and to accept reasonable limits and boundaries for the overt expression and acting out of these feelings (Barrell & Richards, 1982; Blood & Blood, 1977; Buunk, 1982; Clanton & Smith, 1977; Ellis, 1979; Francis, 1977).

5. You can explore alternative forms of sex-love relating that will satisfy your and your mate's nonmonogamous desires. Thus, one or both of you can be allowed to have limited outside affairs, you both can do some swinging together, or you can have secret affairs which you both "know" about but tacitly ignore (Constantine & Constantine, 1973; Ellis, 1972; Wagner, 1976; Watson, 1981; Westheimer, 1983).
6. You can use systemic cognitive distraction such as progressive relaxation, meditation, or yoga to keep yourself from worrying obsessively about actual or imagined infidelities. This is not an elegant philosophic method, but it may temporarily deflect you from anxious rumination.
7. You can engage in thought stopping by forcing yourself to stop thinking about or imagining what your sex-love partners are doing.
8. Think about having or getting engaged in outside affairs yourself and keep reminding yourself that by giving yourself leeway to do this you can derive some real advantages from the nonmonogamous involvements of your mate.
9. Focus on the ideals and virtues of freedom and democracy, and realize that by tolerating your mate's affairs you are giving him or her one of the greatest gifts one person can give another—the freedom to be himself or herself without needless criticism and restraint.
10. Work on caring so much for your mate that you actually *want* this partner to love and to engage in sex in the manner that he or she *naturally* wants. By *wanting* this kind of freedom for your beloved you can become more loving and more caring yourself. Show yourself that your partner deserves whatever additional sex and love he or she can harmlessly get (Barrell & Richards, 1982; Ellis, 1965a, 1972; Hawkins, 1976).
11. Try to feel a form of universal love for all people—including your beloved—rather than monolithic, possessive love for only one partner (Veereshwar, 1983).
12. Remind yourself that this too shall pass, and that your mate's involvements and infatuations with others will probably be short-

lived and that if you wait these out, this mate will distinctly (and often gratefully) return to being more interested in you again.

13. Make greater efforts to be more loving and more exciting to your mate and thereby perhaps win back some of the interest and involvement you may have lost (Ellis, 1985).
14. Try to see the situation your mate is involved in more objectively and see how dangerous it really is to largely or completely lose this mate (Buunk, 1982).
15. Consider the possibility of finding another mate who is likely to be and to remain more involved with you than your mate now is and consider taking some steps toward seeking such a partner.
16. No matter how strong your feelings of jealousy are, realize that you create and indulge in these feelings and that therefore you have the power to control and diminish them. You *make* your feelings of love for your beloved and your beloved's feelings for you important; and you can always diminish their importance in your own eyes, mind, and heart. You largely feel the way you think, and *you* control your thinking (Barrell & Richards, 1982; Ellis, 1962b, 1971, 1973, 1985).
17. Work at being less egoistic and less attached to self-aggrandizement. Much jealousy, as La Rochefoucauld noted, stems from self-love—vanity and ego-aggrandizement—rather than love of another. If you learn, in line with the teachings of RET, to fully *accept* yourself rather than to try to *rate* and *deify* yourself, you will be able to see that your beloved's caring for someone else does not in the least diminish *you,* but at worst reduces some of your *pleasure* (Ellis, 1972, 1973, 1976b; Ellis & Harper, 1975; Veereshwar, 1983).
18. Understand and accept the fact that you rarely can control your mate and that you most likely will sabotage rather than help your relationship with him or her if you seriously try to do so. You can sometimes force your beloved to *act* more lovingly toward you, but how he or she underlyingly *feels* about you is much more likely to be enhanced by your permissive rather than your jealously restrictive attitudes and behaviors.
19. Acknowledge that your rivals are deserving of your beloved's affection too because they have made a real effort to win it and because all humans are deserving of being loved (Barrell & Richards, 1982).
20. See that you do not own or possess your beloved because that person is an individual like yourself who cherishes a sense of personal autonomy and integrity (Seidenberg, 1967).

21. Temporarily escape from the situation. Take a short vacation, as Schoenfeld (1980) points out—across the street, across town, or across the country—according to your personal tastes and preferences.
22. At times take a sedative or a few—but only a few!—drinks. Releasing your tensions via physical methods (baths, sauna, or massage) may also be good (Schoenfeld, 1980).
23. Communicate your feelings to others who will empathically listen—or to a tape recorder or to your private journal.
24. Face up to your jealousy and don't try in any way to avoid it. Desensitize yourself to it by looking it right in the eye and showing yourself that it is not as agonizing as you think it is and that you can live with it and still be a happy person.
25. Keep busy! Get involved in work, art, science, exercise, games, hobbies, or anything else. Better yet, get yourself a vital, absorbing interest in some project or cause that is complex, ongoing, and highly involving (Ellis & Becker, 1982; Ellis & Harper, 1975).
26. Use humor to stop taking yourself and your relationship too seriously. Emotional disturbance largely consists of exaggerating the significance of things—of taking them too seriously (Ellis, 1977b, 1981). And viewing events and feelings with a sense of humor is good prophylaxis and therapy against a prolonged indulgence in rational (and irrational!) jealousy. One of the techniques that has been found especially useful in this respect is to have clients sing rational, humorous songs (Ellis, 1977b, 1977c) to themselves when they are anxious, depressed, hostile, self-downing—or jealous. If you are rationally—or irrationally—jealous, you can try singing one of these songs:

    LOVE ME, LOVE ME, ONLY ME! (Sung to the tune of "Yankee Doodle")
    Love me, love me, only me or I'll die without you!
    Make your love a guarantee, so I can never doubt you!
    Love me, love me totally really, really try, dear;
    But if you must rely on me, I'll hate you till I die, dear!
    Love me, love me all the time, thoroughly and wholly!
    Life turns into slushy slime 'less you love me solely!
    Love me with great tenderness, with no ifs or buts, dear;
    For if you love me somewhat less, I'll hate your goddamned guts, dear!
    (Lyrics by Albert Ellis, copyright 1977, Institute for Rational-Emotive Therapy)

    I AM JUST A LOVE SLOB (Sung to the tune of Lady Scott, "Annie Laurie")
    Oh, I am just a love slob,
    Who needs to have you say
    You'll thrill and still adore me
    Forever and a day!

If you won't guarantee
Forever mine to be
I shall whine and scream and make life stormy,
And then la-ay me doon and dee!
(Lyrics by Albert Ellis, copyright 1977, Institute for Rational-Emotive Therapy)

27. Become philosophic. Read philosophic and contemplative literature and poetry. Develop your own sensible philosophy of life by figuring out that this too shall pass, nothing is sacred, life has many possible satisfactions and so on (Schoenfeld, 1980).
28. Accept jealousy as a legitimate aspect of relationships and one that is rarely completely avoidable if you intensely love someone. Understand what jealousy is and what place it plays in normal human affairs (L'Abate, 1983; Daher & Cohen, 1979).
29. See that your mate's love for you is not necessarily limited and is not diminished if he or she also loves others (Daher & Cohen, 1979).
30. Explore the payoffs for jealousy such as renewed sexual excitment and try to preserve these without using jealous mechanisms to do so (Seeman, 1981).

THE TREATMENT OF IRRATIONAL JEALOUSY

Most theories of irrational jealousy tie it, as the Freudians do, to childhood experiences or conditioning. If, for example, you are sure that your mate is being unfaithful, you are obsessed with the horror of infidelity, and you keep spying on him or her and making paranoid accusations that are figments of your imagination, your psychoanalytically oriented therapists will almost certainly (and quite paranoically!) "discover" that this obsessive-compulsive jealousy stems from the "fact" that you had great "separation anxiety" when your mother left you alone in your crib at the age of two. Or you were insanely jealous of your father's attention to your younger sibling when you were three. Or your childhood sweetheart deserted you at the age of five.

Even if these childhood events actually occurred and had a dramatic influence on your life, they hardly *made* you upset because (as virtually all psychoanalysts unscientifically forget) millions of other children had essentially the same "traumatic" experiences and did not neuroticize themselves about them in the first place. Or even if they did, they did not *continue* to plague themselves about these "traumas" in the second place. Early "traumas" or "conditioning" therefore are superficial explanations for disturbed feelings of jealousy (and of anything else). They fail to explain what cognitive and emotional *predispositions* you *bring* to early conditions which *make* you think and feel that these experiences are so "traumatic," and they also fail to show what *persistent* thoughts and feelings you bring to your recollections of these early events that *make* you continue to bother yourself about them.

Psychoanalytic and conditioning explanations for irrational jealousy are superficial and are rarely relevant to treating this feeling. They omit the deep philosophies that more directly and importantly "create" or "cause" both the original and the present-day self-defeating feelings. The more relevant and useful causal explanations lie in the basic, irrational beliefs or crooked thinking which irrationally jealous people are innately prone to invent, *and* which they partly learn from their parents, teachers, and culture.

According to Rational-Emotive Therapy (RET) these irrational beliefs (IBs) practically always take the form of escalating one's desire and preferences into absolutistic, all-pervasive musts and demands. If, for example, you strongly believe "I'd very much prefer my mate to be interested in and sexually relate only to me, but he or she doesn't have to and it will only be frustrating and unfortunate (and not horrible) if she or he leaves me," you will feel rationally or sanely jealous; you will be somewhat concerned about losing this mate; and you will presumably act well in your relationship so that you will ward off your partner's neglecting you or leaving you. But if you absolutistically and dogmatically believe, "Under no condition *must* my mate ignore or leave me. It's awful if this occurs! I won't be able to stand it! His or her loss would make me an inadequate, unlovable person," you will tend to be exceptionally anxious, insecure, self-downing, dependent—and therefore insensately jealous.

Most irrational jealousy then stems from needing rather than preferring your mate's love and from feeling like an inadequate person (rather than a person with some inadequacies) in case you lose it. It often also includes hostility: "My mate *must* love only me and *never* deprive me of affection; and if I am depressed she or he is a rotten, loathsome *person* for making me suffer!" And it usually includes a strong element of low frustration tolerance and depression: "Because I *must* not be deprived of sex and love, and because I *can't stand* the discomfort of deprivation, life is awful and horrible, I can't be happy *at all*, and I may well have to kill myself to rid myself of this impossibly painful condition!"

RET provides people with a number of cognitive, emotive, and behavioral techniques to discover, clarify, and surrender their absolutistic musts and perfectionistic demands and to change them to realistic rational preferences or desires (Ellis, 1962b, 1971, 1973; Ellis & Whiteley, 1979). In addition to the techniques you can teach your clients to minimize their feelings of *rational* jealousy, some of the main RET methods that you can teach them to overcome their *irrational* jealousy and its self-defeating and relationship-sabotaging consequences include the following:

1. Discover your musturbatory, irrational beliefs (IBs) that tend to create insensate jealousy and actively and persistently dispute and challenge them. As noted in *A New Guide to Rational Living* (Ellis

& Harper, 1975), and *A Guide to Personal Happiness* (Ellis & Becker, 1982), some of the main irrational beliefs and their jealousy-inciting derivatives that people in our culture tend to hold are: (*a*) "I *must*—yes, *must*—have love or approval from all the people I find significant, particularly from the one I especially love." (*b*) "I must be thoroughly competent, adequate, and achieving, and my beloved must find that I am." (*c*) "When people act obnoxiously and unfairly toward me, and particularly when they deprive me of my beloved's affection, I must blame and damn them and see them as bad, wicked, or rotten individuals." (*d*) "When I am seriously frustrated, treated unfairly, or rejected, especially by the person I love most, I must view this kind of treatment as awful, terrible, horrible, and utterly catastrophic." (*e*) "My emotional misery, particularly when things go wrong with my love life, stems from external events and pressures, and from the horrible ways in which people treat me, and I have little ability to control or change my anxious and depressed feelings." (*f*) "If something seems dangerous, such as the possible loss of my mate, I must preoccupy myself with it and make myself exceptionally anxious about it." (*g*) "My early and past life are all-important and caused my present problems. If I have been previously rejected by my parents or lovers, I must be completely unlovable and unable to relate to those I love today." (*h*) "Things should turn out better than they often do and people ought to treat me kindly and lovingly at all times. And if things are bad or people treat me unlovingly, it is awful and horrible and I will never be able to find good solutions to life's grim realities."

After discovering irrational beliefs such as these which significantly contribute to your extreme feelings of jealousy, use the logical, empirical, and antidogmatic methods of scientific thinking to dispute them. Thus, ask yourself: "Where is the evidence that I *must* have my beloved's total interest and affection? Why is it *awful* if things go wrong and if I am not fully loved? Although I certainly do not like being unloved, in what way can I not *stand* being amatively deprived? How does my being ignored by my mate make me an *inadequate* person? Where is it written that my beloved has *no right* to care for others besides or instead of me? Why *must* life be totally joyless and not worth living if I am not loved in exactly the way I want to be?" By continuing to dispute your irrational beliefs in a vigorous, consistent manner, you will tend to minimize them, accept the view that monogamous love may be highly preferential but not *necessary,* and thereby become at worst rationally instead of irrationally jealous of your mate (Ellis, 1972, 1985; Hibbard, 1975).

2. You can replace your irrational beliefs that create insensate jealousy with rational or coping self-statements which you can repeat to

yourself many times and which you keep thinking about until you really believe them. For example: "I do not *need* love, no matter how strongly I *want* it!" "If my beloved is treating me unfairly, that's too damned bad but hardly awful!" "No matter how often I fail in love, that never makes me a rotten, undeserving person!" "Though I'll never like my beloved's neglecting me, I can definitely stand it!"

3. You can practice rational-emotive imagery (Ellis & Becker, 1982; Maultsby, 1975; Maultsby & Ellis, 1974) to change your inappropriate feelings of anxiety, self-downing, or hostility about your partner's real or imagined infidelities into appropriate feelings of concern, disappointment, or frustration. Thus, you can vividly imagine your partner caring for someone else, let yourself feel horrified about this, work on changing your feelings of horror to keen disappointment (mainly by changing your irrational ideas to more rational ideas), and keep practicing the appropriate feeling and the rational ideas for 30 or 60 days in a row until you retrain yourself so that whenever you think of or actually experience your partner's neglect, you feel sorry and disappointed but not obsessively horrified.
4. You can do in vivo desensitizing homework assignments which will let you take the risks of feeling jealous (instead of avoiding them) and, while taking them, actively work on yourself to ameliorate your irrational jealousy. Thus, you can deliberately date a very attractive and nonmonogamous sex-love partner to give yourself actual practice in coping with your feelings of insensate jealousy.
5. You can use techniques of behavioral reinforcement when you think and act less jealously. For example, you can reward yourself with a pleasant activity (music, food, socializing, or what you will) *after* you work on changing those irrational beliefs that are making you obsessively jealous. Or you can reinforce yourself with something you enjoy *after* you have stopped yourself from compulsively checking up on a mate about whom you are irrationally jealous.
6. You can use negative reinforcers—that is, stiff penalties—whenever you foolishly succumb to your irrational jealousy and thereby train yourself to indulge in that jealousy less frequently. If, for instance, you want to stop plaguing your partner about his or her supposed infidelities, you can do something very unpleasant such as burn a $20 dollar bill or eat some obnoxious food every time you plague him or her.
7. You can role play situations in which you often feel and act very jealous, and in these role plays, you can practice acting differently. If, for example, you are a male who is insanely jealous of your wife's flirting with other men, you can arrange for one of your fe-

male friends to play your wife's part and practice feeling less jealous by speaking to your "wife" less angrily about her "flirtation."

8. In real life situations, you can use Kelly's (1955) technique of fixed role playing and force yourself to act unjealously for a whole week with a mate about whom you are actually very jealous until you become habituated to more rational feelings of jealousy with him or her.

The foregoing are some of the main RET techniques that you can teach clients to use when they exhibit obsessive-compulsive, violent, irrational forms of jealousy. With these same clients, you can also show them how to use and encourage them to employ some of the many methods listed in the previous section of this chapter which may be effective for rationally jealous people.

Summary

Feelings of jealousy may be rational or irrational and are so ubiquitous in love and marital relationships that they seem to be a natural part of the human condition. Rational jealousy largely arises when lovers strongly *prefer* reciprocation and companionship from their partners, while irrational jealousy stems from their thinking that they absolutely *must* have the degree of affection that they strongly desire. Feelings of jealousy stem from innate predispositions interacting with social learning. There are many important causes of both rational and irrational jealousy, most of them connected with feelings of frustration, possessiveness, ego involvement, and the importance given to love in general and to the continuation of a particular relationship. Intense feelings of jealousy have been a problem for people in Western civilization for many years but have recently been exacerbated by conflicting attitudes toward monogamic union. Many methods of dealing with both rational and irrational jealousy exist and they have been particularly used in rational-emotive and cognitive-behavioral therapy. As these techniques continue to be used and evaluated, even more effective treatment methods will probably be discovered.

References

Adams, V. (1980, May). Getting at the heart of jealous love. *Psychology Today*, pp. 38–47, 102–105.

Adler, A. (1928). *Understanding human nature*. London: Allen and Unwin.

Arnold, M. B. (1960). *Emotion and personality*. New York: Columbia University Press.

Barrell, J. L., & Richards, A. C. (1982). Overcoming jealousy: An experiential analysis of common factors. *Personnel and Guidance Journal, 61*, 40–47.

Beecher, M., & Beecher, W. (1971). *The mark of Cain: An anatomy of jealousy*. New York: Harper & Row.

Bergler, E. (1952). *The superego*. New York: Grune & Stratton.

Bernard, J. (1971). Jealousy in marriage. *Medical Aspects of Human Sexuality, 5*(4), 200–215.

Berscheid, E., & Fei, J. (1977). Romantic love and sexual jealousy. In G. Clanton & L. G. Smith (Eds.), *Jealousy* (pp. 101–109). Englewood Cliffs, NJ: Prentice-Hall.

Blood, R., & Blood, M. (1977). Jealousy workshops. In G. Clanton & L. G. Smith (Eds.), *Jealousy* (pp. 199–207). Englewood Cliffs, NJ: Prentice-Hall.

Bohm, E. (1961). Jealousy. In A. Ellis & A. Abarbanel (Eds.), *Encyclopedia of sexual behavior* (pp. 567–574). New York: Hawthorne.

Boylan, B. (1971). *Infidelity*. Englewood Cliffs, NJ: Prentice-Hall.

Bringle, R. G. (1981). Conceptualizing jealousy as a disposition. *Alternative Life Styles, 4*, 274–290.

Bringle, R. G., & Evenbeck, S. E. (1979). The study of jealousy as a dispositional characteristic. In M. Cook and G. Wilson (Eds.), *Love and attaction: An international conference*. Oxford: Pergamon Press.

Buunk, B. (1981). Jealousy in sexually open marriages. *Alternate Lifestyles, 4*(3), 357–372.

Buunk, B. (1982). Strategies of jealousy. *Family Relations, 31*. 13–18.

Clanton, G. (1981). Frontiers of jealousy research: Introduction to the special issue on jealousy. *Alternate Lifestyles, 4*(3), 259–273.

Clanton, G., & Downing, C. (1975). *Face to face to face: An experiment in intimacy*. New York: Dutton.

Clanton, G., & Smith, L. G. (Eds.). (1977). *Jealousy*. Englewood Cliffs, NJ: Prentice-Hall.

Constantine, L. L. (1976). Jealousy From theory to intervention. In D. H. L. Olson (Ed.), *Treating relationships*. Lake Mills, IA: Graphic Publishers.

Constantine, L. L., & Constantine, J. J. (1973). *Group marriage*. New York: Collier.

Daher, D. M., & Cohen, M. (1979). Jealousy workshop. A conceptual base and format. *Personnel and Guidance Journal, 57*, 480–483.

Davis, K. (1936). Jealousy and sexual property. *Social Forces, 14*, 395–405.

Ellis, A. (1949a). A study of human love relationships. *Journal of Genetic Psychology, 75*, 61–76.

Ellis, A. (1949b). A study of the love emotions of American college girls. *International Journal of Sexology, 3*, 15–21.

Ellis, A. (1962a). *The American sexual tragedy*. New York: Lyle Stuart and Grove Press. (Original work published 1954)

Ellis, A. (1962b). *Reason and emotion in psychotherapy*. Secaucus, NJ: Citadel Press.

Ellis, A. (1965a). *Sex without guilt*. (rev. ed.). New York: Lyle Stuart and North Hollywood: Wilshire Books.

Ellis, A. (1965b). *Suppressed: Seven key essays publishers dared not print*. Chicago: New Classics House.

Ellis, A. (1971). *Growth through reason*. North Hollywood, CA.: Wilshire Books.

Ellis, A. (1972). *The civilized couple's guide to extramarital adventure.* New York: Wyden.

Ellis, A. (1973). *Humanistic psychotherapy: The rational-emotive approach.* New York: McGraw-Hill.

Ellis, A. (1976a). *Sex and the liberated man.* Secaucus, NJ: Lyle Stuart.

Ellis, A. (1976b). *RET abolishes most of the human ego.* New York: Institute for Rational-Emotive Therapy.

Ellis, A. (1977a). *Anger: How to live with and without it.* Secaucus, NJ: Citadel Press.

Ellis, A. (1977b). Fun as psychotherapy. *Rational Living, 12*(1), 2–6.

Ellis, A. (1977c). *A garland of rational songs.* Songbook and cassette recording. New York: Institute for Rational-Emotive Therapy.

Ellis A. (1979). *The intelligent woman's guide to dating and mating.* Secaucus, NJ: Lyle Stuart.

Ellis, A. (1981). The use of rational humorous songs in psychotherapy. *Voices, 16* (4), 29–36.

Ellis, A. (1985). Love and its problems. In A. Ellis & M. E. Bernard (Eds.), *Clinical applications of rational-emotive therapy* (pp.31–53). New York: Plenum Publishing Corp.

Ellis, A., & Becker, I. (1982). *A guide to personal happiness.* North Hollywood, CA: Wilshire Books.

Ellis, A. & Gullo, J. (1972). *Murder and assassination.* Secaucus, NJ: Lyle Stuart.

Ellis, A., & Harper, R. A. (1975). *A new guide to rational living.* North Hollywood, CA: Wilshire Books.

Ellis, A., & Whiteley, J. M. (Eds.). (1979). *Theoretical and empirical foundations of rational-emotive therapy.* Monterey, CA: Brooks/Cole Publishing.

Ellis, H. (1936). *Studies in the psychology of sex.* New York: Random House.

English, O. S. (1968). Values in psychotherapy: The affair. *Voices, 3*(4), 9–14.

Farber, L. H. (1973). On jealousy. *Commentary, 56,* 50–58.

Fenichel, O. (1955). *The psychoanalytic theory of neurosis.* London: Routledge & Kegan Paul.

Francis, J. L. (1977). Toward the management of heterosexual jealousy. *Journal of Marriage and Family Counseling, 3*(4), 61–69.

Frazer, J. G. (1910). Totemism and exogamy. London: Macmillan.

Freud, S. (1950). Certain neurotic mechanisms in jealousy, paranoia and homosexuality. In S. Freud, *Collected papers* (Vol. 2). London: Hogarth. (Original work published 1922)

Fromm, E. (1947). *Escape from freedom.* New York: Rinehart.

Garrity, J. (pseudonym: J.) (1969). *The sensuous woman.* Secaucus, NJ: Lyle Stuart.

Hansen, G. L. (1982). Reactions to hypothetical, jealousy producing events. *Family Relations, 31,* 513–518.

Hawkins, R. G., Jr. (1976). Jealousy: A solvable problem. *Journal of Sex Education and Therapy, 2*(1), 39–42.

Hibbard, R. W. (1975). A rational approach to treating jealousy. *Rational Living, 10,* 25–27.

Hupka, R. B. (1981). Cultural determinants of jealousy. *Alternate Lifestyles, 4*(3), 310–356.

James, W. (1951). *Psychology*. New York: Dover. (Original work published 1980)

Jones, E. (1937). *Papers on psychoanalysis*. London: Baliere, Tindall and Cox.

Jung, C. G. (1928). *Contributions of analytical psychology*. New York: Harcourt Brace Jovanovich.

Kelly, G. (1955). *Psychology of personal constructs*. New York: W. W. Norton.

Kerista. (1979). *Kerista Village handbook*. San Francisco (P.O. Box 1174), CA: Kerista Village.

Klein, M., & Rivière, J. (1964). *Love, hate and reparation*. London: Hogarth.

L'Abate, L. (1983). Jealousy. *Medical Aspects of Human Sexuality, 17* 121–122.

Libby, R., & Whitehurst, R. N. (1977). *Marriage and alternatives: Exploring intimate relationships*. Glenview, IL: Scott, Foresman.

Malinowski, B. (1913). *The family among the Australian aborigines*. London: Macmillan.

Mathes, E. W. (1983). Jealousy. *Medical Aspects of Human Sexuality, 17*(4), 99–102.

Maultsby, M. C., Jr. (1975). *Help yourself to happiness.* New York: Institute for Rational-Emotive Therapy.

Maultsby, M. C., Jr., & Ellis, A. (1974). *Technique for using rational emotive imagery*. New York: Institute for Rational-Emotive Therapy.

Mazur, R. M. (1973). *The new intimacy: Open-ended marriage and alternative life-styles*. Boston: Beacon Press.

Myers, L., & Leggitt, H. (1975). *Adultery and other private matters*. Chicago: Nelson-Hall Publishers.

Neubeck, G. (Ed.). (1969). *Extramarital relations*. Englewood Cliffs, NJ: Prentice-Hall.

O'Neill, N., & O'Neill, G. (1972). *Open marriage*. New York: Evans.

Otto, H. (Ed.). (1970). *The family in search of a future*. New York: Appleton-Century-Crofts.

Pao, P. (1982). Patholic jealousy. *Medical Aspects of Human Sexuality, 16*(5), 126–132.

Peele, S. (1975). Love and addiction. New York: Taplinger.

Pines, A., & Aronson, E. (1981). Polyfidelity: An alternate lifestyle without jealousy? *Alternate Lifestyles, 4*(31), 373–392.

Ramey, J. W. (1975). *Intimate friendships*. Englewood Cliffs, NJ: Prentice-Hall.

Reik, T. (1944). *A psychologist looks at love*. New York: Rinehart.

Rimmer, R. (1966). *The Harrad experiment*. New York: Bantam Books.

Rimmer, R. (1972). Structural group marriage will become a common experience. *Sexual Behavior, 2*(3), 10–11.

Robbé-Grillet, A. (1959). *Jealousy*. New York: Grove Press.

Rogers, C. R. (1972). *Becoming partners: Marriage and its alternatives*. New York: Delacorte.

Schoenfeld, E. (1980). *Jealousy: Taming the green-eyed monster*. New York: Holt, Rinehart & Winston.

Seeman, M. (1981). Coping with jealousy. *Medical Aspects of Human Sexuality, 15*(5), 52b–52p.

Seidenberg, R. (1967). Fidelity and jealousy: Socio-cultural considerations. *Psychoanalytic Review, 54* 583–608.

Sokoloff, B. (1947). *Jealousy: A psychiatric study*. New York: Howell, Saskin.

Stayton, W. R. (1984). Lifestyle spectrum 1984. *Siecus Report, 12*(3), 1–4.

Stekel, W. (1938). Jealousy. In A. Forbath (Ed.), *Love and marriage*. New York: Liveright.

Sumner, W. G. (1940). *Folkways*. Boston: Ginn and Company.

Vaughan, J., & Vaughan, P. (1980). *Beyond affairs*. Hilton Head, SC: Dialog Press.

Veereshwar, S. A. (1983). Jealousy and the abyss. *Journal of Humanistic Psychology, 23*(2), 70–84.

Wagner, J. (1976). Jealousy, extended intimacies and sexual affirmation. *Etcetera, 33*, 269–288.

Walster, E., & Walster, G. W. (1977). The social psychology of jealousy. In G. Clanton and L. G. Smith (Eds.), *Jealousy* (pp. 91–100). Englewood Cliffs, NJ: Prentice-Hall.

Watson, M. A. (1981). Sexually open marriage: Three perspectives. *Alternative Lifestyles, 4*(1), 3–21.

Westheimer, R. (1983). A little jealousy is not a dangerous thing. *Forum, 12*(5), 72–73.

White, G. L. (1980). Inducing jealousy: A power perspective. *Personality and Social Psychology Bulletin, 6*, 222–227.

White, G. L. (1981a) Jealousy and partner's perceived motives for attraction to a rival. *Social Psychology Quarterly, 44* 24–30.

White, G. L. (1981b). Relative involvement, inadequacy, and jealousy. *Alternative Lifeystyles, 4*(3), 291–309.

SEVENTEEN

The Ego-Analytic Approach to Sexual Apathy

Bernard Apfelbaum, Ph.D. and Constance Apfelbaum
Berkeley Sex Therapy Group

"We have made many mistakes. A lot of the work we have done has been inadequate, but our greatest failure has been the failure to convince medicine first and the behavioral sciences second, that sex is a natural function. Everyone of you know it, but none of you live it and very few of you practice it. And until we accept the concept of sex as a natural function . . . we will always be in difficulty in our therapy." (Masters, 1983)

Masters is saying here, at the end of a *Three Decade Restrospective of the Masters and Johnson Institute* (1983), that his greatest failure has been to convince his colleagues of this simple dictum that they not only already know but that is seemingly so obvious and uncontroversial as to be impossible *not* to be convinced of. Although this may look baffling at first it should be clear that it is hard to convince people of something they think they agree with. What may be less clear is that it is hard to *live* in accordance with the seemingly obvious dictum that sex is a natural function. (This is the reverse of Freud's famous remark to the effect that his critics attacked his theories by day but confirmed them at night.) It was perhaps a measure of Masters's pessimism that he did not elaborate on this comment and made it almost in passing at the end of his address.

Since we all "know," in Masters' words, that sex is a natural function, what prevents us from "living" this knowledge? The answer is performance anxiety. It is performance anxiety that drives us to try to summon up sexual arousal from within rather than to appreciate its conditional and dependent nature. However, performance anxiety alone would not create the widespread and intractable resistance to which Masters refers.

Although it has yet to be noted, what has subtly undermined the Masters and Johnson insight is the whole climate of opinion best represented by the doctrine of self-responsibility, according to which one must indeed summon up sexual arousal from within. This doctrine underlies both commonsense and professional thinking about sex, and among professionals underlies the thinking of both sex therapists and general psychotherapists.

Helen Singer Kaplan (1974b) is the most well known exponent of the self-responsibility doctrine in the field, as well as one of the most influential contributors to the field. The work in which she makes her position most explicit, *Disorders of Sexual Desire* (1979), is also one of the few discussions of sexual apathy in the field and is still the only book-length treatment. In contrast to Masters and Johnson's stimulus-dependent conception, Kaplan's view is that sexual arousal is self-generated, even arbitrary, dependent only on the individual's willingness to make the necessary mental effort required to focus on physical sensation or on sexual fantasies. In her perspective sexual apathy represents an unconscious unwillingness to make this effort, a *withholding* of sexual response.

The idea that sexual arousal is choosable and also may require effort is at odds with Masters and Johnson's conception of sex as a natural function, that is, with the idea that sexual arousal happens spontaneously if it is not blocked by performance anxiety. Kaplan asserts that the Masters and Johnson approach is ineffective in the treatment of sexual apathy and that this is so because they do not deal with the unwillingness to become sexually aroused. It is *their* view that is unique. Kaplan's conception underlies the standard psychodynamic formulation of sexual apathy as a withholding response motivated by anger, by wishes to punish and thwart the partner expressed passive-aggressively. This formulation coincides with the commonsense view of *frigidity*, a condition typically thought of as motivated by stubbornness or spite, especially when it is chronically refractory to well-meaning efforts.

This is the conception of sexual apathy that is also held by those who are sexually apathetic. Self-attribution of responsibility for the condition is always present, we believe, although it may be vigorously denied and externalized. Lack of sexual arousal, especially when it is chronic, is experienced by the afflicted person as a humiliating failure, an incriminating perverseness. The sexually apathetic person exemplifies Masters' observation that one can know that sex is a natural function and yet not know it. In other words, people suffering from this condition have the idea that sex is a natural function but that *they* are unnatural.

Attribution of responsibility to oneself is what creates performance anxiety, leading to desperate efforts to work at sexual arousal (or, eventually, to resignation), as can be seen from this client's self-talk:

Nan: *[reading from her notes on the second sensate focus assignment]* Up 'til now, if you asked me how I felt when Len touched me,

I'd say "Blank." I'd say that I had no feelings at all. Then the first time we did the assignment I noticed that it wasn't so much a blank feeling as that I was turning it off—that I didn't want to think about it or feel about it.

I realized that when Len is touching me I don't want to be aware of anything, especially my feelings, my emotions. I seem to focus all my thoughts on how I should be reacting to what he's doing, and nothing of what I'm feeling.

As I started to write about the passive front [meaning the sequence in which she was supine and Len did the touching] and I thought about it—I didn't really think about it while he was doing it, but when I started writing about it—I started to feel really angry at having to be touched, and I didn't know if it was at him or men in general. I couldn't define it in myself. I was downright mad at having to be touched.

Then what confused me even further is that I knew I wanted to be touched, and I wanted to be loved—but the two don't seem to coincide—and with this normal-type life that I want to have it wouldn't work.

I sat and thought about it a long time and I couldn't get at what was causing it, or the root of it. I think the argument we had earlier in the day might have something to do with it, but I would say there is a sense of—I would say most of the time—when Len first starts to touch me I feel angry or irritated or hostile at the touch. I guess that's why I would rather touch *him*.

Then a lot of questions started going through my mind, like: "Why can't I just enjoy making love?" "Why can't I just accept it for what it's supposed to be: an expression of love and closeness, a fulfillment of needs and desires?" I got very frustrated with myself at that point.

This is a description of performance anxiety, or as we prefer to call it, "response anxiety" (Apfelbaum, 1984a,b). Nan has been hoping to get by by being compliant and by being the aggressor, in order to lead "this normal-type life that I want." Noticing that she's angry when Len touches her makes her feel "very frustrated" with herself. She wonders why she can't just accept sex for what it is, especially since she has never thought it was that important. She feels she is being mysteriously wayward. After all, she does want to be touched. She's even afraid that Len will give up on her, that he will feel rejected and will stop approaching her. He might even leave her to find a woman who responds normally.

Len: She's always been real slow to get into it, and I knew from the beginning—I've had to be real patient, real careful. At first [in high school, at the beginning of the relationship] she would just freeze up. The other guys, they would back off, but I knew what I wanted.

> So, I just took plenty of time and all, and she would gradually come around.
>
> She really enjoys it once we get started, but there's this resistance she's got. Once she gets over it there's no problem and she's the best in bed I've ever had. I know she really wants it; she's just afraid of being a bad girl. *[Laughs.]* I don't need to tell *you* about all that.
>
> I just wish by now [after 14 years, 11 of them married] it wasn't still always so much work to get her into it, but I know she really wants it.

Len has no doubt that Nan suffers from a neurotic resistance to sex. It would be hard for him to have thought anything else, especially since Nan agrees with him. Her upbringing, as might be expected, was strict and cloistered, offering a seemingly obvious explanation for her problem.

Beyond that, both Len and Nan are influenced by the climate of opinion that holds Nan responsible for her apathy. Although the self-responsibility doctrine is now widespread among psychotherapists generally, as we have noted, as well as in the recent self-help literature and in self-mastery training programs (Mind Dynamics, est, Visualizations), it is especially well received in the sex field because it is thought that the alternative is *partner* responsibility, and partner responsibility raises the spector of the harried husband who must somehow divine his wife's sexual wishes, a legacy of the pre-Masters and Johnson marriage manuals. (In the present case example, Len already is a conscientious and dedicated sex partner.)

However, even when the husband supposedly was responsible, sooner or later it was up to the wife to respond. More to the point, both the self-responsibility and partner-responsibility doctrines assume that one or the other partner must *do* something. Either Nan must discover what she wants and learn to ask for it, or Len must discover it and give it to her. Both doctrines rest on the assumption that our sexual needs are simple and local, an assumption so familiar that it is built into the DSM III (1980) in which it is expected that even a third party, the clinician, can determine whether stimulation is sufficient for sexual arousal: "If there is *inadequate sexual stimulation* [in boldface in the original], in either focus, intensity, or duration, the diagnosis of Psychosexual Dysfunction involving excitement or orgasm is not made" (p. 278). Notice that "stimulation" here is unapologetically specified in purely local, physical terms. "Focus, intensity, and duration" do not, of course, refer to mental or emotional stimulation.

The DSM III's concept of inadequate sexual stimulation is integral to the self- and partner-responsibility doctrines. The message is that beyond a certain point you have gotten your due, and beyond that point sexual arousal is up to you. This point even has a public verifiability. It can be certified by the clinician that your partner has done all he or she can. Lack of arousal then calls for the diagnosis of "Psychosexual Dysfunction," meaning that you are inhibiting or resisting sexual response.

In contrast, it is our position that stimulation is inadequate in all cases of psychosexual dysfunction. It only appears adequate if assessment is restricted to physical stimulation. Stimulation can be adequate in "focus, intensity, and duration" while also being coercive, timid, overly conscientious, or mechanical. Also, arousal and orgasm can be responsive to emotional stimulation alone, happening even when physical stimulation is inadequate. However, as we will discuss later, the dependency of sexual response on the emotional climate of the encounter can be difficult to detect. Also, we are arguing that there is a general antipathy to such dependency. To paraphrase Masters, everyone knows that mental and emotional stimulation are crucial to sexual arousal and may even be what sexual arousal is all about, but "none of you live it and very few of you practice it."

Again the problem is response (performance) anxiety. We do not have much patience with those who persist in not becoming aroused and both our diagnoses and our therapies reflect this. Solutions are offered on the level of slogans about responsibility because we *feel* responsible for our own and our partner's arousal. Marital partners, especially, feel that sexual response is something they owe one another, and so they look for moral rather than psychological guidance, for rules that they can appeal to allay feelings of guilt and inadequacy. The psychological answer, that sexual arousal is no one's responsibility or, better put, is not a matter of responsibility, offers no immediate, obvious relief from response anxiety.

To say that someone is frigid or is nonresponsive in sex is to make a moral, not a psychological, statement. The idea is that the person *should* be responding to sex in one particular way: affirmatively.

If we put aside our assumptions about how one *should* respond in sex it becomes apparent that the sexually apathetic person is highly responsive, a feature of this condition that both we and Kaplan focus on, although our effort is to encourage this responsiveness, hers to discourage it. Little or no attention is paid to the way that a patient like Nan actually *is* responding, either by sex therapists or by general psychotherapists. Nan's initial report that she was "blank," that she "had no feelings at all," is accepted and taken as a point of departure. Her apathy then is explained as an expression of anger, or as a power play, or as a holdover from childhood. The psychodynamic therapist then looks for collateral examples of this reaction pattern in other areas. The sex therapist attempts more directly to promote affirmative responses. In other words, there is general agreement that what Nan is doing is withholding or inhibiting response and hence her symptomatic experience is not unpacked.

We introduce the term *unpacking* because we think that the necessary clarifications are conceptual as well as experiential. We think that what

Nan is responding to is the whole climate of opinion we have just reviewed. She is a victim of the belief that stimulation can be adequate even when it is not, and so she must conclude that she is resisting arousal. She fully embraces the doctrine of self-responsibility, being unable to think of Len as in any way contributing to her lack of arousal. Any awareness of Len's role is blocked by their shared expectation that she should be responding affirmatively. This whole train of thought is the cognitive structure of Nan's response anxiety.

Recall that Nan only began to notice the responses she actually was having when she did the second sensate focus assignment, and even then it was not until she wrote her notes on it that her experience began to unfold. First she saw that the state that she had always called blank was the consequence of her not wanting to have the reactions she was having. Then she saw that she was trying to summon up the right response, to "focus all my thoughts on how I should be reacting to what he's doing." This is the beginning of some recognition of how much pressure she is under, although she does not yet feel entitled to call it that.

This pressure leads to the momentary irritation that Nan then detects in herself. She then notes how she ordinarily blocks this response by immediately touching Len (although this solution is, of course, prevented by the structure of the assignment). The irritation also is disqualified by Nan telling herself that there is no reason to feel irritated, that she is just being touched, something that she knows she wants, and why "can't I just accept it for what it's supposed to be?" She tells herself that Len is just expressing love and closeness, meaning that her response is neurotic and perverse. This makes her feel "very frustrated" with herself.

It should be clear even from this brief snapshot that sex for Nan was a punishing experience. Perhaps it also is clear that to skip over the details of Nan's experience, to construe it as some kind of withholding or even as representing a wish not to be aroused, risks intensifying Nan's response anxiety and her punitive self-attributions. What made the details of Nan's experience available to us (and to her) was, we believe, not only that we require detailed write-ups but also that we attempt to maintain a position of neutrality rather than of advocacy, an essential feature of the Masters and Johnson approach.

In asserting the centrality of response (performance) anxiety we appear to many to be confining our explanations to the surface of the problem since such anxiety is typically thought of as conscious. Thus, Kaplan (1979) refers to "deeper" sexual fears which, "in contrast to performance fears . . . are not usually recognized by patients" (p. 29). To us, this is a critical misperception on the clinical level. As we see it the prevalence of unconscious response (performance) anxiety not only vastly outweighs its conscious forms but is the anxiety that is by far the most difficult to bring to consciousness.

The very fact that response anxiety is thought of as a conscious and easily demonstrable anxiety is itself evidence of how difficult it is for the patient or the clinician to detect its unconscious forms. Those who can report response anxiety are a tiny fraction of those who feel it. Few feel entitled to think of themselves as under pressure in sex. Everyone, including Nan, thinks that she should be able to respond affirmatively. It is her responsibility. Who is there to notice the oppresive effect of this universal expectation? It is part of Nan's oppressed position in sex that she does not feel entitled to the experience of oppression itself.

As can be seen from this next excerpt, response anxiety is especially difficult to detect in the patient who is aware of and expresses complaints, the patient who acts rejecting but nonetheless does not feel entitled to act this way. The pressure to respond affirmatively is still there, as is the self-attribution of responsibility and the self-condemnations, but their effects are only to make the patient feel trapped when faced with a sexual initiative. Typically, the patient also does not feel entitled to the experience of being trapped and is only aware of the end product, an aversive response (often accompanied by nausea, as if something is being forced down one's throat), or may have tantrumlike reactions which make response anxiety all the more difficult to detect and to demonstrate to the patient.

Pat, unlike Nan, is aware of feeling oppressed and complains that sex with her husband has gotten impersonal and obligatory. She does seem to feel entitled to her complaints but then she, in effect, gags on them. On closer examination we find that it is the resulting nausea that strengthens her resolve to avoid all sexual contact with her husband:

Pat: The cuddling and the touching is all right, but when it turns to more—like french kissing, it's like when we're cuddling or touching or something, that's all right as long as I know that that's all there's going to be. I don't want actual intercourse. I don't feel good about making love now.

It's like it's an obligation: I'm supposed to do this; I'm his wife. And I don't like it to be that way.

Therapist 1: That sounds like a *decision,* but before you made it sound more like a gut reaction.

Pat: That's it. Now that I'm talking about it it's kind of a decision, but when we're together—it's. . . .

Therapist 1: Automatic?

Pat: It's automatic. It's like there's never been a conscious decision or anything like that. When we're together, a good example is, we could be kissing or touching, but the minute he holds on and tries to make it a quote-quote passionate kiss or a french kiss or something like that, my stomach actually just ties up in knots, just—

[makes twisting/wringing motion with both hands]—and I don't like that. I don't like that at *all.*

Therapist 2: What do you anticipate?

Pat: Not enough touching. And I like to be held. It seems so impersonal when we make love. It used to be we would lay there in bed together and just hold for a while, you know, afterwards and everything.

Therapist 1: It's important that you get *revolted.* You're saying it's a real—you made that gesture *[imitates it]*, a real twisting. . . . You really get repelled. It's really like strong feeling.

Pat: It is. It's a very strong feeling. That's what I can't understand.

Therapist 1: Oh, you don't understand that; you mean it surprises you that you feel that strongly.

Pat: Uh-huh.

Therapist 1: My guess is that it's real hard for you to reject Bill. It's like you're swallowing it.

It is our impression that in cases like this the clinician will agree with Pat that her aversion is caused by her dissatisfactions. After all, she says that it "seems so impersonal when we make love," that "I don't want actual intercourse," and even that it feels "like it's an obligation . . . and I don't like it to be that way." But these dissatisfactions are not sufficient to account for the way that Pat is literally sickened by her husband's sexual approaches.

Although sexual revulsion and disgust are generally taken simply as indicative of the intensity of the client's negative reactions, we detect in these responses the presence of unconscious response anxiety. These clients are especially susceptible to the universal expectation that they will respond affirmatively to sex. For example, the vaginismic woman's whole pelvic area (or even whole body) may be flinching in anticipation of penetration, but she does not feel entitled to voluntarily resist or even to think that she just is not ready for it. Thus the vaginismic flinch is not simply a negative response. Indeed, in our experience it can best be relieved by the client's learning to tolerate having a negative response.

Take the proverbial woman who pleads a headache. She is thought of as a nay-sayer. Thus, one cartoonist had a middle-aged couple browsing in a pornographic bookstore, he meek and slight, eyeing the erotica, she a formidable battle-ax, with her gaze fixed on a book titled *One Thousand and One Excuses.* No caption was needed. Although the fact that she needs excuses to get out of sex is right there in print in front of us, it is nonetheless invisible. The fact that she is unable to say no (without a pretext) is so "superficial" as to pass unnoticed. What makes her response anxiety so invisible?

Thus far, in answering this question we have appealed to the universality of the expectation that sexual responses should be affirmative (universal, that is, in those societies in which the sex-as-intimacy model has emerged, in contrast to non-Western and premodern authoritarian societies in which the sex-as-possession model is still dominant). This is to say that the pressure to respond is hard to see if everyone takes it for granted that they must respond this way. We also have pointed out that response anxiety is difficult to detect in those who respond negatively to sex even if, like the woman in the cartoon, they need an excuse. But there is an additional habit of thought that makes this woman's response anxiety invisible even when, as in the cartoon, her need for an excuse is transparent: *Everyone looks at her from her husband's position.* The point for everyone is that she is refusing him, never mind with what degree of guilt.

FRIGIDITY

Our diagnostic nomenclature in this area consists of thinly veiled admonishments which can be seen to represent the position of the partner, the affected party. Thus, sexual apathy and aversion, now usually called "desire disorders," are more familiarly known as *frigidity,* a term that one of us (Apfelbaum, 1977a) noted elsewhere "seemed more like a complaint than a diagnosis." Masters and Johnson (1966, 1970) wrote the first books in the sex field in which the term frigidity did not appear, and they made a heroic effort to get the sneer out of the diagnosis by defining this condition solely on the basis of only one of its two loosely related meanings, as orgasmic dysfunction. However, this definition did not account for sexual apathy, at least when this condition is not associated with orgasmic dysfunction. (Sexual apathy is not a term in general use, but we use it because, like orgasmic dysfunction, it is purely descriptive.)

Helen Kaplan (1974b) was quick to point out that frigidity and anorgasmia are overlapping but not identical conditions, suggesting "general sexual dsyfunction" as an additional diagnosis. It was hard to get the sneer out without losing the whole condition. The DSM III's "inhibited sexual desire" brings back specificity only to reintroduce a more subtle version of the old, disqualifying, term (at least as we see it), since it suggests that desire is present but held back, "inhibited," rather than suggesting that the desire is not present because the conditions necessary for its appearance are unavailable.

Frigidity, after all, meant that responsiveness was being held back. It meant being withholding: ungiving and even spiteful. Here is where to find the explanation for the fact that only women are called frigid: It is the woman, not the man, who gives (the man takes). This view is now in the process of revision as we begin to think psychologically rather than morally, and as the psychological view gives us a way to be more dispassionate.

However, those who might be expected to be custodians of the psychological view, the psychoanalytic thinkers, have proved to be prisoners of the moral view, so much so that we can use them to show what social disapproval looks like when it is the basis for psychodynamic explanations. (For a more general application of the idea that psychotherapy represents an elaboration of social disapproval, see Apfelbaum & Apfelbaum, 1973; Apfelbaum & Gill, in preparation.) Bennett Simon (1975), a well-known representative of the Boston Psychoanalytic Institute, given a sketchy outline of a hypothetical case of "frigidity" was asked to epitomize the psychoanalytic version of the diagnosis and treatment of this condition. He compressed both into a single paragraph:

> Following periods of repeated and prolonged silence by the patient, punctuated by a rather sweeping, negativistic response to everything the therapist said, the therapist interprets: "Your silence and your negativism are a way of being frigid to me. You have made yourself and your mind as unresponsive to me as your body and your vagina are to your husband. You do this with me because you are afraid of the sexual arousal you feel while lying on my couch." (p. 202)

Notice the readiness here to buy the whole notion of frigidity. This woman is *negativistic:* she refuses to *give.* She *makes herself frigid* (she is responsible for it) by resisting the sexual arousal available to her both on the analytic couch and in bed with her husband (thus "desire" is "inhibited" rather than that the conditions for it are unavailable).

As we see it the causal picture is quite the reverse. The sexually apathetic woman, rather than being negativistic, is too compliant. Rather than being unable to give, she is unable to refuse (like the proverbial woman who pleads a headache). Simon is in a sense right that she is turning herself off; however, this is in a superficial sense (although it is thought of as "deep"). Looked at more closely, she is turning herself off in the effort to turn herself on, as Nan came to realize. She is driven to this effort by response anxiety.

Of course, the chief point which we have been developing is that none of the sexually apathetic woman's reactions would necessarily create a problem if they were not so flatly contradicted (disqualified) by the popular consensus and by its psychodynamic elaboration. Bennett Simon's belief that this woman is a nay-sayer is just as well entrenched as is Nan's husband's (and her own), and Simon's sense of his own lack of complicity is just as serene. The alternative explanation is not considered—even if just to be rejected. Karen Horney (1933), thought of as a liberal and even a feminist analyst, said that "You can in these cases get a more or less distinct impression that frigidity is *a direct expression* [italics added] of undercurrent streams of hostility" (p. 166), meaning of course that responsiveness is being withheld to punish the partner, a "distinct impression" keenly felt by most partners.

The behavior therapist gets to the heart of the matter by suggesting bribing the woman, as in the instance where "a husband gets fellatio five times a week and the wife [in exchange] gets French Provincial furniture" (Koch & Koch, 1976). Thus, through a kind of vulgar realism, the complaint that sexual apathy means withholding is made into a way of life.

Presumably, the same solution could be applied to cases of sexual harassment in the workplace by offering to give the victim a raise. This parallel is not idly drawn. The woman suffering from sexual harassment has much the same experience as the sexually apathetic woman. Perhaps the signal difference is that where the sexually apathetic woman's plight at least had a name—frigidity—the sexually harassed woman's plight, until recently, did not. Sexual harassment is not new, but the recognition (ego-integration) of this experience is so new that the latest instances appear in the daily newspaper, and the term *sexual harassment* had to be coined to give us a way to refer to the phenomenon.

We find the key to this difference in our point that sexual apathy is conceived of from the partner's position. Frigidity, coldness, withholdingness, and spite all reflect that position. This is to say that the very *existence* of the concept of frigidity is a consequence of the partner's experience; frigidity is something that happens to the partner. But sexual harassment happens to the woman herself, and, since her experience was disqualified, the condition itself was invisible.

We are saying that the moral (coercive) nature of the idea of frigidity is made apparent by the explanations it engenders. To interpret sexual apathy as withholdingness and hostility, no matter how benevolently the interpretation is made, is ultimately to express the same impatience most people feel toward victims of sexual harassment or rape.

It is all too easy to forget that prominent among those who condemn the sexually oppressed are the victims themselves. Indeed, what we have been saying is that sexual oppression is in large part created by the victim's being a member of the chorus of her (or his) accusers. This is to say that there is a complicity on the part of harassment or (nonviolent) rape victims, not in the usual sense that they secretly wanted it but in the sense that they were unaware of *not* wanting it. This is not a simple matter of lack of assertiveness. A woman may say that she was raped, but that it took her several days or even years to realize it.

What so often makes it difficult for the victims of "acquaintance" or marital rape to realize what has happened is that their partners are far from realizing it. Their partners may well believe that what they have done is an act of love, affection, or appreciation which was shared by the victim, however reluctantly. This brings us to a dimension of sexual relationships that we believe to be crucial to an understanding of sexual apathy: the way that many people are able to experience a sexual encounter as loving and intimate even though the partner may be feeling oppressed as well as guilty about not sharing the experience. (Thus, in our introductory vignette, Len thought he was being considerate and loving, and Nan believed this too. She thought that her flashes of anger and her apathy represented her inability to appreciate Len's advances.)

Further, the way all of us conduct ourselves in sex is designed to minimize awareness of sexual oppression and to foster the illusion of mutuality—of intimacy. In postindustrial Western societies sex has become a ritual of mutual affirmation rather than the one-sided ritual of possession that typifies personal relationships in premodern, non-Western, authoritarian societies. Interestingly enough, even among the most rulebound and impersonal societies (tribal-level societies in which personal relationships are exclusively matters of property rights and status), courting behavior often is organized around shows of appreciation and narcissistic displays that require appreciation from the partner, behavior that is not limited to official sex partners but may include concubines as well (and that is reminiscent of infrahuman mating rituals).

BYPASSING

What is it about sex that requires these shows and displays even when it is a simple act of possession? Why in more liberated societies does sex become even more closely associated with mutual appreciation? In short, what is it about sex that requires an ego boost? This question has not been asked, much less answered. By way of entertaining this question, let us consider the way that sex partners usually behave. They work at being mutually reassuring and at keeping everything as smooth as possible. They suppress all complaints and criticisms and try to concentrate on what they like and admire about one another. Sex talk is all encouragement and flattery. It is as if sex partners try to eliminate the distance between them by eliminating the differences between them.

This is the time for candlelight, wine, low lights, soft music, and murmured tones, the work of trying to create the erotic ego state. The same reassuring murmurs and narrowed focus are characteristic of hypnotic trance induction, and the hypnotic subject also tries to suspend disbelief and to think of the hypnotist as a powerful and benevolent authority. When the process of romantic induction works, what emerges is the erotic ego state, with its altered state of consciousness. For the most susceptible there may be deep trance phenomena: loss of consciousness (*le petit mort*), automatisms of speech and movement, and a heightened pain threshold. More commonly, the experience can be one of total possession, of and by the partner—a merging. Although there are many who never have experiences of this intensity, they nevertheless experience a degree of acceptance of and by the partner that is rarely felt otherwise.

There are others who can only generate this state by invoking a fantasy partner, but the fantasy too is one of total acceptance in some form. Then there are those who are sexually apathetic or aversive and may never have had this experience. They remain aware of the distance between them and their partners. The general belief is that they are resisting erotic arousal, that they are unwilling or unable to *let go*.

The idea that sexual arousal means letting go is one of the anchors for the notion of frigidity and the disqualification of sexual apathy. The idea is that the sex drive is powerful enough to scare people and therefore that getting turned on is easy if you will only allow it. This is the drive that Freud argued had to be repressed to make civilization possible—although this was not observable. What Freud did observe was the weakness of the sex drive and it was from this that he made his inferential leap. This drive is relatively unconnected to externals; it arises from within.

Many people experience sex in exactly this way, and for them the drive metaphor is entirely convincing. They are what we call good *bypassers* (Apfelbaum, 1977b). In order to bring on the erotic ego state, sex partners work to bypass any discordant note. When they succeed in generating the merging experience it feels as if they have surrendered their controls and allowed their bodies to take over. What has actually happened is that they have gotten high on *agreement*, and the state they have created can be quite fragile, vulnerable to the slightest sign of whatever real-life discord has been temporarily kept at bay.

Imagine the soldier who carries out an act of extraordinary valor. He later reports that his consciousness was narrowed to the task at hand. He experienced neither fear nor a sense of his own mortality. Both were bypassed. He had the motivation and the ability to lose himself, perhaps even in some sense to let go. But to describe the whole process as one of letting go is to miss the narrowing of consciousness that is essential to it. The soldier who cannot block out his awareness of his own mortality and of his personal priorities and is overcome with fear can also be said to be letting go.

To return to the parallel with hypnosis, the good hypnotic subject has the motivation and the ability to trust the hypnotist (meaning to suspend realistic disbelief), to narrow consciousness to the task at hand, and thus to bring on the trance state in which he or she experiences a merging with the hypnotist. The good sexual subject has this same ability, being someone who, when touched, feels instantaneous rapport (the practiced hypnotic subject can go under at the snap of a finger). Others, like pornographic movie stars, have the motivation and the ability to deliberately narrow consciousness to sensation and fantasy when their partners or the context turns them off (Kronhausen & Kronhausen, 1975).

The Sexual Consciousness of the Good Bypasser

Although bypassing is a complex mental act, it is *experienced* by the good bypasser as "letting go." This is especially true of the person who is accustomed to the experience of instantaneous bypassing, but it even is true of those who must work to accomplish it. In a rather paradoxical way, they both feel fully capable of "taking responsibility for their own sexuality," while simultaneously feeling that they are simply allowing the sex drive to take over.

Ann: I know very well that I'm pretty much in charge of whether I'm turned on or not, you know, to a massive extent. I can turn myself on or off sexually, to a great extent. I feel I have that kind of control a lot.

Therapist 1: How do you do it, with fantasies or. . . .?

Ann: Yeah, sure. Just allowing myself. Fantasize, or allow myself to be more relaxed, if I force my mind to stop thinking in a sort of circular or negative kind of way and away from issues of why Tom is acting the way he is.

I can sometimes force my mind onto maybe a visual image of past really good sexual experiences we've had or, you know, do something to *focus* in another area.

There are times when I'm able to throw myself into it wholeheartedly and with a good attitude, but nowadays something will happen and it'll break the image, and I'll go back to the crummy image of "Here we are, *groping* again."

Therapist 2: So there is always a point at which you *become* dependent on Tom.

Ann: Mm-hm. Well, yeah, as soon as I see him acting nervous or tense or rigid, then it clicks *[snaps fingers]* me out of my fantasy or my image that relaxes me—brings me sort of back down to earth.

Notice the way Ann mixes "just *allowing* myself" with "I . . . *force* my mind." She has a clear sense of letting go, despite being keenly aware that she is actively blocking out a reality that constantly threatens to "click" her out of the erotic ego state she has conjured up. It is no wonder that as the good bypasser thinks of it, erotic arousal is created by applying oneself "wholeheartedly and with a good attitude," in Ann's words. To the good bypasser it really *is* all a matter of taking responsibility for your own sexuality; erotic arousal is relatively autonomous—a simple matter of letting the sex drive take over.

The good bypasser has no way to understand the sexual consciousness of the person who does not have the motivation or the ability to bypass. Since turning on is easy—a simple matter of letting go—the person who is unwilling or unable to bypass is seen as either motivated to thwart the partner or as out of touch with bodily imperatives.

The good bypasser overlooks not only the mental work required to bypass but also overlooks the effect on the partner. Thus, Ann had no idea that her ability to ignore Tom and to get turned on in spite of him was contributing to his sexual anxiety states. More likely, she probably thought that her ability to rise above Tom's anxieties would be encouraging to him, possibly even contagious. After all, it is a common observation that a turned-on partner is the most potent aphrodisiac.

This observation is, of course, consistently borne out in most people's experience. However, like most common sense wisdom it rests on the disqualification of negative instances and thus is not susceptible to disproof. Those who experience being turned *off* by a turned-on partner do not question the rule; they just think there is something wrong with *them.* The actuality, at least from what we have been able to infer, is that a turned-on partner can either be the most potent aphrodisiac or the most potent turn-off, and that what determines which it will be is whether or not you think that your partner is turned on to *you.* If you believe that your partner is turned on to something about you or to something that you have done, this is likely to be a heady experience, but if you think that you had nothing to do with it or, worse, that your partner is turned on in spite of you, this can be the most potent turn-off.

The latter is all the more a turn-off because the experience of being bypassed is disqualified. In other words, everyone thinks that a turned-on partner is the stuff of Eros. To feel left out or ignored by a turned-on partner is a nonexperience. Feeling left out may be one of the most common sexual experiences, but it typically has no way to be registered and so is not thought of as part of sex. The experience of being left out, that is, bypassed, is typically a crucial influence in the creation of sexual apathy, especially because the apathetic partner does not feel entitled to it—all the more so if the functioning partner is a good bypasser, someone whose sexual style seems not at all dependent on being responded to and who thinks that turning on is a simple matter of being able to let go.

> **Harold:** Even when we have what seems like a sexually satisfying episode for her, her attitude back to me is, "Gee, that was good, but it's only once. Why hasn't it been this way all the time?" [Or she says,] "It's good, but it could be better." It's very difficult to talk to her about a comment like that. She gets very upset. She says, "Well, if you had been different, I wouldn't have to comment like that." It kind of defeats me. It makes me feel like I can't please no matter what. She says, "That's your problem." She says, "If you cared enough for me you would be willing to make more of an effort."
>
> We have had arguments about sex, really big blast arguments, and we would go to bed and I would be angry, and at the same time she would be angry, and yet she expects me to want to have sex with her.

Therapist: I suspect that she has a sexual style that does rationalize her position. Some people have what we call a bypassing sexual style, meaning that they are very good at performing sexually by ignoring what's going on. So they can respond relatively automatically, despite whatever feelings are going on.

A person who can do that, even though they may not be all that highly aroused themselves, still feels like something sexual is happening and tends to expect that of the other person. Whereas if you're sensitive to the emotional climate and can't block it out, can't just focus on sensation, then it seems like you're unwilling.

The trouble with that way of looking at it is that it makes seduction unnecessary. She'd be thinking there isn't anything she really has to do to interest you.

Harold: Now she lies with her back to me. I tell her, "That's not very stimulating." She says, "There's no reason to face you."

Therapist: She doesn't see how she can be turning you off because *she* can react sexually relatively independently.

Harold: Yeah, I think she can, just because of some comments she has made. A couple of times after we'd had a big argument, she came back with comments like: "Yeah, it was really lousy, but I just sat there and thought of something else."

Therapist: So what she's thinking is that "if you just put your mind to it you could block this stuff out and get into it, and if you cared for me you'd make the effort."

Harold's wife does not excite the sympathies of the reader, nor of the therapists who have heard this tape. She is thought of as a castrating bitch, meaning that she shouldn't treat Harold this way and that she has no position. Yet, as we see it anyone in her situation would feel the way she does if they looked at Harold from the point of view of a good bypasser. What is writ large in her reactions is the prototypic intolerance of the good bypasser for those who are unable to bypass.

Harold's wife had no way to comprehend his lack of sexual interest. This was both the cause and the consequence of her intolerance. Like Ann in the previous example, she undoubtedly has a keen sense of being at the control panel of her own sexuality. Her position is "I just sat there and thought of something else," so why can't Harold? Harold is no help here. Intimidated by her no-nonsense style, he can only offer the weak rejoinder that when she lies with her back to him, "That's not very stimulating."

Harold was no better at understanding his own lack of interest than his wife was since, like almost all bypassed partners, he did not feel entitled to his experience of feeling left out and ignored, as well as being intimidated by her scorn. He felt that he deserved what he got. His interest in sex had never been that strong, and he had never met anyone that he was more strongly attracted to than his wife.

Like almost all bypassed partners Harold thought that he was the abnormal one and that he should be able to become aroused as easily as his wife. After all, she was not dependent on *him* to become aroused, so why should he need anything from her? Given this reading, Harold then tried to conform to his wife's sexuality—again, as do almost all bypassed partners. He tried to perform and managed to "do ok," as he put it, about twice a week.

In other words, Harold was unable to bypass but he nevertheless did his best in this direction. The bypassed partner typically keeps a low profile, trying to at least create the appearance of normal sexuality. In fact, if the bypassed partner did not keep a low profile, he or she could not be bypassed. If Harold had made his distress plain, his wife could no longer have ignored it, just as Ann was brought "back down to earth" when her husband acted too "nervous or tense or rigid." The fantasies (or the sensations) that the good bypasser needs in order to trip out are typically reinforced by their partners.

This is why men are usually better bypassers than women (why, as we are told, women want love and men want sex). Although men are given a material assist by the ejaculatory reflex, women's readiness to look accommodating despite conditions of low erotic arousal often provides men with the necessary encouragement. This effect transcends the individual partner, since by virtue of lifelong exposure, a man can more easily imagine an accomodating partner. (This is our explanation for why women's pornography, in contrast to men's, is almost exclusively concerned with character development. Women begin with the expectation that they will have to be accomodating, so it takes some imaginative effort for them to build a male character who will be patient enough to cater to them, or at least sadistic enough to not require them to minister to the male ego.)

Since men are usually better bypassers than women they also are expected to be. This is what especially disqualifies the male partner's experience when, like Harold, he is the one being bypassed. As a consequence Harold did his best to fit everyone's expectation. He was successful only in concealing his distress from his wife. She probably was entirely unaware of how terrified he was of her, how much sex felt like a disaster area to him, how hard he actually was trying (not to disrupt her concentration)—in a word, how he was getting screwed.

Of course, what we are saying is that Harold's wife could not *afford* to be aware of her husband's distress. Like Ann, she needed him to provide the sensation. Also like Ann, she needed him not to interfere with the mental work that bypassing requires. If her partner did not provide the sensation and also required her attention, she had to feel left in the lurch, grounded, stuck with the tensions of the relationship.

Indeed, if we look a little closer at Harold's wife's sexual "demandingness" (women who want sex a lot are often called demanding, in contrast to men who want sex a lot but are simply thought of as behaving the way men are expected to behave), we find that she is driven to sexual consummation by the same tensions that cause her husband to withdraw. What makes the difference is that through sex she can get away from these tensions. Through sex she can close the growing chasm between her and Harold, and she can be transported into the merging experience, feeling affirmed and affirming rather than rejected and rejecting.

Unfortunately for Harold, her very ability to use his touch as a way to launch the erotic ego-state leaves him feeling all the more distant and all the more abnormal for feeling that way. She can get away from the real relationship through sex. He can get away from the real relationship only through withdrawal.

BYPASSING SEX THERAPY

Thus far we have presented the dynamics of sexual apathy as seen from what for many will be a novel vantage point. We are now in a position to consider the more familiar bypassing approach to sex therapy, as exemplified by its most vigorous and prominent advocate, Helen Singer Kaplan (1974b, 1979). Kaplan's contribution is in its own way novel in that even though her position is shared by many if not most sex therapists (and by almost everyone else), she alone has been daring enough to advocate blocking out the partner and to embrace an autonomous sexual style. She alone does not feel constrained to cloak her position in sex-as-intimacy rhetoric. Without her contribution the sexual philosophy she represents—although it is the majority view—would still be submerged and we would have been obliged to use much of our space just to demonstrate not only that it exists but that it underlies much of sex therapy.

Although she presents it as a quip, Kaplan (1974b) remarks: "It may be said that sex is composed of friction and fantasy" p. 122. That this formulation has more than passing significance is indicated by Kaplan's (1974a) use of it as the title of a popularized summary of her approach, "Friction and Fantasy: No-Nonsense Therapy for Six Sexual Malfunctions." Your partner provides the friction, and you provide the fantasy (Kaplan, 1976): "When a patient is experiencing anxiety during stimulation, the advice usually is, 'Get into a fantasy while she's stimulating you; it doesn't matter what it is.' " She adds that "We encourage the use of fantasy because it is the best tranquilizer people have." She would, of course, get a heartfelt second on this from the good bypassers we have quoted (Harold's wife and Ann), and it also follows that her description of healthy sexuality focuses exclusively on the ability to bypass (Kaplan, 1979).

> The person who is conflict-free about sex mentally does the opposite of the inhibited one, in the sense that he does *not allow* negative feelings or thoughts or distractions to intrude upon his sexual pleasure. . . . When he is in a sexual situation, he does not criticize his partner's taste in bedroom furniture, or see figure flaws, or comment on less than brilliant conversation. His behavior instinctively maximizes his erotic experience. (pp. 84–85)

No one else in the field has so baldly made the case for bypassing. Kaplan feels no need to appeal to intimacy or liberation rhetoric. This is at odds with the prevailing ideology. For example, primary anorgasmic women typically are taught to have orgasms by focusing narrowly on sensation and blocking out the partner. They are taught, that is, to bypass, but they are told that what they really are doing is getting in touch with (taking charge of, or responsibility for) their own bodies (reclaiming them from men, as it were).

The Conditions for Bypassing

Much as we appreciate Kaplan's candor, we believe that her use of the good bypasser as her reference model for healthy sexuality is based on a far-reaching misunderstanding. The bypassing style is not as elective as it seems or as the good bypasser can feel it to be. Typically, the good bypasser *cannot help* bypassing, like the person who falls in love with whomever he or she happens to be in bed with, at least as long as they are in bed. We also maintain that just as the good bypasser automatically bypasses, there are those who can never bypass.

What also makes it difficult to recognize the involuntary nature of bypassing is the experience most people have of working to bypass, that is, working to focus on sensation and on fantasy, or on what they like and appreciate about their partners, and working to tune out what turns them off. We would even say that although no one has yet attempted to determine what is meant by "working" at sex, it could be summarized in one word: bypassing. This is the work of sex, and if everyone took the advice to not work at sex zero population growth would be at hand.

However, those who have difficulty bypassing may be working just as hard at it. As Nan said in our introductory excerpt, "I seem to focus all my thoughts on how I should be reacting to what he's doing," even though the most she could accomplish was to feel blank. Kaplan nevertheless would interpret Nan's failure to become aroused as an unconscious *unwillingness* to become aroused, despite her conscious willingness, even desperation. In fact, Kaplan would take the intensity of Nan's desperation to be a measure of the degree to which Nan must defend against awareness of her unwillingness.

What drives Kaplan to this interpretation, at least as we infer it, is the fact that she works so exclusively from the position of the good bypasser. Thus, for Kaplan bypassing is what sex *is*—friction plus fantasy. From this position there is no way that she would be likely to consider the possibility that some people can never bypass. Kaplan (1974b) even goes so far as to speculate that "there must be naturally occurring bypass mechanisms or modifying factors or defenses which protect the delicate sexual functions from the destructive influences of neurosis and disruptive marriages" (p. 191). "Naturally occurring" here means occurring in nature, which is to say that what makes population growth possible is the evolution of "bypass mechanisms" that protect "the delicate sexual functions" from the destructive effects of our feelings.

Nothing could better express the belief that the good bypasser is truly independent of the partner. If one, far-reaching misunderstanding is that bypassing is elective, a more serious misunderstanding is that it is autonomous. Harold's wife was able to transcend both her hurt and anger, and the tensions in her relationship with her husband, but she was under the good bypasser's illusion that she was doing it all herself—that she was taking responsibility for her own sexuality. She did not know how dependent she was on Harold to be an unobtrusive and supportive or at least nonaccusatory presence.

The erotic ego state typically is fragile, and it is a rare person who can "take responsibility" for it in the face of the partner's expressed distress. No matter how good the bypasser, he or she is dependent on the partner not to strike a discordant note. If this does happen and the spell is broken, it usually is not possible to regenerate the spell without a substantial mending period just as with the hypnotic trance. If the hypnotic subject is jarred out of a trance, that usually is it for that session.

Requiring the partner to be unobtrusive is, of course, a minimum requirement for bypassing. The partner may help to facilitate the needed fantasy. This fantasy is usually about the real partner and may be deliberate or spontaneous. Ann (above) deliberately called up "a visual image of past really good sexual experiences we've had," but the fantasy is usually spontaneous, in the sense that the person believes it is the reality. The fantasy is of the real partner in the present, but the partner is imagined (perceived) as responding positively and as being turned on when in fact he or she is not. This fantasy obviously is facilitated by the partner who fakes feelings, a much more frequent occurrence than faking orgasms.

The good bypasser who looks the most spontaneous is the one who stays aroused despite the partner's expressed protests, as may be typical of acquaintance or marital rape. This is only an apparent invulnerability to the partner's reaction. The nonviolent rapist (the rapist whose motive is not primarily punitive) reinterprets the partner's protests as signs that she really is enjoying it. Another example is the typical "john," who believes that the prostitute enjoys it. This belief has all the strength of a reality perception. Thus, we have had a number of cases in which the wife, after years of faking feelings or at least passively allowing the husband to believe that she was aroused and involved, works up her courage to confess to her husband that she really has been apathetic all along, only to find that he flatly refuses to believe it and even accuses her of playing games.

These husbands were not only being asked to disbelieve what they thought they had seen with their own eyes but they would have had to suddenly adjust to thinking of themselves as inadequate lovers, and even more threatening, they would have had to see themselves as having been sexually exploitive. It would be hard to overestimate the intensity and prevalence of guilt about sexual exploitation. It seems apparent that it is this guilt that causes sex therapists other than Kaplan who push for bypassing to cloak their advice in the rhetoric of intimacy. Some sex therapists have become adroit moral philosophers in their efforts to convince the guilty client that it is ok to have fantasies about another woman while having sex with his wife (he must be turned on to his wife in the first place—or at least it is she that he chooses to be with; to have such a fantasy shows that he must *trust* his wife and anyway he is trying to get turned on for *her*).

It seems to us that this guilt about bypassing creates the most potent hidden dependency in the bypassing style. It is instrumental in motivating the good bypasser to insist on the naturalness and inevitability of his or her style and to disqualify the experience of the bypassed partner. Indeed, the rare person who is free to be explicit about wanting to bypass has a much less oppressive effect on the partner, since the partner then feels entitled to his or her own experience and also does not feel obliged to be reassuring by acting turned on.

Kaplan is well aware of the guilt about bypassing, especially among women, and this is in fact her target population. It is not too much of an inference to say that her whole emphasis on bypassing is aimed at overcoming this guilt about leaving the partner out. However, consistently enough with her approach, she never mentions the guilt from which she wants to free people. Yet, at least as we look at it, difficulty in being able to bypass, in being able to ignore the partner and to focus on sensation, cannot be adequately relieved unless clients appreciate their reluctance to do it and the consequences of this reluctance: the overconscientiousness and oversolicitousness that creates an oppressive dependency on the partner's responsiveness.

Intervening from the Side of the Good Bypasser

If bypassing is indeed less elective and more dependent on the partner than it appears to be, what are the consequences of working from the position that the good bypasser has a truly autonomous sexual style and can be taken as our reference model for healthy sexuality? Kaplan (1974b, pp. 169–172) reports her analysis and treatment of a couple much like Harold and his wife. The wife is defined as a strikingly good bypasser. "She was a large, active, ebullient person who was very free and responsive sexually. She had no sexual difficulties, being easily multiorgasmic in almost any situation." Thus, this woman's ability to respond independently of the "situation" is stated at the outset by Kaplan to establish the fact that she "had no sexual difficulties" and was "very free" sexually.

Unlike Harold, this woman's husband suffered from impotence (although this may have been symptomatic of sexual apathy). He made progress in the treatment and they were able to have intercourse. Then he had an argument with his wife which created "an ambience of rejection, strife, and bitterness." Despite this tension and "contrary to explicit instructions that she avoid pursuing him for sex when he appeared to experience difficulty, she had insisted on having intercourse and attaining coital orgasm," with the result that "he promptly lost his erection on entering." Kaplan concluded that "she had expressed her hostility to him by her sexual demands, which she unconsciously knew he could not meet."

Kaplan's conclusion follows directly from her view of the wife as the healthy one. This leaves no way to explain the wife's pressing her husband for sex under such trying circumstances except as some need to sabotage the treatment. However, our guess is that it is just such trying circumstances that *compel* her to want sex and that she is not as "free" as Kaplan believes.

The more trying the circumstances, the more she would be likely to need her escape into the experience of closeness and mutual acceptance that sex makes available to her—in her case intercourse and coital orgasm. It is precisely at such times that to her sexual arousal feels like the expression of a drive. More to the point, we are convinced that the good bypasser cannot move into the erotic ego state without the illusion of partner receptivity. This is the hidden dependency that is overlooked by those who would take the wife in Kaplan's case as their model of healthy sexuality.

It is hard for such a woman to believe that her husband cannot share her experience. It can even seem like he *must* be sharing it since it is such a convincing experience for her, or at least that he easily could be sharing it if he would only *let go*. Since the experience is so automatic for her, it is hard for her to believe that it cannot be as automatic for him.

It is even harder for such a woman to realize that her reaching out to her husband not only fails to evoke the experience of oneness but is instead experienced by him as a demand that evokes his impotence. In any case performance (response) anxiety is not a credible experience to the good bypasser since sexual initiatives are just experienced as performance *opportunities*. Thus, from this woman's point of view what her husband needs is a partner who is aggressive and passionate enough to overcome his resistance to the sex drive. This may well have been why she was so ready to disregard the therapist's instructions.

Her "resistance" may have represented an inability to openly disagree with the therapist. It is likely that hers was the venerable view that what the frigid woman (or man) needs is a partner who will override her protests. In other words, this woman may, in effect, have been trying to rape her husband in the heartfelt belief that this would free him (we call this the Big Bang theory of frigidity).

However, Kaplan's (1974b) belief is that this woman's actions do not reflect a point of view, and that she simply is able to freely allow the sex drive to take over even under the most adverse conditions: "While rejection upset her very much and caused her to behave destructively towards him, it did not affect her sexual responsiveness adversely. She was perfectly orgastic even when feeling rejected." Our belief is that she was able to use sex as a way to escape from feeling rejected and that this is the hidden dependency that made her sexual responses seem so autonomous.

We have made the point that Kaplan represents the majority view and should be seen as a spokesperson for it by virtue of her readiness to eschew intimacy rhetoric and her prominence in the field. It seems safe to say that almost everyone would agree with Kaplan that the wife she treated was indeed "very free and responsive sexually." Our patient Harold, with his lifelong, low level of sexual interest, wuld be thought of as having "low libido" as compared with his wife's "high libido." In the past, known as "sexual incompatibility," this was often considered an essentially constitutional difference and therefore largely untreatable. Even now some sex therapists (Kilmann & Mills, 1983) assert that "a sexual desire discrepancy is one of the most, if not the most difficult of sex problems to treat" (p. 149).

Summarizing current practice, Kilmann and Mills (1983) find that "typically, the goal of treatment is to increase the frequency of sex in the relationship to meet the expectations of the partner with the higher desire" (p. 149). Our impression is that this problem is a difficult one to treat only when it proceeds in this way, that is, from the position of the high-drive partner. Zilbergeld and Ellison (1980) have been the first to question the sexuality of the high-drive partner, suggesting that he or she is too narrowly focused on sex as a way to feel close. Their approach is to train such a person to find closeness in other ways. However, their treatment of the low-drive partner is more conventional, consisting of encouragement to label slight feelings as sexual and to accumulate these feelings through the development of an anticipatory erotic mental set. This approach is reminiscent of Heiman's (1977) argument that a woman's belief that she is not aroused may be a failure of labeling, since women who show signs of physical arousal will rate themselves as unaroused. This is less likely to be the case with men, the logic runs, because they can see their erections. (We think that the relation between reflexogenic and psychogenic arousal is a complex one and that for some people physical arousal is not accompanied by subjective arousal, Apfelbaum, 1977b, 1980.) Similarly, Crenshaw (1983) advises that women who complain that they feel nothing have "edited out" sexual sensations in the process of devoting themselves to daily chores, and that they therefore should make the effort to attend to those sensations.

Response Anxiety

It looks to us like these exhortations to work at becoming aroused inadvertently rely on response anxiety to motivate the client, and that the sexually apathetic client would typically be too discouraged to make the effort, even in the face of jibes like Crenshaw's (1983) "the lady in waiting" (p. 124). Although all of these authorities are well aware of the apathetic or low-drive partner's oppressed position, they appear to take it as an inevitable consequence of response failure. Our experience is that this condition is easier to treat if it is approached with the idea that the oppressed position is what creates sexual apathy rather than the reverse. This is not easy to see if the oppressing partner is taken as the normal one.

If, instead of urging the apathetic partner to work at becoming more aroused (as by collecting sensations or sensory awareness exercises such as bubble baths and leisurely masturbation), we focus more closely on the apathetic state itself, we discover that it is not simply a state of low desire. Feeling apathetic or aversive is considered to be synonymous with feeling unaroused. However, apathy, or its more intense form, aversion, is a state of emotional withdrawal that can evaporate when the person is capable of an *active dislike* of sex. Thus Pat, the client quoted near the beginning of the chapter who said that "my stomach just ties up in knots," can be thought of as suffering from an almost literally swallowed dislike. Pat could *say* that she doesn't like it, but in an actual sexual encounter she had to submit. (This is the most immediate reason why she had to avoid anything sexual; she had no way to stop things after they became sexual.)

The apathetic person does not feel entitled to be unaroused. Exhortations to become more aroused only strengthen this sense of lack of entitlement. Becoming aroused is even met with resistance because of a fear that this will raise the partner's (and the therapists') expectations (wrongly interpreted by the therapist, we think, as signifying a fear of arousal or even, see Kaplan below, an unconscious wish to stay unaroused in order to thwart the partner). Thus, the therapeutic objective should be to help the person to feel entitled to be unaroused.

This is not accomplished by telling the client that it is ok to not be aroused, since it is not ok, as we have here been at pains to make clear. It is accomplished by helping clients to see the validity of their unaroused state. Essential to establishing the validity of their experience in sex is the kind of reframing that we have been attempting to do in this chapter. If our argument has been successful up to this point, we have established the validity of the apathetic partner's response anxiety.

The apathetic partner does not feel entitled to feel pressured in sex and therefore even when the pressure is intense it is invisible to both partners, both of whom simply believe that the apathetic partner really is failing and really should be aroused. This obliges us as one of our first moves to begin to demystify the good bypasser's sexual style (the "high-drive" partner has to be a good bypasser in order to avoid being turned off by the "low-drive" partner's oppressed state, although the apathetic partner may aid considerably in this, as by faking feelings, in order to avoid humiliation or an attack by the then guilty bypasser). This is what one of us began to do with Harold (see excerpt above). (Ordinarily we would do this with both partners, but his wife had refused to accompany him to therapy on the grounds that he was the one who had to make the effort.) We make the same points we have made in this chapter, beginning by asking the apathetic partner whether he or she has ever wondered how the other person could be so turned on when the apathetic partner felt so turned off. The answer always is yes, which leads to an investigation of what both partners are doing that makes bypassing possible.

The picture will look quite different depending on whether the partners are spontaneous or deliberate. The bypassing partner may be deliberately conjuring up a fantasy "of past really good sexual experiences we've had." Or he may always have believed that his image of the partner as turned on represented reality. The partner being bypassed may be actively working to promote this illusion or may be entirely unaware of how he or she passively promotes it by keeping a low profile.

The next step is to make visible to both partners the bypassed partner's response anxiety, especially as it is intensified by the bypasser's seemingly autonomous style. We would explain that it is response anxiety that makes sexual apathy look so deep-seated (the Masters & Johnson insight) and that makes it look constitutional (since the more patient, seductive, or aggressive and uninhibited the bypassing partner is, the more turned off the other person becomes).

In some cases this reframing is all that is required to establish the necessary reversal of perspective, and a single session is sufficient. With this reorientation the couple's efforts are more likely to relieve the problem than to intensify it. More often, additional sessions are needed to establish this new perspective. The bypassing partner is likely to feel inadequate, guilty, and defensive as the other person's experience is validated, thus generating renewed pressure on the bypassed partner to respond in an affirming way.

Jill: *[reading from notes on the third assignment]* I thought, I don't know how much longer Jack will be able to stand this. He has been trying so hard, and I know how much it means to him. I was going to stop there, but then I thought, no—why can't I just *respond?* And then, to my surprise, I did.

Therapist: How did you do it?

Jill: I just thought: "This is my husband and the father of my children. This is the person I am committed to for the rest of my life. This is the person I want to take care of and who takes care of me, and who I have this good life with." And then I felt something; it began to feel good, and it did for the rest of the time, although that was only a few minutes.

Although Jill had been the bypassed partner, at least in this relationship, she found herself willing and able, under intense response pressure, to formulate what amounted to a catechism, calling up a different image of her husband (than the one she was having in the reality of the moment) as a way of bypassing. We found this to be convincing evidence for Jack that Jill really was "trying" (his complaint had been that she just wasn't trying hard enough). It not only made her experience much more tangible to him, he was taken aback by the grimness of the effort it took for her to accomplish even a modest degree of bypassing. Our case of Jill parallels Kaplan's (1979) case of Donna.

> She now began to deliberately focus on the positive aspects of the marriage and of her husband. When about to make love, she focused on his very real intelligence and sensitivity and on the good life he offered her. At first it was an effort, but gradually she began to give herself to the sexual situation in a spontaneous manner. His impotence cleared rapidly and she began to experience the best sexual response she had ever had in her life. (p. 112)

Donna was under intense pressure from the therapist to bypass, and Jill was under intense internal pressure (guilt in reaction to her partner's increasing distress as he became aware of her unaroused state). The point for us is that when response anxiety is sufficiently intense it may forge the mental set necessary for bypassing. Donna has been trained to become aroused by working at sex, meaning she has learned to *perform*. Even if with practice the performance becomes largely spontaneous, it still seems unlikely that she will crave sex when she is harassed by other responsibilities. She may well only want sex when she is prepared to devote herself wholeheartedly to the task.

Does Sex Mean Always Saying Yes?

It is our impression that the push for performance characterizes mainstream sex therapy (here we do not include the Masters & Johnson model; their influence on other treatment models in the field is not widespread even though the other models came in on the coattails of theirs), although this typically is done ambivalently by those therapists who also are concerned with promoting intimacy and authenticity. Thus, Hartman and Fithian (1972), under the heading "Accentuating the Positive—Always Saying Yes," try to hold the line for authenticity by advising couples to always say yes "genuinely" and to accomplish this by only doing what they enjoy.

> The couples who seem to function best are the ones who are always saying yes to the lovemaking activities in which they are involved. The implicit suggestion here [meaning the lesson to be learned from this observation] is that couples encourage their partners, and engage in those activities which they do enjoy, reaffirming by saying yes that they are enjoying the activity. We strongly encourage all our therapeutic couples to lead their partners into positive and pleasurable activities to which they, with complete abandon, can say yes because they are genuinely enjoying those particular activities. A negative response often seriously inhibits further lovemaking efforts and should be avoided wherever possible. (p. 186)

Hartman and Fithian might well deny that they are pushing for performance (and that they risk intensifying performance anxiety) while making it clear that there is only one right way to behave. More typically, therapists appear to impose (or reinforce) this restrictive set without realizing it, believing that their instructions are having a liberating effect. A good place to look for this performance bias is in the instructions for sensate focus. Stuart and Hammond (1980), in what is intended to be a straightforward, noncontroversial coverage of sex therapy techniques in a behaviorally based, couples therapy handbook, offer instructions in which they state that:

> Your responsibility to each other is from time to time to communicate how you feel: "Your rubbing makes me feel warm and secure;" "I like what you are doing now;" "Your kisses make me tingle." If your partner caresses you in a manner that does not please you, you must take the responsibility for indicating this. However, instead of making a complaint, you might say, "It feels better when you press my lips more gently," or "I would enjoy a soft touch more." (p. 318)

After they go on to advise handriding, being free to experiment, and to "selfishly soak up every sensation," as well as to urge the client to "enjoy your here-and-now experience," they add: "Remember, though, that whatever or however you feel is ok" (p. 318). In other words, after giving examples of how to communicate which all suggest positive responses, after advising the client to not communicate discomfort, and after a point-blank exhortation to enjoy the experience, the client is told, with no apparent sense of inconsistency, to remember that whatever you feel is ok.

Again, Helen Kaplan (1979) is atypical only in being more explicit.

> Britt was instructed to "practice feeling good," i.e., to selectively focus on positive elements in nonsexual situations. She succeeded in doing this and

> found that she was having a very good time on trips, on weekends, and at social occasions. Her increasing pleasure was encouraged by the therapist. (p. 139)

What makes it possible for Kaplan to so openly push Britt into working at always saying yes, even outside of sex, whereas other therapists are more ambivalent or even inadvertent in pursuing the same objective? We have already suggested that mainstream sex therapy takes the good bypasser (the person who is willing and able to always say yes to sex) as its reference model. We have also suggested that behind this model is all the social pressure that makes sex a ritual of mutual affirmation and that makes sex problems a matter of moral weakness, a failure of resolve—an unwillingness or inability to take responsibility for one's responses. Further, we have argued that psychoanalysis, which Kaplan takes as the source of her explanatory constructions at least in its best-known version (id analysis), represents an uncritical elaboration of this moral view. What makes it possible for Kaplan to openly insist that someone like Britt try harder to be a more agreeable and supportive person is that Kaplan has worked her way through to a logically consistent schema that incorporates what for other therapists have been largely submerged assumptions.

Here is how this schema was applied to Britt. Like Nan, our patient who speaks in the excerpt that begins this chapter, Britt felt angry whenever her husband approached her sexually. Where to us this meant that Nan was suffering from having her experience disqualified by both her husband and herself (and almost everyone else), for Kaplan (1974b) it means that Britt "was unconsciously taking vengeance" (p. 138). Her unconscious need for vengeance was a reaction to her husband's "controlling style," but she also was taking out on him "old angers at her father and at other men who had rejected her."

Negative Bypassing

Britt "had no insight into the fact that she was actively conjuring up old memories and injustices when sex was contemplated." In effect, Kaplan arrives at the stunning conclusion that Britt was engaged in *negative bypassing.* She was blocking out what would turn her on in her sexual encounters just as good bypassers block out what turns them off. "The mechanism of focusing on negatives to suppress desire is the mirror image, or the opposite, of conjuring up sexual fantasies in the service of liberating sexual desire" (Kaplan, 1979, p. 37). (Note here that "conjuring up" sexual fantasies "liberates" sexual desire, just as our patient Ann, above, "allowed" herself to relax by "forcing my mind to stop thinking in a sort of circular or negative kind of way.")

Thus, if negative reactions to sex are conjured up, there can be no reason to object to conjuring up positive reactions. They are just as arbitrary.

Since this equation is the linchpin of Kaplan's position, it requires her to *disqualify all negative reactions to sex*—to show that they are conjured up just as arbitrarily as the bypasser conjures up positive reactions. *Disorders of Sexual Desire* is singlemindedly devoted to that effort. "Inhibited sexual desire" (ISD) is a term tailor-made for the Kaplan (1979) version, since for her the cause of this disorder is "the involuntary and unconscious but active suppression of sexual desire" (p. 83). She goes on to say that:

> Most of the patients I have studied tend to suppress their desire by evoking negative thoughts or by allowing spontaneously emerging negative thoughts to intrude when they have a sexual opportunity. They have learned to put themselves into negative emotional states by selectively focusing their attention on a perception or thought or by retrieving some memory or allowing an association to emerge that carries a negative emotional valence. In this manner they make themselves angry, fearful, or distracted, and so tap into the natural physiologic inhibitory mechanisms which suppress sexual desire. . . .
>
> A patient will focus his/her attention on one of the partner's unattractive physical features—his pot belly, her unkempt hair, her fat thighs, the odor of his breath, or his genitals, etc.—in the service of shutting down the sex centers. Or the memory of the partner's unacceptable behavior or past injustices may be employed. The evening that lovemaking is in the air, he will focus on her overspending or her neglect to purchase some needed household item, and she will allow herself to be irritated by evidences of his immaturity or anxiety or suddenly recall that he did not buy her an anniversary present. (p. 83)

Kaplan appeals to the familiar fact that many people persist in bringing their problems to bed with them or even in being reminded of their problems when touched. This has always seemed to their partners to be unnecessary, perverse, and vindictive. Kaplan also links this sexual disposition to fears of intimacy. However, as we have proposed, good bypassers cannot help blocking out all worries and grudges, and for them intimacy is no hazard just because they can become instantly oblivious of their partners.

What we think Kaplan is missing here is the way that the poor bypasser is nevertheless *trying* to be oblivious in return, trying, ironically, even harder than the good bypasser, for whom bypassing is second nature. Indeed, this is our version of the cause of what we prefer to call sexual apathy rather than ISD. People who are sexually apathetic are trying too hard to be oblivious of the experience of being ignored, let down, or used by their partners. They do turn themselves off in this way. Here we agree with Kaplan. But where she argues that they turn themselves off by dwelling on their complaints, we argue that they turn themselves off by trying to get rid of their complaints.

We even agree with Kaplan that it is not their complaints, as such, that create their apathy. Feeling ignored, let down, or used cannot by itself cause sexual apathy, as we suggested earlier. It can only cause lack of sexual arousal. What causes sexual apathy is the *disqualification* of these complaints as a consequence of response anxiety. This brings us to the crucial question of what it is that makes Kaplan, as well as most other therapists and almost everyone else, think that the *cure* for sexual apathy is to disqualify the patient's complaints.

Self-disqualification of Sexual Complaints

We propose that people who suffer from sexual apathy are *inadequate complainers*. Like everyone else, they think that turning on should be easy, automatic, and relatively independent of the partner. They have already disqualified their complaints and are trying to bypass them, but they only get as far as feeling "nothing" (apathy). That is, they succeed only in losing track of their complaints. At best, all they can do is think in the language of pot bellies and fat thighs. The more brazen patient may be able to blurt out that "she (or he) doesn't turn me on," just as our patient Pat, whom we quoted near the beginning of the chapter, was able to say that she didn't like sex with her husband because it was so impersonal. But as we tried to demonstrate in discussing her case, this did not mean that she actually felt entitled to feel turned off. She could say the words, but on closer inspection it was clear that she did not think that her lack of arousal was *valid*.

Sexually apathetic patients are in a withdrawn state in which they typically are unaware of having any complaints. When they do have them, they are aware of only trivial vestiges of the real complaints. Kaplan's (1979) case of Roberta was a woman "who became enraged [at her husband] if he stirred his tea too vigorously or ate rapidly" (p. 177). This is a good instance of the ignominious faultfinding that to us characterizes the poor complainer. However, Kaplan's interpretation is that Roberta "had 'protected' herself from sexual intimacy with him by focusing on some trivial, unpleasant personal habits" (p. 177). Whereas can we infer from her reaction to her husband's hasty way with food his hasty way with her.

For us Roberta fits the picture of the conscientious wife who does not feel entitled to be turned off by her husband's sexual ways, believing, as does Kaplan, that she should be able to focus on his good qualities and on "the good life he offers her." She only gets as far as feeling that there is something wrong with her and accepting him sexually without enthusiasm (and only sporadically). Then when he rapes his food she can't stand it.

People like Roberta can only talk in the language of pot bellies and fat thighs, which earns them no credibility whatever, especially with themselves, and puts them at an even greater disadvantage in their sexual relationships. Clearly, they have done a poor job of convincing themselves or anyone else of their plight. (Perhaps it is only out of kindness that we are now to think of them as suffering from ISD rather than as being frigid.)

As we see it Roberta would be roused from her sexual apathy if she were able to *have* her complaint—that is, to feel entitled to it. Suppose for discussion's sake that her husband was as unsensual with her as he was with his food. Our experience is that when she can see the validity of her complaint she no longer feels apathetic. Then she merely is not aroused, an entirely different state and one typically amenable to quite simple remedies.

To establish the validity of such a complaint requires an investigation of the couple's *sexual reality*. Kaplan is so concerned with disqualifying sexual complaints and establishing that patients with ISD are turning themselves off that she gives no consideration to sexual reality other than to deny its immportance. There are only two cases in which she acknowledges the validity of a partner's complaints. In one woman's case Kaplan speaks of "the reality of the lack of intimacy and sexuality in her marriage," the outcome being that the woman got a divorce, since "she did not want to accept this kind of emotional deprivation (1979, p. 192)."

In the other instance in which Kaplan (1979) grants the validity of a parter's turned-off state, the only reason given is that the husband was "extremely obese (350 lbs., 5′3″)" and "unkempt," whereas his wife was "shy and petite" (p. 69). (Nothing is said about their sexual relationship except that he complained "that she did not desire him sexually.") The implication is that when complaints are valid rather than self-induced or conjured up, the case is hopeless.

Resistance

Pronounced resistance is apparently one effect of Kaplan's attempts to get patients to accept the interpretation that they are conjuring up negative reactions and that their complaints are invalid. Kaplan's first book was organized around this problem, but *Disorders of Sexual Desire* is almost exclusively devoted to it. Resistance to assignments that push for positve responses is endemic, but Kaplan has considerably increased the moral pressure. She says that if the patient does not respond to sensate focus assignments alone (structured to promote bypassing):

> The therapist becomes more actively confrontive. He creates a series of minicrises. For instance, he may create a crisis by confronting the patient with his resistance to pleasure, with his unconscious but active role in suppressing his feelings, and with the fact that he evokes negative feelings to suppress his sexuality. (1979, p. 110)

> The patient is now confronted with the fact that this "negative thinking" is under his control, that he has a choice, and that it is up to him if he wants to change. (1979, p. 106)

> Further insight can then be fostered by confronting the patient with the consequences of his inhibition. The crisis created by his realization that his marriage is in jeopardy, that his spouse is suffering, that he himself is being deprived of a normal life, can sometimes be used to unblock desire without further insight. (1979, p. 107)

> When they resist they are actively confronted. They cannot be allowed to "get away" with any sabotage, with any evasion, with any self-destructive act, with any obsessive thought, with the slightest rationalization, with anything that does not make sense. (1979, p. 120)

Kaplan (1979) points out that these "confrontations are at times intense and even audacious" (p. 121). Haley (1976) states that he finds it useful to tell patients that they are deliberately resisting, even though he does not believe this is the case, just because it often is a potent way to overcome resistance. Whether or not Kaplan's treatment effect is created by this moral pressure, she herself is pessimistic about the outcome with desire disorders, stating that "a full return of desire is exceptional" (1979, p. 196), and although she does not specifically give a success rate, it is apparently no better than 50 percent.

Outcome

What permits Kaplan to advocate her model despite this low success rate is her estimate that the success rate of the Masters and Johnson approach is only 10 percent to 20 percent (1979). Kaplan (1979) advises that "many treatment failures, frustrating to the clinician and discouraging to the patients, can be prevented by limiting traditional sex therapy [her term for the Masters and Johnson approach] to patients complaining of genital phase disorders [that is, to dysfunctions]" (p. 122).

However, Kolodny, Masters, and Johnson (1979), in a publication that appeared two weeks before Kaplan's book, included a chapter on sexual aversion and ISD in which they reported that in their treatment of ISD "satisfactory therapeutic outcomes are the rule rather than the exception" (p. 574). Also, shortly after this Kolodny (1979) delivered a paper in which he reported a provisional success rate of 80 percent for the treatment of sexual apathy at the Masters and Johnson Institute. Thus, their outcome statistics are the exact reverse of Kaplan's for their own therapy.

This discrepancy is easily accounted for. Kaplan's estimate is based on *her own success* with the Masters and Johnson approach. As we suggested earlier, it is easy to give instructions for sensate focus that push for performance, despite Masters and Johnson's own sensitivity to the risks of thereby increasing performance (response) anxiety. Our impression is that this can nullify its effectiveness.

Although these are soft figures (neither Kaplan nor the MJI group give outcome criteria or even the number of patients on which these figures are based), a difference as large as that between a 20 percent and an 80 percent success rate appears to be a real difference. Even the difference between Kaplan's approximately 50 percent success rate with sexual apathy and Masters and Johnson's 80 percent suggests a real difference. The MJI figure corresponds with our own success rate and raises a question about both Kaplan's approach and her contention that desire problems are the most difficult sex problems to treat.

Our impression is that sexual apathy poses the limiting case for bypassing sex therapy in general. It poses special difficulties for the Kaplan model only because her approach is uniquely singleminded and consistent in taking the side of the good bypasser, disqualifying the experience of the sexually apathetic patient, and treating sexual reality as irrelevant. The following vignette from *Disorders of Sexual Desire* (1979, pp. 108–109) serves to show how this approach can overlook simpler solutions:

Hilda: I started to feel good when he stroked me and then I had a rush of anger—I wanted to strangle him.

Therapist: Why? Was he doing something unpleasant?

Hilda: No—he was fine—he was trying hard to please. It's happened before. I get into a rage. . . . It is involuntary and inexplicable. . . . I feel very badly about that.

Therapist: Sounds like you manage to think of something that makes you angry when you two make love.

Hilda: I know, I've come to realize that. It's crazy. . . . I don't know why I do that. I get furious. I thought it was because of his erections, but it happened anyhow. He is so good to me—it doesn't happen with other men. Why?

Therapist: That's a good question.

Kaplan follows this vignette with the comment that Hilda "is confronted with the fact that she . . . is evoking negative responses in her self . . . [and] that in this way she spoils her sexual pleasure or 'protects' herself against the 'dangers' of sexual openess . . . [and] that, although she complains to the contrary, she on some level *does not want* to feel sexual" [italics in the original] (p. 109).

COUNTERBYPASSING SEX THERAPY

We would not be so ready to accept Hilda's own disqualification of her anger. We are less interested in why she is angry than in why she feels unentitled to her anger. It appears as a rush out of the blue, an indication that her anger is usually warded off (meaning that she detaches herself, i.e., withdraws in order to avoid it). We then would note how unjustified Hilda feels to be angry at her partner because "he is so good to me."

We might then introduce Hilda to what we consider to be a piece of sexual reality: People typically do feel that turning on should be easy and that it should not matter that much how your partner is treating you in bed if he is good to you out of bed. We might also add that it sometimes seems to us that there are two causes of sex problems: inconsiderateness and considerateness. It can be especially difficult to have a complaint about conscientious partners since one feels the pressure to like everything they do. This is to say that conscientious partners often intensify response pressure, making the other person feel guilty rather than aroused. Their unselfishness makes it harder for the partner to be selfish (sometimes causing the partner to have sadomasochistic fantasies, which only makes him or her feel all the more guilty).

The Hildas are always in danger of becoming apathetic, which then makes the conscientious partner try even more desperately to approach them in just the right way, perhaps even encouraged by their "low profile." Yet, after laying all this out we would want to add that none of this is necessarily the cause of Hilda's sexual apathy. This whole system we have sketched owes its preservation to the fact that Hilda and her husband do not talk about it.

Mindful of the reflexlike tendency for people to respond to this formulation by feeling remiss for not talking and by holding themselves responsible for it, we would assure them that no one talks in sex, at least with any intent to communicate anything other than verbal strokes. We would say that it seemed clear to us that like most people, Hilda and her husband had no way to talk because they had no way to make it safe and because they had no verbal repertoire in this area, no bank of shared meanings, just because all their energies had gone into blanking out any negative reactions.

Once Hilda and her husband grasped the way we had reframed the problem, they needed to talk from this perspective *during* their sexual encounters. We would suggest to them that talking about their sexual relationship is of value only if it helps them to share their experiences during sex. Toward the end of helping them to develop a repertoire we would give them a checklist (along with our written instructions for the sensate focus assignments) that consists of 50 typical, "negative" experiences in sex (in sex anything not strongly positive is considered negative. See appendix). We have the couple check the items that apply to them each time they do the assignment. We also require them to write notes on what they experienced in the assignments and to read these back to each other and to us at the next session.

The use of the checklist makes it clear that we are not pushing for positive responses and our experience is that this all but eliminates resistance to the assignments. In fact, when we do encounter resistance it is most likely to be from patients who still believe that we expect them to enjoy the assignments. It is not unusual for clients to laugh with relief just on reading the checklist.

Clearly, we do not believe that Hilda has a choice. We also do not believe that she does not want to feel sexual. We think that she is trying too hard to feel sexual. This is why so much resistance is engendered by telling her that she does not want to feel sexual, but this interpretation can also create a powerful ally in the patient's guilt, thereby creating an additional incentive to work at bypassing.

However, it is our experience that interpretations that *relieve* guilt and relieve response pressure are more likely to initiate a rapid resolution of the problem. Hence, we do not find that sexual apathy is necessarily a difficult problem to treat. As Masters (1979) once informally put it: "ISD is the one symptom that can be cured with just an idea." Such reframing typically is based on presenting to the couple the sexual realities we have reviewed here. (Kaplan considers sexual reality to be so irrelevant that she does not refer to the fact that of the 18 cases presented at length throughout *Disorders of Sexual Desire*, 15 are women.)

Although what we call counterbypassing usually consists of introducing the couple to their warded-off experiences and helping them to see the ways these experiences are valid, on some cases we find it useful to work with the couple to develop specific statements that express what they need to share, and that they can take with them into their sexual encounters. (We call these "script lines," and we chose the 50 lines that appear most frequently to construct our checklist.) A case illustration of this technique can serve to make our model plainer. To illuminate by contrast, we have chosen a case that would be least likely to be treated ego-analytically by other therapists.

> This is a case of a latent aversion that was brought out by the first sensate focus assignment and that was resolved in the second, in part, through the use of script lines. The presenting complaint was that despite what both partners described as an enjoyable sex life, the husband frequently felt compelled, immediately following sex with his wife, to go to a public men's room and perform fellatio. He said that the act did not arouse him, and that he often stopped in the middle because he would gag or feel disgusted. His leaving would trigger his wife's alcoholism, despite his protest that it had nothing to do with her.
>
> Rudy, age 27, a Chicano, was raised in a Mexican ghetto in a nearby large city, and had been married for two years to Tina, age 46, a black who was raised in a black ghetto in the local area. They said that they had no other complaints about their relationship and that it was clear to them that the

problem could have nothing to do with their sexual relationship since they cuddled a lot and people would even comment on how they were always touching.

They thought that Rudy's compulsion must have been caused by his having been repeatedly anally raped at age 7 by a babysitter, his 16-year-old uncle. (He said he hated it but was afraid to tell anyone.) However, his compulsion appeared only when this couple's sexual relationship began. Rudy's sexual orientation had always been ambiguous. He had had a long-term heterosexual relationship in high school, followed by a long-term homosexual relationship with one of his high school teachers (he said that he just endured the sexual side of that relationship).

The one clue that we did unearth about their sexual relationship was that even though they did a lot of touching, when it became sexual, and when Rudy wanted to reach orgasm, it was only by means of what Tina called a "quickie," during which there was little or no caressing.

Upon returning from the first assignment Rudy reported that he had been shocked that when his wife first touched his back (he was supine) he had felt an acute aversion for the first time in his heterosexual experiences, a reaction of phobic intensity that went far beyond anything he had felt even in his homosexual experiences. He said that he felt "the shudder of being groped," and that it reminded him of nightmares he had of hands grabbing him. He then panicked; he felt nauseated, his heart pounded, and he hyperventilated. He "prayed for deliverance."

We immediately remarked on the curious fact that Rudy had remained supine despite his gross distress, and could only pray to be released from the experience. We said that he really must have hated it. Why couldn't he say, "Stop, I can't stand it?"

Rudy was instantly relieved. His relief made it clear that he had expected us to be concerned only with the seeming inappropriateness of his reaction, not for us to locate his problem in his inability to cope with this reaction. It almost seemed witty to him for us to say that he hated it, he was so far from feeling entitled to the experience. He also laughed with relief at the thought that he could have told Tina to stop. It now also seemed funny to him that he could never have thought of that.

We found that neither Rudy nor Tina had ever been free to stop a sexual encounter. Tina was no freer to interrupt the assignment even though she could not help but notice signs of Rudy's distress, and even though this made it difficult for her to continue and, as we pointed out, even though there was then no way Rudy *could* have enjoyed it. We explained that almost everyone feels this compulsion to reciprocate in sex, that it is a symptom of response anxiety, and that the Masters and Johnson assignments are designed to block this compulsion and thus can quickly bring out the anxiety that ordinarily is bound by it.

As it happens, the instructions for our second assignment provide for what we call talk breaks and note breaks, and this gave Rudy and Tina some practice in stopping and talking as a way to relieve tension. We also worked with Rudy on script lines that he could refer to (and say) when touched. The lines that he got the most relief out of saying were, as usually is the case, quite simple: (1) "I feel tense"; (2) "I'm not getting anything out of this"; and (3) "This doesn't feel good but I don't know what would."

They were seen twice weekly for six weeks, but by the third session Rudy was no longer experiencing anxiety in the assignments and no longer felt the compulsion to visit public men's rooms. He seemed to enjoy being touched and had no trouble reaching orgasm while being touched. He also reported the relief of other symptoms he had not told us about: he had been phobic about driving in traffic, elevators, standing in lines, and answering the phone. Even more than we realized, his was the mentality of the trapped, although this is pathognomonic of both phobias and sexual apathy (and aversion). Both Rudy and Tina were excited about the fact that one day, after feeling aroused, but then not wanting to go on, they could stop and talk. Surprisingly, Tina said she felt free, like she could make an advance "without having to go all the way." On six-month and two-year follow-up the picture had not changed.

Lest the impression be gained that we did not help Rudy to deal with the effects of the rape experience (since this has been a frequent response to presentations of this case), we want to add that from the vantage point of the ego-analytic model the interventions we have already reported were intended to have that effect, even though from the vantage point of the standard, psychoanalytic model this is not at all apparent.

From our vantage point Rudy's problem was not that he was reliving the rape experience but that he was avoiding reliving it. He was afraid of how Tina would take it if he reacted aversively. As a result he had always felt somewhat apathetic in response to Tina's touch but he would compensate by immediately reciprocating. Thus, Rudy's apathy had been hidden, even from himself, by his quickness to touch Tina when she touched him. (This was only exposed because we used instructions that adhere closely to the Masters and Johnson version, in which the partners take strict turns at being giver and receiver.)

Rudy's previous female partners had apparently avoided touching him once they realized that he was responding apathetically. What created a greater strain for Rudy with Tina and hence may have generated his compulsion was that she responded by trying harder to arouse him (the good bypasser's reaction). This had the effect of making Rudy reciprocate even more compulsively, which was at least partly why they could never stop touching. Tina took his apparent responsiveness at face value (again like a good bypasser) and believed that she had been successful in arousing him. Yet he could only become aroused when they developed their quickie routine, in which she would avoid touching him.

As for why he had had the compulsion that brought him to us, his life was full of obscure, expiatory compulsions. This one appeared to reflect his feeling that by not reciprocating during their quickies he was using (screwing) Tina and that he then deserved to be used (screwed) in return. It was almost like a stab at mutuality. When sex was no longer so one-sided, he no longer felt this guilt (which also meant that he was freer to enjoy it).

A case like this is likely to be screened out by sex therapists working from the bypassing model not only because Rudy appears to be suffering from sex-role confusions that would be resistive to brief treatment, but because Rudy and Tina already were good bypassers and had taken that style as far as it can go. However, even if successfully applied, this strategy would risk increasing rather than relieving Rudy's response anxiety and hence would generate resistance, making the course of therapy longer and more arduous.

Summary

Sexual apathy is a state of withdrawal created in susceptible individuals by the pressure to respond affirmatively in sex. This response pressure is generated by a whole climate of opinion, one that most therapists share. We argue that most diagnostic concepts, from frigidity to inhibited sexual desire, reflect this climate of opinion, representing veiled admonishments of the kind that create sexual apathy. Sexually apathetic patients are considered (and consider themselves to be) "nonresponsive," meaning only that their actual responses are disqualified.

What reinforces the pariahlike status of those who are sexually apathetic is the seeming ability of the good bypasser to create a self-turn on. This autonomous sexual style has fostered the self-responsibility doctrine, best exemplified by the work of Helen Kaplan. Through exhortations to think positively she explicitly aims to disqualify the sexually apathetic patient's negative responses as a form of treatment. We propose that it is this kind of approach that creates the intense resistance and significantly lowered success rate that have thus far been attributed by many to the condition itself.

We propose that the treatment of sexual apathy is best carried out by the consistent application of Masters and Johnson's fundamental insight: that relieving response anxiety alone reverses the withdrawal that sexual apathy represents, thereby removing the block to sexual arousal, and that what makes sexual apathy seem intractable is the way that attempts to enhance sexual arousal can intensify response anxiety.

To most definitively relieve response anxiety requires reframing, meaning making the patient aware that sexual apathy is not a simple lack of sexual arousal but is a withdrawn state created by the pressure to respond affirmatively and the atmosphere of moral censure that the idea of frigidity and its derivatives represents. This moral censure can be seen to underlie therapeutic approaches that treat sexual apathy as a failure of responsibility by the apathetic person or by the partner. Training either partner to take responsibility is in effect to superimpose an administrative solution on the problem that creates an obstacle to the further development of our understanding of sexual arousal and sexual relationships. Approaching the problem on a psychological level offers the opportunity to expand our awareness of sexual reality and of the unrecognized stresses endemic to normal sexuality.

References

American Psychiatric Association. (1980). *Diagnostic and statistical manual of mental disorders* (3rd. ed.). Washington, D.C.: Author.

Apfelbaum, B. (1977a). On the etiology of sexual dysfunction. *Journal of Sex and Marital Therapy, 3,* 128–138.

Apfelbaum, B. (1977b). Sexual functioning reconsidered. In R. Genne & C. C. Wheeler (Eds.), *Progress in sexology* (pp. 93–100). New York: Plenum.

Apfelbaum, B. (1980). The diagnosis and treatment of retarded ejaculation. In S. R. Leiblum & L. A. Pervin (Eds.), *Principles and practice of sex therapy* (pp. 263–296). New York: Guilford.

Apfelbaum, B. (1984a). The ego-analytic approach to individual body-work sex therapy: Five case examples. *Journal of Sex Research, 20,* 44–70.

Apfelbaum, B. (1984b). Ego-analytic sex therapy: The problem of performance-anxiety. In R. T. Segraves & E. J. Haeberle (Eds.), *Emerging dimensions of sexology: Selected papers from the Sixth World Congress of Sexology* (pp. 127–132). New York: Praeger Publishers.

Apfelbaum, B., & Apfelbaum, C. (1973). Encountering encounter groups. *Journal of Humanistic Psychology, 13,* 53–67.

Apfelbaum, B., & Gill, M. M. (in preparation). [Ego analysis, id analysis, and standard psychoanalytic technique].

Crenshaw, T. L. (1983). *Bedside manners.* New York: McGraw-Hill.

Haley, J. (1976). *Problem-solving therapy.* San Francisco: Jossey-Bass.

Hartman, W. E., & Fithian, M. A. (1972). *The treatment of sexual dysfunction.* Long Beach, CA: Center for Marital and Sexual Studies.

Heiman, J. R. (1977). A psychophysiological exploration of arousal patterns in females and males. *Psychophysiology, 44,* 266–274.

Horney, K., (1933). Psychogenic factors in functional female disorders. In H. Kehnan (Ed.), *Feminine psychology* (pp. 162–174). New York: W. W. Norton, 1967.

Kaplan, H. S. (1974a, October). Friction and fantasy: No-nonsense therapy for six sexual malfunctions. *Psychology Today,* 76–86.

Kaplan, H. S. (1974b). *The new sex therapy.* New York: Brunner/Mazel.

Kaplan, H. S. (1976, June). *Recent developments in sex therapy.* Transcript of paper presented at the Nineteenth Annual Meeting of the Society for the Scientific Study of Sex, San Diego.

Kaplan, H. S. (1979). *Disorders of sexual desire.* New York: Brunner/Mazel.

Kilmann, P. R., & Mills, K. H. (1983). *All about sex therapy.* New York: Plenum Press.

Koch, J., & Koch, L. (1976). *The marriage savers.* New York: Coward, McCann & Geoghegan.

Kolodny, R. C. (1979). *The diagnosis and treatment of male inhibited sexual desire.* Paper presented at the Fourth International Congress of Sexology, Mexico City.

Kolodny, R. C., Masters, W. H., & Johnson, V. E. (1979). *Textbook of sexual medicine.* Boston: Little, Brown.

Kronhausen, P., & Kronhausen, E. (1975). *The sex people.* Chicago: Playboy Press.

Masters, W. H. (1979). Personal communication.

Masters, W. H. (speaker). (1983). *Three decade retrospective of the Masters and Johnson Institute.* (Tape No. 434-83, Audio-Stats). Los Angeles. Address to the Annual Meeting of the Society for the Scientific Study of Sex, Chicago.

Masters, W. H., & Johnson, V. E. (1966). *Human sexual response.* Boston: Little, Brown.

Masters, W. H., & Johnson, V. E. (1970). *Human sexual inadequacy.* Boston: Little, Brown.

Simon, B. (1975). Psychoanalytic approach. In C. A. Loew, H. Grayson, & G. H. Loew (Eds.), *Three psychotherapies: A clinical comparison.* New York: Brunner/Mazel.

Stuart, F. M., & Hammond, D. C. (1980). Sex therapy. In R. B. Stuart (Ed.), *Helping couples change.* New York: Guilford.

Zilbergeld, B., & Ellison, C. R. (1980). Desire discrepancies and arousal problems in sex therapy. In S. R. Leiblum & L. A. Pervin (Eds.), *Principles and practice of sex therapy* (pp. 65-101). New York: Guilford.

APPENDIX

*Script Lines Checklist**

Check the lines that apply to experiences you have had and that you've said or could imagine saying.

_____ 1. I feel uncomfortable.

_____ 2. I think your stroking feels mechanical.

_____ 3. I feel I'm supposed to like everything you are doing.

_____ 4. I'm worried about what you're thinking.

_____ 5. That doesn't feel good, but I don't know what would.

_____ 6. It feels like you're being too careful.

_____ 7. It feels like you're trying too hard.

_____ 8. I resent that you're not enjoying this more.

_____ 9. I don't know why we're doing this.

_____ 10. I wish it was OK to ignore you.

_____ 11. I feel hopeless about ever turning you on.

_____ 12. Right now my mind is a blank.

_____ 13. I wish I felt more like stroking you.

_____ 14. I wish I could enjoy your stroking.

_____ 15. This is a chore for me.

_____ 16. I'm not feeling anything.

_____ 17. I don't feel like talking.

_____ 18. I feel a million miles away.

_____ 19. This seems difficult and complicated.

_____ 20. I feel turned off.

_____ 21. I'm afraid you're going to feel rejected if I don't enjoy this more.

_____ 22. I feel like you need me to be more involved.

_____ 23. I want something, but I don't know what it is.

_____ 24. I don't think I'm going to like anything we're doing today.

_____ 25. I think I'm mostly doing this because I'm supposed to.

_____ 26. I'm beginning to feel impatient.

_____ 27. You seem preoccupied (or far away).

_____ 28. I feel like there's something else I want to say, but it's not on any of these scripts.

_____ 29. I'm afraid I'm not going to do a good enough job.

_____ 30. I'm afraid you're going to be disappointed.

_____ 31. I keep getting distracted.

_____ 32. I wish we could play hookey from this.

_____ 33. My mind keeps going off into fantasies.

_____ 34. I feel obliged to do as much for you as you've done for me.

_____ 35. I'm afraid you're getting bored.

_____ 36. I'm afraid you won't tell me if you don't like something.

_____ 37. I feel like we both have to succeed at this.

_____ 38. I'm feeling lazy, but like I'm not allowed to.

_____ 39. I'm feeling that there's too much I don't like.

_____ 40. I'm afraid of discouraging you.

_____ 41. I'm feeling too finicky.

_____ 42. I'd feel like a pest if I said everything I wanted.

_____ 43. I'd like to take a break.

_____ 44. I'm afraid you'd get mad if I stopped doing this.

_____ 45. I wish this wasn't so important.

_____ 46. I feel like there's something you want, but I don't know what it is.

_____ 47. I feel like I should appreciate what you are doing more.

_____ 48. It feels like something just went wrong, but I don't know what it is.

_____ 49. I can't seem to concentrate on what I'm doing.

_____ 50. I hate these script lines.

SECTION 4

Uncoupling and Beyond

EIGHTEEN

Separation and Divorce: Clinical Implications for Parents and Children

Nathan W. Turner, Ed.D.
Assistant Professor of Psychiatry and Human Behavior
Jefferson Medical College
Sandra Strine, Ph.D.
Private Practice

INTRODUCTION

Separation and divorce create more changes for parents and their children than most other life events. Only death creates a more permanent change. The stress level for parents and children is greater than the casual observer might consider (Wallerstein & Kelly, 1980). While the stress might be quite high, the changes for the parents and children can be either positive, negative, or a combination of both (Kurdek & Siesky, 1980; Wallerstein and Kelly, 1980).

Although there are many stages to the separation and divorce process (Turner, 1980), we will confine our discussion in this chapter to four basic stages of the divorce process in which parents and children have opposing needs: (1) deterioration, (2) separation, (3) consolidation, and (4) divorce. The energy demanded to resolve conflicting needs is often not available in the emotionally overloaded family system. Hence, a clearer understanding of predictable trouble spots, with possible effective interventions, can be of value. Areas of complementary needs will also be discussed to aid the clinician in working for win/win solutions as often as possible.

It will be our purpose to trace some of the more important, opposing needs of parents and children and to provide a framework in which these needs may be understood and dealt with by the therapist relating to the case.

Just as the parent(s)' needs change through divorce, the child(ren) need stability in the family. Parents need to fight and assign blame while the child needs to find peace and take a neutral position. While children require lots of affection, parents who are moving toward separation and divorce feel less than affectionate toward anyone (at least on certain days). It is a given then that parents and children will have different needs during the various phases of separation and divorce.

DETERIORATION

Psychological violation of known but unverbalized contracts is what is commonly termed *disenchantment* in a deteriorating marital relationship (Sager, 1976; Turner, 1980). Among the most common sources of relationship disenchantment are (1) growth or change in self or spouse, (2) impact of major life events, (3) social comparison of one's marriage with other marriages, (4) shift in the reward/cost ratio in the marriage, (5) attraction to a third party, and (6) beginning of a gradual withdrawal leading to disenchantment (Turner, 1980).

Other possible variables which may contribute to the demise of a marriage are: (1) developmental differences between the spouses' rate of personal growth (Berman & Lief, 1975); (2) differences in reactions to stressful situations and in one's ability to cope (Peterson, Leigh, & Day, 1984); (3) marrying for different reasons and coming to the realization that the marriage was a mistake; and (4) arrival of the first child within the first two years of marriage. Clearly, there are still other variables that contribute to the demise of a marriage but it is not the purpose of this chapter to explore them all.

According to Bohannon (1970) the first step in the divorcing process is the "emotional divorce," or the painful realization that the emotions once directed toward the other spouse are now being directed away from or against the spouse. Feelings of marital equilibrium begin to change to feelings of disequilibrium (Kolevszon & Gottlieb, 1983).

As marital conflict heightens and the deterioration of the relationship is acknowledged by the spouses, time and energy are directed toward the major decision of whether or not to separate (Turner, 1980). Some parents have less energy and attention to give to their children at this time. They often become less loving and affectionate and may cease setting limits for their children because they are too emotionally exhausted to enforce them. Other parents may move to the opposite extreme and overcontrol their children, using them as scapegoats for the rage they feel toward their spouses (Isaacs, 1981). In our experience, a few parents do draw closer to their children at this time in anticipation of the impending loss of the marital relationship.

Most parents do not tell their children what is "really going on" during the deterioration phase for fear of upsetting them needlessly (Kurdek & Siesky, 1979). Even though the emotional climate of the home may have changed dramatically, parents typically want children to behave as if nothing has changed. Parents need to have their children's behavior be stable while they focus their own energy on the marital crisis. Parents also often need to accelerate the conflict with each other in order to break through their ambivalence and come to a decision about whether or not to separate (Turner, 1980, 1982). A separation that does not occur with the help of a professional therapist will in most cases become a de facto contribution to the deterioration of the marriage to an even greater degree than before.

When disenchantment begins the children, sensing the emotional climate in the home changing radically, begin to search for explanations. Younger children tend to blame themselves for the conflict and older children begin to wonder if their family will be breaking up. At this time children have a strong need to be reassured that they are loved and are not responsible for the turmoil they see and/or hear around them. They want to know what is actually going on since their fantasies are often worse than the reality, as this case illustrates.

CASE ONE

Six months after the separation of his parents, a six-year-old only child who had become extremely accident prone confided to the female therapist that he knew why they had *really* broken up. About a week before the breakup the child had brought home a report card containing negative comments about his classroom behavior. Later that same night he had heard his parents fighting about him. In the week that followed he had tried to be very, very good, but his mother kept yelling at him and then breaking into tears and his father totally ignored him. When the father moved out without even saying goodbye to the son, the child became convinced that his bad report card had caused the father to become angry and to leave. No other explanation was even offered to the child because, as the parents later explained, they thought he was "too young" to know the reasons for the separation.

Parents tend to avoid telling children the total story since they intuitively know that children want to keep the family intact. They may see leveling with children as adding another crisis to the marital trauma. Children can become anxious and upset by living with parents who are anxious and upset themselves. Therefore, children's anxiety may induce regressive behavior, acting out tendencies, or simply increased demands for parental attention. Parents who set firm, clear limits help to reduce the anxiety of worried children.

Research findings suggest that children who are totally shielded from marital conflict have a harder time understanding the need for separation (Wallerstein & Kelly, 1980). On the other hand, parents who air all their conflicts in front of their children induce needless parentification and loyalty splits. Yet, if children are protected from the fact that serious marital discord is brewing, they may feel forever confused by the later announcement of an impending separation. Children need time to prepare emotionally for a separation. Therefore, the parents' need to postpone making major announcements to children until late in the decision-making process runs counter to a child's need to be fully informed and have time to prepare for a major life change. Children's questions deserve candid, trustworthy answers such as "Yes, we are having marriage problems," or "We just don't know yet whether we will work out our problems or not. We are really trying."

Therapists need to bring honesty and clarity into the family communication system during this period of marital and family deterioration. One role of the clinician is to assist the parents in being aware of how their decision making can impact on the children. By delaying telling the children for too long, parents disenfranchise their children. Children may lose the right to make their own decisions, to become emotionally prepared on their own level, and to have a legitimate part in the family's systemic processes.

SEPARATION

The decision to separate is a complicated one. There are known stages in the decision-making process which Janis and Mann (1977) have described in their five-step model. The five steps are:

1. Appraising the challenge (what are the risks if I don't change?).
2. Surveying alternatives (have I surveyed all possible alternatives?).
3. Weighing alternatives (which alternative will best meet my goals?).
4. Deliberating about commitment (will I act on the best alternative?).
5. Adhering to decisions despite negative feedback (what are the risks if I change or don't change?).

"Once the individual decides to act, she/he will begin to search for alternatives" (Turner, 1980). It may be assumed in most cases that once the perceived costs are greater than the rewards for remaining in the marriage, the individual will decide to leave the marriage (Kitson, Holmes, & Sussman, 1983).

An understanding of decision-making steps and dynamics is essential for the clinician to offer sage and supportive counsel during the intricate steps the individual is navigating. For example, it is crucial that the therapist realize that vacillation is the hallmark of the third step, weighing alternatives. "The concern is to make the best possible decision in light of all the alternatives. The person tends to remain at this stage until completely ready to make a commitment to one alternative and carry it out" (Turner, 1980, p. 159). If a therapist prematurely urges a person to "get on with it" and to unduly shorten this third step, thereby meeting the therapist's rather than the client's needs to continue to vacillate as a normative process, unnecessary regression and/or depression may occur. Further, during the fifth step it is very important for the clinician to monitor the client's capacity to cope with negative feedback about the decision to separate and/or divorce (Janis & Mann, 1977; Turner, 1980).

Finally, it should be kept in mind that the five-step process might not proceed in a clear, linear sequence.

> It is important to note that although decision-making processes generally appear to move from stage one to stage five, reversion to a prior stage may occur not only once but several times from either stage three or four, during the complex process of deciding about a separation or divorce. The decision to separate or divorce is not a simple or an easy one to make. (Turner, 1980, p. 160)

It should be noted that people often stay in unrewarding marriages because the comparison level of alternatives is unacceptable (Thibaut & Kelley, 1959). For example, if dissatisfaction seems preferable to loneliness or poverty, a spouse may decide to stay in an unhappy marriage. This notion of the comparison level of alternatives explains the prime motivation of many who need an affair or a serious relationship as a precursor to deciding to leave a marriage.

When parents have decided to separate they need to tell their children that they have made a decision to physically separate. Children need to know as much as parents can tell them at that time about where they will live, with whom, and for how long. Children also need to have some explanation about why the parents are separating. It is important for parents to make it clear that the children are not the cause of the separation or problems.

Many adults have difficulty sharing the painful news about separation with their children. Some deny that very young children even need an explanation. Some leave it to the other spouse to do the telling. We recommend that parents inform their children together and model parental cohesiveness despite the marital rift. Studies indicate that how a child is told that his/her parents will be separating can have a dramatic effect on the child's adjustment (Kurdek & Siesky, 1981). Children who are told that the reasons behind the decision have to do with the parents' having grown apart from each other so much that they can no longer be happy living with each other will be *less* likely to keep hoping that their parents will reconcile. The children will have a clearer understanding of the meaning of divorce in terms of the parents' "psychological separation."

When a decision to separate has been made, concerns about informing family, relatives, and friends often surface. Disapproval by one's children only serves to complicate the decision and, for some, children's unhappiness may act as a deterrent to the actual separation. For these reasons the decision to separate is usually tested out first with persons from whom approval and understanding are expected. Those from whom disapproval is expected tend to be told last.

An important variable to be monitored by clinicians is the capacity of the individual to cope with negative feedback received about the recent decision and to adhere to the decision in spite of opposition (Turner, 1980). Also of concern to the clinician should be those individuals who totally deny feelings of grief over ending a marriage. Many people become overly elated and flee into an affair or a second adolescence. Others become overly angry and blame the partner for everything. In our experience, full recovery from divorce depends on one's ability to experience the sadness of the loss, to take responsibility for one's own contribution to the demise of the marriage, and to begin to direct attention to building a new life and a new relationship with one's children.

During the separation stage, custody decisions and visiting arrangements are determined. Children need to know that they will still have regular contact with both parents (Wallerstein & Kelly, 1980). It has been found that how the custodial parent defines his/her situation and continues to cope with child-rearing responsibilities influences the social competence of children (Peterson, Leigh, & Day, 1984). Many studies suggest that custodial parents often define their situation as being untenable when extensive role conflicts develop (Hetherington, Cox, & Cox, 1979; Peterson, et al., 1984; Spanier & Castro, 1979).

Upon separation, role diffusion often erupts within the custodial home. The custodial parent is called upon to be more of a disciplinarian than is desired and more of an emotional support to the children than is possible. He or she must often function as two parents since one is missing. It is important for parental agreement about such matters as discipline, house rules, homework, special events, holiday observances, and the like to be high in order for clear messages to be given to the children. However, parental agreement in most matters is notoriously low during the process of separation (Hetherington et al., 1979).

It is important to observe that recent literature notes that several personal skills help custodial parents to handle increased role demands and to view their new role in a positive way. These capacities include marketable skills, nontraditional sex-role attitudes, the ability to establish new social relationships, high levels of education, substantial income, emotional maturity, and the capacity to define new role demands as being rewarding (Hetherington et al., 1979). To illustrate, certain divorced women have the capacity to assign a *positive* definition to their circumstances; that is, to see divorce as an opportunity to pursue new careers and/or to engage in parent-child relationships free of interference from their former partners. Furthermore, women who possess nontraditional sex-role attitudes seem more capable of viewing their divorced situation as one of increased autonomy (Peterson et al., 1984).

Money is usually a major issue in newly separated families. The increased living expenses of two households, extra commuting, and unexpected bills all add to the stress level for the family system. Parents often have to adjust their own standard of living downward in order to maintain an adequate and satisfying lifestyle for the children. Minimal depletion of financial resources is seen as one variable in children's positive divorce adjustment (Desimone-Luis, O'Mahoney, & Hunt, 1979; Hodges, Wechsler, & Ballantine, 1979).

Sometimes parents have a need to express their sadness and vulnerability to their children in the early stages of separation. Some children find it frightening to see their parents cry or be upset since they have a need for their parents to be strong and "in control." In our experience however, the parent's need to draw close to the children is *only* accomplished through this willingness to be vulnerable. This parental vulnerability and honesty has nothing to do with using children as confidants or go-betweens, a clear exploitation of one's offspring. The latter has the danger of placing children of varying ages into social/emotional roles far beyond their years and abilities.

Parents need to begin a single life with new interests, new friends, and possibly new intimate relationships. These needs often conflict with the children's needs for parental companionship and for reassurance of the parent's love to counter their fears of more loss and abandonment. Children who see that their parents are more nurturing and giving after developing new friendships are less threatened and fearful as time goes on. Clinicians need to encourage a balance in the lives of newly separated parents between time for giving to self and time for giving to their children.

As parents find ways to care for themselves in order that they can be more emotionally available to their children, they begin to find themselves in what we term the consolidation phase.

CONSOLIDATION

The consolidation phase is one in which spouses gradually achieve emotional distance from each other, thereby confirming their decision to remain separated. During this time of diminishing parental ambivalence about the decision to separate, the children may continue to have hopes of parental and familial reconciliation. Children need their parents to be unambiguous about the decision to separate. The "on again, off again" quality of so many marriages is confusing and upsetting to children who want and need predictability in their lives. Their parents' problem is not their problem, yet they are directly affected by it as the following case illustrates.

CASE TWO

> A 12-year-old girl in our separation/divorce workshop was extremely upset by the coming and going of her father who had moved in and out of the family home three times in the past six months. "I don't know why she keeps taking him back!" she complained. A slightly older girl offered, "Maybe your mom still loves him. After my parents split up they stopped fighting. I noticed that Mom would comb her hair and put lipstick on before my Dad would come over. And now he's going to move back in." "Maybe you're right," replied the 12 year old. "Mom keeps saying how much Dad has changed since the separation."

Working out the details of a single, coparenting or visiting type relationship with the spouse can produce conflict or, occasionally, a confusing kind of closeness. While children have a need for their parents not to fight over them (Hess & Camara, 1979; Rosen, 1979; Wallerstein & Kelly, 1980), an overly friendly relationship between parents can trigger children's reunion fantasies, especially if there are no other romantic interests in the lives of the parents. Persistent reunion fantasies need to be handled by parents with statements such as, "It must be odd for you to see Dad (or Mom) and me talking without fighting. We're only able to do that because we don't have to live together anymore."

For adults, building a new life in terms of career, education, and new friendships is a primary task of the consolidation period. Finding new ways of adapting to a single lifestyle is a continuing challenge for the newly separated adult. Adapting to the primary role of being economically self-supporting is a major challenge, especially for the woman without a career or marketable skills. The style of one's decisions as well as their ultimate effectiveness will determine much of one's future. (Weiss, 1975; Janis & Mann, 1977). "Decisions pertaining to a new career, further education, relating to family and friends, and even how to relate to children and the former spouse involve social arenas of potential success or failure" (Turner, 1980, p. 161). For many the consolidation phase can be compounded by a mixture of feelings such as feeling guilty over being so relieved, joyful, and peaceful after years of marital conflict.

During the consolidation period children, especially those under age 10, need their parents to be interested, involved, and available to help them build a new life. Therapists need to encourage parents to plan special things to do with each child as well as activities with all the children. A typical feeling on the part of parents is "there is not enough of me to go around." Clinicians can facilitate the need of both parents and children to build and improve relationships by pointing out the need for balance and advance planning around the allocation of time. Parents with active support systems can more readily give to needy children.

During the dating time of each parent with new "friends" the more open sexuality of each spouse will raise issues and questions for the children about sexuality (Wallerstein & Kelly, 1980). Therapists can facilitate values clarification for both adults and children during family therapy sessions. Children often feel that their parents should not be dating others even when the parents themselves have agreed to do so. The clinician must help children to understand that it is natural and healthy for parents to go out and have a good time with friends. It is equally important to help adults temper their enthusiasm for bringing dates home prematurely and/or behaving in a sexually provocative manner in front of children who are still adjusting to marital separation. Questions such as "Who to bring home? When? What is appropriate to share with children?" need to be considered.

Children may also experience a parent's freedom to be close to other adults as yet another painful rejection. The expression of adolescent sexuality is often triggered at this time as illustrated in the following case example.

CASE THREE

> As the custodial father began to deepen his relationship with the woman he had been dating for several months, he began to receive some good-natured kidding from his 16-year-old son who had been "going steady" for more than a year. Indeed, the parallels of open affection and delight in each other's company were obvious to all. Eventually, the father and his new woman friend began to stay overnight openly at each other's homes. One morning when the father went in to awaken the son (as was his custom), he found the boy missing. When it was discovered that the son had been secretly meeting and sleeping with his 15-year-old girlfriend, the boy's retort was in effect, "Well, Dad, this is what you're doing!"

The larger family system includes the extended family on both sides of the marriage. During separation and divorce parents often tend to minimize contact with ex-in-laws due to friction, judgments, or pressures to continue the marriage rather than separate and divorce. But children tend to do best when cordial and supportive relationships with kin can be sustained (Jacobson, 1978; Kurdek & Siesky, 1980). Stagnated relationships do not benefit either generation. Therapists need to encourage the continuity of all possible extended family relationships and the working through of problems for the sake of all (Boszormeny-Nagy & Spark, 1973; Bowen, 1961). Both parents and children can benefit from avoiding further losses of supportive relationships. Family therapy sessions that include necessary members of the extended families who are geographically available would be the clinical intervention of choice. The importance of social system variables that can assist the therapist in diagnosis and treatment choices are noted by Green.

> In regard to divorce adjustment counseling and therapy, the identification of the effects of the predivorce relationship, the level of alternative attractions, and the amount of external pressures to remain married in the post divorce environment may prove to be valuable diagnostic indicators for professionals aiding individuals cope with the adjustment to divorce. (1983, p. 72)

Once the period of consolidation (whether short or long) has been experienced, each spouse at some point determines that the marriage is not worth reconciling and decides to terminate it in divorce. "Divorce is more likely to occur when the material, symbolic, and affectional rewards of remaining married are low and the costs are high. Withdrawing the divorce petition is not a random event. It is more likely when the potential rewards of the divorce are low, the costs are high, and the alternatives available elsewhere are limited" (Kitson, Holmes, & Sussman, 1983, p. 53).

DIVORCE

Once the decision has been made one spouse may feel a sense of relief while the other spouse may feel "left" and rejected (unless it was a mutually determined decision). Parents often need to express frustration about divorce and related decisions such as custody, support, finances, and visitation (Turner, 1980). Children, in contrast, need to feel that they are not caught in the middle of parental disputes again. Ironically, once the decision to divorce has been made by parents (closure for adults), a series of new issues arise for the children (open issues for children) including "Where will I continue to live and with whom?" "Do both parents still love me?" "Was it my fault?" "Will I have to change schools and leave my friends?" and "Will I get to live with my other siblings or will we be divided up between our two parents?" Therapists therefore need to encourage the parents to vent their strong feelings of loss, helplessness, and despair to friends, peers, and clinicians out of respect for the children's need for closure on their parents' marital problems. Triangulation of children into the marital dynamics during separation and divorce is often an underdiagnosed variable. Family therapy is the preferred form of therapeutic intervention for dealing with the total system at one time and for dealing with the "secrets," triangulations (using children as "messengers"), and the unhealthy venting of negative feelings onto children.

Divorce impacts on all generations involved in a family system, from children to grandparents. The need for grandparental support (support from one's own parents) remains a factor throughout the divorce process. It is typical for grandparents to perceive divorce as a reflection on their own parenting skills ("Where did I go wrong in raising my child?"). Hence, they are often understandably not able to accept or support the demise of their offspring's marriage. If grandparents are willing to be involved in their offsprings' therapeutic process, then family therapy with the extended family system may effectively deal with their hurt and disappointment.

Middle-aged adults who divorce need support from their adult children who are often outraged at having the context of their emotional security (intact family) stripped away at a time when they are experiencing important individual and marital development (Turner, 1980). Therapists need to facilitate communication between the generations in order to reduce the threat of relational stagnation and retarded recovery of the divorcing adult.

Among the issues the adult moves through in reconstructing her/his personal life after divorce are (1) identity and personal reorganization, (2) family realignment, (3) social role reconstruction, (4) vocational change or reappraisal, and (5) assessment of one's values (Turner, 1980). In an analogous manner, children move through similar issues at their own level of development and maturity.

Identity and personal reorganization issues which are raised for the adult are typified by questions like "Who am I?" and "Who am I to become?" Either a partial or complete life reorganization is triggered for the adult including being single again, living with new financial realities, and having to start a new form of social life. In family realignment one's ties with the family of origin may be strained or broken. Certainly, strains may occur with one's former in-laws, children, and other relatives depending on the strength of the original relationship. In moving into the singles world again the adult has to reconstruct social roles and build skills including dating, learning how to deal with rejection(s), and learning to handle uncertainty about whether to ever trust the opposite sex again. Divorce usually impacts females more than males with a need to reappraise their vocational plans and careers. Further education and training may be needed by the female who has been out of the working world for years. All of the preceding changes can trigger a need to reassess one's values regarding marriage, family, sex, lifestyle, money, career, and education (Turner, 1980).

The parent's recovery from divorce is often synchronized with the development of a new intimate relationship. Remarriage can be a hasty decision without appropriate deliberation with one's self or one's children. Children, seeking to minimize change and further adjustments to new adults or new children in their lives, frequently oppose the idea of remarriage for either parent. Therapists need to encourage ex-spouses to move very slowly toward a new commitment; full recovery from divorce often takes from two to five years (Weiss, 1975). Relationships among potential step family members need to be built gradually for optimal adjustment later by all concerned (Visher & Visher, 1982). Family therapy sessions can be very helpful in the facilitation of building potential step family relationships in an open, healthy manner.

Clinical Applications

The following tables list in summary fashion (1) the parent's need, (2) the child's need, and (3) a potential therapist's role for the guidance of the busy clinician (see Tables 1, 2, 3, and 4). Obviously there are many more methods of therapeutic intervention. We have only listed a few, generic ones for the sake of general illustration. Hopefully, this listing will serve to stimulate the therapist to think about the unique dynamics occurring between parent(s) and child(ren) and the need for thoughtful forms of therapeutic intervention for the sake of the total family system.

TABLE 1 Deterioration Phase

Parent's Need	*Child's Need*	*Therapist's Role*
To acknowledge deterioration of marriage; to take time deciding whether or not to separate	To have parents get along; to be reassured he/she is loved and not responsible for the change in emotional climate	Encourage honest sharing about conflict and reduce blaming between spouses
Not to tell the children for fear of upsetting them needlessly	To know what is really going on; fantasies worse than reality	Deal with fantasies of children; get parent to answer honestly
To have children behave well so personal crisis can be handled	To have parents set firm limits and not be angry when child's anxiety induced regression occurs	Point out process: misbehavior following increased anxiety; help parents resolve crisis; set firm limits with children via family therapy
To accelerate marital conflict (and discharge anger on kids if they misbehave!)	To have parents not fight; to have increased parental attention, understanding, and patience	Help children see parents' need to try to resolve problems; encourage parents to save some energy for the children via family therapy

TABLE 2 Separation Phase

Parent's Need	*Child's Need*	*Therapist's Role*
To tell children a physical separation will occur and why	To know the truth; to know he/she is not responsible for the decision; to have both parents together	Encourage two-sided, honest explanation with no scapegoating of children; to tell children parents cannot live happily together with both parents present or in a family therapy session
To have the children be OK	To talk about separation with family and friends; to react to the news and reality of the separation; to have freedom to regress, be sad, be depressed, be afraid	Point out to parents that children must go through their own process and often need to deal with layers of feelings including fear, anxiety, anger, depression, and hostility
To decide on custody and visiting arrangements; work out relationship with spouse and children	To know he/she is loved; to know he/she will see both parents and when; to have parents not fight, (reunite?), agree on discipline	Facilitate parental disputes about custody and visitation; keep children out of the middle; coordinate child-rearing practices of parents; capitalize on desire of parents and children to have better relationship
To decide on changes such as standard of living, schooling, and/or career plans	To keep things as much the same as possible; to not have money problems	Help reality test with family; initiate problem solving around common issues; minimize changes at child level (e.g. allowances, treats, etc.)
To express sadness; to draw close to children	To have the parents be OK; to get extra comfort and nurturing from parents	Facilitate honest sharing; prevent dumping and parentification; encourage mutual nurturing
To begin a single life with new friends and new interests	To have companionship of parent and reduce threat of further loss	Help children understand adult needs to have peers and outlets so he/she can be more giving to children

TABLE 3 Consolidation Phase

Parent's Need	*Child's Need*	*Therapist's Role*
To consolidate decision to divorce; achieve emotional distance from spouse	To have parents be unambiguous about separation or to have parents reunite	Help spouses resolve ambivalence; deal with children's reunion fantasies
To work out the single, co- or visiting relationship with spouse	To have parents not fight	Help parents resolve visitation issues, so children experience minimal friction
To build a new life; career and education; improved parent-child relationship	To have parent interested, involved, and available to help child build new life; to be able to express deep feelings or act them out	Encourage parents to plan special things to do with and for each child; capitalize on desire of both parent and child to improve relationship
To date; to have outside interests; to change values to fit new life; to work out relationships with extended family	To have parent to him/herself; to have parent stay the same; to have continuity, avoid further loss; to have cordial and supportive relationships with extended family	Mediate conflicting parent-child needs; point out when children are adults' priority; help adults and children with values clarification; facilitate working out relationships with extended family—a win/win situation!

TABLE 4 Divorce Phase

Parent's Need	*Child's Need*	*Therapist's Role*
To express frustration about divorce decisions such as custody, support, visiting	To have parents be happy; not to be in the middle of parents' disputes	Encourage parents to ventilate frustration to friends, therapist; keep children from being triangulated
To have parental support; to have support of grown children	Not to be in the middle of extended family arguments; to have family intact	Help adults work through issues with family of origin; facilitate communication between parent and grown children
To express broad range of feelings toward former spouse	Not to be confused about finality of the divorce	Encourage parents not to ventilate these confusing feelings to vulnerable children
To perhaps remarry and enter into a stepfamily relationship	To minimize change and need for further adjustments and concessions	Encourage adults to move very slowly toward a new commitment; to allow relationship to build gradually

Summary

This chapter has covered four stages of separation and divorce in which parents and children often have oppositional needs: (1) deterioration, (2) separation, (3) consolidation, and (4) divorce. Differences in parents' and children's energy levels, parents' emotional ability to give and receive, levels of discipline needed, and levels of decision making were discussed.

Different levels of anxiety, fear, overreactions, and need for reassurance were discussed as they varied according to the needs of the adult or of the child. Separation dynamics, custody issues, single-parenting binds, and economic pressures were discussed. Characteristics of divorced women who cope better than average were noted. Decision-making dynamics were enumerated at key junctures during the separation and divorcing processes.

Finally, the impact of divorce on all generations was covered, with special emphasis placed on the value of family therapy for the total familial system as the treatment method of choice.

References

Berg, B., & Kelly, R. (1979). The measured self-esteem of children from broken, rejected and accepted families. *Journal of Divorce, 2*, 363–370.

Berman, E. M., & Lief, H. I. (1975). Marital therapy from a psychiatric perspective: An overview, *American Journal of Psychiatry, 132*(6), 583–592.

Bohannan, P. (Ed.) (1970). *Divorce and after.* New York: Doubleday Publishing.

Bowen, M. (1961). The family as a unit of study and treatment. *American Journal of Orthopsychiatry, 31*, 40–60.

Boszormenyi-Nagy, I., & Spark, G. M. (1973). *Invisible loyalties*. New York: Harper & Row.

Desimone-Luis, J., O'Mahoney, K., & Hunt, D. (1979). Children of separation and divorce: Factors influencing adjustment. *Journal of Divorce, 3*, 37–42.

Green, R. G. (1983). The influence of divorce prediction variables on divorce adjustment: An expansion and test of Lewis' and Spanier's theory of marital quality and marital stability. *Journal of Divorce, 7*(1), 67–81.

Hess, R. D., & Camara, K. A. (1979). Post-divorce family relationships as mediating factors in the consequences of divorce for children. *Journal of Social Issues, 35*, 79–96.

Hetherington, E. M., Cox, M., & Cox, R. (1979). The development of children in mother-headed families. In D. Reiss & H. Hoffman (Eds.), *The American family: Dying or developing* (pp. 117–145). New York: Plenum Press.

Hodges, W. F., Wechsler, R. C., & Ballantine, C. (1979). Divorce and the preschool child: Cumulative stress. *Journal of Divorce, 3*, 55–68.

Isaacs, M. B. (1981). Treatment for families of divorce: A systems model of prevention. In I. Stuart & L. Abt (Eds.), *Children of separation and divorce* (pp. 242–254). New York: Van Nostrand Reinhold Company.

Jacobson, D. S. (1978). The impact of marital separation/divorce on children: III. Parent-child communication and child adjustment. *Journal of Divorce, 2,* 175–194.

Janis, I. L., & Mann, L. (1977). *Decision making: A psychological analysis of conflict, choice and commitment.* New York: The Free Press.

Kitson, G. C., Holmes, W. M., & Sussman, M. B. (1983). *Withdrawing divorce petitions: A predictive test of the exchange model of divorce. Journal of Divorce,* 7(1), 51–66.

Kolevzon, M. S., & Gottlieb, S. J. (1983). *The impact of divorce: A multivariate study, Journal of Divorce,* 7(2), 89–98.

Kurdek, L. A. (1981). An integration perspective on children's divorce adjustment. *American Psychologist, 36,* 856–866.

Kurdek, L. A., & Siesky, A. (1979). An interview study of parents' perceptions of their children's reactions and adjustments to divorce. *Journal of Divorce, 3,* 5–18.

Kurdek, L. A., & Siesky, A. (1980). Effects of divorce on children: the relationships between parents' and child's perspectives. *Journal of Divorce, 4,* 85–100.

Lebow, J. L. (1984). On the value of integrating approaches to family therapy. *Journal of Marital and Family Therapy, 10*(2), 127–137.

Peterson, G. W., Leigh, G. K., & Day, R. D. (1984). Family stress theory and the impact of divorce on children. *Journal of Divorce,* 7(3), 1–20.

Porter, B., & O'Leary, K. D. (1980). Marital discord and childhood behavior. *Journal of Abnormal Child Psychology, 8,* 287–295.

Raschke, H. J., & Raschke, V. J. (1979). Family conflict and children's self-concepts. *Journal of Marriage and the Family, 41,* 367–374.

Rosen, R. (1979). Some crucial issues concerning children of divorce. *Journal of Divorce, 3,* 19–26.

Sager, C. J. (1976). *Marriage contracts and couple therapy.* New York: Brunner/Mazel.

Santrock, J. W., & Warchak, R. A. (1979). Father custody and social development in boys and girls. *Journal of Social Issues, 35,* 112–125.

Spanier, G. B., & Casto, R. F. (1979). Adjustment to separation and divorce: A qualitative analysis. In G. Levinger & O. C. Moles (Eds.), *Divorce and separation: Content, causes, and consequences* (pp. 211–227). New York: Basic Books.

Stolberg, A. L., & Anker, J. M. (1983). Cognitive and behavioral changes in children resulting from parental divorce and consequent environmental changes. *Journal of Divorce,* 7(2), 23–41.

Thibaut, J. W., & Kelley, H. H. (1959). *The social psychology of groups.* New York: John Wiley & Sons.

Turner, N. W. (1980). Divorce in mid-life: Clinical implications and applications, In W. Norman & J. Scaramello (Eds.), *Midlife: Developmental and clinical issues* (pp. 149–177). New York: Brunner/Mazel.

Turner, N. W. (1982, December). Conflict utilization in marital-dyadic therapy. *Psychiatric Clinics of North America, 5*(3), 503–518.

Visher, E., & Visher, J. (1982). *How To win as a stepfamily*. New York: Dember Books.

Wallerstein, J. S., & Kelly, J. B. (1980). *Surviving the breakup: How children and parents cope with divorce*. New York: Basic Books.

Weiss, R. S. (1975). *Marital separation*. New York: Basic Books.

NINETEEN

Gender Differences in Postmarital Adjustment

Hettie B. Frank, Ph. D.
Private Practice

INTRODUCTION

With the dramatic rise in the divorce rate in the last decade has come an equally dramatic increase in research related to marital dissolution and its consequences (Raschke, 1977). One focus of interest that has emerged is a comparison of the effects of separation and divorce upon men and women. The general results of this research have pointed to an interesting pattern: While the women reported greater degrees of emotional distress, the men were found to have higher incidence rates of serious physical and emotional disorders, violent accidents, and suicide. This finding has left social scientists free to make their own interpretations regarding who was most distressed based upon the particular definition of distress that was used.

The focus of this chapter is also upon gender differences in the adjustment to marital dissolution, but the emphasis has been shifted away from who suffers more to what problems separated women and men encounter, how they cope with these problems, and what consequences they may face. Beyond this it is suggested that the study of gender differences is perhaps too general and therefore not sensitive enough to provide a clearer understanding of the personal factors involved in postmarital adjustment.

MARITAL SEPARATION AND STRESS

Marital separation continues to become an increasingly commonplace phenomenon in American society. While there has been increased legal, religious, and social sanctioning of marital dissolution, the impact upon those who undergo separation appears to have in no way diminished.

This is most clearly demonstrated by the consistency of findings in the association of marital status with physical disorders and psychopathology. Bloom, Asher, and White (1978), in their review of the literature, have noted that the separated and divorced, as compared with those married, never married, or widowed, have the highest rates of admission to in and outpatient psychiatric and alcoholism facilities, the highest incident rates for motor vehicle accidents, disease morbidity, disease mortality, and the greatest number of homocides and suicides. In studies comparing the separated and divorced, the separated have higher incident rates.

How is it that the relation between marital status and the incidence of emotional and physical disorders is so strong? As Bachrach (1975) has noted there is greater certainty of the fact of such associations than about the reasons. Bloom et al. (1978) have reviewed the various theories and models proposed to explain this association and have distilled them into two hypotheses. The first is that preexisting disabilities can serve as stressors to precipitate marital dissolution. It is suggested in this hypothesis that whether an individual enters into a marriage with a physical or emotional disorder or develops such a condition while married, not every marriage is strong enough to endure such stresses (Briscoe, Smith, Robins, Marten, & Gaskin, 1973; Srole, Langner, Michael, Opler, & Rennie, 1962; Turner, 1972).

The second hypothesis is that marital disruption, is itself a significant stressor in adult life, and "can serve to precipitate physical and psychiatric difficulties in some persons who might otherwise not develop such problems" (Bloom et al., 1978, p. 886). Support for this hypothesis may be found in two different areas of research. The first is in the reports of increased vulnerability to physical and emotional disorders found in those individuals whose spouses have died (Helsing, Szklo, & Comstock, 1981; Maddison & Walker, 1967). The other is in the rate of first admissions to psychiatric inpatient facilities. Bloom (1975) reports on a three-year study of admissions in Pueblo, Colorado. First admission rates for men with disrupted marriages were approximately nine times higher than for men with intact marriages. For women with disrupted marriages these rates were three times higher.

While Bloom et al. (1978) state that "marital disruption and physical and emotional disorders are clearly interactive in the sense that one has the potential to influence the other" (p. 885), the dramatic increase in the marital dissolution rate in the last decade suggests that more people who can be considered healthy and normal are separating and divorcing. This being the case, it is important to more fully understand the sources of stress surrounding separation and the factors associated with successful coping strategies and adaptation to single life.

With the significant loss, disruption of lifestyle, and transition involved in marital disruption, Holmes and Rahe (1967) consider it one of the major stressors in adult life. Many separated persons must confront the realization that, perhaps for the first time, the course of their lives will now drastically change from the one they had planned long ago. Separation requires considerable reassessment and adjustment in important life spheres, as well as in self-concept. Bohannan (1970) describes six spheres which people confronted by marital disruption must deal with: legal, emotional, economic, coparental, community, and psychic. While most people weather the pain, crises, and transitions of separation and make the necessary adaptations to single adulthood, others have considerable difficulty coping with their life changes long after these changes have become reality.

The separation period appears to constitute a distinct phase in the process of marital dissolution and adjustment to that dissolution (Bloom et al., 1978; Chiriboga, Coho, Stein, & Roberts, 1979; Kraus, 1979). While the actual separation may signal the end of living with constant marital dissatisfaction and conflict, it marks the beginning of life alone in what may suddenly feel like a married world. However, by the time the divorce decree is finalized, enough time has elapsed so that for many, a considerable degree of adjustment to living as a single adult has been made (Rose & Price-Bonham, 1973).

THE ADJUSTMENT TO SEPARATION

Perhaps the major reason the separation period is experienced as such a stressful one is that during this time the individual must make assessments and decisions about almost every aspect of everyday life in the midst of an atmosphere of intense emotional conflict and loss. This period most often begins even before the couple actually separates, but while they are in the process of deciding whether or not to separate (Bloom & Caldwell, 1981). Spanier and Casto (1979) describe the necessity of one's making "two distinct but overlapping adjustments" (p. 213) to separation. One involves adjusting to the break-up of the marriage, and the other the establishment of a new life as a single adult.

Emotional Adjustment

The first adjustment, facing the dissolution of one's marriage, is a painful but vital emotional adjustment. It involves dealing with powerful and conflicting feelings in many spheres. While the individual undergoing a separation may feel a great sense of relief that the decision to part has finally been made and feel a sense of freedom and excitement about making a new start in life, that same person most often experiences strong feelings of resentment, failure, regret, bitterness, injury, victimization, anger, and fear over the end of the marriage and the beginning of life without the mate. Similar conflicting feelings are experienced regarding the spouse. The individual often feels both love and hate, concern and fury, and guilt and blame.

The feelings of sadness and regret over the dissolution of one's marriage and of great caring and concern toward the spouse are often surprising and disconcerting to the individual, but are a normal part of the separation adjustment process. The presence of these feelings appears to have little relation to one's perception of the quality of his or her marriage (Weiss, 1979b) or to who initiated the separation (Goode, 1956). These feelings are attributable to the powerful emotional bond which develops over time between marriage partners and which supersedes the quality of their relationship. This bond or attachment that the husband and wife experience is akin to that of the child and the parent, which is seen as a biological instinct (Bowlby, 1969, 1973). In fact, the marital bond is seen as the natural, developmental extension into adulthood of basic, vital early bonding which is necessary for emotional sustenance and relatedness (Erikson, 1959; Pincus, 1960).

However, as Weiss (1979b) points out, once established, the feeling of attachment appears to be quite separate from the feelings that make up love, and are far more difficult to erase.

> It would appear that in many unhappy marriages most of the components of love fade, sometimes to be replaced by their opposites. In this way trust may change to mistrust, idealization to disrespect, liking to disdain. Attachment, however, seems to persist. It seems that most components of love are modifiable by negative experience, but attachment once developed can be sustained by proximity alone and fades only slowly in response to absence. (p. 204)

It is often only in literature, as in Simenon's (1976) *The Cat*, that we can capture the depth and power of attachment as it can exist alongside the contempt and mistrust of a marriage in which love is long dead.

The feelings of longing for the lost spouse, guilt, anger, and regret over the end of the marriage, panic over the prospect of living alone, and fear concerning one's ability to do so are some responses to the loss of attachment (Bowlby, 1980), and for a time they may compete with and even overshadow the feelings that precipitated the separation in the first place. Krantzler (1973) and Wiseman (1975) liken the process of adjusting to the dissolution of a marriage to an individual's reaction to his or her impending death. Wiseman goes further by paralleling the process of separation adjustment with Kubler-Ross's (1969) stages in the acceptance of one's death, with the difference that the dissolution of a marriage involves rejection and the necessity of building a new life.

Other important losses must also be faced with separation. They include the relinquishing of old and familiar patterns of living (Weiss, 1975), social and familial ties, and an identity as a wife or husband—a label given great value in society and for many one that is a measure of self-esteem and acceptance.

The process of adjusting to separation involves coming to terms with these great emotional losses. Horowitz (1979) describes this adjustment process most sensitively and focuses upon a key factor in dealing with it.

> An ideal adjustment to loss . . . is to accept it, to replace that which is lost, and to go on living. But there is an important, painful interval between the first pangs of recognition of loss and the adaptation to circumstances as they must be. (p. 236)

The interval Horowitz speaks of is that of mourning or grieving. Marris (1974) describes this grieving as a wish to "consolidate all that is still valuable and important in the past, and preserve it from loss; and at the same time, to reestablish a meaningful pattern of relationships, in which the loss is accepted" (p. 31).

While mourning has its recognized and valued place in one's reaction to the death of a spouse, many view mourning over the dissolution of a marriage as puzzling and perhaps aberrant since separation is often seen as a choice. Continued feelings of attachment, and grief over the losses of a married identity, familial and social ties, and established patterns of living coupled with the knowledge that the marriage must end for the greater good of the individuals involved produce feelings of great ambivalence. This ambivalence most often causes considerable distress for the separating partners, as well as frustration for those around them who want to be helpful. It is enormously difficult for separating individuals not to act on their ambivalence.

Weiss (1979b) describes the management of ambivalence as a very emotionally trying process. Some people suppress one set of feelings—either the positive or negative, while others alternate between experiencing both the good and bad, leaving them frustrated and often locked in the ambivalence. A good percentage of separated couples continue to see each other socially and some maintain sexual relations. Others become so frightened by the intensity of their attachment feelings and by their ambivalence that they attempt to maintain their equilibrium by continuously dwelling on the past and present injuries, disappointments, and anger that they perceive as being caused by the spouse. The intensity of their negative feelings may well reflect the strength of their continued attachment. For many separated couples the presence of children enables them to maintain contact and the feeling of attachment but to keep the focus away from themselves.

The major set of factors in the emotional adjustment to separation is the recognition, acknowledgment, and acceptance of both the continued feelings of attachment to the former spouse and the mourning over the many personal losses inherent in the process of marital dissolution. Allowing oneself to grieve over the end of a marriage appears to be very difficult for many people. The need to see themselves as doing "fine" and in control is closely linked with their feeling of self-esteem and with their belief that the decision to separate was indeed the correct one.

Establishing a New Life

While the newly separated person is undergoing considerable emotional stress, major decisions and changes must be made involving almost every aspect of everyday life. These involve changes in living arrangements, economic adjustment, new parental roles, occupational decisions for some and for most new social and familial roles.

It is not until a couple lives separately that each partner becomes aware of how interdependent they were in maintaining their home and family life. This is especially true of the majority of families in which the husband's role was chiefly that of breadwinner and the wife's major responsibilities centered around homemaking and child care. For such couples their roles and responsibilities fall for the most part within rather traditionally defined sex role categories. The husband's role orientation is seen as "instrumental," with its focus on goals and mastery, while the wife's is considered "expressive," emphasizing social bonding, nurturance, and the maintenance of relationships (Barry, Bacon, & Child, 1957).

Within this schema the husband's energies are mainly directed out of the home and into the workplace. His income and occupational status provide the family with its financial support and most often determine the family's social environment. The greater part of the wife's energies are directed into the home and toward the family members. Within this context it is often the wife's role to be the keeper of the couple's social calendar, the one who maintains their familial and social ties. While many family related decisions are jointly made, many traditionally oriented couples perceive the wife as the first to compromise and the husband as having the final decision-making authority.

With marital separation the expressive-instrumental role balance maintained by both partners is destroyed. Each spouse becomes separately responsible for both the instrumental and expressive demands that arise in starting a new life as a single adult. Each individual must take on new responsibilities and role changes which may not have been anticipated in the early stages of separation. Among these responsibilities are establishing and running a separate household, maintaining child care, and managing finances. One is also faced with major role changes and must adapt to becoming a former spouse, a single parent, and a single adult among family, friends, colleagues, and strangers.

The degree of success with which the separated person meets these new demands appears to be associated with his or her ability to incorporate both the masculine-instrumental and feminine-expressive role orientations. For example, in order for a man to establish a viable, ongoing relationship with his children he must not only provide a home but he must also take on the responsibility for being their sole caretaker for longer periods of time than when he was married. And for the woman the financial stresses of separated life may require that she work outside the home and integrate the new role and responsibilities of worker with those of being a single mother and head of household.

In establishing a new life the individual's social and familial roles are often dramatically altered. For example, while a couple may choose to share custody of their children upon separation, how each spouse feels regarding ability and satisfaction as a single parent is quite another matter. One's role with friends and extended family may also change drastically. While many separated people experience some of their married friends withdrawing from them for a variety of reasons, there is also a tendency which is not recognized by some separated individuals to themselves withdraw socially. This is often due to their own sense of discomfort, self-consciousness, and feelings of failure heightened by their being perhaps the lone single among married couples. And while one may understand or rationalize the reasons why such friendships may end, the experience is often a painful reminder of the extent to which one's life changes after marital separation. In addition, family members' reactions toward the separation and their feelings about the causes of the separation have a strong influence upon one's role and degree of comfort within the family for a long time.

The need to establish and maintain a new social network is a recognized and important part of becoming a single adult. The presence and availability of such a network may serve as a mediating or coping resource on the effects of stress (Berkman, 1977; Folkman, Schaefer, & Lazarus, 1979; Hirsch, 1979). As Weiss (1979a) points out, "single adults, more than the married, need to establish ties outside their homes, for they are without that fellow adult within the household who can provide the married with assistance and companionship" (p. 167). Berkman (1977) goes further by stressing the importance of social ties and confidants for the well-being of single adults. She has found that unmarried people with a high degree of social connectedness and support have significantly lower mortality rates than those single adults who are more isolated.

The social network is seen as a source of emotional and material support, information, services (Caplan, 1964), new social contacts (Walker, McBride, & Vachon, 1977), and alternative perceptions of the sources of stress (Lazarus, Averill, & Opton, 1974). Hirsch (1981) describes the social network as a personal community in which the individual embeds and expresses his or her social identity. To most fully benefit from what social networks have to offer, the separated often need to integrate old and new associations to aid in the transition from married to single adulthood (Wilcox, 1981).

Separated individuals report feeling surprised and disappointed with friends who choose to maintain a relationship with the spouse and not with them. In addition, they themselves choose to end friendships that had been strongly based upon the relationship between the couples. With the loss of old friends it is important to make new friends. It is with new friends, especially if they are unmarried, that the separated person's reference group begins to alter and concomitantly his or her identity from that of a married to a single adult. The creation and maintenance of a social network is seen as requiring both expressive and instrumental skills. Not only must the person initiate new relationships, but he or she must provide such elements of friendship as support to old and new associates.

The role of the family in the social network of the separated is a complex one. While family members are often perceived as sources of emotional and material support, it has been found that in times of transition such as marital separation or the death of a spouse, friends are often perceived as being more helpful than family (Hirsch, 1980; Procidano & Heller, 1979). Hirsch elaborates by saying that friends as opposed to family groups help the person to reorganize his or her life in an adaptive manner by being more encouraging about "establishing alternative social identities and . . . providing more opportunity to find temporary refuge from reminders of problematic family relationships and events" (p. 170).

Other components of social networks have been identified as contributing to satisfaction. It has been found that large networks (Pattison, Llamas, & Hurd, 1979) are more satisfying as are relationships that are reciprocal (Blackman & Goldstein, 1976; Coyne & Lazarus, 1981) and complex or multidimensional—meaning that there is more than one basis for the relationship, such as someone being both a co-worker and a social friend outside the job (Hirsch, 1979; Tolsdorf, 1976). These components comprise the quality of the social network and the quality of one's social network is associated with the degree to which the network can serve as a potential buffer against the effects of stressful life events.

With the social transition from married to single adulthood most individuals both fear and desire getting involved in new dating relationships. It is often through such relationships that the separated person begins to feel a rekindling of self-esteem in terms of being seen as attractive, interesting, desirable, and lovable. One's feelings about dating may often reflect one's emotional adjustment to being separated. Weiss (1975) suggests that in order to feel a sense of comfort and enjoyment with dating, the individual must feel ready to lessen his or her attachment to the past and the former spouse, feel emotionally able to make new associations and attachments, and be willing to risk the possibility of new problems and rejection.

Sex Differences in Separation Adjustment

In assessing the various spheres of transition involved in marital separation, patterns have emerged to indicate that sex differences exist in the perceptions of stresses, ways of coping with those stresses, and the mental and physical health outcomes experienced (Brown & Fox, 1979). While marital separation forces both men and women to assess and make changes in almost every area of their lives, men's and women's perceptions have been found to differ with respect to the stressors that they experience.

Economic adjustments. The economic resources of couples in intact households are often insufficient to support two households. Women and men both feel the consequences of this but somewhat differently. Brown and Fox (1979) note that "one of the few areas in which fairly consistent sex differences emerge involves the post-divorce economic adjustment of men and women: women experience more downward economic mobility and simply have less income after a divorce" (p. 105).

With much less money available, women often must turn to the workplace to supplement their support payments. However, for a majority of these women their earning potential is and remains limited due to lack of marketable skills, limited experience in the career market, and the high cost of child care. Limited income is seen as creating several sources of stress for women. Many working women are often forced to continue to remain economically dependent upon their former spouses and families thus limiting their sense of autonomy. In addition, downward mobility often forces women to change their own and their children's lifestyles and at times, living environment, thereby lessening their hope for a better future. For most separated women their only hope of regaining a sense of economic security is through remarriage, which creates increased pressure and stress in the adjustment to marital dissolution.

While most men also experience the financial stresses of separation, they have greater potential to increase their earnings and most often they do so. However, a continued source of distress for many men is the loss of decision-making power about how their former wives spend the money they provide for them and their children. These men begin to feel like nothing more than cash registers and they perceive their wives as seeing them as using the dollar to control and to be withholding and sadistic.

Relationships with children. As Wallerstein and Kelly (1980) observe fathers and mothers both experience increased anxiety regarding the welfare of their children after separation. The anxiety appears to be caused more by concern over each spouse's ability as a single parent to provide nurturance, guidance, and support than by second thoughts about the wisdom of the separation.

While many more fathers appear to be seeking custody of their children and joint custody has become a more acceptable option for separating parents, a great majority of mothers still receive custody. Whichever custodial arrangement is settled upon, each parent becomes responsible for providing what the other parent provided in the past. It is suggested that this is a greater source of anxiety for men than for women as it requires the father to assume the nurturant, emotionally supportive role, a role that has traditionally been the mother's. This role shift must often occur over short time spans such as during visitation periods and vacations. This is often made more difficult by the father's also having to react to and deal with his children's often problematic reactions to the parents' separation.

In addition, noncustodial fathers most strongly feel their loss of familial identity in that they most often have to return home to an empty house at the end of the workday, and can no longer enjoy the traditional role of head of household (Weiss, 1975). This role loss, coupled with feelings of increased alienation from family life and limited ongoing involvement in the lives of their children, causes many fathers to feel frustration and resentment over their loss of influence in the raising of their children. Many fathers try to win back their children by taking on the role of weekend Santa Claus and by being overly lenient about rules and discipline, providing constant entertainment and diversions, and buying many gifts. This role soon proves to be quite exhausting and no substitute for a real relationship, which would require a greater role shift. Other fathers, as Hetherington, Cox, and Cox (1976) found, become increasingly less involved in the lives of their children and by the end of two years have significantly decreased contact with them, becoming both physically and emotionally absent parents.

Separated parents with custody—usually mothers—feel stressed by the need to expand their responsibilities concerning their children to include providing greater financial support and being the sole adult decision maker in the household. These mothers are often concerned with the changes in their relationships with their children that have taken place out of necessity. For example, with fewer financial resources available to them and less time for working single mothers to devote to household duties, they must have their children take on more responsibilities and demand less of their time. These mothers become concerned that their children will begin to view them as demanding disciplinarians who are forcing them to grow up too quickly. This fear is heightened by many mothers' perceptions that in contrast the fathers, with greater financial ease and less demanding lifestyles, will make their children become more resentful of their mothers. Hetherington et al. (1976) did find that single mothers do respond to increased responsibilities with fears of loss of control and inability to adequately handle the pressures they are experiencing. To compensate they become more controlling and restrictive with their children, who in turn often have greater behavior problems. As these mothers gradually feel better able to handle their new life responsibilities they become less authoritarian with their children.

Social networks. Following separation both spouses undergo changes in their relationships with friends, family, and colleagues. Men and women appear to experience different patterns of social network change, with different stresses inherent for each.

Families appear to be more protective of separated women than of men. Women tend to retain their relationships with their families and in-laws more often than do men, regardless of whether or not there are children (Spicer & Hampe, 1975). Families tend to offer and extend financial support and housing more to women undergoing separation than to men. While at crucial times this type of support is invaluable to the separated woman's well-being, it too has its stresses. Weiss (1975) notes that such dependency upon family may require the woman to play a passive, infantilized role and to relinquish some of her decision-making power and autonomy. In addition, as noted by Hirsch (1980), such reliance upon family may further embed the woman into a problematic family structure without offering her new alternatives to help ease the transition to single adulthood.

Just as many men lose ties with their families and in-laws after separation, they also tend to lose ties more readily than women with their old married friends (Hetherington et al., 1976). Part of the reason for this may be seen as a traditional function of the woman's role in the marriage—that of the couple's social coordinator working to maintain relationships and planning time to see friends. The loss of the familiar old friendship and family ties is often very unsettling to men after separation as it emphasizes their reliance upon their former wives for important social connections and heightens their feelings of loneliness and isolation (White, 1979).

While men, traditionally the noncustodial parents, tend to have more leisure time and more money to spend than their former wives, their feelings of loneliness and isolation give their seeking new contacts a desperate quality, driving them to get out and meet new people—especially women—

even if they feel no pleasure from this pursuit. This heightened sense of loneliness and isolation may be a factor in understanding why divorced men remarry sooner than divorced women. Women on the other hand tend to report that time and financial constraints, as well as child-rearing responsibilities, limit their social accessibility beyond old ties (Hetherington et al., 1976).

Sex differences in coping styles. Sex differences have been noted in the ways people deal with the stresses leading up to separation and those they experience after the separation.

Women have traditionally been seen as the emotional backbone of the home, sensitive to the needs and feelings of family members, working to promote familial harmony. In contast to this image more women than men report favoring divorce as a solution to a failing marriage, and more women than men feel that the children in such a family would be better off if the couple separated (Roper Organization, 1974). Consistent with these findings women have traditionally been the initiators of marital dissolution. While some reasons for this have had to do with legal and financial considerations (such as the mother's claim for child support once the husband has left the home), even with the liberalization of grounds for divorce and more equality in the division of property, a greater percentage of women still initiate separation leading to divorce.

One possible consequence of women's greater tendency to seek marital dissolution is the heightened degree of distress they report experiencing during the preseparation stage (Albrecht, 1980; Bloom & Caldwell, 1981). It is during this time that they must weigh the potential consequences of separation—loss of financial security and increased responsibilities within the family—against the consequences of remaining married. With their decision they are determining the future direction of their own and their families' lives. Men on the other hand report greater distress during the early, postseparation period (Bloom & Caldwell, 1981). It may be during this time that the significant life disruptions, disappointments, and loneliness which most often come with separation are first realized and experienced as opposed to the fantasies of mastery and quick adjustment to single adulthood which accompany preseparation.

While women are the greater proponents and initiators of marital dissolution, they also tend to report greater degrees of postseparation distress than do men (Albrecht, 1980; Gurin, Neroff, & Feld, 1960). This is not contradictory, but as suggested by Brown and Fox (1979) among others instead points to the effects of early socialization on both women and men. In keeping with their expressive role orientation, women have been trained to be highly sensitive to emotional nuances, dependent upon others, and socially motivated. Men, trained in an instrumental role orientation, have been encouraged and forced to strive and compete and not to admit signs of weakness, vulnerability, or distress. As a result men appear to derive their self-esteem from mastery, and women from social acceptance.

Men and women appear to have developed different sets of response patterns to many types of stress. For example, regarding emotional stress, both sexes appear to react to similar stressors and on clinical examination have similar reactions and symptoms, but their subjective experiences appear to be quite different. Men are more apt to deny experiencing distress in the face of evidence to the contrary and tend to avoid seeking help, even from friends on an informal basis (Dohrenwend & Dohrenwend, 1976; Kessler, Reuter, & Greenley, 1979; Padesky & Hammen, 1981). Women on the other hand tend to define their problems in mental health terms, report more psychological symptoms when interviewed, and seek help more readily from a variety of sources (Coie, Pennington, & Buckley, 1974; Gove & Tudor, 1973; Gurin et al., 1960).

Within this socialization schema men and women appear to demonstrate different styles of coping with the stresses of marital separation. Women, traditionally taught to rely more upon others than upon themselves, often question their ability to adequately handle their new life situations, feel overwhelmed by it, and seek help from friends, family, and professionals very quickly. In contrast, men, trained toward rationality and self-reliance, tend to turn to their work for mastery gratification in the face of stress and avoid reaching out to others for assistance and companionship. Carlson (1971) suggests that some men are so mastery (or "agency") oriented that they are not aware of experiencing feelings of distress.

Sex Differences in Health Outcomes after Separation

As was noted earlier the separated appear to be a group that is highly vulnerable to stress related physical and emotional disorders (Bloom et al., 1978). When the sexes are compared a pattern begins to emerge which indicates that while separated women report greater degrees of distress, separated men have the highest incidence rates of mental and physical illnesses, as well as of deaths.

While women's early distress warning system may cause them to experience heightened senses of agitation, fear, and helplessness, this same stress warning system also appears to be a long-range asset in preventing more serious disorders. Because women tend to seek professional assistance relatively quickly after experiencing distress, the nature of the help they receive can be preventive in nature. Men on the other hand are more apt to deny early symptoms of stress or to minimize their significance (Monat & Lazarus, 1977). And by the time men seek treatment it is more often on an emergency basis, thus involving greater risks to health and life.

There exists a growing body of literature describing how the process of marital separation affects both spouses. These data have been very valuable to clinicians in helping them to better assess and understand the needs, conflicts, stresses, and goals of individuals and couples struggling to adjust to marital dissolution, and to gear their treatment closer to those needs. At this point however it appears advantageous to go beyond the examination of unitary gender groups to explain differences in such adjustment areas as perceived stressors and coping styles. The study of a variable such as sex role attitude may further broaden our understanding of how men and women with very different personal orientations adjust to separation and how their orientations may have a relation to their adjustment. Such a study was recently conducted and will be described.

Several researchers have investigated the association between sex role attitude and reported postseparation distress, and have obtained results that have for the most part greater consistency than the results of investigations focusing solely upon contrasting groups of separated women and men. The results of the sex role attitude studies point to a significant correlation between a traditional sex role orientation or lifestyle and the subjective report of greater emotional postseparation distress compared to less emotional distress related to an androgynous or nontraditional orientation or lifestyle (Brown & Manela, 1978; Chiriboga & Thurnher, 1980; Felton, Brown, Lehman, & Liberatos, 1980; Meyers, 1976). In one investigation where the focus was specifically upon men (White, 1979), this correlation was not found to be significant (this may be due to the very small size of the sample used in the study). In an expansion of the above investigations a study was recently conducted in which the sex role attitudes of separated women and men were related to several adjustment factors (Frank, 1983).

A study examining sex differences in postmarital adjustment

Background. Marital separation is "disruptive and traumatic" (Spanier & Casto, 1979) for all involved in the experience. In the transition from married to single adulthood two major areas of adjustment have been identified. These are dealing with feelings of emotional loss due to the end of the marriage and the loss of attachment, and establishing a new life. Within these two areas of adjustment several tasks need to be accomplished: *(a)* the acknowledgment and mourning over the emotional losses involved in marital separation; *(b)* the taking on of the responsibilities and role changes involved in becoming a single adult; and *(c)* the creation and maintenance of an available social network that is perceived as sensitive and responsive to the needs of a separated person.

In order to accomplish these vital adjustment tasks the individual must call upon both masculine oriented instrumental skills and feminine oriented expressive skills. In an attempt to go beyond an examination of dichotomized male-female patterns, it was proposed that those men and women who endorse both masculine and feminine characteristics and values in themselves—androgynous individuals—would have greater flexibility in adapting to new situational demands and have relatively easier adjustments to single adulthood than those men and women who identified exclusively with masculine values or feminine values—masculine sex-typed men and feminine sex-typed women.

Hypotheses and research questions. It was first hypothesized that feminine sex-typed women would report greater postseparation distress in the areas of emotional functioning and responsibilities and role changes than would androgynous women and men. It was then hypothesized that masculine sex-typed men would report less postseparation distress than the androgynous women and men.

Regarding the social networks of this sample of separated adults, it was asked whether the sex role attitudes of the respondents have an association with the quality of their networks.

In order to examine these issues all the research participants were first classified according to sex role attitude, using the Bem (1981) Sex-Role Inventory, short form. Three groups were formed: masculine sex-typed men, feminine sex-typed women, and a combined group of androgynous women and men. (Cross sex-typed and undifferentiated individuals were not included in this part of the study.) They then completed the Post-Separation/Postdivorce Problems and Stress Scale (Raschke, 1974, 1978) and a two-part social network questionnaire (Jones & Fischer, 1978; McCallister & Fischer, 1978).

Results. Regarding the report of postseparation distress, the feminine sex-typed women reported experiencing a significantly greater degree of distress in both the areas of emotional functioning and responsibilities and role changes than did the group of androgynous men and women. The masculine sex-typed men presented a more complex but revealing picture of adjustment after separation. In every category of adjustment pertaining to responsibilities and role change this group reported *greater* degrees of distress than did the androgynous group, but in the area of emotional functioning they reported (as predicted) a significantly lesser degree of adjustment distress.

Regarding the creation and quality of postseparation social networks, it was found that the group of androgynous women and men had scores indicative of higher quality social networks than the masculine sex-typed men and the feminine sex-typed women. The androgynous group's networks were found to be significantly larger, more complex, and perceived as being more satisfying. It was also found that in addition to size, complexity, and degree of satisfaction derived from the social network, feelings of reciprocal support from network members and a higher percentage of friends than family members in the network were associated with increased postseparation distress.

Conclusions from the research study. The results seem to indicate that without the instrumental-expressive flexibility needed to successfully take on the new responsibilities and role changes that are a part of adjustment to single adulthood and parenthood, feminine sex-typed women and masculine sex-typed men reported elevated degrees of distress and showed indications of impairment of functioning in these areas. In addition, both of these groups reported having social networks that were not perceived as adequate or particularly satisfying. These traditionally sex-typed individuals had not increased their social base in size or richness of relationships and did not appear as satisfied with their networks as did the group of androgynous people.

While the groups of feminine sex-typed women and the masculine sex-typed men both reported greater degrees of adjustment distress in the area of responsibilities and role changes and had more constricted and less satisfying social networks than the androgynous women and men, it was in the reporting of emotional distress that they differed significantly. The feminine sex-typed women reported heightened emotional distress around separation while the masculine sex-typed men tended to deny such distress. These two groups appear to reflect the stereotypic views of women and men facing stress: Such women tend to question their ability to meet the challenges facing them and react by feeling helpless and emotionally distressed (Pearlin & Schooler, 1978). For such men their self-esteem appears to be associated with their perception of maintaining control and remaining emotionally invulnerable in the midst of distressing life circumstances (Jourard, 1964). It can be speculated that for a proportion of such men the loss of support from their wives and the loss of social contacts, coupled with difficulties adapting to single adulthood and denial of emotional distress may over time increase their susceptibility to stress related emotional and physical disorders.

In contrast, it appears from the results that the group of androgynous women and men have for the most part reached an adaptive balance between mourning the loss of the old and working toward establishing the new. With the androgynes' relative ease and flexibility in performing in both masculine and feminine roles, they appear to be better able to face the complex tasks in the adjustment to marital separation and single adulthood.

TREATMENT IMPLICATIONS

There appears to be a growing trend for more people both women and men considering separation or having recently separated to consult professional counselors and psychotherapists. This may be due to a variety of reasons: a greater tendency on the part of matrimonial attorneys and family physicians to recommend such services; more media reportage on stress and the health consequences of such stressful life events as separation; and referrals by school personnel for services for children of separating couples—to name a few.

In working with the separated individual the clinician may find it useful to maintain two points of reference. One is the tasks involved in the transition to single adulthood: *(a)* mourning the end of the marriage and loss of attachment, *(b)* adjusting to new responsibilities and role changes, and *(c)* integrating a new social network. The other point of reference is sex role attitude. One's sex role attitude does appear to be associated with the quality of adjustment to marital separation as seen in relation to the areas of postseparation adaptation. More specifically, androgynous individuals appear to have greater emotional and role flexibility and adaptiveness in the transition to single adulthood than do traditionally sex-typed people.

Traditional masculine and feminine sex role attitudes are based upon identification with rather narrowly drawn sets of characteristics that, depending upon the given circumstances, can be adaptive or maladaptive. With an adaptive adjustment to single adulthood requiring increased emotional and role flexibility, traditionally sex-typed individuals may experience difficulty in adapting to life after separation without understanding why. A clinician with an understanding of both the positive and negative ramifications of sex role attitude can be very helpful. For example, the masculine sex-typed man may quickly and decisively handle the legal and financial arrangements involved in his separation, but in a situation calling for an expressive mode of behavior, such as when he has the children for a whole weekend, he may lose his sense of mastery and experience heightened anxiety. Conversely, for feminine sex-typed women to suddenly be faced with masculine-instrumental demands stirs feelings of inadequacy and helplessness.

Brown, Perry, and Harburg (1977) suggest that "it may be useful to discuss sex role attitude as a diagnostic tool and as a possible means of intervention because of the strong relationship of sex role ideology to self-esteem and other psychological outcomes" (p. 560). In working with feminine sex-typed women, clinicians may find them to be a particularly distressed group. They appear to have a tendency to experience strong feelings of helplessness and anxiety in the face of marital separation. This is partly due to their viewing themselves as primarily nurturers and supporters with little ability to assert authority or to defend their beliefs. Such women often feel it is a tremendous blow to their sense of identity and self-esteem to lose their role as wife and see their only solution as being a quick remarriage. However, their confidence in themselves is so diminished that they see little prospect of this occurring, thus increasing their sense of hopelessness.

In focusing upon the tasks of adjustment with feminine sex-typed women, the clinician may formulate some goals such as the expansion of the social network away from a small, tight, family dominated unit to one that includes more friends from different sources, as well as helping these women to assert their feelings and beliefs and increasing their feelings of self-reliance and self-respect.

With masculine sex-typed men clinicians often are faced with their most reluctant patients/clients. For these men self-esteem is associated with mastery, rationality, and invulnerability to excessive emotionality. Because of the images of decisiveness, leadership, and assertiveness associated with traditional masculinity, this role orientation has been perceived by men and women to be a model of maturity and mental health. However, it has been demonstrated that when forced to lose control, masculine sex-typed persons and feminine sex-typed persons exhibited equally high degrees of helplessness (Baucom & Danker-Brown, 1979). This situation may be closely analogous to what is experienced after marital separation when there have been significant personal losses in many life spheres.

Because masculine sex-typed men tend to deny feelings of hurt and vulnerability, it may be very difficult for them to adequately mourn the end of their marriage and the loss of attachment. The clinician may decide that such grieving may more effectively come later in the process of counseling/therapy after the individual becomes more comfortable exploring and speaking about emotions. The clinician may find that the area of role changes and responsibilities may be best explored first as it is the least emotionally loaded and may prove the least threatening to the patient/client. It is also important for the clinician to keep in mind that while traditionally sex-typed men may have many acquaintances, they have few if any close friends or confidants aside from their wives (Brown & Felton, 1978; Chiriboga et al., 1979; Tognoli, 1980). With increased postseparation stress they may isolate themselves further from family and friends.

This raises an important issue regarding treatment goals for the separated and divorced. Given the data on the greater role flexibility and emotional adaptiveness of androgynous individuals, should the clinician have as a goal the alteration of a traditional sex role orientation to a more androgynous one? This may be viewed in two ways. First, an androgynous orientation appears to be one that is most adaptive during periods of transition, and can serve as a coping function during such times (Felton et al., 1980). It would seem then that the promotion of an androgynous sex role attitude for patient/clients would be advantageous.

However, from another perspective, the shift from a traditional to a more androgynous orientation appears to be inherent in the nature of counseling and psychotherapy. As the data of Abrahams, Feldman, and Nash (1978) indicate, sex role attitudes are not fixed personality traits, but are adaptable to changing life circumstances. When an individual separates and in the course of living alone must develop and use both instrumental and expressive skills in order to function effectively as a single adult, that person should adapt his or her sex role attitude to reflect the changes in his or her life. In addition, counseling or psychotherapy is a process in which the person spends considerable time assessing and exploring alternative feelings, actions, ideas, and attitudes. In the process of counseling or psychotherapy the individual often begins to loosen emotional and cognitive rigidity. A very similar process seems to occur when a person makes adaptations in his or her sex role attitude. So it appears that the individual becomes more androgynous within the counseling or psychotherapy setting without androgyny having to be identified as a specific goal.

Ross and Sawhill (1975) indicate that within an average of three to six years after divorcing a majority of the divorced women and men do remarry. It is a goal of therapy with separated people to help them make the most of the time they are living alone, to help make it a meaningful, productive, and rewarding interval during which the individual learns to relinquish the old and welcome the new. It is also a time in which the person learns most profoundly about the power of human adaptation.

Summary

The view of marital dissolution as a major stressor is by now generally accepted by mental health professionals. The process of adaptation to separation and divorce however is not a universal one, and there appear to be differential patterns of adjustment that are gender and sex role related. These patterns fall within perceptions of stresses and problems related to the ending of a marriage and the beginning of a single life, responses to the problems and stresses experienced, and the emotional and physical health related consequences of marital dissolution

While some areas of adjustment are related to such external issues as custody arrangements and economic changes, others are centered around emotional and attitudinal issues such as the experience of grief and mourning and the creation and maintenance of a new social network. It is suggested that a more adaptive adjustment to marital dissolution is associated with greater flexibility in both the feminine-instrumental and masculine-expressive domains as seen in psychological androgyny.

References

Abrahams, B., Feldman, S. S., & Nash, S. G. (1978). Sex-role self-concept and sex-role attitudes: Enduring personality characteristics or adaptations to changing life situations? *Developmental Psychology, 14*, 393–400.

Albrecht, S. L. (1980). Reactions and adjustments to divorce: Differences in the experiences of males and females. *Family Relations, 29*, 59–68.

Bachrach, L. L. (1975). *Marital status and mental disorders: An analytical review* (DHEW Pub. No. [ADM] 75-21). Washington, D.C.: U.S. Government Printing Office.

Barry, H., Bacon, H. K., & Child, I. L. (1957). A cross-cultural survey of some sex differences in socialization. *Journal of Abnormal and Social Psychology, 55,* 327-332.

Baucom, D. H., & Danker-Brown, P. (1979). Influence of sex roles on the development of learned helplessness. *Journal of Consulting and Clinical Psychology, 47,* 928-936.

Bem, S. L. (1981). *Bem Sex-Role Inventory: Professional manual.* Palo Alto, CA: Consulting Psychologists Press.

Berkman, L. (1977). *Social networks, host resistance and mortality: A follow-up study of Alameda County residents.* Unpublished doctoral dissertation, University of California, Berkeley.

Blackman, S., & Goldstein, K. (1976). *Reciprocity networks in the community and manifest psychological anxiety.* Paper presented at the 58th annual meeting of the Eastern Psychological Association, New York.

Bloom, B. L. (1975). *Changing patterns of psychiatric care.* New York: Human Sciences Press.

Bloom, B. L., Asher, S. J., & White, S. W. (1978). Marital disruption as a stressor: A review and analysis. *Psychological Bulletin, 85,* 867-894.

Bloom, B. L., & Caldwell, R. A. (1981, August). Sex differences in adjustment during the process of marital separation. *Journal of Marriage and the Family, 43,* 693-701.

Bohannan, P. (Ed.). (1970). *Divorce and after.* Garden City, NY: Doubleday Publishing.

Bowlby, J. (1969). *Attachment and loss, I: Attachment.* New York: Basic Books.

Bowlby, J. (1973). *Attachment and loss, II: Separation.* New York: Basic Books.

Bowlby, J. (1980). *Attachment and loss, III: Loss.* New York: Basic Books.

Briscoe, C. W., Smith, J. B., Robins, E., Marten, S., & Gaskin, F. (1973). Divorce and psychiatric disease. *Archives of General Psychiatry, 29,* 119-125.

Brown, P., & Felton, B. J. (1978). *Coping with marital disruption in later life: The role of social supports.* Paper presented at the annual meeting of the American Orthopsychiatric Association, San Francisco.

Brown, P., & Fox, H. (1979). Sex differences in divorce. In E. S. Gomberg & V. Franks (Eds.), *Gender and disordered behaviors* (pp. 101-123). New York: Brunner/Mazel.

Brown, P., & Manela, R. (1978). Changing family roles: Women and divorce. *Journal of Divorce, 1,* 315-328.

Brown, P., Perry, L., & Harburg, E. (1977). Sex role attitudes and psychological outcomes for black and white women experiencing marital dissolution. *Journal of Marriage and the Family, 39,* 549-561.

Caplan, G. (1964). *Principles in preventive psychiatry.* New York: Basic Books.

Carlson, R. (1971). Sex differences in ego functioning: Exploratory studies of agency and communion. *Journal of Consulting and Clinical Psychology, 27,* 267-277.

Chiriboga, D. A., Coho, A., Stein, J. A., & Roberts, J. (1979). Divorce stress and social supports: A study in helpseeking behavior. *Journal of Divorce, 3,* 121–135.

Chiriboga, D. A., & Thurnher, M. (1980). Marital lifestyles and adjustment to separation. *Journal of Divorce, 3,* 379–390.

Coie, J. D., Pennington, B. V., & Buckley, H. H. (1974). Effects of situational stress and sex roles on the attribution of psychological disorder. *Journal of Consulting and Clinical Psychology, 42,* 559–568.

Coyne, J. C., & Lazarus, R. S. (1981). Cognitive style perception, stress, and coping. In I. L. Katush & L. B. Schlesinger (Eds.), *Handbook of stress and coping* (pp. 144–158). San Francisco: Jossey-Bass.

Dohrenwend, P. B., & Dohrenwend, B. S. (1976). Sex differences and psychiatric disorders. *American Journal of Sociology, 81,* 1447–1454.

Erikson, E. H. (1959). Identity and the life cycle. In *Psychological Issues* (Monograph 1). New York: International Universities Press.

Felton, B. J., Brown, P., Lehmann, S., & Liberatos, P. (1980). The coping function of sex-role attitudes during marital disruption. *Journal of Health and Social Behavior, 21,* 240–248.

Folkman, S., Schaefer, C., & Lazarus, R. S. (1979). Cognitive processes as mediators of stress and coping. In V. Hamilton & D. M. Warburton (Eds.), *Human stress and cognition* (pp. 265–300). Chichester, England: John Wiley & Son.

Frank, H. B. (1983). *The adjustment of men and women to marital separation: The relation of sex-role attitudes to social support networks and distress.* Unpublished doctoral dissertation, New York University.

Goode, W. J. (1956). *After divorce.* Glencoe, IL: The Free Press.

Gove, W. R., & Tudor, J. F. (1973). Adult sex roles and mental illness. *American Journal of Sociology, 78,* 812–835.

Gurin, G., Veroff, J., & Feld, S. (1960). *Americans view their mental health.* New York: Basic Books.

Helsing, K. J., Szklo, M., & Comstock, G. W. (1981). Factors associated with mortality after widowhood. *American Journal of Public Health, 71,* 802–809.

Hetherington, E. M., Cox, M., & Cox, R. (1976). Divorced fathers. *The Family Coordinator, 25,* 417–428.

Hirsch, B. J. (1979). Psychological dimensions of social networks: A multi-method analysis. *American Journal of Community Psychology, 7,* 263–277.

Hirsch, B. J. (1980). Natural support systems and coping with major life changes. *American Journal of Community Psychology, 8,* 159–172.

Hirsch, B. J. (1981). Social networks and the coping process: Creating personal communities. In B. H. Gottlieb (Ed.), *Social networks and social support* (pp. 149–170). Beverly Hills, CA: Sage Publications.

Holmes, R. L., & Rahe, R. M. (1967). The social readjustment scale. *Journal of Psychosomatic Research, 11,* 213–218.

Horowitz, J. M. (1979). Psychological response to serious life events. In V. Hamilton & D. M. Warburton (Eds.), *Human stress and cognition* (pp. 237–264). Chichester, England: John Wiley & Son.

Jones, L., & Fischer, C. S. (1978, January). *Studying egocentric networks by mass survey* (Working Paper NO. 284). Institute of Urban and Regional Development, University of California, Berkeley.

Jourard, S. (1964). *The transparent self.* Princeton, NJ: Van Nostrand Company.

Kessler, R. C., Reuter, J. A., & Greenley, J. R. (1979). Sex differences in the use of psychiatric outpatient facilities. *Social Forces, 58,* 557–571.

Krantzler, M. (1973). *Creative divorce.* New York: M. Evans & Company.

Kraus, S. (1979). The crisis of divorce: Growth promoting or pathogenic? *Journal of Divorce, 3,* 107–119.

Kubler-Ross, E. (1969). *On death and dying.* New York: Macmillan.

Lazarus, R. S., Averill, J. R., & Opton, E. M. (1974). The psychology of coping: Issues of research and assessment. In G. V. Coelho, D. A. Hamburg, & J. E. Adams (Eds.), *Coping and adaptation* (pp. 249–315). New York: Basic Books.

Maddison, D., & Walker, W. (1967). Factors affecting the outcome of conjugal bereavement. *British Journal of Psychiatry, 13,* 1057–1067.

Marris, P. (1974). *Loss and change.* New York: Pantheon.

McCallister, L., & Fischer, C. S. (1978). A procedure for surveying personal networks. *Sociological Methods and Research, 7,* 131–148.

Meyers, J. C. (1976). *The adjustment of women to marital separation: The effect of sex-role identification and stage of family life, as determined by age and presence or absence of dependent children.* Unpublished doctoral dissertation, University of Colorado.

Monat, A., & Lazarus, R. S. (1977). Introduction. In A. Monat & R. S. Lazarus (Eds.), *Stress and coping: An anthology.* New York: Columbia University Press.

Padesky, C. A., & Hammen, C. L. (1981). Sex differences in depressive symptom expression and help-seeking among college students. *Sex Roles, 13,* 68–80.

Pattison, E. M., Llamas, R., & Hurd, G. (1979). Social network mediation of anxiety. *Psychiatric Annals, 9,* 56–57.

Pearlin, L. & Schooler, C. (1978). The structure of coping. *Journal of Health and Social Behavior, 19,* 2–21.

Pincus, L., & Tavistock Institute of Human Relations (Eds.). (1960). *Marriage: Studies in emotional conflict and growth.* London: Methuen.

Procidano, M. E., & Heller, K. (1979, September). *Toward the assessment of perceived social support.* Paper presented at the annual meeting of the American Psychological Association, New York.

Raschke, H. J. (1974). *Social and psychological factors in voluntary postmarital dissolution adjustment.* Unpublished doctoral dissertation, University of Minnesota.

Raschke, H. J. (1977). The role of social participation in postseparation and postdivorce adjustment. *Journal of Divorce, 1,* 129–140.

Raschke, H. J. (1978, October). *The development of a Post Separation/Post Divorce Problems and Stress Scale.* Paper presented at the annual meeting of the

National Council on Family Relations, Philadelphia. (ERIC Document Reproduction Service No. ED 170 619)

Roper Organization, Inc. (1974). *Virginia Slims American women's opinion poll* (Vol. 3). New York: Roper Organization, Inc.

Rose, V. L., & Price-Bonham, S. (1973). Divorce adjustment: A woman's problem. *Family Coordinator, 22*, 291–297.

Ross, H., & Sawhill, I. (1975). *Time of transition: The growth of families headed by women.* Washington, D.C.: The Urban Institute.

Simenon, G. (1976). *The cat.* New York: Harcourt, Brace, Jovanovich.

Spanier, G. B., & Casto, R. F. (1979). Adjustment to separation and divorce: A qualitative analysis. In G. Levinger & O. C. Moles (Eds.). *Divorce and separation* (pp. 211–227). New York: Basic Books.

Spicer, J., & Hampe, G. (1975). Kinship interaction after divorce. *Journal of Marriage and the Family, 37*, 113–116.

Srole, L., Langner, T. S., Michael, T. S., Opler, M. K., & Rennie, T. A. C. (1962). *Mental health in the metropolis.* New York: McGraw-Hill.

Tognoli, J. (1980). Male friendship and intimacy across the life span. *Family Relations, 29*, 273–279.

Tolsdorf, C. C. (1976). Social networks, support, and coping: An exploratory study. *Family Process, 15*, 407–417.

Turner, R. J. (1972). The epidemiological study of schizophrenia: A current appraisal. *Journal of Health and Social Behavior, 13*, 360–369.

University of Colorado (Boulder), Department of Psychology, Separation and Divorce Program. *Personal Data Survey Questionnaire.*

Walker, K. N., & MacBride, A., & Vachon, M. L. S. (1977). Social support networks and the crisis of bereavement. *Social Science and Medicine, 11*, 35–41.

Wallerstein, J. S., & Kelly, J. B. (1980). *Surviving the breakup.* New York: Basic Books.

Weiss, R. S. (1975). *Marital separation.* New York: Basic Books.

Weiss, R. S. (1979a). The emotional impact of marital separation. In G. Levinger & O. C. Moles (Eds.), *Divorce and separation* (pp. 201–210). New York: Basic Books.

Weiss, R. S. (1979b). *Going it alone.* New York: Basic Books.

White, S. W. (1979). *The adjustment of men to the process of marital separation.* Unpublished doctoral dissertation, University of Colorado.

Wilcox, B. L. (1981). Social support and adjusting to marital disruption: A network analysis. In B. H. Gottlieb (Ed.), *Social networks and social support* (pp. 97–115). Beverly Hills, CA: Sage Publications.

Wiseman, R. S. (1975). Crisis theory and the process of divorce. *Social Casework, 56*, 206–212.

TWENTY

Remarriage: Repetition versus New Beginnings

Martin Goldberg, M.D.
Professor of Psychiatry
University of Pennsylvania Medical School

OVERVIEW

As with any sort of marriage, remarriage has its own advantages and disadvantages. Whether a remarriage can be a truly new beginning and not a repetition, depends on many factors not the least of which is the extent to which the couple has resolved their previous ties—ties to the former spouse as well as to the families of origin. In reality such ties are never totally resolved. But it is possible to gain understanding and perspective and to utilize these in developing a new contract, a new scenario, and new behavior in a new marriage. Doing all of this is nothing less than a lifetime endeavor. When people are flying blind they certainly cannot correct their course. Thus, the resolution of past ties can only be accomplished when these ties are first recognized and acknowledged—no mean task at best. Past errors and mistakes can only be resolved if one becomes aware of them, accepts and acknowledges them as things of the past, and establishes and pursues a course of not repeating them. The rule of thumb which I recommend to my patients on this matter is as follows: If you believe you have resolved your past ties, you are in trouble and it is certain that you have not! If you recognize that they are there and need further work and attention, you are ready to proceed!

Understanding and perspective about each person's past and present needs are required in order to deal successfully with the various, dynamic interactions that shape and form any relationship, any system, any family. These interactions involve basic areas of power and control, nurture, intimacy and privacy, trust, fidelity, lifestyle, and sense of order. In most instances interactions in these areas in remarriages are similar to those in first marriages, but they carry additional complexities. Principal among these are the complexities of step-families and of households in which children of a previous marriage are involved.

Most people who remarry have high expectations and demands of marriage. If they did not they would more likely have stayed in devitalized, prior marriages in a passive resigned manner, or they would have remained single after divorce or widowhood occurred. Consequently, it should not surprise us that one of the major tasks that needs to be accomplished by any remarried family is the development of realistic expectations.

When the remarried couple can develop or deepen their mutual trust sufficiently to establish order in the new family and to promote realistic expectations, they can then go on to lead the family into new and appropriate scenarios and solutions. The task of the therapist is to catalyze and facilitate these actions in every way possible.

Remarriage has been part and parcel of the American scene for a good many years now. This is so much the case that it may be possible in an article on remarriage to skip over the usual, awesome bundle of statistics presented for the purpose of demonstrating what a commonplace matter remarriage is. Without all the facts and figures (often misleading or misinterpreted), we can all readily agree that marriage, divorce, and remarriage are everyday phenomena in our lives. *Most* Americans who can get married do so. *Many* first marriages end in divorce. Most people who get divorced (or who are widowed) eventually remarry if they possibly can do so. And a sizable number of remarriages also end in divorce. We will presently consider whether remarriages are, on the whole, more or less satisfying or durable than first marriages—and other such intriguing questions.

Just as statistics on remarriage abound, so do articles, books, and graduate dissertations. (It was possible to identify 21 such dissertations written between 1967 and early 1984.) Consequently, there is grave danger that yet another piece of writing on the subject will only repeat twice-told tales and perhaps proffer another debatable set of theoretical assumptions. In an effort to avoid these pitfalls at least partially, I am hoping to concentrate on some aspects of remarriage that have been given shorter shrift. For example, in reading over the literature I get the general impression that more attention has been paid to the remarried family with children than to the remarried family that is childless. (Indeed, Sager et al., 1981, seem to define the remarried family in such a way as to exclude the remarried couple without children from being considered a family.) Since my own work is primarily though not exclusively couples therapy, I have more interest in focusing on the *remarried couple*—with or without children.

In 30 years of practicing psychotherapy with couples I have worked with over 250 couples in which at least one spouse had been previously married. Almost one third of these couples have been childless or have had no children presently living with them. Of the remaining couples with children, I have worked with some in a combination of couples and family therapy, and I have referred others (after some basic couples therapy) for further work with the entire family. About 90 percent of the remarried couples who have consulted me have done so because their relationships were in real trouble. The balance have been couples who wished to take a prophylactic approach to their new marriages and wanted marital enhancement, marital enrichment, or whatever you may choose to call it. Inasmuch as my general approach is psychodynamic with a systemic orientation, most of the couples I have seen have worked relatively intensively and extensively with me. Usually, this has involved one or two weekly sessions for a period of time that may have been as brief as a month or as long as a year or more; the overall mean number of sessions has been around 20.

There are other aspects of remarriage that have received relatively little attention, and I will try to highlight some of these in the course of this chapter. Now, however, I would like to comment on another impression I gained from reviewing the literature on remarriage. This is the marked tendency to come up with generalizations—often fairly sweeping—that tend to contradict other generalizations and thus lead to a fair degree of confusion. As an example consider the simple question of whether remarriages are different from first marriages. Most of the literature presents the generalization that indeed they are. Occasionally someone says, "no, they are not different, they are really the same." Or consider a more debatable question: Are remarriages more satisfactory or more durable than first marriages? Here, we get generalizations in both directions and what is more confusing, statistics to back all of these up (Albrecht, 1979; Cherlin, 1978; Day & Mackey, 1981; Glenn & Weaver 1977; White, 1979).

A different viewpoint on these questions ensues if we consider the proposition that perhaps we truly cannot generalize even with the aid of statistics. Are remarriages different from first marriages? Some are and some are not. Some remarriages are remarkably similar to first marriages. For example, remarriages in which neither spouse has had children previously are apt to be virtually identical to first marriages. Remarriages in which a family is reconstituted with "his, her, and our" children are something else altogether and often bear little similarity to first marriages. (But note the word *often:* I have seen a few such marriages that did not conform to this axiom.) Are remarriages more satisfactory? It depends. And it depends on *many* things such as the age at remarriage, the length of the previous marriage, the number of children at the time of remarriage, and perhaps even whether we are examining the wife's satisfaction or the husband's satisfaction (Spanier & Glick, 1980; Spanier & Furstenberg, 1982; Vinick, 1978; White, 1979; Glenn & Weaver, 1977). Are remarriages as durable as first marriages? My clinical experience would lead me to agree with the conclusions reached by Glenn and Weaver (1977) in their very sizable questionnaire study. If a remarried couple can make it through the first year or two their marriage has a good chance of enduring. But the mortality rate in those initial years (the legendary "period of adjustment") is considerable. The redivorce rate also varies depending on many other matters, age at the time of remarriage again being one of these.

MATE SELECTION IN REMARRIAGES

Why and how people choose each other seems to me a basic question in remarriage as it is in any form of coupling. Elsewhere, I have written of the significance of first encounters and initial reactions in this respect (Goldberg, 1982). A great deal of important information can be gained if the clinician pursues the question: When, where, and how did you first meet your spouse, and what were your very first impressions of him/her?

CASE EXAMPLE

Dr. A., a surgeon, met his second wife, Mrs. A.2, when she came to work in his office as a nurse. At the time each was married. Dr. A.'s initial impression of Mrs. A.2 was that she had considerable strength and competence but was basically unattractive. He also found her very cooperative and understanding. For her part Mrs. A.2's initial impression was that her new employer was a man of great strength and individuality, with considerable charm and a fierce determination to do things his own way. Mrs. A.2 found these qualities quite appealing: The man she was married to at the time she met Dr. A. was weak, passive, and excessively dependent upon her.

Several years later Dr. A.'s first wife, Mrs. A., became seriously ill and after a protracted period of sickness died, leaving her husband with the care of their four children. Dr. A. was devastated by the loss of a woman he had always found to be extremely attractive and desirable. He felt he could never possibly replace her. Nonetheless, the care of his children weighed heavily upon him. Within not too many months of Mrs. A.1's death he began to court Mrs. A.2, who had recently divorced her husband. After a brief courtship they were married.

When Dr. A. and Mrs. A.2 came to my attention they had been married for about a year and were having severe marital problems. Mrs. A.2 felt that her husband was simply exploiting her by thrusting all the care and

> responsibility of his four children upon her. She also complained that Dr. A. ignored her sexually in terms of any real intimacy and was always preoccupied with his surgical practice. When she did see him he was dictatorial, critical, and unloving. For his part Dr. A. complained that his second wife was nowhere near the woman that Mrs. A.1 had been. He lamented Mrs. A.2's unattractiveness and felt that she was quarrelsome, petty, and ineffective with his children. Despite couples therapy, which involved eight conjoint sessions, matters went from bad to worse, and within three months they had separated and were eventually divorced.

The process of mate selection in this couple, as is so often the case, is rather clearly revealed by their initial interaction. They met as boss and employee, and no matter what else ensued, their relationship remained one of boss and employee. Dr. A. chose a second mate who could not possibly compete with the cherished first wife he was still mourning but who would ostensibly be an efficient "employee" in caring for his children and running his household. Mrs. A.2 chose a second mate who would be reparative of her first marriage in that he would bring her the strength and assertiveness her first husband so notably lacked. In making this choice she was quite unaware that Dr. A.'s personality closely resembled that of her father, a strong, dominant, self-preoccupied individual, and that she had chosen her first husband precisely because he was so much the opposite of father!

Given this sort of selection in the coupling process, there is little likelihood that a satisfactory and enduring relationship can eventuate. Indeed, the outcome here was preordained. Having chosen a woman who could not in his eyes have possibly competed with his first wife in desirability, Dr. A. then went on to prove that this was the case by distancing Mrs. A.2 and treating her as the employee she had always been. And having married her boss Mrs. A.2 got just that—a boss for a husband who indeed did show great individuality, a fierce determination to "do things his own way," and was thus utterly uncooperative as a spouse.

The case of Dr. A. and Mrs. A.2 illustrates several different but closely related agendas that people often bring into second marriages. Incomplete resolution of a prior marital relationship ostensibly ended either by divorce or death may then be carried into a subsequent marriage, which it is bound to affect profoundly. (Garfield, 1982, has elucidated this clearly in his writings on mourning in marital separation, divorce, and remarriage.) Compulsive repetition of a conflicted and ambivalent relationship with a parent is a prime reason for marital choices in both first marriages (Goldberg, 1982) and remarriages. Mrs. A.2 brought this agenda into her second marriage just as she had brought it into her first marriage. The same agenda resulted in the choice of two husbands who were polar opposites, but in each instance Mrs. A.2 was flying blind as to the reasons for her ultimately unsatisfactory choices.

CASE EXAMPLE

A somewhat different instance is furnished by Mr. B., a man in his mid-50s who is now in his second marriage. He met his first wife at a campus mixer when they were both students at a large midwestern university. He was struck by a certain objectionable quality in her demeanor, which was arrogant and conceited, and by her attempt to monopolize attention at the party. So impressed was he that at the end of the evening he told her in no uncertain terms how "repulsive" he thought she was. A year later they were married. There ensued some 20 years of conflict ridden marriage characterized by incessant power struggles in which Mrs. B. almost always had the upper hand. These struggles took place everywhere but most of all in the bedroom, where Mrs. B. was often sexually denying.

In his early 40s, after having been sexually faithful for many years, Mr. B. became involved with another woman who was new and exciting, very personable, and very sexually stimulating to him. After a relatively brief but torrid love affair the situation was discovered by Mrs. B., who quickly put a stop to it. Confronted with an ultimatum Mr. B. gave up his lover and returned to the fold only to become involved in a second affair about a year later. Again, the circumstances of his first meeting and his initial impression of this new lover are worthy of note. He met this woman by striking up a conversation with her while at a bar. She was considerably younger than he (15 years) and seemed from the very first moment of their conversation to be pleasant, compliant, and cooperative to an extreme. She struck Mr. B. as someone who would go along with him and not involve him in the kind of constant struggle he suffered in his marriage.

This affair developed apace and ran a very different course from his first extramarital liaison. After a year Mr. B. left his wife and home and announced to Mrs. B. his intention to get a divorce. As one might well imagine that did not prove easy. Just as Mr. and Mrs. B. had reveled in their power struggle in marriage for some 20-odd years, so they proceeded to battle with great gusto during the divorce process by involving themselves, their five children, and anyone else who got too close to the scene. Meanwhile, Mr. B. had moved in with his young lover, and when after much carnage he finally obtained his divorce, he quickly entered into a marriage with her. Today, some five years later, Mr. B. and Mrs. B.2 are living in a marriage which in substance if not in form closely duplicates Mr. B.'s first marriage. The power struggles are still there but with an interesting (and possibly age-appropriate and culture-related) switch. It is now Mr. B. who withholds sex as a means of controlling his wife. And Mrs. B.2, a few years older and wiser, is no longer so compliant, particularly as she has become aware of the feminist movement and has grown resentful of male domination.

Mr. B.'s marital choices can be viewed as follows. In his first wife he chose someone who mirrored his own being. What he found "repulsive" (and obviously attractive) in her were the very qualities that were in him: arrogance, self-centeredness, and a need for power and dominance. These qualities, probably introjected into his own personality through identification with his father, had an ambivalent hold on him. By choosing Mrs. B.1, he had married someone on whom he could project this ambivalence. In fighting *her* arrogance and narcissism he could forget his own. In his second wife he ostensibly chose a polar opposite—to himself and to Mrs. B.1—only to wind up with basically the same sort of mate. But it should be noted that this first marriage lasted over 20 years, so something substantial must have held it together. Consequently, I would guess that Mr. B.'s second marriage will "work" for him and will endure if Mrs. B.2 does not get fed up with the power struggle and sexual deprivation and opt out.

We may also ask about the person one does *not* choose in marriage or remarriage. Why did Mr. B. marry his second lover and not his first? One theory that is widely held at the level of a sort of folk wisdom is that it is not wise to marry the person with whom you have the kind of emotional involvement that seems to lead you out of a prior marriage. An experienced (and female) divorce lawyer put it to me thus: "Men never marry the springer when they leave a marriage." Other bits of advice are not to "marry the catalyst" and, of course, never to go from the frying pan into the fire. In point of fact, however, some men and some women do "marry the springer." Unfortunately this is a phenomenon for which statistical data are all but totally lacking. It is quite impossible to obtain honest data on this, but my clinical experience indicates the phenomenon to be relatively common, particularly for men. (Honest data will likely never be available, for there is much motivation for concealment. Social disapproval and unfortunate legal consequences generally mitigate against the admission that one is leaving a marriage specifically to marry another person. Consequently, most couples conceal the length of their attachment and insist that they met "long after John left his wife," or "when Mary's first marriage had been totally dead for years.")

Here is a factor in mate selection in remarriages that may be of considerable import, but we can draw no firm conclusions about it. Are remarriages to a lover who was the springer or catalyst out of the first marriage apt to be satisfactory or unsatisfactory? How do they compare to remarriages contracted some years after the end of a prior marriage and in which the second spouse was not on the scene at all during the first marriage? My own limited data drawn from clinical impressions leaves me with the rather surprising and unexplained conclusion that springer remarriages are no less satisfactory than other remarriages and may even tend to be more successful. I have some suspicion, however, that this is more the case for the husbands in these remarriages than for the wives. (White's questionnaire study, 1979, would indicate that remarried men in general are happier with their second marriages than are remarried women.)

Not all the factors in mate selection in remarriages are unconsciously determined. Just as with first marriages "proximity and propinquity" exercise considerable influence. Desire for financial security and increased social status are also factors in both first and remarriages. Certain items seem to fade in import. For example, in a first marriage one generally tends to select a spouse with a similar or compatible religious affiliation. In remarriages Peters (1976) reports—and I would concur—that this seems to matter less and that there is greater likelihood of choosing someone from a very different religious background. Peters also reports that "rationalism" is a greater influence in mate selection in remarriages. I can only dissent and voice the suspicion that there is very little in the process of choosing a mate for any marriage that is truly reasonable or rational.

AREAS OF CONFLICT IN REMARRIAGES

In terms of surface issues it is said that couples battle most commonly (in decreasing order of frequency) about: (1) money, (2) sex, (3) child-rearing, (4) in-laws, and (5) pregnancy. Let us consider this checklist in considering what remarried couples fight about. My experience indicates that money would still be a very solid number one on the list. Alimony and child support are usual accompaniments of remarriage and furnish additional fuel for financial conflicts. The complexities of family structure in the remarried family may also add to the intensity of money battles.

CASE EXAMPLE

Lisa, aged 40 and a divorcée, and Ben, a 56-year-old wealthy executive and widower, met and fell in love some years ago. After a fairly brief courtship they were married. Moving into the new household were Lisa and her two children, ages 12 and 10, plus Ben. His three adult children were all living on their own.

Even before the marriage there were certain financial concerns. Lisa had been receiving approximately $150 a week in support for herself from her first husband, but this support was to end if she remarried. She wanted assurances from Ben not only that he would support her in marriage, but that if *they* were divorced for any reason he would then pick up the $150 weekly support tab. Ben agreed to this only after some grumbling about taking on "another man's burden." An additional problem involved the matter of work. Lisa had been working regularly at an unpleasant but necessary job that paid her approximately $10,000 a year. Ben wanted her to be free to spend time at home with him, and he insisted that she give up the job. Lisa feared that this would leave her entirely financially dependent on him. Finally, there was the matter of Ben's three children. They had been anticipating that some day they would inherit the proceeds of their father's very sizable estate, and they expressed grave concerns that a new wife would deprive them of what they (and Ben) considered to be rightfully theirs.

Because of all these problems Ben had a prenuptial agreement drafted. The basic provisions of this agreement were:

1. Lisa would not be entitled to any share of the financial estate that Ben had accumulated prior to their marriage.
2. Lisa would receive $8,000 a year tax-free from Ben to compensate her for the loss of salary on giving up her job. She could use this money for whatever purposes she chose.
3. Ben would provide "all reasonable" support for Lisa and her two children.
4. In the event of divorce or of Ben's death Lisa would receive ongoing support of $150 weekly.

Of course there were other clauses and fine print in the agreement, but these major provisions give the flavor of it. Lisa was reluctant to sign, but when she expressed reservations she was told by Ben to "sign or else." So sign she did.

Not at all surprisingly, a year after their marriage Ben and Lisa were in my office in the thick of a marital war that revolved around money. Lisa was furious that Ben had forced her to give up her fair share of things, and Ben was equally furious at what he regarded as Lisa's rank ingratitude and at her attempt to take something away from his children, "something that I and my first wife worked so hard for so many years to build up." This attitude on his part was provoked by the fact that Lisa was insisting on a renegotiation of their prenuptial agreement. Unfortunately, that renegotiation never occurred, for after an abortive attempt at counseling involving just two sessions in the office Ben announced that he was having no part of any counseling, mediation, or renegotiation and that Lisa could accept his terms "or else." Today, several years later, they are still married but are living in a bitter, loveless, and conflict-ridden marriage.

Prenuptial agreements are a way of attempting to minimize financial misunderstandings and financial conflicts in remarriages. I am certain that they do serve those functions in many instances. In other cases, however, like that of Ben and Lisa, the prenuptial contract only serves to perpetuate mistrust and becomes just another weapon in an ongoing financial battle.

Sexual conflicts are said to be almost as common as financial battles in first marriages. In remarriages it is my impression that the sexual arena is less lively and that sex is less often a major source of concern. A fairly frequent pattern is that in which both husband and wife in a remarriage give a relatively low priority to sex. In these instances each spouse will complain about the lack or infrequency of sex but will do little to change or correct it. The conclusion soon becomes evident—that neither spouse is really discontented with this state of affairs. There are, of course, many other remarriages in which a sexual problem or dysfunction that existed in the first marriage has been corrected because of a new and better marital/sexual interaction. There are also some instances in which the very same problem reappears in the remarriage. All in all, however, I would conclude that remarriages are a bit less sexually troubled because the spouses tend to be a bit older, a bit more experienced, a bit more realistic, and somewhat more mellow (or is it burned out?) in their sexual dimension.

Battles over *child rearing* seem to be even more common in remarriages, where they can take on additional intensity because of the increased complexity of the family structure and the looser definition of family functions and roles. These matters have been so well elucidated by Sager (Sager, Steer, Crohn, Rodstein, & Walker, 1980; Sager, Walker, Brown, Crohn, & Rodstein, 1981) and by many others that I will not elaborate on them here.

In-laws provide an immensely popular source and reason for marital conflict. It is my belief that this issue is quite often a projection of a more pertinent, underlying conflict. For example, when a man reports to me that he hates his mother-in-law and cannot stand her dominating ways, I find that one or more of the following are true: (1) he hates his wife and cannot stand her dominating ways; (2) he hates his own mother and cannot stand her dominating ways; and (3) he hates himself and cannot stand his own dominating ways. In any case it is generally far safer to express hostility toward in-laws than to express it toward closer targets, so in-laws become scapegoats *par excellence.*

This state of affairs carries over into remarriages with some additions and elaborations. I conceptualize the situation in remarriages to be one in which "the in-laws" include not only the other spouse's family of origin, but also the other spouse's former wife or husband and the children of the first marriage. This is a functional rather than a structural definition. All these people are not really in-laws, but I regard them as such because they all have the capacity to interfere or attempt to interfere in family functioning (just as in-laws do) and because they can all be scapegoated and blamed for everything that is wrong (just as in-laws can).

I cannot even estimate whether arguments over *pregnancy* are as common in remarriages as in first marriages, nor have I seen any studies on this question. The sort of disagreement about pregnancy that I have encountered in remarriages involves situations in which husband and wife are at different points in their lives, chronologically or otherwise. For instance, consider Art and Susan. Both were married previously. Art is 48 and has a 26-year-old daughter, and two sons, ages 24 and 22, by his first marriage. Susan is 32 and has no children Her prior marriage lasted only a year or two, and she and her first husband never really tried to have children. Before Art and Susan got married he made it clear to her that he did not want any more children. Art's outlook is that he has had three kids and has gone through the trials and tribulations of raising them and the expense of educating them; thus, he has done his part and wants no more of it. Susan reluctantly agreed to Art's stipulation but is continuing to debate it now that they are married. At age 32 she feels that her child-bearing years are passing and that she is being deprived of a normal part of marriage and family life. The question of pregnancy thus continues to be the major focus of conflict for this couple.

THE DYNAMICS OF CONFLICT IN REMARRIAGE

Elsewhere (Goldberg, 1982), I have suggested that it is fruitful to consider conflict in marriage in terms of the following dynamics: (1) power and control, (2) nurture, (3) intimacy/privacy, (4) trust, (5) fidelity, and (6) lifestyle and sense of order. These same dynamics shape any relationship, be it marriage, remarriage, living together, or whatever. There are distinctive aspects to the expression of these dynamics in remarriage however, so we will now proceed to consider some of the most striking of these aspects.

Power and control. The issue of power in first marriages is a predominant one and is most often expressed in terms of the power struggle; that is, the fight to see who is going to dominate and who is going to submit or at least who is going to control whom in what areas.

Such power struggles are, of course, not uncommon in remarriages. Often they are complicated by an overlap with power struggles from previous marriages.

CASE EXAMPLE

> Ezra and Connie have been married for several years. For Connie this is a first marriage, but Ezra had a previous marriage of almost 25 years' duration to Gail. The relationship between Ezra and Gail was a chronically conflicted one in which there were constant battles for control and in which each spouse seemed to thrive on the struggle. Eventually, however, Ezra apparently wearied of it and sought and finally won a hard-fought divorce. Throughout the process of separation and divorce Ezra and Gail battled mightily. It was a common occurrence for Gail to call Ezra at his office 10 to 15 times a day to berate him and to disturb him during his nonworking hours on an even larger scale. Today, three years after their divorce, this behavior continues almost unabated. The serenity of Ezra and Connie's life together is constantly interrupted by phone calls and even by personal visits from Gail, who continues her power struggle with her ex-husband. In addition, events are beginning to occur that are quite predictable. Connie and Ezra are now involved in a power struggle of their own, one that apparently centers around Connie's demands that Ezra take more effective action to put an end to the ongoing dilemma with Gail. The net result is that this remarriage now has a sort of double (or should we call it triangular?) power struggle.

Even more complex power struggles are possible, however, where both spouses in a remarriage have previous partners who may still be involved or where the children of a previous marriage become involved in the battle for control.

While complex power struggles are often seen in remarriages, an even more common dilemma is the *power vacuum.* In this scenario, the family interactions are marked by an absence of effective power and a consequent lack of control. Husband, wife, children all seem to be relatively powerless and events seem to transpire in a chaotic, haphazard style in which one complication is heaped upon another. No one is in control; no one acts; everyone reacts. This sort of picture is encountered particularly in remarried families that bring together in abrupt fashion a complex cast of characters, often including teenage or younger children from the prior marriages of both spouses.

Dealing with the power/control issue (and with the attendant chaos) is one of the major tasks in the treatment of the remarried couple and will be discussed subsequently. Suffice it to say here that successful treatment generally involves empowering the couple to take charge, in some agreed upon fashion, of their marriage and their family.

Nurture. As I define nurture, it is the issue of who takes care of whom (rather than who controls whom) and in what ways. The dynamic of nurture is not different in remarriages than in other relationships, but it is again more complex and often more distressing. So often, there are many more mouths to feed: the husband, the wife, the ex-spouse or ex-spouses, the children (maybe his, hers, and theirs), and so on. Everyone needs nurturing—physically and emotionally—and often the need goes unmet.

John is a 55-year-old widower who recently married Eileen, a 40-year-old divorcée with three teenage children. All of them now live together. In my office, where they have come for help with their already ailing marriage, John is almost in tears as he complains of the bad behavior of the children. "I always keep some fine, small filets of beef in the freezer. I've done so for years. Then, if there is some unexpected company or if I just want a very special treat, I can grill those steaks. Now, I can't keep a damn thing in the refrigerator or freezer because those kids just go in there, grab it, and eat it or give it to their friends." John is feeling very unnurtured and the real problem of course is not the food. Food is simply the perfect metaphor for the areas in which he can feel the children's needs competing with his own for his wife's attention, love, and tenderness.

The additional complexity presented in a remarriage such as this is one of disagreement on *priority of nurture.* Nurture involves not only the question of "who takes care of whom?" but also the question "in what order"? In recent generations most middle-class American families formed by first marriages are child-centered, to the extent that nurturing the children has the very highest priority. But remarriages often do not have such a clear ordering of needs. A husband and wife who are in considerable harmony on other issues may still differ markedly on the question of who gets taken caare of *first.*

Intimacy and privacy. I would define intimacy as the need for closeness and contact, again both in the physical and the emotional spheres. It is a need for *togetherness.* Privacy, on the other hand, can be defined as a need for *apartness.* In one sense these two needs can be visualized as being at different ends of a spectrum, yet they are not mutually exclusive. Some people have tremendous needs for intimacy and little or no need for privacy. Others (not many) have great need for apartness and virtually no need for togetherness. Most of us, however, have both of these needs to a considerable extent and seek, at different times and in different ways, both contact with and distance from others. In a given marriage intimacy and privacy may or may not be areas of serious conflict depending on how the needs of husband and wife fit together. These are areas where similarity of needs make for harmony, whereas dissimilarity may make for considerable unhappiness. (Consider, for example, the all-too-common American marriage in which a woman with a great need for closeness, contact, touching, and so on chooses a husband who has to hold her—and the world in general—at arm's length.)

In remarriages, the intimacy-privacy axis is very often a conflicted one, and the most characteristic sort of complaint is one involving a lack of privacy in the family. Reconstituted or blended families often throw together combinations of husband, wife, and children that do not make for easy comfort or harmony. For example, consider the sort of household (not rare today) in which there dwells a husband and wife plus *his* 14-year-old daughter and 10-year-old son, plus *her* 13-year-old daughter and 9-year-old son, plus their two children, ages 3 and 1. The older children compete with each other and complain bitterly at the room-sharing arrangements in the house but vent their deepest dissatisfaction on the two "babies," who are perceived as noisy, intrusive, and disruptive. The husband and wife are constantly juggling to somehow keep this eight-member family comfortable in a home that does have four bedrooms but never seems adequate. The constant complaint of all the family members (except for the babies) is "there's no place I can be alone!"

CASE EXAMPLE

A more serious sort of conflict is exemplified in the remarriage of Jon, a 40-year-old widower, and Bette, a 26-year-old divorcée. Living with them in their luxurious but compact two-bedroom condominium is Jon's 18-year-old son, Robin. A year after marrying and setting up these living arrangements, Jon and Bette are in my office complaining of Robin's erratic behavior, moodiness, and uncooperative attitude. It does not take me terribly long to diagnose the problem, which becomes almost visually evident after meeting

> with all the family members. Robin is a strapping, late-adolescent youngster who, in a totally age-appropriate manner, is bursting with energy and vitality, much of it sexual in nature and only thinly veneered. He is living in a situation where he is thrown into intimate contact with his stepmother. Bette, a striking, blonde woman, emanates a degree of sexual energy and attractiveness that is not much less than Robin's. Robin has to go to sleep each night in the bedroom next to his father and stepmother, has to see Bette around the apartment in various stages of dress and undress, has to kiss her hello and goodbye each day like a good little son, and is expected somehow to keep his cool in the midst of all this. Robin does not remain cool but rather develops temper tantrums in which he becomes angry with Bette or with Jon. He begins to fail in his studies at school and often absents himself from the household without notice or explanation. He has become a problem, and Jon, for one, is totally mystified. "The boy has everything. A nice home, a good father, a lovely stepmother who cares for him. I just can't understand it." Jon is a physician by occupation and is obviously not unintelligent, but he is much too caught up in the problem to see it with any clarity.

This case, along with many others, seems to substantiate Jones's (1978) conception that the unmarried family situation is most difficult for the stepmother and for adolescent children. Even more serious problems along the intimacy/privacy axis may develop in remarriages where sexual feelings erupt into actual incestuous behavior or various forms of sexual abuse within the family (Perlmutter, Engel, & Sager, 1982).

Trust. This is the dynamic in marital and family interaction that may underly virtually all others. Struggles over power, nurture, intimacy/privacy, and so on may go on for years and years, but marriages most often founder and fail due to this most basic issue. Does each spouse *know* and *feel* to the fullest extent that the other one is *for* him or her and has beneficial rather than harmful intent in heart and in mind. Trust is difficult to define in adult words. It is not an adult concept or feeling. It is one developed in earliest childhood. Is the other person good? Is he or she *for* us? If so, we may trust. Problems of trust in marriage are not totally distinctive, but they do tend to have their own style and again their own complexities.

One of the most sizable obstacles to the establishment of trust is past history—past history of betrayal or of deep hurt. Many of those entering into remarriages have had just such past histories. Not only is this true of husbands and wives who have suffered pain in their first marriages, it is equally true of many children in remarried families. Often, these children carry with them the scars inflicted by painful family situations in the past, scars that contribute to an attitude of considerable mistrust (Goldstein, 1974).

Somehow, the remarried family needs to establish a degree of mutual trust that is seldom present at its inception. (Needless to say, legal instruments such as prenuptial agreements do not help at all in this area but rather tend to foster an atmosphere of caution, self-preservation, and suspicion.)

Fidelity. This is an item that is certainly related to trust, but one which I choose to regard as a separate dynamic. I do so because the two items are not necessarily coexistent. As I have written elsewhere (Goldberg, 1982), "Fidelity implies the keeping of vows: generally to love, honor, and cherish, and to place no other one above the spouse. (Oddly enough, a man who totally distrusts his wife may carry out all these vows out of conscience and she may do the same, whereas a man who has a fine, trusting, marital relationship may still be unfaithful. Hence, my inclination to view trust and fidelity as separate dynamics)" (p. 463).

Fidelity is often a major area of conflict in remarriages but not in terms of sexual faithfulness. Far more frequently the issue is one of faithfulness to a spouse versus faithfulness to some other family member, that is, to a child of a previous marriage or even to the ex-spouse.

Kitty and Ed exemplify this sort of remarriage problem. They came to see me due to Kitty's complaint that "there is a triangle." This triangle, it emerged, involved Kitty and Ed plus Gwen, Ed's 14-year-old daughter from his first marriage. Gwen does not live with Ed, but on her regular visits (twice weekly and every other weekend) a situation develops in which Kitty feels that Ed gives his daughter all his time and attention. Kitty is very bitter in enumerating the "6 days out of every 14" when she feels that Ed is lost to her because of "another woman" (i.e., Gwen). The bitterness and anger engendered by this situation could compare with any extramarital triangle.

Lifestyle and sense of order. This final dynamic of marital interaction and conflict involves differences in style, in temperament, and in approach to life. A great many significant factors are subsumed under this heading including differences in lifestyles, differences in cognitive styles, differences in styles of dealing with anxiety (mental defense mechanisms), differences in assertiveness, differences in activity/passivity, and differences in sense of order. Sense of order has to do with how we choose to order our lives and our universes in terms of spatial arrangements, time, and so on. It is revealed in the degree to which we thrive or shrivel at the sight of overflowing ashtrays and uncapped toothpaste tubes, how troubled we are by lateness or punctuality, and other such mundane matters that fill our lives. Differences in style need not be divisive in a marriage; theoretically, at least, it is possible to visualize such differences as having a complementary, strengthening effect. Quite often, however, the actual effect is otherwise, and much strife results from the interaction of a neat, punctual, mildly anxious and apprehensive individual with a spouse who is far more casual about time and neatness and who will revel in any new challenge or risk.

Conflicts in these areas in remarriages are not particularly distinctive if there are no children involved. But in the many instances where children *are* involved and where we are dealing with reconstituted or blended families, situations develop in which multiple *family* styles may be at variance and may contribute to severe conflicts.

In discussing the dynamics of nurture we mentioned the case of John who was profoundly disturbed because his step-children raided the refrigerator and freezer and consumed his prize steaks. The style and order of things in John's first marriage was such that his own children would never have dared to do something like that. But his second wife, Eileen, had raised her children in a free and easy style. They could have friends over at any time and unannounced, and whatever was in the household larder was as much at the children's disposal as it was at the parents'. Needless to say, this difference in style made for constant tension in John and Eileen's marriage and in their reconstituted family.

CASE EXAMPLE

Fred, a 55-year-old divorced attorney and his fiancée, Lily, aged 34 and also divorced, were seeing me for premarital counseling as they went through the process of preparing to join themselves and Lily's three small children (ages 3, 5, and 8) in a new family and a new household. They arrived at my office one day in a state of obvious tension and hostility, the reasons for which were not immediately apparent; gradually, the story emerged. They had spent the day house hunting and had been looking at a very attractive home in the Main Line suburban area of Philadelphia. It was a gracious and elaborate property with beautiful rooms, beautiful features, and lovely, manicured grounds. Both of them were enthralled by the house, and as they left the real estate agent who had been showing it to them, Lily could contain herself no longer. "What a wonderful, wonderful place to raise children," she said. "Oh, my Gawd," Fred answered, "I never really thought of that. They would rip that place to shreds and just ruin it in no time at all." During the next hour, while they were driving to my office, both maintained a stony silence as Lily retreated into wordlessness and Fred wondered what in the world she was angry about.

This vignette illustrates several conflicts of style and related matters that are not uncommon in remarriages:

1. Lily was much more permissive with her children than Fred was with his own offspring. There was a generational difference reflected here. At age 34 Lily was part of a child-centered generation, whereas Fred, 21 years older and from a rural, more conservative background, still believed in the old doctrine of children being seen but not heard.

2. Lily and Fred were at different points in their respective life cycles, and this resulted in very different needs and desires. Lily was at a point of wanting to build a strong, beautiful home for the family. Fred had been through all that for many years and really wanted to simplify life and have a smaller, plainer household with fewer complications.
3. Carrying this one step further it could be said that Fred, having raised several children of his own, did not really want to go through the process of childrearing all over again. His love for Lily was carrying him into a marriage wherein he was to resent her children by considering them a burden and an interference.

TREATING THE REMARRIED FAMILY

A detailed examination of treatment methods and modalities for the remarried family is beyond the scope of this chapter. Instead, I will emphasize the approach that I have found to be most helpful in dealing with the remarried. This approach attempts to accomplish the following goals more or less in sequence:

1. The elimination of chaos and confusion and the establishment of order in the family.
2. The building of trust in the marital dyad.
3. The extension of this trust to the entire remarried family.
4. The resolution of past allegiances and ties.
5. The revision of unrealistic expectations.
6. The development of ways and means whereby the newfound family relationship may be used to help all family members to express and meet their needs.

In attempting to achieve these goals the therapist must decide where to concentrate the therapeutic effort and whom to include in the therapy. True family sessions in which every member of the remarried family is included may be quite large and cumbersome in many instances. Such meetings may include husband and wife along with "his, her, and their" children and may also encompass previous spouses, grandparents, in-laws, and so on. If the therapist can assemble such a complete cast of characters the ensuing session is often very instructive in highlighting all the various forces and conflicts at play in the family. For that reason I like to have such a session very early in the therapy. However, I do not generally find it advisable to continue such sessions even if it is possible to do so. (In fact, there is a tendency for family members to absent themselves from ongoing sessions as a means of resistance to the therapeutic process.)

What seems to work more effectively is to concentrate the ongoing therapy on the marital dyad. As I conceptualize it this is of great importance precisely because the marital bond is relatively weak in many remarriages (as it is in many first marriages), and that weakness makes for confusion and disorder in the family. Husband and wife have to take control of life in the remarried family, whether the family consists of just them or whether it consists of them plus four or five children. Needless to say, in order to establish such control they must develop clear and effective communication, and they must be able to agree together on new solutions, new compromises, and new trade-offs to deal with the new problems they are facing.

In working with the remarried pair the therapist generally has to establish some order and take some control in the early sessions in order to begin to promulgate the first goal of reducing chaos and confusion. Thus, the therapeutic triad gradually develops effective power that can then be utilized in the family by the marital dyad. As this happens generational boundaries are established or restored, and confusion gradually subsides.

For this to happen, of course, mutual trust must be developed. Husband and wife generally bring to the office much distrust which is built on previous hurts and betrayals, many or most of which antedate the present relationship. Under these circumstances I find it most effective if *I* am able to develop a trusting relationship with each spouse. I am then able to use that trust to encourage and solidify a growing trust between husband and wife as they come to understand each other's fears and vulnerabilities. When this does happen there is virtually always a simultaneous or only slightly subsequent development of increasing trust in the entire family unit. One of the things that happens, I believe, is that all members of the family come to realize that this new marriage and this new family *is for real* and that the bond between husband and wife is genuine and lasting. As this realization occurs stepchildren, who have previously doubted this new reality, can be less anxious and guarded and can cease their attempts to either perpetuate or interfere with this marriage. The same is true for the previous spouses who in many instances have been intervening strongly in family matters just because they sensed the weakness or impermanence of the new unit.

As trust is developed husband and wife are encouraged to work together in the resolution of past ties that have interfered with the marriage. In addition to the previous spouses, these ties include allegiances to the families of origin. Describing these connections as ties or allegiances that need to be broken may give the mistaken impression that husband and wife are encouraged to dissolve positive connections with their past families and others. This is not the case. The ties in question are often ties of anger, hatred, fear, and revenge which need to be resolved so that healthier interactions may evolve all around.

The emerging equanimity that develops in the remarried pair when therapy is successful allows them to reevaluate their original, usually unrealistic expectations of what marriage and family life can and should be

(Visher & Visher, 1982). One of my patients put this so eloquently that I will quote him more or less verbatim. "Inside you, in the back of your head, there is always this dream—this fantasy. You come home at night from work or maybe it is Sunday and the whole family is already home. You're all sitting around in the den having a conversation. It's friendly and relaxed and funny. Your wife is lovely and understanding and everyone is crazy about her, and the kids are all amusing but perfectly behaved. Everyone loves and admires you and everyone gets on so well together. Everyone can just be happy and enjoy life."

This dream—this fantasy—is very touching indeed because it does exist in each of us: father, mother, child. Sadly, it is seldom realized outside of novels, television shows, or "B" movies. Life is rarely this lovely, placid picture we would make it. But as couples develop more realistic expectations they can still be optimistic and realize that life,—particularly life together—while seldom serene, remains interesting, intriguing, and rewarding.

Remarried families often do very well with some effective counseling or therapy. Isaacs (1982) has advocated early intervention as being of great importance if such therapy is to be successful. Fortunately, remarried families are often willing to accept such intervention. The process of going through previous marital failures does often incline people to seek help and to seek it at an early time. It remains for marital and family therapists and other mental health professionals to promulgate more realistic expectations of marriage and of remarriage, expectations that will further encourage families to go for the help they need at the earliest possible time. It remains for us additionally to develop ever more effective means of helping troubled families.

References

Ahrons, C. R., & Perlmutter, M. S. (1982). Therapy with remarriage families: III: The relationship between former spouses: a fundamental subsystem in the remarriage family. *Family Therapy Collections, 2,* 31–46.

Albrecht, S. L. (1979). Correlates of marital happiness among the remarried. *Journal of Marriage and the Family, 41*(4), 857–867.

Brady, C. A., & Ambler, J. (1982). Therapy with remarriage families: X. Use of group educational techniques with remarried couples. *Family Therapy Collections, 2,* 145–157.

Cherlin, A. J. (1978). Remarriage as an incomplete institution. *American Journal of Sociology, 84*(3), 634–650.

Cherlin, A. J. (1981). *Marriage, divorce, remarriage.* Harvard University Press, Cambridge, MA.

Crohn, H. et al. (1982). Therapy with remarriage families: XI. A basis for understanding and treating the remarried family. *Family Therapy Collections, 2,* 159–186.

Davids, L. (1982). Divorce and remarriage among Canadian Jews. *Journal of Comparative Family Studies, 13*(1), 37–47.

Day, R. D., & Mackey, W. C. (1981). Redivorce following remarriage: A re-evaluation. *Journal of Divorce, 4*(3), 39–47.

Duffy, M. (1981). Divorce and the dynamics of the family kinship system. *Journal of Divorce, 5*(1–2), 3–18.

Espenshade, T. J., & Braun, R. E. (1982). Life course analysis and multistate demography: An application to marriage, divorce, and remarriage. *Journal of Marriage and the Family, 44*(4), 1025–1036.

Garfield, R. (1980). The decision to remarry. *Journal of Divorce, 4*(1), 1–10.

Garfield, R. (1982). Therapy with remarriage families: I. Mourning and its resolution for spouses in marital separation. *Family Therapy Collections, 2,* 1–16.

Glenn, N. D., & Weaver, C. N. (1977). The marital happiness of remarried divorced persons. *Journal of Marriage and the Family, 39*(2), 331–337.

Goldberg, M. (1982). The dynamics of marital interaction and marital conflict. In M. Goldberg, (Ed.), *Marital Therapy Psychiatric Clinics of North America, 5*(3), 449–467.

Goldner, V. (1982). Therapy with remarriage families: XII. Remarriage family: Structure, system, future. *Family Therapy Collections, 2,* 187–206.

Goldstein, H. S. (1974). Reconstituted families: The second marriage and its children. *Psychiatric Quarterly, 48*(3), 433–440.

Gurak, D. T., & Dean, G. (1979). The remarriage market: Factors influencing the selection of second husbands, *Journal of Divorce, 3*(2), 161–173.

Isaacs, M. B. (1982). Therapy with remarriage families: IX. Facilitating family restructuring and relinkage. *Family Therapy Collections, 2,* 121–143.

Jones, S. M. (1978). Divorce and remarriage: A new beginning, a new set of problems. *Journal of Divorce, 2*(2), 217–227.

Kalish, R. A., & Visher, E. (1981). Grandparents of divorce and remarriage. *Journal of Divorce, 5*(1–2), 127–140.

Messinger, L., & Walker, K. U. (1981). From marriage breakdown to remarriage: Parental tasks and therapeutic guidelines. *American Journal of Orthopsychiatry, 51*(3), 429–438.

Messinger, L. (1976). Remarriage between divorced people with children from previous marriages: A proposal for preparation for remarriage. *Journal of Marriage and Family Counseling, 2*(2), 193–200.

Mitchell, K. (1983). The price tag of responsibility: A comparison of divorced and remarried mothers. *Journal of Divorce, 6*(3), 33–42.

Mott, F., & Moore, S. F. (1983). The tempo of remarriage among young American women. *Journal of Marriage and the Family, 45*(2), 427–436.

Nadler, J. H. (1983). Effecting changes in stepfamilies: a psychodynamic/behavioral group approach. *American Journal of Psychotherapy, 37*(1), 100–112.

Parish, T. S. & Dostal, J. W. (1980). Evaluations of self and parent figures by children from intact, divorced, and reconstructed families. *Journal of Youth and Adolescence, 9*(4), 347–351.

Perlmutter, L. H., Engel, T., & Sager, C. J. (1982). The incest taboo: Loosened sexual boundaries in remarried families. *Journal of Sex and Marital Therapy, 8*(2), 83–96.

Peters, J. F. (1976). A comparison of mate selection and marriage in the first and second marriages of the remarried divorced. *Journal of Comparative Family Studies*, 7(3), 483–490.

Price-Bonham, S., & Bolswick, J. O. (1980). The noninstitutions: Divorce, desertion, and remarriage. *Journal of Marriage and the Family, 42*(4), 959–972.

Sager, C., Steer, H., Crohn, H., Rodstein, E., & Walker, E. (1980). Remarriage revisited. *Family and Child Mental Health Journal, 6*(1), 19–33.

Sager, C., Walker, E., Brown, H., Crohn, H., & Rodstein, E. (1981). Improving functioning of the remarried family system. *Journal of Marital and Family Therapy*, 7(1), 3–13.

Santrock, J. W., Warshak, R., Lindbergh, C., & Meadows, L. (1982). Children and parent's observed social behavior in stepfather families. *Child Development, 53*(2), 472–480.

Spanier, G. B., & Glick, P. C. (1980). Paths to remarriage. *Journal of Divorce, 3*(3), 283–298.

Spanier, G. B., & Furstenberg, F. F. (1982). Remarriage after divorce: A longitudinal analysis of well-being. *Journal of Marriage and the Family, 44*(3), 709–720.

Thies, J. M. (1977). Beyond divorce: The impact of remarriage on children. *Journal of Clinical Child Psychology, 6*(2) 59–61.

Treas, J., & Vanhilst, A. (1976). Marriage and remarriage rates among older Americans. *Gerontologist, 16*(2), 132–136.

Vinick, B. H. (1978). Remarriage in old age. *Journal of Geriatric Psychiatry, 11* (1), 75–77.

Visher, E. B., & Visher, J. S. (1982). Therapy with remarriage families: VIII. Stepfamilies in the 1980's. *Family Therapy Collections, 2*, 105–119.

Walker, K. N., & Messinger, L. (1979). Remarriage after divorce: Dissolution and reconstruction of family boundaries. *Family Process, 18*(2), 185–192.

Walker, K. N., Rogers, J., & Messinger, L. (1977). Remarriage after divorce: A review. *Social Casework, 58*(5), 276–285.

Walker, L. et al. (1979). An annotated bibliography of the remarried, the living together, and their children. *Family Process, 18*(2), 193–212.

White, L. K. (1979). Sex differentials in the effect of remarriage on global happiness. *Journal of Marriage and the Family, 41*(4), 869–876.

Whiteside, M. F. (1982). Remarriage: A family developmental process. *Journal of Marital and Family Therapy, 8*(2), 59–68.

Yoder, J. D. & Nichols, R. C. (1980). A life perspective comparison of married and divorced persons. *Journal of Marriage and the Family, 42*(2), 413–419.

AUTHOR INDEX

SUBJECT INDEX

This book has been set Compugraphic, in 10 and 9 point Palatino, leaded 2 points. Section numbers are 48 point Frutiger 55 and section titles are 36 point Palatino Bold Italic, Chapter numbers are 28 point Frutiger 55 and chapter titles are 24 point Palatino Bold Italic. The size of the type page is 26 by 46½ picas.